Antisemitism Through the Ages

Edited by
SHMUEL ALMOG

Translated by
NATHAN H. REISNER

Published for the

Vidal Sassoon International Center for
the Study of Antisemitism, The Hebrew
University of Jerusalem

by

PERGAMON PRESS

OXFORD · NEW YORK · BEIJING · FRANKFURT
SÃO PAULO · SYDNEY · TOKYO · TORONTO

U.K.	Pergamon Press plc, Headington Hill Hall, Oxford OX3 0BW, England
U.S.A.	Pergamon Press, Inc., Maxwell House, Fairview Park, Elmsford, New York 10523, U.S.A.
PEOPLE'S REPUBLIC OF CHINA	Pergamon Press, Room 4037, Qianmen Hotel, Beijing, People's Republic of China
FEDERAL REPUBLIC OF GERMANY	Pergamon Press GmbH, Hammerweg 6, D-6242 Kronberg, Federal Republic of Germany
BRAZIL	Pergamon Editora Ltda, Rua Eça de Queiros, 346, CEP 04011, Paraiso, São Paulo, Brazil
AUSTRALIA	Pergamon Press Australia Pty Ltd., P.O. Box 544, Potts Point, N.S.W. 2011, Australia
JAPAN	Pergamon Press, 5th Floor, Matsuoka Central Building, 1-7-1 Nishishinjuku, Shinjuku-ku, Tokyo 160, Japan
CANADA	Pergamon Press Canada Ltd., Suite No. 271, 253 College Street, Toronto, Ontario, Canada M5T 1R5

First edition 1988

Library of Congress Cataloging in Publication Data
Śin'at-Yiśraél Le-doroteha. English.
Antisemitism through the ages.
(Studies in antisemitism)
"Based upon lectures and symposia held in 1978 in Jerusalem by the Zalman Shazar Center for Jewish History"—Pref. Translation of: Śin'at-Yiśrael Le-doroteha.
Includes bibliographical references and indexes.
1. Antisemitism—History. I. Almog, S. II. Merkaz Zalman Shazar le-ha 'amakat ha-todo 'ah ha-historit ha-Yehudit. III. Title. IV. Series.
DS145.S5813   1987   909'.04924   87–7276

British Library Cataloguing in Publication Data
Antisemitism through the ages.—(Studies in antisemitism).
1. Antisemitism—History
I. Almog, Shmuel II. Sinat Israel ledorotea. *English* III. Series
305.8'924   DS145

ISBN 0–08–034792–4 (Hardcover)
ISBN 0–08–035850–0 (Flexicover)

This edition is a translation of *Sin'at Yisrael ledoroteha* © 1980 The Zalman Shazar Center, Jerusalem

Printed in Great Britain by A. Wheaton & Co. Ltd., Exeter

Contents

vi   *Contents*

Contents vii

Preface

The publication of the English version of this volume was inspired by a series of summer courses held in Jerusalem on "Antisemitism as a Historical Phenomenon." The favorable response to these courses indicated a growing concern with the nature of antisemitism and a renewed interest in understanding more about it. The vast corpus of publications on the Holocaust left many questions unanswered, and a desire was expressed for a general text that would probe deeper into the roots of antisemitism.

Many books and articles have been published on this subject in recent years, but they usually confined themselves to one particular aspect, or to a certain country during a definite period. However, an attempt to present an overall study of this phenomenon poses serious methodological questions: For example, can a common denominator be found between the ancient hatred of Israel as it appears in the Bible ("Haman plotted to do away with all the Jews," Esther 3:6) and the struggle of the Christian Church against Judaism? Are these to be placed alongside the lowly status of the Jews under Muslim rule? Furthermore, can all these be connected with modern antisemitism and especially with the annihilation of the Jews in Nazi Europe?

There are two diametrically opposed approaches to the continuity of anti-semitism. One approach is that which has crystallized to some extent in Jewish tradition, namely, "All the nations hate Israel." The other approach tries to see each specific occurrence in its historic context, or even to counterpoise – as does Salo W. Baron – the hatred of Israel and the love of Israel as the two pivots of Jewish history.[1] In his view, it is somewhat comparable to a country's foreign relations. Relations between states are sometimes friendly, sometimes hostile. Yet foreign relations are generally conducted with many countries; thus, it may be possible to balance hostility in one direction with friendship in another. Unfortunately, no such balance has been reached so far between philosemitism and antisemitism.

Another question refers to the antiquity of Jew-hatred. Many see it as a constant concomitant of Jewish history. Jules Isaac, in his volume on the roots of antisemitism, enumerated a long list of authors – Jewish and non-Jewish, antisemitic and philosemitic – who held this position. He himself claimed that the Christian Church's hatred of Israel was different from that of its predecessors, even though the Church itself made use of the pagan tradition it had inherited.[2] Thus, two different kinds of Jew-hatred joined together and were from then on inseparable, because one layer was built upon the other. This, then, created a *continuity of antisemitic consciousness*, although its roots were originally anchored in different historical circumstances (see the essay by Shmuel Ettinger in this volume).

At first glance, it may be difficult to distinguish between the continuum of antisemitic consciousness and the claim of its essential timelessness. The very old tradition of Jew-hatred seems to suggest that antisemitism has always existed, has never ceased, and apparently never will. However, it is imperative for historical understanding to be able to distinguish between the two; otherwise we are doomed to thrash around in the thicket of charges and counter-charges from which there is no exit.

Against the ancient accusation that the Jews themselves are to blame for the hatred against them, one hears the traditional motif that Judaism is "the lamb amidst seventy wolves." Occasionally, there are modern authors who elaborate on this position, such as George Steiner, for example, who described the Holocaust as some sort of revenge against the Jews for having brought the world the message of monotheism, early Christianity, and social Messianism.[3]

The present collection does not claim to offer the definitive answer to antisemitism through the ages, but rather to follow closely its metamorphoses in varied and varying circumstances. At the same time one should pay attention to the historical sediment which has accumulated from ancient times and left its imprint upon the relationship between Israel and the nations (in the widest sense).

This collection is based upon lectures and symposia held in Jerusalem by the Zalman Shazar Center for Jewish History, and has been updated for the present volume. It is not a systematic work but a collection of studies by renowned Israeli scholars working in various fields, who share neither a common ideology nor any particular school of thought.

The publishers attempted to include in its program the totality of Jewish history – in antiquity and the Middle Ages, in the Christian world and the Muslim countries, and, of course, in modern times – and, in most instances, actually did succeed in comprehensively covering the major subjects germane to the topic. However, readers may notice a subject missing which they feel relevant to the area under discussion, or judge the balance of the topics discussed as inadequate. On the other hand, there is an advantage to this collection in that it brings together a wide range of studies by scholars normally occupied in disparate fields and thus it covers a broad area. Though the essays generally appear in chronological order rather than being geographically grouped, it was not possible to ignore the differences between Christian Europe and the Muslim world. Therefore, a separate chapter was devoted to antisemitism in the Orient, including the traditional Muslim society as well as the Arab response to Zionism and the State of Israel.

Finally, a word on terminology: The term *antisemitism* is attributed to Wilhelm Marr, about whom there is an article by Moshe Zimmerman in this volume. This term quickly came into such widespread use that it no longer refers to a specific category of Jew-hatred, such as racial antisemitism, or even modern antisemitism as such. On the contrary, one now usually designates as antisemitism all phenomena of Jew-hatred without any particular distinction. We have acted accordingly and used the term antisemitism as a synonym for all Jew-hatred whenever it seemed more in keeping with current usage.

The publication of this book was made possible by the cooperation of the Zalman Shazar Center for Jewish History with the Vidal Sassoon International Center for the Study of Antisemitism, The Hebrew University, Jerusalem. It is part of a series of studies on antisemitism to be published jointly by Pergamon Press and the Vidal Sassoon Center. Many thanks are owed to all those who were helpful in the preparation of the book: Dr Richard I. Cohen, Ms Sue Fox, Mr Yohai Goell, Dr Nathan H. Reisner and Ms Irit Sivan.

Shmuel Almog

Notes

1. Salo W. Baron, "World Dimensions of Jewish History," in *Simon Dubnow: the Man and his Work*, ed. Aaron Steinberg (Paris, 1963), p.36.
2. Jules Isaac, *Genèse de l'antisémitisme: essai historique* (Paris, 1956), pp.29–35, 327.
3. George Steiner, *In Bluebirds' Castle: Some Notes Toward the Redefinition of Culture* (London and Boston, 1978), pp.36–41.

1

Jew-Hatred in its Historical Context*

SHMUEL ETTINGER

There is little doubt that after World War II and the Holocaust that befell the Jewish people, new approaches began to develop with respect to the phenomenon known as antisemitism. In the wake of Nazi Germany's attempt to put into practice an abstract theory – "The War against the Jews" – which involved the indiscriminate murder of millions and which at times conflicted with political and military needs, the *Weltanschauungen* of both Jews and non-Jews were badly shaken. This historical experience without a doubt served as the turning point in the renewed discussion of antisemitism, its roots, manifestations, and continuity over the course of time. Prior to World War II, despite the intensity of attacks on Jews, antisemitism was looked upon as a marginal or secondary phenomenon, a propaganda device, discussed seriously only in Zionist circles.

Moreover, attempts that were made before the Holocaust to explain antisemitism, usually dealt with isolated manifestations, concentrating on particularly historical situations (government persecutions or outbursts of pogroms), placing the accent on an examination of the Jews' condition in a given country, and so forth. Under the influence of the Holocaust many attempts were made by psychologists, sociologists, and historians to find some general significance in antisemitism, and in some extreme cases, to discover something universal in it. And from here it is just one more step to the central problem – perhaps the decisive matter in understanding the essence of antisemitism – the problem of its historic continuity. Is the hatred and rejection of both Jews and Judaism – known as *antisemitism* since the last quarter of the nineteenth century – the same phenomenon throughout history in all of its manifestations or, perhaps, is this term simply an umbrella for all social, political, and psychological phenomena which caught on thanks to terminological or ideological convenience?

*This translation first appeared in *Immanual* 11 (1980): 81–94.

1

1. Some Theories Explaining Antisemitism

In order to examine this problem properly, one should note that the source of the discussion was primarily emotional, and stemmed from the need for introspection once the full scope of the Holocaust became clear. In this respect it resembles the state of mind following World War I when public opinion was shaken by the horrible slaughter of millions which, in retrospect, seemed contrary to all ethical and logical considerations. Once again the search for the guilty ones, for those who bore the responsibility, began. As a result, the German people and their national characteristics were carefully scrutinized in order to view their relations with the Jews in historical context.

In a similar manner, the histories and cultures of the Eastern and Central European peoples on whose territory the slaughter was carried out and who were among its more important perpetrators: Ukrainians, Lithuanians, Croatians, and Hungarians were also examined. Before long voices began to be heard alleging that the guilt of the murdered is no less than that of the murderers; that they were partners in crime, so to speak. The main supposition was that a large share of the guilt falls on the Jews themselves and, in particular, on their pre-Holocaust leaders who did not understand the political map of their times and even saw in antisemitism a factor contributing to Jewish unity – a sort of ally. Jewish leaders under Nazi rule were deemed to be especially guilty in that they aided their persecutors in their attempts to register, concentrate, and ultimately deport Jews to the death camps. However, this very preoccupation with the problem of guilt led scholars to examine the Holocaust in a broader historical perspective. They began searching for its historical roots, its connections with antisemitism in earlier periods, and in this manner arrived at an examination of Jew-hatred in its various forms and manifestations.

Under the influence of the Holocaust three approaches to the study of antisemitism's causes emerged. One approach claimed that the issue of Jewish–non-Jewish relationships (between majority peoples and the Jewish minority that lives among them) is not a real problem but a deception exploited by propagandists for their own purposes, be they psychological, social, or political. Proponents of this approach maintain that there never was a real Jewish problem, not even in Germany, and therefore there was no real antagonism between Jews and non-Jews. Antisemitism came about, in their opinion, as a result of the manipulation of historical prejudices and from the focusing of the public's bitterness on an imaginary enemy. In this manner, antisemitism was reduced to a sort of historical digression. No doubt, apologetics and nostaliga, as well as the desire to preserve the lovely dream of German–Jewish coexistence, played a major role in the formulation of this idea which found expression in Eva Reichmann's book.[1]

Another approach is evident in Hannah Arendt's book which places a significant share of the blame for the growth of antisemitism and even for the extermination of the Jews upon the Jews themselves, their leaders, their conduct, and their course of action.[2] According to her, at a certain stage in modern European history Jews ceased to perform a meaningful social function and only derived benefit from their wealth and status. Thus a real conflict was created between Jews and all other social classes who subsequently identified the Jews with the State. Had it not been for the blindness of these Jews who did not understand the roots of this social development, antisemitism would not have taken on the forms that it did. Moreover, had Jewish leaders not becomes so enmeshed in the enemy establishment, the Holocaust would not have taken on the dimensions and shape that it did.

Without getting into a detailed discussion of Hannah Arendt's argument (and others of similar viewpoint) as expressed in *The Origins of Totalitarianism* which deals with the sources of antisemitism and her volume on the Eichmann trial which deals with the Holocaust[3], one can say that her reasoning was influenced by assumptions that were widespread in German society, and to a certain degree by antisemitic and even Nazi attitudes. After all, the anti-semites' argument over the course of time has been that since hatred for Jews existed in different periods and among different peoples, the reason for it cannot be posited in the temporal or social conditions in which the Jews live, but in the Jews themselves. The acceptance by students of antisemitism of non-Jewish attitudinal patterns including, among other things, the image of the Jew as perceived by the non-Jewish world, is not so amazing. Among many Jews the Holocaust did bring about a change in values and made for a more independent view, but Hannah Arendt was not one of their number. She is set apart from other scholars by the extremism inherent in her use of the negative stereotype of the Jew.

A third approach, diametrically opposed to the first two, was advanced by my late mentor and teacher, Professor Ben-Zion Dinur in his article "Diaspora Communities and their Destruction"[4] which was written under the immediate influence of the Holocaust. In his opinion, there is no real novelty in the Holocaust since hatred and destruction of the Jewish people have always been a part of Jewish and Gentile history. Proof of this is the decline of the Jews in the Greco-Roman world when millions disappeared during the transition to the Middle Ages, presumably due to annihilation, although there is no explicit evidence to support this contention. The process which Dubnow picturesquely called "The Migration of Jewish Centers" is, according to Dinur, nothing more than the disruption and destruction of Jewish life. What happened in the Greco-Roman world happened again in the Middle Ages during the Black Death; the Chmielnicki massacres; once again, in the Modern Era toward the end of World War I in the Ukraine; and twenty years later in the Holocaust. The destruction of the Jewish people was, from the beginning, the rule in the relationship of large parts of the Gentile world towards the Jews, with the Holocaust of our time being only more radical and systematic. Thus Dubnow's talk of migrations in the Diaspora and transfers of Jewish centers[5] are nothing but an embellishment of historical reality: these were not wanderings of Jewish centers but their destruction.

More than a generation has passed since the formulation of these views, and still it seems that we will never entirely succeed in detaching ourselves from the terrible trauma of the Holocaust. Nonetheless, those who attempt to examine antisemitism and its place in the life of the Jews and other peoples of Europe must strive to shield themselves from the emotional pressure of the Holocaust. Moreover, we must remember that despite the Holocaust and the great shock that it caused among large segments of public opinion in Europe and America (and even in other parts of the world), and despite the establishment of the State of Israel which was to be the final answer to this problem, antisemitism to this day has not ceased to be an important factor in various countries and in many areas of life. Even today these antisemitic arguments exude freshness and vitality. Those who have recourse to them do so with great fervor, despite their literal reliance, occasionally, on things that were said hundreds of years ago. Indeed, anyone who reads antisemitic writings of ancient times and then examines anti-Jewish arguments of the Middle Ages and the nineteenth and twentieth centuries will be astonished by the similarity of their arguments and reasoning. This fact alone is enough to stimulate us to study antisemitism, not just as Jews trying to understand a phenomenon which still plays a central role in our lives, but as civilized people contemplating an unusual and amazingly persistent phenomenon.

2. Socio-psychological Theories

Let us now take a look at some explanations of Jew-hatred and antisemitism as they appear in the scholarly literature of the post-World War II era. The more accepted explanations are those that derive from the field of psychology, that attempt to draw a causal or statistical connection between antisemitism and people of a particular psychological make-up (such as those who experienced some sort of trauma or exhibit antisocial attitudes), and there to look for the roots of antisemitism.[6] Similar to these are several sociological studies whose point of departure is the assumption that a certain degree of aggression exists in every group of people and finds expression in their relations with aliens. According to these scholars, antisemitism is just another expression of this complex.[7] In the same vein, attempts were made to explain antisemitism in the context of minority- and majority-group relations, between in- and out-groups. In the words of Professor Salo W. Baron we discern the old motive – the dislike of the unlike – which supposedly is the universal key to understanding antisemitism. Its intensity is explained by the concurrence of several factors which determine relations of a minority group under conditions of group tension. The opening section of the entry "Antisemitism" in the *Encyclopaedia Hebraica*[8] explains its peculiarity by the combination of several negative attitudes toward a minority: hatred of the different, of the weak, and of the alien. Since these three find a common focal point in the Jewish people, the roots of antisemitism must be engendered in them. Several of these explanations have been supported by wide-ranging field studies and systematic investigation. But even so there is a fundamental difficulty in accepting them. After all, it is a fact that the measure of adverse feeling toward Jews is not equal in all countries and cultures.

Indeed, there are great differences in the attitudes toward Jews on the part of their "host" peoples. Logically speaking, if the basic psychological factors that are grounded in the individual's personality were the main reason for their attitude to Jews, and if this stemmed from the psychological or social make-up of groups, cultures, economic classes and the like, then such manifestations should be more or less similar between peoples who find themselves in similar stages of cultural and social development. But it is a fact that there are differences in various peoples' relationship with the Jews and the degree of intensity involved. An even greater problem derives from the fact that the very definition of these negative attitudes raises doubts. Many antisemites describe the Jew not as being weak but rather as possessing satanic powers which threaten the structure of the surrounding society, its economy, culture, and so forth. According to their arguments, the struggle with the Jews is a crucial struggle *because* of their tremendous power. Scorn for the weak appears in only a few instances.

Even more complicated is the conception of the Jew as someone who is different from other human beings. According to this thesis, the principal manifestation of hatred for the Jews should have been depicted in terms of their different life-style and appearance (the observant Jew replete with earlocks and traditional dress). And so it was at times, for example, in placards and caricatures. However, in the ideological and theological literature of antisemitism, hatred is directed at Jews whose life-style and appearance *resemble* that of the non-Jewish world. In real life, hatred for the Jew who tried to pass as a Gentile was more intense than the hatred for Jews who represented the traditional image. As the ideology of modern antisemitism gained strength, the negative attitude toward the assimilated Jew who resembled the Gentile in life-style, dress, and sometimes even in religion (converts), became exacerbated on the basis of the claim that the really great danger stems from those of Jewish origin who join the monastic order, or become European radicals, from those who look as if they have altogether broken with Judaism. One of the paradoxes of modern antisemitism is that it was the "non-Jewish Jew" – the Jews who divorced themselves from their ethnic surroundings and culture and attained conspicuous success in non-Jewish society, such as Disraeli, Sarah Bernhardt, Marx, and Trotsky – who served in the antisemite's eyes as symbols of ascendent and inimical Jewry, "the different and the alien." That is to say, the antisemites represented as the embodiment of Judaism and as its leaders, people of total or partial Jewish origin, at times even those not at all of Jewish origin, who did not see themselves as Jews, and in truth were much closer to the

Gentile than the Jewish world. Baron Rothschild, the so-called "King of the Jews," was not deemed offensive in Gentile eyes because of his refusal to eat pheasant and snails. In fact, the life-style of members of the House of Rothschild had much more in common than not with that of their Gentile neighbors.

Similar to this is the matter of peculiarity. It was accepted among various antisemites that the peculiarity of Jews as opposed to non-Jews, Semites as opposed to Aryans, causes instinctive opposition, revulsion, and recoiling – all of which stem from "racial fear" (*Rassenangst*). However, it has already been proven that "racial fear," even in Nazi ideology, was not a real fear but a propaganda slogan. Had this been a phobia whose source was "racial dissimilarity," then those who subscribed to it would have distinguished between people according to objective criteria, that is tall, blond-haired, blue-eyed people would have been thought of as Aryan and short, dark-skinned people with long noses as Semites (and, according to jokes that were often told in the 1930s, a majority of Nazi leaders would have been classified as Semites). But devotees of the racial doctrine, supposedly repulsed by "the other," did not determine "race" according to biological properties but according to affiliation with religious congregations and by legal definitions. And that is yet another proof that "peculiarity" is not an unmediated reaction to a particular person or group but a social or cultural convention. Thus, it is difficult to exlain antisemitism on the basis of these attitudes which themselves demand explanation.

Furthermore, in connection with the attempt to explain antisemitism by means of socio-psychological hypotheses – even if we agree that potential aggression exists in individuals and groups, finding expression with respect to groups defined as "external" or "marginal" – the question still remains: Why does it assume such a constant and extreme form toward Jews? Explanations of this sort deal very little with the question of the Jews' specific character or even with their status in the surrounding society, and direct most of their attention to the psychological, social, or political structure of the surrounding majority of peoples. Such explanations from the outset turn Jews into a marginal or even casual element and, by doing so, make the problem one of explaining the phenomenon in the framework of world history rather than as a factor in Jewish history.

The widespread claim is that Jews, as a minority group dispersed among many countries, serve as a convenient outlet for the release of the majority peoples' tensions and anxieties. Those who argue so are not disturbed by a problem which is central from the standpoint of Jewish history, which is: What forges minorities in many countries into parts of a single body, and what then gives this conglomerate its sense of unity? As is known, there is no lack of tension and hatred between majority- and minority-groups in any given place, yet none of this has ever developed into a continuous and persistent phenomenon as has Jew-hatred over the course of its existence. An additional difficulty in explaining antisemitism as a function of Jewish dispersal is the fact that Jew-hatred existed in places where there were no Jews at all for hundreds of years, as in Spain after the expulsion, or in Muscovite Russia. In sum, one can say that these explanations miss the target in spite of the importance of the studies on which they are based. They explain the *exploitation* of the hatred for Jews by individuals or groups in psychological or social distress, or for the sake of attaining political objectives, but do not grapple with the factors and causes involved in the *genesis* of this hatred.

3. Socio-economic and Religious Theories

Perhaps those scholars are correct who argue that tension between non-Jews and Jews does not stem primarily from the psychological make-up of individuals or from socio-psychological factors, but from real socio-economic causes such as competition, conflicts or interest, and so forth. According to this approach, the conflict that prevails, for instance, between the working or peasant class and their exploiters gives rise to antagonism between the former and the Jews because the latter belong to the parasitic and exploitative classes. The hatred of the middle class for the Jews who are merchants and middlemen, finds its basis in the competitive relationship with the urban elements. The same can be said for the hatred of the upper classes toward the Jewish plutocracy of the nineteenth century, those newcomers who used to be described as "pushing their way to the head of the line" in order to grab positions of influence. All in all, antisemitism is an expression of the real social tension that exists between Jews and other classes.

The problem with this explanation is that in spite of the conflicts between various classes, they have stood united in their hatred for the Jews who in almost no situation appear as allies of a non-Jewish group. Therefore, it is doubtful that these classes would have distinguished the Jews as their enemies merely from the standpoint of their interests had there not been a deeply rooted image of the Jews as an undesirable group. Moreover, despite the supposedly realistic nature of this approach, the facts contradict its basic supposition that Jews constituted a class of exploiters. This view was disseminated in the nineteenth century just when the pauperization of the Jewish masses was growing greatly not just in Eastern Europe but even in Central and Western Europe – as Jews moved from service and brokerage occupations to physical labor; and a class of Jewish workers came into being (in Eastern Europe and in immigration centers) which played an active role in Jewish society. Moreover, that the negative image of the Jew is antecedent to the social class factor is demonstrated by the fact that adherents of this approach do not see anything wrong in an overall increase in the number of lawyers, scientists, or artists, whereas a rise in the number of Jewish practitioners of these same professions represents an alleged danger to society in that it distorts society's character, upsets the social equilibrium, and so on.

The failure of the above-mentioned explanations led some scholars back to the traditional, time-honored explanation, that is, to the basic conflict between

Judaism and Christianity. From the very start, Christianity appeared on the historical stage as a negation of Judaism and, when it attained power in affairs of State, it turned opposition to Judaism and oppression of the Jews into an official slogan. It pushed Jews to the margins of society, forcing them into economic activity and a social class that aroused their neighbors' hatred. There is no doubt that this argument has a good deal of truth to it despite the fact that Jew-hatred – both literary and popular – preceded the advent of Christianity. Not a few of the early Christians bore it within themselves as a result of their pagan upbringing. However, Christian Jew-hatred is only one component of a multifaceted phenomenon, decisive proof being the fact that antisemitism did not lessen with the decline of Christianity's influence on government, culture, or society. One can even say that the opposite is true: that the strengthening of modern antisemitism was concomitant with the decline of the influence of religious belief, and that the antisemitic movement won its successes through secular and, at times, anti-Christian arguments.

4. Theory of Intrinsic Antisemitism

We conclude with an additional explanation, one that is traditionally popular among antisemites who see the cause of antisemitism in the Jews themselves. So claimed Servatius, Eichmann's attorney during the trial; and Dostoevsky who, in his famous article on the Jewish question, asked: Why has everyone always hated the Jews? Can some general meaning be imputed to this phenomenon? After all, we are speaking of societies that have existed throughout history, from the Hellenistic era up to the present time. The peoples who persecuted the Jews had different social systems, cultures, and governments, yet common to all was their hatred of the Jews. The only possible explanation for this is that the cause of antisemitism is inherent in the Jews themselves: in their way of life, law, and deeds. The Jews have always persevered in their historic existence as a socio-religious group, the majority of them abstaining from intermingling with Gentiles and rejecting assimilation. During various periods in history, Jews appeared as the competitors of non-Jews and claimed spiritual supremacy. According to the doctrine of election, they saw themselves as bearers of the religion of truth, of supreme ethics. As a result, the Gentile world reacted adversely by withdrawing from them, and eventually looked upon the Jews with revulsion.

There is nothing surprising in the fact that a socio-religious group possessing separate goals would arouse hatred and opposition. But it is difficult to accept this explanation. If antisemitism had been an instinctive revulsion toward the Jewish people or an unmediated reaction to them, the acceptance of Jews by the surrounding society would not have been possible. Moreover, how was it that many countries and groups in Christian Europe declared the Jews' integration and their equality as an accepted legal and social principle?

Let us compare the status of the Jews – their occupational distribution and cultural level – at the end of the eighteenth century and at the end of the nine-teenth (or beginning of the twentieth) century. We will see one of the great success stories of European (and perhaps even American) history. This is the story of a marginal group cut off from society by being engaged in a limited number of occupations and by living in areas which geographically and culturally were remotely situated; a group which was thus denied access to the surround-ing world (an access which for the most part it did not even desire). In the course of one hundred years, the Jews become a group whose members reside, to a great degree, in the large cosmopolitan centers of the world and occupy a respectable place in several important areas of modern society: in economic life, scientific and artistic creation, political activity, and so on. Had this recoiling of the Gentile from the Jew really been a decisive factor in their relations, it would be difficult to explain this sort of development which did indeed take place in the nineteenth century.

Therefore, there can be no substance to the simplistic ideas advanced by antisemites and Jews alike who claim that the very existence of the Jewish people arouses the Gentiles' hatred, or to sayings such as "Esau hates Jacob" or "the eternal hatred for the Eternal People." They are contradicted by the very course of Jewish history. It is a fact that many Europeans were prepared to ignore the Jews' religious and social peculiarities and accept them in their society. There are examples of aid and friendship toward Jews, or philosemit-ism, and even sacrifice for their sake. In sum, the popular explanations of the causes of antisemitism are based on a partial or limited perception of this com-plex phenomenon. Moreover, most of these explanations derive from the assumption that modern antisemitism is a recent development, and thus fail to stress sufficiently its context of prolonged and complex relations between Jews and non-Jews – that is, its context of a very long heritage of cultural variance and socio-religious conflicts.

5. The Historical Approach

The conclusion is, therefore, that an investigation of the causes of antisemit-ism cannot be attempted without first discussing the hatred of Jews in terms of its historical development. As a point of departure one must ask: When did the special adverse attitude to Jews first appear, not merely as a conflict between tribes or nations, but as a fundamental and conceptual denial of their worth? An attempt to answer this question brings us back to the Hellenistic Era when a widespread diaspora came into being – either as a result of immigration or proselytism – and a monotheistic minority took its place among the nations as a fixed factor and, in the course of time, as a competitor. This religious conflict and competition, together with the difference in life-style and social and ethical values, created the basis for the rejection of the Jews. In order to justify this hostility, an attempt was made to prove the superiority of the polytheistic majority's convictions and social doctrines. The advent of Christianity as a monotheistic religion only changed the form of the competition and the character of the conflict. As already mentioned, it was not Christianity that determined the primary patterns of the fundamentally negative attitude toward the Jews, in spite of the fact that from a theological point of view, the polemic against the Jews served as a vital basis for Christianity, more so than for any other religion or culture.

In the struggle to increase its influence, Christianity began to exploit the hostility to Judaism already widespread in Greco-Roman society in order to win support and popularity among the very extensive circles in which scorn or opposition to Judaism were already deeply rooted. In the writings of several Church Fathers – canonists as well as schismatics – the denial of the Jews' religious and cultural values became the central motif. They devoted great effort to locating defects in the Jewish people, finally portraying Jews as the sum total of all negative characteristics. As Christianity spread among the people of Europe, the clergy became the bearers of the religious, cultural, and ethical values of the entire people and consolidators of an educational network. Thus the negative stereotype of the Jews, crystallized in their writings and sermons, became the cultural "baggage" of medieval Europe. Moreover, because their method of transmitting cultural assets was based on rote memorization and reliance on established authorities, this negative stereotype became embedded in Christian Europe's consciousness and a central image in its ideational and conceptual world, finding expression in theological writings, sermons, the plastic arts, drama, and ballads. Thus the negative stereotype penetrated geographical and cultural areas where there were no Jews and no basis for real human relationships.

It is worth noting that just as new features were added to the existing stereotype in the time of the Church Fathers – the Jews being portrayed as unscrupulous, as deicides, and foresaken by God – so, at the height of the Middle Ages, were added usury, black magic, and ties with the Devil. A study of the stereotype's individual components as they changed over the course of time would be a worthwhile project. This is especially important for the transition from the Middle Ages to the Modern Era with respect to the changes that came about under the influence of cultural and religious transformations in sixteenth and seventeenth century Europe. Looking at the image of the Jew in theological and polemical literature, in sermons, plays, fiction, and the plastic arts, one realizes that certain features of the medieval image had been cast off. Nonetheless, the basic image remained the same, the only difference being that its characteristics were better adapted to the ideas of the Modern Era. Indeed, the Europeans – in particular, the enlightened Europeans – continued to bear the negative stereotype of the Jew in their consciousness, and if certain features had become blurred with the passage of time, others came to replace them.

It is clear that, in itself, the persistence of the negative stereotype in the European consciousness is not enough to explain Jew-hatred as an active social phenomenon in the Modern Era. We must also consider an added factor: the justification and rationalization of this same negative image. Because of the intellectual and ethical change in values and the antitradition revolt which saw in human reason the ultimate criterion for determining humankind's relation to nature and society, the negative image found itself in need of moral and ideological justification and explication if it was to persist. In the Hellenistic Era, too, there had been attempts to seek a justification of this attitude in the Jews' self-segregation and isolation which marked them as *odium generis humani*. In the Middle Ages, the crime of deicide, which bore eternal punishment, provided this justification against the enemies of Christianity. But one should consider that another prejudice also played a role in this process: the suspicion of Jews as potential traitors ever ready to deliver state secrets of the Christian nations to the Mongols, Arabs, or Turks.

In the Modern Era the accent has shifted to the "instinctive feeling of revulsion," that is, to the feeling of aversion to the alien Jew or to the social protest of the "exploited masses." Those who relied on historical studies argued that over the course of European history, Jews were parasites exploiting their fellows and living at the expense of others. This sort of argument began to appear toward the end of the 1870s in the German ecclesiastical press[9] and in the 1880s, as in Karl Buecher's study of Frankfurt.[10] With the spread of social Darwinism and the concepts of biologic determinism, the justification shifted to the sphere of the natural sciences, as if antisemitism apparently revealed the basic conflict between two elements, the Aryan and Semitic races. That is to say, this time, a supposedly scientific justification and explanation was found for the ancient negative image of the Jew.

An additional factor which explains the influence of Jew-hatred, one which converted it into an active force in modern antisemitism, is the deliberate exploitation of the negative stereotype in the political arena for political and social ends. This was made possible by the great transformation that took place in European society during the second half of the nineteenth century when the importance of ideological movements arose in the political arena. It is true that in the past, antisemitic elements and the negative stereotype were exploited by the ruling class, the clergy, and the burghers, to attain various political objectives: in the struggles that took place in the Middle Ages and the beginning of the Modern Era between Church and Crown, in the cities' struggle for freedom, and during the Reformation. However, this became a widely used weapon only in the Modern Era when a majority of European countries adopted democratic political practices thus giving considerable influence to political parties and their programs; and when ordinary people, in their quest for a supposedly rational ideology to guide their daily behavior, were given the possibility of increasing their self-esteem through scorn and hatred for the Jews. It is worth noting that radicals were no exception, earning a prominent position among those who exploited the stereotype and the ideology which justified it. As with other ideological problems, a positive correlation exists between the intensity of antisemitism and the degree of its exploiters' extremism, whether of the left or right.

In conclusion, let us say that in order to understand antisemitism in all its aspects one must take three factors into account: (1) its historical roots and character as it developed over the course of time; (2) the rationalization and justification of the existing negative image; (3) its deliberate exploitation for political and social purposes. Because of the nature of modern society, not only has the use of the stereotype not diminished, but in fact its exploitation is on the increase. With the growing influence of the mass media, one cannot reasonably expect it will be otherwise. It is only natural that people today, exposed to an incessant stream of information with which they cannot possibly cope adequately, will attempt to bring order to this confusion by using stereotypes. In any case, the discussion of antisemitism in terms of its historical development is essential if we are to understand this very significant phenomenon.

Notes

1. Eva G. Reichmann, *Hostages of Civilization: The Social Sources of National-Socialist Anti-Semitism* (London, 1950).
2. Hannah Arendt, *The Origins of Totalitarianism* (New York, 1956).
3. Idem, *Eichmann in Jerusalem* (New York, 1963).
4. In Hebrew, *Knesset* 8(1944):46–60. Now also in his collected studies, Historical Writings (Heb.), IV (Jerusalem, 1978), pp.175–192.
5. Simon Dubnow in *Nationalism and History: Essays on Old and New Judaism*, ed. Koppel S. Pinson (New York, 1970), pp. 328–331.
6. D. J. Levinson, "The Study of Anti-Semitic Ideology," in T. W. Adorno *et al.*, *The Authoritarian Personality* (New York, 1950), pp.57–101;
7. For example, Perez F. Bernstein, *Jew-Hate as a Sociological Problem* (New York, 1961).
8. B. Netanyahu, "Antisemitism," *Encyclopaedia Hebraica* (Heb.), 4 (Jerusalem, 1952).
9. Cf.: L. Erler, "Historische-kritische Uebersicht der national-oekonomischen und social-politischen Literatur," *Archiv fuer katholisches Kirchenrecht* 42–48 (1879–1882).
10. Karl Buecher, *Die Bevoelkerung von Frankfurt am Main im 14 und 15 Jahrhundert* (Tuebingen, 1886), pp.526–601.

2

Antisemitism in Rome

MENAHEM STERN

1. Introduction

There are various aspects to the relationships between Rome and the Jews throughout history. As early as the sixties of the second century B.C.E., in the very earliest stages of the Hasmonean Revolt, a pattern of regular political relationships was established between Judaea and Rome. During this period, Rome was the friendly power which offered its assistance to the Jews in their effort to remove the yoke of Seleucid rule. Judah the Maccabee sent representatives to Rome and the first treaty was drawn between Judaea, in its state of revolt, and the Roman Republic (161 B.C.E.), which was already the rising power in the Mediterranean world, casting its shadow over political developments in the Eastern Mediterranean Basin. In 1 Maccabees, chapter 8, we still hear echoes of the naive enthusiasm of the Jews at the show of force exercised by Rome against world powers, whereas a Roman historian of the Augustan period saw the establishment of the first ties between Rome and Judaea as granting legitimacy to the establishment of a Jewish State, as almost a grant of independence to the Jews by the Romans: "When they (the Jews) revolted against Demetrius, they sought the friendship of the Romans and, of all the peoples of the East, they were the first who gained their freedom" (Justin, Epitome 36, 3:9). This first treaty was ongoing and Judah's three heirs renewed it.

A hundred years later things had changed completely, after Rome's expansionist policy had been revived and Pompey annexed Syria. This sealed the fate of Judaea. Jerusalem, unlike Antiochia, strongly opposed the annexation, and in 63 B.C.E. the Temple Mount was stormed and taken by the Roman legions. Active opposition in the first stage of the conquest was a widespread and natural phenomenon in other lands as well, but in Judaea it continued in the repeated rebellions of the fifties of the first century B.C.E. and with Mattathias Antigonus joining the Parthian invaders (40-37 B.C.E.). The establishment of the Province of Judaea (6 C.E.) and the Roman census taken by Quirinius, the legate (governor) of Syria, caused new ferment. During the rule of Pontius Pilate

(26-36 C.E.), spirits became most heated and in the days of the last procurators before the rebellion there were continuous disturbances. In the year 66 the rebellion erupted which was to become open and protracted warfare. For four years this war kept the best of the Roman forces occupied in Judaea with Vespasian and Titus personally involved.

Their victory in this war was considered the greatest military exploit of the Flavius dynasty, as attested by the various allusions to it in the Latin poetry of that generation; a famous inscription of 80 C.E. in honor of Titus hails him as the one who subjugated the Jewish people and the city of Jerusalem – something which no general, king, or people had ever before accomplished.

The Bar Kokhba Revolt was certainly no less fierce than the Great Rebellion and constituted the most serious military effort of the Roman Empire in the days of Hadrian. Reinforcements were summoned from all parts of the Empire and the best Roman generals took part in the war which lasted three and a half years. The historian Dio Cassius (69, 14:3) emphasized the fact that in his announcement to the Senate the Emperor omitted the customary formula "I and my legions are well." In the course of the actions the Roman legions had suffered heavy losses, one legion (the 22nd "Deiotariana" legion) was completely wiped out, and memory of the Roman losses in the revolt was still alive a generation later (as evidenced by Fronto in the days of Marcus Aurelius).

Undoubtedly the Roman authorities and Roman public opinion were alert to the continuous struggle against the Roman Empire in Judaea. This phenomenon was absolutely exceptional, especially in the Hellenistic East which showed little rebellious military activity against Rome in the period after the war of Mithradates. To be sure, here and there in the mountains of Asia Minor there were some military actions against tribes which did not willingly accept Roman rule; the prolonged resistance to Roman rule by the Greeks of Alexandria, which never came to military expression but was expressed in the so-called "Acts of the Pagan Martyrs of Alexandria," is also known; but none of this is comparable to what took place in Judaea. In the West, too, we hear of clashes and rebellions but primarily in the early stages of the Roman domination or on the outskirts of the Empire. In most instances, the provinces of the Latin West became the main components of Roman civilization even though, here too, there is a difference between the Spanish provinces, Africa and Gallia Narbonensis, on the one hand, and Northern Gaul and Britain on the other.

The continued military clashes between Rome and the Jews, then, emphasized all the more the uniqueness of the Province of Judaea and its population within the Roman Empire and Greco-Roman civilization. The Romans were not blind to the fact that the instigators of the rebellions and the wars drew their inspiration from the sense of Jewish uniqueness; the faith that the East would be victorious and that leaders coming from Judaea would rule the world (Tacitus, *Historiae* 5, 13: *"ut valesceret Oriens profectique Iudaea rerum potirentur"*) was an important factor in the outbreak of the Great Rebellion. This was the Latin formulation of the Jewish Messianic belief.

2. Jewish Communities in the Roman Empire

Relations between Rome and Judaea were certainly influenced by the existence of a large Jewish diaspora throughout the Roman Empire and particularly in its eastern sectors. In the cities of the large, wealthy, Roman provinces – Asia, Syria, and Egypt – there were masses of Jews, organized in their communities, living according to their customs, and demanding privileges based upon their religious tradition and a way of life molded by that tradition. The Hellenistic world, as well as the Oriental world which preceded it, was accustomed to the existence of well-organized groups of ethnic communities in foreign lands. Much was written about the concept of the *politeuma* in the Hellenistic world; the Jewish community itself was a *politeuma*, for example in Alexandria and Berenice, or else it took on some other organizational form acceptable in the Hellenistic world. However, along with the great spread of the Jewish communities throughout the Mediterranean world, their very close ties with the religio-national center in Judaea should also be emphasized. This connection was institutionalized to a great extent and was recognized by the Roman government which allowed the *half-shekel* monies to be forwarded to the Temple in Jerusalem. Already in the Hellenistic period the Jewish communities in the various kingdoms had gained the freedom to worship God and the right to refrain from participating in the official State religion. The struggle for the rights of the organized Jewish community and of the Jews within the framework of the Hellenistic cities runs as a scarlet thread throughout the history of the Jews in the Hellenistic-Roman East.

The religious and social separatism of the Jews was an argument used by their opponents. From the standpoint of Rome, the matter was sometimes complicated. On the one hand, the Romans were interested in the support of the many Jews in the eastern lands and thus they preserved the *status quo* which had existed before the Roman domination. On the other hand, it must be remembered that the Hellenized affluent classes were the mainstay of Roman rule in the East and the situation at times was most delicate as, for example, in Egyptian Alexandria about which one can learn from the famous letter of Claudius (CPJ. No. 153). In the cities of Asia Minor and Greece itself, the arrangement of Augustus continued to exist for centuries, whereas in Egypt, Cyrenaica, and Cyprus we are witness to the outbreak of one of the greatest catastrophes in Jewish history.

3. Greek Literature

Rome's culture was, in great measure, bilingual – equally Latin and Greek. The Romans were able to learn about the Jews very specifically from contact in their everyday life, with concentrations of Jewish population in the various countries where the Romans were active. But for anything having to do with scientific knowledge about the character of Judaism, about the origins of the

Jewish religion, about the personality of Moses, the history of the Jews, and the nature of their country, there was ready material available from the Greek sources. One fundamental fact must be stressed: In their great creative age, from Homer to Demosthenes and Aristotle, classical Greek literature and philosophy did not deal with the Jews and Judaism, and hence even in the later generations, anti-Jewish points of view could not be attributed to the giants of Greek philosophical literature. The classical literature which could provide ammunition for the later generations was the Latin, not the Greek. Jews of the Hellenistic period sometimes described Pythagoras and Plato as disciples of Moses and as influenced by the Jewish Torah, but no modern antisemite has attributed anti-Jewish ideas to the Greek spiritual giants of the classical period.

Greek literature, after Alexander, continued to be interested in ethnography and the history of the foreign peoples, but this interest was significantly limited: the Greeks revealed themselves as being neither willing nor ready to learn foreign languages and use them as primary sources in describing these peoples. Generally, they preferred mythological constructions which combined the histories of the various peoples within the Greek tradition with the authentic traditions of the peoples themselves.

Already in the first stages of the development of the literature of the Hellenistic period, as we may learn from the fragments of the writings of Theophrastus, Hecataeus, Clearchus, and Megasthenes, there are references to Jews. The picture which emerges is basically positive. The Jews are described as a group of people embodying the wisdom of the East and whose order is based upon principles which match the best aspirations of Greek thought. In time, the image underwent a change which can be particularly connected to the development which began in Ptolemaic Egypt and is reflected in the remnants of the Greco-Egyptian literature which have reached us via the *Contra Apionem (Against Apion)* of Josephus.

Likewise, it seems that the decrees of Antiochus and the wars of the Hasmoneans against the Seleucid Kingdom and the strongholds of Hellenistic civilization also contributed their share. Egypt was a country with an anti-Jewish tradition. We already hear of an anti-Jewish outbreak in that country in the Persian period. We have information about tension between a number of Ptolemaic kings and the Jews; also a papyrus from the first half of the first century B.C.E. containing a letter of a man named Heracles, in which the following sentence appears: "You know that they detest the Jews" (CPJ No. 141).

The account of the Exodus from Egypt, related in the Book of Exodus, was made available to the Greek reader by the *Septuagint* and perhaps reached the Egyptian priests even earlier. This account demanded an Egyptian rebuttal and the Egyptian priests rose to the challenge. The first name known to us of the anti-Jewish polemicists is Manetho (third century B.C.E.). Manetho described the Exodus in a hostile manner, connected the Jewish Patriarchs to the Hyksos and emphasized their hatred for Egypt, her religion, and her temples. A similar version is to be found in Chaeremon of the first century C.E., and takes on an extremely anti-Jewish tone with Lysimachus, whose exact time we do not know, and with Apion. It is also quoted by enemies of the Jews in the entourage of Antiochus Sidetes, who also refer to the Exodus story. It is brought in at the beginning of Book 34 of *The Historical Library* of Diodorus of Sicily.

Manetho was an Egyptian priest who wrote the history of Egypt in Greek; Chaeremon was also an Egyptian priest but of a new breed. He was also a Stoic philosopher, thought to have been one of Nero's instructors. Apion was rooted in the Egyptian tradition, on the one hand, but, on the other, he was also an Homeric exegete active in Rome and in Greece. Apion even served as one of the Alexandrian delegation at the time of Gaius Caligula whereas Chaeremon represented Alexandria at the beginning of Claudius's time.

From this, then, one may draw the far-reaching conclusion that as early as the beginning of the Roman period, the Greco-Egyptian and the Greco-Alexandrian approaches were in effect identical. Yet is is interesting to note that the Greco-Alexandrian historian Timagenes – who was not of the Egyptian priestly circles – in one of the few fragments which have remained of his writings which relates to the Jews, revealed an objective attitude to the Hasmonean King, Aristobulus I. He did not even deplore the forced conversion of the Itureans by the King. Still, it seems that he included in his historical work the hostile Greco-Egyptian version of the origin of the Jews alongside other more sympathetic versions. In any case, Egypt was the birthplace of most of the traditions hostile to the Jews. The Jew-hatred which characterizes the "Acts of the Pagan Alexandrian Martyrs" corroborates the impression one receives from the remains of the Greco-Egyptian literary tradition reflected in the *Contra Apionem*. These Greco-Egyptian traditions easily found their way to Rome.

4. The Settlement in Rome

The growth of the Jewish settlement in Rome and even in other places in Italy can be traced in general outline. The first source about Jews in Rome deals with events of 139 B.C.E. and refers to the expulsion of people who were spreading the Jewish faith in Rome (Valerius Maximus 1, 3:3). The expulsion of the Jewish propagandists was not an unprecedented step in the Roman history of those generations. The Roman authorities also took similar actions against the penetration of other alien cults into the city of Rome (*the Pomerium*) and also against other phenomena which in the eyes of the Roman administration endangered the welfare and stability of Roman society. Thus, for example, the popularity achieved by the astrologers in Rome was a thorn in the flesh of the authorities and the astrologers were also expelled in the same year as the Jews. The rhetors and the philosophers had been expelled earlier, in 161 B.C.E., and, in 154 B.C.E., Epicurean philosophers had been banished from Rome. It may be that the atmosphere steeped in the social tension which had begun to undermine the structure of Roman society in those years also influenced the expulsions.

As the capital of the Mediterranean world, Rome had attracted Jews even before Pompey took Jerusalem (63 B.C.E.). When Cicero made his defense of Flaccus (59 B.C.E.) there were masses of Jews residing in Rome. Julius Caesar was considered the great benefactor of the Jews and when he banned associations, he explicitly excluded the Jews from that ban. We hear of large numbers of Jews in Rome from the period of Augustus. Philo even singles out Augustus for praise for having set an alternative time for the distribution of money and corn should the general distribution happen to fall on the Sabbath (Philo, *On the Embassy to Gaius* 158). During the days of Augustus a number of synagogues were established in Rome. One was even named for him, and a second – for his son-in-law, Marcus Agrippa.

However, in the days of the Emperor Tiberius (19 C.E.) there was a regression. The immoral behavior of the Egyptian priests in sexual matters and some corruption in financial matters by Jews who had misappropriated silver and gold which had been dedicated to the Temple by a female convert, served the Senate as a pretext for deciding on a series of steps against the Egyptian and Jewish worships (Josephus, *Antiquities* 18, 65–84; Tacitus, *Annals* 2, 85; Suetonius, *Life of Tiberius* 36; Dio Cassius 57, 18:5a). The Egyptian priests were crucified and the holy objects of Isis were burned. The Jews were punished in a different way: four thousand of military age, of the freedmen class, were sent to the island of Sardinia to fight brigands. Jews and converts alike were driven from Rome but the results of the expulsion were not felt for long, and after a while masses of Jews were in Rome once more.

Claudius (41–54 C.E.), like Augustus before him, was interested in fostering the ancient Roman religion and its tradition, in putting a halt to its corruption, and its being overshadowed by the alien worships. Thus, as one loyal to the Roman tradition, Claudius tried to revive the ancient Etruscan lore of the *Haruspices*, outlawed the Gallic Druids, and took steps against the spread of astrology. It seems, therefore, that Jewish religious propaganda was not to his liking from the outset. He was especially angered by the spread of Christianity in Rome, accompanied by the appearance of Christian preachers and rifts and quarrels among the Jews of Rome themselves. Basically one should accept the version of Dio Cassius (60, 6:6) who argued against those who were of the opinion that Claudius expelled the Jews from Rome. He explained that the Emperor became convinced that the difficulties he would face in doing so would be too great and was content merely to forbid the existence of organizations. In any case, the growth of the Jewish community in Rome did not cease because of the events at the beginning of Claudius's reign. Moreover, we hear no more of any attempts whatsoever to expel the Jews, in whole or in part, from the Empire's capital.

Nero's reign brought no basic changes in the policy of the Emperors toward the Jews. We read that Poppea Sabina, the Emperor's wife, even evidenced a sympathy for the Jews and their religion. With Paul's arrival in Rome, in Nero's day, and the spread of Christianity among Jews and non-Jews, the Roman government gradually realized that it had here a new faith originating from Judaea whose aim was to undermine the foundations of the existing order and traditional Roman society. The destruction of Jerusalem by the Flavian dynasty brought many Jewish captives to Rome. At the same time, a number of Jewish personalities settled in Rome, such as the historian Josephus Flavius who wrote his works in Rome. The legal status of the Jews in Rome was not damaged. It should also be pointed out that, unlike Egypt and Cyrenaica, Rome and the other cities of Italy never served as foci of armed Jewish opposition nor, similarly, was there ever a pogrom in Rome or Italy as there was in Alexandria (38 c.e.) or in Seleucia on the Tigris.

It is sometimes assumed that the period of Domitian (81–96 c.e.) was a more difficult one for the Jews than the reign of the Flavian dynasty which preceded it, because of the strict collection of the "Jew tax" and the persecution of members of the Roman aristocracy, including some very close to the Emperor himself, because of their tending toward Judaism.

The number of Jews in Rome was relatively large. Josephus uses the figure of 8000 as the number of the Jews of Rome demonstrating before Augustus after the death of Herod. The number of Jews exiled in the days of Tiberius, in 19 c.e., reached 4000. One may then estimate that the Jewish population of Rome came to some tens of thousands, perhaps 50,000 out of a general population of 750,000 or 800,000. They were organized around the synagogues in their various quarters but, first and foremost, in Trastevere on the right bank of the river Tiber.

We know very little of the economic situation of the Jews of Rome and Italy in the first centuries of their settlement there. The existence of Jewish poor and impoverished is reflected in the *Epigrams* of Martial and the *Satires* of Juvenal. Very little about their means of earning a livelihood emerges from either the inscriptions or the literary sources. There must certainly have been not a few artisans among the Jews but information on this is scant. Of Aquila the Jew we read that he was a tent-maker by profession. In the inscriptions there appear a Jew who is a butcher and another defined as an artist (painter). A Jewish actor, Aliturus, was of assistance to Josephus (*Vita* 16) and another actor appears in Martial (*Epigrams* 7, 82). Nevertheless, there is no denying that there were well-to-do people among the Jews of Rome and Italy, as is attested by some of the graves and inscriptions in Rome, carved by professional craftsmen. One may assume that the affluent Jew from Ostia, Gaius Justus, of whom we learn from one of the recently published inscriptions, was not the only slave-holder. It is a certainty that the sources of the period bear no specific reference to the wealth of the Jews nor criticism of their becoming affluent. Jewish indigents and beggars were a target for the contemptuous barbs of the Jew-haters more than were the wealthy Jews.

5. References to Jews in Latin Literature

In the first century B.C.E., for the first time in Latin literature, there appears a reaction to Jews and Judaism in two of the most outstanding representatives of Latin culture in the last days of the Republic: Varro and Cicero. A fragment of what Varro wrote of Jews in his large work *Antiquitates Rerum Humanarum et Divinarum* has been preserved by Augustine. Varro identified the Jewish God with Jupiter, head of the Roman deities, and compared the Jews to the ancient Romans in that, like the ancient Romans, the Jews, too, worshipped their God without a statue or likeness. Whoever invented the statues for the gods deprived people of the fear of heaven. Varro's words dovetailed with the traditional Stoic criticism of worshipping idols and images. In this Varro reminds one of the Greek geographer and historian, Strabo. We do not know who served as Varro's source for this view, Posidonius or perhaps Antiochus of Ascalon.

Cicero differed from Varro. The Jews do not appear in any of his philosophical works. He did not refer to them in his voluminous correspondence, and only called Pompey "Hierosolymarius" because he captured the city. The Jews appear only twice: in his oration (59 B.C.E.) "In Defense of Flaccus" (28:66–69) and in his oration "On the Consular Provinces" (5:10–12). In both instances, the Jews are in the camp of Cicero's opponents. The first oration was in defense of his friend Flaccus who served as propraetor of the province of Asia and was accused of improper behavior by the cities of the province. The Jewish representatives joined with Flaccus's accusers because he had confiscated the "half-shekel" monies destined for the Temple in Jerusalem. Cicero defended Flaccus in two ways: by intending to prove that what Flaccus did was not against the law and by stressing the failings of his opponents. The Jewish religion he defined as "superstition" and explained to the panel of judges that Pompey refrained from plundering the Temple not out of any feeling of respect for the Jews, the enemies of Rome, but because of the kind of person he was, and out of political considerations. Cicero concluded his outburst by emphasizing the difference between the Jewish religion and the traditional institutions of Rome and by recalling the war which the Jews had recently waged against the Romans.

To evaluate the anti-Jewish outburst in Cicero's speech properly, we must attend to its juridical context and the lawyers' practice of defaming their opponents as the situation warranted. In other speeches he had directed his slurs against the Sardinians or the Gauls, and in the *Pro Flacco* oration he dealt this way with the witnesses from Asia Minor, the Phrygians, the Mysians, the Carians, and the Lydians, who were not treated any more sympathetically than the Jews. It should be noted that Cicero himself pointed out the difference between his true opinions and those he expressed as an attorney (*Pro Cluentio* 139). Nevertheless, it is of interest to note two points in his charges against the Jews, points later repeated by other writers in the Greco-Roman world:

their blatant unity (*concordia*) and the fact of their political-military failure which proves that the gods are not favorably disposed to them. In his oration "On the Consular Provinces," Cicero charged the proconsul of Syria, Gabinius, with having turned the *publicani* over to the Jews and the Syrians, "peoples born for slavery." Hence we know that in that generation many slaves came from Judea and Syria, but there is not the slightest indication that his comments against the Jews were motivated by the competition prevalent between the Jewish business classes and those of the Roman equestrian class whose interests Cicero himself represented.

The poets and historians of the Augustan period were aware of the Jews' presence in Rome. Tibullus and Ovid knew of the Sabbath. Horace knew of the Sabbath and circumcision and even pointed out the missionary zeal which characterized the Jews. He also laughed at the tendency of the Jews to believe everything (*Sermones* 1, 5:96–104). As we can learn from Livy's epitomes (*The Periochae*), the historian, in his great Roman history dealt with the capture of Jerusalem in the days of Pompey and Antony, and while doing so described the Jewish religion and the Temple in Jerusalem. Like Varro, he too was impressed by the fact that the Jews made no statue or image of their God and did not think that God has a bodily form.

Livy was the national historian of Rome from the period of Augustus. His contemporary, Pompeius Trogus, on the other hand, was the universal historian who described the world outside of Rome, the world of the Macedonian-Hellenistic kingdoms. In the 36th book of his great history, the *Historiae Philippicae*, he devoted a lengthy, detailed discussion to the clash with Antiochus Sidetes, which has come down to us in Justin's summary. Preserved for us here is the fullest discussion of the Jews in the Latin literature before Tacitus. Most scholars assume that Pompeius Trogus was dependent upon the large historical work of Timagenes, the Greco-Alexandrian historian who lived in the Rome of Augustus.

Pompeius Trogus described the origin of the Jewish nation and the geography of Judea and reviewed the development of the nation and its history from the Persian period to the struggle against the Seleucids. Three different sources are discernible: the Biblical one, the source which connects the origin of the Jewish nation and Damascus, and the third, hostile to the Jews in the spirit of the Greco-Egyptian tradition with which we are familiar from the time of Manetho onward. All of these components left their imprint on the work of Pompeieus Trogus who apparently was unsuccessful in combining the three to form a consistent picture. In any event, his description concludes with a sympathetic summary emphasizing the effectiveness of the Jewish order.

Pompeius Trogus's description can serve as an example of what a Roman intellectual of his time found fit to report about the Jews. In the arrangement of the material the description is somewhat similar to the more famous one of Tacitus. But the significance of this similarity is not necessarily that Tacitus drew upon Pompeius Trogus or even upon those same available sources used

ATA—B

by Pompeius Trogus in his day. There is also a basic difference in their approaches: Pompeius Trogus sounds basically objective whereas Tacitus sounds hostile. They both drew upon the same Greco-Hellenistic tradition but in a different spirit. One can clearly see the great difference in the atmosphere of Rome in the period of Augustus and that which characterized Rome in the time of Trajan.

Actually, the philosopher and writer Seneca (who died in 65 c.e.) is the first among those Latin authors whose views have been preserved who attacks the Jewish religion on principle. His approach is not even to be explained by special circumstances of any kind, such as affected the comments of Cicero. Seneca was very strongly opposed to the spread of the Oriental cults in the Roman world. He was angered by the fact that the customs of this sinful people, (the Jews) should have gained such great influence and been accepted throughout the world: the victors enacted the laws of the vanquished. He added that the Jews at least knew the sources of these customs whereas those who joined them did not as a rule know why they did what they were doing. He also criticized the custom of the Jewish Sabbath by which they waste a seventh of their lives. Elsewhere (*Epistulae Morales* 95:47) he even protests against the custom of lighting Sabbath candles because gods do not need them. There is a special significance to Seneca's criticism of the ceremonial Jewish religion which sounds like a response to the Jewish challenge of presenting the Jewish monotheistic faith as an abstract form of divine worship in step with philosophy (as in Josephus, *Contra Apionem* 2:190 ff.). Seneca presented Judaism as one of the superstitions characterized by a worship which is contrary to the philosophic concept of abstract religion.

Similar views were expressed by a contemporary of Seneca's, the great satirical poet Persius who was influenced by Stoic philosophy and championed exalted views of religious principles. He, too, saw in Judaism one of the superstitions which had come to Rome from the Orient. In his fifth satire (verses 176–184) he attacks Jewish customs as he did those of the Phrygians or the Egyptians.

Jew-hatred was perhaps more prominent in the authors of the Flavian period and reached its peak in some of the great authors of the time of Trajan and Hadrian. When the great rhetorician Quintilian (in the days of Domitian) wished to bring an example of city-founders who were infamous for concentrating in their cities people who brought a curse on their fellows, he recalled the founder of the Jewish *superstitio*, Moses, (*Institutio Oratoria* 3:7,21), whereas Pliny the Elder saw the Jews as a nation outstanding for its hatred of the gods (*Naturalis Historia* 13:46).

6. Tacitus

The historian Tacitus was the one who went farthest. In the fifth book of his *Histories* (written in the first decade of the second century c.e.), he included a

lengthy excursus on the Jews which is the most detailed description we have in
Latin literature of the origin of the Jewish people, its religion, history, and land.
As was the practice of the ancient historians, Tacitus deals with the Jews in the
context of the decisive military confrontation with them, the siege in the days
of Titus (*Histories* 5:2–13): "Since I have come to tell of the last days of the
famous city, I should tell you of its beginnings." Because of his fame as one of
the great figures of Latin culture, especially from the days of the Renaissance
onward, Tacitus's words received an extraordinary hearing.

Tacitus suggested a few versions of the origin of the Jews: Some were
neutral; one even praised them and sought to anchor their origin in the tradition
of the Homeric epic; while the last one was completely hostile. Apparently,
Tacitus transmitted six versions of the origin of the Jews and the development
of Judaism seriatim and, after citing them, even commented (paragraph 4) that
he is not responsible for their reliability, for example, "these practices, whatever the nature of their institution." However, the relatively great length of
the last version as compared to the other five, the abundance of its descriptive
material, the inclusion of etiological explanations, as well as the fact that Tacitus then moved directly to his own views – all of these gave this version
special weight as the one preferred by him. Basically this is the one we know
from the Greco-Egyptian tradition, and in some aspects Lysimachus most
approximated Tacitus in this version. Tacitus even presented the sixth version
as the one to which most authors subscribed. It contains the account of the
plague which broke out in Egypt and the advice which Bocchoris received from
the oracle to cleanse the kingdom and remove the people who hated the gods;
of the seizure of the leadership by Moses, and the practices he instituted to
strengthen his rule. These practices are the opposite of those of all other
human beings. What to us are the most sacred, are to them the most profane.
And conversely, what is impure in the eyes of others is to them permissible. In
the sanctuary he erected as a scared gift an image of the animal (the donkey)
which had been their guide and put an end to their wanderings and their thirst.
They offered up the ox as a sacrifice because the Egyptians worshipped Apis.
They abstained from eating pig as a reminder of the plague of leprosy transmitted by that animal.

Tacitus sketched the character of the Jewish nation in his generation and
specified that this was his opinion. He declared that all the dregs of humanity,
after detesting the religions of their fathers, would gather monies for the
Temple in Jerusalem and, as a result, the wealth of the Jews grew. Among
themselves they are faithful and merciful but towards others they evidence
animosity. They are different in their foods, enslaved to lust, do not marry
non-Jews, but among themselves nothing is forbidden. They instituted the
practice of circumcision in order to separate themselves from others. And
those who have taken on their practices also undergo circumcision. Those who
join them (the proselytes) have first become scornful of the gods, have detested their native land and ridiculed their close relatives. With these harsh

words Tacitus condemns the proselytizing movement which had brought many Romans to abandon their religion and society and join the Jews. Judaism is characterized by misanthropy and separatism, and the proselytes follow in the Jews' footsteps and cut their ties with Roman society. Tacitus was aware of the abstract Jewish monotheism and the refusal of the Jews to participate in the worship of the Emperor, but he confined himself to a description of the facts without expressing his own opinion of the phenomena. The comparison of Jewish practices and the Dionysus cult known from Plutarch, he rejected in disgust. However, his outlook was far from racial and he approved of King Antiochus' attempt to free the Jews of their superstitious faith and bestow Greek culture upon them though he was prevented from reforming the detested nation because of the Parthian War.

It is of interest to point out that in his description of Jewish history in the Province of Judaea under Roman rule, Tacitus did not deprecate the Jews for their rebellious character nor did he even see them as responsible for the Great Rebellion. The Roman procurators such as Felix or Florus bore a greater share of the blame. The Jews took up arms in the days of Gaius Caligula but they did so only after the Emperor ordered that the statue be brought into the Temple. The procurator, Felix, was brutal, steeped in lust, and "yet the patience of the Jews nevertheless continued until the time of the procurator Gaius Florus; in his day the war erupted" (Tacitus, *Histories* 5:10).

The *Annals* were written later, the last of them after the Jewish uprisings in the time of Trajan. But it is difficult to estimate the degree to which these events effected Tacitus' attitude toward the Jews. The loss of Jewish life was to him of very little import (*Annals* 2:85; *vile damnum*), however in his description of the disturbances in Judea during the procuratorships of Cumanus and Felix, he fixed the blame squarely upon the procurators and not upon the Jews (ibid. 12:54). In the famous chapter on the rise of Christianity (ibid. 15:44) he designated Judea as the land which is the origin of this scourge (*origo eius mali*) but did not add any comments about Judaism. It is clear that for him, as for Seneca and Juvenal, it was the spread of Judaism and its influence threatening the integrity of Roman society which counted. As far as he was concerned, this constituted a more significant danger than the military threat and the political nuisance the Jews were to the Roman Empire. The proselytism and the sympathy for Judaism in various circles were the factors goading the enmity of Tacitus more than the Jewish uprisings to which he was witness.

The greatest historian of the period was here complemented by the greatest of the Roman satirists, Juvenal. He expressed his wrath at the penetration of foreign elements which changed the face of the capital of the Empire; he could not bear the Greek atmosphere, and even less the Oriental, which had come to dominate Rome, and the fact that the Syrian Orontes was being poured into the Tiber (*Saturae* 3:60–63). He detested the *parvenu* Syrian and Egyptian and, like Tacitus, emphasized the misanthropy of the Jew and the deterioration of

Roman youth attracted to Judaism; "the father observes the Sabbath; then the son is circumcised" (ibid. 14:96–106).

Misanthropy was placed atop the list of Jewish characteristics by both Tacitus and Juvenal. In the works of Seneca, as in those of Tacitus and Juvenal, the spread of Judaism and the destruction of Roman society thereby are what prodded them to the attack. Horace, also, already knew of the enthusiastic proselytizing by the Jews, and their religious propaganda was a motive force in their expulsion from Rome both in 139 B.C.E. and in the days of Tiberius. It certainly is not accidental that antisemitism in Latin literature became fiercest in the period that Jewish penetration of the various levels of Roman society reached its peak. The influence of Judaism was felt not only in the eastern provinces of the Roman Empire and the royal courts in the East. It encompassed not only many members of the lower classes but even spread into the upper echelons of Roman society among men and women of the senatorial class, to the unhappiness of the conservatives and those loyal to Roman tradition. In the wake of Judaisim came Christianity which was to them, at first, indistinguishable from Judaism. Flavius Clemens, a relative of the Flavian dynasty emperors who was put to death by Domitian on the charge of slipping into the ways of Judaism, can serve as an outstanding example of Judaism's penetration into the highest strata of Roman society (*Dio Cassius* 67, 14:1–2).

After the Bar Kokhba Revolt, the hostility which had characterized the earlier period abated. The proselytizing movement weakened and Christianity replaced Judaism as the missionary faith fighting paganism and undermining the sacred Roman tradition. The spokesmen for the Greco-Roman civilization who fought Christianity, revealed an ambivalent attitude toward Judaism. On the one hand, they were prepared to recognize it as a national religion and, as such, a possible component of the existing civilization and order. They were even prepared to value the Jews' devotion and loyalty to the tradition of their fathers. On the other hand, in order to injure Christianity and do harm to its conceptual foundations, the guardians of the Greco-Roman civilization could not refrain from a polemic of principle against Judaism as expressed in the Bible. Furthermore, anti-Jewish motifs from the classical Latin literature also continued to appear in the later Latin literature (Rutilius Namatianus). To what extent the anti-Jewish tradition of the Christian Church at the beginning of the fifth century C.E. was influenced by the anti-Judaism of the classical tradition is another matter.

Undoubtedly, the anti-Judaism of the leading lights of the Latin culture of the Silver Age – Seneca, Quintilian, Tacitus, and Juvenal – was of greater significance to the following generations than the unrestrained anti-Jewish polemic of the representatives of the Greco-Egyptian tradition in Alexandria or the expressions and frame of mind of forgotten Greek authors in Syria or Asia Minor.

3

The Sages' Reaction to Antisemitism in the Hellenistic-Roman World

MOSHE DAVID HERR

1. Antisemitism in the Roman Empire

In the Midrash we find the following story:

> Said R. Pinhas: Two women prostitutes were quarreling with each other in Ashkelon. Said the one to the other: "If you do not leave here, for you look Jewish – I do not forgive or pardon you." After a while they became friendly again. Said the second to the first: "I forgive and pardon you for everything, but not for saying to me that I look Jewish."[1]

The instructive barb in this account is that it does not specify that it was indeed a Jewess – it may well have been a Gentile woman – who was insulted by the defamation that she looks Jewish. However, there are many proofs that "Jew" was an insulting term in the Roman Empire. One such will suffice here – the refusal of Vespasian and Titus to accept the honorific title of "Judaicus"[2] after having suppressed the great revolt and their victory in Judaea. For, unlike other titles such as "Africanus,"[3] "Asiaticus,"[4] "Britannicus,"[5] or "Germanicus,"[6] one who accepted that title was likely to be considered a Judaizer, with all of the negative connotations attached to it. Hence, we understand this to mean that "Jew(ess)" was an opprobrious epithet in the Roman Empire.

The Jews in the Roman Empire knew well what their Gentile contemporaries thought of them.[7] For that, they did not need to read the writings of the Greek Jew-haters (in Alexandria or Syria) or of the Roman ones. They could hear and register these things from the lips of any Gentile in the cities of the Land of Israel with mixed populations and, all the more so, from the Gentiles outside it. If they chanced to go into the theatres and circuses, they could see plays there, whose whole point was antisemitism.[8] Therefore, in the literature of the Sages

27

not only echoes of what was being said by the antisemites but even excellent imitations – both in form and content – of their writings. Proof of this is in the excursus of hatred in the *Targum Sheni* (lit. "Second Translation") to the *Book of Esther* (3:8), a sort of composition in itself – a monograph on the Jewish religion and the history of Israel – a carefully contrived collection of falsehoods and half-truths for defamatory purposes.[9]

A characteristic example of the polemic between the Jew-haters and the Jews can be found in the following dialogue:[10]

> A certain heretic said to Rabbi Judah the Prince: "We are better than you. Of you it is written: 'for Joab and all Israel remained there for six months, until he had cut off every male in Edom'[11] whereas you have been with us many years yet we have not done anything to you." He answered: "If you please, a student will join you (and give you the answer)." He was joined by R. Oshaia who said to him: "Because you do not know how to act – you would like to kill them all, but you don't rule over them; should you kill those you rule, you will be called a truncated kingdom." Replied the heretic: "By the Agape of Rome! With this (care) we lie down and with this we get up."

This is a reply to the Gentile's charge[12] that the Jews hate the human race – which exposed the truth. The Gentile admits that the Jews do not plan to eradicate humandkind but that it is the Gentiles, the Romans, who plan to destroy the Jewish people, and it is this thought which gives them sleepless nights.

The Sages were well aware of the real reasons for the hatred of Israel, including the charge that the Jews hate humankind; thus they relate:[13]

> It is like the king who married a matron. Said he to her: "Do not speak to your (former) companions; neither borrow from them nor lend to them.[14] Once, the king became angry with her and drove her from the palace. She went to all of her neighbours but they would not have her. [(So she returned to the palace and) the king said to her: "You have acted impudently (by coming back!)"] Replied she to him: "You are the one who caused this by saying: 'Do not borrow anything from your neighbours nor lend anything to them.' Had I lent to them and borrowed from them, one of them would have seen me in the house and (then) would they not have received me?!" . . . Said Israel to the Holy One, blessed be He: "Did you not cause this by telling us: 'neither shalt though make marriages with them: thy daughter thou shalt not give unto his son, nor shalt thou take his daughter unto thy son'? . . . If we married our daughters to their sons or their daughters to our sons, one of them would see our daughter (in his home) or one of us would see our daughter in his home, would he not accept her?! . . . Hence, 'For Thou hast done it.'"

Tacitus[15] had previously described the Jews in the following words: *"Sed adversus omnes alios hostile odium. Separati epulis, discreti cubilibus, proiectissima ad libidinem gens; concubitu alienarum abstinent; inter se nihil illicitum* (but toward every other people they feel only hatred and enmity. They sit apart at meals, and they sleep apart, and although as a race they are prone to lust, they abstain from intercourse with foreign women; yet among themselves nothing is unlawful.)"

The Jews' separation and isolation from the gentiles in dining and drinking and especially in marriage was, for many of the latter, a primary factor in accusing the Jews of being misanthropic.[16] Thus the Sages concluded: "Do not the gentile nations go into exile?! (Certainly.) But even so, for them it is no real exile; but for Israel it is. The exile of the gentile nations, who eat their bread and drink their wine, is not real exile; but for Israel, who do not partake of their bread nor drink of their wine, theirs is real exile."[17]

2. Reaction of the Sages

The Sages' response to antisemitism was not uniform. Different Sages reacted in different ways and, on occasion, the very same Sage changed his stance – all according to the subject and the circumstances.

The reactions were most varied. For example, we find in the Midrash: "R. Samuel b. Nahman said: 'None of the nations should really have scabs. Why then are there such among them? So that they should not taunt Israel and say to them, Are you not a nation of lepers?' "[18] Here we have a specific response to the prevalent charge that the Jews were afflicted with leprosy.[19]

Quite often we have hostile words directed at the Gentiles and their ways as compared to those of the Jews: "The power which Thou grantest us is not the same as that which Thou grantest them, for when Thou grantest us power, we deal with them mercifully; but when Thou grantest them power, they treat us ruthlessly."[20] The Sages expand on this: that the nations of the world do not have civilized laws[21] and are steeped in murder, incest, adultery, lewdness, plunder and theft, and other abominations. These, of course, are precisely the charges the Greeks and Romans levelled against the Jews.[22] Is there no direct connection between these things or are the claims of the Jews only in reaction to the accusations of the antisemites? Thus, for example, Berenice is said to have had relations with her brother, Agrippa II.[23] Both the Jewish-Hellenistic literature, which detailed the sins of the Gentiles in general and those of the Romans in particular,[24] and the literature of the Sages, reacted to this. Thus, for example, R. Nehemia said: "This is the wicked Titus, son of the wife of Vespasian."[25] And thus we find: "R. Judah said in the name of Samuel in the name of R. Hanina: 'I saw a gentile buy a goose at the market, use it immorally, and then strangle it, roast and eat it.' "[26]; for it was said of the Gentiles that "they prefer the cattle of Israelites to their own wives"[27]. And "R. Akiba said:[28] 'I saw a gentile bind his father and place him before his dog

ATA—B*

who ate him.'"[29] And the Sages fixed the rule of law that "a gentile has no (legal) father"[30] because the law of matrimony does not apply to a Gentile.[31] And even when they seemed to praise the Gentiles, they derided them as addicted to pederasty.[32] Therefore they ruled:

> Cattle may not be left in the inns of the gentiles since they are suspected of bestiality; nor may a woman remain alone with them since they are suspected of lewdness; nor may a man remain alone with them since they are suspected of shedding blood. The daughter of an Israelite may not assist a gentile woman in childbirth since she would be assisting to bring to birth a child for idolatry, but a gentile woman may assist the daughter of an Israelite. The daughter of an Israelite may not suckle the child of a gentile woman, but a gentile woman may suckle the child of the daughter of an Israelite in this one's domain. (An Israelite) may accept healing from them for his beasts but not for his person, and in no place may he have his hair cut by them. So R. Meir. But the Sages say: In the public domain it is permitted, but not if they are alone.[33]

Similarly there is a parallel text:

> Cattle may not be left in the inns of the gentiles, even males near males or females near females, because the male draws the male and the female draws the female; nor, needless to say, males near females or females near males. Cattle may not be committed to a herdsman of theirs nor does one commit a child to him for instruction or to learn a craft or to remain alone with him. A daughter of an Israelite may not suckle the child of a gentile woman since she is raising a child for idolatry, but a gentile woman may suckle the child of an Israelite daughter in the latter's domain; a daughter of an Israelite may not assist a gentile woman in childbirth because she would be assisting in bringing to birth a child for idolatry; nor may a gentile woman assist an Israelite daughter in childbirth because they are suspected of murder. So R. Meir. But the Sages say: a gentile woman may assist an Israelite daughter in childbirth when others are standing by; if the two are alone, it is forbidden because they are suspected of murder. (An Israelite) may accept healing for his beasts but not for his person. A gentile woman may not cut up an embryo in its mother's womb nor give her a cup of root-water (to cause barrenness) because they are suspected of murder. Nor may an Israelite remain alone with a gentile in the bath-house or urinal. If an Israelite chances to travel with a gentile, he should keep the gentile on his right, not on his left; R. Ishmael, the son of R. Johanan b. Beroka, says: with a sword in his right hand; a walking-stick in his left. If the two are ascending or descending a slope, the Israelite ascends (first) and the gentile descends (first); nor should (the Israelite) bend down in front of (the gentile) lest (the gentile) bash his skull; and (the

Israelite) should mention a much longer journey, if (the gentile) asks his destination – he should reply evasively, as Jacob did to Esau: "until I come unto my lord unto Seir" and went on his way to Succoth. An Israelite having his hair cut by a gentile should be looking in the mirror.[34]

Also:

An Israelite circumcises a gentile for proselytization but a gentile may not circumcise an Israelite, because they are suspected of murder. So R. Meir. But the Sages say: a non-Jew may circumcise an Israelite when others are present nearby. If the two are alone it is forbidden, because they are suspected of murder.[35]

All of these laws date from the mid-second century c.e., that is, from the generation after the suppression of the Bar Kokhba Revolt and Hadrian's persecutory decrees. There is a connection.

3. A Change in Concepts

A further question is whether other laws which discriminated against the non-Jews[36] also stem originally from a reaction of this kind or do they perhaps really represent an immanent, internal development.[37]

It is clear that the turning point which led to the change of law in this regard was based upon the desire to prevent an even more serious reaction by the non-Jews when they became aware of these things, as is related explicitly in the account of the two commissioners whom the Government of Rome sent to the House of Study.[38] This turnabout was expressed in a series of laws.[39] Almost all of the Sages who forbid robbery from a non-Jew, and even more, retaining the lost article of a non-Jew, do so because of desecration of the Name (of God) or, phrased differently, for the sanctification of the Name.[40] Similarly, they issued many regulations against discrimination between Israelites and non-Jews "for the sake of peace."[41] "A town in which Israelites and gentiles live—the administrators collect from both for the sake of peace. One supports poor gentiles with poor Israelites for the sake of peace. One delivers funeral orations for, and buries dead gentiles for the sake of peace. One condoles gentile mourners for the sake of peace." Thus they ruled: "Whosoever sees a (lost) ass of a gentile must deal with it as he would were it of an Israelite."[42]

Moreover, the absolutely opposite phenomenon existed alongside antisemitism in the ancient world – a great regard for Jews and Judaism and a flourishing, growing movement of conversion to Judaism, including partial conversion.[43] And the Sages were also well aware of this phenomenon: "Said R. Hanan: What was perpetrated by the coastal cities was not perpetrated even by the generation of the Flood, for it is written: 'Woe unto the inhabitants of the sea-coast, the nations of the Cherthites,' which means that they deserved to be annihilated (*kareth*). Yet for whose sake do they stand? For the sake of one gentile and one God-fearing person whom the Holy One, blessed be He, receives from their hands."[44] And here too there was an awareness by the Sages of the echoes emanating both from the proselytes and the peoples of the world. Thus, for example, the concept embodied in the ruling that "a proselyte is like a child newly born,"[45] created the reality in which when the proselyte, Neophytos, had married the wife of his maternal brother and the matter was submitted to the Sages they ruled: "The law of marriage does not apply to a proselyte."[46] The same applies in the account of Ben Yasyan: "When I went to the coastal cities I came across a certain proselyte who had married the wife of his maternal brother. Said I to him: Who permitted you (this marriage)? Replied he to me: Behold the woman and her seven children; on this bench sat R. Akiba when he made two statements: a proselyte may marry the wife of his maternal brother . . . "[47]

However, later they ruled against incest among proselytes, that it should not be said that "they exchanged a (religion of) stricter for (one of) more easy-going sanctity."[48] This reason is in full agreement with that of Paul, who reacted to a similar situation in his *Letter to the Corinthians*: "It is commonly reported that there is fornication among you, and of a kind that is not found even among gentiles; for a man is living with his father's wife. And you are arrogant! Ought you not rather to mourn? Let him who has done this be removed from among you."[49] That is to say, Paul was also shaken by the fact that, of all people, the new Christians, who had abandoned paganism, had gone, as it were, from a stricter state of holiness to a less stringent one. Moreover, it is clear from these rulings of the Sages that they agree that the non-Jews are generally disciplined about incest. And, in fact, during the period of the *Amoraim*, there was a change in the concept that a non-Jew "has no father."[50]

It is likely that there is even a connection between the very complex reality of the non-Jewish ambience in the Hellenistic-Roman world, including its attitude to Jews and Judaism, and the evolution of the concepts of "righteous among the nations"[51] and "commandments of the children of Noah."[52] In other words, it seems that the Sages' perceptions of "righteous among the nations" and "commandments" obligatory upon "the children of Noah" basically derive not only from an immanent internal development but also from the bilateral relationship between the Gentile world and that of the Sages. Fundamental to this is the recognition that, on the one hand, not all non-Jews are licentious and unbridled, and that, on the other, there is a sort of program, theoretical for the time being, but with practical potential for the future, to fix the immoral status of the non-Jew who is not in the world of the Halakha.

Antisemitism, then, had a serious place in the consciousness and reactions of the Sages. The reactions of the Sages to antisemitism, it turns out, were not uniform but varied and most complex. The differences and distinctions are recognizable, not only from period to period, but even from Sage to Sage within the same period.

Notes

1. *Lam. Rabba* (hereafter *R.*) 1:11 (as in the 1st edition [Pesaro, 1509]); cf. the corrupt version in ms. Rome, ed. S. Buber, (Wilna, 1899), p. 75; and see , ibid., n. 342, in which the antisemitic significance of the account is not grasped.).
2. Dio Cassius, *Roman History*, 66, 7.
3. The title given both to Publius Cornelius Scipio the Elder, for his victory over Hannibal at Zama (201 B.C.E) and to Publius Cornelius Scipio Aemilianus the Younger who defeated Carthage and destroyed it (146 B.C.E.).
4. The title given to Cornelius Scipio who defeated Antiochus III.
5. The title given, for example, to Germanicus (see below, n. 6), the son of Claudius and Messalina, after his father's victory over Britain.
6. The title given, for example, both to Decimus (Nero) Claudius Drusus, son of Livia, Augustus' wife, after his defeat of the Germans – to him and his sons after him – and to Vitellius.
7. See: J. Bergmann, *Jüdische Apologetik im neutestamentlichen Zeitalter* (Berlin 1908); I. Heinemann, "The Attitude of the Ancients Toward Judaism" (Heb.), *Zion* 4 (1939): 269–293 [*Hellenistic Views on Jews and Judaism* (Heb.) (henceforth: *Hellenistic*), (Jerusalem, 1974), pp.7–31]; M. D. Herr. "Antisemitism in Imperial Rome in the Light of Rabbinic Literature" (Heb.), in *Benjamin De Vries Memorial Volume*, ed. E. Z. Melamed (Jerusalem, 1968), pp.149–169 [=*Hellenistic*, pp.33–43]. The reactions to antisemitism in Babylonia (in Parthia and Sassanid Persia) are not within the scope of this article.
8. See *Lam. R.*, Proem 17 (ed. Buber, p.14); and compare the version in the Geniza ms. published by Z. M. Rabinovitz, *Ginze Midrash: The Oldest Forms of Rabbinic Midrashim According to Geniza Manuscripts* (Heb.), (Tel-Aviv, 1977), pp.122–123; and see my article "Antisemitism in Imperial Rome", pp. 150–151.
9. Cf., ibid., pp.149, 158–159.
10. *T.B. Pes.* 87b (according to ms. Munich 6 – see R.N.N. Rabbinovicz, *Dikdukei Soferim: Variae Lectiones in Mischnam et in Talmud Babylonicam* [München, 1867], ad locum, pp.267–268).
11. This verse, in 1 Kings, 11:16, like similar verses, is put in the Midrashim, into the mouths of Jew-haters as charges of misanthropy on the part of the Jewish people; see J. Bergmann, *Jüdische Apologetik*, p.146 ff. And cf.: "When they had their kingdom, a king arose over them named David, who had evil designs against us, wishing to destroy us, and wipe us off the earth. Two lengths he killed but one he left alive, and those left he enslaved, as is written: ' . . . and he measured them with the line, making them to lie down on the ground.'" (*Targum Sheni on the Book of Esther*, 3:8 [ed. M. David (Krakau, 1898), p.24]) [the verse is 2 Sam., 8:2, and speaks of David's war with Moab]; or, similarly: "And thereafter a cruel king arose named David, who killed the Philistines, the Edomites, the Ammonites, and the Moabites and no one stood before him." (*Abba Guryon* 3, Aramaic version in ms. British Museum [ed. S. Buber, in *Sammlung aggadischer Commentare zum Buch Esther* (Vilna, 1886), p.31]); and further: "And again they had a king named David who would go forth, destroy and wipe out all the nations and had mercy on no creature, as is said: 'And David left neither man nor woman alive' (1 Sam. 27:11). (ibid., p.30); and similarly in *Esther R.*, 7:13.
12. See S. Lieberman, *Greek in Jewish Palestine* (New York, 1942), p.141; E. E. Urbach, *The Sages: Their Concepts and Beliefs* (Jerusalem, 1975), pp.543–544.
13. *Lam. R.*, 1:21 (ed. Buber, pp.93–94) =*Pesikta de-Rav Kahana*, 19 (anokhi), 2 [ed. B. Mandelbaum, (New York, 1962), p.303][Eng. translation by W. G. Braude and I. J. Kapstein (Philadelphia, 1975), p.324.]; and see Heinemann, "The Attitude", p.284 (=*Hellenistic*, p.22).
14. Till here, according to the reading of the 1st edition [Pesaro 1509]; thereafter, according to the text of ms. Rome, and cf. the text in *Pesikta de-Rav Kahana*. The material in the square brackets has been added in accordance with the *Pesikta de-Rav Kahana*.
15. *Histories*, 5:5. And cf. the account of R. Akiba and the beautiful women a governor sent him for the night (*Aboth de Rabbi Nathan*, version A, 16 [ed. S. Schechter, (London, 1887), p.63; Eng. translation in *The Fathers According to Rabbi Nathan* (New Haven, 1955), p.84] and what I wrote about this in my articles: "Persecutions and Martyrdom in Hadrian's Days," *Scripta Hierosolymitana* 23 (1972): 87; "The Historical Significance of the Dialogues between Jewish Sages and Roman Dignitaries", *Scripta Hierosolymitana* 22 (1971): 136–137.
16. See Heinemann, "Antisemitismus" (n. 22 below), pp.19–20. And cf. his article "The Attitude": 283–284 [=*Hellenistic*, pp.21–22]; V. Tcherikower, *Hellenistic Civilization and the Jews* (Phi-

ladelphia, 1959), pp.366–367; Herr, "Antisemitism": 151–152, 155–157 [=*Hellenistic*, pp.35–36, 39–41].

17. *Lam. R.*, 1:3 (ed. Buber, p.62).
18. *Midrash Bereshit Rabba* [hereafter *Gen. R.*], ed. J. Theodor and Ch. Albeck (Jerusalem, 1965), pp.1077–1078; and cf. Bergmann, *Jüdische Apologetik*, p.147.
19. See Manetho, *Aegyptiaca*, apud: Josephus, *Contra Apionem*, 1: 229, 233ff. (M. Stern, *Greek and Latin Authors on Jews and Judaism 1;* [Jerusalem, 1974];p. 78ff); Lysimachus, *Bibiotheca Historica*, 34–35, 1:1–2, Stern, ibid.; Pompeius Trogus in Justin's *Historiae Philippicae*, Epitoma of Book 36, 2:12; (Stern, ibid., p. 335) Diodorus, *Aegyptiaca*, apud: Josephus, *Contra Apionem*, 1:304–308 (Stern, ibid., p. 383); Tacitus, *Histories*, 5:3. And cf. Josephus, *Contra Apionem*, 1: 257ff., 279–284; *Antiquities*, 3: 261, 264–268. On the Jews as a plague, cf. Claudius in his letter to the residents of Alexandriar: *"koinen teina tes oikoumenes noson* etc.,*"* V. A. Tcherikover and A. Fuks, *Corpus Papyronum Judaicarum*, 2 (Cambridge, Mass, 1960, No. 153, 5:99–100 (p. 41).
20. *Sifre on Deuteronomy*, 323 [ed L. Finkelstein (New York, 1969), p. 373].
21. See S. Lieberman, "Roman Legal Institutions in Early Rabbinics and in the 'Acta Martyrum',*"* *Jewish Quarterly Review* 35(1944/5): 1–57.
22. See I. Heinemann, "Antisemitismus", Pauly-Wissowa, *R-E der Classischen Altertumwissenschaft*, Supplementband 5 (Stuttgart, 1931), pp.19–22.
23. *Antiquities*, 20:145; Juvenal, *Satires*, 6:156–158. The satire was composed in 116 C.E. and is completely suffused with antisemitism.
24. For the charge against the Gentiles of bloodshed, theft, fornication, and pederasty, see the *Fourth Sibylline Book*, 31–34; not only Nero was charged with matricide (ibid. 121; the *Fifth Sibylline Book*, 31–39,142,145,363),but also all the Romans (ibid. 386). Rome is described not only as a city of fornication and pederasty (ibid. 166,429–430), but also as a place of robbery and violence, prostitution – both male and female – coercion, incest, buggery, and other such abominations (ibid. 386–394; verse 392 seems to be directed against the deeds of Tiberius in his old age [cf. Suetonius, *The Life of Tiberius*, 45.])
25. *Sifre on Deuteronomy*, 328 [ed. Finkelstein, pp.378–379]; cf. *Aboth de Rabbi Nathan*, Version B, 7 (ed. Schechter [n. 15 above], p.20): "and there was there a wicked man, Titus, the son of Vespasian's wife (in ms. H. the text reads: 'the son of his sister'). And see further, *Midrash Debarim Rabbah*, ed. S. Lieberman, (Jerusalem 1965^2), pp.21–22; and his *Greek in Jewish Palestine* (n. 12 above), pp.164–166.
26. *T. B., Tractate 'Abodah Zarah* 22b (according to ms. Jewish Theological Seminary of America, New York, ed. S. Abramson)(New York, 1957).
27. Ibid.
28. This is the reading of ms. Rome (Assemani 32), Berlin and London, in *Midrash Tannaim* (Heb.)(collected from *Midrash Haggadol*) 12:31 (ed. D. Hoffmann) [Berlin, 1908], p.55) and in the ms. *Midrash Hakhamim* however in ms. Oxford, 1st edition, and the *Yalkut Shimoni* "Jacob".
29. *Sifre on Deuteronomy*, 81 (ed. L. Finkelstein [n. 20 above], p. 147); cf. *Midrash Agur: The Mishnah of Rabbi Eliezer* 1:3 (ed. H. G. Enelow [New York, 1933], p. 16).
30. *Gen. R.* 18:5 (ed. Theodor and Albeck, p.165); *T. B. Yeb.* 98a; ibid. *Nazir* 61a: "except for the gentile who has no father." And cf. the earlier *Mishna Yeb.* 2:5; *M. Qiddushin* 3:12. And see below in n. 46.
31. *T. B. Yeb.* 98a: "there is no law of matrimony for the proselyte." And cf. I. M. Hacohen Guttman, entry: "father", in *Key to the Talmud*, 1 (Heb.) (Budapest, 1906), pp.15–23.
32. Cf., for example, the exaggerated ironic tone in Ulla's statement: "These are the thirty commandments which the sons of Noah took upon themselves but they observe only three of them, namely, (1) they do not draw up a *kethubah* document (marriage deed) for males, (2) they do not weigh flesh of the dead in the market . . . " (*T.B. Hullin* 92a–b). Of the three commandments strictly observed by the children of Noah (cf. infra n. 52), the first attests to the fact, that though pederasty was rife, yet they cringed at the writing of a *ketubah* for males; and it has already been noted (see M. Joel, *"Einige Notizen als Erganzungen zum Zweiten Theil meiner Schrift:'Blicke in die Religionsgeschichte',"* in *Jubelschrift zum siebzigsten Geburtstage . . . H. Graetz* (Breslau, 1877), pp.174–175, n. 1; E. E. Urbach, *Sages* (n. 12 above), pp.533–534 and p.927, n.30) that even this phenomenon of homosexual marriages was not absent in Rome, alluding to Dio Cassius, *Roman History*, 62 (not 63 as in Joel):13 (and cf.,

even earlier, Suetonius, *The Life of Nero*, 28). There the story is told of Nero, who married his lover Spurus, whom he called Sabina, in a legal marriage ceremony (which included payment of a dowry, a wedding hymn, prayers, and blessings for the birth of legitimate children) to which all the members of the court were invited. Then Spurus was brought to the residence of Nero, who castrated him, dealt with him as with a woman, clothed him in the raiment of the Emperor's wife, and he was called, among other things, "*kyria*" (feminine form of Lord). Thereafter, Nero had two male bed companions simultaneously: Pythagoras was the "husband" and Spurus was the "wife" (Dio Cassius, ibid. 1–2; cf. also supra, ibid. 12:3. Likewise, *mutatis mutandis*, there was the account of Nero's freed slave, Doryphorus, who married Nero, who moaned and cried during the wedding night like a virgin being taken to wife for the first time (Suetonius, ibid. ibidem).

33. *M. Av. Zar.* 2:1–2.
34. *Tos. Av. Zar.* 3:2–5 (ed. M. S. Zuckermandel [repr. Jerusalem, 1963], p.463); *Talmud Yerushalmi Av. Zar.* 2:1 (fo. 40:col. 3); ibid., 2:2 (fol.41:col.1); *T.B. Av. Zar.* 26a–b; 29:a; and cf. further, *Massekhet Kutim* 1:10 (ed. M. Higger in *Seven Minor Treatises* (New York, 1930), p.63.
35. *Tos. Av. Zar.* 3:12 (ed. Zuckermandel, p.464).
36. For example: "If the ox of an Israelite gored the ox of a gentile, the owner is not culpable. But if the ox of a gentile gored the ox of an Israelite, whether it was accounted harmless or an attested danger, the owner must pay full damages." *(M. Baba Kamma* 4:3; and this is the opinion of R. Meir who is of the mid-second century C.E. [*Tos. B. K.* 4:3 (ed. Zuckermandel, p.351)]); "robbery of a gentile is permissible but of an Israelite is forbidden" (*Sifra on Deuteronomy* 344 [ed. Finkelstein, pp.400–401); *T.Y. B.K.* 4:3 [fol.4:col.2]; "For murder, whether of a gentile by a gentile, or of an Israelite by a gentile, punishment is incurred; of a gentile by an Israelite, there is no punishment incurred; for robbery, if one stole or robbed, and likewise if he finds a beautiful woman or committed similar offenses – a gentile against a gentile and a gentile against an Israelite is forbidden, but an Israelite against a non-Jew is permitted" (*Tos. Av. Zar.* 8[9]:5 [ed. Zuckermandel, p.473]; *T.B. Sanhedrin* 57a; *T.Y. Shabbat* 14:4 [fol.14:col.4] = *T.Y. Av. Zar.* 2:2 [fol 40:col.4]; and what was written by S. Lieberman, *Hayerushalmi Kiphshuto: A Commentary based on the Manuscripts of the Yerushalmi* . . . , 1 [Jerusalem 1934], p.188); and further cf. *M. Sanh.* 4:6 and what was written by E. E. Urbach: "'Kol Ha-Meqayyem Nefesh Ahat . . . ': Development of the Version . . . " (Heb.), *Tarbiz* 40 (1970–71): 268–284; and see further: *M. Sanh.* 9:2; *Tos. Sanh.* 12:4 (ed. Zuckermandel, p.443); *M. Yoma* 8:7; *Mekhilta de Rabbi Ishmael*, Nezikin 4 [ed. H. S. Horowitz and I. A. Rabin (Jerusalem, 1960), p.263]; *Mekhilta de Rabbi Simeon bar Yohai* (*R.*) 21:14 [ed. J. N. Epstein and E. Z. Melamed (Jerusalem, 1955), p.171]; *Sifre on Deuteronomy* 16 [ed. Finkelstein, pp.26–27] and *T. B. Baba Kama* 113a (on Rabbi Ishmael); *Midrash Haggadol:* Exodus 23:6 [ed. M. Margaliot (Jerusalem, 1956), p. 535; *Sifra*, Kedoshim, Chap. 4:12; *T. B. Baba Metzia* 111b; *Tos., B.M.* 2:26 (ed. Zuckermandel, p.375): "as to non-Jews and (Jewish) shepherds and breeders of small cattle, even though one is not bound to get them out (of a pit), one must not throw them in (to a pit to endanger their lives)" (ibid. 33 [ibid.]; *T.B. Sanh.* 57a; *Av. Zar.* 13b; ibid. 26a–b.)
37. See M. Guttmann, *Das Judentum und seine Umwelt*, 1 (Berlin 1927), p.101, n.1; Z. Falk, "Non-Jew and Resident Alien in Hebrew Law" (Heb.), *Mahalkhim* (1969):9–15; D. Rokeach, "On the Relationship of the Sages to Gentiles and Proselytes" (Heb.), ibid. 5(1971):68–75.
38. *Sifre on Deuteronomy* 344 (ed. Finkelstein, p.401); *T.Y. B.K.* 4:3 (fol.4:col.2); *T.B. B.K.* 38a. And see our article, "The Historical Significance" (n. 15 above): 132–133, and in n.45 there we indicated the previous literature.
39. "At that time, Rabban Gamaliel issued a decree forbidding theft from a gentile as a desecration of the Holy Name" (*T.Y. B.K.* 4:3); "One who steals from a gentile must return (the theft) to the gentile; theft from a gentile is more severe than from an Israelite because of profanation of the (Holy) Name" (*Tos. B.K.* 10:15) [ed. Zuckermandel, p.368]; R. Akiba differs with R. Ishmael (n.36 above) and argues that "we should not attempt to circumvent him (the gentile) on account of the sanctification of the Name" (*T.B. B.K.* 113a); and R. Simeon, his disciple, stated that "the following was expounded by R. Akiba when he arrived from Zifrin: 'Whence can we learn that the robbery of a gentile is forbidden? From the significant words "After that he is sold, he may be redeemed again," which implies that he could not withdraw and leave him (without paying the redemption money). You might then say that he may demand an exorbitant

sum for him? No, since it says: "And he shall reckon with him that bought him" to emphasize that he must be very precise in making the valuation with him who had bought him.'" (*T.B.* ibid., 113a–b; and cf. *Sifra*, Behar Ch. 9:2–3); "'Thou shalt not oppress thy neighbour.' Your neighbour is as your brother. And your brother is as your neighbour. Hence you learn that robbery from a non-Jew is (considered) robbery. And, needless to say, even from your brother." (*Seder Eliyahu Rabbah* (Heb.) 15 [16], ed. Meir Ish-Shalom, (Wien, 1902), pp. 74–75); "Hence they said: Let a man remove himself from theft from an Israelite and from a gentile, even from anyone in the marketplace. For whoever steals from a gentile will finally steal from an Israelite; and whoever robs a gentile will finally rob an Israelite. Whoever swears (falsely) to a gentile will finally swear (falsely) to an Israelite. Whoever deals deceitfully with a gentile will finally deal deceitfully with an Israelite. Who sheds the blood of a gentile will finally shed the blood of an Israelite. And the Torah was not given for this but to sanctify His great Name. 'I will set a sign among them, and send from them survivors to the nations . . . ' What is said at the end of the verse? 'They shall declare My glory among these nations.'" (ibid., 26 [28], p. 140) – Even for those who claim that "the robbery of a gentile is prohibited—an article lost by him is permissible" (*T.B. B.K.* 113b); but there were those who differed even on this: 'R. Pinhas b. Yair said that where there was a danger of causing the desecration of His Name, even the article lost by a gentile is forbidden' (ibid.); and thus, on the topic, in the *Jerusalem Talmud (T.Y.) B.M.* 2:5 (fol. 8:col. 3) we read that 'even according to the one who is of the opinion that theft of a gentile is forbidden, everybody admits that his lost article is permitted' yet, nevertheless, R. Simeon b. Shetah returned the lost article of a gentile and 'was not a barbarian' but sought to hear 'blessed is the God of the Jews.' And it is interesting to compare the Halakha that 'a baby sucks a gentile woman' (*Tos. Niddah* 2:5 [ed. Zuckermandel, p. 642; and cf. S. Lieberman, *Tosefeth Rishonim: a Commentary . . .* (Heb.), 3 (Jerusalem, 1939), p. 259]; *T.Y. Av. Zar.* 2:1 [fol. 40:col. 3]; *T.B. Yeb.* 114a) to the opposite law: 'one does not suck the breast of a gentile woman' (*Tos. Shab.* 9 [10]: 22 [ed. Lieberman, p. 40], except that in both those instances what is discussed is not the danger involved but the impurity, for, in both the opposing laws, the (matter) of suckling from the gentile woman is juxtaposed with suckling from an unclean beast (and see the note in I. Levi's commentary on the *Jerusalem Talmud, B.K.* 4:3, p. 114; S. Lieberman, *Tosefta Ki-fshutah* (Heb.), 3 [Moed] (New York, 1962), pp. 149–150), and cf., further, the printed *Tanhuma*, Exod. 7; *Exod. R.* 1:25 (ed. Shinan [Jerusalem and Tel-Aviv, 1984], p. 80.

40. For the original meaning of these concepts see our "Persecutions and Martyrdom" (n. 15 above), p. 106, n. 72* where we have indicated the earlier literature.

41. *Tos. Gittin* 3 [5]:13–14 (ed. Lieberman [New York, 1973] p. 259); *T.Y. Gittin*5:9 [fol. 47:col. 3]; *T.Y. Demai* 4:6 [fol. 24:col. 1]; *T.Y. Av. Zar.* 1:3 [fol. 39:col. 3]; *T.B. Gittin* 61a.

42. *Tos. B.M.* 2:27 (ed. Zuckermandel, p. 375); *T.B. B.M.* 32b; and cf. also *T.Y. B.M.* 2:11 (fol. 8:col. 4). The *T.B.* there gives the reason as "lest there be hatred," which is a Babylonian argument (cf. *T.B. Av. Zar.* 26a).

43. See, *inter alia*, A. S. Herschberg, "The Great Proselytization Movement in the Period of the Second Temple" (Heb.), *Hatekufah* 12(1921): 129–148; 13(1922):189–210; Heinemann, "The Attitude", p. 269ff. (=*Hellenistic*, p. 7ff.); M. Stern, "Sympathy for Judaism in Roman Senatorial Circles in the Period of the Early Empire" (Heb.), *Zion* 29(1964):155–167; and also cf.: L. H. Feldman, "Jewish 'Sympathizers' in Classical Literature and Inscriptions," *Transactions of the American Philological Association*, 81(1950):200–208.

44. *Gen. R.* 28:5 (ed. Theodor and Albeck, p. 264).

45. In *T.B. Yeb.* 48b the statement is brought in the name of R. Yose.

46. Ibid., 98a, also quoted in the name of R. Yose; and cf. the earlier *Mishnah Yeb.* 11:2: "If the sons of a female proselyte became proselytes with her, they are not subject to the law of *halitzah* or of levirate marriage . . . So, too, if the sons of a bondswoman have been freed with her"; and cf. *Tos. Yeb.* 12:2 (ed. Lieberman [New York, 1967], pp. 39–40); *Sifre on Deuteronomy*, 289 (ed. Finkelstein, p. 308); *T.Y. Yeb.* 11 (fol. 11:col. 4–12:col. 1); *Gen. R.* 18:5–6 (ed. Theodor and Albeck, pp. 165–167); *Massekhet Gerim* 3:5 (ed. M. Higger (n. 34 above, p. 74); *T.B. Yeb.* 97b–98b; *T.B. Sanh.* 57b–58b; and further cf. *Mishnah Ketubot* 4:3. And cf. supra nn. 30–31.

47. *T.B. Yeb.* 98a.

48. Ibid. 22a; and there the question which was raised in Palestine in the days of the *Amoraim* is cited: Are proselytes subject to the law of incest in the second degree? And cf. also *T.B.*

Qiddushin 18a: "R. Hiyya bar Abin said in R. Johanan's name: A non-Jew succeeds his father by Biblical law;" and ibid., above, 176: "Rava said: by Biblical law, a non-Jew is his father's heir . . . But the succession of a proselyte (to the estate of) a gentile is not in accordance with Biblical law but by the law of the Soferim . . . A gentile (succeeds) a proselyte, or a proselyte (succeeds) a proselyte, neither by Biblical law nor by the law of the Soferim . . . ".

49. *1 Corinthians* 5:1ff.
50. See, for example, *T.Y. Yeb.* 2:6 (fol.4:col.1); *T.B. Yeb.* 62a; *T.B. Bekhorot* 47a–b.
51. See *Tos. Sanh.* 13:2: "R. Eliezer says: 'None of the gentiles have a place in the World to Come for it is said: "Let the wicked return to Sheol," these are the wicked of Israel; ["all the nations who ignore God!" – these are the wicked of the gentiles']. Said R. Joshua to him: 'If Scripture had said: "Let the wicked return to Sheol all the nations" and ceased, I would agree with you [that these are the wicked of Israel and the nations], but since the verse reads "who ignore God" – there are righteous among the nations who have a share in the World to Come." (ed. Zuckermandel, p.434 [the bracketed texts are according to the Vienna ms.]); cf. *Otiyyot de-Rabbi Akiba* version A:7, ed. S. A. Wertheimer in *Batei Midrashot: Twenty Five Midrashim* . . . , 2, pp.368–369 – on "the righteous among the nations of the world." And of Job it was said: "R. Hiyya taught: 'In my world there was one righteous gentile . . . ' " (*T.Y. Sotah* 5:8 [fol.20:col.4]); and the parallel in *Gen. R.* 57:4 (ed. Theodor and Albeck, p.618); 'One righteous man arose among the nations'; while in *T.B. Baba Batra* 15b: 'There was a certain pious man among the nations of the world' (according to mss.; see *Dikdukei Soferim* (n.10 above) for *B. B.*, ad locum, p. 69). And see M. Guttmann. *Das Judentum*, (n. 37 above), pp.168–194; E. E. Urbach, *Sages* (n. 12 above), pp.412, 543–544. From here the concept developed to: "the pious among the nations of the world are called pious because they punctiliously observe the seven commandments given to the children of Noah." (*Midrash Agur* [n. 29 above], 6, [ed. Enelow, p.121]); and see the *Talmudic Encyclopedia* (Heb.), 6, entry "ger toshav", p.290, n. 11; J. Katz, "The Vicissitude of Three Apologetic Passages" (Heb.), *Zion* 23–24 (1958–1959): 174–193.
52. *Tannaim* of the second century C.E., after the Bar Kokhba Revolt and the persecutory decrees, speak of the "Seven Noahide Laws" (*Tos. Sotah* 6:9 according to the ms. Vienna [ed. Lieberman (New York, 1973), pp. 188–189); and see his commentary, ad locum, p. 674]; *Seder Olam Rabbah* 5 [ed. A. Marx (Berlin, 1903), p.13]; *Tos. Av. Zar.* 8(9):4–8 [ed. Zuckermandel, pp.473–474]; *T.B.Sanh.* 56a–59b, 74b; *T. B. Yeb.* 48b; *Massekhet Gerim* 2:5; (ed. Higger, p. 73]; *T. B. Av. Zar.* 64b; *Mekhilta de Rabbi Ishmael*, Bahodesh, 5 [ed. H. S. Horowitz and I. A. Rabin (Jerusalem, 1960), pp.221–222]; *Sifre on Deuteronomy* 343 (ed. Finkelstein, p.396); *Midrash Tehillim* 2:5 [ed. S. Buber (repr. New York, 1947), pp.26–27; Eng. trans. by W.G. Braude, *The Midrash on Psalms* (New Haven, 1959), p.39]). For the six commandments given to primeval Adam see *Gen. R.* 16:6 (ed. Theodor and Albeck, pp.149–151 where parallels are indicated; and see Theodor's notes there); and cf. *Mekhilta de Rabbi Ishmael*, ibid. 3 (ed. Horowitz-Rabin, p.211), and on the "thirty commandments" of the children of Noah and their connection with the "thirty righteous" in the world, see *T.Y. Av. Zar.* 2:1 (fol.40:col.3); *Gen. R.* 98(99):9 (according to the ms. Vatican [ed. Theordor and Albeck, p.1260]); *Midrash Tehillim* 2:5 (in ms. [ed. Buber, p.26, notes and emendations, 31]); *T.B. Hullin* 92a (and the text there: 'thirty righteous men among the nations of the world,' but the ms. Munich reads: 'thirty righteous,' omitting 'among the nations of the world'). And see E. E. Urbach, *Sages*, pp.533–534 and n.30 on p.927. The "children of Noah" concept is already found in the *M. Nedarim* 3:11. For the commandments of the children of Noah cf. further *Tos. Demai* 2:24 (ed. Lieberman [New York, 1955], p.72) and the parallels in the *Talmud Babli: Pesahim* 22b and *Av. Zar.* 6b (and see S. Lieberman in his *Lengthy Explanation* ad locum, p. 220); *Tos. Shehitat Hullin* 7:9 (ed. Zuckermandel, p.509); *Sifre on Deuteronomy* 76 (ed. Finkelstein, pp.141–142); *Tos. Oholoth* 2:1 (ed. Zuckermandel, p.598); *T. B. Hullin* 102a; *Sifra*, Hovah portion 1:1,8; ibid. Zav portion 10:1; ibid. Shemini portion 4:5; Chapter 6:6; ibid. Emor Chapter 19:4. And see M. Joël, "Einige Notizen" (n. 32 above), pp. 174–175, n. 1; and cf. M. Guttmann, *Das Judentum* (n. 37 above), pp. 98–114, and there is a great measure of apologetics in what he says. As for the basic concept of universal commandments incumbent upon all the Gentiles, i.e., upon all people insofar as they are human beings, see already the *Fourth Sibylline Book*, 24ff. dating from about the end of the First century C.E. (which speaks of the blaspheming of God, refraining from idolatry, bloodshed, theft, fornication, and pederasty); and cf. *Acts of the Apostles* 15:20,29; 21:25 (an instruction to the Gentiles to abstain from idolatry, from

prostitution, from the meat of what is strangled, and from blood.) cf. further *Sifra, Aharei Mot,* Chapter 13:10 (the incest scroll). In praise of the Gentiles who have accepted the commandments, extreme things are said: "Whence (do we know that) even a gentile who does as the Torah prescribes is as a High Priest? Scripture says: 'which if a man do, he shall live by them' . . . " (ibid. 13; *T. B. B. K.* 38a; *T. B. Sanh.* 59a; *T. B. Av. Zar.* 3a. And see Urbach, *Sages,* pp. 543–544).

4

The Church Fathers and The Jews in Writings Designed for Internal and External Use

DAVID ROKÉAḤ

Before we deal with our subject, a brief comment on the purpose of this study and the biographical-chronological background is necessary.

Between the second and the fifth centuries C.E., more than a hundred Church authors wrote hundreds of volumes on various subjects, including commentaries on the Bible and the New Testament; works on ethics and theology; appeals, reactions, and apologetic-polemic attacks addressed to Roman Emperors, to their official representatives and to the pagan world as a whole; and writings against the various heretical Christian sects and against the Jews. We will focus here primarily on four personalities: Justin Martyr, Melito of Sardis, Origen, and Tertullian, and will also consider some of the Christian martyrs.

1. Biographical Background

Justin Martyr was born about 100 C.E. in Neapolis-Shechem in Samaria. His parents were pagans. There is nothing to indicate that he knew about the Jews or the Samaritans in the Land of Israel or that he had any special contacts with them. According to Justin, during his search for the truth, he became familiar with some contemporary schools of philosophy, being especially attracted by the teachings of Plato, but he finally became affiliated with Christianity. He emphasizes the great influence that the courageous stand of the Christian martyrs had upon his decision.[1] In about 165 C.E., he was denounced and then put to death when he refused to abandon his faith. About 155 C.E., Justin had written his *First Apology* (directed to Emperor Antoninus Pius) and, shortly thereafter, *The Dialogue with Trypho the Jew*, which is supposed to have taken

place during the Bar Kokhba Revolt. The *Second Apology* was written after
Marcus Aurelius became Emperor (161 C.E.).[2]

Melito, from Sardis in Asia Minor, died about 190 C.E. Some twenty years
earlier, he wrote an *Apology* directed to Emperor Marcus Aurelius and his son
Commodus, brief excerpts of which were quoted by Eusebius in his *Ecclesiastical History* (1,26:5–11). A papyrus containing a flowery homily by Melito,
On the Passion, featuring a comparison between the account of the Exodus and
the death of Jesus, was recently discovered. It should be noted that Melito was
a Quartodeciman, that is, one whose practice it was to celebrate Easter on the
fourteenth day of the month of Nisan – as the Jews celebrated Passover – and
not to postpone it to the following Sunday.[3]

Origen was born about 185 C.E. and died about 254 C.E., a few years after
suffering great torture during the persecutions in the time of Emperor Decius.
He came from Alexandria in Egypt where he was educated, but he spent time
in the Land of Israel, and even established a school in Caesarea, where he did
his literary work and preached. Origen, first and foremost, was a mystical-
allegorical exegete of the Bible and New Testament. For "external" use, he
wrote *Contra Celsum*, his reply to Celsus, a pagan polemicist who flourished at
the end of the seventies of the second century C.E. This reply was prepared – unenthusiastically – in response to the pleas of Origen's friend
Ambrose, and dealt with the attacks on Christianity in Celsus's *The True Discipline*.

Among the selections from Celsus's work that Origen brings for refutation
are some sharp words against Jesus and the Christians that Celsus puts in the
mouth of a Jew. Not all of the Jew's charges have a Jewish source, and some of
them are not appropriate at all for a Jew, but two of them at least do derive
apparently from a Jewish source, and they represent varying reactions to the
Virgin Birth and to Jesus's flight to Egypt.[4] The "Jew" puts it thus:

> You [that is, Jesus] falsified (the matter of) your birth from a virgin: for
> you come from a Jewish village and a native woman, improverished and
> wretched, earning her living from spinning, who was driven out by her
> husband, a carpenter by trade, when it was discovered that she had com-
> mitted adultery. After she had been cast out by her husband and was
> wandering disreputably, she secretly bore Jesus by a soldier named Pan-
> thera. Jesus (subsequently) hired himself out to Egyptians because of his
> poverty and there acquired experience with specific (magical) powers in
> which the Egyptians excel. And when he returned, he became arrogant
> because of these powers, and on account of them declared himself God.[5]

As we shall see, Origen's restrained reaction to the slurs of the "Jew" is most
instructive.[6]

Tertullian lived and worked between 160 and 220 C.E., approximately. He
was born in Carthage in North Africa, received a pagan education, and was

learned in the law. After he became a Christian, he took a radical stand against anything smacking in the slightest of paganism, and his ascetic tendencies brought him into the Montanistic camp. Like Justin, Tertullian was very much influenced by the ability of the Christians to endure suffering during the persecutions.[7] Accordingly, in his work *Scorpiace* (i.e. a serum against scorpion bites), he presented a merciless attack on the Gnostics and on those Catholics who claimed that the Christians should not volunteer for martyrdom. In about 200 C.E., Tertullian wrote his *Adversus Iudaeos* ("Against the Jews"). A few years earlier, about 197, he had written his most important work, the *Apologeticum* ("Apology"), which was addressed to the governors of the provinces. In this work he championed the cause of the Christians who were persecuted for no fault of their own and, at the same time, attacked polytheism in harsh, cutting language.[8]

Two accounts of Christian martyrs are of special interest to us, both for what they do and what they do not contain. Bishop Polycarp, the highest ranking Christian personage in the Province of Asia, was burned at the stake in Smyrna in the middle or end of the fifties of the second century. The account of his martyrdom was transmitted in a letter sent by the Christian community of Smyrna to that of Philomelium. This letter expressed a perception of the martyrdom as an imitation of Christ in the torture and death of the martyr, and provided the basis for the creation of martyr worship. Polycarp was a Quartodeciman, which suggests that he was close to Jewish practices, at least on this point: it makes the opposition and enmity of the Jews of Smyrna toward him more understandable. For the closer the ties, the greater was the danger of the Christian missionary activity that the Jews feared. The Jews therefore were bitterly opposed to Polycarp. The martyrdom of Pionius, which also occurred in Smyrna, but about a hundred years later (250 C.E.) during the Decian persecutions, is recorded in a way that also calls to mind Jewish-Christian relations in Smyrna; a comparison with what is reported to have happened at the martyrdom of Polycarp is most instructive (see below). Of course, one must not forget that these works were intended as propaganda.[9]

2. The New Testament

Just as the homilies of the Sages generally reveal faithfulness to the Biblical approach,[10] it was natural for the Church Fathers to express their solidarity with the position of the New Testament toward the Jews. And although one may find positive statements and a favorable attitude toward the Jewish people and the Jewish Torah expressed in the Gospels, the dominant note is still negative and hostile. This is indeed to be expected, if we remember that the Gospels were compiled in the Yavneh (Jamnia) period, which saw a sharp conflict between the Jews' Pharisaic leadership and the Christian sect. On the other hand, the Church strove to improve its image in the eyes of the Roman authorities and, accordingly, sought to soften the impression of the Crucifixion by transferring the guilt as well as the responsibility for it from the governor Pontius Pilate to the Jews – even though, as is well known, crucifixion was a punishment inflicted on rebels by the Roman authorities as a matter of course. The guilt associated with the Crucifixion had handicapped the Church in attracting pagans, particularly those in governmental positions. The process of rehabilitating Pilate, and thereby the Roman Empire, as we shall see, was intensified in the second and third centuries. Were it not for the fact that the (Catholic) Church had reached a ruling position in the Empire, Pilate would have become a saint of the Church; Pilate and his wife are, indeed, enumerated among the saints of the Coptic Church.

There are, of course, variations in the texts of the four Gospels. We will consider some of them in order to produce the most damning statements about the Jews and delineate the involvement and responsibility of the Roman authorities.[11] Matthew 26:3–4 reads: "Then were gathered together the high priest, who was called Caiaphas. And they took counsel together how they might seize Jesus by guile and put him to death." John 18:3 reads: "Judas, therefore, having received the cohorts, and attendants from the high priests and the Pharisees, cometh hither with torches and lanterns and weapons." John 18:12 puts it this way: "The cohort therefore and the tribune and the attendants of the Jews seized Jesus and bound him." Matthew 26:59–60 states: "Now the high priests and the whole Sanhedrin sought false witness against Jesus in order that they might put him to death; and they found none . . . " while Matthew 26:67 adds: "Then did they spit in his face, and buffet him, while others cuffed him." Matthew 27:2–5 expands: "And they bound him and led him away and delivered him to Pilate the governor. Then Judas, who betrayed him, upon seeing that he was condemned, repented and took back the thirty pieces of silver to the high priests and the elders, saying, 'I have sinned in betraying innocent blood.' But they said, 'What is that to us? Look thou to it.' And flinging down the pieces of silver into the temple he withdrew, and went away and hanged himself." The version of John 18:28–31 is as follows: "They bring Jesus therefore from Caiaphas to the praetorium. Now it was early; and themselves entered not into the praetorium, that they might not be defiled, but might eat the passover. Pilate therefore went out to them and saith, 'What charge bring ye against this man?' They answered and said to him, 'If he were not a criminal, we would not have delivered him up to thee.' Pilate therefore said to them, 'Take him yourselves, and judge him according to your law.' The Jews said to him, 'It is not lawful for us to put anyone to death.'"

We read in Matthew 27:15–31:

> Now at the feast the governor was wont to release to the multitude any one prisoner whom they would. And they had at that time a notorious prisoner called Barabbas. When therefore they were gathered together, Pilate said to them, "Whom will ye that I release to you, Barabbas, or Jesus who is called Christ?" For he knew that it was out of envy that they

had delivered him up. And whilst he was seated upon the tribunal, his wife sent to him saying. "Have thou naught to do with that just man; because I have suffered many things in a dream today because of him." But the high priests and the elders persuaded the multitude to ask for Barabbas and make away with Jesus. And the governor answered and said, "Which of the two will ye that I release to you?" They said, "Barrabbas!" Pilate saith to them, "What then shall I do with Jesus who is called Christ?" They all say, "Let him be crucified." He said, "Why, what evil hath he done?" But they cried out all the more vehemently saying, "Let him be crucified!" Now when Pilate saw that he was gaining nothing, but rather that a tumult was arising, he took water and washed his hands before the multitude, saying, "I am innocent of this blood; do ye look to it." And all the people answered and said, "His blood be upon us and upon our children!" Then he released to them Barabbas, and after scourging Jesus delivered him to be crucified. Then the soldiers of the governor took Jesus into the praetorium, and gathered together about him the whole cohort. And stripping him, they put on him a crimson mantle; and they plaited a crown of thorns and placed it upon his head, and a reed in his right hand. And falling upon their knees before him they mocked him, saying "Hail, king of the Jews!" And they spat upon him, and took the reed and struck him on the head. And when they had mocked him, they stripped him of the mantle and clad him in his own garments and led him away to be crucified.

According to John 19:11–12,19,38:

Jesus answered "Though wouldst have no power over me were it not given thee from above; for this cause he that hath delivered me to thee hath the greater sin." After this Pilate sought to release him. But the Jews shouted aloud saying, "If thou release this man, thou art no friend of Caesar's; every one who maketh himself a king setteth himself against Caesar" . . . Pilate also wrote an inscription and put it upon the cross; and there was written *Jesus the Nazarene, the King of the Jews.*" And after these things Joseph of Arimathae, who was a disciple of Jesus, though secretly for fear of the Jews, asked of Pilate that he might take away the body of Jesus; and Pilate gave him leave. He came therefore and took away his body.

The Acts of the Apostles contain the account of the imprisonment of Stephen, his trial before the Sanhedrin, and his stoning. Stephen had addressed the Sanhedrin, concluding with the following words (Acts 7:51–53): "Stiff of neck, uncircumcised of heart and ear, ye always resist the Holy Spirit; as did your fathers, so do ye. Which of the prophets did not your fathers persecute? And they killed those who proclaimed beforehand the coming of the just one, of whom now ye are become the betrayers and murderers, ye who have received the Law as promulgated by angels and have not kept it."

3. Status of Christians

How did the relations that prevailed between the Roman authorities and the Christians throughout our period, that is, until the accession of Constantine the Great, contribute to the attitude of the Church to Judaism? The problem of these relations has been excellently analyzed and summarized in Molthagen's dissertation.[12] Without entering into detailed discussion, the situation may be described as follows: The imposition of the death penalty for adherence to Christianity (*nomen Christianum*) dates most probably from 64 C.E., when Nero attempted to blame the Christians for setting Rome ablaze. The relevant order (*mandatum*), sent by Nero to the magistrates of the city of Rome, was later inserted into the collection of instructions (*mandata*) received by governors before they left for their provinces.[13] From the correspondence between Pliny the Younger and Emperor Trajan of 112 C.E.,[14] we learn that this order was still being observed by the governors at that time. In the second half of the second century, however, we find the governors attempting to persuade the Christians who were handed over to them to renounce Christianity and thereby save themselves. Nero's "mandate" classified the Christians as a subversive group, politically dangerous to the State and an enemy of the emperor and the empire. Therefore, members of this group were condemned to death even though they had not committed any crime.[15] The only change introduced in this policy by Trajan was implemented following the sending of his rescript to Pliny, and was not made primarily for the benefit of the Christians: Trajan ruled against the admissability of anonymous accusations as a matter of general policy.[16]

The brief reign of Emperor Decius (249–251 C.E.) caused trouble for Christians throughout the empire. He issued an edict that all the inhabitants of the empire were to sacrifice to the gods of the State. Committees were even established to supervise the implementation of the edict. Decius had wished to attract the favor of the gods for the empire through this form of worship – it was a political-religious move. While Decius's edict was not intended to serve as a means for persecuting the Christians, such indeed was its result.[17] In the year 257, Emperor Valerian and his son Gallienus issued an edict repeating Decius's earlier demand that all must worship the gods of the State.[18] This time, however, it was directed against the Christian clergy, probably because Valerian and Gallienus realized that the most stubborn resistance to such worship was concentrated in the leadership of the Church. In any event, Gallienus cancelled the edict in 260 C.E. It must be remembered that, during the time of Decius and Valerian, as well as after the repeal of the edict by Gallienus, the legal status of Christianity underwent no basic change: Adherence to Christianity was prohibited on penalty of death.[19] The last persecutions of Christianity began in 303 C.E. when Emperor Diocletian began a war of annihilation against the Church. He ordered the destruction of churches and the burning of Christian holy writings. In his fourth edict, issued in 304, Diocletian again raised the demand that all the inhabitants of the empire worship the gods.[20] The Jews were exempted from this decree as is evident from the tradition in the Jerusalem Talmud (*Avodah Zarah* 5:4 [44d]: "When King Diocletian came here, he decreed and said: All the nations shall pour out libations except for the Jews; the Kutim offered libations and their wine was forbidden." In the year 311, shortly before his death, Galerius published an edict which not only put an end to the persecutions of the Christians but even surpassed the tolerance of Gallienus in that for the first time, Christians were allowed to be Christians. In other words, for the first time since the days of Nero, there was a decisive change in the legal status of Christians.

In light of the above, it is clear why the Church leadership wished to change its image in the eyes of the Roman authorities. One possible way was to rehabilitate Jesus, the founder of the sect, which might be accomplished by exonerating Pontius Pilate of the charge of responsibility for the Crucifixion. As we have noted, the presentation of Pilate as wishing to spare the life of Jesus and trying to save him from the hands of the Jews had appeared even in the Gospels.[21] Such a description of Pilate is at total variance with the description of his character and deeds in Josephus Flavius; Philo of Alexandria sums up Pilate's behavior by saying that he was both callous and merciless (*Embassy to Gaius* 301). As was to be expected, the Church Fathers followed the tendency of the Gospels and blamed the Jews for the death of Jesus. In his *Apology* (21:24), Tertullian even saw fit to remark that, when Pilate allegedly reported about Jesus to Emperor Tiberius, Pilate himself was already a Christian at heart.[22]

This tendency was clearly illustrated in Melito's *Homily on the Passion*. On the one hand, Pilate was mentioned only once in the treatise, despite his decisive role in the events leading to the Crucifixion. On the other hand, Melito expanded the tradition of the Gospels to ascribe to the Jews both the preparations for the Crucifixion (such as the furnishing of the nails, the rods, the vinegar, and the gall), and the actions involved in it (such as the flogging, the crowning with thorns, the chaining, and the offering of the gall to drink).[23] Melito's forgiving of Pilate goes hand in hand with the sympathetic attitude toward the Roman Empire expressed in the fragments of his *Apology* which stressed that of all the emperors, only the infamous Nero and Domitian believed the slanderous stories circulated about the Christians. On the other hand, like most Church writers, Melito never tired of pointing repeatedly to the close chronological connection, as it were, between the birth of Christianity and the founding of the Principate by Augustus. To him, this conjunction was a good omen for the Romans who grew in strength and flourished thereafter, enjoying an age of peace and prosperity for the empire.[24]

This was the second point made by the Christians. Their third theme was the rebelliousness of the Jews and the Christians' dissociation from it. As is well known, the Christian community of Jerusalem left for Pella (in Transjordan) on the eve of the Great Revolt (66–70 C.E.), while the Christians refused to join the rebellion of Bar Kokhba and were probably punished for their refusal.[25] This wish to enlighten the Romans as to the difference between the seditious Jews and the peace-loving Christians explains the appearance of the destruction of Jerusalem and of the Temple in the apologetic works written by Justin, Origen, and others for pagan audiences.[26]

Indeed, mention of the Destruction served other propaganda purposes. First, the Christians argued, it proved the fulfillment of Jesus's prophecy. Second, the Destruction was connected by the Christians with the Jews' rejection and execution of Jesus, and the persecution and deaths of the Apostles (such as Stephen, James son of Zebedee, James brother of Jesus, and Paul) in the period before the Temple was destroyed. The Christians argued that not even one generation passed between the killing of Jesus and the punishment suffered by the Jews. Similarly, their presentation of Pilate and the Crucifixion served a double propaganda purpose. On the one hand, it was intended to win over the Romans and, on the other, to limit the influence of Jews upon Christians and, especially, upon pagans who wished to join the Church. Such an accusation would alienate them from Judaism.

4. Relations between Christians and Jews

This brings us to the question of the relations between Jews and Christians during those centuries: did these relations contain points of friction which generated antisemitic reactions among Church writers? Three other questions are associated with this one: Had there been a continuing and real conflict between the Jews and the Christians, or was there only empty bickering between them while the real conflict was taking place between the pagans and the Christians? Did the Jews collaborate with the pagans in their anti-Christian struggle? And did the Jews compete for the souls of the pagans and thereby clash with Christian missionary activity? All of these questions are controversial. We therefore have no option but to review briefly the various positions and arguments and determine our own stance.

Let us begin with Marcel Simon. His work[27] excels in extensive reviews of the relevant literature. He himself holds the generally accepted positions and tries to support them to the best of his ability. He sees the period from after the Bar Kokhba Revolt until the end of the Patriarchate in Israel (135–425 C.E.) as one of propaganda wars between the Jews and the Christians. In these centuries, Simon claims, the self-isolation of Judaism had not yet begun and its proselytizing activity was a thorn in the flesh of Christianity (ibid. 15–16). On the other hand, he feels, we witness a change in the attitude of pagan opinion toward the Jews as a result of the growing strength and disturbing spread of the Church. After the tensions and crises of 70–135 C.E., favorable and even wholly positive attitudes toward Judaism developed among the pagans, nurtured by their hostility toward the common enemy as well as by an awareness that Judaism and paganism were on the same conservative, ideological side against an innovative, revolutionary Christianity (ibid. 61–62 and cf. 436). Simon mentions that Celsus exploited the figure of a Jew alongside his harsh criticism of the Jewish faith, whose only merit he saw in the antiquity of its tradition. The praises of Judaism are much more abundant in Prophyry's work and, needless to say, in Julian's. Furthermore, the Roman authorities recognized the Jewish people and tolerated their religion. According to Simon, the threat of seditious Christianity[28] led to the pagans looking upon a pagan's conversion to Judaism as a lesser evil than conversion to Christianity, while a Christian's becoming a Jew was seen as pure profit. There is reason to believe that, in the criticial situation created by the interference of Christianity, the pagans allowed the Jews the freedom to spread their religion provided they did so at the expense of Christianity. This Simon derives from Jewish propagandizing during the execution of martyrs as, for example, in the *Martyrdom of Pionius*. There is reason to assume, adds Simon, that under certain circumstances the Roman authorities played the Jewish card against Christianity: this would explain the fact that a Christian anti-Jewish polemic would malign the Jewish community for its dependence upon the scepter (of the emperor) and the legions.[29] What is in the realm of plausible speculation for the third century becomes, to Simon, indisputable fact in the case of Emperor Julian.[30]

As for the Christians' attitude toward the Jews, says Simon, even if their very existence were justified theoretically in various ways (for example, they are witnesses to the truth of Christianity), in practice their existence was fraught with danger. In stressing the fall of Israel, the Church Fathers and the apologists addressed the Christians as much as the pagans and the Jews. By such a charge (and others), they sought to counter the attractiveness of the Jews and their propaganda, and to prevent the Christians from "Judaizing."[31]

As for the reality of the Jewish-Christian debate, the crucial question is whether the Jews waged an active proselytizing campaign.[32] Simon tries very hard to prove that they did; yet even he admits that the Jewish sources are inconclusive, while the Christian sources can be interpreted as a defense against the considerable attractiveness of the Jews even in the absence of propaganda on the Jews' part, as can be deduced, for example, from the eight vitriolic sermons of John Chrysostom against the Jews.[33] Certainly Halakhic leniencies in the acceptance of converts would attest to tendencies to convert, more than would laudatory statements whose value is neutralized by derogatory comments. Yet, even at the end of the first and the beginning of the second centuries, when we hear of converts in Jewish and pagan sources,[34] the Sages are not prepared to forego any of the legal restrictions concerning conversion, while they take an even more determined stand later on. The silence of the pagan sources in this period (from 150 C.E. on) is very telling.[35]

Simon expected to find considerable support for his views from Jewish funerary inscriptions, but he was bitterly disappointed: of seven hundred Jewish inscriptions in Frey's *Corpus Inscriptionum Judaicarum*, only nine referred to converts and four to *metuentes* (God-fearers). In order to explain away this contrary evidence for his hypothesis, Simon was forced to offer various rationalizations: that, in epigraphy, arguing from an absence of positive evidence can have no real significance, since finds are accidental and new discoveries are liable to change the picture; that the source of almost all the inscriptions is Rome, where the authorities presumably checked on forbidden proselytizing activity, and where it may also be possible that converts were not so indicated on their gravestones in order to avoid unpleasantness or difficulties for their surviving relatives and descendants; and similar arguments. After exhausting the explanations, Simon reaches the surprising conclusion that, in the light of what Juvenal writes, one must be cautious in interpreting the epigraphic evidence.[36] It would seem that the opposite is correct: Satire is not more valuable than simple inscriptions having no ulterior motive and, therefore, the satire should be interpreted in the light of the inscriptions.

Simon tries to strengthen his position, that the Sages actively proselytized the pagans, by indicating the sources that deal with "Greek wisdom," as well as the translation of the Torah into Greek, synagogue art, and so forth. His explanation is somewhat involved: The liberal stand of the Sages to the adaptation of pagan culture stems from their interest in conversion and its purpose was to influence the pagan world which, therefore, had first to be understood.[37] However, it is simpler and more correct to say that the position of the Sages reflects a consideration of their material needs along with the recognition that idolatrous influences no longer constituted a real threat to the Jews.[38]

Parkes (pp. 106–107,120), for all the paucity of references that he finds to Christianity in the Talmudic literature of the second-third centuries, a paucity that indicated to him that the Jews ignored Christianity after it became the religion of the Gentiles, still stresses the fact that the most serious motivation for the polemic between the two faiths was Jewish proselytism, which was competing with that of the Christians for the souls of the pagans.[39]

Vogt,[40] on the other hand, did not accept the conclusions reached by Parkes's studies of the *Acta* (the accounts of martyrdom). Vogt thought that his conclusions require criticial examination, and claimed that the Christian threat created a pagan-Jewish coalition which, as he put it in picturesque and prejudiced langauge, " . . . was a combination of unequal forces and a common feeling of helplessness in the face of Christianity's creative power: a union of the blind and the halt" (p.9).

Two scholars, Williams (above n.2) and Blumenkranz,[41] make an indirect contribution concerning our problem with their survey of the Christian literature whose concern, as its name suggests, is to attack the Jews. Simon states (p. 167) that Williams thinks that these writings faithfully reflect actual conflicts. However, it seems that both these scholars vacillate in their views. Williams (Introduction p. 17) says that the reader of these works gets an impression of "sameness" but that a closer inspection reveals something unique in each work. Further on (p.43) he notes that Tertullian's work, *Against the Jews*, had two aims: to defend the Christians against the Jews, of whom there were a great number in North Africa, and to convert the Jews, an aim that interested many Christians. This missionary aim, which Williams attributes to Tertullian's and similar works, is hard to accept because the very language of these works indicates that their authors had given up all hope of converting the Jews to Christianity. On the contrary, these authors feared the influence of the Jews: they sought to distance the Christians from them, and to keep the Christians from imitating their Jewish neighbors in Sabbath and holiday observances and other practices. Williams himself attributes this goal to Aphraates (p. 96) and emphasizes that Chrysostom's homilies, *Against the Jews*, were intended primarily for the Christians.[42]

Blumenkranz asserts at the outset that a considerable number of these pamphlets, especially those written at the end of the third century, were meant not only for the Church's war against the Jews but also for its war against other enemies, such as the pagans, the heretics, and the schismatics. These pamphlets also served internal Christian catechetical purposes. Since the hope of converting the Jews was gone, it could not have been a fundamental premise of these works. Rather they were meant to assist Christians in their disputations with Jews (debates which have always taken place), in their struggle against the influence of the Jews on the faithful, or on those seeking to join the Christian fold. Works whose sole function was the polemic against the pagans and heretics even contained an open apology for the Jews of the pre-Jesus period (Blumenkranz, p. 2 and n. 6; pp. 3–4), whereas Augustine's assertions about the relative and temporary authority of the ceremonial-ritual law were directed not only against the Jews but also against the "Judaizers" (ibid., pp. 133, 145, 151, 153, 155; cf. pp. 204, 210–211). Blumenkranz asserts (p. 85) that, so long as the pagan masses were a target for recruitment by Jews and Christians, the two faiths were compelled to engage in constant debate. Much literary evidence of these disputations, he notes, has been preserved among the Jews and the Christians. On the other hand, we read (p. 165) that until the destruction of the Temple the Jewish "mission" operated on a large scale and that converts were warmly received; thereafter, however, especially in the first centuries of Christianity's ascendance, there was a certain withdrawing inward upon itself of Judaism, which in the nature of things did not allow for its absorbing new elements. But Blumenkranz does not attempt to clarify the reasons for this withdrawal, being satisfied with leaving the impression that Judaism gave up its "missionary" thrust and left the field open to Christianity.

On this matter, Harnack takes an entirely different position.[43] He claims, unlike Williams, that these writings are not to be seen as a realistic response to the claims that were actually formulated by the Jews, and that the figure of the Jewish opponent in the dialogues and of the anonymous rival in the doctrinal writings is wholly artificial. This opponent's horizons are no different from those of his partner in dialogue: He is a Jew unlike any in real life, a product of the imagination. Harnack suggests that what purports to be a polemic is in reality an apologetic defense of Christianity intended for internal Church use. It refutes the reservations held by the Christians themselves or those likely to be put forth by pagans who had been influenced by the Gospels but had not as yet accepted Christianity. The aim of these works is to convince the pagans of the veracity of Christianity, using proofs from Biblical passages, while their being directed against Jews is a device. Such writings, he points out, cannot be expected to shed any light whatsoever upon the actual relationships of the two religions.

To these arguments (which he derived from an analysis of the relevant texts), Harnack adds one more, perhaps the most important of all. In his opinion, the Christians could not have been familiar with actual Jewish argumentation because, from the time of Domitian, the relations between Hellenistic Christianity and Judaism had lost all of their importance. There is no doubt that the Rabbinic literature was still speaking of contemporary debates in the second century, but, as far as Palestine and Syria were concerned, this activity was quite exceptional. In fact, Judaism did not concern the Christians; Judaism was not interested in them nor did it interest them itself. The two faiths were oblivious to one another and did not engage in active polemics.

This perception of Harnack's is supplemented and strengthened to a degree by Hulen's article.[44] Hulen drew up a classification of the contents of the anti-Jewish writings which indicates that works of the fourth century at least, such as Chrysostom's, are not concerned with defending Christianity or with detaching Jews from Judaism but with the defamation and calumniation of Judaism *per se*.

We conclude this survey with the new interpretation suggested by Yitzhak Baer.[45] His intention is clear: to prove that the Jews were a party of equal weight in the polemic within the pagan Empire. This thesis is formulated in the very first sentence of his article: "During its first three hundred years of existence, the Christian Church appears as the rival of the Jewish religious community competing with it *even while simultaneously engaged in a common struggle against the pagan Roman Empire.*" Later, Baer complains that "standard history books dealing with the epoch which is the subject of this article, describe the Christian Church as standing singlehanded in its holy struggle against paganism and the kingdom of evil [i.e., Rome] while the Jewish community's role in the political and intellectual reality of this world is forgotten." And on his p. 102 (in connection with R. Isaac's commentary in *The Song of Songs Rabbah* on 1:5–6, cf. his p. 114): "The Christian Church appears on the side of the congregation of Israel as her rival of the near past and has still to prove the achievements and credits due to her at Israel's side in the great historic struggle against paganism, *a struggle which doubtless demands its victims from Israel no less than from her young rival.*"

Baer attempted to show that the Jews were a target of religious persecution (as were the Christians) through his interpretation of Talmudic sources (for example, R. Johanan's statement to Bar Drossai, *Jerusalem Talmud, Avodah Zarah* 4:43d end), as well as of Christian and Roman sources.[46] However, it is difficult to accept Baer's view just as there is no foundation for the diametrically opposed theory which sees the Jews as collaborators with the Roman authorities against the Christians (for which, see below).

5. Frend's Theory

In 1965 Frend published his book on the persecutions of the Christians (see above, n. 9). Frend argues repeatedly that the Jews were active partners of the pagans in the persecution of Christians during the second century and for at least the first half of the third (see *Martyrdom and Persecution* pp. 168, 288, 334). Here is one example (pp. 258–259):

> In Asia [Minor] the pagans and Jews were threatened by the same enemy, and for the first time for many generations united against him.
>
> This strange alliance dates from after the defeat of 135. It was one of the means by which Israel saved itself from destruction, but at the cost of forfeiting for ever its claim to the universal allegiance of mankind [i.e., that all the nations shall flow unto it]. From now on, the domestic struggle between the Old Israel and the New becomes merged in the general conflict between Church and Empire. In the persecutions which were to wrack Asia in the reign of Marcus Aurelius the Jew was often in the background. For nearly another century he continued to stir up trouble wherever he could.

In his note 148 *ad locum*, Frend refers for confirmation of his statements to the charges made by Tertullian in the *Scorpiace* and by Origen in *Contra Celsum* as well as to the *Martyrdom of Pionius*.[47]

In 1966 Fergus Millar published a review of Frend's book[48], half of which was devoted to the refutation of Frend's thesis (as quoted above). Millar mentions, apparently with approval, the words of Professor Baer on the confrontation of both the Jews and Christians with their idolatrous environment (p. 233). Millar then proceeds to ask on what evidence Frend relies, other than general statements in Christian sources about the hostility of the Jews. Examining the evidence adduced by Frend, he indicates its weaknesses, before commenting (p. 234):

> It is necessary to conclude, with M[arcel] Simon, that the evidence for Jewish responsibility for the persecutions is very scanty. This is not to say that there was not polemic (though we know far more of Christian anti-Jewish polemic), hostility and on occasion violence. It is simply to say that, after the first half-century at least, the Jewish communities of the Diaspora were, given that we know very little about them, largely irrelevant to the principal conflict, that between Christianity and its pagan environment.

Let us now examine in more detail the two central and clearest statements concerning the participation of the Jews in the persecution of the Christians. After attacking the Gnostics and the Catholic Christians, who recoil from martyrdom, Tertullian addresses those outside the Church who take part in terrorizing the Christians, saying (*Scorpiace* 10): "Will you count here both the synagogues of the Jews – the sources of the persecutions, in which the Apostles were whipped – and the assemblies of the Gentiles with their circus, in which they shout and cry enthusiastically 'death to the third race' [that is, to the Christians]?" Frend deletes a few words from this sentence and states in his book (p. 334): "Tertullian's outburst '*synagogae Judaeorum fontes persecutionum . . .* ' [the synagogues of the Jews, the sources of the persecutions] . . . cannot be dismissed as mere rhetorical flourish." On this Millar remarks tersely and aptly: "It would be better to quote it more fully ' . . . *fontes persecutionum, apud quas apostoli flagella perpessi sunt*' [in which the Apostles were whipped]. Millar meant that the ending ties Tertullian's words to the "briefing" given by Jesus to his apostles. This link weakens the force of the conclusion that Frend wishes to draw from the *beginning* of the sentence as to the behavior of the Jews *at the time of Tertullian*. The words of Jesus are as follows (*Matthew* 10:17–19): "But beware of men: for they will deliver you up to the councils and *they will scourge you in their synagogues*. And ye shall be brought before governors and kings for my sake, for a testimony before them and the Gentiles. *But when they deliver you up*, take no thought how or what ye shall speak: for it shall be given you in that same hour what ye shall speak."

Millar's criticism seems to have pressed heavily on Frend for, after four years, Frend published a short article (see n. 8 above) in which he attempted to answer Millar and to strengthen his own statements on the accusations of Tertullian against the Jews. In this article, Frend presented every statement of Tertullian that points a condemning finger at the Jews and argued that these statements had a realistic background. As for our sentence, Frend argues (in his article, p. 295) that "If one takes the sentence as a whole, however, together with its mention of shouts of 'Death to the third race,' it must be obvious that Tertullian was thinking of what was happening in Carthage there and then. He was a journalist, not an antiquary, and the reference to the apostles is there for emphasis." Further on, Frend asserts: "Carthage at the turn of the third century held the same peril for the Christians as Smyrna in the time of Polycarp. It is not unreasonable to suggest, following Tertullian, that in both cities 'Jews and pagans were united in common action,'[49] for very different motives certainly, but for the Christians it meant a simmering hatred liable to break out on any trivial pretext in savage acts of persecution . . . Curiously enough Smyrna again provides a parallel situation with Jews and pagans making common cause against the confessor Pionius" (p. 296). Frend finishes by saying: "The pages of Tertullian enlighten both the positive and negative sides of the Jewish Christian relationship. The latter was hardly, as has been claimed [by Millar], 'largely irrelevant to the principal conflict between Christianity and its pagan environment.' On the contrary, *synagogae Judaeorum fontes persecutionum* was a fact."

Frend's having repeated his assertions in forceful and uncompromising language does not make them more convincing. Even if we accept the words of the *Acta Martyrum* literally[50], we cannot compare a tradition about deeds that occurred (whatever the degree of exactness that we ascribe to it) with the abstract and sweeping assertions of Tertullian, who found himself obliged to look for support to the authority of the Gospels. The comparison remains invalid.

As for the second proof brought by Frend, from Origen, it is easy to show that it is based on an error.[51] In *Contra Celsum* 6:27, Origen says:

> . . . . He [Celsus] seems to have behaved in much the same way as the Jews who, *when the teaching of Christianity began to be proclaimed*, spread abroad a malicious rumour [*dysphêmia*] about the gospel, to the effect that Christians sacrifice a child and partake of its flesh, and again that when the followers of the gospel want to do the works of darkness they turn out the light and each man has sexual intercourse with the first woman he meets. This malicious rumour *some time ago* unreasonably influenced a very large number and persuaded people knowing nothing of the gospel that this was really the character of Christians. And even now it still deceives some who by such stories are repelled from approaching Christians even if only for a simple conversation.

Surprisingly, Origen does not mention the things that were raised by the Sages against Jesus, his birth and actions, but only the false charges brought against the Christians concerning ritual murder and fornication. There is no doubt that Origen's accusations are baseless, for otherwise apologists of the second century such as Aristides (*Apology* 17), Athenagoras (*Embassy for the Christians* 3), Justin Martyr (*First Apology* 26, *Second Apology* 12), Tertullian (*Apology* 4:11), and others, who put up a defense against such accusations widely accepted among the pagan multitudes, would not have refrained from noting their Jewish origin. Such immoral deeds were ascribed to the Christians by the people and the authorities because they were an illegal religious sect; it was only natural, in their eyes, that criminal acts should be committed in the secret gatherings of the Christians. This may be inferred from Pliny the Younger's letter (Book 10, Epistle 96), and is also conspicuous in the report on the martyrs of Lugdunum (Lyons) in Gaul (in the *Acta Martyrum*, chap. 14). The Jews are not mentioned there at all with respect to the whole affair; the accusations of "dinners in the manner of Thyestes and sexual intercourses in the manner of Oedipus"[52] were extorted by torture from the pagan household servants of the Christians. The full charge was that, in their ritual gatherings, the Christians would envelop an infant in dough and then eat it, and that after feasting, they would extinguish the lights and commit adultery and incest (cf. Minicius Felix, *Octavius* chap. 9). In his *Dialogue with Trypho the Jew* (chap. 10), Justin asks Trypho if he believes this slanderous account about the Christians, and Trypho replies that something which is repugnant to human nature is not worthy of belief. Clearly, then, Origen's claim ascribing to the Jews such false charges against the Christians is wholly unfounded.

ATA—C

6. Writings on the Martyrs

From the Acts of the Apostles we learn of widespread missionary activity developed by the Christian apostles in the period from the death of Jesus to the war of the Destruction of the Second Temple. The bases for their activity outside of the Land of Israel as well as the sources of their recruitment were the Jewish communities and their synagogues. The apostles provoked unrest and confusion within the Land of Israel as well, and it is therefore understandable that the leadership institutions in Jerusalem[53] could not sit idly by, but persecuted and suppressed them as much as possible. During the seige of Jerusalem in the Great Revolt, the Jewish Christians left and went to Pella in Trans-Jordan (see above, section IV and n. 25). This was the first clear sign of the separation.

After the Destruction, the Pharisaic leadership, headed by the Patriarchate and the Sanhedrin, faced the task of suppressing the Jewish sects such as the Sadducees and the Christians. The Jewish Christians were strengthened in their faith in the Messianism of Jesus after his prophecies about the destruction of the Temple were fulfilled. Since the Jewish Christians fulfilled religious injunctions as did all Jews and were part of the houses of worship – while propagandizing for their faith – the Sages felt compelled to counter-attack in two ways: one, by a rebuttal of the faith in the power and divine inspiration of Jesus, through saying that his mother was an adulteress and that his father was a Roman soldier named Pandera-Panthera[54]; they claimed that all of Jesus's power came from the magic that he had learned in Egypt when he was there[55]. The second way involved sealing off the avenues of influence of the Jewish Christians on the Jews; for this reason, the *Birkat ha-Minim* (that is, the curse [literally, the blessing] of the heretics)[56] was instituted in Yavneh (Jamnia). These steps almost certainly brought an end to contact with, and the elimination of danger from, this sect. Thereafter, the "Ebionite" sects were a constant problem for the Christian-pagan Church. The distance became even greater because of the dispensations from observing Halakhic demands granted by the apostles to the pagans who wished to become Christians. From this point on, the pagan element of the Church became stronger and stronger, and the Church itself sought out the lines of demarcation from Judaism. The Jewish Christians were persecuted by the Jews for the last time when they refused to join the Bar Kokhba Revolt; Christianity in the Empire went its own way, with its development involving a struggle with Roman authority and even persecutions from time to time. The Sages and the Jews of the Diaspora had no further interest in this process because they no longer had anything to fear from it.[57] Even when the preferential status that the Jews – unlike the Christians – had enjoyed under pagan rule gave way to an inferior, degrading one, the very fact that the Church Fathers strove to validate Christian theology by recourse to the edicts and decrees of the secular arm contributed to strengthening and extending the separation. It may be then that, from the point of view of the contemporary Jewish leadership, there was a positive aspect to this legislation.

The stories contained in the collections called the *Acts of the Christian Martyrs* are not objective works. They seek to glorify and exalt the heroism of the martyrs and also to strengthen the hearts of the Christians who might themselves be similarly tried one day. In this instance, therefore, we are warranted in placing great weight on the silence of these sources. From our point of view, the compelling fact is that, in the *Acts* from the second century onward, one cannot find a single instance of a specific charge that the Jews collaborated with the authorities in capturing the martyrs or that they informed against them.

It is also instructive to compare the account of the martyrdom of Polycarp, from the middle of the second century, with that of Pionius, from the mid-third century. Both martyrdoms took place in Smyrna. In the first instance[58] the Jews are presented as active participants in gathering the wood for Polycarp's burning "as is their custom." They guard his body and prevent the Christians from taking it for burial. Incidentally, on this point, there is a suspicious similarity between this reported behavior of the Jews of Smyrna and the behavior attributed to the Jews at the time of the Crucifixion of Jesus. Compare *The Martyrdom of Polycarp* 17: " . . . Nicetes, Herod's father . . . was moved, then, to beseech the governor not to turn over his body [Polycarp's] saying: 'lest they leave the Crucified One and begin to worship this one.' He said this after he had been subverted and influenced by the Jews who even guarded (the body) when we were about to remove it from the fire," with Matthew 27:62–66: "And the next day, that following the day of preparation, the high priests and the Pharisees gathered together unto Pilate, saying, 'Sir, we have remembered how that impostor said, when still alive, "After three days I will rise again." Command, therefore, that the sepulchre be made secure until the third day, lest haply his disciples come by night and steal him away and say to the people, "He hath risen from the dead"; and thus the last imposture would be worse than the first.' Pilate said to them 'Ye have a guard [of soldiers]; go, make it secure as ye know how.' And going they made the sepulchre secure, sealing the stone and setting a guard." In short, the enthusiasm of the Jews was no less and was perhaps even greater than that of the pagans. It is worth noting the expression "as is their custom" (in Polycarp 13) regarding the Jews; it indicates that the Jews had behaved in this way previously. This is not so in the second case, in the martyrdom of Pionius. There it says only that the Jews flocked to the market square since they were free from work on "a great Sabbath." They go, then, to see the special spectacle of the trial of the martyrs, watching and laughing at the desolation of the Christians.[59]

It may seem paradoxical, but the stand of the Jews at the death of Polycarp can be explained precisely by the friendly tone (*philoi* etc.) taken by Justin when he addresses Trypho and the Jews in general[60]. For this reason, I classify the *Dialogue with Trypho the Jew* as the last Christian work which, like the Synoptic Gospels, tries hard by friendly means to influence the Jews to stop being obstinate and to acknowledge Jesus.[61] This would mean that it is likely that the last missionary efforts to convert the Jews were undertaken in the middle of the second century; Polycarp was almsot certainly one of those directing this policy, hence the great enmity shown him by the Jews. After the Christians had despaired of the Jews and left them to their own devices, the Jews dealt with them calmly, as the account of Pionius shows a century later.

In his article on Melito of Sardis (n.3 above), Noakes analyzes some polemical parallels found in the works of Justin and Melito. For example, both react to the question of the Jews asking: Why blame us for the death of Jesus if, in any case, he had to suffer and die in order to redeem humankind? Justin's response lacks the strength of Melito's rebuke.[62] In Melito we also have explicitly stated the tendency to blame the Jews instead of Pilate[63] for Jesus's Crucifixion. According to Noakes, "Melito's work *On the Passion* reflects the conflict between the Jews and the Christians in Asia Minor. In paragraph 72 there, he turns to the Jewish people and reprimands them harshly for the killing of Jesus. Nearly a third of *On the Passion* (paragraphs 72–99) is devoted to attacks on the Jews in this matter. The Jewish people is accused as a murderer, even by its own admission, as an ingrate, etc. The intensity of Melito's polemic undoubtedly testifies to the antagonism which prevailed between the Jewish and Christian communities of Sardis."[64] Yet, if this were so, why was it not expressed in Justin's *Dialogue* when the martyrdom of Polycarp testified so much more powerfully to the strong hatred of Jews for Christians in Asia Minor? It seems to us that the explanation offered above is valid here as well. Justin still entertains the hope of winning the Jews to Christianity[65] whereas Melito has already despaired of them and his entire desire is to neutralize their dangerous influence on the Christians and on the pagans inclining to Christianity. Therefore, Melito is not afraid to use a wounding, uncompromising style while Justin uses mild, seductive language (see, for example, the Epilogue in the *Dialogue* 142).

7. Treatises against the Jews

The *Dialogue with Trypho* can, for practical purposes, be considered the pioneer work in the category of "*Adversus Iudaeos*" (against the Jews) treatises. The outline of these works, such as *The Dialogue*, or the *Against the Jews* works of Tertullian and Augustine, or the various *Altercationes* of the second to fourth centuries, is a very simple one: Jesus and the religious injunctions. Therefore those verses continually reappear which, according to the claim of the Christians, allude to Jesus, the time of his coming, his divine origin, the Jews' attitude toward him, and the like. The Christians are also compelled to explain on what basis they reject the injunctions concerning circumcision, the Sabbath, forbidden foods, laws of purity and impurity, and so forth. The personality of Jesus, as might be expected, is the central target of the attacks by the pagan philosophers since he was the "founder of the sect" ("*archêgetês tês staseôs*") as Celsus put it (8:14). Porphyry and Julian frequently comment on

Biblical texts in order to refute Christian exegesis. The revocation of the injunctions of the Torah by the Christians who depended upon radical allegorical exegesis riddled with contradictions is also a polemical motif used repeatedly by the pagans. It was therefore convenient and perhaps even necessary for the Christians to direct their efforts at self-defense against the Jews, because the very existence of the Jews and their determined opposition to the system and pretensions of the Christians gave the greatest of weight to those charges of the pagans. They were a serious obstacle as well as a weak point in the Christian effort to convince the pagans to accept Christianity. If we find that the Christians, in their polemics against the heretics and schismatics, raise the same reasons as are found in the treatises *"Adversus Iudaeos"* (see in section V above), and that these last have a clear catechistic function and were of value in the internal struggle to forestall the "Judaizers,"[66] then, inevitably, their anti-Jewish importance diminishes; the titles of these works should not be allowed to mislead us. It is possible, therefore, to say that the *"Adversus Iudaeos"* treatises were *also* directed against the Jews. On the other hand, the picture of Judaism which emerges from the polemic literature against the pagans is quite clear.

The treatise of Tatian, Justin's pupil, is outstanding in its frank, acerbic, and daring language. Like Justin, Tatian wishes to give the impression that he is expert in every aspect of Greek culture: philosophy, poetry, history, and so forth, and that his choice of the Law of Moses has come after he considered and weighed the value and truth of all of these teachings. Except for the final chapters (36ff.) in which Tatian deals with proving that Moses and his Law preceded Homer and even Homer's predecessors, Orpheus and Musaeus for example, (it should be pointed out that on this matter of precedence the Christian apologists, almost without exception, repeat Josephus), Tatian's words clearly indicate the enormous importance attributed to the Biblical accounts by people of little education who were barely familiar with the teachings of the philosophers and who found the mythological stories repugnant. The simplicity and authority with which the Torah recounts the most complicated and difficult problems were understood by the pagans of this intellectual type and convinced them. In his article, "Judaism in the Eyes of the Ancient World," after noting the sources which deal with conversion and with the influence of the Bible on the conversion of pagans, Yitzhak Heinemann says:[67]

> The public statements of people who were attracted to Christianity in the period when the Church had no sacred scriptures other than the Bible are in consonance with these accounts. The most important of them is that of Tatian [=*To the Greeks* 29]: "When I seriously examined what might be of use to me, I chanced upon some barbaric [i.e., non-Greek] writings of earlier date than those of the Greeks. They succeeded in convincing me – by the simplicity of their expression, by their description of Creation which is easy to understand, by foreseeing the future, by their good laws,

and because they teach the rule of the one god dominant over all." All of these statements confirm the evidence of our literature that the advantage of Judaism was based on the books of the Bible. There were none such in the official religion or in the mystery religions. Here, Tatian supplements the information of the Aggada, that even the simple form of the Bible, different from the involved style of rhetoric, attracted many of the readers. It is interesting that it was the account of Creation which influenced Tatian as it did Aquila.[68]

Tertullian's sharp, scourging language against the pagans and the heretics is famous. However, his attitude to the Jews in his *Apology* is completely different (see ibid., 16:1–3). He contradicts Tacitus on their worship of a donkey's head and calls him "the most talkative of liars" (*loquacissimus mendaciorum*). It is not difficult to understand why Tertullian was constrained to defend the Jews and he even states it openly: "From this, it seems to me, it was assumed that we, too, being close to the Jewish religion, also worship this image [that is, a donkey's head]."[69] To be sure, Tertullian does not deny that there are differences and even points of opposition between Christians and Jews: The Christians do not abstain from forbidden foods, do not celebrate the Jewish festivals, do not practice circumcision, and so on (ibid., 21:2); the most important controversy between them is over the coming of the Messiah whom the Jews are awaiting and who the Christians claim has already come (21:15). But, on the other hand, their Torah is true and their prophets are true. Under the auspices of Judaism, the most sublime faith, Christianity grew.[70] Tertullian goes out of his way to repeat the account of the preparation of the Septuagint translation (18:5) and, of course, expands upon the antiquity of the Mosaic Law and the faith which it warrants since its prophecies have been fulfilled (19:1). In summing up, Tertullian points out that his proofs are principally dependent upon the reliability and antiquity of the Scriptures (44:1).

Origen's lengthy work *Contra Celsum* is intended to nullify the influence of Celsus's arguments on the pagans who tended to Christianity, and to provide the Christians with rebuttals for the objections and attacks provided the pagans by Celsus. In addition to using Josephus and Philo in accordance with the usual Christian practice,[71] Origen makes every effort to defend Judaism and glorify it. He makes it clear that Christians and Jews join in believing that the Bible was written and informed by the holy spirit even though the Christians do not observe the injunctions of the Torah and differ in its interpretation (5:60). This does not prevent him from praising the Jewish constitution (*politeia*) which is based, according to him, for the most part on worthwhile things, such as the forbidding of prostitution, laws concerning Hebrew slaves, and so forth; because in the realm of ethical-social matters, as opposed to ritual-worship matters, the Christians continued to base themselves upon the laws of the Torah as a guiding and binding codex. On that same issue Origen says (5:42) that the wisdom of the Jews is superior not only to that of the pagan masses but also to that of the philosophers; because the latter, for all their wisdom, were snared by the worship of idols and daemons whereas even the least of the Jews worships only the God of the universe. In reply to Celsus's argument that it is unreasonable that the Jews be especially beloved of God and that to them alone He sends His angel-messengers – for their condition and the kind of country they attained are proof to the contrary – Origen says (5:3) that the Jews were the beneficiaries of God's special grace in that he never forsook them and that, though they were few in number, they have been protected by the power of God. Other proofs of this sort can be cited, and it can also be shown that Origen attacks the Jews (in this treatise) only when forced into doing so. One explicit paragraph should be enough to indicate his sentiments clearly. At the beginning of his treatise, Celsus presented a Jew in sharp, heated debate with Jesus and the Christians. One would expect that this provocation by the Jew would infuriate Origen and that he would be drawn into a specific, bitter debate with Judaism; to our surprise, Origen shows great restraint and puts an end to the exchange with the Jew which he had just begun by saying:

> However, it is not my task here to explain the meaning of circumcision which began with Abraham and was stopped by Jesus as he did not wish his disciples to do the same. For it is not now the right time to explain his teaching on this matter, but rather to endeavour to destroy the accusation brought by Celsus against the doctrine of the Jews; for he thinks he will more easily prove Christianity to be untrue if he can show its falsehood by attacking its origin in Judaism. (Chadwick's translation of 1:22).

The statistical picture emerging from Origen's writings is most instructive.[72] On the one hand, the number of expressions sympathetic to Judaism in *Contra Celsum* alone (about thirty) is almost the same as in all of his other works put together. On the other hand, the number of hostile expressions in his other works is almost identical with the number of positive ones, whereas in *Contra Celsum* the number of hostile comments is only about a tenth of the number in the other works. This statistic speaks for itself and attests to the fact that Origen's approach to the Jews, as with the other Church Fathers, was a direct result of theological and political necessity.[73]

8. Works Intended for Christian Audiences

The preceding review has shown us only one side of the coin as it is reflected in works written for an external audience. True, in the works meant for internal consumption, the Church Fathers had completely different goals and therefore the picture of the Jew in their works became progressively darker. Even Justin, whose motives for employing a soft tone vis-à-vis the Jews we discussed above, does not refrain from attacking the Jews harshly. To his mind, they are wicked, worse than the people of Nineveh who, at least repented, (*Dialogue* 30,93,107). Their wickedness had been revealed in the killing of righteous people in the past, and was outstandingly evident in the persecution of Jesus's followers (*Dialogue* 93). Justin's sharpest formulations appear in his *Dialogue* 123, just before Trypho's bursting out with the question: "What, then? Are you Israel?!" Here is an example of them: "You are not ashamed to hear these words time and again [before this Justin had cited from Deuteronomy 32:20: ' . . . children with no loyalty in them,' and from Isaiah 42:20: 'Seeing many things, he gives no heed; with ears open, he hears nothing'], and you do not tremble when God threatens, but rather are you a foolish and hard-hearted people. 'Truly I shall further baffle that people with bafflement upon bafflement; and the wisdom of its wise men shall fail, and the prudence of its prudent men shall vanish' [Isaiah 29:14]. And rightly so! For you are neither understanding nor wise, but rather insidious and scoundrels (*panourgoi*); clever only at doing wrong [see Jeremiah 4:22] and not fit to recognize the hidden counsel of God or the faithful covenant of God or to discover His eternal paths." Above all, Justin is furious with the Sages who, he thinks, are responsible for the refusal of the Jewish people to acknowledge Jesus, and he presses Trypho not to place his trust in the Sages because they are leading themselves and their followers into error (ibid., 32,68).[74] What is most striking in Justin, and in others who followed suit, is his blending of Biblical and New Testament verses with contemporary claims into a single entity. This created the misleading impression of a commentary reflecting contemporary events but which was one-sided since it presented only the negative aspects of the Jewish Bible about the Jews while the positive aspects were used, as shown above, only in the works directed to the outside, pagan world.[75]

This system, of course, is also used by Origen. We cannot – nor is there any reason to – repeat the well-known motifs also appearing in Origen, such as the killing of Jesus by the Jews, their punishment, and the like.[76] We will deal with the development of only one motif, which subsequently achieved great popularity: Satan and the Jews. In the Gospel of John (13:2) it says: "And as supper was beginning, when the devil (*diabolos*) had already put it into the heart of Judas Iscariot the son of Simon to betray him . . . " Origen stresses this point in response to the Jews' claim that it was Jesus's disciples who handed him over. According to Origen, the Jews acted as the agents of the Devil in the killing of Jesus, though this fact did not, of course, erase their own responsibility. He even adds, with no support whatever from the Gospels, that it was the Devil who put the idea of asking Pilate that Jesus's grave be sealed and placed under guard into the hearts of the priests and scribes.[77]

In the year 386, John Chrysostom was appointed preacher of the principal church in Antioch. Chrysostom occupied this post for the next twelve years. At the beginning of his ministry, in 386 and 387, he delivered his eight sermons *Against the Jews*[78] All scholars agree that the sermons of Chrysostom (the "golden mouth") were intended almost exclusively for his Christian audience. It is clear from their content that the Jewish influence in Antioch was considerable in the social and even in the religious sphere. Chrysostom was appalled by the fact that the Christians, members of his flock, frequented the synagogues, joined in the Jewish festival celebrations and, in general, were drawn to everything related to Judaism and open to its influence. This concern appears in all of his sermons whose leitmotif is the attempt to dissuade his hearers from any dealings whatsoever with Jews, whether in the religious or economic-legal sphere. It is interesting that the tables have now been turned: In the second century, Justin had Trypho state that the Sages prohibited the Jews from having anything to do with the Christians (*Dialogue* 38): "And Trypho said: 'Sir, it were good for us if we obeyed our teachers, who laid down a law that we should have no intercourse with any of you, and that we should not even have any communication with you on these questions.'" This is confirmed by a Talmudic source, by a Sage who was a contemporary of Justin (*Abot de Rabbi Nathan* version B, ch. 3, Schechter ed., 7[13]:

> Another explanation: 'Remove,' etc. (Proverbs 5:8). R. Joshua ben Korha says: this is naught but the way of heresy (*minuth*). You tell a person not to go to the heretics (*minim*) and not to hearken to their words, so that he will not stumble over (because of) their deeds. He says to them: 'Although I do go, I do not listen to their words and I will not stumble over (because of) their deeds.' They say unto him: 'Although you have confidence, do not go, for of this it was said, "Remove thy way far from her," (Ibid.) and it says, "For she hath cast down many wounded" (Prov. 7:26).'

Now, however, at the end of the fourth century, John Chrysostom makes desperate efforts in the opposite direction, to no avail. The difference between the two situations is that, while in the first half of the second century the Christians still strove to convert the Jews, by the time of Chrysostom there was no Jewish initiative to convert the Christians or the pagans; it was only the Jews' very existence and their behavior as an established and unified religious group that were seen as a danger then. The hatred toward the Jews that permeated Chrysostom's work is in inverse proportion to Chrysostom's knowledge of Judaism.

In his book dealing with the *Adversus Judaeos* works, Williams remarks several times that the Christians argued "rightly," that is, he sets himself up as a judge between the Jews and pagans and their Christian adversaries, and passes sentence in favor of the Christians. In view of this, Williams's critical view of Chrysostom is very instructive. In his opinion, the absence of an "evangelical spirit" from Chrysostom's attitude toward the Jews is even more serious than his ignorance of Jewish matters (including his ignorance of the Hebrew language). Williams therefore thinks that Chrysostom's sermons do not deserve to be summarized as he summarizes the other treatises of this kind; instead he only quotes some of Chrysostom's utterances. Typical paragraphs from two of Chrysostom's sermons will serve to illustrate their character:

> *First Sermon*, 7: What sort of folly, what kind of madness, to participate in the festivals of those who are dishonored (*êtimomenous*), turned over by God, and who provoked the Lord? If someone killed your son, tell me, could you bear the sight of him?! Could you stand to hear him speak? Would you not rather flee from him as from an evil demon, or as from the devil (*diabolos*) himself? They killed the son of your Lord, and you dare to gather together with them under the same roof? When the one who was killed by them so honored you by making you his brother and fellow-heir, you heap such dishonor upon him (*atimazeis*) by revering (*timan*) his murderers and crucifiers, and flatter them (*therapeuein*) by attending their festival assemblies. You enter their profaned places, you cross the thresholds of their defiled houses and you recline at the table of daemonic powers. That is what I am persuaded, after their God-slaying, to call the Jewish fast. What else are they who work against God but doers of the will of the daemons?[79] *Sixth Sermon*, 6: Because of this I myself hate the Jews for, though holding the Law (*nomos*), they commit an outrage (*hybrizousin*) against the Law; in this way they attempt to ensnare the simple folk. This charge would not have been so grave *had they not disobeyed Christ while believing in the Prophets*. But now they have forfeited all forgiveness for, on the one hand, they assert that they accept the words of the latter [the Prophets] and, on the other hand, they commit an outrage (*kathlybrizousin*) against the one [Christ] about whom they prophesied.[80]

Incidentally, the same attitude – but from a Jewish point of view – arguing that the Christians were worse than the pagans because of their belief in the Torah and the Prophets, is expressed by R. Tarphon of Yavneh (see below, n. 81).

9. Summary

Let us now attempt to summarize our discussion. In the period before the destruction of the Second Temple, as well as in the Yavneh period (that is, from the Destruction to the Bar Kokhba Revolt), the Christian sect was seen as a thorn in the flesh of the Jewish national leadership which (before the year 70) attempted to eliminate the irritant or at least expel its adherents from Jewish society and combat their influence and propaganda. Toward this end, the *Birkat ha-Minim* (that is, the curse [literally, the blessing] of the heretics) was instituted, and polemical barbs were hurled at Christian theology (as, for example, calling Jesus "ben Stara" or "ben Pantera").[81]

After the Bar Kokhba Revolt, the Jewish-Christian conflict faded away in an era of increasing Christian estrangement from Judaism. This withdrawal from

Judaism became more powerful in the Church with the increased power and numbers of Christians of pagan origin. It also appears that the eagerness of the Jews to convert their neighbors, a missionary eagerness that could have caused friction, decreased. As a matter of fact, the Christians now had a free hand among the pagans (apart, of course, from persecutions by the Roman authorities, which must have deterred many and caused others to desert).

As for these persecutions by the authorities, it is clear that in no instance did the Jews initiate them; they did not inform on the Christians, nor did they hand them over to the authorities. The *argumentum e silentio*, especially the silence of the compilers of the *Acta Martyrum*, is very strong in this case. Jesus's warning on this subject (see *Matthew* 10:17–18) might have served as a stimulus for raising such charges against the Jews had there been any basis whatsoever for them in reality.

But even after the strong rivalry had passed, there remained negative residua against Judaism which were formed in and sanctified by the New Testament, and this determined the attitude of the Church Fathers in subsequent generations.

The position of the New Testament was also influenced by the Christians' relations with the Roman authorities, which the Church sought to improve. One of the ways to achieve this improvement was to rehabilitate the image of Pontius Pilate, the representative of the Roman authorities, and to limit or deny entirely his responsibility for the trial and crucifixion of Jesus. The other side of Pilate's rehabilitation was, of course, the condemnation of the Jews. As the illegal status of Christianity in the Empire did not change until the edict of the year 311, it was only natural that the Church Fathers of the second and third centuries should continue to work for this desired change, doing so perforce at the expense of the Jews by, for example, throwing all of the blame for the killing of Jesus on them.

But it was not this alone that led the Church Fathers to an anti-Jewish position. They were forced into such a stance by the very existence of the Jews and their attachment to their Law, their customs, and their traditions. Christianity was absolutely dependent on the Jewish Bible and on the connections between it and the New Testament for its theology and ethics. Christianity needed this connection in order to prove the antiquity of its belief; also it had to contend with the influence exerted by the Law and the Prophets on pagans who were attracted to the Church and wished to become Christians. This dependence raised many embarrassing questions for the Christians. Since the origins of Christianity and the path to Christianity were intertwined with the Holy Scriptures of the Jews, the Jews' very existence, even without any action on their part, constituted a problem for the Church.

This situation forced the Church Fathers to come forth to defend Christianity and explain its stand. As I see it, this was the fundamental cause of the attacks on the Jews made by the Church Fathers: they had to make Judaism unattractive, even repulsive, to Christians and to pagans. On the other hand, we encounter many words of praise and defense of the Jews and Judaism (though they refer to the period *before* the time of Jesus) in various apologetic treatises intended for pagans or Gnostics and heretics.[82]

The question which we must now confront is this: are we dealing here with legitimate attacks within the framework of mutual rivalry and polemic – bitter though it might be – or did these attacks perhaps exceed these limits and ought they accordingly to be defined as antisemitic?

In his discussion of "The Epistle of Barnabas" which, in his opinion was "probably written after the uprising of Simon Bar Cochba," J. Alvarez argues that this work was in fact the first treatise of the *Adversus Judaeos* series, and that it served as an apologetic model for the second and subsequent centuries.[83] Its author, says Alvarez, "desires at any cost that Christians divorce themselves from the Synagogue, and suggests the keeping of the eighth day of the week in place of the Jewish Sabbath (15,8)," for he "saw how some Christian communities wavered between both religions and so kept up Jewish practices, and this he wishes to eliminate." Alvarez adds (p.74) that "with the Pseudo-Barnabas is born the scorn for the Jewish People and their [title of] pride as the chosen people passes over to the Christians." The "Pseudo-Barnabas attributes Jesus's death to the Jews, even the Crucifixion, lance, insults, and spittle which the Gospels attribute to the Romans." Still, Alvarez draws two somewhat surprising conclusions (p.76): first, "the Apostolic Fathers propose a separation between Synagogue and Church" and, second, "they are anti-Jewish but not antisemitic in the sense that history has given to this word."

Alvarez focused his dicussion on the early Church Fathers (second century); of this group, the author of the "Epistle" is exceptional because of his hostile language, hostile perhaps because of the goal he set for himself: the removal of the Christians from the influence of Judaism. But there is no doubt that *in general* the tone of the attacks on the Jews became, paradoxically, ever more acute as the distance in time increased from the period of sharp, actual conflict between Jews and Christians. This means that the more the contact between the two religions diminished, the stronger became the hatred expressed toward the Jews. The explanation of this phenomenon is, I suggest, that the Christians now despaired of ever converting the Jews, and therefore saw no point in imposing self-restraint. Because of this, the real, flesh-and-blood image of the Jew was lost, and replaced by an abstract, one-dimensional, negative and Satanic figure, delineated in a mosaic of derogatory verses and statements from the Jewish Bible and the New Testament. At the root of the matter lies, then, not the actual condition or behavior of the Jews, but rather the image of the Jews required for the purposes of Christian theology. The theologians created this image according to the New Testament, on the one hand, and the allegorical interpretation of Biblical heroes personifying the wicked and sinful Israel who persecutes the true and good Israel, that is, Christianity, on the other. In this way, expositional exercises and unbridled, hate-filled denunciations, written and expressed in response to contemporary conditions, established a long-enduring attitude toward the Jews – and this because of the authority of their authors and the prestige they enjoyed in subsequent generations. This attitude, together with the New Testament, formed the approach of Christianity to the Jewish people in the Middle Ages and in modern times, when Judaism was at the mercy of the Christian Church, and when the causes that had engendered antisemitism in the early Church had long since passed from the world.

Notes

1. See Justin Martyr, *Dialogue with Trypho the Jew* 1ff.; *The Second Apology* 42. Cf. the effect of the martyrdom of R. Hanina ben Teradyon on the Roman officer as described in the *Babylonian Talmud, (hereafter T.B.) Avodah Zarah* 18a.
2. On Justin and his treatises see: J. Quasten, *Patrology* 1 (Utrecht, 1950), p.196ff., which includes a detailed bibliography. For specific discussions of his attitude toward the Jews, see: A. Lukyn Williams, *Adversus Judaeos: A Bird's-Eye View of Christian Apologiae until the Renaissance* (Cambridge, 1935); R. Wilde, *The Treatment of the Jews in the Greek Christian Writers of the First Three Centuries*, (Washington D.C., 1949).
3. On him see Quasten, *Patrology* 1,p.242ff. On his attitude toward the Jews see the article of K. W. Noakes, "Melito of Sardis and the Jews," *Studia Patristica* 13(1975) [=*Texte und Untersuchungen* 116]:244–249.
4. On this see my article: "Ben Stara is Ben Pantera — Towards the Clarification of a Philological-Historical Problem" (Heb.), *Tarbiz* 39(1970):9–18 and Ernest I. Abel, "The Virgin Birth: Was it a Christian Apologetic?" *Revue des études juives* 128(1969):395–399.
5. *The True Discipline* 1:28,32.
6. On Origen and his works, see Quasten, *Patrology* 2(Utrecht, 1953), p.37ff. and the above-mentioned works of Williams and Wilde; also in the introduction of H. Chadwick to *Origen Contra Celsum* (Cambridge, 1965).
7. See *Ad Scapulam* 5.
8. See Quasten, *Patrology* 2(1953), p.246ff.; Williams, *Adversus Judaeos*; and W. H. C. Frend, "A Note on Tertullian and the Jews," *Studia Patristica* 10(1970) [=*Texte und Untersuchungen* 107]:291–296.
9. See Quasten, *Patrology* 1,p.77ff., the full texts and the introduction in H. Musurillo, *The Acts of the Christian Martyrs* (Oxford, 1972); W. H. C. Frend, *Martyrdom and Persecution in the Early Church* (Oxford, 1965).
10. Cf. my article "On the Attitude of the Sages towards Gentiles and Proselytes" (Heb.), *Mahalkhim* 5(1971):72–73.
11. On the legal-governmental aspects of the trial and crucifixion, see Haim H. Cohn, *The Trial and Death of Jesus* (New York, 1971), p.71ff.
12. J. Molthagen, *Der roemische Staat und die Christen im zweiten und dritten Jahrhundert* (=*Hypómnemata* 28) (Goettingen, 1970).
13. See Molthagen, ibid, p.23ff. In his article "The Ban on Circumcision and the Bar Kokhba Revolt" (Heb.), *Zion* 41(1976):145–146, J. Geiger argues that "until a few generations ago the prevalent assumption was that there had been some general law which forbade the existence of Christianity, whether as an *Institutum Neronianum* or in some other form. Today there are no serious objections to the assumption that the legal aspect of the persecutions stemmed from the power of *coercitio* of the provincial governors . . . " I have no doubt that had Geiger been aware of Molthagen's clear and convincing interpretations which logically reconcile the entire complex of the available sources, he would not have hastened to pronounce so absolute a judgment and would not even have drawn an analogy between the persecution of the Christians and Hadrian's edict on circumcision.
14. See *Epistolae* 10: Letters 96–97. Cf. Molthagen, pp.20–21.

15. Molthagen, pp.30–33.
16. Molthagen, pp.35–36.
17. Molthagen, p.61ff.
18. Molthagen, pp.85–88.
19. Molthagen, pp.98–100.
20. Eusebius, *On the Martyrs of Palestine* 3:1; Molthagen, pp.105–109.
21. See especially *Luke* 23:25; *John* 19:16.
22. *Pilatus, et ipse iam pro sua conscientia Christianus.*
23. See *On the Passion* lines 571–574, 676–678; cf. 695–710 and 690–694 (for the confrontation of Gentiles and Jews). Cf. Matthew 27:26,29,30,34. See also Noakes on this (above, n. 3), pp.247–248.
24. See Eusebius, *Ecclesiastical History* 4, 26:7–9.
25. See Eusebius, *Ecclesiastical History* 3, 5. Justin Martyr (*The First Apology* 31) says: "For in the Jewish war which lately raged, Barchochebas, the leader of the revolt of the Jews, gave orders that Christians alone should be led to cruel punishments, unless they would deny Jesus and utter blasphemy . . . " (trans. M. Dods, Ante-Nicene Christian Library). In contrast to the religious motive ascribed by Justin to the persecution of the Christians by Bar Kokhba, Jerome speaks of a national-military motive. This motive seems more reasonable although, because of their belief in Jesus as Messiah, the Christians were unable to join the army of Bar Kokhba, of whom Rabbi Akiba said: "this is the King Messiah." The words of Jerome (in Eusebius's *Chronicon* under the year 133 c.e.) are as follows: "Cochba, the leader of the Jewish gang, used various tortures to kill the Christians who refused to help him against the Roman forces."
26. See Justin, *The First Apology* 47,53; Origen, *Contra Celsum* 4:73. Cf. Minucius Felix, *Octavius* 33:2–5; Tertullian, *Apology* 20:3.
27. M. Simon, *Verus Israel: Études sur les relations entre Chrétiens et Juifs dans l'empire Romain, 135–425* (Paris, 1948).
28. M. Simon, pp.143–144. Judaism was also threatened directly by Christian preaching. Julian wished to shake the faith of the Christian believers by rebuilding the Temple; since he could not bring them back to their ancestral religion (polytheism) as he wished, he undoubtedly hoped to bring them to Jewish worship (which he thought similar to Hellenism), and hoped that by their return to the religious tradition (Judaism) which they had left, denying it, an end would be put to their existence as a *tertium genus* (a third race).
29. *Sceptro et legionibus fulta.* Ps. Aug., "Altercatio Ecclesiae et Synagogae" *PL* 42:1131.
30. See M. Simon, pp.138–139. The conclusion to be drawn from Simon, then, is that there was no pagan-Jewish polemic but that the pagans and Jews formed a single bloc against Christianity. If the pagans did in fact see the Jews as allies, this does not mean that the feeling was necessarily mutual. On this point related to the question of the Jews' responsibility for the pagan persecutions of the Christians, Simon seems to disagree with Allard and Harnack who, with almost no objections, accepted the opinion that the Jews had a not insignificant share in them. Simon generally supports the conclusions of Parkes's studies on this matter, although Simon feels that Parkes is overly philosemitic (see pp.144–155, especially 149, 152, 153; cf., on the other hand, pp.237–238).
31. M. Simon, pp.118–120. On the problem of the "Judaizers," see pp.356, 368, 382–383. From what Simon says here, a slightly different conclusion can be drawn: that Christianity in its debate with the Jews took a defensive line forced upon it by the very fact of Judaism's existence, and that Judaism had no need for the polemic or for proselyting.
32. See Simon on p.315.
33. Simon's reliance upon Braude's *Jewish Proselyting in the First Five Centuries of the Common Era* (Providence, R.I., 1940) is undermined by the criticism of G. Alon who says (*Studies in Jewish History* 2 [Heb.][Tel-Aviv, 1958], pp.282–283): "The difference of opinion between R. Joshua b. Hananiah and R. Eliezer about the proselyte who was circumcised but not immersed (in the ritual bath) or immersed but not circumcised should not be brought here in the Babylonian Talmud version – *T.B. Yebamoth* 47a. The tradition in the *Jerusalem Talmud Kiddushin* 3 [64d] and *Massekhet Gerim* is decisive in the rejection of the Babylonian version and in establishing the tradition of the Land of Israel, according to which R. Joshua never said that circumcision is not an [essential] prerequisite."

34. Judah the Ammonite proselyte, and Keti'a bar Shalom; similar information appears in Juvenal and Tacitus. Cf. Josephus, *Contra Apionem* 2, 10:123: "From the Greeks we are separated more by our geographical position than by our institutions, with the result that we neither hate nor envy them. On the contrary, many of them have agreed to adopt our laws; of whom some have remained faithful, while others, lacking the necessary endurance, have recanted."

35. See Simon pp.315–328. From what Dio Cassius (37:16–17) writes, i.e., that people of other nations who observe the commandments of the Jewish faith are also called Jews, Simon concludes that there was still vigorous Jewish proselytizing in this period. Simon does mention Justin's words to Trypho and those who wish to be proselytes, that is, to become Christians (*Dialogue* 23:2), and notes that Tertullian, at the start of his treatise, *Adversus Iudaeos*, reports a debate that he purportedly heard between a Jewish proselyte of pagan origin and a Christian. Finally, Simon remarks that Origen pointed out that proselytism was still very active in his time (In Matth. Comm. Ser. 16=PG 13, p.621). Simon argues that what is true of the time of the composition of the Gospels (*Matt.* 23 :15; cf. 23:13), namely that after the Destruction Pharisaism and Judaism are to all intents and purposes identical, is also true for the centuries thereafter: "Le temoignage d'Origène *pour qui l'invective évangélique est toujours actuelle, en fait fois*" (Simon, pp.328–330; my italics).

   Simon's proofs are weak. His conclusion does not necessarily follow from what Dio Cassius writes; Justin reflects the last of the real struggles of the first and second centuries C.E.; Tertullian himself states that he presents the Jewish proselyte of pagan origin in order to challenge the claim of the racial election of Israel, that is, his proselyte is tendentious and artificial. As for Origen, it is precisely his dependence upon the Gospels which detracts from his credibility, for this is how the "theological" antisemitism of the Church was created. For Origen, see: J. Parkes, *The Conflict of the Church and the Synagogue: A Study in the Origins of Antisemitism* (London, 1934) p.148.

36. Simon, p.330. By way of summary he adds: "*Rien n'authorise à conclure de la penurie des épitaphes explicites à la pauvreté du recrutement prosélytique.*" Cf.p.335.

37. Simon, pp.347–348: "*Il y a plus dans ces dispositions libérales qu'opportunisme ou snobisme. Elles reflétent sans doute une souci prosélytique: pour agir sur le monde paien il faut le connaitre et le comprendre.*" S. Lieberman says approximately the same in his *Greek in Jewish Palestine* (New York, 1942), p.51. And see the criticism of G. Alon, *Studies* (above n.33) 2, p.264).

38. Cf. E. E. Urbach, "The Rabbinic Laws of Idolatory in the Second and Third Centuries in the Light of the Archeological and Historical Facts," *Israel Exploration Journal* 9(1959):151–156; 234–237.

39. On this Parkes (p.107) relies upon the article of Israel Levi, "Le prosélytism juif", *Revue des études juives* 50(1905):1–9; 51(1906):1–31. Levi differentiates between the approach of the Halakha and that of the Aggada regarding proselytes, arguing that sympathy for the proselyte appears more strongly among the Aggadists and that it is this spirit which represents the ideal of Judaism, just as the spirit of Christianity is to be sought in the Gospels, not in the *Corpus Iuris*. Against this view, see my article, "On the Attitude of the Sages towards Gentiles and Proselytes" (Heb.), *Mahalkhim* 5 (1971):71ff.

40. J. Vogt, *Kaiser Julian und das Judentum* [=Morgenland, Heft 30] (Leipzig, 1939), pp.6–9, 32.

41. B. Blumenkranz, *Die Judenpredigt Augustins* (Basel, 1946).

42. Williams, p.133: "Chrysostom's sermons were intended almost entirely for his Christian listeners, and only exceptionally for Jews."

43. A. Harnack, "Die Altercatio Simonis et Theophili," *Texte und Untersuchungen* 1, 3:75ff. For Simon's summary of Harnack's position, see pp.167–168.

44. A. B. Hulen, "The Dialogues with the Jews" *Journal of Biblical Literature* 51(1932):58–70. See Simon pp.172–174.

45. Y. Baer, "Israel, the Christian Church, and the Roman Empire from the Time of Septimius Severus to the Edict of Toleration of 313 A.D.," *Scripta Hierosolymitana* 7 [*Studies in History*, eds. A. Fuks and I. Halpern] (1961) :79–149. My italics.

46. Baer retracted his comments on this after Lieberman's note which pointed out that the tradition in the *Letter of Rav Sherira Gaon* (Heb.) fixed the year 279 as the time of R. Johanan's death, i.e., five years before Emperor Diocletian came to power. It was to the persecutions of Diocletian's reign that Baer had attributed the account of Bar Drossai and its significance. Cf. Justin's words to the Jews (*Dialogue* 44) which for our argument can be taken at face value:

"But if you [the Jews] remain hard-hearted, or weak in [forming] a resolution, and are unwilling to accept the truth on account of death, which is the lot of the Christians, you shall be responsible for your own fate." And cf. the criticism of E. E. Urbach, "The Rabbinical Laws of Idolatry," (above, n.38): 234, n.80 and his comments in the Hebrew version in *Eretz-Israel* 5(1958):202, n. 16.

47. These sources are also cited, *inter alia*, by Wilde (above, n. 2; see p. 145) and others as proof that the Jews had a hand in the persecutions of the Christians.

48. Journal of Roman Studies 56(1966):231–236.

49. The last words are taken verbatim from Frend's book, p.323; there, Frend made this assertion in regard to the cities of Rome and Smyrna.

50. It is reasonable to assume that their formulation was intended to serve propagandist aims. Thus, for example, the words put into the mouth of Pionius about the land of Judaea and its destruction are no more than Biblical descriptions. The presentation of the Jews as opposing the burial of Polycarp's body and the reason offered for this seem tendentious, being presented in order to draw a comparison between the behavior of the Jews in Smyrna and their behavior at the time of the Crucifixion of Jesus (and see below).

51. Frend does not even mention it again in his article, although Tertullian accused the Jews of slandering the Christians. The following quotation from Origen is from Chadwick's translation (above, n. 6).

52. *Thyesteia deipna kai Oidipodeioi mixeis.*

53. The High Priest and his Sanhedrin. See E. Bickerman, "The Sanhedrin" (Heb.) *Zion* 3(1937–38):356–359.

54. See, for example, *Tosefta Hulin* 2:24; Munich MS.in *Dikdukei Soferim: Variae Lectiones*, ed. R. Rabbinovicz (München, 1867), for *T.B. Shabbat* 113b; Origen, *Contra Celsum* 1:28,32 (=the Jew in Celsus). And see my article (above, n. 4).

55. *T. B. Shabbath* 104b; Origen, ibid. Likewise, Arnobius, 1:43; Eusebius, *Praeparatio Evangelica* 3:6, 28.

56. *T.B. Berakhot* 28b; Justin, *Dialogue* 15;47 et al.; Epiphanius, *Panarion (Haereses)* 29:9. See also R. Kimelman, "*Birkat Ha-Minim* and the Lack of Evidence for an Anti-Christian Jewish Prayer in Late Antiquity," in *Jewish and Christian Self-Definition* 2, ed. E. P. Sanders with A. I. Baumgarten and A. Mendelson (Philadelphia, 1981), pp.226–244, and W. Horbury, "The Benediction of the *Minim* and Early Jewish-Christian Controversy," *Journal of Theological Studies* 33 pt. 1 (April, 1982):19–61.

57. The heretics' skill in magic apparently led Hananiah, the nephew of R. Joshua b. Hananiah astray, and the Sages were forced to send him away to Babylonia (*Eccles. R.* 1:24). But in the Land of Israel people continued to turn to them for cures, despite the opposition of the Sages. After the Ben Dama incident (*T.B. Av. Zar.* 27b), we hear about the son of R. Joshua b. Levi (*Eccles. R.* 10:7). The Christians brag especially about their power to exorcise demons; see, for example, Eusebius, *Praeparatio Evangelica* 3: 6,35: "Who does not know that by invoking the name of Jesus and with very pure prayers we fend off the deeds of the demons?" Cf. 3:6,36. About the conversion of the Jews to Christianity, it may be that we can conclude from what Eusebius writes in the *Praeparatio Evangelica* 2:3,43 that the results of the Christian mission to the Jews were negligible, even though he is referring to the past: " . . . very few of them believed in our Lord and Savior . . . "

58. *The Martyrdom of Polycarp* 13 and 17.

59. *The Martyrdom of Pionius* 3:6, 4:8.

60. Cf. G. Alon's comments on his points of disagreement with S. Lieberman in *Studies in Jewish History* (above, n. 33), 2, p.266 and n.31 on p.267.

61. Cf. *Dialogue* 23 and 28: "You [i.e., the Jews] have but a short time left to accept Christianity" (=*prosêlyseôs*) . . . " In connection with the martyrdom of Polycarp and the emotional bitterness of the Jews which it reveals, Wilde (p.143) suggests that the Jews opposed the Christians because they viewed the Christians as polytheists despite the strong Christian pronouncements about the monotheistic character of their faith. But if this explanation be valid, one must ask why it finds no expression in Justin's *Dialogue* written at the same time.

62. Cf. Justin, *Dialogue* 95 with Melito, *On the Passion* pars. 74–75.

63. In *The First Apology* 35, Justin also states briefly as fact that Jesus was crucified by the Jews. Cf. Origen, *Contra Celsum* 2:34.

64. For all of the above, see Noakes, "Melito of Sardis," above, n.3:246–247.

65. See his reaction in *Dialogue* 95: "And let none of you say: 'If his father wished him to suffer these things, so that by his bruising [Isaiah 53:5] the human race might be healed, then we have done no wrong.' If, indeed, you say such things while you repent of your sins, and recognize him to be the Messiah [=Christ], and observe his commandments, remission of sins will be yours, as I said before. But if you curse him . . . "

66. It is interesting that among the works of Clement of Alexandria (of the end of the second century), Eusebius lists a treatise against the "Judaizers" (*Ecclesiastical History* 6 13:3): *ho epigegrammenos Kanôn ekklêsiastikos ê pros tous Ioudaîzontas.*

67. (Heb.) *Zion* 4(1939):269–293, esp. 273.

68. As for Aquila, see *Shemot R.* 30. On the study of the Bible, especially of the Prophets, and its influence, see *The Acts of the Apostles* 8:27–28; Justin, *Dialogue* 7–8; Clement of Alexandria, *Strom.* 6:15; Theophilus, *To Autolycus* 1:14; 2:34–35; 3:9; Origen, *Contra Celsum* 1:15; Tertullian, *Apology* 18.

69. 16:3: *atque ita inde praesumptum opinor, nos quoque, ut, Iudaicae religionis propinquos, eidem simulacro initiari.*

70. See 18:2,5–6: *quasi sub umbraculo insignissimae religionis.*

71. On Origen's use of Biblical verses as a counter-weight to Plato, see: *Contra Celsum* 6:18.

72. See Wilde, *The Treatment of the Jews* above, n. 2, pp.192–202.

73. This phenomenon is found in the apologetic work of Eusebius (*Praeparatio Evangelica*) directed to the pagans. In that work Eusebius argues the superiority of the Law of Moses and the Prophets over the philosophy, theology, and ethics of the pagans. See the discussion of this issue in its entirety in my article, "The Jews and Their Law (Torah) in the Pagan-Christian Polemic in the Roman Empire" (Heb.), *Tarbiz* 40(1971):462–471.

74. See: Wilde, pp.126–127; and cf. 129–130, which is a summary of Justin's approach to the Jews.

75. Cf. R. R. Reuther, "The *Adversus Judaeos* Tradition in the Church Fathers: The Exegesis of Christian Anti-Judaism," in *Aspects of Jewish Culture in the Middle Ages*, ed. P. E. Szarmach (Albany, 1979), pp.27–50.

76. See Wilde, p.187 ff.

77. Cf. *Matt.* 27:62–66, and above, beginning of section VIII. And see *Comment. in Matthaeum* 13:9 (=*PG* 13:1117); *De Principiis* 3:2,4 (=2:310).

78. See J. Juster, *Les Juifs dans l'empire romain . . .* (New York, [1914]. 1, p.62; Williams, pp.132–133; Quasten 3(1960), p.424ff. (On the *Adversus Judaeos* homilies see pp.452–453).

79. =*PG* 48:854.

80. =*PG* 48:914.

81. And cf. the furious words of R. Tarfon and R. Ishmael in *T.B. Shabbath* 116a (according to the *Dikdukei Soferim* [above, n.54]): "Come and hear: the parchments and the books of the *minim* [heretics] must not be saved from a fire [on the Sabbath] but they must burn where they are, they and the Divine Names occurring in them . . . R. José says: on weekdays one must cut out the Divine Names which they contain, place them in a repository, and burn the rest. R. Tarfon said: may I bury my children if I would not burn them [the heretics' writings] including their Divine Names if they came to my hand! For even if one pursues him to slay him, and a snake pursues him to bite him, he [may] enter a place of idolatry [for refuge] but not the houses of these [people], *for the latter recognize [God] yet deny [Him] whereas the former are ignorant and deny [Him]*, and of them Scripture saith [Isaiah 57:8]: 'And behind the doors and the posts hast thou set up thy memorial.' R. Ishmael said: [one can reason] *a minori.* If in order to make peace between man and wife the Torah decreed, 'Let my Name, written in sanctity, be blotted out in water,' these, who foment jealousy, enmity, and wrath between Israel and their Father in Heaven, how much more so; and of them David said (Ps. 139:21–22) 'Do not I hate them, O Lord, that hate Thee? And am I not grieved with those that rise up against Thee? I hate them with perfect hatred; I count them mine enemies.'" See also n.4 above.

82. For this phenomenon, see my recent *Jews, Pagans and Christians in Conflict* (Jerusalem and Leiden, 1982).

83. See J. Alvarez, "Apostolic Writings and the Roots of Anti-Semitism," *Studia Patristica* 13(1975) [=*Texte und Untersuchungen* 116]:69–76.

5

Hatred of the Jews or Love of the Church: Papal Policy Toward the Jews in the Middle Ages

KENNETH R. STOW

> In the spreading of the Gospel they are treated as God's enemies for your sake; but God's choice stands, and they are his friends for the sake of the patriarchs. (What is more), if their rejection of Jesus has meant the reconciliation of the world, what will their acceptance mean? Nothing less than life from the dead!

This citation from Paul's Epistle to the Romans[1] epitomizes both the dilemma and the polarity of medieval Christian theology in its dealing with the Jews. Put succinctly, although Jews were their theological enemies, Christians were nevertheless obligated to treat the Jews according to the tenets of *Caritas*, or Christian love. More disturbingly, Christians had to confront the paradox of their dependency on the Jews. There would be no resurrection of the dead at the Second Coming and no dawning of the World to Come, until the Jews embraced Christianity.

1. Two Schools of Thought

The necessity of loving one's enemies, and being dependent on them as well, did not augur a placid relationship between Christians and Jews. Elaborating on Paul's declarations and fashioning a program from them that would make coexistence with the Jews possible would be most difficult, so difficult, in fact, that a consensus within the medieval Church on the subject of the Jews would never be achieved. Circumstances, nevertheless, made it necessary to formulate both a program and an outlook. And it would not be incorrect to say that during the course of the Middle Ages two schools of thought emerged, each with its own program – the first emphasizing exclusively the negative, and the second both the positive and the negative aspects of Paul's writings on the Jews.

The principal exponent of the first school was the late fourth century Bishop of Antioch, John Chrysostom. For Chrysostom, the Jews were a source of pollution and defilement. Their synagogues, he argued, are seats of drunken banqueting and houses of prostitution that must be avoided by Christians at all costs. Indeed, it would be preferable to avoid all contacts with Jews, since Christians who join the Jews in fellowship at the "table of Satan" and from there proceed to the altar of Christ defile the sacrament of the Eucharist and transfer to it the impurities they contract from the Jews. Anyone with knowledge of such goings on, therefore, is to be admonished and called upon to denounce them in public, as well as this perpetrators, for the safety of the Christian community.

Chrysostom, however, was an extremist, and his ideas were not quickly adopted. Nor were they universally known, especially in early medieval Europe. Still, his thinking did have its exponents. The ninth and tenth century bishops Agobard of Lyons and Ratherius of Verona both declared war on Jews, whom they considered guilty of subverting Christian officials and kings and whom they charged with creating an *impedimentum* to the Church no less dangerous than the threat posed by Antichrist himself. Even if Agobard insisted that Jews must not be harmed, his goal was undeniably to restrict their activities as much as possible.[2]

A similar position was adopted by the late eleventh century Abbot Guibert of Nogent. Reviving the sexual imagery of Chrysostom with lewd particulars, Guibert described a Jew who agreed to initiate a monk into the secrets of the Devil, but only after the cleric first proved his perversity and his denial of the faith by spilling his seed on the ground and treating it as though it were the flesh and blood of Christ. Guibert never accompanied these descriptions with calls for reprisals, violent or otherwise, yet he did not disguise his pleasure when telling of a Jew who was burned for being an accomplice to a fictitious and heretically tainted murder.[3]

But there were some who did call for action, in particular, fifteenth century Italian Franciscans like Bernardino da Feltre, whose sermons against the "crime" of Jewish lending invariably ended with a call for expulsion.[4] Bernardino's zeal was only one step removed from that of the wandering bands of crusaders who attacked the Jews of the Rhineland in 1096 moved by the slogan: Why should we go to the East, the enemies of Christ thrive here among us.[5]

One school of Christian thought on the subject of the Jews thus predicated its teachings on the theme of contamination and its avoidance. If one feels a need to speak of "Religious Hate" – although I believe this term should be invoked with only the greatest of caution as a sole or as a self-sufficient historical explanation – then that term may be applied here. Because of their fears and insecurities, churchmen like Chrysostom, Agobard, Guibert, and Bernardino da Feltre did hate Jews. Agobard even said he did, in just so many words.[6]

By contrast, the second school of Christian thought on the Jews built its theology and programs on *all three* aspects of Pauline thinking noted earlier. Carrying the implications of that thought to its limits, Augustine, in the early fifth century, presented a two-sided picture. On the one hand, he depicted the Jews as carnal, preferring their unregenerate earthly ways, those of the Old Testament, to the spiritual path of those who had achieved salvation and peace of the soul through Jesus, the way of the New Testament. Accordingly, the Jews were punished and considered enemies. But their punishment was that of Cain; they were to be seen and learned from, yet never to be harmed. Like Cain, moreover, and through their ancient scriptures, which they preserved, and in allegorical testimony to the true faith of Christ, the Jews served as witnesses to the coming apocalypse. Hence, despite their insistence on remaining in their stubbornness and living behind a veil of blindness, the Jews were to be approached with love. For it was their defection that first enabled the grafting of Gentiles onto the "olive tree" of God. Like Paul, therefore, Augustine believed that the Jews would be regrafted onto this "holy tree" – but only at the end of days. Indeed, Augustine is most explicit that present day efforts at conversion of the Jews, if praiseworthy, would not be very successful.[7]

Augustine was perhaps the primary vehicle for the transmission of Pauline thought to the Middle Ages. And in many ways it is legitimate to describe medieval culture as an Augustinian-Pauline culture.[8] Thus, it is no surprise to find that even in the sixteenth century, the common opinion of Christian theologians and jurists insisted that Jews should not be expelled; such an act would operate against the fulfillment of the prophecies concerning the End of Days when the Jews would "see the light," and there would be "one flock and one pastor."[9] Going further, in 1569 the Council of Trent declared as dogma that the conversion of the Jews was one of three necessary events foreshadowing the world cataclysm.[10] In short, although the Jews were seen as theological adversaries who epitomized the opposite of Christian virtue, their presence in Christian society was indispensable. As no thinker after Paul had phrased it so openly, that society was dependent on the Jews for the achievement of its ultimate goal.

This state of affairs seemed to place the Jew in what the canons of the Church would call a state of "honor," implying a measure of precedence of Jews over Christians and bordering on denying the fundamental Pauline claim that Christianity had superceded Judaism. Augustine's emphasis on the carnal and rejected Jew, who was the living incarnation of Cain, was thus designed to counterbalance this potential esteem and lessen the sense of dependency and insecurity. It was necessary to show that Christianity, and not Judaism, was the True Israel, and that Christians enjoyed complete mastery over Jews.

This was not a task for theological exhortations alone. Augustine could, however, rely on the Imperial Jewry law that had been developing for over one hundred years and was now about to be published in the 438 Theodosian Code.[11] Indeed, Roman Imperial law almost certainly helped shape Augustine's two-sided picture of the Jews. Its existence allowed him to stress the need to love (his word) the Jew as much as to emphasize Jewish carnality. Adhering to ancient Roman law and custom, the Theodosian Code treated the Jew as a citizen (*cives*) of the Empire;[12] the Jews' ritual, and even certain of their jurisdictional privileges, thus were to remain intact. Their actions, however, especially those that might raise them to a position of authority over Christians, as judges, masters, or military officials, were to be severely limited lest they resulted in insult and the "pollution" of the faith. As the Code succinctly put it: "They shall maintain their own rites without contempt of the Christian law, and they shall unquestionably lose all privileges that have been permitted them heretofore, unless they refrain from unlawful acts."[13] Jews, consequently, were to live integrally in Christian society, but their status was to be defined and their actions delimited in order to promote the honour and prevent the defamation of the Christian faith and the individual Christian. As legal inferiors, Jews were to live like the elder – a figure first used by Paul and then Augustine – serving the younger.[14]

This was also the position adopted by the founder of the medieval papacy, Gregory the Great. The near identity of the above citation with the universally cited dictum of Gregory: "Just as one ought not to grant any freedom to the Jews in their synagogues beyond what is decreed by law, so should the Jews in no way suffer in those things already conceded to them,"[15] is obvious. A one-by-one analysis of the two dozen or so letters of this pope on matters concerning Jews shows unequivocally that he saw himself as an administrator of the laws of the Theodosian Code. But Gregory was also a spiritual son of Augustine, and his adaptation of the Code's formula to characterize Jewish status indicates that he saw the Code and Augustine's theology as complementary. Jews were to be restrained, but without violating their fundamental rights.

Gregory was not alone: Perhaps in direct imitation of his lead, his successors on the throne of Peter, with a few notable exceptions in the eighth, ninth, and tenth centuries, made the principles of Paul, Augustine, and the Roman law the basis of their dealings with the Jews. Neither favorable, moderate, nor harsh, nor rooted in personal whim, nor, above all, in religious animus, their policies were characterized almost without exception by an effort to weld the diverse requirements of theology into a consistent and unified whole. The goal was to create an efficient Jewish status – one that would consign the Jews to a position of unmistakable inferiority by emphasizing their rejection, degradation, and servitude, yet would also protect them and respect their lawful privileges, so that ultimately they would be able to fulfill their necessary role in Christian soteriology.[16] What motivated the popes was the fundamental Christian principle of spreading of the Gospel message "until its sound reached to the four corners of the earth."[17] In other words, the popes were motivated by a love of the Church.

2. Ninth to Eleventh Centuries

In the following statement of Gregory the Great, the centrality of the Church is indisputable. "I praise your missionary intentions,"[18] he wrote to the bishops of Arles and Marseilles, "but you have erred in using force to baptize Jews.[19] Those converted by force remain unconvinced of the Christian truth and eventually go back to their old superstitions to die unrepentant." What Gregory really meant was that such converts soon become apostates, threatening the integrity of the faith and making a mockery of the sacrament of baptism. For the good of the Church, forcible conversion had to be rejected.

The Church would be placed in a similar predicament if a Jew acquired mastery over a Christian. A Sicilian Jew named Nasas had purchased a Christian slavewoman, whom he then forced to pray before an altar he was supposed to have erected. In reaction, Gregory wrote to his prefect in Sicily that to conciliate the Grace of God Nasas must be punished and the woman freed. Otherwise, the Christian faith would be "polluted" through "subservience" to the Jews.[20] Why Gregory spoke of the "faith" rather than the individual Christian is explained in a letter to Queen Brunhilda of the Franks. Jewish possession of Christian slaves, he lamented, is tantamount to "giving the boot" to Christ.[21] Through baptism individual Christians become joined to the body of Christ, as if Christ were the head and they the members. To end the slavery of Christians to Jews, therefore, is to liberate Christ's faithful from his enemies; by implication, it is to liberate Christ himself.

Besides defending the Church, these letters on slavery seem to recall the words of Chrysostom. Nonetheless, the references to enemies and pollution, like the language of the Nasas letter, are based on the laws and the language of the Theodosian Code.[22] As much as the Code spoke of Christian slaves being polluted by Jewish ownership, it still scrupulously defended what it considered the Jews' legitimate rights. This was also true of Gregory the Great. His references to the legal rights of the Jews are ubiquitous, even to the point of stating explicitly that Jews are to live according to the tenets of Roman law.[23] A clear example of this is his instructions to the Bishop of Luna in Liguria, ordering him to press for the release of Christian slaves working on Jewish *latifundia*, but at the same time warning that if the manumitted *colonii* continue working on the *latifundia* following their release, then they must remain on the soil – since they have bound themselves by the law of *colonii*.[24] To own a *latifundium* and to have *colonii* on it is a civil right that no law had ever denied to the Jews; nor would Gregory. His Jewry policy, based on the teachings of Augustine and the tenets of the Roman law, was thus consistent. If that policy tilted in any direction, it was in the direction of what Gregory would have considered the defense of the Church.

What Gregory called Jewish mastery over Christians, or Christian subservience to Jews, was expressed by others in terms of Christian superiority and Jewish inferiority. The theme of the Jew as Esau and the Christian as Jacob – the Jew and Judaism as rejected and the Christian and Christianity as chosen in the place of the Jew: the Jews as the elder who was to serve the younger – had grown from a hint in Paul into a staple of theology.[25] Apart from its symbolic importance, this issue of relative status was emphasized to maintain barriers between Jews and Christians, lest the latter be exposed to Jewish claims that might breed Christian doubt. One of the most sensitive issues of the Jewish-Christian encounter, the dual problems of excess familiarity and Jewish superiority, created emotional responses in the papacy even at the height of Church power in the thirteenth century. How much more then in the eighth century, a period of enormous insecurity throughout Christian Europe, when the issue was not merely the proper order of society, but its continued existence? "What," wrote Pope Stephen IV (768–772) to the Archbishop of Narbonne, "has the society of light (that of the Christians) to do with the society of darkness (that of the Jews), the conventicle of Christ with Belial, and the consensus of the Temple of God with idols?"[26] An end, he insisted, must be brought to the aberration of Christian *colonii* who labor in Jewish fields and vineyards and live under the same roof as their Jewish employers in the towns, where they are exposed day and night to "Jewish lies and blasphemies." As pope, Stephen concluded, it was his task to provide the balm for any pestilence that might strike the divine flock.

With the exception of the perplexing letter of Pope Leo VII (936–939) sent in response to the query of Archbishop Frederick of Mainz in 937 and declaring that if preaching should fail to convert them, the Jews may be expelled from the city: "For why should light be joined to darkness and that which is holy be given to dogs"[27] – the letter of Pope Stephen may be the most extreme statement ever made by a pope concerning the Jews. Indeed, the later canon law rejected its premises. Labor in the fields of Jews was expressly permitted; what was prohibited was to serve Jews as domestics.[28] As for the rough language, Stephen's citation of Corinthians has no parallel, even in the vituperations of Innocent III on the subject of Christian wetnurses. The intensity and specificity of Stephen's arguments, moreover, expose his anxieties. If, rather than being punished for their role in the Crucifixion, he wrote, Jews are openly allowed to insult Christianity, who can refrain from questioning Christian claims of Jewish rejection; and who can refrain from questioning fundamentals of the Christian faith!

In the ninth and tenth centuries, therefore, papal anxieties originated in the same apprehensions that had motivated Agobard and his school: the fear of the Jews as the enemy of society and the belief that as minions of Antichrist capable of corrupting Christian officials the Jews were being allowed to pursue their threatening machinations unchecked.[29] In a period in which Christian Europe was menaced by invasions from all sides and in which the Christianization of the home populus was either incomplete or overlaid with pagan syncretism, such apprehensions about a Jewish fifth column are comprehensible. Yet, it is notable that even in this time, papal attitudes never abandoned traditional principles. Frederick of Mainz had asked whether he could force the Jews into choosing between baptism and exile, reminiscent of Agobard who had tried to kidnap Jewish children and forcibly baptize them. Leo VII replied by accepting the possibility of exile but, following the lead of Gregory the Great, refusing to consent to the use of force as an instrument of conversion.

In addition, by the eleventh century, the situation of the Church had changed for the better. Not only had Europe itself become more thoroughly Christianized, but so too had the old invaders – to the extent that the Normans, once pagan Scandinavians, had now set out under the papal banner to conquer Sicily and Southern Italy from the Saracens and Byzantines. The Church, in other words, was finally in a position to identify its real enemies, distinct heretical sects from within, and the Saracens without. To be sure, it would still be two hundred years before heresy was successfully contained, but within the confines of Europe at least the fight against the Saracens was clearly being won. It was in these circumstances that in 1063, Alexander II congratulated the bishops of Spain who had helped prevent Jewish bloodshed during an offensive against Spanish Muslims and made a point of stressing: "Different indeed is the case of the Jews from that of the Saracens. The latter persecute Christians and drive them from their towns and lands; warfare against them is just. The Jews, in distinction, are universally ready to be subservient."[30] Papal attitudes since the days of Stephen IV and Leo VII had thus altered. If anyone is identified as the enemy of society, it is not the Jews, but the Saracens. However, the reason for this change was not so much a heightened awareness of the Saracen threat, as the fact that the Jews had demonstrated their "subservience", by which Alexander meant that the Jews had accepted their fate and agreed to live in peace, according to the demand of Christian theology that the "elder serve the younger." In contrast to the Saracens, who were active enemies and against whom a "Just War" could be legitimately waged, the Jews were considered by Alexander to be passive and submissive. If they were still enemies, it was only in the Pauline theological sense. In practice, they caused no harm and, indeed, were "different."

Yet, with this declaration Alexander II was not returning unqualifiedly to the policies of Gregory the Great nor, especially, to his thoroughgoing observance of Roman law and its fundamentals. Despite the warnings of the Theodosian Code about the consequences of excess, Roman law had otherwise guaranteed Jewish toleration and physical protection virtually without precondition. Alexander, in distinction, had predicted these fundamental rights on subservience and on the recognition of and consent by the Jews to the servile status that their role in the Crucifixion merited. Otherwise, the Jews would not be "different" from the Saracens. Alexander's premise thus appears to be the obverse of that of Agobard. An active and threatening Jewish presence could not be tolerated; a passive and submissive one could be.

3. Legislation from the Eleventh Century

By pointedly electing to define the Jewish condition as "subservient," Alexander was aligning himself, as had Gregory the Great before him, with the witness theories of Paul and Augustine. But he was also innovatively superceding the strict terms of his predecessors, and the precise concerns of the Roman law, too, by welding toleration, and not merely privilege, to subservience and restriction. Only the subservient Jew exemplified the teachings of the Church, and under that condition alone was it correct to tolerate the Jews and offer them protection. Neither concession nor compromise, it was Church interest and theology that underlay both continuity and change in papal Jewry policy.

Alexander's forceful articulation of the previously inchoate idea that toleration and subservience must go hand in hand would typify papal policies and dealings with the Jews from the eleventh through the sixteenth centuries. The papacy furthermore would now be able to put Alexander's thinking into practice throughout Christian society, because its role in that society was becoming increasingly stronger. Indeed, what has so often been identified as an escalation of papal anti-Jewish activity in the thirteenth century must be perceived as the implementation of that which had long been in existence in one form or another. Those few specific actions of the papacy for which there was no explicit precedent, namely, the wearing of special clothing, the limitation of usury, and involvement in the burning of the Talmud at Paris in the 1240s,[31] are best understood as outgrowths of traditional theological and canonical concerns over social separation, mastery over Christians, and blasphemy and a willingness to tolerate a Judaism that supposedly foreshadowed Christianity but not the allegedly perverted Judaism of the Talmud. And, even then, the resolution of the questions of dress and usury was ambivalent in both theory and practice, and the ultimately ambiguous involvement of the papacy in the Talmud episode was, at the most, supportive of local forces rather than initiative.[32]

What was new in the thirteenth century was the scope of the papal Jewry policy. But that only matched the scope of all papal policies. If the proper place of Jews in Christian society required careful definition, so too did that of the clergy, the religious orders, the laity, the Emperor, the secular powers, heretics – and, indeed, the Church itself. Despite pressures to the contrary on the part of the growing kingdoms, the Church held fast to its ideal of a unified society, *Christianitas*, the *patria communis* of all Christians, which was synonymous with the *Corpus mysticum Christi*.[33]

The way to achieve these all-encompassing definitions was through law. Accordingly, the final decades of the twelfth century and the opening decades of the thirteenth were marked by new conciliar legislation, including that passed at two ecumenical councils, an unprecedented quantity of legal editing, a vastly increased output of papal letters, and the establishment of bodies deemed appropriate to control the life of the Church – all under the supervision of the papacy. The goal of this activity was to cull and update the legal past of the Church to achieve a complete and efficient legal synthesis that would serve as both a constitution and an all-embracing body of ecclesiastical law. This constitution was achieved in 1234 with the publication of the *Decretals* of Gregory IX, which would serve as the official body of Church law from that time until 1918. The papacy had sought to establish its universal juridical competence since the late eleventh century, and it considered its decretal letters binding on all.[34] But in the sphere of codified law there had been only the decisions of local councils and compendiums drawn up by local jurists (some more and some less favorable to papal controls), and both had only local applicability. The conciliar and codifying activities of the papacy leading up to 1234, therefore, must be perceived as preparatory steps for bringing all aspects of Church life under papal jurisdictional competence.[35]

With respect to the Jews, all of this means that the large quantity of thirteenth century legal texts concerning them, including those papal edicts that have the appearance of innovation, may not be seen *ipso facto* as indicating an intensification of the so-called anti-Jewish activities of the Church, and especially of individual popes. This material indicates, rather, that the centralization and control the papacy was seeking in other spheres was also being sought with regard to those activities of the Jews which the papacy believed should come under its direct supervision.[36]

A review, however brief, of papal legislation on the Jews as it was formalized in 1234 reveals a continuity with the past, with earlier Church law, Christian theology, and the actions of previous popes. As stated, its novelty lay principally in its quantity and comprehensiveness and not in increased repressiveness. No better illustration of this point exists than the Jewry policy of Innocent III, the prime papal mover of the thirteenth century, which is clearly outlined in two well-known letters, *Sicut Iudaeis non* and *Etsi Iudaeis*, both of which were edited and incorporated into the *Decretals* (X.5,6,9 and X.5,6,13 respectively).

Since approximately 1121, during the reign of Calixtus II, popes had repeatedly issued the Jews an all-encompassing bull of protection, *Sicut Iudaeis non*. The text of this bull varied little from pope to pope,[37] and the version incorporated into the 1234 *Decretals*, that of Clement III, mirrors faithfully the original text of 1121. The version issued in 1199 by Innocent III, however, contains some notable additions intended to amplify and clarify the texts of his predecessors.

In discussions of this bull, stress is normally placed on the *Sicut iudaeis* clause, first used by Gregory the Great, indicating that just as the privileges of the Jews must be preserved, so must the Jews themselves obey the limits imposed on them. The rest of the letter is then seen as an elaboration on this clause. Nevertheless, even more important than the *sicut* clause is a second one asserting that the pope is granting the Jews protection (*defensio*) in response to their own request. That protection includes the right not to be forcibly baptized, not to have property violently taken away, and not to be punished except by the courts of the land. Such *defensio* clauses were present in every charter obtained by Jews from the secular powers since Louis the Pious in the ninth century. However, Jewish charters of privilege were by no means the only place where the clause was to be found; nor, for that matter, was the clause invented for the sake of the Jews. Originally, it was a prefeudal legal formula in which inferiors asked for and received the protection of superiors. In return, the inferiors placed themselves under the juridical purview of the superiors. In a rough sense, therefore, the clause created a contractual agreement.[38]

This notion of contract is not surprising. Innocent III and his predecessors were the secular lords of the Jews who lived on the papal estates, and the use of the *defensio* clause in *Sicut iudaeis* may have grown out of this relationship. The contract Innocent III had in mind, nevertheless, was not one between a lord and his retainers or his wards, but a purely spiritual one; accordingly, the Pope took great pains to explain its spiritual conditions. First, he repeated the dicta of his predecessors, namely, the core *sicut* clause of Gregory the Great and the common principle that Christian piety commands the acceptance of Jews despite their refusal to accept Christian truth. For emphasis, he also added the Augustinian theory of Jewish witness. This addition was calculated to strenghten and supplement the notion implicit in the principle of acceptance on the basis of piety: The toleration of Jews in Christian society, no matter how rooted it was in Christian tradition, was not an absolute; it had to be justified and its conditions stipulated. By their very presence, Jews had to demonstrate and promote the good of the Christian faith.

To guarantee that these conditional terms be appreciated – for some reason no pope ever adopted the unequivocally contractual (and negative) phrasing of the Theodosian Code, perhaps Alexander II's emphasis on subservience had refined and superseded it[39] – Innocent appended innovative provisions to the bull threatening Christians who did not live up to the requirements of protection. His commitment to fulfilling his side of the contract was sincere. "Nevertheless," he concluded "we wish to protect by the buttress of this protection (i.e., this contract) only those who do not presume to plot the subversion of the Christian faith."[40] Minimally, this clause – borrowed almost verbatim from the Pact of Umar, which guaranteed Jewish security in Moslem lands – meant that Jewish violations of the canons limiting their behavior would have to be corrected. In broader terms, it implied that under certain conditions, namely, an irreversible violation by the Jews of the terms of the contract, expulsion was a possibility. Before the fifteenth century, however, this possibility, among Churchmen at least, was rarely considered.

How Innocent III himself pictured this contract and the intent of its final clause may be seen in the 1205 bull *Etsi iudaeos*. Extrapolating from the terms used by Alexander II in his own conditional statement of protection and perfecting Alexander's concept of the linkage between toleration and subservience,[41] Innocent demanded that the Jews live in "Perpetual Servitude."[42] Had Innocent III coined this term by 1199 when he issued his text of *Sicut iudaeis*, he doubtlessly would have used it to define Jewish actions harmful to Christian wellbeing as plots to subvert their Perpetual Servitude.

Perpetual Servitude thus referred not so much to a formal legal status as it did to the need for making the Jew embody Christian theological truths. Concretely, this meant that the Jew had to be restrained by means of canons like those prohibiting a common table and Christian slaves, or mandating special clothing, whose clear intention was to establish in fact the relative inferiority of the Jew to the Christian. Reality was thus to mirror the belief that Christianity had superceded Judaism, liberating the Christian through grace while the Jew remained enslaved under the "Law." Each piece of restrictive canonical legislation is lucid about this intention. Only through their Perpetual Servitude and inferiority to Christians could the Jews serve as a true witness to Christian liberation.

Paradoxically, however, only through Perpetual Servitude was the contract established by Innocent III possible. For this "servitude" supplied a rationale explaining why the Jew had a definite place within the Christian world and, more important, why and under what conditions the Jewish presence had to be maintained. In addition, following the thought of Innocent III, Perpetual Servitude also explained why the papacy was obligated to preserve traditional Jewish rights and privileges once the Jew had acquiesced to Christian dominion.

4. Varying Papal Attitudes

In this light, it is possible to understand the bull *Etsi iudaeos*.[43] Although various researchers have seen it as either an outpouring of gratuitous wrath and hatred or the product of a perverse understanding of early Christian theology, or, alternately, as an expression of a desire to eliminate the Jew from society and an attack on the foundations of Jewish existence,[44] *Etsi iudaeos* must, rather, be seen as an outburst of papal anger at Jews who have broken the terms of the *Sicut* contract. (To avoid misunderstanding, it must be stressed that this is only an explanation, not a justification, of the pope's actions.) Innocent thus castigated as a "snake around the loins" those Jews who "hurl unbridled insults at the Christian faith" and "bring confusion upon it" through their actions. At Eastertime when the Christian wetnurses of Jewish children "take in the body and blood of Jesus Christ, the Jews make these women pour their milk into the latrine for three consecutive days."[45] The addressee of the letter, the Archbishop of Sens, was thus to prevail upon the king and his nobles to force the Jews to dismiss these nurses (as the canons prescribe). As for the Jews themselves: "Bowed under the yoke of perpetual slavery . . . by the effect of this action (the dismissal of the nurses and the enforcement of the canons), they shall recognize themselves as the slaves of those whom Christ's death set free, at the same time that it enslaved them."[46] As much as Innocent was concerned with uprooting uncanonical practices, he was also preoccupied with Jewish behavior in general. The Jews, he insisted, must recognize and assent to their status; they must realize they have no choice other than to abide by the contract the Church has made with them in the clauses of *Sicut*.

It is precisely here that the nature of the basic alteration in papal attitudes between the eighth and thirteenth centuries may be discerned. In *Etsi iudaeos* the anger of the pope was directed against Jews who had broken the *Sicut iudaeis* contract. Stephen IV had been animated by apolcalyptic anxieties, apprehensive of what might possibly occur. It is a fair assumption that had the Jews lived by the contract of *Sicut iudaeis* and not insulted the Eucharist, doubtlessly believing it to be black magic that would gravely harm their offspring by way of the nurses' milk, Innocent III would have remained silent. But by acting as they had, the Jews had threatened the faith with confusion . . . "For as soon as they being to gnaw in the manner of a mouse and to bite in the manner of a serpent, one may fear lest the fire that one keeps in his bosom burn up the gnawed parts."[47] At least temporarily, the Jews had begun to act like the Saracens, active enemies whose actions did not bespeak Christian truth. Those actions had to be contained.

Careful consideration must also be given to the nature of the demands made in *Etsi iudaeos*. Despite the opprobriousness of terms like Perpetual Servitude, not to mention their objectively measurable pernicious effects, Innocent's basic assumption in this letter was that the contractual equilibrium could be reestablished – even though the Jews had blasphemed against the Eucharist itself. His specific demand was limited to the restoration of canonical rigor and the dismissal of Christian nurses. Likewise, his anger in likening the Jews to a serpent or a gnawing mouse is clearly metaphorical and even aphoristic; it certainly lacks the cataclysmic overtones heard in the eighth and ninth century. Innocent III, in other words, like Alexander II before him, believed a *modus vivendi* with the Jews was possible.

This belief would continue to be espoused. As put by the one time Dominican General, Cardinal Humbert of Romans, drawing up guidelines for the Second Ecumenical Council of Lyons in 1274: "We allow the Jews to live with us because they neither know how to cause us harm, nor are they capable of it; rather, (explicitly citing Alexander II) they are ever prepared to serve." In phrasing his words in this way, Humbert was foreshadowing the bulk of later medieval juristic opinion[48] which held that Jews living peacefully within the bounds of the status assigned them in law were to be considered *fideles* of the Roman Church – not as believers and participants in the *Ecclesia triumphans*, to be sure, but as members of the *Ecclesia militans* who did not plot against the Church and bring confusion upon the faith.

The Christian world, however, was not united in this opinion. As was indicated earlier in outlining the positions of the two basic schools of Christian thought on the subject of the Jews, it is impossible ever to speak in an all-embracing way of the policy of *the* Church – unless perhaps the reference is to the official institution of the Church as represented by the papacy and the canon law. Rather, there is a need to specify individuals and organized bodies *within* the Church. To make this point, one need go no farther than to refer to the extended debate on the question of the permissibility of baptizing Jewish children without parental consent, in which Thomas and Duns Scotus took opposing sides in the thirteenth century, the jurists Marquardus de Susannis and Ulrich Zasius in the sixteenth century, and the whole western world in the nineteenth century during the course of the Mortara case. Not every churchman, in other words, may have preached the necessity of expulsion or taken part in fomenting dangerous libels, but, by the same token, not every churchman was convinced that the Jews were passive *fideles* of the *Ecclesia militans*.

Divergent opinions on the Jews were to be found among the popes themselves. To borrow from American Constitutional jurisprudence, there were going to be strict and loose interpretations of the contractual terms of Jewry law and status. But no pope would ever consider voiding the contract. Hence, in 1288, Nicholas IV reissued *Turbato Corde*,[19] demanding strict punishment for Jews who aided and abetted heretics or sought to promote conversion from Christianity to Judaism. Yet in the same year, he also issued *Orat Mater Ecclesia*,[50] declaring that the Church tolerates Christian injury to Jews under no circumstances. Recalling the words of Paul in Romans 11:25, he tellingly reasoned that such injury operates against the prayer of the Church that the veil of blindness preventing the Jews' illumination be eventually removed. In these two bulls, therefore, *Turbato Corde* and *Orat Mater*, the lines of the contractual policy are finely drawn.

Nowhere may papal Jewry policy be seen more clearly, however, than in that truly comprehensive statement of the papacy and its vision, the *Corpus Iuris Canonici*. Space prevents a complete examination of the more than one hundred canons regulating Jewish life. Still, a paraphrase of the main themes of these canons will make their purpose clear. Jews, the canons declare, are tolerated by Christian piety to live within Christian society. Consequently, they should not be expelled unless they prove themselves to be enemies who plot and act criminally against Christians or their faith. On the contrary, Jews who live peacefully must be treated justly and always in accordance with the laws; they are, after all, citizens of their places of residence. This does not mean that Jewish rights and privileges are the same as those enjoyed by Christians; the Jews are restrained by numerous limitations. In particular, they may not benefit from the appurtenances, sacraments, or rituals of the faith. However, in instances where Jews are delinquent in morals or fail to punish offenders who have violated the Law of Moses, Church courts may intervene directly. The Church must also strictly insure that social intercourse with Jews, which is permitted in theory, does not become dangerously excessive. To this end, Jews are to be distinguished in their clothing, Jews and Christians are never to dine at a common table, and, at certain times, especially Holy Week, Jews may not move freely among Christians. All these limits have been established to prevent Jewish superiority and the resulting insult to the faith. Insult is indeed the gravest offense a Jew may commit, and it must never be permitted. Usury and Jewish testimony against Christians should, accordingly, also be prohibited, although there are moments when both prohibitions may be beneficially ignored. Nevertheless, such official ignorance may not be countenanced should a Jew acquire any form of jurisdiction over a Christian, whether through the exercise of public office or the ownership of a Christian slave. Jews may certainly never bear titles of nobility. On the other hand, Jews do have their privileges, most notably the right to observe their own law, especially ritual law, and, concommitantly, they maintain their synagogue buildings in repair and marry according to Jewish use. Jewish civil law, too, may be observed – if it does not contradict the canons or general civil law.[51] A Jew who converts to Christianity becomes a "new man" and his material status should improve. The conversion of the Jews is, after all, the ultimate goal of the law and all Christian thought. Still, this desire does not excuse the use of force. By the same logic, no Jews should be accepted for conversion until their legitimate intentions and true beliefs have been determined beyond question. Otherwise, converts might soon backslide to Judaism and become heretics, bringing eternal damnation upon themselves and scandal upon the Church. Needless to add, conversion to Judaism is a capital offence.[52]

Papal Jewry policy was thus a blend of toleration, restriction, and the hope for ultimate Jewish salvation, presupposing a constant equilibrium between all three of these elements and never limited to any one of them alone. Yet, had not papal Jewry policy evolved to vivify that thinking? Even in anger, the popes retained their awareness of the dual social function of the Jews and counselled against arbitrary measures. In a letter to the Count of Nevers asking him to restrain the Jews from taking excess usury, from giving testimony against Christians, and from selling the unkosher hindquarters of slaughtered animals, Innocent III produced a lengthy array of theological principles to justify his demands. The Jews, he declared with force and no little agitation, must live in the servitude they have brought upon themselves, and they must never be favored with privileges allowing them to oppress the servants of God. They are to live as Cain, marked and wandering in ignominy. Yet, he added, like Cain, too, they are to live unharmed, "so that the origins of the divine law not be forgotten, and seeking the name of the Lord, Jesus Christ."[53]

On this last point, Innocent III, like his papal colleagues, remained a bit vague. To "seek the name of the Lord" meant that besides testifying to the spreading of the Gospel message by means of the scriptural texts, the Jew was eventually to embrace that message too. Yet, although preambles to papal letters might recall this point and the canons might elaborate a complete set of guidelines on how to deal with converts, medieval popes rarely took any action to implement the goal of Jewish conversion – and when they did, their actions were never consistent.[54] Here again, they were following the lead of Paul and Augustine.

5. Sixteenth Century Millennarianism

The mass conversion of the Jews, Paul had said, would mean life from the dead, meaning that the Jews were to convert on the eve of the Second Coming. Accordingly, papal attempts actively to promote conversion could be expected only when speculations that the end was near had become common and penetrated the Church hierarchy. That occured only in the sixteenth century.[55] Then, in a studiedly revolutionary formula in the 1555 bull *Cum nimis absurdum*, reflecting a half-century and more of new thinking on the subject of the conversion of the Jews, Paul IV – who indeed believed that the millennium was fast approaching – insisted that the Church tolerates the Jews not so much out of Christian love, as had always been said, but for the express purpose of leading them to convert.[56] Unexpectedly, however, in order to attain this end, *Cum nimis* ordered the implementation of the most comprehensive set of restrictive regulations ever decreed, including one calling for the erection of walled ghettos in which, for the first time, the Jews living under papal jurisdiction were to be enclosed. This was no contradiction in terms. According to Paul IV, these regulations were to act as catalysts awakening the Jews to Christian truth. Through their recognition of the status of Perpetual Servitude and, more important, through their assent to the justice of that status – or so Paul IV believed – the Jews would finally awaken to the truth of Christianity. At which moment, as Paul had prophecied in the Epistle to the Romans, the advent of the millennium would be near.

In promulgating his decrees, it must be stressed, Paul IV had not gone against tradition. He had made a point of reiterating the traditional stance that Christian piety justified the toleration of Jews. What differentiated Paul IV from his predecessors was his willingness to confront the basic unity of the elements of Christian thought applying to the Jews. Carrying the implications of chapter eleven in the Epistle to the Romans to their logical conclusion, he recognized that Perpetual Servitude and the ultimate redemption of the Jews were bound together no less strongly than were Perpetual Servitude and the justifications for continued toleration. But, then again, Paul IV was convinced that the time had finally arrived to turn the perennial hope for Jewish conversion into fact.

Yet, like all millennarian hopes, that of Paul IV, too, was based on illusion. His policies did succeed in increasing significantly the number of converts, but they never produced the mass conversions he had hoped for. Regrettably, the

Jews, and not objective factors, were held responsible for this failure. The result was that in 1569, Pius V, a follower of Paul IV and his policies, expelled the Jews from all regions of the Papal State except Rome and Ancona. Explaining his actions, Pius V declared in nebulous terms that the Jews were guilty of heinous crimes and irreparable violations of the conditions of their contract of servitude. Still, he was not expelling the Jews in their entirety, because he was convinced that the remnant in Rome and Ancona would be easily converted. As for those who had been expelled, they had proved themselves by their crimes to be "dead sheep," who were not destined to form part of that universal flock that would arise under the one messianic pastor at the end of days (John 10:16).[57]

Even at this critical moment, therefore, the basic Pauline teaching on the salvation of the Jews had to be upheld, regardless of the fact that what the popes really wanted to achieve was a unity of believers at all costs and irrespective of the particular fate of the Jews. Put otherwise, the complex linkage of toleration, subservience, and dependency had persisted over the centuries. So persistent was it, in fact, that at the end of the medieval epoch it led a papacy, seeking by all means to reassert and prove Catholic truth, simultaneously to expel the Jews and to seek large scale conversions, and so to adopt a Jewry policy that was at once self-contradictory, yet still consistent with the past. It was, perhaps, this inherent self-contradiction, already present in the writings of the Fathers and the earliest popes, and in many ways still in force in our own day,[58] that created the unceasing tension which students have always considered decisive in the molding of papal–Jewish relations.

Notes

1. Romans 11:28 & 11:15. To be sure, Paul's intentions in these verses are not transparent. There can be no question, however, that they assign the Jews a necessary role in Paul's soteriology, as, indeed, later commentators understood him to mean; see below, n. 10.
2. On the origin of these statements, see M. Simon, "La polemique antijuive de S. Jean Chrysostome et la mouvement judaisant d'Antioche," *Recherches d'Historie Judéo-Chretiènne* (Paris, 1962), pp.140–153; and the texts themselves in Migne, P.G., 48: 843 et seq. And see the translation and introduction in W. Meeks and R. Wilken, *Jews and Christians in Antioch* (Missoula, 1978). See also K.R. Stow "Agobard of Lyons and the Origins of the Medieval Conception of the Jew," *Conservative Judaism 29* (1974): 58–65.
3. On Guibert, see B. Monod, "Juifs, sorciers, et hérétiques au Moyen Age, d'Après les Mémoires d'un Moine du XIe Siècle," *Revue des Etudes Juives* 46 (1903):237ff; and J.F. Benton, *Self and Society in Medieval France* (New York, 1970), pp. 134–137, 209–211.
4. As yet these Franciscans and their anti-Jewish activities have received no monographic treatment. See, among others, P. Browe, *Die Judenmission im Mittelalter und die Paepste* (Rome, 1942), p.237ff; and especially Renata Segre "Bernardino da Feltre, i Monti di pietà e i banchi Ebraici," *Rivista Storica Italiana 90* (1978): 818–833.
5. The Jewish Crusade texts in *Persecutions in Germany and France*, ed. A. M. Habermann (repr. Jerusalem, 1971). The Latin chronicles also record this slogan.
6. *Monumenta Germaniae Historica, Epistolae* (M.G.H., Epist.) 3, 190.
7. A thorough study of Augustine's views is found in B. Blumenkranz, *Die Judenpredigt Augustins* (Basel, 1946). The essential texts are the *Adversus Iudaeos, Contra Faustum* Bk. 12, and *City of God* Bk. 18, chaps. 45–47 and Bk. 20, chap. 30, where the role of the Jews at the end of days is explained.

8. Any study of Augustine reveals the conscious link he saw between himself and Paul. On the centrality of Augustine for medieval culture, see, e.g., C. N. Cochrane, *Christianity and Classical Culture* (New York, 1957), pp.359–516, and H. Marrou, *St. Augustin* (Paris, 1949).

9. John 10:16, a locus classicus for referring to eschatological hopes.

10. See J. Donovan, trans., *The Catechism of the Council of Trent* (New York, 1829), p.64.

11. Most of the Jewry law of the Code is found in Bk. 16, chap. 8. (C.T. 16, 8). See here, Amnon Linder *Jews and Judaism in Roman Imperial Law* (Heb.) (Jerusalem, 1983).

12. Justinianic Code, Bk. 1, Title, 9, par. 8 (C.1, 9, 8).

13. C.T. 16, 8, 18 (an. 408).

14. Genesis 25:23.

15. *M.G.H. Epist.* II, 123, 15.

16. A number of the elements of papal Jewry policy now to be discussed have already been identified, especially in the following three studies: S. Grayzel, *The Church and the Jews in the XIIIth Century* (Philadelphia, 1933), E.M. Synan, *The Popes and the Jews in the Middle Ages* (New York, 1965), and G. La Piana, "The Church and the Jews," *Historia Judaica 11* (1949): 117–144. These studies, however, do not take into account the essential unity of the elements of papal Jewry policy, nor do they address the issue of the soteriological necessity of Jewish conversion.

17. Romans 10:18. On the symbolic importance of this verse, see L. Caperan, *Le problème du salut des infidèles* (Toulouse, 1934), esp. pp.216–218, 255–298.

18. See G. Schnurer, *Church and Culture in the Middle Ages*, trans. G. Undreiner, (Patterson, N. J., 1956), pp. 336–382, on the missionary activities of this pope.

19. *M.G.H. Epist.* I, 1, 47.

20. *M.G.H. Epist.* I, 3, 38: "*Ne quod absit, Christiana religio iudaeis subdita polluatur.*"

21. *M.G.H. Epist.* II, 9, 213: "*Quid enim sunt Christiani omnes nisi membra Christi? Quorum videlicet membrorum caput cuncti novimus, quia fideliter honoratis. Sed quam diversum sit, excellentia vestra perpendat, caput honorare et membra ipsius hostibus calcanda permittere. Atque ideo petimus, ut excellentiae vestrae constitutio de regno suo huius pravitatis mala removeat, ut in hoc vos amplius dignas cultrices omnipotentis Domini demonstretis, quod fideles illius ab inimicis eius absolvitis.*"

22. *C.T.* 16, 8, 18 & 22.

23. *M.G.H. Epist.* I, 2, 6: "*Romanis vivere legibus permittuntur.*"

24. *M.G.H. Epist.* I, 4, 21. As with other estate owners, the Jew may also not remove the *colonius* from the soil.

25. On this subject, see G. D. Cohen, "Esau as Symbol in Early Medieval Thought," in *Jewish Medieval and Renaissance Studies*, ed. A. Altmann, (Cambridge, Mass., 1967), pp.19–48.

26. II Corinthians 6:14–15. The letter is found in Migne, P.L. 129, 857.

27. In truth, Innocent III would remark: "*Herodes diabolus, Iudaei daemones; ille rex iudaeorum, iste rex daemonum,*" (*P.L.* 217, 561), but this was in the course of a sermon. With their effects on the popular mentality, the importance of sermons may not be minimized. Nevertheless, they are not legal determinations, as were the letters of Leo and Stephen, and their language always tends to extremes, especially in metaphors such as the above.

28. Marquardus de Susannis, *De Iudaeis et Aliis Infidelibus* (Venice, 1558), Part I, chap. 4, and Thomas Aquinas, *Summa Theologica*, IIa, IIae, 10, 10, obj. 3 & reply; and see n. 24 above.

29. See Stow, "Agobard," n. 2 above.

30. *P.L.* 146, 1386D–1387A: "*Dispar nimirum est Judaeorum et Sarracenorum causa. In illos . . . iuste pugnatur; hi vero ubique parati sunt servire.*"

31. This is not the place to explain this assertion in full. Suffice it to say that in the thirteenth century the nature of the special dress was rarely specified, and papal exemptions from this requirement exist in numbers from the thirteenth through the sixteenth centuries. In papal letters and conciliar decisions, only excessive usury is forbidden; K. R. Stow, "Papal and Royal Attitudes Toward Jewish Lending in the Thirteenth Century," *AJS Review* 6(1981):161–184. In practice, even Paul IV (see below) allowed some interest to be taken. Banking in the Papal State by Jews was not suppressed until the late seventeenth century; see Ermanno Loevinson, "Les concessions des banques de prêt aux Juifs par les Popes des XVIe et XVIIe siècles," *Revue des Études Juives 92* (1932): 1–30, etc. The problems of Christian servants of Jews and Jewish witness against Christians were given special attention in the thirteenth century; but, here again the issue was not without precedent, for legislation on these subjects had been passed in early French and Spanish councils, as well as in local charters of privilege. See

Bernhard Blumenkranz, *Juifs et chrétiens dans le monde occidental, 430–1096* (Paris, 1960); and see, too, K. R. Stow, *The "1007 Anonymous" and Papal Sovereignty: Jewish Perceptions of the Papacy and Papal Policy in the High Middle Ages*, [Hebrew Union College Annual, Supplements. vol. 4] (Cincinnati, 1984); and for an opposite opinion, Jeremy Cohen, *The Friars and the Jews* (Ithaca, 1982).

32. The subject of the Talmud in the thirteenth century has been treated at length by Merchavia, *The Church versus Talmudic and Midrashic Literature* (Heb.) (Jerusalem, 1970). It is clear from the texts that every papal initiative came only *in response* to requests from Paris. The original spark likely came from one Nicholas Donin, a convert, and was pursued by clergymen at Paris like Odo of Tusculum; See Stow, *1007*, pp. 62–63.

33. See the discussion by E. H. Kantorowicz, *The King's Two Bodies* (Princeton, 1957).

34. See K. F. Morrison, *Tradition and Authority in the Western Church, 300–1140* (Princeton, 1969), p. 273ff.

35. An exception to this statement is the *Cinque Compilationes Antiquae* of the late twelfth and earlier thirteenth century. Although papally sanctioned in part, especially the Third Collection, they were not as comprehensive as the *Decretals*.

36. A fundamental examination of this problem may be seen in J. Rambaud *et al. L'Age classique, 1140–1378: sources et théorie du droit* (Paris, 1965), pp. 222–264 and 133–166.

37. See S. Grayzel, "the Papal Bull, Sicut Iudaeis," in *Studies and Essays in Honor of A.A. Neuman* (Leiden, 1962), pp. 241–280; and Synan, *Popes*, p. 97ff.

38. On the *defensio* or *tuitio* clause, see V. Colorni, *Legge Ebraica e leggi locali* (Milano, 1945), pp. 32–66; on charters and their development see G. Kisch, *The Jews in Medieval Germany* (New York, 1970), pp. 135–153.

39. See the text cited above.

40. See Synan, *Popes*, p. 98, on the change in formulae, and Grayzel *XIIIth Century*, (above, n. 16) 92ff. for the full text.

41. Compare *"parati servire,"* as explained above," with *"perpetua servitudo."*

42. Perpetual Servitude must not be confused with Chamber Serfdom and other similar secular statues; Gavin Langmuir, *"Tanquam Servi*: The Change in Jewish Status in French Law about 1200,"* in *Les Juifs dans l'histoire de France*, ed. M. Yardeni (Leiden, 1980), pp. 24–54. Consequently there is a need to rethink the claim that the origin of these two serfdoms is to be sought in the struggle between popes and emperors in the thirteenth century, notably, Gregory IX and Frederick II. See esp. S. Baron, "Plentitude of Apostolic Powers and Medieval Jewish Serfdom," in *Yitzchak F. Baer Jubilee Volume* (Heb.), ed. S. Baron *et al.* (Jerusalem, 1960), pp. 102–124. Popes did indeed argue with emperors over Jews (e.g., Grayzel, XIIIth Century, pp. 192); nevertheless, on fundamental questions of sovereignty over the Jews and their "serfdom" to princes in particular, canonists, civilians, and theologians were unanimous. See some of their opinions in summary in de Susannis, *de Iudaeis*, Part I, chap. 7.

43. The text appears in Grayzel, p. 114ff.

44. Such views may be found in H. Graetz, *History of the Jews*, where he misses no opportunity to speak of the popes as the sworn enemies of the Jews (e.g., [Philadelphia, 1894], 4, pp. 496–521); in Synan, *The Popes*, pp. 87–97, where he speaks of erring theology underlying *Etsi*; and in Grayzel, p. 41ff., where he argues that the thirteenth century Church established a "Policy of Degradation," through which it "attacked the very foundations of the economic, political, and social life of the Jews" and was moving "in the direction of eliminating the Jew from Society." In fairness, Grayzel does argue that the aim of this policy was to prove the Church's fundamental teaching "that God had spurned Judaism." Nevertheless Grayzel's emphasis is clearly on degradation as a primary policy goal.

45. Grayzel, p. 114.

46. ibid.

47. ibid.

48. For Humbert, see J. D. Mansi, *Sacrorum Conciliorum Collectio*, 59 vols. (Venice, 1779–1782), 24, p. 115; and see, too, Baldus *de Ubaldis*, Consilia (Venice, 1608), no. 428, par. 5, along with de Susannis' elaboration on Baldus, *de Iudaeis*, Part II, chap. 2, par. 2.

49. See the texts in *Bullarium Romanum* (Turin, 1858), 3, p. 796 and 4, p. 88.

50. See the text in E. Langlois, *Les registres de Nicolas IV*, (Paris, 1886), p. 93.

51. Specifically, *ius commune*, the reworked Roman Law in force in Italy through the Middle Ages.

52. For a detailed discussion of this legislation and the sources of contemporary commentaries,

see K. R. Stow, *Catholic Thought and Papal Jewry Policy* (New York, 1977), pp.80–183 and 299–393.

53. See the text in Grayzel, pp.126–131.

54. A perusal of Browe's *Judenmission* leaves no doubt about both the infrequency and inconsistency of papal conversionary efforts.

55. The short lived, early fifteenth century policies of Benedict XIII may be seen as a precedent and precursor of Paul IV's policies; see Stow, *Catholic Thought*, pp.278–289.

56. On Paul IV, see Stow, *Catholic Thought*, pp.3–13.

57. On Pius V, See Stow, *Catholic Thought*, pp.24–26, 34–37, 220, and 225–277 on eschatology, including that of Paul IV.

58. See the "Declaration on the Relation of the Church to non-Christian religions" from the 1965 Vatican II conference, pars. 2 and 4; although see the advances now made in Eugene J. Fisher, "The Evolution of a Tradition: From *Nostra Aetate* to the 'Notes'," *Christian Jewish Relations* 18 (1985): 32–47. However, in *Il Sabato* (Oct. 24, 1987), pp. 37–39, Card. Jos. Ratzinger restated the traditional Church view unambiguously: "Il dialogo con gli ebrei? Il papa ha offerto rispetto ma anche una linea teologica: Cristo è il compimento di Abramo." ("The dialogue with the Jews? The pope has offered respect, but also a theological approach: Christ is the fulfillment of Abraham.") Ratzinger no doubt was referring to John Paul II's appearance in the Roman Tempio Maggiore in 1986.

6

The Devil and the Jews in the Christian Consciousness of the Middle Ages*

ROBERT BONFIL

Of the many elements characteristic of antisemitism, one of the most wide-spread and persistent is the motif connecting the Jews with the Devil. An example of this motif appeared in a 1941 issue of Julius Streicher's Nazi journal *Der Stürmer* which speaks of "the annihilation of this people, whose father is the Devil." Streicher certainly was employing an existing stereotype, one which had deep roots in the past. As such it had accumulated through the ages a substantial number of meanings and associations, both ideological and emotional, in the Christian consciousness.

Discovering the origins of stereotypes is a difficult task at best. Seeking the roots of the Jew-Devil stereotype presents some special problems. For example, one must first try to ascertain whether the medieval patterns of thought which associated the Jews with the Devil were of a basically rational or irrational nature. One must also ask whether they were an outgrowth of popular fears and superstitutions or were they, perhaps, the product of a systematic ideology formulated by the Church. These are but a few of the questions which must be confronted when considering the role of the Devil motif in the long history of Christian antisemitism.

1. Characteristics of the Devil

Who is the Devil in Christian belief? In the New Testament the Devil is depicted as the enemy of God and of Jesus, His son (Matthew 13:39). He puts

* This article appeared in English in an adapted version as part of the Jewish Studies University Series of the International Center for University Teaching of Jewish Civilization (Jerusalem, [1983]).

believers to the test and tempts them to sin (Matthew 4:1; John 3:8). He disrupts people's relationship with God, appearing in his Old Testament role as adversary and accuser. In the New Testament and in the writings of the Church Fathers he also appears as the leader of a group of angels who have fallen from grace for rebelling against God. As Jesus described it to his disciples, "I watched how Satan fell, like lightning, out of the sky" (Luke 10:18). And why did Satan fall? Because he "is not rooted in the truth; there is no truth in him" (John 8:44). The Devil embodies all the forces of heresy and rebellion against God. He poses a constant challenge to believers, threatening their faith with doubt and temptation. Until the end of time, it is the Devil's role to trick the faithful into straying from the path of truth, so that he may gain power over the world.

An examination of the basic characteristics that Christianity attributed to the Devil will reveal that they bear more than a passing resemblance to those attributed to the Jews. This resemblance derives from the Christian perception of the Jewish people as those who rejected Jesus and brought about his death on the cross. The Jews, therefore, were the enemies of God – first they rejected Him, and then they murdered Him. As punishment for this crime, the Chosen People lost their birthright and were superseded by the "true" Israel (*Verus Israel*), that is, the Church of the Christian faithful. But Christianity still reserved an important role in history for the Jewish people. By means of their very degradation the Jews were to bear eternal witness to the truth of Christianity.

The link between the Jews and the Devil appears explicitly in the New Testament. This is illustrated in the following passage from the Gospel according to John (8:43-44):

> Jesus said (to the Jews), "If God were your father, you would love me, for God is the source of my being, and from Him I come. . . Your father is the devil and you choose to carry out your father's desires. He was a murderer from the beginning, and is not rooted in the truth; there is no truth in him."

Here we are but a short step away from identifying all Jews with "Satan's synagogue" (Revelation of John 2:9; 3:9), that is to say, the Church of Satan, as opposed to the true Church. This concept was to serve as a model for the antagonism between the Church and its enemies. In the Middle Ages this antagonism found potent expression in the antithetical concepts *Ecclesia* and *Synagoga*. During the course of time the tendency to connect the Jews with the Devil became a fundamental and persistent aspect of Christian attitudes toward Jews and Judaism. It received considerable and varied expression in both the written and spoken word and served as a motif in painting and sculpture for hundreds of years.

2. Changes in Concepts and Attitudes

During the Middle Ages, the Christian conception of Satan underwent substantial changes. Many of these changes were matched by similar developments in the Christian perception of the Jew. While superficial comparisons should be avoided, it nevertheless seems clear that there is a basic, structural similarity between the image assigned by Christianity to the Devil and that assigned to the Jews. It should also be pointed out that this similarity encompasses a wide range of different motifs.

As a case in point, let us begin by examining the changes in attitude toward the Jews of Christian Europe during the eleventh and twelfth centuries, changes which became particularly noticeable following the First Crusade (1095). While the Christian attitude toward Jews before the Crusades was not a very positive one, anti-Jewish outbursts were generally sporadic, like the symptoms of a disease in its early stages. Ghettos, Jewish badges, blood libels, and accusations of well-poisoning had not yet appeared. Jews had not yet been pushed out of their livelihoods and forced into money-lending. For the time being the Jew was considered to be like a rebellious brother who, under certain circumstances, could be made to reform his ways. In other words, the basic humanity of the Jews was not in question.

This began to change from the twelfth century. During this period the Church was gaining strength, but social antagonisms and heretical sects were also spreading. Against this background, Christian attitudes toward Jews became more negative. The image of the Jew as the brother who had lost his birthright was supplanted by the stereotype of the fratricidal brother, sentenced to wandering with the mark of Cain on his forehead. More and more, the Jews were viewed in the master-slave relationship – a fact which had important ramifications on their legal and political status. Greater emphasis was now placed on the alien nature of the Jews in a homogeneous Christian world. This was expressed in dramatic performances, especially the Passion Plays, in which the actors portraying Jews would stammer incoherent Hebrew or even utter nonsense syllables. In the plastic arts, as well, the Jew became increasingly caricatured and even repulsive.

By the twelfth century, if not earlier, the Christian portrayal of the Devil was also undergoing a radical change. No longer did the Devil appear in works of art with the attributes of an angel. Now his features were designed to cause revulsion. He was portrayed as a dwarf or as a giant, with an oversized head and bulging eyes. To these were added long, flame-like hair (a symbol of the fires of hell), long fingernails, horns, a tail, and the like. Those attributes of the Devil which most sharply contrasted with the Divine, those which inspired fear, were the ones which were emphasized. During the thirteenth, and especially during the fourteenth century, the emphasis was transferred from the frightening to the hideous and grotesque.

On the surface, it would seem that the changing attitude toward the Jews and the new portrayal of the Devil were unrelated. The deterioration of the Jews' status in Christian Europe may be attributed to a number of factors. For one thing, the Jews often became pawns in power struggles between the Church and the temporal rulers. Whichever side could enforce its authority over the Jews could feel that it had made a tangible gain in the quest for power. The Church even employed theological arguments to justify their progressive subjugation. To make matters worse, the emerging stereotype of the Jew as the exploiter of the poor was reinforced by the fact that more and more Jews were being forced to turn to moneylending for their livelihood. All of these trends helped make it convenient for Christian society to exploit the Jews as scapegoats.

Entirely different factors were responsible for the changes in the Christian conception of the Devil. First of all, the Church wished to stress the negative aspects of the Devil in order to teach its followers to beware of his temptations. Here, Church art fulfilled an important function since it could convey to the illiterate masses messages unavailable to them through books. In addition, a major portion of the scholastic philosophy in vogue at the time was devoted to investigating the nature and source of evil in the world. Exhaustive study and debate were dedicated to the ancient traditions which told of the angels who fell from grace after having disobeyed God at the time of Creation. This preoccupation with evil was often reflected in the socio-religious issues of the time. For example, the temptation to join a heretical sect was portrayed as one of Satan's stratagems. It was not easy to resist Satan because his arguments were clever, yet it was imperative not to succumb to him for he could lead one to hell.

As mentioned above, there is no obvious connection between the change in attitude towards the Jews and the development which changed the Christian conception of the Devil. Nevertheless, the Devil's new image would henceforth be inextricably tied up with the stereotype of the Jew along the lines set down in the New Testament. The Devil would be depicted both in painting and sculpture as riding on the back of a Jew or the back of *Synagoga*, the maiden whose blindfolded eyes are incapable of perceiving the true light of Christianity. In Christian thought and folklore, in sermons and in art, the Devil's new attributes would also be assigned to the "Church of Satan," that is, the Jews.

The writings of the thirteenth-century monk Caesarius of Heisterbach may provide an illuminating example. He tells of a Jewish woman who wished to bring her daughter back to Judaism after she had been baptized. The woman tried to negate the effect of the holy waters by "baptizing" her daughter in excrement. Scholars agree that there is an unmistakable parallel here between the Devil motif and the Jewish stereotype. A folk legend tells about how the Devil, after having fallen into the holy waters, tried to free himself of their influence by means of a similar "baptism" in excrement. There is also a clear connection between the motif in these legends and the idea of the "Jewish stench" which can only be washed away by the baptismal waters.

In the Christian art and folklore of the Middle Ages, a considerable number of Devil motifs appeared as symbols of Jews and Judaism. These included the familiar dark, bulging eyes. Occasionally horns appeared on the heads of Jews. (Horns were also employed to indicate "bad Christians," especially heretics.) Goatees and tails were appended to the portrayals of Jews. The insistent depiction of the Jew as a nonhuman creature tended to reinforce the stench motif. In addition to these concrete symbols, the Jew was often tied in with more abstract and mythical symbols. One example is the mythical basilisk who often appeared in conjunction with the Devil in Christian literature. Half-serpent and half-bird, the basilisk exuded a death odor, and one glance from him was sufficient to kill. There was only one way to protect oneself from the creature's fatal powers – a pure crystal ball. Similarly, there was only one defense against the Devil. That was to call out the name of the Virgin Mary, the symbol of absolute purity. One can find both the Jews and the blind *Synagoga* compared to the basilisk in the anti-Jewish literature of the Middle Ages.

There were additional seemingly unrelated motifs which converged in Christian thought, reinforcing the link between the transmuted new perceptions of the Devil and of the Jews. For one thing, Judaism was perceived as posing a dangerous challenge to Christianity. What was the nature of this challenge? First of all, the Jews were stubbornly and uncompromisingly proud, despite their degradation. Second, there was a logic to the Jewish arguments about Christianity a logic so powerful that it produced fear and helplessness in the hearts of Christians. At times it even seemed that Truth itself was in danger. For both of the stereotypes described above – that of the Jews as masters of logic (a skill, acquired, no doubt, as a result of their constantly occupying themselves with the Talmud), and that of the Jews as arrogant – we can find parallels in the characteristics attributed to the Devil. In the Middle Ages many people considered logic to be *ars diaboli*, the art of the Devil. Satan would overwhelm believers with "logical" arguments in order to entrap and frighten them to death. See, for example, Dante's *Divine Comedy* – Inferno 27, 123.

The Devil was also portrayed in the Middle Ages as a proud figure whose self-love was boundless, following the notion of the scholastic philosophers that the angels who fell from grace were banished for the sin of arrogance. These ideas are reflected in the *Summa Theologica* of Thomas Aquinas (1225-1274), and in the writings of the Scottish theologian Duns Scotus (1265?-1308). The latter even ascribed the sin of lechery (*luxuria*) to the Devil. The Jews were also accused of unbridled lechery. This was a stereotype which had appeared as much as a millennium earlier, in the preachings of John Chrysostom of Constantinople (345?-407) who interpreted the New Testament phrase, "the Church of Satan," as referring to the Jews, and claimed that the synagogue of the Jews was really a brothel and a dwelling place for demons.

One may argue that this is merely a coincidence, that there really is no connection between the two phenomena. It seems clear, however, that there are deep underlying factors which connect the Jew and the Devil in the Christian consciousness of medieval Europe.

3. Pugio Fidei

In order to substantiate this thesis it may be useful to examine one of the outstanding anti-Jewish tracts of the Middle Ages – *Pugio Fidei* (The Dagger of Faith) by Raymond Martini (1220-1285). Written toward the end of the thirteenth century, it in time became one of the foremost weapons in the Christian polemic against Judaism. The book was produced following intensive research undertaken in Spain in order to discover and delete anti-Christian references in Jewish books. Martini's "researchers," most of them former Jews, knew Hebrew and provided him with a compilation of sources from the Talmud and the Midrash. *Pugio Fidei* belongs to the type of literature which tried to prove the truth of Christianity from within the Jewish tradition. Needless to say, the use of the Hebrew sources as well as the translations was tendentious and often arbitrary. Basically Martini seems to be asking the ancient question: "If even the Jewish tradition testifies to the truth of Christianity, why do the Jews not accept it?" His answer is simple: "The Jews do not accept Christianity because of their ancient pact with the Devil, to which even the Talmud attests." One of the examples which Martini brings is from the Tractate Me'ila, 17a-b:

> The Roman Government once issued a decree prohibiting the Jews from observing the Sabbath and circumcising their children, and requiring that they have intercourse with menstruating women . . . The Jews then pondered: "Who shall go [to Rome] to work for the annulment of the decree? Let R. Simeon b. Yohai go, for he is experienced with miracles" . . . Then Ben Temalyon came to meet him. "Is it your wish that I accompany you?" he asked. Thereupon R. Simeon wept and said: "My forefather's handmaid [Hagar] was found worthy of meeting an angel three times, yet I – not even once! Nevertheless, let the miracle be performed no matter how." Then Ben Temalyon possessed the Emperor's daughter. When R. Simeon arrived there he called out: "Ben Temalyon – leave her! Ben Temalyon – leave her!" When he proclaimed this, Ben Temalyon left her. Then [the Emperor] said to them [R. Simeon and R. Jose]: "You may request whatever you desire." They were led into the treasure house to take whatever they chose. They found the decree, took it, and tore it to pieces.

If that is the case, Martini concludes, the writings of the Jews prove that:

> God employed the Romans [who were considered both by the Jews and the Christians to be the progenitors of Christianity] to keep the Jews from observing the Sabbath, performing the rite of circumcision, and keeping all of the other ritual commandments. Ben Temalyon, i.e., Satan, restored circumcision, the Sabbath, and the other rites by some demonic miracle, in order that the Jews might pray and study Torah.

This becomes the basis for an entire doctrine: Whereas Christians interpreted the ritual commandments of the Bible allegorically, the Jews, misled by Satan, observe them literally. By restoring the ritual commandments to the Jews, Satan blinded them to the true meaning of Scripture, which points to the truth of the Christian faith. Thus it is the Devil who inspired the Jews to reject Jesus with such arrogance and stubbornness. They, as a result, have been reduced to an inhuman state, and that is the reason for their unnatural attitude toward Christianity. Everything believed by the Jews to be Divine revelation is, therefore, really nothing other than the revelation of Satan. Even those Jews who chose to die to sanctify the Holy Name (*kiddush hashem*) were really "martyred" for the glory of the Devil.

In Martini's tract, the ancient motif connecting the Jews with the Devil no longer appears as a metaphor. For him the matter is one of ideological conviction with a compelling inner logic of its own. It is this ideology which provided the theoretical basis for the tendency, described above, to dehumanize the Jews. Stated simply, the Jews, who lived among the Christians as a distinct religious community, were perceived as embodying the will of Satan. With their demonic poison they endangered the very well-being of Christianity. The challenge which Judaism represented for Christianity was nothing less than the challenge of the Devil. *Pugio Fidei* was widely circulated and had a significant impact, not only on the Christian polemic with the Jews, but also on the theological debate over the place of the Pentateuch within Christianity. Contemporary research has found that Martini's book was influential through the end of the Middle Ages and even into the Renaissance.

4. Conclusions

What has just been described may be considered a central theme around which numerous variations evolved. It would seem that we are still far from being able to unravel the many ramifications of the Jew-Devil motif in the history of Christian behavior towards the Jews in the Middle Ages. It stands to reason, however, that a careful examination of this complex issue will take us far beyond the theological confrontation with the Jews and will reveal motifs integral to the development of Christian culture and consciousness.

A basic concept inherent in Christian thought is the dichotomy of God versus Satan. From here it is only a short distance to the formula: the human race as servant of God versus the human race as rebels against God. Taken yet one step further, there emerges a world in which God is supreme, limiting, and even able to suppress human desires versus a world in which people have unbridled freedom and power. What we have here is essentially the age-old dichotomy between God and sorcery, between the Divine and the satanic, which found expression in the contradictory conceptions of worldly success and enjoyment as both desirable and sinful. This basic contradiction creates ideological tension in every system of religious thought (including Judaism) – yet it is especially marked in Christianity.

Beginning with the New Testament itself, the Jew was perceived within the context of that tension. It is not surprising, therefore, that the Jew-Devil motif appeared repeatedly in Christian culture in subsequent generations, undergoing metamorphoses with the passage of time. For example, in the literary version of the story of Doctor Faustus, dating from the Renaissance, the drawing of circles and the chanting of cabbalistic formulas are employed in an attempt to arouse the Devil. A man enters into a covenant with the Devil in order to gain control over the world and exploit it for his own pleasures. The Jew appears in the story not only through the obvious symbolism of the cabbalistic formulas, but also through the deeper symbolism of the circles. In addition to representing the Devil who encircles and overpowers human beings, the circle symbolizes the Jews who, since the thirteenth century, could be recognized throughout the Christian world by the round patch they were forced to wear on their breasts.

The Devil also appears in Christian literature and sermons as a seductive woman. Symbols drawn from the recesses of human sexuality were applied to the Jews as well. In this regard, the writings of John Chrysostom have already been mentioned, as well as the fact that unrestrained sexual desires were also attributed to the Jews. Another symbol fraught with sexual connotation was the yellow badge which Jews had to wear since, in many places, yellow was the color associated with prostitution.

The themes discussed above have found expression in various forms until our own day. On the socio-economic plane, the Jews have been portrayed as symbols of the ambition to succeed in business at any cost, even to the destruction of the ideological foundations upon which the continued existence of society depends. In the political sphere, the Jew has become the symbol of revolution: one whose behavior contradicts the very principles of morality and justice. Antisemitism has thus equated the Jew with all those forces which undermine human society and disrupt the course of history.

In any event, the Jew seems to symbolize something which simultaneously attracts and repels the Christian spirit. The Jews must be oppressed but not annihilated, for they possess something which is both attractive and repugnant, human and bestial, beautiful and ugly, a source of pleasure and a source of misery. The Jew symbolizes the existential dialectic of the Christian culture which has not succeeded in linking the human and the Divine yet still strives to attain that goal.

7

The State, the Church, and the Jews in Medieval England

ZEFIRA ENTIN ROKÉAH

In 1290 C.E., the whole of the Jewish community was expelled from England, producing a *Judenrein* state for some 350 years to come. This community had existed for over 200 years prior to this first, lasting, national expulsion of Jews in Western Europe. In this expulsion, as in the earlier discovery or – more correctly – revival of the charge of ritual murder at Norwich in 1144 C.E., England initiated a pattern to be imitated throughout medieval Europe in the years that followed. The expulsion from England necessarily and naturally raises many questions in the mind of the student of medieval Europe, of England, and of antisemitism: why and how the expulsion occurred; how it affected the Jews; the effect on medieval England first of the presence, and then of the absence, of the Jews; and so on.

1. Life of the Jews before the Expulsion

Various researchers have put forward suggestions as to the nature and role of English Jewry before the expulsion of 1290; some examined what little is extant and known of literary works (such as the poems of Meir of Norwich) or scholarly, religious works (such as the glossaries of Anglo-Jewish writers on the Talmud), while others delved into the rich evidence of the economic activity of medieval English Jewry in its Christian setting (such as debt bonds and the records of the Exchequer of the Jews.[1] Another scholar, who called for a study of prejudice in order to clarify the history of medieval Jewry, has begun to publish material reflecting contemporary prejudice in England.[2]

Similarly, both contemporaries and modern scholars have offered a variety of descriptions of, and explanations for, the expulsion itself. The Waverley chronicler, who calls them *"Judaeorum exasperans multitudo,"* indicates that they were expelled from England with their wives, children, and movables forever,

100 Zefira Entin Rokéah

under threat of forfeiting all their goods, at the instigation of Queen Mother Eleanor.[3] The Dunstable chronicler states that the king expelled the Jews because of the blasphemies the Jews had uttered frequently about the faith of the Christians; the Osney annalist calls the Jews "*inimici crucis Christi et blasphematores fidei Christianae*" who have impoverished the populace, and notes that any Jew found in England after the appointed time of departure would be beheaded or hanged.[4] Bartholomew Cotton, a Norwich monk, notes the drowning of Jews and the carrying off of their gold, silver, and other possessions by many who were later taken into custody and subsequently executed.[5] Modern students of the period have tended, however, to stress the economic aspects of the expulsion, suggesting that Jews were no longer necessary to the country, having been systematically impoverished by Henry III and Edward I, and having been replaced by "Cahorsins," Italian bankers, and the like who could carry out their functions in England's developing national economy. The valuable work of these researchers has presented a picture of the Jewish community that is perhaps rather more dependent on economic records than is desirable; their canvas has too many blank areas. As Salo Baron has noted,

> the extant rich documentation on Jewish moneylenders in medieval England has almost completely diverted the attention of scholars from the pulsating life of what probably was the non-moneylending majority of English Jews, just as the one-sidedness of sources relating to kings, nobles, clerics, and patrician burghers made many historians oblivious of the life of the overwhelming inarticulate majority of villeins and urban proletarians.[6]

The Jews of medieval England, even those who were indeed moneylenders and pawnbrokers, had family and community lives; they ate, drank, dressed, and dwelt in ways of which the abundant records offer a fascinating glimpse. Some of them were scholars, some professional men, and some – rogues and knaves. Since it was rather more difficult of access and analysis than some of the economic evidence, much of which is in print, the manuscript evidence concerning other aspects of the lives of English Jews of the twelfth and thirteenth centuries – especially judicial records and the related financial ones – has tended to be ignored by certain historians of English Jewry, Cecil Roth foremost among them.[7] However, even Roth, when confronted with such materials in print, acknowledged that records like the Tower receipt rolls for the years 1275-1278 present "a segment of the population that does not seem to figure elsewhere and therefore never to have had significant business dealings. . . ."[8] It is to these other Jews that my attention has been drawn in the course of my work on the materials in the Public Record Office, London, and elsewhere, and with whom I have dealt in several articles examining one sort or another of extra-legal activity in which English Jews were involved in the years leading up to the expulsion.[9]

But who and what the Jews were must be seen against the ba\
English medieval society, and so some general comments on pre-e\
England are necessary at this point.

First and foremost: in the twelfth and thirteenth countries, England \ .s
among the most orthodox countries of Europe in religious matters. Heresy was
both exceedingly rare and decisively dealt with when it appeared, with steps
being taken to prevent the arrival of heretics from the Continent. It was not
found necessary to import the Inquisition into England although the Dominicans
– known on the Continent for their orthodoxy and services to the Inquisition –
were present and capable of acting as its agents. [10]

In this period, England was a more united and more effectively governed
country than any other in Western Europe; its national institutions, most
especially its financial and administrative ones, were some one hundred years
ahead of those of, say, France. The Norman conquerors of England had found a
system of government well-supplied with techniques (such as the writ or the
court system) which were not fully exploited by the Anglo-Saxons, but from
which the Normans could select those most likely to be effective and then
realize their full potential. There was an amazing degree of communication
between the central government and the localities, through the sheriffs, the
nobility, and the meetings of the county courts, and this despite the notorious
difficulties of communication in the medieval period, with its bad sea facilities
and worse overland systems. Instructions were sent to sheriffs in every expectation that they would be carried out – eventually – the sheriffs being past
masters of the art of excusing inaction. Nonetheless, the sheriffs knew that
they themselves might be subject to heavy financial penalties for dereliction
of duty if they did not do as instructed. This relative strength of England's
medieval administrative system is reflected in the documentary riches that
today make medieval England both so tempting and so overwhelming to the
researcher. [11]

A third point about medieval England: with the exception of the rare poll-
taxes, financial obligations were seen as obligations imposed upon property,
usually immovable property, rather than upon persons. Thus, if a national tax
such as Danegeld were imposed, it was paid at the rate of so many pence per
unit of land rather than as so many pence per person. (From the late twelfth
century on, a new sort of tax was levied, assessed on movable property and set
at a particular percentage of the individual's worth.) Just as the traditional taxes
had been tied to the land, loans of money were seen as financial obligations tied
to an individual's land.

A borrower who received a loan from a Christian or Jewish moneylender
signed or sealed a bond acknowledging that, if the debt were not paid when
due, the money owed could be levied for the benefit of the lender from all the
lands and property held by the debtor at the time the debt was incurred –
regardless of who held the property at the time the debt was paid. Such, for
example, was the case of Gilbert Conan, who had borrowed money from the

Jews, Benedict of Winchester and Sweteman son of Licoricia, against his bond for eighty pounds sterling. In order to recover the money in 1272-1273, Benedict impleaded Stephen of Edworth, a current tenant of lands formerly held by Gilbert. The court decided that, as the lands that Stephen now held were indeed in the hands of Gilbert at the time that Gilbert contracted his debt, Stephen would have to pay the Jews (and might, if he wished, recover the money from Gilbert, whose debt it really was, in another court case).[12] (It has been suggested that this obligation of landed property rather than of persons had its roots in Jewish legal procedure as developed over the previous centuries, rather than in English law, but this is by no means certain.)[13]

Thus, especially in the thirteenth century, as the Crown taxed the Jews ever more heavily, increasing numbers of tenants of lands were called into court by Jews in order to pay debts incurred by their lords. The Christian resentment of the Jews that this caused can readily be imagined, as the Jew rather than the Crown was the visible and immediate cause of the tenants' financial difficulties.[14] In this process, whereby large sums were extracted from the populace and passed on to the Crown by the Jews, there was considerable benefit for the Crown. English kings of the thirteenth century faced significant opposition from their barons concerning the raising of money for the Crown's benefit, especially in the wake of the royal extravagance, bungling, and indulgence of foreign favorites which had brought the royal reputation and coffers to a new low in the middle of the century. Instead of the king's having to justify new taxes to the rebellious baronage, he was able to obtain money from the same source without constitutional difficulties by taxing the Jews, who then foreclosed on their clients, who were as a rule in arrears. Many financially embarrassed debtors turned to the large religious houses for help; these would pay their debts in return for the gift of their lands to the monastery (and, as often as not, the debtors would become the monastery's tenants for the lands they had held formerly in their own right). Great landowners, too, acted in this manner to aid debtors, swallowing up their lands in the process. Thus, in addition to being the royal sponge for the absorption of funds, the Jews were middlemen in a process whereby the greater religious houses and lay lords encompassed ever larger quantities of landed property at the expense of the lesser nobility and knights.[15]

When we deal with the English Jewry of the Middle Ages, we cannot but be aware of various aspects of that community's history from the Norman Conquest to the nation-wide expulsion of 1290. Not the least important aspect of this history is the factor of antisemitism, which still awaits its historian.[16] Anyone dealing with this subject must consider the ritual murder libel (as we will below), as well as other factors: how and why the Jews went from being a flourishing community, whose members lent money even to the king, to being an impoverished group made poorer and poorer by the Crown's shift to arbitrary taxation (tallage) from the late twelfth century on; the application of canon law and procedures to limit the Jews' participation in general community life, even to the extent of pronouncing them excommunicates from the Church and Christian society;[17] the Jews' being in a special position vis-à-vis the Crown; and, not least, the Jews' monetary activities. In this connection, one may note Gavin Langmuir's suggestion that "the stronger the central government, the more rapidly were Jews assigned a quasi-servile status, and the greater became their social isolation . . ." along with the comments made above on England's relatively efficient and strong government.[18] At the time of the expulsion, as we have noted, various explanations of the king's action were offered by a range of chroniclers; contemporary comment on the *scelera* or crimes of the Jews (although it is not clear whether the reference is to the Jews' rejection of Jesus and to the events surrounding his crucifixion, or to their contemporary crimes), as on the Jews' monetary offenses (including the clipping and counterfeiting of coins), is to be found both in English records and chronicles as well as in the responsa of Rabbi Meir son of Baruch of Rothenburg.[19] The comments of Rabbi Meir condemning coin-clipping and "currency falsifiers who have led to the destruction of our brethren, the inhabitants of France and the island [England]" are very much to our point: in order to understand the Jewish community of medieval England more fully, one must consider the extra-legal activities of which the Jews were accused. However, considerations of time and space prevent us from dealing with all of these questions here; we will touch only on the questions of ritual murder and the attitude of the Church in England towards the Jews.

It is worth noting, however, what is remarkable in the records concerning English Jewry of the Middle Ages: the matter-of-fact tone of the writers, whether they are dealing with coin-clipping, ritual murder, debts, or anything else. There is very little *overt* hatred of Jews expressed in private records (such as chronicles and letters); antisemitic feeling must be gathered from their credulity concerning stories about the Jews, for example about ritual murder, or from their repetition of clichés about the Jews, rather than from specific and new vitriolic statements. The public records may occasionally indicate a certain degree of prejudice against Jews in the judgments handed down by the courts but – with the exception of certain records connected with the charges of coin-clipping of the late 1270s and of some marginal sketches drawn by bored scribes – there is no specifically anti-Jewish statement to be found in them.[20] We must distinguish between the antisemitism inherent in a system such as the English medieval one, where Jews had to live according to the so-called Law and Custom of the Jewry, which set definite limits on their actions simply because they were Jews (e.g., Jews might not live wherever they chose; Jews' oaths in court were of less weight than those of Christians; and so on), and a system that is not only intrinsically antisemitic but which openly and regularly oppresses Jews physically and slanders them in official statements issued to the public, as in twentieth-century Europe.[21] However, in the years that preceded the expulsion of 1290, and particularly in the years that followed the accession of Edward I (1272), a changed attitude towards the Jews became apparent.

apparent. This attitude became ever worse; its culmination was their exile. But even this altered approach was ambivalent: on the one hand, hundreds of Jews were imprisoned and very many of them were hanged on possibly false evidence of their coinage violations; on the other, the authorities endeavored to ensure the safe passage of Jews abroad during the expulsion itself and punished those who robbed or abandoned them to their death. [22]

2. The Ritual Murder Libel – William of Norwich

It is well known that England had the dubious distinction of being the first country in medieval Europe to be the scene of the renewed ritual murder libel against the Jews. From the time of the events at Inmestar, Syria, of 415, when Jews were accused of committing a ritual murder, and which came ten years after the provisions in the Codex Theodosianus forbidding Jews to burn Haman's image or mock the cross on Purim, there is no record of such charges being brought against the Jews. [23] The story of the events of 1144 in Norwich appears in *The Life and Miracles of Saint William of Norwich by Thomas of Monmouth*, Thomas being a Benedictine monk who came to Norwich Priory after the alleged crucifixion. [24] His opinion of the Jews may be gathered from what he calls them: "Christian-slaying Jews" (*christianicidarum iudeorum*). [25] Inasmuch as this story provided the impetus for numerous additional charges, it is worth examining in detail.

Thomas related that William, the twelve-year-old son of farmers, had been apprenticed to the skinners of Norwich from the age of eight; he did good and inexpensive work, and so had many dealings with Jews. On Monday of Easter week, a man pretending to be the cook of the Archdeacon of Norwich bribed William's mother with three shillings to let William come and work in his kitchen. The two were seen entering a Jew's house. [26] On the Wednesday of that week, which Thomas tells us incorrectly was the Passover, after the Jews finished their prayers, they gagged William elaborately with a wooden gag fastened with many knots, three of them on his forehead. [27] Thereafter, they shaved his head and lacerated it with thorns before holding a mock trial. They then fastened him to the middle of three upright poles connected by a horizontal one, partly by nails and partly by bonds. They stabbed him in the left side, and poured boiling water over the body to stop its bleeding. The child died.

On Good Friday, after they had been seen by a Christian carrying the corpse in a sack to a site far from the Jewish neighborhood, two Jews hanged the body from a tree in a wood and fled back to Norwich, where they hastily bribed the sheriff to protect them and silence the witness. The corpse was seen by various individuals, who planned to bury it the day after Easter Sunday. However, rumors spread in Norwich and many townspeople came out and saw the body on Sunday. The body was buried and reburied on the same site in the wood. William's mother and aunt went throughout the town accusing the Jews of the crime. Nearly two weeks later, the dean summoned the Jews before the Church synod. The Jews turned to the sheriff, who notified the bishop that he (the bishop) had no jurisdiction over the Jews; the Jews refused to appear, claiming they were subject only to the king and not to the Church, and ignoring repeated summonses. Finally, the Jews were threatened with a peremptory sentence and extermination if they failed to attend. At the synod, the Jews denied their guilt, but refused to clear themselves by the ordeal. The deliberations continued until nightfall; under cover of night, the Jews fled to the royal castle in Norwich (which was under the sheriff's command).[28] The child's body was moved into the monks' cemetery. The Jews were not, apparently, brought to trial before a royal court on the accusation of murder (murder was one of the crimes reserved for the royal courts), and there were no riots or violence against the Jews in the wake of the accusation.

Many local residents disbelieved the story, but the Cluniac prior of the house of Saint Pancras at Lewes – who was then visiting Norwich – tried in vain to receive the body of the child-martyr from the bishop of Norwich.[29] Various miracles were associated with William in 1144; only after six years had passed, in 1150, were additional miracles recorded – at a time when Thomas of Monmouth himself could act as their witness.

A monk who was a convert from Judaism, Theobald of Cambridge, told Thomas that the Jews had a written tradition that, in order to regain their freedom and their fatherland, they must sacrifice a Christian every year. To this end, he reported, the Jews of Spain met yearly at Narbonne in order to cast lots for the chosen country; in that country, lots were then cast to choose the city that would furnish the victim. In this manner, Norwich had been chosen for 1144.[30] (This story is reminiscent of those of Apion and Damocritus concerning the periodic sacrifices of non-Jews by Jews.)[31]

It is important to note that no valid evidence was produced and that the Jews were neither tried nor punished for this alleged crime. It was only some five years later, when a Jew – apparently one of those supposedly seen removing the corpse – was murdered by his debtor's esquires, that the story was revived; the bishop, one of William's most devoted adherents, insisted that, before the esquires of his mesne tenant be tried, the Jews be tried in connection with the child-martyr. The beginning of this murder trial is known to us only from Thomas's admittedly conjectural account of it; no official court record of it has been preserved. Even according to Thomas's version, the continuation of the trial was postponed to an unknown date, a date never arrived at.[32] It cannot be doubted that Thomas would have mentioned punishments meted out to the martyr's murderers if such had been imposed at a later stage of the trial. From this time forward, William's cult grew.

Modern scholars have suggested varying interpretations of the finding of William's body. Strack suggested that William had been buried by his relatives while in a cataleptic fit; M. R. James thought it not impossible that William had died in the Jewry, possibly because of an accident or the act of an "insane or superstitious Jew."[33] M. D. Anderson, in *A Saint at Stake*, indicated that the Jews' unwise "cruel horseplay" connected with a Purim masquerade's hanging of Haman might have led to William's being told to keep away from Jews, and that his sudden absence might have led the Jews to fear a possible attack on them. They might, she said, have questioned him brutally about this possibility, smuggled him out of town and then killed him following their being seen by the Christian witness, in order to ensure his silence and forestall a possible attack.[34] Lipman, in *The Jews of Medieval Norwich*, on the other hand, noting that there is no evidence of such Purim horseplay in medieval England, thought that William's death was probably the result of a sexual crime against a child by a deviate with sadistic impulses – who was not necessarily a Jew.[35] Lipman also noted various reasons for the revival of the charge of ritual murder in Norwich: the poor relations of Norwich Jews and their Christian neighbors; the increasing indebtedness of the local populace to the Jews. Anderson underlined Norwich's need of a local saint, especially in the light of the expected income from his shrine, and stressed that no one could become a saint who had not suffered for Christ (and what better than to suffer in this way at the hands of those arch-unbelievers, the Jews?).[36] I suspect, however, with M. R. James, that the presence of the convert Theobald was the prime factor. We know that the rash of accusations of a similar nature that followed occurred in places (such as Gloucester and Bury St Edmunds) that had a clear connection with Norwich, to which Theobald had moved.[37]

3. Later Accusations

Let us examine the later accusations briefly. The Jews of Gloucester were accused in 1168 of a similar crime. (Note that this is before Thomas's *Life* was "published," but at a time when the story of Saint William was "notorious" at Pershore, near Gloucester, which had connections with Norwich.) It was alleged that the Jews had secretly enticed the boy Harold away, on 21 February, and had concealed him until 17 March. Then, using the excuse of celebrating a circumcision, they held a great celebration at which they tortured the child. The story indicates that the Jews placed thorns on his head and in his armpits, and liquid wax in his eyes and ears; they also knocked out some of his teeth, and placed him between two fires to scorch him while they poured boiling fat over him. Not surprisingly, the boy died. The Jews bound his feet with his own girdle and threw him into the Severn River on Friday, 17 March. On the next day, his body was recovered by fishermen. A procession of monks from the nearby religious house received the corpse, washed, and then buried it, after noting the wounds.[38]

In the 1170s, there were several similar accusations in France, at Orleans, Blois, and Paris. These accusations may have reflected the presence in France of the bishop of Norwich and his party (Bishop Evorard died at the Abbey of Fontenay): it is quite possible that one of the party spread the story.[39]

In 1181, at Bury St Edmunds, near Norwich, the martyrdom and burial of the boy Robert is noted by the local chronicler, Jocelin of Brakelond. Unfortunately, he provides no other details of the event; other chroniclers noted that Robert was killed cruelly and secretly in May or June. However, we have no additional contemporary testimony concerning the events in Bury.[40]

In a British Museum manuscript, which has been dated at about 1280, there appears the story of the murder of another child, this time in Bristol. The manuscript includes a drawing of a Jew stabbing a crucified child. The associated events are alleged to have occurred circa 1183. Samuel, a Jew of Bristol, who had crucified three other boys in the previous year, we are told, now tortured and crucified Adam, son of William the Welshman of St Mary Radcliffe parish, in his (Samuel's) house. Upon Samuel's crucifying the boy, a loud voice proclaimed in Hebrew: "I am the God of Abraham and the God of Isaac and the God of Jacob whom thou hast for a fourth time nailed to a cross . . . ." Samuel's wife confessed her guilt, and she and her son expressed their desire to be baptized the following day – whereupon Samuel killed them both.[41] This little-known episode does not, apparently, appear in contemporary records, and the child was not revered as a saint. The story seems even less likely than the earlier ones.

The chronicler Richard of Devizes noted with pride that, in 1190, the residents of his beloved city Winchester had not – unlike those of many other cities – been caught up in the wave of riots against the Jews at a time when the Londoners, for example, had begun to "immolate the Jews to their father, the Devil."[42] But in 1192 the ritual murder charge appeared in Winchester. As Richard tells the story, the Jews of Winchester, being "zealous, after the Jewish fashion, for the honour of their city," decided to martyr a boy there.[43] The chosen victim was a young French boy who had been a cobbler's apprentice in France. He was sent by a French Jew, along with a letter in Hebrew, to the Jews of Winchester, the "Jerusalem of the Jews" in those parts. (The chronicler adds some nasty comments on various English towns, remarking that in London, a most evil place, the Jews are less perfect than elsewhere because of their bad environment.)

The French boy was employed by a certain Jewish cobbler in Winchester, being given good wages for very little work. He and a young Christian friend from France always slept at the ramshackle hut of a poor, old woman. On Good Friday, the boy failed to return to the hut. His friend had terrible dreams all night; after several days' search had failed to reveal the missing boy, he turned to the Jewish cobbler, who was very unpleasant to him (unlike his previous manner). The boy quarrelled with the Jew, charging him with loud cries of having crucified and perhaps even eaten his friend. A Christian woman servant in the Jew's household declared that she had seen the missing boy go down into the Jew's storeroom, but had not seen him return from it. Before the judges, the accusations of the two failed, as the boy was a minor and the woman "infamous" because of her employment by Jews. The accused Jew asked to be

permitted to clear himself by oath. Then, "Gold won the judges' favour . . . ,"
as the chronicler put it, "and the matter was dropped." It may be noted in
passing that Richard of Devizes himself noted that the citizenry of Winchester
"greatly indulged" in one vice only, that of lying "like sentries." In this case,
where there was neither a corpse nor a body of evidence, one can only assume
that they were acting in character.[44]

In 1202, the Jews of Lincoln came under suspicion when a child's body was
found near the town. In 1202, also, Bonefand, a Jew of Bedford, was accused of
the emasculation and death of Richard, the young nephew of Robert of Sutton.
Bonefand, denying the charge, offered the king one mark for an inquiry to be
made by a jury. The jurors declared that Bonefand was innocent; Robert
accordingly would have to satisfy the king's demands for having made a false
accusation.[45] It is worth noting here that some contemporary Christians believed that Jews were likely to circumcise the Christian children they proposed
to crucify, perhaps in order to make them resemble Jesus, the day of whose
circumcision was celebrated on 1 January.

In the years 1225 and 1232, a number of charges connected with the killing
of children were made against the Jews of Winchester. In one of these cases,
the child was found alive and well; in a second case, the child's own mother was
taken into custody pending trial; in a third instance, two of the five Jews
charged were convicted. It would seem that, in these episodes, formal judicial
proceedings forestalled charges of ritual murder being made or violent action
being taken by an enraged citizenry.[46]

A number of Jews at Norwich were accused of having circumcised the five-
year-old son of a Christian physician in 1230.[47] The Norwich circumcision case
is of particular interest to us for several reasons. First, it is quite likely that
the affair was important to the Church because it assumed that the Jews had
intended to crucify the circumcised boy. This assumption is supported by the
phrases used by the chronicler Roger of Wendover and by his successor,
Matthew Paris.[48] The Church, it would seem, saw the act of circumcising the
child not only as a crime in its own right, but as part of a far more serious
procedure – the preparations for a contemptuous crucifixion – which had been
stopped in time. For this reason, the Norwich circumcision case is included in
our survey of ritual murder charges in medieval England. It appears that the
leaders of the Norwich Jewish community knew nothing about the circumcision
of the child, as they paid the king for the privilege of examining the allegedly
circumcised boy themselves.[49] The community leaders declared (in somewhat
obscure language), following their examination, that the child was not fully circumcised; it may be that they hoped to have the charge reduced from circumcision to the less dangerous one of bodily harm by indicating that the circumcision
was not valid according to Jewish law. But their declaration did not help the
accused Jews, at least three of whom were executed following legal proceedings that dragged on for many years.[50] The proceedings also raise the question
as to why the Norwich Jewish community's leaders asked to examine the child

themselves. One historian, Walter Rye, suggested that the boy had been cir-cumcised by Jews, and that it was other Jews, who were ignorant of their act and disbelieved the charges made against their coreligionists, who asked for the examination. Rye also thought that the child might have been the son of a convert to Christianity whom the Jews involved wished to "save" for the Jewish community. (This suggestion was based on the child's father's name – Benedict – and his profession: medicine; both had Jewish associations.)[51] But another possibility, hinted at above, should be kept in mind: after they exa-mined the child, the court records show, the Jews stated that the child had been seen, and that the top of his penis was covered by a membrane in its front portion (*"Et visus est puer, et membrum ejus visum est pelle coopertum ante in capite"*). It is entirely possible that the Jews gave their ruling here according to Jewish law (*Halakha*) in stating that, since it was not complete, the child's circumcision was invalid.[52] It is not impossible that the community's leaders hoped, as suggested above, to reduce the charge from circumcision to one of ordinary bodily harm, in order to limit the potential danger to the community. But they failed to prevent a tragic end to the proceedings.[53]

In 1244, it was the turn of the Jews of London to be accused. On 1 August, the body of a boy was found in the churchyard of St Benedict's, with what interpreters from the House of Converts alleged to be Hebrew letters incised upon its arms, legs, and chest; these letters supposedly showed that the child, after having been sold to the Jews, had been killed ritually by them. The canons of St Paul's, perhaps in response to the assertions of some that the bodies of children crucified by Jews had – after being received in churches – become famous for miracles, hurriedly buried it in their church.[54] All the Jews of England were told that they would have to pay an enormous sum (allegedly 60,000 marks, or 40,000 pounds sterling) as compensation for the crime.

In 1255, the Jews of Lincoln were accused concerning the boy known the-reafter as Little St Hugh. It was alleged that the Jews enticed this eight- or nine-year-old boy away, concealed him for a time (varying from ten to twenty-six days), either starving him meanwhile (according to the Burton Annals) or feeding him on milk foods alone (as reported by Matthew Paris), while issuing an invitation to the Jews of the kingdom to attend – supposedly to help celebrate a wedding. Then, in council, the Jews decided to put the child to death. The monastic annalist of Burton tells us that they circumcised the child, stripped him, beat him and spit in his face, cut off his lower nose and cut his upper lip, and then broke his teeth. He was crowned with thorns, knifed, pierced by nails, forced to drink gall, crucified, and speared. During all these tortures, we are told, he did not utter a single moan or cry. After he died, the Jews cast him into a pit (or well). Miracles occurred following the discovery of the child's corpse nearly a month later, on 29 August. The canons of Lincoln Cathedral buried him with great pomp.

Following the child's mother's appeal to the king, Henry III, the matter was investigated. One of the judges promised the Jew Jopin (=Copin, =Jacob), near whose house the child had been found, that he would not be executed if he confessed and revealed details of the crime; the Jew "confessed," but was put to death at the order of Henry III. An additional ninety-one Jews were sent to London for imprisonment. Eighteen of them were executed, and the rest pardoned only after the (unsuccessful) intervention of the friars (Burton calls them Dominicans, Matthew Paris says they were Franciscans) and the efforts of the Earl of Cornwall, who held the Jewry in his hand then (and who may have received a large bribe).[55]

A similar accusation concerning London is mentioned only after years had passed since the alleged occurrence, in the late 1260s. In 1276, King Edward I sent two orders within a two-week period to his itinerant justices then dealing with offenses supposed to have been committed by various Londoners. The first order states that the Jews declared that they had been acquitted in the time of Henry III of charges connected with the death of a Christian boy found dead in the Dovegate district of London, and that, if their declaration were truthful, the judges were not to trouble them again concerning the affair. In their reply, the judges told the king that "a Christian boy, who was crucified by them [the Jews], and who was irreverently and miserably slain, in offence of the name of Jesus Christ and against the peace of the realm," had been thrown by the Jews into the Thames and had been washed ashore at Dovegate. The king said he wished to consult with the itinerant justices, the justices of the Jews, and also his councillors, about this "detestable . . . deed," and told the itinerant justices to adjourn the case until a month after Easter (when what had been decided would be made known in parliament), and to leave the Jews alone meanwhile.[56] I have been unable to find evidence as to the fate of the accused Jews, but it is not impossible that the whole accusation was a convenient tool for the king to extort money from the Jews, both before sending the first order and after dispatching the second: the Jews may have found it worthwhile to "purchase" a permanent adjournment of the case so as to avoid the anticipated and terrifying outcome of such judicial proceedings, especially in the light of what followed the 1255 Lincoln charges.

The last charge of this kind before the expulsion of the Jews from England in 1290 is that of 1277 (or 1279) in Northampton. The chronicler of Bury St Edmunds reported that on Good Friday – the day of Jesus's crucifixion – on 31 March, the Jews of Northampton had crucified a boy who did not die. As a result, many Jews were dragged at horses' tails after Easter (2 April) before being hanged at London.[57] Cecil Roth, the historian of English Jewry, suggests that this story derived from the chroniclers' confusing the dates of the Adoration of the Cross (Good Friday) and the Exultation of the Cross (14 September), and their "muddled attempt to explain the confiscations and executions known to have taken place at this period, actually the outcome of the allegations of clipping the coinage, ..."[58]

A number of conclusions can be drawn from this unhappy history of ritual murder accusations:

(a) in most of the cases, there was inadequate evidence of such a crime and Jews were not put on trial;

(b) in only three instances, including the case in which the child remained alive, were the Jews punished and/or executed. In another instance, and without trial, a heavy financial penalty was imposed;

(c) in nearly all the cases reported, the events are associated with the Passover-Easter season, and there is a clear effort to associate the events with Jewish attempts to express contempt for the crucifixion of Jesus;

(d) certain Jews or converts played a significant part in publicizing such charges against Jews: in one case, it was a convert who was responsible for spreading such charges against the Jews and perhaps also of creating the relevant myth, while in another a Jew "confessed" a number of "facts" that brought many of his coreligionists to the gallows along with the confessor himself. In a third episode, converts "deciphered" letters incised on a child's corpse, thereby causing the Jews to be suspected and to face a severe financial penalty;

(e) once the idea of ritual murder became part of the thought patterns of Christians living in medieval England, it became an inseparable part of their view of Jews and might be resurrected each time the body of a dead child was found;

(f) in many cases in which a dead child was elevated to the status of martyr, the hope of financial gain played a considerable part, whether the anticipated profits would accrue to the king or to local churchmen, for whom the donations of pilgrims to local shrines could not but be important.[59] In this connection, M. D. Anderson comments in *A Saint at Stake* (pp. 199-200) that "rich rewards could be reaped from honours paid to the most unlikely saints . . ." and that "while it was thus of great importance to every religious house that its church should house the shrine of a wonder-working saint, the fact that few people had been killed for their faith in pagan England limited the number of local martyrs" available. It seems reasonable that some would try to adapt supply to demand, especially with a considerable income from shrines being likely to result;

(g) it must be stressed that there is no indication in these early cases that the *blood* of the victim was needed for any purpose at all – unlike the emphasis on this point to be found in later centuries.

4. English Jews and the Church

The relations of the Jews of England with the Church had always been somewhat complicated, from the early years of their settlement. Among the earliest references to Jews in England are those from the reign of William Rufus (1087-1100) indicating that the king had encouraged converts from Judaism to Christianity to recant. At least one disputation between Jews and Christians took place in his time; the king even stated jokingly that, if the Jews won in this disputation, he himself would join their faith – to the scandal of all beholders.[60] In this period, there was a famous public disputation of a Jew from

Mainz with Gilbert Crispin, the abbot of Westminster, which led, apparently, to one Jew's conversion.[61] Anselm, the archbishop of Canterbury, expressed his concern for the well-being of the convert and called upon Christians to aid him.[62]

At about the same time, Prior Philip of St Frideswide's, Oxford, tells the story of a young Jew of Oxford, Deulecresse, the son of Mossey of Wallingford, who had mocked St Frideswide, saying that he could cure as well as the saint, and mocking her cures by pretending to be crippled and then "curing" himself in public. The saint, so the story goes, caused him to become insane, and he hanged himself in his father's kitchen. Yelping dogs ran behind the cart in which his body was brought to London for burial.[63]

In 1144 and frequently thereafter, as we have seen, English Jews were accused of the ritual murder of children. Whereas there had been relatively little disturbance in England at the time of the First Crusade (other than a possible large influx of Jews from Rouen following the 1096 disturbances there),[64] at the time of the Second Crusade, we find St Bernard of Clairvaux appealing to the people of England, as well as to those of France and Germany, not to molest the Jews in their crusading fervor. This may hint at unrest in England at that time.[65]

Throughout this period, despite the specific interdiction of such practices, various religious foundations borrowed money from the Jews, pledging church vessels, books, and vestments as security for their loans; even relics were used in this way.[66] During the twelfth century, many religious houses went into debt to the Jews in order to finance their grandiose building projects and land purchases. The Jewish financier Aaron of Lincoln alone financed building projects in nine Cistercian abbeys as well as the cathedrals of Lincoln and Petersborough and the great church at St Albans.[67] However, after 1188, the Cistercians were forbidden to borrow from the Jews.[68] In keeping with the clearly expressed policy of the Church, Jews were forbidden to take usury from crusaders. But the great religious foundations and churches served the Jews, among others, as depositories for their valuables (and even, on occasion, as places of safety for themselves).[69] This practice, as well as many others, was condemned by the synod at Oxford in 1222, to which we shall return.

The great turning points in the attitude expressed by the Church in England towards the Jews were the great Lateran councils of 1179 and 1215, which echoed and expanded the ancient restrictions on the Jews. Stephen Langton, the archbishop of Canterbury, among the most prominent participants in the Fourth Lateran Council, was extremely energetic in implementing its decisions in England. Even before Langton's 1222 synod, the bishop of Worcester had issued statutes forbidding the Jews to take church books, vestments, or ornaments in pledge, and had – echoing the provisions of the council of 1179 – forbidden Christian wetnurses to nurse Jewish children and female Christian servants to sleep in the houses of their Jewish employers. He further forbade the safekeeping of Jewish valuables in churches.[70]

But it was at the Oxford synod of 1222 held by Langton that the fullest expression was given to the anti-Jewish measures of the Fourth Lateran Council of 1215, while those present added some touches of their own. As these canons "came in fact to form the basis of the local law of the English Church in the later middle ages,"[71] their nature was of considerable importance. *Inter alia*, this synod declared that Jews were henceforth not to have a Christian woman dependent (*mancipia*) serving them; that no new synagogues were to be built; that Jews had to pay the church tithes due from lands they obtained.[72] In addition, Jews were to wear a special, distinguishing badge on their outermost garments: the badge was to be two fingers wide by four fingers long and of a color other than that of the garment.[73] The object, of course, was to prevent unwitting intercourse of Christians with Jews. (It should be noted that as early as 1218 the central government had issued orders to the sheriffs of various counties concerning the wearing of such a badge by the Jews. There are numerous references in 1221 to Jews' being fined for failing to wear the badge.)[74]

Just as the Fourth Lateran Council had decreed that the weapon of excommunication was to be used against Jews who took exorbitant interest or refused to pay church tithes on land, so the zealous Stephen Langton and the bishop of Lincoln had seen to it that the Jews of Lincoln were excommunicated in effect and cut off from supplies of food and other necessities. The government found it necessary to order the authorities of Canterbury, Oxford, Norwich, and London to see to it that Jews were supplied with foodstuffs and other essentials.[75]

Provisions similar to those of the 1222 Oxford synod are to be found in the canons of other local synods held in England throughout the thirteenth century, forbidding Jews to receive Church goods as pledges for loans, forbidding the deposit for safekeeping of Jews' valuables in churches, and so on. The prevailing note was that of the Fourth Lateran Council: to separate the Jews from Christian society and prevent them from taking advantage of Christians. But these attempts were unsuccessful, at least in part. The violation of Church edicts in various fields apparently continued throughout the century, with the repeated violations being reflected in the repeated legislation on these points. For example, concerning the Jews' employment of Christian women as servants, we find Archbishop Walter Giffard of York dealing with the excommunication of nine Christian women in 1276. Five of the nine noted in the records are stated specifically to be *ancillae* (servants) or *nutrices* (wetnurses) of Jews. All nine women had refused for more than forty days to comply with Church directives concerning their forbidden employment, and the secular arm was now to act against these excommunicants.[76] We noted above the possibility (in the Church's eyes if not in the king's) of using the threat of excommunication in order to force the Jews to pay church tithes, cease collecting usurious interest, and the like. In this connection, there are several documents extant indicating that persons identified clearly as Jews (*not* as converts) have been excommunicated by the Church. They include Manser, Jew of Oxford; Floria of Northampton, a Jewish widow; and Peter Le Franceys of Strigull (Chepstow), a Jew; they were excommunicated in the 1260s and 1270s for reasons not specified in these records.[77] F. D. Logan, in his article on thirteen London Jews, suggested that in these cases the use of the excommunication had probably been dictated by the desire to have the secular arm act against the Jews and force them into compliance with the wishes of the ecclesiastical authorities.[78] In the list of their grievances drawn up in the 1250s, the clergy complained *inter alia* that, when the ecclesiastical courts proposed to deal with recalcitrant Jews who refused to wear the Jewish badge or to dismiss their Christian servants, the king's agents would step in to announce that jurisdiction over the Jews belonged to the king and force the churchmen to readmit the Jews to communion with their Christian neighbors, friends, and suppliers.

The 1222 Council at Oxford is also renowned for being that in which a deacon who had apostasized for the love of a Jewess was degraded by the Church, handed over to the secular authorities, and promptly executed. The other scandalous conversion of the century was that of the Dominican, Robert of Reading, some fifty years later; Robert, now known as Haggai, embraced Judaism and married a Jewish wife. Throughout the period, we find Jews jesting with churchmen as their equals, Jews depositing their valuables in churches for safekeeping (as we noted above), and so on.[79] But we also find expressions of contempt for Christianity attributed to Jews throughout the period. Jews were punished, even executed, for blasphemy, for the circumcision of Christian boys, and for similar offenses. We know, for example, of the Norwich Jew, Abraham son of Deulecresse, who was dragged and then hanged for blasphemy and other offenses about a decade before the expulsion of all Jews from England in 1290.[80] An Oxford Jew seized a cross from its bearer in a religious procession at Oxford in 1268 and trod the cross underfoot; he could not be found in the town after committing the offense. A story is also told of the defiling of an image of the Virgin by the very wealthy Abraham of Berkhamsted in 1250 and of his subsequent imprisonment until the Earl of Cornwall interceded on his behalf.[81]

Whereas until 1253 royal legislation affecting the Jewry had been essentially financial in character, the statute of 1253 dealing with the Jews confirmed the provisions of the 1222 Oxford council. Thus the full force of secular authority was put behind the Church's actions concerning the Jews. Jews might not have synagogues in any towns but those they had previously inhabited; no Jews were to remain in England unless they had guarantors and the wherewithal to pay taxes; Jewish prayers were to be said in a low voice, and no Christian women were to be servants of Jews. No Jew was to buy or to eat meat during Lent; no Jew was to disparage Christianity nor debate religious matters with a Christian; Jews and Christians were forbidden to have sexual relations with each other. Jews were to wear the identifying badge on their chests; Jews were not to be allowed in the churches and none was to act in order to dissuade would-be converts to Christianity, while no Jews were to live in any but the recognized towns for settlement without special license.[82] This piece of legislation, so much influenced by the Church, was very appropriately the work of Henry III, that overly pious king with no real understanding of his religion, so constantly at the mercy of papal whims and the super-religiosity of his consort, Alienora of Provence.

In his important article dealing with "The Jews and the Archives," Langmuir indicated that, in dealing with such complicated questions as the nature of medieval prejudice against Jews, it was not enough to be content with examining archival evidence while overlooking the findings of social scientists (as, he indicated, H. G. Richardson did in his work on Angevin Jewry).[83] Langmuir suggested that "the relations between medieval Jews and non-Jews [which] have usually been viewed as readily understandable consequences of religious antagonism rather than a product, at least after 1100, of prejudice" should be seen in the light of the nature of contemporary Christian society in all its aspects. He added: "It is difficult to imagine a more perfect screen on which might be projected the dissatisfactions, the anxieties, the hostility, and the repressed fantasies of the delights and powers of evil brewed by all the tensions of a rapidly developing and increasingly institutionalized society" than the Jews.[84] As we noted earlier,[85] Langmuir indicated a possible parallel in development between population growth (or stasis or contraction) and a sense of opportunity, on the one hand, and increasing antisemitism on the other. He suggested that with considerable economic advance, there was less antisemitism (as in the twelfth century), and with gradually limited economic opportunities (as in the thirteenth and fourteenth centuries), antisemitism prospered ever more in an atmosphere of frustration and disappointment. This process was expressed in the spreading of increasingly irrational ideas about Jews from the second half of the twelfth century on – with a peak being reached in the fourteenth century (ironically, "when the Church was at one of its lowest points"), that is, *after* the Jews were expelled from England.[86] Furthermore, Langmuir pointed out a connection between the strength of the central government, and the status of the Jews and their willingness to engage in the risky business of money-lending: a stronger government could exploit and oppress Jews more effectively. At the same time, a strong government administering justice through a network of local and central courts provided a sense of security for the money-lenders, who could pursue reluctant debtors in the courts.[87] Langmuir noted that while "the majority of the little evidence that there is suggests that it was primarily those who lived in close contact with Jews who were friendly with them, . . . that is poor evidence of the general climate of opinion . . ." in medieval England; he suggested – on the basis of the findings of the students of modern prejudice – that those Christians "who had fairly frequent contact without intimacy [with the Jews] would have been the most hostile" to them. By 1190, he added, "there is indubitable evidence of widespread hate"; the wave of ritual murder accusations from about 1130 on, he proposed, "may have been, in part, a popular reaction" to the settlement of Jews outside of London.[88] Langmuir's views seem reasonable on the whole, but the interpretation he offered of ritual murder seems not to fit into the framework of his expanding society theories.

Unfortunately, there has not yet appeared a serious study of the influence of the Franciscans and Dominicans on the attitude of the English to the Jews.[89] However, it is known that the friars did not sit idly by, but intervened in political as well as social matters in England from about 1220 C.E. on. In the case of at least one ritual murder charge (Lincoln, 1255), friars intervened to protect the accused Jews, as we have seen (above, and n. 55); but, as Jeremy Cohen has noted in his study of the friars and anti-Judaism in medieval Europe, "the most predominant attitude of the friars toward the Jews was marked by an aggressive missionary spirit and often violent animosity."[90] My own researches into the charges made against Jews and Christians concerning coinage violations, especially the coin-clipping charges of the 1270s, make it clear that a definite anti-Jewish bias informed the proceedings. Christians convicted of the same violations of the coinage as Jews were, as a rule, subjected only to financial penalties; in many cases, the Jews were executed by hanging.[91]

A full study of the various factors that brought about the expulsion of the Jews from England has not yet been made. As a rule, historians have concentrated on the economic aspects of the problem – primarily the impoverishment of the Jews and their replacement in economic life by Italian bankers. There is no question that the attitudes of various groups in English society must be studied, including the lords, the knights, the townsmen, and clergymen of all ranks, before we can begin to understand the many-faceted background of the expulsion. There is similarly no question that medieval prejudice must be understood, for anti-Jewish feeling played a key role in these events.

England had a special relationship with its Jews in the Middle Ages, a relationship based on clearly recognized modes of behavior, laws, and customs, yet it was precisely in the midst of this recognized status pattern that a wave of ritual murder charges appeared for the first time in medieval Europe with its accompanying anti-Jewish sentiment. It was England, too, that set the pattern for the rest of Europe with the first, nation-wide, and long-lasting expulsion of the entire Jewish population of the country. It is clearly worthy of further study.

Notes

1. See A. M. Habermann, ed., "Hebrew Poems of Meir of Norwich," in V. D. Lipman, *The Jews of Medieval Norwich* (London, 1967), p. 359 ff. [=pp. 1–45 of Hebrew section]; *Tosfoth Hachmei Anglia (Glossaries by Anglo-Jewish Scholars)* (Heb.), eds. A. Schreiber, S. Sofer and E. D. Pines (Jerusalem, 1968 ff.); all of these glossaries are based on MS De Rossi 933 of the Biblioteca Palatina di Parma. See also I. Epstein's "Pre-Expulsion England in the Responsa," *The Jewish Historical Society of England, Transactions* [hereafter *JHSET*] 14:187–205, or A. Marmorstein, "New Material for the Literary History of the English Jews before the Expulsion," *JHSET*, 12:103–115; cf. E. E. Urbach, ". . . Scholarship by the Rabbis of England of

the Pre-Expulsion Period," (Heb.) in *Essays presented to Chief Rabbi Israel Brodie . . .* , eds. H. J. Zimmels, J. Rabbinowitz, and I. Finestein (London, 1967), 2, pp. 1–56, and E. Kupfer, "A Contribution to the Chronicles of the Family of R. Moses ben R. Yom-Tov 'the Noble' of London," (Heb.) *Tarbiz*, 40(1971): viii [=English summary], 385–387. See also *The Etz Hayyim* (Tree of Life) of Rabbi Jacob Hazan (Heb.), ed. I. Brodie (Jerusalem, 1962–1967), 3 vols.; *Dodi Ve-Nechdi (Uncle and Nephew): The Work of Berachya Hanakdan*, ed. H. Gollancz (London, etc., 1920), and *The Sepher hashoham (The Onyx Book) by Moses ben Isaac haNessiah* (Heb), ed. B. Klar (London, 1947).

The scholars stressing economic matters include Peter Elman, "Jewish Trade in Thirteenth-Century England," *Historia Judaica*, 1(1938–1939):91–104; see also his "The Economic Causes of the Expulsion of the Jews in 1290," *The Economic History Review 7*(1937): 145–154, and his unpublished University of London M.A. thesis of 1936, "Jewish Finance in Thirteenth Century England . . . ." H. G. Richardson's remarks on the expulsion in *The English Jewry under Angevin Kings* (London, 1960), pp. 213–233, especially pp. 225–229, stress Edward's need of money as the primary motive for the expulsion of Gascon Jewry and of English Jewry; the rest of his work deals largely with the economic evidence. V. D. Lipman's *The Jews of Medieval Norwich* (London, 1967) delineates the Norwich community, using economic records as the principal source of information. All students of medieval English Jewish history depend on the *Calendar of the Plea Rolls of the Exchequer of the Jews . . . ,I.: . . . 1218–1272*, ed. J. M. Rigg (London and New York, 1905), as well as on *II.: . . . 1273–1275*, ed. J. M. Rigg (Edinburgh, 1910), *III.: . . . 1275–1277*, ed. H. Jenkinson (Colchester, London and Eton, 1929), and *IV.: . . . 1272 . . . 1275–1277*, ed. H. G. Richardson (London, 1972). Equally indispensable are *Select Pleas, Starrs, and Other Records from . . . the Exchequer of the Jews, A.D. 1220–1284*, ed. J. M. Rigg (London, 1902), and *Shtaroth: Hebrew Deeds of English Jews before 1290*, ed. M. D. Davis (London, 1888), and *Starrs and Jewish Charters preserved in the British Museum* 1, eds. I. Abrahams, H. P. Stokes, and H. Loewe (Cambridge, Eng., 1930); vol. 2, ed. H. Loewe and others (London, Colchester and Eton, 1932); vol. 3, ed. H. Loewe (London, etc., 1932). But there is a very considerable body even of economic evidence (such as taxation records) that is still not in print.

2. See Gavin Langmuir, "The Jews and the Archives of Angevin England: Reflections on Medieval Anti-Semitism," *Traditio* 19(1963):183–244, and also his "The Knight's Tale of Young Hugh of Lincoln," *Speculum* 47(1972):459–482. Langmuir suggests ("The Jews . . . ," pp. 242–243) the possible significance of the population curve and the view of society as having or lacking opportunities related to it for the state of contemporary antisemitism. See my comments below. Langmuir's suggestion that the growth of the population to the thirteenth century, its stasis during the thirteenth, and contraction in the fourteenth, may parallel the "relative tolerance towards Jews in the twelfth century, the severity of the thirteenth, and the virulent anti-Semitism of the fourteenth century," while provocative, seems to over-simplify a complex subject. Langmuir is now preparing a study, "Historiographic Crucifixion," which will deal with Norwich; see his "Thomas of Monmouth: Detector of Ritual Murder," *Speculum* 59(1984):820–846, esp. n. 4; his "Thomas" deals with the Norwich events in detail.

3. "An exasperating multitude of Jews." *Annales Monastici II: . . .Annales Monasterii de Waverleia (A.D. 1–1291)*, ed. H. R. Luard (London, 1865), p. 409.

4. "Enemies of the cross of Christ and blasphemers of the Christian faith." *Annales Monastici III*, ed. H. R. Luard (London, 1866), pp. 361–362. The annalist also records the fate of some of the Jews who were drowned through the deceit of sailors, as well as the gratitude of the clergy and baronage at the expulsion (expressed in money granted the king). For Osney, see *Annales Monastici IV*, ed. H. R. Luard (London, 1869), pp. 326–327, where the robbery and drowning are described vividly, and it is noted that the fifteenth was "extorted" from the Catholics because of the enemies of the cross. The Dunstable chronicle, like that of Waverley, supported the baronial cause; it was clearly antagonistic to the Lord (later King) Edward. Both are contemporary and original. The Osney chronicle's section for 1278–1293 apparently was written by Thomas Wykes – a royalist – who was rather more sympathetic to the Jews than most of his contemporaries. See, for all of these, Antonia Gransden, *Historical Writing in England c. 550 to c. 1307* (London, 1974), pp. 424–432, 466–469.

5. *Bartholomaei de Cotton Monachi Norwicensis Historia Anglicana (A.D. 449–1298)*, ed. H. R. Luard (London, 1859), p. 178. Bartholomew's account may refer to the events reported in contemporary records. See my "Crime and Jews in Late Thirteenth-Century England," *Hebrew Union College Annual* 55(1984):131–132 and n. 120. Cf. the version of *The Chronicle*

of Walter of Guisborough Previously Edited as the Chronicle of Walter of Hemingford or Heming-burgh, ed. H. Rothwell (London, 1957), pp. 226–227; Walter's dramatic, detailed, description of the Jews' drowning follows his comments on the Jews' "malice" and "perfidy," and their usuries and false records that had impoverished many magnates. He adds that the Jews had corrupted the coinage throughout the land. Gransden indicates that Walter respected documents and had "excellent sources of information," but also a "love of the dramatic." (*Historical Writing*, p. 473.) Rothwell indicates (p. xxvi) that Walter used, for 1198–1291, anything he had, uncritically; his later entries are fuller but not wholly accurate (pp. xxvii–xxix). *The Chronicle of Pierre de Langtoft . . .*, ed. Thomas Wright (London, [1866] 1964), also, it seems, by a northern chronicler, notes briefly that the clergy and barons asked that the land be cleared of Jews, in return for a fifteenth granted the king; no one opposed the exile of the *"Jues de la mescréauncye,"* or *"misbelief."* (He seems to have used the same sources as Guisborough; see Gransden, *Historical Writing*, pp. 475–476.) The most dramatic versions of the 1290 events are those of Osney and Guisborough.

6. *A Social and Religious History of the Jews* 11 (2nd ed.; New York, London and Philadelphia, 1967), pp. 6–7. Baron also notes (in vol. 12, p. 141): "the vast majority of English Jewry eked out a meager livelihood, while many lived in dismal poverty." Baron suggests that it was "England's growth into a national state" that was the main reason for the expulsion of 1290 (11, p. 210). It may be noted that some Jews, at least, one of them a physician, tried to get the king's permission to return to England in 1310; they seem to have had no success. See *Chronica Johannis de Oxenedes*, ed. Sir H. Ellis (London, 1859), p. xiv and n. 1; this information is from the British Museum MS known as MS Hargrave, 179, fol. 295, which was copied from the Cottonian MS Otho B iii, burned in 1731. (Gransden, *Historical Writing*, pp. 402, 439, thinks this chronicle is "almost valueless" because it is "so closely related to the chronicle of Bury St Edmunds" for the years 1258–1290; however, Ellis indicates that this item about the proposed reentry of Jews in 1310 is probably unique. It is not clear who was its author, as the chronicler who wrote the major part of the chronicle died in 1293.)

7. *A History of the Jews in England* (3rd ed.; Oxford, 1964); this edition, replete with changes made on the basis of the findings of H. G. Richardson, still depends on published materials. Unfortunately, even when using published materials, Roth did not always evade pitfalls, as in his *Jews of Medieval Oxford* (Oxford, 1951), p. 159 and n. 3, where he refers to the house of Bonevie f. Vives in his text, and to the *Hundred Rolls*, pp. 790–791, reading " *'Vives filius Ben'. . ."* in n. 3, where he also refers to an apparently non-existent work of Thorold Rogers, *"Ancient Records relating to the City of Oxford,"* p. 208, when his reference is clearly Rogers' *Oxford City Documents, 1268–1665* (Oxford, 1891), p. 208. When Dr. Redcliffe Salaman called Roth's attention to a Jewish caricature in a Memoranda Roll in the Public Record Office, London, Roth seems not to have examined any other rolls in the series; see my article, "Drawings of Jewish Interest in Some Thirteenth-Century English Public Records," *Scriptorium* 26(1972):58 and n. 8. Roth seems to have used only such manuscript evidence as was available to him in Oxford or in his own collection. The Rev. Michael Adler, in his *Jews of Medieval England* (London, 1939) and other works, did make use of archival materials, but his research time was limited; he found some materials but not others equally important in the same series of records. See my "Some Accounts of Condemned Jews' Property in the Pipe and Chancellor's Rolls," *Bulletin of the Institute of Jewish Studies* 1(1973):19–20 and nn. 1, 2 on p. 19.

8. "Why Anglo-Jewish History," in *JHSET*, 22(1970):21–29, esp. p.26. (The rolls in question are now in print, in vol. IV of the *Calendar of the Plea Rolls of the Exchequer of the Jews* [above, n.1], p. 148ff.)

9. For example, the *HUCA* article (above, n. 5), and "The Jewish Church-Robbers and Host Desecrators of Norwich (ca. 1285)," *Revue des études juives* 141(1982):331–362. The *REJ* article deals at length with ritual murder.

10. For heresy in England, see Felix Makower, *The Constitutional History and Constitution of the Church of England* (London and New York, 1895), pp. 183–185; F. Pollock and F. W. Maitland, *The History of English Law before the Time of Edward I.* (2nd ed.; Washington, D.C., 1959), 2, pp. 544–552.

11. On English governmental techniques, see the summary of S. B. Chrimes, *An Introduction to the Administrative History of Mediaeval England* (Oxford, 1959), *passim*; N. F. Cantor, *The English: A History of Politics and Society to 1760* (New York, 1969), ch. 3, pp. 68–135, deals with the centralization of government. David Douglas stresses that the Normans depended on

local institutions and customs in all the lands they conquered, and governed splendidly as a result (in his *The Norman Achievement* [London, 1969], pp. 183–191). See also H. G. Richardson and G. O. Sayles, *The Governance of Mediaeval England* . . . (Edinburgh, 1974), ch. 8, esp. pp. 166–172.

12. E. 13/2, m. 9 dorse (=the Exchequer court roll for 1272–1273), in the Public Record Office, London.

13. By, for example, Jacob Rabinowitz, *Jewish Law: Its Influence on the Development of Legal Institutions* (New York, 1956), esp. chaps. xviii and xix, pp. 250–289; however, as Roth suggested (*Hist. of Jews in Eng.*, p. 282), Rabinowitz may have overemphasized the influence of Jewish on English procedure.

14. See the important comments of G. I. Langmuir, "The Jews and the Archives of Angevin England . . ." (above, n. 2), pp. 223–224. The resentment derived from the financial difficulties of many found its expression in the wave of anti-Jewish riots that followed the coronation of Richard I, as well as in the killing and destruction that befell the Jews of London in the 1260s during the baronial rebellion. It must, however, be remembered that the background of these events was rather more complicated, even though it had a substantial financial motive (the same may be said of the expulsion of Jews from various English towns in the 1270s and the 1280s).

15. See n. 1 above for P. Elman's various works, esp. his "Jewish Finance," pp. 82, 122–127; and his "Economic Causes," pp. 145, 148–150. H. G. Richardson, *Eng. Jewry* (n. 1 above), ch. 5, "Jews and the Land," pp. 83–108, examines the process delineated by Elman.

   Jews also lent money to the lower classes, indirect evidence of which is provided by the Patent Rolls: a commission was issued to John of Louvetot (*Luvetot*) to inquire about Christians who were *judaizantes*, "acting like Jews . . . in lending money and other goods to indigent Christians, in taking money after the return thereof, and detaining the pledges." (*Calendar of the Patent Rolls . . . 1272–1281* [(1901) Nendeln, Liechtenstein, 1971], p. 172, and cf. p. 176.)

16. See n. 2 above.

17. H. G. Richardson, *Eng. Jewry*, pp. 182–186; F. D. Logan, "Thirteen London Jews and Conversion to Christianity: . . ." *Bulletin of the Institute of Historical Research* 45, no. 112 (Nov. 1972): 214–229. See also J. Shatzmiller, "Jews 'Separated from the Communion of the Faithful in Christ' in the Middle Ages," in *Studies in Medieval Jewish History and Literature*, ed. I. Twersky (Cambridge, Mass. and London, 1979), pp. 307–314. In addition to the cases mentioned by Logan of Jews having been declared excommunicate, there are, in the class of *Significavit* writs (C. 85) at the Public Record Office, Christian servants of Jews being so declared (see C. 85/170. m. 70). Walter Giffard, the Archbishop of York, declared that the Christian maids and wetnurses of the Jews Isaac Amgan, Abraham of Germany (*Alemannia*), Mireylda the Jewess, Isaac of Colchester, and Abraham Thurk had been contumacious against the ecclesiastical courts for more than forty days, and asked (in the usual way) for the assistance of the secular arm. See also F. D. Logan, *Excommunication and the Secular Arm in Medieval England* . . . (Toronto, 1968), *passim*, and my n. 77 below.

18. Gavin Langmuir, "The Jews and the Archives," (n. 2 above), pp. 240–241. The influence of the two queens named Eleanor (Alienora), the mother and wife respectively of Edward I, will also have to be considered, as well as the presence of the friars in all of its ramifications.

19. See above, n. 5, for Walter of Guisborough. "*Scelera*" are noted, for example, in the 1290–1291 Lord Treasurer's Remembrancer's Memoranda Roll, E. 368/62, m. 20, at the Public Record Office, London. See also Aron Owen's "The References to England in the Responsa of Rabbi Meir Ben Baruch of Rothenburg, 1215–1293," *JHSET* 17(1951–1952): 73–78, and Salo W. Baron, *A Social and Religious History of the Jews* 12 (2nd ed.; New York, London, and Philadelphia, 1967), pp. 128, 304 n. 66. Baron stresses the "Jews' relative non-involvement in currency manipulations . . ." in medieval Europe (p. 304 n. 66), and indicates "it is truly remarkable how few of them were, rightly or wrongly, accused of mutilations" of the coinage (p. 128). He suggests that the figures given for Jews hanged in London in 1279 (280 or 293) are "almost certainly exaggerated" (p. 127). I will have more to say on this point in a forthcoming paper on the coinage trials of the late 1270s.

20. For the grotesques, see my "Drawings of Jewish Interest," (above, n. 7), pp. 55–62 and the works noted in n. 2 on p. 56; for anti-Jewish sentiment, see H. G. Richardson, *English Jewry* (n. 1 above), pp. 217–223, and my forthcoming paper.

21. There is no question that the authorities used force to make English Jews do what they

wished; for example, Jews were imprisoned if they failed to pay their tallage on time and not released until they had paid what was due (see Richardson, *English Jewry*, pp. 153, 168–170). But far more serious was the case of a Jew, seven of whose molars were reportedly extracted at the order of King John, one after another, until he gave in to the king's financial demands. The story appears in *Rogeri de Wendover liber . . . flores historiarum . . .* , ed. H. G. Hewlett (London, 1889), 2:54–55, and was repeated by Matthew Paris in the *Chronica Majora*, ed. H. R. Luard (London, etc., 1874), 2, p. 528. The status of these chronicles lent credibility to the story, but doubts of its accuracy have been raised. Sidney Painter has noted the cruelty of King John to his subjects – Christian and Jewish alike – but indicates that "While the stories of the tortures used to persuade the Jews to contribute adequately to the tallage of 1211 may well be exaggerated, it is hard to believe that they are purely imaginative." See his *The Reign of King John* (Baltimore, 1966), pp. 236–237. Cf. Michael Adler, *Jews of Medieval England* (above, n. 7), pp. 202–203. This cruelty is exceptional in the web of ties between the Crown and English Jews: the extortion of money from the Jews was normal; a deliberate and directed course of torture was not, as a rule.

22. See H. G. Richardson, *English Jewry*, pp. 217–225; M. Adler, "Inventory of the Property of the Condemned Jews (1285)," *Miscellanies of the Jewish Historical Society of England* (London, 1935), 2: 56–58; Z. E. Rokéah, "Some Accounts of Condemned Jews' Property in the Pipe and Chancellor's Rolls," *Bulletin of the Institute of Jewish Studies*, 1(1973):19–42; 2(1974):59–82;3(1975)41–66. For the expulsion, see Richardson, p. 228 and n. 4. The king and his agents were, of course, interested in filling their role as the protectors of the peace as of the law.

23. See the bibliography in n. 16 of my "Jewish Church-Robbers" (n. 9 above). It is the view of Jean Juster, *Les Juifs dans l'empire romain* (New York, n.d.; reproduction of 1914 ed.), 2, pp. 204–205, that the Inmestar occurrence was not a ritual murder but, rather, a killing that resulted from drunken horseplay (at Purim). To the above-noted bibliography may now be added Gavin Langmuir's "Thomas of Monmouth" (above, n. 2), pp. 822–827.

24. *The Life and Miracles of Saint William of Norwich by Thomas of Monmouth*, ed. A. Jessopp and M. R. James (Cambridge, Eng., 1896), pp. x–xiii. (Hereafter referred to as *Saint William.*) See also my "Jewish Church-Robbers" (n. 9 above).

25. *Saint William*, p. 6.

26. *Saint William*, pp. 15–19.

27. In 1144, Passover was on 25 March, not on 22 March; Easter Sunday was 26 March (*Saint William*, p. 20 n. 1).

28. *Saint William*, pp. lxv–lxx, 20–49.

29. *Saint William*, pp. 49–59.

30. *Saint William*, pp. lxxi, 93–94. The late Professor H. H. Ben-Sasson commented to me some years ago that such accusations against the Jews made by converts were not to be found in that period, and that converts customarily told the truth about their former coreligionists (as was the case, for example, when, in the wake of the Fulda blood libel of 1235, former Jews stated emphatically that Jews did not injure Christian children or need their blood). Accordingly, he doubted that Theobald told such a story. However, it is not impossible that one convert was exceptional in this, and that, in an excess of new convert's zeal (and perhaps seeking to justify his having left the Jewish fold), he made up his story. Thus, Theobald should be seen as the story's inventor (G. Langmuir sees Thomas of Monmouth as due the credit for creating the crucifixion myth; see his "Thomas of Monmouth," p. 846).

31. See David Flusser's "The 'Blood-Libel' against the Jews in the Light of the Views of the Hellenistic Period," (Heb.) in *Commentationes Iudaico-Hellenisticae in Memoriam Iohannis Lewy*, ed. M. Schwabe and I. Gutman (Jerusalem, 1949), pp. 104–124.

32. See my "Jewish Church-Robbers" (n. 9 above), pp. 337–338 and nn. 20, 21; and *Saint William*, pp. 97–110.

33. *Saint William,*pp. lxii–lxxiii; see also the article in the *Jewish Encyclopedia*, 3, pp. 260–261.

34. M. D. Anderson, *A Saint at Stake* (London, 1964), pp. 98–99, 101–108.

35. V. D. Lipman, *The Jews of Medieval Norwich* (London, 1967), pp. 55–56.

36. Anderson, *A Saint at Stake*, p. 200.

37. *Saint William*, pp. lxxi–lxxii, lxxvi–lxxix.

38. It should be noted that no ritual purpose is noted here, but the date is close to that of Passover. See *Historia et Cartularium Monasterii Sancti Petri Gloucestriae*, ed. W. H. Hart (London, 1863), 1:xxxix–xl, 20–21, and *Saint William*, pp. lxxiv–lxxv.

39. This is the view of M. R. James, *Saint William*, p. lxxvi.
40. *Cronica Jocelini de Brakelonda de rebus gestis Samsonis Abbatis Monasterii Sancti Edmundi: The Chronicle of Jocelin of Brakelond concerning the acts of Samson*, transl. H. E. Butler (London, Edinburgh and Paris, 1949), p. 15 n. 6, p. 16 and n. 1. See *Saint William*, p. lxxv, for the Melrose Chronicle's version: ". . . *Robertum quem quidam Iudaeus occulte crudeliter neci tradidit.*" The Rev. Joseph Stevenson, who edited and translated this chronicle, stated that, from about 1140 on, this work is "possessed of the highest credibility, being the testimony of individuals who lived seldom later than half a century from the occurrence of the events which they record." (See Stevenson, *The Church Historians of England: Vol. IV–Part I.* [London, 1856], pp. xvi, 138–139.) Antonia Gransden, *Historical Writing* (n. 4 above), p. 319 n. 7 concurs, saying: "The Melrose chronicle, . . . , is Scotland's principle monastic chronicle; . . . has much information not found elsewhere, and is particularly useful for the history of Scotland and northern England in the thirteenth century." Gransden adds that Brakelond's saint's life of Robert is "now lost" and that his passion appears in the *Annales Sancti Edmundi* in Felix Liebermann's *Ungedrückte anglo-normannische Geschichtsquellen* (Strassburg, 1879), p. 135 (Gransden, p. 381). However, the *Annales* entry is brief and uninformative. Gervase of Canterbury suggested that Robert was martyred at Easter-time (*ad Pascha*), by Jews (*a Judaeis*); see *The Historical Works of Gervase of Canterbury*, ed. William Stubbs (Wiesbaden, 1965 [1879]), 1, p. 296. (Easter Sunday of 1181 was 5 April.) For the May and June dates, see *Saint William*, p. lxxv.
41. B. M. Harleian MS 957, no. 7. See Adler, *Jews of Medieval England* (n. 7 above), pp. 185–186, and Joseph Jacobs, *The Jews of Angevin England* (London, 1893), p. 152 (=illustration from MS).
42. *The Chronicle of Richard of Devizes of the Time of King Richard the First; Cronicon Richardi Divisensis De Tempore Regis Richardi Primi*, ed. J. T. Appleby (London, etc., 1963), pp. 3–4.
43. Ibid., p. 64.
44. Ibid., pp. 64–69. See Roth, *History of the Jews* (n. 7 above), p. 22 n. 1, which suggests that Richard of Devizes's "sarcastic account, which has led to the suspicion that the whole story is fictitious, is grimly confirmed by a record of the expenses for escorting the Jews of Winchester to Westminster" in the pipe roll for 1193–1194. *Why* they were sent to Westminster is not noted there; see *The Great Roll of the Pipe for the Fifth Year of the Reign of King Richard the First . . .* , ed. D. M. Stenton (London, 1927), p. 134, for this entry. Patricia Allin's "Richard of Devizes and the Alleged Martyrdom of a Boy at Winchester," in *JHSET*, 27(1978–1980): 32 39, does not deal with it. For Richard's attitude towards the Jews, see Gransden, *Historical Writing* (n. 4 above), p. 251, where it is suggested he had "pro-Jewish sentiments," and N. F. Partner, *Serious Entertainment: The Writing of History in Twelfth-Century England* (Chicago and London, 1977), p. 178, whose considered opinion is that he had "nothing good to say" about Jews.
45. Roth, *History of the Jews*, p. 22 n. 1 gives the relevant sources; the Bedford case also appears in Jacobs, *Jews of Angevin England* (n. 41 above), pp. 216–217.
46. Roth, *History of the Jews*, p. 273; [D. H. Gifford], *The Jews of England; Exhibition of Records* (London, 1957), pp. 7–8; *Annales Monastici, II: . . . Annales Monasterii de Wintonia (A. D. 519–1277)*, ed. H. R. Luard (London, 1865), p. 86 (=1232). See also my "Crime and Jews" (above, n. 5), n. 13 on pp. 100–101.
47. For a more detailed summary of the Norwich case, see my "Jewish Church-Robbers" (above, n. 9), pp. 340–345. The circumcised child was shown by his father to local government and ecclesiastical officials; however, it was only after four years had passed that court proceedings were undertaken against thirteen accused Jews. The father charged that the child had been circumcised "in contempt of the Crucified [Jesus] and of Christianity" (*in despectu Crucifixi et Christianitatis*"). See *Select Pleas, Starrs and Other Records . . .* , ed. Rigg (above, n. 1), pp. xliv–xlvii; Lipman, *Norwich* (above, n. 1), pp. 59–62; *Curia Regis Rolls . . . (1233–1237)* (London, 1972), pp. 333–335.
48. The matter was transferred from a royal to an ecclesiastical court on the grounds that no felony was involved but rather matters of religious moment such as circumcision and baptism. The various legal proceedings took a decade or so to complete, a decade during which Jews' houses were set on fire and Jews attacked; castle sergeants attempting to help the Jews were attacked themselves (see *Select Cases of Procedure without Writ*, ed. H. G. Richardson and G. O. Sayles [London, 1941], p. 121). But the royal officials were none too likely to intervene, and this encouraged the rabble. In 1231, a Jew of Norwich named Senioret was outlawed for

circumcising the child, and his house was granted to the child's father. The Jews tried, by means of payments to the authorities, to have the matter dealt with by the royal courts (only), but in vain. See Lipman, *Norwich* (above, n. 1), pp. 59–60 and p. 60 n. 1; [Gifford], *Jews of England* (above, n. 46), p. 7 (par. 16) (=Chancery, Miscellaneous Inquisition C. 145/18/22). For the reports of the chroniclers about these events, see *Rogeri de Wendover . . . flores historiarum*, ed. H. G. Hewlett (London, 1889), 3, pp. 101–102; *Matthaei Parisiensis . . . Chronica Majora*, ed. H. R. Luard (London, 1876), 3, pp. 305–306, and (London, 1877) 4, pp. 30–31: *The Chronicle of Bury St Edmunds*, ed. A. Gransden (London, 1964), p. 10; and pp. 341 n. 28 and 344–345 of my "Jewish Church-Robbers." See also F. Liebermann's comments on *Select Pleas*, ed. Rigg, in *The English Historical Review* 17(1902):554.

49. See *Select Pleas*, ed. Rigg, pp. xlvi–xlvii, and n. 30 on pp. 342–343 of my "Jewish Church-Robbers."

50. Lipman, *Norwich*, p. 61, notes the names of the two Jews who were hanged: Mosse f. Abraham (Mosse Mokke), and Isaac Parvus (f. Solomon). He mentions another Jew, Theor (=Diaia?), who was hanged because of the circumcision and whose house was given to the child's father (ibid., p. 61 and n. 4). He mentions additional Jews; one, having been charged, was dead; another had been condemned; a further eleven were fugitives.

51. Walter Rye, "The Alleged Abduction and Circumcision of a Boy at Norwich in 1230," *The Norfolk Antiquarian Miscellany* (Norwich, 1877), vol. 1, pt. 2, p. 319 and n. 3, p. 320.

52. See *Select Pleas*, ed. Rigg, p. xlvi and n. 2. Jewish religious literature dealt with the possibility that a circumcised male might seem not to be so: "These shreds [of the foreskin, if they remain] render the circumcision invalid: flesh that covers the greater part of the corona . . . ; if he waxes fat [and the corona is covered anew] this must be set right for appearance's sake. If one is circumcised without having the inner lining torn, it is as though he had not been circumcised" (*Mishnah*, Shabbat XIX:6; = *The Mishnah*, transl. H. Danby [Oxford, 1933], p. 117). The *Gemara* states that recircumcision must be performed if the infant seems uncircumcised when straining at stool (Babylonian Talmud, Shabbat, 137b; *The Babylonian Talmud: Seder Moed: Shabbath II*, transl. H. Freeman [London, 1938], pp. 691–692). See also Tosefta Shabbat XVI:9 (=XV in *The Tosefta*, ed. Saul Lieberman [New York, 1962]), and Jerusalem Talmud, Yevamoth VIII:1 (9a). Maimonides, *Mishneh Torah* (Hilkhot Milah, ch. II, 3–5), also dealt with the problem, but it is not clear whether Norwich Jews were then familiar with the work, first used extensively during this period in England by Master Moses of London; see E. E. Urbach, "Contributions to Rabbinic Scholarship by the Rabbis of England of the Pre-Expulsion Period" (Heb.), in *Essays presented to Chief Rabbi Israel Brodie* (London, 1967), p. 10, and E. E. Urbach, *The Tosaphists: Their History, Writings and Methods* (Heb.) (Jerusalem, 1968), pp. 401–403.

53. The Bury St Edmunds chronicle and that of Matthew Paris both state that in 1240 four Norwich Jews were dragged through the city streets while tied to horses' tails, and were hanged thereafter. Roger of Wendover, on the other hand, notes for 1235 that seven Jews convicted in this connection had been imprisoned, their lives and limbs being subject to the king's pleasure.

54. It was customary in England for all of a convert's property to be confiscated for the benefit of the royal coffers: the new Christian remained penniless. In order to prevent such penury (and perhaps to encourage would-be converts), Henry III founded a House of Converts in London in 1232, ordering that all its residents receive a fixed daily income for the rest of their lives. On this institution, see "The History of the Domus Conversorum" in Michael Adler's *Jews of Medieval England* (n. 7 above), pp. 279–379, esp. pp. 279–287. It may be noted that in this instance, too, converts acted in a manner that endangered their former coreligionists (see n. 30 above). But, according to Matthew Paris, the converts were adjured, "as they loved their life and members, and for the honour, the love, and the fear they had for the king, and with no deceit of untruth . . . ," to decipher the inscription on the child's corpse (*Chronica Majora* [n. 48 above], 4, pp. 377–378). Matthew Paris adds there that the Jews, "in order to taunt and revile Jesus Christ, as it was reported frequently, either crucified that little boy or – intending to crucify him – baited him with various torments, and, when he died prematurely, and thinking him unworthy of a cross, threw him there" (" . . . *Judaei ipsum puerulum in Jesu Christi improperium et contumeliam, quod frequenter relatum est accidisse, vel crucifixerant vel crucifigendum variis tormentis exagitaverant, et cum jam exspirasset, eum cruce indignum illuc projecisse*"). Paris emphasizes that there were signs of torture on the boy's body. The converts had difficulty in deciphering the writing because of the contraction of the child's

skin but succeeded in the end in reading the first names of the child's parents as well as a statement that the child had been sold to the Jews; they were unable to "read" why or by whom. Paris adds that some suspected London Jews had fled, and that, even though the corpse did *not* bear signs of the five wounds (of Jesus), the canons of St Paul's quickly buried it near their great altar.

For a description of the founding and nature of the *Domus Conversorum*, see *Matthaei Parisiensis, . . . , Historia Anglorum, sive, . . . Historia Minor . . .* , ed. F. Madden (London, 1866), 2, pp. 362–363 (*s. a.* 1233).

55. See Gavin Langmuir, "The Knight's Tale" (n. 2 above), pp. 459–482. He notes there (pp. 461, 464, 478) that the version of the Burton chronicler is more reliable for events at Lincoln in 1255 than that of Matthew Paris. He stresses (p. 464) that, before the events of Lincoln of 1255, no responsible representative of the *lay* authorities acted on reports made charging the Jews with ritual murder (unlike local churchmen). In 1255, however, immediately after arriving at Lincoln, King Henry III himself ordered the sheriffs to prevent Jews from leaving the kingdom, and ordered Jopin's execution despite the promise to the contrary made to Jopin by John of "Lexinton" (=Laxton), who was the brother of Henry, then the bishop of Lincoln. (It was John of "Lexinton" who had received Jopin's "confession"; John's family was highly clerical, and "came to focus its ambitions on Lincoln Minster," according to Langmuir, ibid., p. 474.) Langmuir notes that Pope Innocent III had forbidden Christians to accuse Jews of using Christian blood; he stresses that Innocent did *not* condemn the "crucifixion libel," which was "still the best known charge" made against Jews (ibid., p. 480). See also Joseph Jacobs, "Little St Hugh of Lincoln," in *Jewish Ideals and Other Essays* (London, 1896), pp. 192–224. Jacobs did not succeed in his diligent efforts to find the judicial records connected with the 1255 events (ibid., p. 203); the impression derived from Langmuir's work is that he did not seek manuscript evidence but contented himself with published records only. It is not impossible that documentary evidence may yet be discovered in English archives. The chroniclers of the Lincoln events are: *Annales Monastici*, ed. H. R. Luard (London, 1864), 1, pp. 340–348 (=Burton); *Annales Monastici*, 2, pp. 346–348 (above n. 2) (=Waverley); *Matthaei Parisiensis . . . Chronica Majora* (London, 1880), 5, pp. 516–519, 546, 552.

56. See *Calendar of the Close Rolls . . . Edward I: 1272 1279* (Liechtenstein, 1970), pp. 271–274. Ritual murder charges made against the Jews are *not* mentioned in *The London Eyre of 1244*, ed. H. M. Chew and M. Weinbaum (London, 1970), which deals with the years 1244–1246, and which was taken from Misc. Rolls AA of the Corporation of London Records Office (=Guildhall); the manuscript Guildhall Misc. Rolls BB, which has not yet appeared in print, and which includes material about financial penalties imposed by the itinerant justices who sat at the Tower of London in 1276, also does not mention the killing of a Christian child by Jews, though the orders noted above were sent by the king to his justices sitting in judgment there. This may be the result of the adjournment of the matter to the Easter parliament (and its not being dealt with there). Similarly, such ritual killing is not mentioned in the legal records of the time preserved in the Public Record Office in London, including the reports of the gaol delivery justices for Newgate prison for 1272–1276 (=JUST. 3/35A); such records for Newgate for 1276–1286 (=JUST. 3/35B); or the records of prisoners from various counties and the London district for 1272–1278 (=JUST 3/85).

57. Antonia Gransden, in her introduction to the Bury chronicle (above, n. 48), indicates that it is "a valuable contemporary authority for the last years of Henry III's reign and for Edward I's reign to 1301" (p. xvii), and that it "is the only known authority for a number of statements" such as that concerning the conversion to Judaism of the Dominican, Robert of Reading, in 1275, or the alleged crucifixion in 1279 of a boy at Northampton (p. xxii); Gransden also notes that such chroniclers as "Florence of Worcester" depended on the Bury chronicle for their information (ibid., p. xvii); the same is true of Bartholomew Cotton's and "John of Oxenedes' " chronicles (*Historical Writing*, pp. 400, 402), so that Roth's citing these last three chronicles for the Northampton story (*History of the Jews* [n. 7 above], p. 78, n. 3) is somewhat misleading, though he does note that Cotton and Oxenedes repeat Florence of Worcester's version. Roth's *History* should be updated, not least because of later work regarding the filiation and value of various chronicles. See his *History*, pp. 274–275, for the report that fifty Jews were said to have been dragged and then hanged, and that others were sent to London to be punished.

58. See above, n. 22, for works dealing with coinage violations, as well as n. 38 of my "Crime and Jews" (above, n. 5).

59. Income from St William's shrine was considerable in the thirteenth century but decreased gradually and virtually disappeared by the middle of the next century. Nonetheless, considerable sums of money were spent on repairs to his shrine in the cathedral (*Saint William*, pp. lxxxii–lxxxiv). See Lipman, *Jews of Medieval Norwich* (above, n. 1), p. 56, and *Saint William*, pp. 49–50, for the information that it was the request of the visiting prior of St Pancras at Lewes to receive it that showed the value of such a treasure as a martyr's body to a church.

60. *Willelmi Malmesbiriensis monachi de gestis regum Anglorum libri quinque; historiae novellae libri tres*, ed. W. Stubbs (London, 1887–1889), 2, p. 371 (=book iv, ch. 317); *Eadmeri historia novorum in Anglia, et opuscula duo de vita sancti Anselmi et quibusdam miraculis eius*, ed. M. Rule (London, 1884), pp. 99–101.

61. See Bernhard Blumenkranz, *Gisleberti Crispini Disputatio Iudei et Christiani et Anonymi Auctoris Disputationis Iudei et Christiani Continuatio* (Utrecht and Antwerp, 1956), pp. 8, 28; *Patrologiae cursus completus: scriptores latini*, ed. J. P. Migne (Paris, 1854), 159:1007–1036 (hereafter, referred to as *PL*).

62. See *PL*, vol. 158 (=*Sancti Anselmi . . . Opera Omnia*, ed. D. Gabriel Gerberon, vol. 2[Paris, 1854]), *Epistolarum Liber Tertius*, cxvii, col. 153–155.

63. See A. Neubauer, "Notes on the Jews in Oxford," in *Collectanea: Second Series*, ed. Montagu Burrows (Oxford Historical Society, 1890), pp. 282–284, and compare the story of a Jewish youth who killed himself, in E. Kupfer, "A Contribution to the Chronicles of the Family of R. Moses ben R. Yom-Tov 'The Noble' of London" (Heb.), *Tarbiz* 40(1970–71):385–387.

64. On the slaughter of the Jews of Rouen and on the forced baptism of those who survived, see Norman Golb, *History and Culture of the Jews of Rouen in the Middle Ages* (Heb.) (Tel-Aviv, 1976), pp. 15, 19–20, and Appendix 3 (pp. 175–177). Cf. Cecil Roth, *History of the Jews* (n. 7 above), p. 6: he suggests that the remnants of the 1096 slaughter may have fled to England (there is, however, no evidence to this effect).

65. See Roth, ibid., pp. 9–10, and J. Jacobs, *Jews of Angevin England* (above n. 41), p. 22.

66. *Gesta regis Henrici secundi Benedicti abbatis . . . Benedict of Peterborough*, ed. W. Stubbs (London, 1867), 1, p. 106. See also my "Jewish Church-Robbers" (above, n. 9), pp. 333–334 for Jews and churches.

67. Roth, *History of the Jews*, p. 15; but Richardson, *The English Jewry* (n. 1 above), pp. 90–92, finds no evidence to support the notion that the Cistercian abbeys borrowed from Aaron of Lincoln in order to build. He suggests that the monks dealt with him and other Jewish money-lenders in order to acquire landed property of such debtors as could not repay their loans to the money-lenders. Langmuir, in "The Jews and the Archives" (n. 2 above), p. 217, disagrees with Richardson's position, suggesting it has not been proven that, in addition to their acquisition of lands, the abbeys were not going into debt because of their building projects and possible "fiscal incompetence" as well.

68. See David Knowles, *The Monastic Order in England* (2nd ed.; Cambridge, Eng., 1963), p. 656. But cf. Richardson, *The English Jewry*, pp. 98–99, where examples of such transactions dating from *after* they were forbidden appear.

69. For Jocelin of Brakelond's resentment of such practices, see my "Jewish Church-Robbers," p. 333.

70. In 1219. See "Jewish Church-Robbers," pp. 333–335, and *Councils and Synods with Other Documents Relating to the English Church; II: A. D. 1205–1313: Part I: 1205–1265*, ed. F. M. Powicke and C. R. Cheney (Oxford, 1964), 55[6], 121[47]. (Hereafter referred to as *Councils and Synods, 1*.)

71. See *Councils and Synods, 1*, p. 100.

72. Ibid., p. 120.

73. The Jewish badge found on the Continent was most likely to be round in shape; see B. Blumenkranz, *Le Juif médiéval au miroir de l'art chrétien* (Paris, 1966), pp. 28–29, 71. S. W. Baron, *A Social and Religious History of the Jews* 3 (2nd ed.; New York, 1960), pp. 139–141, 298 n. 22, gives the provisions of Mutawakkil's decree of 849–850 C.E. concerning the dress of the *dhimmis* as well as other aspects of their lives: they were to wear honey-colored garments, while the outer garments of their slaves had to bear two honey-colored patches. It seems that "the Almohade legislation, . . . , was far more responsible for the introduction of the European 'badge' than any eastern decree." (Ibid., p. 298 n. 22.)

74. See *Councils and Synods, 1*, p. 121 n. 1. On 30 March 1218, orders were sent to the sheriffs of Worcestershire, Gloucestershire, Warwickshire, Lincolnshire, Oxfordshire, and Northamp-

tonshire, as well as to the mayor and sheriffs of London, according to which Jews had to wear a distinguishing badge in the form of two white "tables" (*tabulas*), made of linen or parchment. (The Jewish badge appears in contemporary English manuscripts in the shape of the tablets bearing the Ten Commandments; for some later examples, see my "Drawings of Jewish Interest" [above, n. 7], p. 61, where one such "badge" appears alongside the drawing of a coin; it has been suggested that the European badge may, in its shape, have been meant to indicate a coin.) See also Richardson, *The English Jewry*, pp. 178–180.

75. The Church threatened to excommunicate the Jews of Worcester in 1219 (see *Councils and Synods, 1*, 55[6]), the Jews of Winchester (in 1224?), the Jews of Oxford in 1222 (ibid., 117[36], 131[32]), and the Jews of an as-yet unidentified diocese as well (in 1222–1225?) (ibid., 149[54]). For the intervention of the lay authorities concerning Hereford and other places in 1218, and concerning Lincoln, Oxford, and Norwich (after 1222), see ibid., 55 n. 1 and 120 n. 2.

76. According to the Public Record Office, London, document, C. 85/170. m. 70, one of the "*Significavit*" writs. (See nn. 77 below and 17 above.)

77. The relevant documents are C. 85/98, mm. 34, 39; C. 85/167, m. 13. See also Richardson, *The English Jewry*, pp. 190–191; he states that the procedures connected with the implementation of the writs "*Significavit*" and "*De excommunicato capiendo*" were "not applicable to a Jew, even to one who had masqueraded as a Christian." The writ of "*Significavit*" (so named for its opening word) was one used by the king to inform his sheriff in one or another shire that one of the bishops had advised him of the excommunication of one of the king's subjects and had asked for the help of the secular arm in dealing with the contumacious individual involved. "*De excommunicato capiendo*" ordered the sheriff to imprison the excommunicated individual(s), until such time as he (they) returned to the fold of the Church. However, the four "*Significavit*" writs we have dealt with here seem to contradict Richardson's views.

78. See F. D. Logan, "Thirteen London Jews" (n. 17 above), esp. pp. 225 and n. 2, 226.

79. See F. W. Maitland, "The Deacon and the Jewess," in *Roman Canon Law in the Church of England* (London, 1898), pp. 158–179; Roth, *History of the Jews*, pp. 83 and n. 6, 276; *Giraldi Cambrensis opera, VI: Itinerarium Kambriae . . .* , ed. J. F. Dimock (London, 1868), p. 146.

80. For Abraham, see my "Some Accounts of Condemned Jews' Property" (n. 7 above), p. 24 n. 1.

81. See Roth, *History of the Jews*, pp. 56, 274(c); *Matthaei Parisiensis . . . Chronica Majora* ed. H. R. Luard (London, 1880), 5, pp. 114–115 (=*s.a.* 1250); D'Blossiers Tovey, *Anglia Judaica . . .* (Oxford, 1738), pp. 168–169. But cf. Langmuir's comments on the Lincoln events (above, n. 2), p. 463.

82. See *Select Pleas, Starrs, and Other Records*, ed. J. M. Rigg (above, n. 1), pp. xlviii–xlix; *Councils and Synods, 1* (above, n. 70), 473–474. The regulations of 31 January 1253 are dealt with briefly by Richardson, *The English Jewry*, p. 191.

83. See n. 2 above.

84. Langmuir, "The Jews and the Archives," (above, n. 2), pp. 189, 192.

85. See n. 2 above.

86. Langmuir, "The Jews and the Archives," p. 238.

87. Ibid., pp. 199, 203, 209, 213–214.

88. Ibid., pp. 222–223.

89. For a general study, with some comments on England, see Jeremy Cohen, *The Friars and the Jews . . .* (Ithaca and London, 1982).

90. J. Cohen, *The Friars and the Jews*, p.43.

91. See my "Crime and Jews" (n. 5 above), n. 38, and the works noted above in n. 22 for the coinage accusations. I hope to deal at length with the coinage trials of the 1270s in the near future.

8

Pablo de Santa Maria on the Events of 1391

MICHAEL GLATZER

1. Introduction

A repeated phenomenon in the history of antisemitism is that of apostates who assist in actions aimed at bringing their fellow-Jews to apostasy, who are informers for the Christians against the Jews, and debate with Jews as representatives of the Church. This phenomenon is especially prominent in Spain: We mention in particular three famous apostates: Abner of Burgos, Solomon Halevi, and Joshua Halorki. We wish to deal here with Solomon Halevi – Pablo de Santa Maria (1352-1435) – the rabbi of Burgos who in time became its bishop. At the beginning of the fifteenth century he served the king of Castile as personal instructor and chancellor and therefore is considered as one of the most successful apostates of the Middle Ages.

When dealing with the history of Jews in Spain, the events involved in the persecutions of 1391 – the persecutions, the flights and, above all, the forced conversions – are usually seen as the crisis which decided the fate of the Jewish people there, which drastically upset the pattern of their lives, and prepared the ground for their expulsion. Therefore it seems worthwhile to examine how the apostate, Pablo de Santa Maria, described that very event, the persecutions of 1391, so that we can understand how he saw it.

Toward the end of his life, in 1434, Pablo de Santa Maria wrote his long work, *Scrutinium Scripturarum*, in which he tried to prove the truth of Christianity and the errors of the Jews. Toward the end of the book he dealt with the events of his lifetime and described the riots and the conversions.

2. The Context

In the tenth chapter of the sixth discourse, in the second part of the book (*Scrutinium Scripturarum*, Pars 2, Distinctio 6, Cap. 10, Ed. Burgos 1591, pp. 521-526), Pablo de Santo Maria attempted to prove that the dates of the

Redemption given by the Pharisees, the Jewish sages of the past generations, referred to events in the lives of the Christian faithful – an argument interesting in itself and with which we shall deal further on. In this connection, Pablo singled out three calculations of the Messiah's coming and identified them with events in the preceding generations: one was that of Maimonides; the second, that of Nahmanides and Gersonides; and the third, of two prophets among the Jews of Spain, the one from Avila and the other from Chillon.

The date of special interest to us is that of Nahmanides and Gersonides, but first let us look at the date of Maimonides, based upon a famous passage in his *Epistle to Yemen*.

Without getting into the debate over the authenticity of the passage, which was proven by Abraham Halkin in his introduction to the *Epistle to Yemen*, suffice it to say that Solomon Halevi had no doubts about it. The date is based upon the prophecy of Balaam: "Now it is said of Jacob and Israel: 'What hath God wrought!' " (Num. 23:23) which is interpreted as if having been spoken midway between the Creation and the Redemption. The basis for this interpretation, found in the *Jerusalem Talmud, Tractate Shabbath*[1] fol. 8/col. 4, is quoted in the commentary on the *Book of Creation* (Heb. "*Sefer Yezirah*") by R. Judah ben Barzillai[2] and R. Abraham bar Hiyya's *Scroll of the Revealer* (Heb. "*Megillat ha-Megalleh*").[3] Maimonides foresaw the renewal of prophecy at the expected time: "From that time one should count the amount of time from the six days of creation until that time and prophecy shall return to Israel."[4]

According to the various manuscripts of the *Epistle to Yemen*, the date was changed from 1210 to 1212 or 1216. Solomon Halevi designated the date as "218 years ago," his way of designating the calculations at the beginning of the book.

Whatever the calculation, it is interesting that the event predicted by Maimonides occurred in the second decade of the thirteenth century which, according to Pablo de Santa Maria, coincided with the estabilshment of the mendicant orders:

> At the time determined by him (Maimonides), two most saintly and religious men became famous in the Church of God, namely, Saint Dominic and Saint Francis, by whose merit and by the merit of their disciples in religion the teaching of the faithful and the practice of the universal Church became radiant, as everyone knows.[5]

If that is so, the Maimonides foretold an event in the redemption, not of the "perfidious Jews," but of the people of God, the Christians: "*ad redemptionem populi Dei, scilicet Christiani.*"

This is a perfect example of "he prophesied but knew not what", namely, that Maimonides foresaw, as it were, the establishment of the mendicant orders. This seems to have nothing to do with antisemitism, except for the "perfidious Jews" phrase, but we shall see later how this expression tied in with the antisemitic phenomena of the fifteenth century.

The date which especially interests us, as we have noted, is that of Nahmanides and Gersonides. It was based upon the interpretation of Daniel 12:11: "From the time the regular offering is abolished, and an appalling abomination is set up – it will be a thousand two hundred and ninety days." On Nahmanides, Solomon Halevi wrote: "Though he was not as great an authority as his predecessor (Maimonides), still he was not a mediocre authority and was known as the greatest among them."[6] The calculation did in fact appear in two places in his works: in *The Book of Redemption* (Heb. *"Sefer ha-Geulah"*)[7] and in his commentary on Genesis 2:3,[8] and is also cited by Gersonides in his commentary on the Book of Daniel.[9] The two commentators said that the year of the redemption is the year of the destruction of the Second Temple plus 1290, i.e., $68 + 1290 = 1358$ c.e. (5118 a.m.).

Thus Solomon Halevi arrived at his contemporary events.[10] The decisive event, the confirmation of the Nahmanides and Gersonides interpretation of Daniel's vision, was the execution of a Jewish courtier by King Pedro the Cruel. This was interpreted as decisive from the point of view of "the departure of the scepter from Judah." Till then the Jews had held so high a position in Castilian society that they could argue against the Christians that "the scepter had not departed from Judah" on the soil of Spain. In Solomon Halevi's words:

> You must know that in Spain and especially in the kingdoms of . . . our lords the kings, the kings of Castile and Leon, and for a long time earlier, the Jews had been of high rank, in many instances higher than that of the faithful, and held great public positions among the Christians and were appointed over many of the faithful.[11]

The situation was so serious that it was:

> *"scandalum seu periculum animarum caedebat fidelium simplicium."* The Jewish unbelievers persisted in their claims; even said and wrote that the fact that Jews in Spain were in the government proved the truth of Patriarch Jacob's prophecy that "the scepter shall not depart from Judah etc.," as stated.[12]

In other words, the status of the Jews in Spain was such that it offended the Christian faithful and encouraged the Jews to persist in their error, since their success attested to the righteousness of their course. And this is the description for the year 1358:

> However, one who will study the history of Spain will note that in the time of which we speak, about 1358, Pedro jailed one who was the most important Jew and very important at the royal court; and while he was in prison the king ordered him killed along with other important personages of the same origin; and since then no other Jew has been appointed to (such high) office at the king's court.[13]

The reference is to Don Samuel Halevi, the courtier of King Pedro I, who was imprisoned along with his relatives and later killed in prison. It is interesting that Solomon Halevi thought the intent was to remove the Jews from their positions, but in Baer's opinion this was not the case here:

> Don Samuel's tragic fate was not in any way connected with a design to debar Jews from the service of the state. Other Jews came in his stead. Most prominent among them were members of the Halevi and Beneviste families of Burgos.[14]

Baer refers here to the family of Solomon Halevi himself! Further on, the apostate pointed out that in the period of Pedro's brother, Henry II, many Jews were killed, especially in Toledo. This king also renewed the restrictions on the Jews:

> He ruled . . . that the Jews should wear a special emblem on their clothes as required by canon law, yet in spite of that it was unheard of in Spain; rather the Jews lived among the faithful with no differentiations, which led to much corruption and violation of the Divine law.[15]

The next step in the decline of the Jews of Spain, as Solomon Halevi described it, was their removal from every public office in the time of John I, Henry II's son, and the revocation of their autonomy in criminal matters, because they had abused it.[16]

3.   The Persecutions of 1391

Thus far we have dealt with the governmental measures against the Jews which began with the Don Samuel Halevi affair in 1358 and continued to harm them for thirty years. The author then turned to the part played by the masses in the anti-Jewish actions:

> (At the start of Henry III's reign), the masses frenzied by the last blood of the Messiah, rose up mightily against them (the Jews) and many were killed throughout Spain; and these riots began in Seville in whose metropolitan church an archdeacon, a person of simple education and a virtuous life (*litertura simplex et laudabilis vitae*) began to preach against the errors of the Jews and their way of life, and against their synagogues recently built in contravention of the canon law – and this started the riots.[17]

Solomon Halevi saw the riots as caused by "a mob frenzied by the blood of the Messiah," incited by an archdeacon of Seville, Ferrant Martinez, the archdeacon of Ecija. He did not identify the archdeacon by name but his description – "of simple education and a virtuous life" – indicates a combination of disparagement and admiration: the disparagement of a learned bishop, a University of Paris diplomate in theology, toward the lowly, simple clergy; and the admiration of an apostate Jew who aspired to the conversion of other Jews and respected the unflagging persistence shown by the archdeacon of Ecija in his energetic preaching against the Jews and their errors. The correspondence between the kings of Castile, Henry II and John I, and Ferrant Martinez about his anti-Jewish preaching thirteen years before 1391 is well known. One can assume that Pablo de Santa Maria, the *canciller* of Castile, was well aware of it and therefore knew that this was not a scholastic theologian like himself but a rank-and-file priest, arguing simplistically against the harm being done to the ordered Christian society. He lists three such injuries: the errors of the Jews, their ostentatious way of life, and their new synagogues.[18] And, indeed, these are exactly the three things against which Ferrant Martinez preached, even spelling them out for John I in his reply to the king, who had chastized him at the behest of the Jews of Seville.[19]

According to Solomon Halevi, the archdeacon of Ecija's preaching was enough to provoke the riots which spread throughout Spain and even beyond. Here is how he described the scope of the disturbances: "And as a result of this (the beginning of the riots in Seville), in the shortest time and with great speed, the *tumultus* spread through all of Spain and even beyond the Pyreness and to the islands of Majorca and Sardinia."[20] This is the accepted description of the scope of the riots and the speed with which they spread as also indicated by other sources.[21] He saw the results of the riots thus:

> But God who is so good brings good out of evil, thus he wished ("*disposuit*") that while the fury raged and when it subsided thereafter, not a few Jews should become introspective, saying (Deut. 31:17): "Surely it is because our God is not in our midst that these evils have befallen us." And so, because of the wrath, they heeded their reason, began to look into the Bible, and with the help of the Divine enlightenment, recognized their error, so that by their return to the Lord, their publicly calling upon the Messiah, and their devoutness, with God's guidance, they turned the hearts of many back to their fathers, as we know happened in all of those areas.[22]

"Out of the strong came something sweet." According to Solomon Halevi, the conversions were not a direct result of coercion but of the soul-searching by the Jews whom the disturbances awakened to a re-examination of their ways. Everything happened under the providence of God who, in his way, wished to bring the erring nation to repentance. The Jews did not agree to baptism to save their lives, but went of their own free will after realizing their error in light of the bitter reality of their lives in Spain.

There are two possible explanations for this description: The first is that Solomon Halevi wished thereby to describe and justify his own apostasy as stemming not from fear but from study, awareness, enlightenment, and voluntary decision. On the other hand, he wished to see the *Conversos* of his generation as true converts and not as hidden Jews, and was trying to persuade the Christians to trust them.

The first explanation was directed at those Jews who found it hard to accept the sincerity of the conversion of a Jewish scholar such as he had been; the second explanation defended the *Conversos* against the accusations of the Old Christians.[23]

We must note that the author termed the events of 1391 as "bad things" ("*Mala*") but saw them as evils from which "good things" ("*Bona*") grew. Therefore he did not say anything derogatory about the riots or their inciter, Ferrant Martinez, whose praise we have already heard. His attitude toward the riots was pragmatic: whatever contributes to the spread of the Christian faith, and especially to the conversion of the Jews, is good; the disturbances that contributed to the holy purpose were evils, to be sure, but evils which produced good results.

4. Developments after the Persecutions of 1391

Following his description of the 1391 persecutions, Pablo de Santa Maria listed another in the series of fateful events which had begun about 1358: the legislation known to us as the Laws of John II or the Laws of Valladolid.[24] Since this legislation was drawn up at the beginning of the reign of John II, who was still king when the *Scrutinium Scripturarum* was composed, the author prefaced his account with praise for his king. He noted that the king had come to the throne at the age of two and had remained under the supervision of his regents until he had attained maturity. Pablo de Santa Maria did not point out that he himself, among others, had been a member of the Council of Regents. He noted that during the period, and even later when John II had assumed the reign: "many things were decided against *Judaicam Impietatem* which for the most part have been observed in councils and kingdoms so that with the help of Heaven we see that heresy, both Jewish and Saracen, has assuredly been repelled."[25] Thus he described a process which had begun about seventy-five years earlier and had continued until the composition of the book, which also played a role in fending off the Jewish heresy. It is worth noting here that the laws are being kept "for the most part" ("*pro maiori parte*"), since the difficulty of enforcing restrictive and separative legislation in practice is well known. It is also known that when John II reached his maturity, he retreated from the radical legislation which his Council of Regents had announced in 1412.[26] The author tried to camouflage this retreat in the phrase "for the most part."

5. The Purpose of the Historical Description

Why did Pablo de Santa Maria describe this whole process? Why did he depart from the study of the scriptural texts for that of recent historical events?

What conclusions did he come to from this study? "And from this we are forced to conclude that at the time determined by the sages of the Jews as the last for their redemption, then there began the destruction of the heresy of the heretics, and from that has flowered salvation, life, and the vitalization of the believers in the Messiah . . ."[27] That is to say, in the year 1358, which according to the Jewish sages was to be the date of the Redemption of the Jews, the process of the destruction of heresy had begun by the removal of the Jewish courtiers from the courts of the kings of Castile: a process which included the imposition of the Church's demands to distance the Jews, remove their authority and influence, deny their autonomy in criminal matters; and to implement their mass conversion, and the drawing of legislation for their degradation. This process is one of redemption because those who repent and accept the Christian faith are redeemed.

Pablo de Santa Maria's thesis was an expansion of the thesis which underlay the mission to the Jews since the thirteenth century: that it is possible to prove the truth of Christianity from the writings of the Talmud and the Midrash. This thesis retained its force even after the Disputation of Barcelona (1263) and was the basis of Raymond Martini's *Pugio Fidei*. But it was made even more absurd because the sages cited were not ancient, unknown or semi-legendary figures from far-off Babylonia or the Land of Israel, but sages of the last few generations, leaders of the Jews in Spain. Thus Pablo de Santa Maria, at one and the same time, derided the perfidy of his Jewish contemporaries and their error; and attributed truth to the pronouncements of their sages and leaders.

6. The Omen in the Time of Abner of Burgos

We have seen Pablo de Santa Maria's explanation of two dates: that of Maimonides, and that of Nahmanides and Gersonides. The third, that of the two prophets, is 1295 (5055 A.M.) and is based upon the words of the prophet of Avila and the prophet of Chillon, of whom we know from the *Responsa of R. Solomon ben Abraham Adret*[28] and from the words of Abner of Burgos quoted in the book *Fortalitium Fidei* ("Fort of Faith") of Alonso de Espina.[29] Solomon Halevi depended upon Abner, and his quotations from Abner's work *Wars of the Lord* (Heb. *"Milhamot Adonai"*) very closely approximate the version of Alonso de Espina, who made considerable use of the *Scrutinium Scripturarum*, as B. Netanyahu has proved.[30] Solomon Halevi recounted that on the day fixed for the expected Redemption the Jews gathered in their synagogues and declared a fast. Then they were privileged with an omen from heaven in the form of crosses on their white silken garments. They reacted to this miracle variously: There were those who interpreted it as witchcraft; others did not dare to judge; and there were those who saw it as an omen and accepted baptism. Halevi related that in his youth he had heard of this from the elders of Burgos and was amazed not to find in Church history any echo of this day which should have been remembered as a special holiday. He attributed this lack to the very great influence of the Jews of that period, who could prevent things both in the kingdom and in the Church.[31] Of the other dates which he had noted in the first part of his book as dates of Redemption, he said that events could be found which had taken place on those dates in similar fashion. But these were events which had transpired in the east and south, whereas his concern was Spain, the west, and the north.[32]

7. Antisemitic Motifs

After this long description, Pablo de Santa Maria's purpose in describing the series of events is clear: He wished to prove his thesis about the Redemption dates of the Jewish sages. However, in this description there are three main motifs which are basic concepts of antisemitism: the derogation of the high social status of the Jews, a call for their degradation and social segregation, and the use of their writings against them.

The first prominent motif was the decrying of the high social standing of the Jews in Spanish society, in the charge that their influence was exaggerated and constituted a disgrace to the Christian faith; furthermore, that their having authority did damage to the faith of the simple masses in that Church laws were being violated. This motif has appeared in antisemitic writing in various forms, and has been especially prominent in modern times, when the wealth of the Jews has been taken as a social injustice and not necessarily as a disgrace to Christianity. It is interesting that in this case the derogation comes from one who was himself an influential Jew at court and whose influence, after his conversion, became even greater.

The second prominent motif was the debasing of the Jews according to the demands of the Church after the Fourth Lateran Council. There were two purposes of this debasement: to protect the faithful from harm by the Jews and to pressure the Jews into changing their religion. The history of antisemitic legislation can be described as a continuity of laws aimed at removing the Jews from society and revoking their privileges. This goal was expressed in the Middle Ages by the cancellation of the Jewish privileges which existed, and in the period of the struggle for emancipation, by the opposition to granting Jews equal rights. The difference stems from the transition from a corporate society to one in which the citizen has a direct link with government. In both instances, however, the goal is the same: to remove the Jew from society.

The last motif is the concept of proving the Christian claim through the writings of the Jewish sages. As we have said, this was not Solomon Halevi's innovation, but rather a continuation of the system which had developed in the thirteenth century in the school of Raymond Martini and had reached new heights in the teaching of Abner of Burgos. Here we must point out that this claim, that the Jewish sages themselves did not understand what they were saying, ties in with the perception of the Jews as a satanic force of real power which they use for evil ends. Had the Jews only been in error, their later sages would not have been privileged to utter their prophecies. They had the power, but used it for negative purposes. There is a continuity here from the blood-and-host libels of the twelfth century to the accusations and libellous documents of the nineteenth and twentieth centuries.[33] The apostate Solomon Halevi used the Jewish writings as a vindication for his deeds which his Jewish education seemingly demanded.

With that, the point should be made be that one element is absent in Solomon Halevi's teaching: There is no trace of antisemitism in its racial sense. For him, a converted Jew is truly a Christian. It will remain for Alonso de Espina's camp to develop the racial side of antisemitism, regarding the *Conversos* with skepticism and looking upon their full participation in Christian society grudgingly. This important aspect of tension between the groups in Spain, which has its parallel in modern antisemitism, did not draw its inspiration from Pablo de Santa Maria.

8.   Pablo de Santa Maria's Attitude toward the Events of 1391-1412

In light of all this one can sum up Pablo de Santa Maria's attitude to the events of 1391-1412:

1.   The persecutions of 1391 were part of a process which had begun with the Don Samuel Halevi affair, included the activities of Kings Henry II and John I restricting the Jews, and continued with the legislation of John II. This process was still going on when the *Scrutinium Scripturarum* was written, and the book itself was part of it.
2.   Ferrant Martinez played an important role in inciting the riots, in rousing the mob to attack the Jews, but he should be honored, not reviled, for his part.
3.   The riots yielded favorable results. They brought the Jews to true repentance and a return to the right path.
4.   The legislation against *Judaicam Impietatem* was a desirable way of fighting heresy.
5.   The anti-Jewish riots and the other steps taken against them were part of a providential plan for Christian Redemption.

These ideas coalesced into an acceptable spiritual stance in Christian Spain and created the atmosphere in which the expulsion of the Jews became a vital and necessary step. Pablo de Santa Maria's political role in implementing the program still requires investigation. For the time being, his contribution can be summed up as providing, out of Jewish sources, an eschatological explanation for the explicit Christian aspiration to convert the Jews.

Notes

1. *T. J. Shab.* fol.8/col.4: "R. Hanina, son of R. Abbahu, said that in the middle of the world's days that wicked one stood up. What was his reason (for saying so)? 'Now it is said of Jacob and Israel: What hath God wrought!' (Num. 23:23)."
2. See R. Judah ben Barzillai, *Commentary on Sefer Yezirah* (Heb.), ed. S. J. Halberstam (Berlin, 1885), p. 239.
3. See R. Abraham bar Hiyya, *Scroll of the Revealer* (Heb.), ed. A. Poznanski (Berlin, 1924), p. 147.
4. According to the Hebrew translation of the *Epistle to Yemen* by Y. Kafih (Jerusalem, 1972), p. 49, and cf. the A. S. Halkin edition (New York, 1952), pp. 82–83, and see the Introduction there, pp. xii–xiii.
5. *Scrutinium Scripturarum* (Burgos, 1591), p. 522.
6. Ibid.
7. Ramban (Nahmanides), "The Book of Redemption," in *Writings and Discourses* 2, ed. C. R. Chavel (New York, 1978), pp. 628–650.
8. Ramban on Genesis 2:3. Cf. *Commentary on the Torah* 1, ed. C. R. Chavel (New York, 1971), pp. 63–64: "This will take place one hundred eighteen years after the completion of five thousand years, that the word of the Eternal by the mouth of Daniel might be accomplished: 'And from the time that the continual burnt-offering shall be taken away, and the detestable thing that causeth appalment set up, there shall be a thousand two hundred and ninety days.' (Daniel 12:11)."
9. Gersonides' commentary on Daniel 12:11: "And for that this number will be completed when there will be one hundred and eighteen years of the sixth thousand."
10. Cf. F. Cantera y Burgos, *Alvar García de Santa María* (Madrid, 1952), p. 286.
11. *Scrutinium Scripturarum*, pp. 522–523.
12. Ibid., p. 523.
13. Ibid.
14. Y. Baer, *History of the Jews in Christian Spain* 1, (Philadelphia, 1961), p. 364.; Cf. "*Cronica de España del arzobispo don Rodrigo Jimenez de Rada, por el obispo don Gonzalo de la Hinojosa*," *Colección de Documentos Inéditos para la Historia de España*, 106, p. 92; Julio Valdeon Baruque, *Los Judios de Castilla y la Revolution Trastámara* (Valladolid, 1968).
15. *Scrutinium Scripturarum*, (n. 5 above); and cf. Baer, ibid., 1, pp. 367–375.
16. See Baer, ibid., 1, pp. 375–378.
17. *Scrutinium Scripturarum*, pp. 523–524.
18. It should be noted that Don Samuel Halevi built in Toledo one of the most beautiful synagogues in Castile, known today as *El Transito*. See F. Cantera y Burgos, *Sinagogas de Toledo, Segovia y Cordoba* (Madrid, 1973), pp. 49–138.
19. See Baer, *History* 2, pp. 95–99 and in his *Die Juden in christlichen Spanien: Urkunden und Regesten*, 2 (Berlin, 1936), pp. 210–218, 231–232.
20. *Scrutinium Scripturarum*, p. 524.
21. See Baer, *History* 2, pp. 95–110, and cf. the letter of R. Hasdai Crescas to the community of Avignon, *Scepter of Judah* (Heb.), 1, ed. Wiener (Hanover, 1855), pp. 128–130.
22. *Scrutinium Scripturarum*, ibid.
23. Defending the *Conversos* and having them considered faithful Christians were among the central purposes of *Defensorium Unitatis Christanae* of Alonso de Cartagena, Solomon Halevi's son. About him, see the Introduction of H. Beinart's *Conversos on Trial by the Inquisition* (Heb.) (Tel-Aviv, 1965).
24. On the laws of Valladolid see Baer, *History* 2, pp. 166–169, and in his documents, 2, pp. 264–272. One should note that these laws were aimed at Jews and Saracens alike.
25. *Scrutinium Scripturarum*, ibid.
26. See Baer, *History* 2, pp. 244–245.
27. *Scrutinium Scripturarum*, ibid.
28. *Responsa of R. Solomon ben Abraham Adret* (Heb.) 1, responsum 148 (Bene-Berak, 1958), pp. 205–209.
29. Alonso de Espina, *Fortalitium Fidei* (Nuremberg, 1485) fol. 91b–c.
30. B. Netanyahu, "Alonso de Espina: Was He a New Christian?" *Proceedings of the American Academy of Jewish Research* 43 (1976):107–165.

31. *Scrutinium Scripturarum*, pp.524–525; and cf. Baer, *History* 1, pp. 227–281, and A. Z. Aescoly, *Jewish Messianic Movements* (Heb.) (Jerusalem, 1956), pp. 211–215.
32. *Scrutinium Scripturarum*, p. 526.
33. Cf. A. Funkenstein, "Changes in the Patterns of Christian Anti-Jewish Polemics in the Twelfth Century" (Heb.), *Zion* 33 (1968):125–144; C. Roth, "The Medieval Conception of the Jew," in *Essays and Studies in Memory of Linda R. Miller* (New York, 1938), pp. 171–190; J. Trachtenberg, *The Devil and the Jews* (New Haven, 1943).

9

The "Black Death" and Antisemitism

MORDECHAI BREUER

1. Introduction

In the Middle Ages, there were three great plagues which broke out and spread beyond the confines of a single region: the series of plagues and events associated with the name of Justinian in the sixth century; the "Black Death," which took many lives from 1346 to 1361; and the Great Plague of London, which also reached the European continent, in 1665-1666. It should be noted that as far as people at the time knew, the plague which occurred in 1346-1361 was a one-time phenomenon and was designated the "Black Death" because of the black spots which appeared on the bodies of the stricken. One of the most famous people to attest to what took place was the poet, Petrarch, whose beloved Laura perished in the calamity. He wrote that the scope of the plague was so dreadful and total that following generations would not believe what happened. It was a universal catastrophe which claimed a huge number of victims. The demography of the Middle Ages is one of the branches of research which is based upon very sparse and imprecise information, but the accepted premise today is that more than a third of Europe's population perished in the holocaust – in absolute numbers, as many as twenty-five million.

What does this mean in terms of a single city? Here are a few figures. At the height of the plague, in Berne, Switzerland, six hundred died daily, and one should remember that no city at that time had more than a few thousand inhabitants. In the German cities of Cologne and Mainz there were one hundred deaths per day. Two-thirds of the students at Oxford were wiped out. Epidemiological research has shown that the transmission of the disease from person to person, due to the density of housing or because people were together for most of the day, increased the number of casualties in the urban centers of population and especially in the university cities. This is also why the mortality rate in the monasteries was among the highest.

Of the many plague scenes recorded we shall mention only that, because the cemeteries were filled to capacity, Pope Clement VI felt obliged to sanctify the waters of the Rhône River (he lived at Avignon) so that the victims could have a Christian burial in the river.

In recent years new research findings have appeared on the causes of the vast scope of the plague and its repeated recurrence. We shall not linger over this other than to note the fact that prior to 1348-1349, at the peak of the plague, there were three very rainy summer seasons. As a result, hunger was rife in Europe and poverty spread extensively throughout society. The frightful scenes of the "Black Death" were preceded by the phenomenon of drought and the distress of famine. There were places, in Breslau, Germany, for example, where Jews were killed not by the plague, which had not yet reached there, but as a result of starvation, for hungry people in their distress turned upon the Jews.

The plague spread in recurring waves along the great trade routes, at the pilgrimage sites, at the fairs, and similar places where people congregate in large numbers. Most of the Jewish communities were located on those trade routes. The first wave reached Europe from the East, first reaching southern France, spreading from there to Spain, and then over western, central, northern, and eastern Europe.

2. The Well-poisoning Libel

As we know, in that generation and subsequently, the destruction of the Jews in the days of the plague was associated with the well-poisoning libel: "The Jews poisoned the wells in order to wipe out the Christians." One should be aware that this libel was not invented during the "Black Death." A number of much earlier instances are recorded: This libel had already played an important role in the days of the First Crusade in 1161 in Bohemia, in 1267 in Vienna, and at the time of the persecution by the lepers in France in 1321. When the horrible killing of Jews was at its height during the "Black Death," many Jews were seized and put on trial because of this libel. Here there was an innovation in the history of antisemitism: The accused were tortured and forced to confess that the Jews were conspiring against the Christians to wipe them out. Among the main motives to which they "confessed" were their hatred for the Christians, their desire to avenge themselves on Christianity, and their aim to establish Jewish domination of the world. They were further forced to "confess" that in the world-wide organization by means of which the Jews intended to achieve their goal, the Rabbis fulfilled an important function; and that the secret organization's center was in Toledo, Spain, from whence messengers went to all of the Jewish communities delivering the packets of poison.

The minutes of the interrogation of the Jews of Freiburg record that after severe torture the Jews confessed that everyone from the age of seven and above in the neighboring Jewish communities knew about the poisoning of the wells; and that a twelve-man committee of Jewish leaders had been set up and had organized the project. To a Jew who had been asked the reasons, they attributed the following: "Because you Christians killed so many Jews, because of what King Armleder did [1336], and because we too want to be masters . . . you have been masters long enough."

There is no doubt that the masses believed all the stories of the atrocities attributed to the Jews. But we must investigate the thinking of the intelligentsia, of the Church leaders, of the chroniclers, of the scientists and doctors who investigated the disease and its circumstances. A German savant, Conrad of Magenberg, summed up the four causes which, in the opinion of many, were likely to cause the disease: One was the astrological constellation which, as everyone knows, is inescapable. As a second cause he listed earthquakes, which is very revealing of the scientific perceptions of the time. In the years prior to the plague there had been earthquakes in Europe. The prevalent opinion was that as a result of earthquakes, poisonous matter is released toward the surface by the inner tectonic activity of the earth and this pollutes the wells; that is to say, the well-waters are indeed the source of the disease, but not because of external poisoning. The third reason for the outbreak of the plague was punishment from on high, God punishing the sinning population. The fourth, last and least, was that the wells were poisoned by the Jews. One must understand that the motivation for searching for causes was wholly theological. Whoever sought or found a physical-medical cause thereby detracted from the significance of the theological one. "In truth and honesty we believe to this day that this death and everything thereunto appertaining is naught but a decree from Heaven," wrote the city council of Cologne to that of Strasbourg at the height of the fatal events. Pope Clement, in one of the bulls which he issued against the persecution of the Jews, stressed most emphatically that the plague was a divine punishment and it is inconceivable to blame earthly or human powers for it. Incidentally, Professor Dinur, in his note on this source, feels that the fact of the Pope's turning to the bishops is proof that they, too, were among those seeking to conspire against the Jews.

Clement added that the source of the plague was definitely from heaven and not from the Jews because the Jews were smitten no less than the Christians, and the plague had originally broken out and was still constantly breaking out in places far removed from any Jewish settlement. The question of whether Jews perished in the plague in the same measure as Christians has been controversial. While none of the documents written by persons living at the time of the plague mention anything about Jewish victims (which would have served as a significant indication of the innocence of the Jews), we feel that S. Guerchberg has succeeded in proving that the Jews perished, if not in the same measure as the Christians, at least in no less significant a measure. Therefore there is no credence to the claim that the Jews knew in advance of the poisoning of the wells, were careful not to drink from them, and hence did not die. The myth of the small number of Jewish victims is of much later origin, appearing not before the beginning of the fifteenth century.

It is important to note that Pope Clement protested against the libel twice, and even more important, that in the lands where his voice was heeded, in Avignon and its environs, as well as throughout Italy, the poisoning libel did not spread and there were no serious incidents against the Jews. This indicates, first, that the official Church did not support the libel and certainly did not institute it; and, second, that a ruler or person of authority could, if he so desired, prevent the killing of Jews in places which were under his direct control. As for the scientists and the university professors, there is no doubt that anyone who considered himself an intellectual or person of understanding did not believe that the Jews had poisoned the wells and that this was the cause of the plague. Except for the Faculty of Medicine of the University of Paris, there was not one of the generation's experts who tried to connect the plague with the drinking of polluted water. Yet the savant, Conrad of Magenberg, was the only contemporary author who specifically disassociated himself from accusing the Jews, although after recounting that the Jews of Vienna died in such great numbers that their cemetery had to be extended, even he added: "But I do not wish to whitewash the wickedness of the Jews." However, in summation he wrote: "There are those who say that this was caused by the Jewish people, but this opinion is without foundation."

It is, however, necessary, taking into account the discussion by S. Guerchberg, to draw a distinction between causing the disease and spreading it. Even those who did not believe that the Jews had poisoned the wells were likely to believe that they had a hand in spreading it from place to place, because they were so widespread. The fact that the plague swept over all of Europe, wave upon wave, could only be explained as something organized and planned by a group which had agents everywhere. An author from Montpellier wrote at the height of the plague that though its causes were "natural," its prolonged duration and immense diffusion were the result of maliciously premeditated, anti-Christian planning. Nevertheless, when the plague finally ended, a German abbot wrote in his chronicle: "As far as this persecution of the Jews is concerned, there are those who think that they were accused falsely."

3. The Flagellants and the Religious Factor

The Jews were not the only victims of the poisoning accusation. Even in places where there were no Jews at all, a scapegoat was sought and found in one of the minorities. In the East, in the Tatar region from which the plague began in 1345, the Christians who were a minority there suffered. In Denmark, two priests suffered; and it is true that at the time there was already, especially in Germany, a suppressed hatred of churchmen which found its release in priests and monks being blamed for spreading the disease. In Narbonne the English who resided there were blamed. In many places where there were no

Jews, wandering pilgrims were blamed. In Spain, not only Jews were blamed but Muslims as well. Everywhere the blame was placed on those residents of the city who were not of the majority group. These varied from place to place. Here and there members of the aristocracy were persecuted and in other places the lepers, the maimed, and the gravediggers were blamed.

Nevertheless, it would not be correct to say that the Jews suffered just as did every other minority group. They suffered inestimably more because they were the most defenseless, and also for economic and political reasons with which we shall deal. But first we must discuss another phenomenon, that of the masochistic flagellants, or "gashers," as Dinur called them, that is to say, people who made their way from place to place, torturing their flesh with whips till the blood flowed, and in this way seeking to prevent the calamity of the plague. It often happened that after such bands of flagellants had appeared, there would be a slaughter of the Jews. This movement was primarily a religious one. Flagellants had already made their appearance in Germany in the thirteenth century, but the movement grew to unprecedented proportions during the "Black Death." As we have said, they sought to prevent the plague and therefore appeared in most places before the plague arrived. Hence, even before the plague claimed its victims, Jews were killed in many places.

The flagellants tormented themselves in order to fend off the plague by substituting their humanly inflicted suffering for that to be imposed by heaven. But from a group moved by a religious fervor and nothing more, they quickly became a group considered by the Church to be sectarians and heretics. The Pope quickly removed his protection from them though, at the beginning, he had personally participated in the whipping ritual. It became clear to him that this was an anti-Church and anti-Establishment group. From the very start, the flagellants did not tolerate priests and clerics because the latter were, in their eyes, sunk in sin. They did not celebrate the accepted Christian rite of the Eucharist (the offering of the bread and the wine), claiming that their offering is of themselves and that their own blood which they shed is commingled with that of Jesus. In the eyes of the Church, therefore, this was a most dangerous phenomenon, for the Eucharist was the central ritual in the Church's liturgy. But this was not all. The movement assumed a social, revolutionary character and turned against the forces making for an ordered society: the wealthy, the nobility, the urban dwellers, and the city leaders, and against those who served them – the Jews. In any case, the religious element in this movement was prominent and clear. In a few places, such as Mainz and Frankfurt, the local residents began to kill Jews as soon as the flagellants entered the city. Their entrance inflamed passions and led to acts of religious zealotry and violence. There is no doubt that the religious factor played a very active part in everything that happened from the beginning of this movement's activity till its end. There were places where the libel of the poisoning of the wells was accompanied by the blood libel against the Jews, as for example, in Zurich. The question is: How important and how central was the religious factor in the atmosphere of the Middle Ages?

It is possible to argue that killing Jews, not directly and specifically out of religious motives but, for example, because they were lending money at interest, is actually motivated by religion. The taking of interest was considered a grave transgression of the laws of the Church and its ethical code, a very base act, an act of necessity at best, which the Church must decry. Therefore it was a crime to accept the existence of money-lenders-at-interest within Christian society which, accordingly, was being punished by heaven. The Jews were bringing the catastrophe upon Christianity because of their sin, and must be excised from Christian society. Even if they were not accused of ritual murders or poisoning of wells, the very readiness to tolerate the Jews was seen as a transgression in the eyes of heaven. When one is searching one's deeds and seeking purification to escape punishment, one might end up killing Jews, and not necessarily because of a conflict of opinions and beliefs.

On the other hand, it must be pointed out that none of the traditional motifs of the various libels, from the eleventh century onward, that is, Jewish plots to degrade Christianity and its symbols, defiling the wafer and so on, appears in the minutes of the interrogations of the Jews accused during the "Black Death." At most, they came up in connection with distant rumors about the matter. All of the investigations focused on the poisoning charge and the attempt to prove that the intent of the Jews was to harm Christians, rather than Christianity. (At the height of the Middle Ages, Jews were accused of being deicides, whereas now they are charged with being murderers of individuals and peoples, with a well-organized and planned world conspiracy. In this there is something of an innovation.)

Could the Jews save themselves from persecution by converting to Christianity? Was this suggested or demanded of them? The consensus of the scholars is that in Spain conversion was acceptable whereas in Germany it was rather rare, not because there were no Jews ready to convert but because it was neither asked of them nor did it help. In contrast to the persecutions of 1096, this time the Jews of Germany were not given the choice of death or baptism, and there is much evidence of this. Even converted Jews, who had been baptized as Christians before the outbreak of the plague, suffered in various places just as did the rest of the Jews. Those Jews who converted to Christianity in the midst of the slaughter were also killed when the rioters returned a few days later. In some places the children were taken for baptism, but the impression is that this was done because it was the tradition, and not because of any clear purpose as to the conversion of the Jews. The attackers had no intention whatever of forcing the Jews to change their faith and this was not the focus of what was happening.

4. Social and Economic Factors

Indeed, an analysis of what occurred during the days of the plague indicates that social, economic, and political factors were of much greater import in fan-

ning the flame of antisemitism than is generally assumed. The first
this was G. Caro, the historian of the economy of the Jews in the Mid
though he did not yet give it its full due. The fourteenth century was a p
major upheavals in the cities. The social conflicts and the economic te ...s
between the patrician families of means and influence, primarily involved in
commerce, and the craftsmen's guilds, continued to intensify. And there was a
third party: the aristocracy, the lords of the land and the manor who dwelt
around the cities. There were two aspects to the struggle between these
groups: economic and political. The merchant's interest was that the craftsman
provide him with inexpensive products; the artisan wanted a higher price. The
merchants wanted an open urban economy, including the import of inexpensive
merchandise into the city; the craftsmen hated imported goods and wanted a
kind of urban autarchy of independent production. They wanted to capture the
entire market for themselves and impose their monopolistic prices upon the
purchasers. The aristocracy, which had lost much of its property and needed
the urban market, supported the mercantile elements. This clash of economic
interests led to a political struggle. The guilds fought the city authorities, and
over the course of the fourteenth century, during the period of the plague and
thereafter, urban authority in many cities passed from the patricians to the
craftsmen.

There was a clearly Jewish aspect to this development. Many documents
report that those who came to kill the Jews in the cities were "the ordinary
folk," and in the eyes of the chroniclers and the urban leadership, these "simple
people," the unrepresented masses without influence in the city council, turn
out to be the craftsmen. They were motivated to conspire against the Jews
because the Jews served the merchants and the aristocrats and, with their
capital and their loans, helped establish the urban economy and the city's growing political and territorial independence. The Jews also aroused hatred
because they lent money to the craftsmen at usurious rates of interest. This
anger was vented in the days of the plague and is an added explanation of the
fact that the anti-Jewish movement was mainly urban.

How did the city councils relate to the Jews during the plague period? Those
were the days when the cities were most deeply in the process of becoming
firmly established and expanding territorially. The cities of Germany, especially
the cities of southern Germany, were successfully expanding their boundaries
by acquiring land from the local nobility living in the vicinity. The relevance of
this to the present topic is that the city paid the noblemen for the lands which
they transferred to it, and the huge sums required for this purpose were raised
from the Jewish lenders and taxpayers. This is another important aspect of the
common interests of the patrician urban leadership and the Jews.

Many city councils spoke out against the poisoning libel. In the Alsation
chronicle of Königshofen there are copies of letters from the city councils of
Cologne, Freiburg, Basel and others. Many expressed the opinion that the
anti-Jewish movement should be nipped in the bud. Cologne's reason was that

this was the start of an uprising against the council's authority and that the anti-Jewish movement would, in the end, become a revolutionary, antipatrician one. In Heilbronn, Strasbourg, Cologne, and Erfurt, they stated explicitly that they had never heard a disparaging word about the Jews and that there was no proof of their guilt. Graetz attributed humanitarian motives to the heads of these cities but, in fact, they were acting according to the rules of practical politics. However, it required great courage to stand up and endanger oneself by defending the Jews, even if only out of selfish, material interests, and many were not ready to do so. The city council of Regensburg saved the Jews of the city, and in a large parchment scroll to which were appended 237 signatures, all the long-standing citizens pledged themselves to hasten to the aid of the Jews. In other cities, precautionary and defense measures taken on behalf of the Jews delayed the disaster for a few months. By the beginning of 1349 it was clear that a number of city councils wished to suppress the popular uprising from fear that the mobs might oust them. This happened, for example, in Strasbourg, where the members of the council were accused of being Jew-lovers and of receiving bribes from them. A day after the Strasbourg council was toppled and replaced, the city's Jews were put to death. In Basel and other places the mobs forced the council to burn the Jews alive.

5. The Attitude of Charles IV

And now for the political-governmental aspect, represented by the Emperor who, in the period under discussion, was still a king, Charles IV. This is a complex matter which is of central and primary importance at least as far as the cities of western and southern Germany are concerned. Charles IV is described by many who have studied his personality and policies as one of the outstanding rulers in Europe, of high caliber, a talented statesman and diplomat, a practical politician, an excellent economist and businessman who made his moves with cold, pragmatic calculation. In 1346 he was chosen to be king by the faction of nobles who supported the Pope in his opposition to King Ludwig of Bavaria. In 1347 Ludwig died and his faction chose Günther of Schwarzburg as king. The two factions prepared for civil war. When the plague broke out, Germany was split between two rival kings and there was no point in talking of a joint military effort to suppress the urban rioting.

Charles established firm foundations for his kingdom in remarkably well-planned ways. He made peace with his opponents, the nobles and the city councils, and with a large sum of money persuaded Günther to relinquish his claim to the throne in favor of Charles. The result was that Charles was crowned at Aachen as king of all Germany. All of this required vast sums of money. These were paid, of course, by the Jews, "the serfs of the exchequer." Charles employed many devices for raising monies from or by means of the Jews. He "sold" the Jews to the cities: That is to say, he gave the cities a mortgage on the taxes from the Jews in exchange for large sums of cash or commitments. The cities, of course, in their turn, took these payments from their Jews. Charles exercised his authority to cancel the debts Christians owed the Jews, in exchange for payment of part of this debt to the king's treasury. When the plague was at its height and the bands of flagellants were sweeping across the country, he sold or transferred the holdings of the Jews, if and when they should be killed, to the cities and nobles who saw fit to support him. Over and above all of this, the Jews paid the city councils hard cash to finance the means of protection and defense which the cities adopted to prevent the disaster. In exchange for all of these payments, the Jews could expect one thing: that the king, the nobles, and the city councils who had benefited from their monies would protect them. Undoubtedly, they were legally and morally obligated to do so and there is no reason to doubt that they would indeed have preferred to protect the lives of their Jews in order to continue to benefit from their money. However, when under the circumstances we have described, it appeared that they would not be successful, they decided to turn the destruction of the Jews to their best advantage.

There was a ramified network of commercial and political relationships between the crown and the cities in which the Jew served solely as a commercial object. The concept, "serfs of the exchequer," which in earlier centuries had meant the king's protection in return for paying him the serf's tax, was now, practically speaking, devoid of any meaning of protection. The Jews of Germany had become merchandise, converted to chattel and profitable property. This was the end of the process which had begun in the days of King Rudolph I who, in 1286, ordered the confiscation of the possessions of Jews who had fled from the Reich, with the justification that the Jews are the serfs of the king's exchequer "in their body and their possessions." In 1343, King Ludwig of Bavaria cancelled the debts owed the Jews of Nuremberg explaining that, "you belong to us and the kingdom in your body and possessions and we are free to deal with you howsoever we wish." Charles IV made a similar declaration in 1347: "All the Jews belong to our exchequer in their bodies and possessions." In Charles's Golden Bull of 1356 a famous paragraph appeared in which the Jews are mentioned in the same breath as natural resources, forests, and mines which belong to the king and which the king may grant to his nobles. This paragraph perfectly expressed the situation wherein the Jews were considered purely as articles of commerce. The legal code of that period saw the possessions of the Jews as something not belonging to them but entrusted to them so long as the ruler so desires. This concept had indirectly been given Church approval by Thomas Aquinas who had written that the possessions of the Jews should be expropriated, since their possessions came to them through usury. To be sure, he was referring only to what the Jews "had amassed for themselves through the vile means of interest," but since the Jews at that time were constrained to deal primarily in money-lending, his words strongly reinforced the tendency to consider all of their possessions as merely a conditional holding.

Therefore, one can not evaluate the deeds of the king and the city councils in terms of hatred or love of the Jews. In the areas which belonged to him or his dynasty directly, in Luxemburg and Bohemia, Charles acted energetically and with obvious success to protect the Jews because there he had no one to whom to sell his Jewish "merchandise," and therefore it was in his interest to protect it and keep it alive; whereas in the other districts he was satisfied to give a lukewarm order not to harm the Jews. Thus it happened that on the very day that the Jews of Frankfurt were burnt to death, less than three weeks after Charles had bought the support of the city and gone on his way, he issued a stern order to his city of Luxemburg to protect its Jewish inhabitants and their possessions, "for both the Pope and he himself believe that the Jews have been accused unjustly." This only shows that Charles dealt with the Jews, in Kracauer's pertinent formulation, as a merchant deals with merchandise which is about to beçome spoiled: He tries to sell it to any bidder at the best possible profit under the circumstances.

Of the plethora of documentation available which shed light upon Charles's commercial attitude toward the Jews, let us treat of one instance, that of the Jews of Frankfurt. As stated, the king turned the townspeople from foes to friends after bestowing upon them a series of income-sources and privileges, the most important of which was the transfer to the city of all of the revenues and services due the king from the Jews. In the document of this transaction signed by the king there are two seemingly contradictory paragraphs. In one paragraph it says that the king commands the city official charged with maintaining order within the city's confines and in charge of its citizens as well, to protect the Jews from any enemy. In the other paragraph the king declares that he releases the city in advance of any claim or demand which would be within his right to make against it should the Jews be murdered – "which far be it from God to desire!" This contradiction does not attest to the cynical character, as it were, of Charles's deeds. They are no more cynical than those of the merchant who tries to save what he can of his merchandise which is about to be lost, as the slaves in the American South at the beginning of the past century were regarded. Merchandise is neither loved nor hated; it is intended for producing profit.

A few days after this document was signed, the bands of flagellants burst into the city in spite of the fortifications and the special precautions, fell upon the Jewish neighborhood, and set it on fire. There are indications that the murderers were helped by craftsmen of the city. The damage caused to the city was great and only the "wise" king emerged unscathed because he had already received his compensation for transferring the Jews to the city's jurisdiction.

The Jews and their possessions, rather than matters of faith and religion, were thus at the center of events in Germany. This can also be seen from an examination of the behavior of the Jews and their reaction. It is a general rule that the attitude of diaspora Jews to the non-Jews is largely a function of the non-Jews' attitude toward them. There is no doubt that the Jews were aware of the negotiations over their bodies and possessions which had taken place between the authorities. Many tried to flee, as the documents clearly indicate. Thus we learn, for example, that Elector Rupert of the Palatinate gave refuge in the city of Heidelberg to the Jews who fled from Worms and Speyer, but generally it was most difficult to escape. During plagues, the city residents were in the habit of locking and bolting their gates; no one was allowed to enter or to leave. Moreover, they also closed off the Jewish section and posted an armed guard over it. Their declared purpose was to protect the lives of the Jews, but it was really meant to prevent their flight so long as their bodies and possessions were commercially and politically negotiable. Nevertheless, at that time many German Jews did reach Eastern Europe where a large Jewish population was destined to develop.

6. Conclusions

When the fury broke upon them, the communities followed the example of their ancestors and suffered martyrdom. However, in contrast to the most impressive, multifaceted saga of heroism in the accounts of the 1096 pogroms, there are almost no traces of martyrdom in 1348-1349 except for the shockingly matter-of-fact lists in the *Memorbücher* and the description of the heroic stand of the Jews of Nordhausen. The argument that there was no one to record the events of those days because nearly the entire generation was wiped out is absurd. The catastrophe of the "Black Death" is mentioned in fifteenth century German-Jewish literature and there are also a few *kinot*, but there are almost no detailed accounts of martyrdom. Jews set their homes on fire out of despair since there was no escape, not in combat as during the slaughters of the 1096 pogroms. Yet, while there were not many instances of armed defense by the Jews during the Crusades, in 1348-1349 there were relatively many more.

All this attests to an atmosphere of cold calculation, without the religious fervor and zeal for the faith which had marked the events at the time of the Crusades. The planned, premeditated, and organized exploitation of what remained of Jewish holdings is more akin to the familiar scenes of the Holocaust in our generation than to the days of 1096, when the Jews threw their money and gold out of the windows in order to gain time for their martyrdom. In his article in the *Jubilee Volume in Honor of Yitzhak Baer*, Professor Jacob Katz has compared the pogroms of 1648-1649 with those of 1096 and stressed the differences between them as events involving *Kiddush Hashem* (Jewish martyrdom). He pointed out that in contrast to the great religious tension which pertained between Jews and Christians during the period of the Crusades, the readiness to perform acts of martyrdom had weakened in the seventeenth century ghetto period. This he attributed in great degree to the fact that in the latter period Jews ignored what was taking place in the non-Jewish world. This comparison should also be applied to the pogroms of 1348-1349 in which there

ATA—F

are also relatively few signs of an active, fervent, religious struggle. From this standpoint, they were more like those of 1648-1649 than of 1096, though they occurred during a period still far from that of the ghetto. If this is the case, Professor Katz's analysis warrants re-examination.

To sum up, the prevailing presentation of the destruction of the Jewish communities of Germany as a result of the well-poisoning libel is only partially correct because it ignores the social, economic, and political factors. Clearly, the horrors of the plague released and activated deep feelings of fear and hatred pent up in the hearts of the masses. The demonization of the image of the Jew reached an unprecedented height in the accusation of a world-wide Jewish plot against the Christian world. This plot, as everyone knows, became part of the arsenal of modern antisemitism. Nor is this the only aspect of fourteenth-century antisemitism heralding the course taken by the antisemitism of recent generations. The combination of zealous, aggressive action and the lust for gain; the transformation of a disliked minority with a distinctive collective identity, scattered through many countries, into a scapegoat to be weighed down with all the ills of the time; the premise that such a group, ostracized and degraded by society, is of necessity bound to rise up at the first opportunity and take a terrible revenge upon that society, even to the extent of obliterating it – all of these motifs are already to be found in the acts of slaughter perpetrated during the "Black Death."

All this is valid, indeed, as far as the dark emotions of the masses are concerned. As for the city and governmental leadership, these operated out of realistic considerations. Of all the reasoning emerging from the official documents and studies by contemporary scholars, weakest of all – in terms of the Middle Ages – is the religious argument calling for the speedy elimination of Judaism as a religion. Anyone interested in exploiting the Jews as a source of revenue would not wish to hasten their conversion to Christianity, for a converted Jew is no longer permitted to loan money at interest. The conversion of a Jew is a loss to the exchequer. The Jews became chattel and as such could not be the object of hatred by those who traded with them. A few years ago, a German scholar wrote that the deal of Charles IV and the city of Frankfurt was, in and of itself, "normal"; and though this expression from the pen of a German scholar may give rise to speculation, he was undoubtedly right in pointing out that this was consistent with the thinking of the period. A number of chroniclers, in summing up the slaughter of the Jews, emphasized that its main cause was the lust for Jewish possessions; and the author of the Alsation chronicle concluded: "The ready cash in the hands of the Jews was also the poison which killed them. Had the Jews been poor, they would not have been burned." In his book, *Emek ha-Bakha* ("Valley of Tears"), Joseph ha-Kohen also writes a number of times: "But they did lay hands on the spoil."

It is very doubtful whether Baron was correct when he argued that, unlike the Nazi plan for the destruction of the Jews, there were never governmentally instigated pogroms against the Jews in the years between 1096 and 1391. Does the source of modern antisemitism really lie in the events of 1348-1349, as Poliakov and Norman Cohn write? We leave the answer to this question to scholars who have specialized in this field.

For Further Reading

D. Andernacht, "Die Verpfändung der Frankfurter Juden 1349," *Udim* 3(1972):9–25.

S. W. Baron, "Changing Patterns of Antisemitism," *Jewish Social Studies* 38(1976):5–38.

G. Caro, *Sozial und Wirtschaftsgeschichte der Juden* 2 (Leipzig, 1920), pp. 192–219.

F. F. Cartwright, *Disease and History*, (London, 1972), pp. 29–53.

N. Cohn, *The Pursuit of the Millenium*, (2nd ed.: New York, 1962), pp. 129–138.

N. Cohn, *Warrant for Genocide* (New York, 1969), p. 22.

G. Deaux, *The Black Death*, (London, 1969).

H. Dicker, *Die Geschichte der Juden in Ulmm*, (Rottwell, 1937), pp. 8–16.

M. W. Dols, "The Comparative Communal Responses to the Black Death in Muslim and Christian Societies," *Viator* 5(1974:269–287.

E. Friedell, *Kulturgeschichte der Neuzeit* 1 (Meunchen, 1929), pp. 97–98.

H. Graetz, *History of the Jews 4* (Philadelphia, 1894), pp. 100–135.

S. Guerchberg, "La controverse sur les prétendus semeurs de la 'Peste Noire' d'après les traites de peste de l'époque," *Revue des Etudes Juives* 108(1948):3–40.

J. F. K. Hecker, *Der Schwarze Tod im 14. Jahrhundert*, (Berlin, 1832).

I. Kracauer, *Geschichte der Juden in Frankfurt a.M.* 1, (Frankfurt a.M., 1925).

E. Littmann, "Studien zur Wiederaufnahme der Juden durch die deutschen Städte nach dem schwarzen Tode," *Monatsschrift für Geschichte und Wissenschaft des Judentums* 72(1928): 576–600.

J. Parkes, *The Jew in the Medieval Community* Ch. 4, (2nd ed.: New York, 1976), p. 264.

L. Poliakov, *The History of Antisemitism* 1, (London, 1974), pp. 107–122.

O. Stobbe, *Die Juden in Deutschland während des Mittelalters* (Braunschweig, 1868; rep. Amsterdam, 1968).

R. Straus, *Die Juden im Wirtschaft und Gesellschaft* (Frankfurt a.M., 1964), pp. 45–68.

H. R. Trevor-Roper, *The European Witch-Craze*, (New York, 1969).

P. Ziegler, *The Black Death*, (London, 1969).

10

Jews and Judaism in the Political and Social Thought of Spain in the Sixteenth and Seventeenth Centuries

JOSEPH KAPLAN

1. The Background

On 31 March, 1492, the Catholic kings expelled all Jews from the Spanish kingdom. Thus came to an end the history of one of the largest, most established, developed, and flourishing of the Jewish communities of the Middle Ages. Did antisemitism disappear from Spanish soil along with the Jews? Baruch Spinoza, in his *Tractatus Theologico-Politicus*, might have been answering this question:

> That they have been preserved in great measure by Gentile hatred, experience demonstrates. When the king of Spain formerly compelled the Jews to embrace the State religion or go into exile, a large number of Jews accepted Catholicism. Now, as these converts were admitted to all the native privileges of Spaniards, and deemed worthy of filling all honorable offices, it came to pass that they straightway became so intermingled with the Spaniards as to leave of themselves no relic or remembrance.[1]

According to Spinoza, the Judaism of the forcibly converted in Spain, descendants of the Spanish Jews, was not raised as an issue by the government and therefore they were assimilated by Spanish society. If that indeed was the case, does this indicate that antisemitism was forgotten by the Spaniards and that, with the Expulsion, the "Jewish problem" stopped disturbing them?

The Spanish reality of the sixteenth and seventeenth centuries was different from the picture painted by Spinoza: Not only were the converts to Christianity not granted "all the rights of a native Spaniard" nor considered "fit for any degrees of honor," but the Hispanic society, including its leaders and institutions, saw the converts as a reincarnation of the Jewish community which had dwelt in Spain before the Expulsion; the "New Christians" of Jewish origin were seen as a caste, different in essence and nature from the "old," "pure," Christian population. After the Expulsion, the forced converts became an object of the hatred hitherto directed against the Jews. From the eighties of the fifteenth century, the many trials of the Inquisition directed against the "New Christians" and their descendants created a hostile public opinion which shunned them. This was expressed in the opprobrious terms applied to them (*marranos*=pigs; *tornadiços*=turncoats; *alboraycos*, after Muhammad's wonder-horse, etc.) and by the creation of a vast number of satires[2] in which the stereotype of the "New Christian" was crystallized, based primarily upon the negative image of the Jew in Christian society; but there were also new elements added relating particularly to the special status of the *conversos* and the characteristics that they had supposedly developed in this situation.

The "Blood Purity" Statutes (Estatutos de Limpieza de Sangre), introduced into many religious and governmental institutions of Spanish society during the fifteenth to seventeenth centuries, expressed in social terms the different value placed upon the "old" as against the "new" Christians. On the basis of there being Jewish blood flowing in their veins, the latter and their descendants were denied entrance to universities and religious orders and the possibility of holding public office.[3] According to those who enacted these laws, the central motivation for these discriminatory regulations was the obligation of Christian society to defend itself against the "negative influences" and "dangerous schemings" of that community whose Christianity, according to the evidence accumulated in the dossiers of those who had been tried by the Inquisition, merely masked a Jewish interior and a deep tie with the faith of Israel. In time, the argument became more and more pointed: that the "polluted blood" of the "New Christians" was sufficient to explain their deceitfulness and heresies and to justify their being ostracized. This is because of the curse carried by the Jews and all of their descendants as a result of "that despicable murder," because then "they lost their claim to their noble lineage, and the blood of the murderers of Jesus was so polluted that their children, their nieces and nephews, and all their descendants, all of them are as if born with polluted blood, and therefore they are denied all honors, offices, and titles . . . the abomination of their ancestors will cling to them forever."[4] This determination made assimilation with the "Old Christians" impossible for the community of "New Christians," and the former's hostility to the "undefiled" Christian was seen by the latter as an integral part of their being.

It is clear that the expulsion of the Jews from Spain was not enough to put an end to the Iberian society's struggle with the Jewish question and it occupied a central place in the political and social thought of sixteenth and seventeenth century Spain.

In order to understand this phenomenon, we shall look not necessarily to works written specifically about the Jews and Judaism but mainly to materials dealing with the political, economic, social, religious, and cultural condition of the Spanish kingdom in general during those centuries. An investigation of the books written about "the virtues of the Spanish kingdom," the characteristics of "the Christian Prince," "the King's Council and his advisors," and even about the health of the community, will reveal that the question of their relationship to the Jews and Judaism did not cease to disturb Spanish circles even after the Expulsion. How to relate to this question became one of the central components of Spanish culture in the sixteenth and seventeenth centuries.

2. The Crystallization of Nationalism and the Idea of a "Chosen People"

After the unification of Spain under Ferdinand and Isabella, modern Spanish nationalism proceeded to crystallize, one of its first expressions being repeated emphasis upon the mission of the Spanish nation to spread Christianity throughout the world. During the period of the Catholic kings, a Messianic fervor gripped Spain, drawing its sustenance from the strong faith in the power of a united Spain to establish the kingdom of heaven on earth. (There were even those at that time who endowed Ferdinand with a Messianic character.) This fervor grew even stronger when, in the days of Charles V, Spain became part of the mightiest power in Europe. Imperial Spain, which spread Christianity to the ends of the earth, the power which fought evidences of heresy within and without, saw itself as the heir of the chosen people of biblical times. The stultification and decline suffered by Spain in the first half of the seventeenth century brought no change in this sense of the "chosenness" and mission of the Spaniards. Not only did the feeling of superiority not weaken, but among a number of Spanish thinkers it strengthened their faith in the mission of their kingdom as the flag-bearer of Catholic Christianity. "A promise was given His Chosen People in the Scriptures; and its heir to this grace is the Spanish nation," wrote Juan de Salazar in 1619, who tried to prove "the almost absolute similarity between these two peoples."[5]

Many in Spain repeated these ideas, particularly in the period of the severe crisis which befell the kingdom in the days of Philip IV. A number of books of those years bear such titles as *The Excellencies of the Spanish Monarchy* or *The Excellencies of the Spaniard* and were written from a conviction of the destiny and mission of the people of Spain, God's chosen. Everything, according to their writings, shows God's preference for Spain and the supremacy of the Spanish: the conquests on the American continent, the transformation of the Indians from savages to human beings, the eminent people with whom Spain is blessed, and so forth. El Cid is the embodiment of Samson; Charles V is the new King David;[6] some saw Spain then as "the chosen land" and Juan de la Puente entitled it "the land of God."[7]

The Spaniard's view of themselves as the chosen people, and the many, repeated parallels with the history of the biblical Hebrews found in the political literature of the time, were enough to rouse the wrath of the Spanish against their Jewish "competitors" whom they condemned with fervid zealotry. These political writers were not satisfied with stripping the Jews of their "chosenness," but they also felt a need to explain and justify the latter's rejection by the Divinity. In their eyes, the expulsion of 1492 indicated both the final rejection of the Jews and the choice of the Spanish in their stead.[8] To be sure, this perception sees the Expulsion as the end of a process, but is also contains within it the faith that the more the Spanish persisted in their struggle against Judaism and succeeded in extirpating any Jewish trace, the more forcefully would they prove that they were chosen instead of the rejected Jews. This is the source of the admiration for the Spanish Inquisition felt by many of the Spanish thinkers of the period under discussion and in the establishment of which they saw a revelation of the divine grace God bestowed upon Spain.[9]

3. Lineage, Honor, and Purity of the Blood

In this Spain, caught up in Messianic fervor and a sense of religious mission, when only those belonging to "Old Christian" families, whose lineage contained no trace of the originally Jewish "New Christians," were considered to be of impeccable Christian origin – the question of one's lineage became a matter of the utmost social urgency. In many respects, the *moriscos*, the "New Christians" whose origins were in the Muslim population, aroused the same reservations as did those Jews who had become Christians, and their descendants. But, in the main, it was the descendants of the ancient chosen people who became despised and regarded as inferior by their supposed heirs, the Spaniards of wholly Christian origin, the bearers of the Christian gospel throughout the world. The "New Christians," with their connection to Judaism, endangered the Christian integrity of Spanish society, a perfection which is a precondition for the Messianic mission. It is from this that, in the sixteenth and seventeenth centuries, the "purity of the blood" (*pureza de sangre*) became a major factor in the "honor" (honra), and the effort to prove "a pure origin" is one of the outstanding marks of Spanish society in these centuries.

We shall not evaluate the functional importance of this conflict about "honor" in the social and class confrontations which took place in Spain during the period under consideration. Yet, one must point out that it served the interests of all the social forces which sought, for various reasons, to fight the middle class, the urban merchant class, a significant portion of which, at least in Castile, was composed of "New Christians"; and it mainly served the lower, folk levels of society which used the conflict to compensate for their feeling of social deprivation. After the Old Christian community had begun to identify specific businesses and occupations as being of a Jewish complexion and content, and after this community had begun to see financial activity, tax farming, commerce, and medicine as clear indicators of Jewish origin, the lower classes in particular could point to their superiority by virtue of their low social class standing. The purpose of "honor" turned the Spanish into a people possessed: Since the raising of a suspicion that people were of "impure origin" could be catastrophic for the suspects and determine their fate, people were compelled to anticipate that possible blow by proving, while there was yet time and as best they could, that their lineage was untainted, that is, that they were "pure in life and origin" (*vida limpia y cuna limpia*).

The tried and effective means of proving "pure origin" was by indicating a "pure life," that is to say, being in an occupation or trade which is neither "Jewish" nor has any "Jewish smell" to it. "It is unseemly for one sporting a beard who could be *a soldier* or *a farmer* (emphasis supplied) to sit in a shop selling thread and cloth," appears in one of the comedies of Juan Ruiz de Alarcón.[10] Indeed, the occupations of soldier and farmer were sufficient to assure "honor," because anyone so engaged could be pointed to with certainty as an "Old Christian" without blemish. The jurist Juan Arce de Otalora wrote in 1559:

> Those whose origin is not with those who fought to expel the Moors from Spain . . . lack the superior qualities and the habits of the Spanish aristocracy, because the *hidalgos* of Spain, in days of yore and always, served and serve the kings and the kingdom in their wars . . . the others never went to war except as doctors and surgeons.[11]

In terms of "honor," they assessed the doctors and the surgeons as inferior not only to the soldiers but also to the farmers. When the jurist Galindez de Carvajal came before Charles V to describe the composition of the royal Council, in a number of instances he pointed out the pure lineage of the members by pointing to their origins in farming families: "Doctor de Oropesa is an Old Christian from a family of farmers; licentiate Santiago is pure by virtue of his parents because on both sides he is descended from farmers." On the other hand, "Doctor Beltrán is learned and sharp . . . but all are of the opinion that it would be good to replace him with someone else because his origin and way of life do not befit the counselor of any lord."[12] Indeed, to be a descendant of farmers assured "honor" because this attribution almost assuredly means "a pure Christian origin"; erudition, on the other hand, was suspect and liable to lead to dreadful disgrace.

"Jewish origin" was indicative not only of social fault but also of physical blemish. One of the important Spanish doctors of the seventeenth century claimed that one of the punishments imposed by God upon the Jews was a pain between the ribs which attacks many of them, though, as he says, not everyone who suffers these pains is necessarily of Jewish origin . . .[13] Another doctor, Juan de Quiñones, wrote a special treatise to prove the claim that male Jews have a tail and, like women, a monthly flow of blood![14]

Claims such as these defects were also heard from jurists. Ignacio del Villar came out strongly against any contact with Jews (meaning the "New Christians" of Jewish origin), no matter to what extent, because Judaism to him was a poisonous seed, and anything sprouting from it was defective and corrupt.[15] In a political tract of 1700 it is stated that it is forbidden for a "New Christian" woman to serve as wet-nurse for the royal children because her milk is polluted since she is of the despised and accursed race.[16] In the eyes of those who were of the aforementioned opinions, baptism was not powerful enough to purify the *Conversos*, the "New Christians," of the terrible sins of their ancestors. Even their Christian education over generations was not enough to eradicate their despicable traits. They still constitute a real danger to the "pure" Spanish society. This danger takes on terrifying dimensions to the extent that they are perceived in the general consciousness as a foreign body which has cunningly managed to penetrate Christian society and which, in its Christian guise, is undermining its foundations. "If only they could kill us with impunity, they would not desist from doing so," Villar charges against the "New Christians."[17] And in a work which appeared in 1594, a hundred years and more after the Expulsion, the author warns against an international conspiracy threatening the integrity of Spain in which, according to him, the Jews are playing a most important role.[18]

4.   Social and Political Criticism and the "Perception of Reality"

In the sixteenth century, other voices were heard in Spain. The humanist from Valencia, Furió Ceriol, came out sharply against the radical nationalistic and religious particularism which had gripped Spanish society: "A sure sign of spiritual stultification is the hot-headed derogatory talk against one's opponent, derogating the Prince's enemies, derogating the members of a different sect or derogating strangers, be they Jews or Moors . . . for the wise man knows that good and evil exist everywhere."[19] The difference between peoples is naught but a result of climatic, social, and historical factors. These factors created "the jealousy of the Jews and their wisdom" as opposed to "the arrogance of the Spanish and their faithfulness."[20] It was not long before Juan de Huarte, one of the most important Spanish thinkers of that period and the most important of its doctors, formulated a similar concept for understanding the external and internal differences between nations. The difficult political circumstances in which the Jews found themselves shaped their character: "For those who live in foreign countries, in servitude, in pain, and in oppression, tend to an angry temperament because they are deprived of free speech and revenge for their oppression; and this temperament is parent to the slyless and the evil."[21]

The works of Furió Ceriol and Huarte and their rational approach undoubtedly influenced those seeking social reforms in the seventeenth century. The decline of the Hispanic Empire in the days of the last two kings of the Habsburg dynasty raised questions for many. "Everything is going to Hell," wrote the Count of Gondomar in 1625 to the Count-Duke of Olivares.[22] As a result of this feeling, a number of the best thinkers of Spain were moved to come out openly against the Messianic ideology and the mystical fervor which had turned Spain, in the words of one of them, into "a republic of bewitched men living outside the natural order."[23]

These thinkers – including the *arbitristas*, those who wrote the memoranda, and the seekers of reforms at the beginning of the seventeenth century – saw in the "status of Blood Purity" and the atmosphere created by the discrimination against "the New Christians," one of the main factors in Spain's decline, its demographic impoverishment, and its economic pauperization. Against those seeking the "excellencies" of Spain, they proposed the need for "triumpho del desengaño" (victory of sobriety):[24] "No one is more noble than his fellow, but he who is the more talented"; "There is nothing in one's origin to stigmatize a person."[25] The descendants of the Jews and the Moors, they argued, are not the ones who brought about the decline of Spain nor are they the ones who endanger its future. The roots of the decline are in the racist fervor, in the fear of being likened to the Jews or the Moors,[26] and in the aversion to any occupation which might make its practitioner suspect of an "impure" origin.

The forces were unequal, and the tolerant-rational approach remained the heritage of the few: The spirit of "sobriety" was overwhelmed. In the eighteenth and nineteenth centuries, many of the "purity of the blood" laws still predominated in many Spanish institutions. (They were officially repealed by the *Cortes* in 1860.) Indeed, not only was hatred of the Jews and Judaism not forgotten by the Spaniards after the Expulsion but it became a very important factor in the crystallization of Spanish nationalism, and its influence on the development of modern Spain was decisive.

Notes

1. B. Spinoza, *A Theologico-Political Treatise* (trans. by H. M. Elwes) (New York, 1951), pp. 55–56. Elwes erroneously translated "renegades" instead of "converts".
2. On this literature see: H. Beinart, *La Inquisición Española* (Buenos Aires, 1976), pp. 17–22.
3. See: A. A. Sicroff, *Les Controverses des statuts de pureté de sang en Espagne du XVe au XVIIe siècle* (Paris, 1960).
4. J. Arce de Otalora, *Summa nobilitatis Hispanicae, etc.* (Salamanca, 1559), p. 187ff.
5. Juan de Salazar, *Política española* (Logroño, 1619), p. 79ff.
6. Ibid., p. 95.
7. Juan de la Puente, *Convenienca de las dos Monarquias Católicas, etc.* (Madrid, 1612), p. 183ff.
8. See, for example, in B. Peñalosa y Mondragón, *Libro de las cinco excelencias del Español, etc.* (Pamplona, 1629), p. 37.
9. See, for example, Pablo Espinosa de los Monteros, *Segunda Parte de la Historia y grandeza de la gran ciudad de Sevilla* (Sevilla, 1630), p. 90.
10. Juan Ruiz de Alarcón, "La crueldad por el honor," in *Comedias* (Madrid, 1916), p. 463 [=Biblioteca de autores españoles, 20].
11. Arce de Otalora, *Summa nobilitatis*, p. 187ff.
12. See: A. Castro, *De la Edad Conflictiva* (3rd ed. Madrid, 1972), p. 180ff.
13. G. de Huerta, *Problemas filosóficos* (Madrid, 1628), p. 16ff.

14. On this treatise and its author, see: Y. H. Yerushalmi, *From Spanish Court to Italian Ghetto* (New York and London, 1971), p. 122ff.
15. I. del Villar, *Sylva responsorum Juris* (Madrid, 1614), p. 54.
16. A. Fernández de Otero, *Tractatus de officialibus Republicae* (1700), p. 17.
17. I. del Villar, *Sylva*, p. 127.
18. M. de Isaba, *Cuerpo enfermo de la Milicia española* (Madrid, 1594), p. 134.
19. F. Furió Ceriol, *Concejo y Consejeros del Principe* (Amberes, 1559), p. 17.
20. See: H. Méchoulan, "L'alterité Juive dans la pensée espagnole (1550–1650)," *Studia Rosenthaliana* 8 (1974):185ff and also see his *Raison et alterité chez Fadrique Furió Ceriol* (Paris and The Hague, 1973).
21. J. de Huarte, *Examen de ingenios para las sciencias* (Amberes, 1603), p. 258.
22. See: J. H. Elliot, "Self Perception and Decline in Early Seventeenth-Century Spain," *Past and Present* 74 (February 1977):41ff.
23. M. González de Cellorigo, *Memorial de la Política necesaria y útil restauración a la república de España* (Valladolid, 1660), fol. 25.
24. So called after the book of F. Matute, *El triumpho del desengaño* (Naples, 1632).
25. F. de Amaya, *Desengaño de los bienes humanos* (Madrid, 1681), p. 93.
26. The criticism of the attitude toward the *moriscos* grew more bitter following their expulsion from Spain in the years 1609–1614.

11

Jew-Hatred in the Islamic Tradition and the Koranic Exegesis

HAGGAI BEN-SHAMMAI

In the middle of the eighth century, most of the world's Jews, including the autonomous Jewish center in Babylonia, were in lands under the rule of Islam. In the central countries under Muslim rule, the Jews were fewer in number than the Christians. This was the case in Egypt, the Land of Israel, Syria, and also Iraq. The Christian majority underwent a gradual process of Islamization which in a few countries was very slow. In a few of the Islamic countries there are Christian minorities to this very day who have to a great extent preserved their status as the backbone of the veteran urban bureaucracy. Across the borders, there were Christian powers such as Byzantium, Ethiopia, and the Frankish kingdom. The fact that they constituted a threat to Islam provided added strength for the Christians living in Muslim lands.

1. The Tradition of anti-Jewish Literature

From the ninth century onward, out of the ancient tradition, there began to develop a literature of polemics against the Jews, "the people of the Book" (or "the protected people" – both terms referring primarily to the Jews and the Christians) or against the non-Muslims. Not inconceivably, this literature followed old Christian examples, extant before Islam, with parallels in ancient Persian literature as well. Several years ago, Professor Moshe Perlmann wrote an article with an interesting and instructive summary of the anti-Jewish polemic literature.[1] This literature in itself, however, is not our concern here but serves merely as one indication of hatred and scorn for Judaism (and Christianity). No less important an indication, and much more useful, are the decrees generally, though erroneously, called the "Covenant of 'Umar." They were not promulgated all at once but gradually took shape over a few centuries, apparently reaching their more or less final form in the ninth century. There is no doubt that the crystallization of these regulations against the non-Muslims, especially against "the people of the Book," was connected with the name of the caliph Al-Mutawakkil, who reigned in the mid-ninth century C.E.

These regulations were intended to degrade and humiliate both the individual non-Muslim (by the different garb they were made to wear) and the religious group as a whole. One of the most important of the regulations, intended to degrade the entire group, forbade the appointment of Jews and Christians to public positions or positions of authority. We know that this regulation (and not only this one) was not always strictly adhered to in practice. In some countries and some periods there were so many exceptions that it seemed they had become the rule.

We do in fact again and again find Jews and Christians in positions of authority in various Islamic countries at different times; Jews or Christians were even appointed to the office of vizier, the equivalent of a head of state today. Generally, whenever such a thing happened, there was always some religious figure of authority who, at the proper moment, would privately or publicly explain to the rulers how they should conduct themselves, and the affair sometimes ended unpleasantly. Let us illustrate with one story.[2] The 'Abbasid Caliph al-Ma'mun (who ruled from 813–833) honored a certain Jew greatly. To be sure, nowhere is it said that he appointed the Jew to an official position but "he seated him higher than those most dignified – al-Ashraf" (perhaps the occurrence of this term indicated that he seated him even over the descendants of Muhammad who are normally designated as a group by this term). "One of them became angry and sent a note to al-Ma'mun on which the following verses were written:

> O Son of him, obedience to whom was incumbent upon all people, and whose truth was decree and law binding (upon us), He whom thou honorest claims that the father of your fathers[3] (=Muhammad) is nothing but a Liar.

Al-Ma'mun answered him: 'You are right! – ordering at once that the Jew be drowned. Then al-Ma'mun told those who were present the story of al-Miqdad ibn al-Aswad, a friend of the Prophet – how, (when he was on one of his journeys), he was accompanied for a whole day by a Jew. When evening came, al-Miqdad remembered the saying handed down from the Prophet: 'No Jew meets with a Muslim in privacy unless he has some scheme to trap him.'" (Incidentally, this is one version of this tradition. There are tens of parallel versions with variations.) After al-Miqdad promised the Jew that he would not hurt him, the Jew confessed to him: "'I did in fact have a trap in mind. All day I have been planning to tread upon the shadow of your head.' (Stepping on the shadow here apparently has some magical significance: the shadow is the soul and stepping on it is a symbolic act of trampling on the soul, i.e., a kind of killing.) "'How right was the Prophet of Allah,' rejoined al-Miqdad."

As already mentioned, there are many variations of the old sayings. For example, "No Jew remains alone with a Muslim unless he plans to kill him," or "No two Jews meet except to plot the death of Muslims," and many more such. The story quoted was intended against the "protected people" in general and is one of a series of similar accounts. Did the Jew have a separate status? As mentioned, legally the status of the Jew was not different in principle. All the "protected people" were equal, especially the Jews and the Christians. There is even an opinion that the fact that the Jewish communities thrived under Muslim rule for over thirteen hundred years while there was a consistent, evident shrinkage of the Christian population is proof enough of Islam's attitude toward Judaism as against its attitude toward the Christians. It seems to me that this fact indicates, no less, and perhaps even primarily, the nature of the Jewish communities everywhere, not only in the Muslim lands, in contrast to that of the Christian communities.[4] However, it is not my intention to discuss the laws and regulations but rather the Islamic tradition which, while it provides an underlying ideological base for the law, also has a developmental dynamic of its own beyond the letter of the law. The polemic literature, especially that which deals with the Jews, is anchored in this Islamic tradition.

The literature of the Islamic tradition in essence constitutes the continuity of the development of Islam as reflected in the Koran. One of the important findings of the famous Orientalist Goldziher was that the oral Islamic tradition, *Hadith* in Arabic, reflects the development of early Islam and its relationship to historical developments during its first two centuries. A large part of the entire spiritual creativity of Islam in that period developed as oral tradition. It is a vast, complex mosaic composed of an infinite number of tiny pieces (including Islamic historiography). Naturally, Koranic exegesis is the first area in which this creativity took on an oral tradition form. An examination of this literature, especially the exegesis of the Koran, indicates that the main core of the attitude toward Jews and Christians had already been almost fully shaped before 750 C.E. If we accept the proposition that the main decrees against the Jews were first institutionalized in the days of the Umayyad Caliph 'Umar b. 'Abd al-'Aziz about the year 100 of the Islamic Era (i.e., about 720 C.E.), then there is no doubt that there is a close connection between this fact and the crystallization of the attitude toward the Jews in the mid-eighth century which we shall describe below. Our examination indicates that the attitude toward the Jews as reflected in this tradition during that period had already been crystallized in the main centers of Islam: in Medina, in Syria, and in Iraq.

This tradition, shaped over a thousand years ago, has continued with a vital dynamism of its own to this very day. There are many instances of it in twentieth-century literature. For example, the publication containing the discussions at *The Fourth Conference of the Academy of Islamic Research* held in Cairo in 1968[5] has very instructive articles about attitudes toward the Jews. Every year sees the publication of scores of books written by Muslims containing anti-Jewish traditions. Their authors are from various circles: In some of the books the religious outlook is the decisive factor; in some, the secular outlook is couched in European antisemitic terms. In this connection, one should mention an example which is a curiosity. About forty years ago, a work of intrinsic interest was printed in Egypt. It is called *Ifham al-Yahud* ("Silencing the Jews"), composed by Samau'al al-Magribi, an apostate Jew, in the middle of the twelfth century C.E.[6] Samau'al explains how he came to the truth of Islam – after a dream one night – and why the religion of the Jews is so contemptible that it deserves to be degraded and suppressed. This treatise was published in one volume, along with a similar one, also by an apostate Jew who converted to Islam apparently at the end of the nineteenth century. The volume has an introduction by a Muslim scholar named Muhammad Mahmud al-Faqi who, at that time, was the head of some Muslim society. The introduction very precisely repeats all the traditions found in the literature for a thousand years, plus an interesting insertion of a number of motifs from *The Protocols of the Elders of Zion*. This is of interest because at that time the "Protocols" had not yet penetrated the Muslim religious circles but were more widespread among people who had access to modern secular literature.[7]

2. The Curse Against the Jews

A central place in the traditions concerning the Jews is held by the words of the Koran in Sura 2:61/58: "And abasement and poverty were pitched upon them, and they were laden with God's anger; that because they had disbelieved the signs of God and slain the Prophets unrightfully; that because they disobeyed and were transgressors."[8] The reference is actually to the Israelites in the wilderness, but to all of the Muslim exegetes, without exception,[9] it was absolutely clear that the reference was to the Jews of their day. The Arabic word translated as "pitched upon them" also means, literally, that the "abasement and poverty" were decreed for them forever.[10] The "abasement" is the payment of the poll tax and the humiliating ceremony involved. As for the "poverty," this insured their remaining impoverished forever. There are traditions which attribute this interpretation to Muhammad himself.[11] The text continues: "and they were laden with God's anger." Here the text is speaking of a fearful rage decreed upon them forever, and many traditions, in parallel versions repeated again and again in different sources, connect this "anger" with the anger in the Koran 1:7 where are mentioned "those against whom Thou art wrathful." In this verse, Muslims ask that God lead them in the right path, not in the way of those who must bear His wrath. This last is connected to Koran 5:60/65 in which it is said of the Israelites: "Say, Shall I tell you of a recompense with God, worse than that? Whomsoever God has cursed, and with whom He is wroth, and made some of them apes and swine, and worshippers of idols[12] – they are worse situated, and have gone further astray from the right way." Who are the people who have incurred perpetual degradation, who suffer God's wrath forever and who have become the apes and swine referred to in this verse? Many Muslim exegetes interpreted this as referring to the Jews, and some cite various stories of Jews who actually became apes or swine.[13] They associate this with another verse. Koran 5:78/82: "Cursed were the unbelievers of the Children of Israel by the tongue of David, and Jesus, Mary's son," and explain it to mean the Jews who were cursed by David when he passed the house of a certain Jew, or by Jesus when he passed the house of a certain Jew, who because of these curses were transformed into swine or apes.

What is the explanation of this fearful decree? Why were the Jews so terribly cursed? The main reason was that from time immemorial the Jews rejected God's signs, the wonders performed by the prophets. They did not accept the prophecy of Jesus whom the Koran counts among the prophets. But this is all part of the Jews' nature: they are by their very nature deceitful and treacherous. In Sura 2:89/83 it says: "When there came to them a Book from God, confirming what was with them – and they aforetimes prayed for victory over the unbelievers – when there came to them that they recognized, they disbelieved in it; and the curse of God is on the unbelievers." In this connection the tradition recounts that at first the Jews truly hoped for Muhammad's victory over the Arab nonbelievers and said: "Would that Allah send this prophet of whom our Book says that his coming is assured." But when the prophet finally came and they saw that he was not of them, they then denied him out of jealousy of the Arabs, though they knew that in truth he is the prophet. Furthermore, this Jewish trait brought them to grave heresy. They thought that they would succeed not only in leading humankind astray but also in fooling God. Sura 5:64/69 reads: "The Jews have said, God's hand is tied." And in the continuation of the verse: "As often as they light a fire for war, God will extinguish it." Exegetes cite traditions which prove that the Jews always hated the true prophets and put them to death. Therefore they always failed in their wars and their Temple was destroyed time and again. According to one tradition: "These enemies of God (mentioned in the verse) are the Jews. Whenever they kindle the flame of war, God extinguishes it. Never are the Jews found in any land but that they are the lowest of the inhabitants. (You know) that Islam came upon the scene when the Jews were under (the rule of) the Majus (i.e., the Zoroastrians) who are, of all creatures, the most detested by God."

The vile characteristics inherent in Jews are also stressed by the commentaries and traditions dealing with Sura 5:41/45 which reads:

> O Messenger, let them not grieve thee, that vie with one another in unbelief, such men as say with their mouths "We believe" but their hearts believe not; and the Jews, who listen to falsehood, listen to other folk, who have not come to thee, perverting words from their meanings, saying "If you are given this then take it; if you are not given it, beware!" Whomsoever God desires to try, thou canst not avail him anything with God. Those are they whose hearts God desired not to purify; for them is

degradation in this world; and in the world to come awaits them a mighty chastisement.

In his commentary, Tabari[14] cites many traditions on this verse of which these are the main ones:

1. 'Abd Allah b. Suraya was the most expert and wisest of the Jews in Medina. When Muhammad reached Medina, he passed the House of Study (*Bayt al-Midras*). The Jewish sages were dealing with the case of an adulterer and adulteress and could not come to a decision. At their request, Muhammad made the decision for death by stoning in accordance with the Torah. The end of the matter was that Ben Suraya admitted that Muhammad was the most expert in the Torah but that the Jewish sages would not admit it out of jealousy.

2. A Jew tried to lie to Muhammad and claim that the penalty for adultery in the Torah is lashes. Only after Muhammad had him swear by the Torah, did the Jew admit that the punishment is stoning; and added that since adultery is widespread among the Jewish dignitaries who were afraid that they might be exposed if they differentiated in the penalty between dignitaries and the simple folk, they replaced stoning with lashes. At that Muhammad said: "My God, I am the first who has revived Your commandment[15] after these have killed it."

3. A combined version of these two traditions – perhaps a later one – opens with the story as in the first version. The Jewish sage finally admitted that the Jews ignored the Torah's proper punishment for adulterers, that is, stoning, and had substituted lashes. Then, after the Jew had confessed, the verses under discussion were revealed to Muhammad (i.e., 41–44/45–49 of Sura 5).

4. An exegetical tradition ties this verse to those called *munafiqun*: according to the accepted interpretation, a Koranic term for those whose mouths and hearts are not one, that is, who stated that they accepted Islam but secretly remained hostile to it and even actively assisted the tribes fighting Muhammad. Tabari opted for this interpretation and even connected it to the first tradition: The verse refers to 'Abd Allah b. Suraya who told Muhammad that he believed in his prophecy (for he had presented the case for his decision), but in his heart he did not believe.

Tabari explains "Those they are whose hearts God desired not to purify"[16] meaning that God wanted to lead the Jews astray and hence created their hearts this way. They will never walk in the straight path. Further on in the Koran, in 42/46, the Jews are described as (the ones) "who listen to falsehood and consume the unlawful." Most of the commentaries explain "the unlawful" as bribery, and there are those (in a tradition ascribed to 'Ali b. Abi Talib, Muhammad's cousin, son-in-law, and the fourth Caliph) who interpret this also to mean the pay for blood-letting, the dowry for an adulteress, the price of a dog, the price of wine, the price of a dead animal (i.e., one not properly slaughtered), and more.

3. Differences in Attitudes to Jews and Christians

The examples cited here are but a tiny fraction of the material which could be quoted on this subject. An interesting question is: Do the Koran and the tradition differentiate between Jews and Christians? In fact, the attitude would appear to be the same. In Sura 5:51/56 we have: "O believers, take not Jews and Christians as friends; they are friends of each other. Whoso of you makes them his friends, is one of them." Interestingly, the traditions cited in connection with this verse[17] deal with the question: What is the law on consuming animals slaughtered by Christian Arabs and marrying their daughters? This is proof that these traditions are early, since they are from a period when the problem was still acute and the process of Islamization was just beginning. One tradition tended to forbid it, specifically mentioning the Arab-Christian tribe of Taghlib which it compared to the "Christians-of-the-children-of-Israel." (Is this merely confusion or is it directed at the Judeo-Christians?) Another tradition set a special law for the Arab Christians and permitted consumption of animals slaughtered by them and the marriage of their women.

However, there is another verse which differentiates between Jews and Christians. In the same Sura, 82/85: "Thou wilt surely find the most hostile of men to the believers are the Jews, and the idolaters; and thou wilt surely find the nearest of them in love to believers are those who say 'We are Christians'; that, because some of them are priests and monks, and they wax not proud." The tradition connects this verse with another, Sura 3:55/48: "When God said, 'Jesus, I will take thee to Me and will raise thee to Me, and I will purify thee of those who believe not, I will set thy followers above the unbelievers, till the Resurrection day,'" about which there is a tradition: "The Christians are to be above the Jews until the day of Judgment, for there is no land where the Christians are not above the Jews, neither in the east nor the west. The Jews are degraded in all the lands."

In these traditions the Christians have a clear priority over the Jews. If we posit that the early tradition reflects the historical development of early Islam and that the political, economic, and social reality was apt to produce this preference, there is no doubt that these traditions reflect this reality.

As has been stated, this tradition has remained alive to this very day. It is interesting to see this tradition of preference for Christians over Jews in nineteenth-century Egypt. The accounts of the orientalist Edward William Lane's travels in Egypt[18], written in 1835, contain interesting confirmation of this. To be sure, Lane was a Christian observer and clearly a concerned party, but his testimony is generally accepted as reliable. Besides which, the Jewish minority in Egypt at that time was too small to create the impression of being an economic or any other sort of power which might arouse antisemitic associations.

On the difference in the Muslims' attitudes toward the Jews and the Christians, Lane first of all mentions the verse mentioned above, Sura 5:82/85, according to which the Jews are the greatest foes of the believers. Apparently, that is what Lane heard in Egypt, and he says that that is the reason why the Jews are most hated. Later on he recounts the tale of the Jew who greeted another Jew and (in error) said to him "Good morning, sheikh Muhammad," for he thought he was a Muslim acquaintance. The Jews seized the Jew and beat him severely because he thought to wish a Muslim well. Lane heard this account from a Muslim who sought to prove to Lane that Jews would beat anyone who means to wish a Muslim well. Lane also cites a standard phrase which he says he heard in Egypt: "Such a one hates me with the hate of the Jews."

Describing the living conditions of the Jews, Lane reports: "Though their houses have a mean and dirty look from without, many of them contain fine and well-furnished rooms. The more wealthy among them dress handsomely at home, but put on plain or even shabby dress before going out." In his opinion, the reason for this is that the Jews thought they must appear condemned to perpetual misery and degradation in keeping with the interpretation of Sura 2:61/58, as mentioned above.

We have cited only a few examples. Tracing the chain of the tradition is a very arduous task in which scholars more able and gifted than I am have already labored, researched, and brought to light much that is new on the subject. The important thing, however, is that if the oral tradition reflects the developments in early Muslim society, then the traditions about the Jews, without doubt, not only formed the ideological infrastructure of the anti-Jewish legislation but were also a reflection of the actual attitude toward the Jews in the first two centuries of Islam's existence. It is not inconceivable that in these traditions something of the Byzantine or the early Iranian legacy was absorbed. It is also not beyond possibility that apostates had a hand in the matter. It may even be that the influence of these traditions on the Arabic speaking Muslims over the generations was greater than their influence upon other Muslims. For all practical purposes, however, it makes no substantial difference.

Notes

1. M. Perlmann, "The Medieval Polemics between Islam and Judaism," in *Religion in a Religious Age*, ed. S. D. Goitein (Cambridge, Mass., 1974, pp. 103–138); and especially the article (mentioned in the bibliography ibid.) of G. Vajda, *"Juifs et musulmans selon le hadit," Journal Asiatique* 229(1937):57–129 which also extensively treats early Islam's attitude to the Jewish Halakha and the laws of Islam suspected to be of Jewish origin.
2. From the treatise by Ghazi Ibn al-Wasiti (end of the thirteenth century), published with English translation by R. Gottheil, "An Answer to the Dhimmis," *Journal of the American Oriental Society* 41(1921):396,429.
3. The Abbasid caliphs claimed descent from Abbas, Muhammad's uncle.
4. See: S. D. Goitein, *Jews and Arabs* (New York, 1967), especially p. 65.
5. The complete text of the Conference was published in Arabic and English in Cairo in 1970. (Its English title is *The Fourth Conference of the Academy of Islamic Research*). Selections from the English edition were published by D. F. Green, *Arab Theologians on Jews and Israel* (Geneva, 1971).

6. The edition under discussion was published in Egypt in 1939 (and apparently was reprinted there in 1961; see Y. Harkabi *Arab Attitudes to Israel* (Jerusalem, 1972), p.492, n. 7). M. Perlmann published a critical edition of the treatise by Samau'al al-Magribi, with English translation, in the *Proceedings of the American Academy for Jewish Research* 32(1964).
7. On the development in Islam from a traditional hatred of the Jews to antisemitism of the European type, see: Y. Harkabi, *Arab Attitudes*, p.218ff. On *The Protocols of the Elders of Zion* and its connection with the Arab-Jewish conflict, see E. Rubinstein's survey "'The Protocols of the Elders of Zion' in the Arab-Jewish Conflict in Erez Israel in the Twenties" (Heb.), *Ha-Mizrah he-Hadash* 26(1978):37–42.
8. The verse numbers cited are from the European edition by G. Flügel. Where these differ from those of the Royal Egyptian edition, the Egyptian numbers are given first and then the numbers according to the Flügel text. The English rendering is mostly that by A.J. Arberry, *The Koran Interpreted*, Oxford 1964.
9. There are interpretations ascribed to Muhammad's companions such as his cousin, 'Abdallah Ibn 'Abbas. These attributions are most doubtful, but by the mid-eighth century the earliest interpretations were already in writing.
10. The identical expression, in the sense of an everlasting decree, also occurs in Sura 3 of the Koran, 108/112.
11. As was apparently done with most of the traditions during the second century of the Hegira. Most of the traditions cited here are from the comprehensive commentary of Muhammad b. Jarir at-Tabari (died in the year 923 C.E.) and are found in parallel versions in most of the collections of the tradition assembled in the ninth and early tenth centuries C.E.
12. The source of the Arabic word (untranslated in the Hebrew by Rivlin) is apparently Aramaic (there are those who think it reached the Arabic language from the Ethiopic) and means worship of the idols.
13. See, for example, Tabari, part 4, p.293.
14. Part 1, p.232ff. With parallels in all the collections of the tradition. These collections are discussed at length by Vajda (see above, n. 1), pp.93–99.
15. That is, he restored it. In this connection the phrase "revitalizing the commandment" or "revitalizing the custom" was widely used.
16. Ibid., p.238.
17. Ibid., p.277ff. On the Christians of the Taghlib tribe see Vajda, op. cit., p.114 n. 4.
18. E. W. Lane, *An Account of the Manners and Customs of the Modern Egyptians* (London, 1860). For this material see pp.554–556.

12

The Economic and Social Background of Hostile Attitudes Toward the Jews in the Ninth and Tenth Century Muslim Caliphate

AVRAHAM GROSSMAN

1. Introduction and Background

The social and legal status of the Jews in the Muslim lands of the Middle Ages is often described in positive terms. This is, in great measure, influenced by the conditions of Jewish life there as compared to those prevailing in Christian Europe. As a rule, the description is correct. The Jews in Christian Europe did generally suffer more severe harm. The comparison is all the more striking in view of the fact that the Christian Church in Europe generally had an important role in establishing attitudes toward the Jews and developed an all-encompassing ideology justifying their degradation. (This ideology greatly influenced the repeated attacks upon the Jews and the repercussions.) The Muslim Caliphate, on the other hand, had no body parallel to the Christian Church.

This comparison, however, has done a great injustice to the historic truth. During Islam's first three generations the attitude toward the Jews was relatively good, but it gradually grew worse. The decline was expressed in their political, legal, social and security positions.[1] From the ninth century on, the Jews were often faced with hostile attitudes, degradation, persecutions, and outbreaks of violence which took a great toll. These events did not always attract the same attention as the Jewish persecutions of western Europe.[2] The truth is that the Jews who lived in many of the lands of the Muslim Caliphate

that the Ishmaelite exile was difficult. Maimonides felt that there had never been a more difficult one.[3]

The anti-Jewish propaganda in the Caliphate was nurtured by two main motifs: religious and socio-economic. This discussion will discuss the second, seeking to determine whether it already existed in the ninth and tenth centuries, and how important it was in the anti-Jewish preaching and the outbreaks against the Jews. As far as the ninth and tenth centuries are concerned, this question has not really been investigated thus far except for a few notes in studies devoted to other subjects. We shall deal with it from two aspects: the attitude of the government and the attitude of the masses, between which a clear distinction should be made. We shall also use sources from the first half of the eleventh century which, to a great degree, also reflect the moods of the preceding period.

In order to understand the background of those inimical relationships, one must describe, even if only by allusion, the revolution which took place in the economic dealings of the Jews and in their social status at that time. The Jews of Babylonia – who constituted the majority of the Jewish people at the time of the Muslim conquests – abandoned agriculture. This is not the place in which to discuss the reasons, but the sources indicate that in 785 C.E. most of the Babylonian Jews were no longer involved in agriculture. Rabbi Moses, the Gaon of Sura, testified that the decree of the Geonim which permits a woman's *ketubah* (marriage contract) and debts to be collected from movables was due to the fact that "here, most people do not own lands." From what Rabbi Sherira Gaon and others wrote, this decree was promulgated in the year 1096 according to the Seleucid Era, that is, 785 C.E.[4] Clearly, most of the Jews in Babylonia ("here") no longer held land. If only one region of Babylonia were involved, it is doubtful that they would have resorted to a general decree such as this. His statement "but in other places where most of the people do hold land" is to be seen as relating to those areas of Babylonia and its surroundings where the Jews continued to be engaged in agriculture, and apparently also to Spain, where most of the Jewish population were agriculturally occupied until the twelfth century. Many of the Babylonian Jews turned to commerce and joined the new stratum of the middle and upper classes of Muslim businessmen, a stratum which arose and developed at the end of the eighth century and especially in the ninth.[5]

Much evidence of this transfer of Jews into commerce is preserved in the internal and external sources, and especially in the *Responsa* literature. Many scores of responsa of the ninth century and later (especially those of Rav Paltoi and Rav Natronai) touch upon the activities of Jews in local and international commerce within the Muslim Caliphate. Some of these Jews amassed great wealth, and evidence has been preserved of the magnificent and opulent lives many of them led. The literature also speaks of the Jewish bankers in Baghdad, and other members of the court, who actually achieved political greatness and held top positions among the leadership of Babylonian Jewry.[6] The sources do not enable us to know their number, but it seems that they were many. The numerous responsa dealing with this matter support this premise. This change of economic structure also greatly affected the Jewish social image. This is well illustrated in Rav Sherira's statement, from the second half of the tenth century, that the Jewish women of Baghdad are no longer used to doing work that the Jewish women of the villages still continue to do: "and these chores of grinding, baking, washing – we treat them according to the importance of the person and local custom. In the villages we compel them to grind, for the women are accustomed to it; but in Baghdad, where the women are totally unaccustomed to grinding, we do not compel them [to do so]."[7] He even used the phrase "a woman important in wealth." Such was also the reality at that time in various cities of North Africa and Egypt, as indicated by various sources preserved in the Cairo *Geniza*.[8]

Our theory that many Jews were busy with commerce and that a recognizable change had taken place in their life-styles is contradicted by one of the best Arab authors of that period, Al-Jahiz, who relates that the Jews of his day (the mid-ninth century) are also involved in "despicable" trades (tanners, dyers, and the like), and that therefore the masses' hatred of them has grown, but the sources do not confirm this and it is absolutely unacceptable. It may be that this was an expression of his tendency to depict them as despicable in order to lower their respect in the eyes of the Muslims.[9]

2. The Status of Non-Muslims

The legal and social status of the Jewish and Christian *dhimmis* was already clearly on the decline in the Muslim Caliphate of the eighth century, and they were being discriminated against, but in the sources which have reached us there is no evidence of a connection between this decline and the economic status of the Jews and Christians. This decline was especially expressed in the days of 'Umar II, son of 'Abd al-'Aziz (717–720). Ancient traditions – including that of Ibn 'Abd Rabbih (869–940) – ascribe to him the *dhimmis'* having to wear special attire, and later sources also ascribe to him the directive not to employ the *dhimmis* in roles of authority. All this in spite of the fact that in the Covenant of 'Umar, which is primarily of this period, there are no restrictions upon the economic dealings of Jews and Christians, upon their holding public office, and there is no accusation of fraudulent economic misdeeds. This is the case in every available version of this "covenant" in spite of its many aims at discrimination and degradation in the religious and social realms.[10]

The seeds of such a charge against the Jews – that is, that they are not trustworthy – exist in the speciual formula of the oath imposed upon them. According to al-Qalqashandi this oath already existed in the time of Caliph Harun-ar-Rashid (786–809). The oath was accompanied by various threats should the Jews violate it and, in this pattern of threats and the basic degradation which flows from them, it parallels – even in its dating – the "Jewish oath" (*more judaico*) instituted in that period by Charlemagne and, somewhat later, by the Byzantine Emperor Basil I as well. With the connections that apparently existed between Charlemagne and Harun-ar-Rashid, one may even assume that there was some sort of connection between these two oaths specifically intended for Jews. In any case, the fact of its imposition indicated a view of the Jews as untrustworthy, people whose word – and even whose oath – is unreliable, hence the need for various threats in order to frighten and deter them as much as possible from violating the oath.[11] One may assume that such a suspicious approach resulted in a perception of the Jews as those to be suspected of improprieties in their economic dealings. It may even be that the oath originated specifically in the economic sphere.[12]

During the Caliphate of al-Ma'mun (813–833), the son of Harun Ar-Rashid, the status of the Jews noticeably worsened; hostile propaganda increased and became more bitter. It was then, for the first time, that the connection between the Jews' rising economic and social status and the opposition to them was clearly evident; and there was even an attempt to stereotype them negatively. These traditions of al-Ma'mun's attitude toward the Jews should be considered as primarily reliable since they were preserved in a varity of sources: Arabic, Hebrew, and also a single Syrian one.

Fourteenth-century Arab writers – Ibn al-Nakash and Ibn-Qayyim-al-Jauzia – recount that "Caliph al-Ma'mun imprisoned twenty-eight hundred *dhimmis* and ordered the expulsion of many Jews who went to the provincial cities." Afterwards, the following order was issued by the Caliph: "The Jews are the most corrupt of all peoples, the worst among them are the Samaritans, and of them, certain unnamed families – and therefore their names shall not be included in the list of officials of the army or tax offices."[13] The description of the Jews as "the most corrupt people" apparently originates in their being charged with fraudulent business dealings, and hence the directive to remove them from government service and expel them from Baghdad to the provincial cities, if this last detail is indeed reliable. Similar traditions of al-Ma'mun's attitude toward the *dhimmis* and the Jews in particular are also preserved in other sources. Razi Ibn al-Wasiti recounts that he ordered a Jew who had risen to greatness and held an honored position at court to be drowned, merely because of his success and his senior position, without any other charges being made against him.[14] Of special interest is the tradition of the *Hadith* which al-Ma'mun related: Al-Miqdad ibn al-Aswad, one of Muhammad's friends, was travelling with a Jew when he suddenly remembered the Prophet's words that a Jew will not be alone with a Muslim unless the Jew has evil designs upon him. Therefore al-Miqdad asked the Jew what was in his heart, promising him that he (al-Miqdad) would not harm him. The Jew admitted that from the time they had set out, he had stepped upon the shadow of Miqdad's head.[15]

Most serious of all was al-Ma'mun's attempt to harm the office of the Exilarch, and perhaps even to abolish it. Bar Hebraeus – the last of the important Syrian authors – writes that as a result of a contest over the Exilarch's position between two Jewish groups, al'Ma'mun issued a directive that any ten men of "any cult whatever" have the right to appoint their own head.[16] The great esteem in which the Exilarchate was held by the Jews kept them from exploiting this directive, but the Exilarch's status was seriously damaged, as indicated by the writings of the Gaons Rav Sherira and R. Samuel b. Ali.[17] The Exilarch's role as the Jews' representative to the government, his importance in the crystallization of the Jewish autonomy and its operation, the great symbolism of his office for the Jews as a reminder of their past glory – all these explain the tremendous damage inherent in that directive. We have no specific knowledge of what moved al-Ma'mun to restrict the *dhimmis*. However, the fact that what he did was intended to harm the Jews perhaps even more than others and was clearly related to their economic activities and their success, indicates that the latter served as an important factor in this aim.[18]

This situation continued under Caliph al-Mutawakkil (847–861) and to a certain extent was even aggravated. Different sources – even such as are entirely independent and did not draw upon a common source – report varied social restrictions which he imposed upon the *dhimmis*. Significant for us is his order to the officials in charge of the districts not to employ Christians or Jews in administrative posts. He accused a number of the officials of preferring *dhimmis* to Muslims as functionaries, despite the fact that the former abuse their status, oppress the Muslims, are hostile to them, and involve themselves in oppression and deceit. Especially severe is his directive that the *dhimmis* place figures of evil spirits upon the entrances of their homes.[19] Here we have the first instance of recourse to the emotions of the masses. The fear of the devil and evil spirits was, at that time, certainly enough to rouse feelings of suspicion, hatred, and withdrawal from the *dhimmis*, even though there was no strict enforcement of this order and others like it. These things are mentioned in Abu Halal al-'Askari's book *Kitab al-Awail*. It was written in 1005 and, therefore, even if the claim is made that the order is not authentic, it reflects the serious charges against the Jews and Christians which were levelled at the end of the tenth century (the author's time) and which could increase the hatred against them among the masses. Yet, we do not have hard evidence of mass Jew-hatred in al-Mutawakkil's day. Signs of such hatred clearly appear hand in hand with the rise of the Jews to senior positions in the administration and their choice of a luxurious life-style. The beginning of such general mass hatred is customarily attributed to the beginning of the eleventh century in Fatimid Egypt when some Jews and Christians achieved the highest levels of authority, but its traces can already be found a hundred years earlier in the Abbasid Caliphate.

A *contemporary* Jewish chronicler described the history of the famous Netira banking family which had achieved a position of very important influence in the court of the Abbasid Caliph al-Mu'tadid (892–902) and his son al-Muktafi.[20] Though the description is of a somewhat legendary character, it undoubtedly contains an historic kernel because the writer draws upon various realistic de-

He describes the attempt by one of the ministers, jealous of Netira's success, to incite the Caliph against the Jews and the fact that they were miraculously saved. Netira, whose power became even greater as a result of this unsuccessful attempt, refused to take the minister's slaves and most of his possessions, despite their being given him as a gift by al-Mu'tadid. From the entire description it is clear that he was concerned about the hatred of the masses and their jealousy of such a successful Jew. For this reason he and his son Sahl – who served at court after him – made it their practice to distribute charity and valuable gifts to the Muslims. This motif, of refraining from benefiting from the wealth of the Caliph and others, and of helping the non-Jews, recurs in this description a number of times. The writer relates that after they were saved, the Jews lived "quietly and peacefully for the remaining nine and a half years of the al-Mu'tadid reign without any difficulty or calamity . . . that the non-Jews left them in peace and did not press or trouble them at all. Only once did some Sufi riffraff attack them and cause trouble near the Menorat Ha-Maor . . . and from that time on no one dared look at a Jew malevolently."[21]

Indeed, the fact that those who tried to harm the Jews were of the Sufi sect (the mystic movement in Islam) indicates that this incident was religiously motivated; but the fact that the writer repeatedly stressed that Netira and his son refrained from living luxuriously, refused to benefit from government property, and aided the Muslim poor, shows how fearful they were lest their wealth and social status provoke the jealousy of those around them. The entire description indicates that there were attempts by people in authority among the Muslims to do them real harm, attempts rooted in jealousy of their success – and it is difficult to assume that there was no basis for this feeling. But neither in this source nor in any other contemporary ones do we find evidence of violent mob outbreaks against the Jews as a result of this jealousy.[22]

3. The Events in Egypt

The events at the end of the tenth and the first half of the eleventh centuries in Egypt and Spain were clearly and explicitly documented, and inestimably serious. Not only did hatred of Jews because of their economic success and their rise to high levels of authority spread widely among the population, but systematic, very acerbic, anti-Jewish propaganda was produced which depicted the Jew as an untrustworthy, treacherous, exploiter and oppressor of the Muslims. In some instances these characteristics were even attributed to the principles of the Jewish faith.

The outburst of hatred in Egypt came in three waves:

(1) At the end of the tenth century and the beginning of the eleventh, in the time of Yaqub Ibn Killis, the Jewish vizier who had converted to Islam, and after that the Christian vizier 'Isa ibn Nestorius, who was assisted by the Jew Manasseh, who served as administrator of Syria and Palestine. Various Arab authors – including Ibn al-Athir who lived approximately at that time – accused

them of being overbearing, of causing deliberate injury and deprivation to Muslims, and of preferring members of their own group. There were those who found it necessary to mention that Ibn Killis's conversion to Islam was for appearance only but that at heart he still remained a Jew concerned with his fellow Jews, and hence, according to them, he discriminated against the Muslims. According to various traditions, 'Isa and Manasseh were executed by Caliph al-'Aziz, because of the bitter complaints of the Egyptians.[23]

(2) In the days of Caliph al-Hakim at the beginning of the eleventh century.[24]

(3) The accusations against the sons of Sahl at-Tustari and the propaganda against them toward the mid-eleventh century.[25]

The second wave, which was of violent character and in which many of the Muslim masses in Egypt participated, is of special importance: not al-Hakim's own persecutions but what happened in those days at the end of 1011. A short, detailed work (*megillah*) about this event, written by a contemporary Jew, has been preserved. I believe that even here the great hatred of the masses can be explained against the background of jealousy at the Jews' economic success and the posts of authority held by some of them:

The *Egyptian riffraff were jealous of them*, stoned and cursed them, and were exercised over them . . . they winked at them, insulted, mocked, besmirched, attacked, and sought to destroy them . . . and the people panicked and fled for their lives . . . and thousands upon thousands surrounded them and Egypt buzzed with excitement over them and the land was sundered by their cries . . . and the population intended to plunder their wealth and wipe them from the face of the earth . . . and in all the towns and villages of Egypt, in the highway garrisons, and in No Amon they sought to lay hands upon the Jews and gathered against them to *loot and plunder*, to kill and destroy.[26]

The writer is describing something of his time and place and therefore his repeated point about the participation of the masses in the attempt to harm the Jews in different parts of Egypt should be taken as reliable evidence of the great and widespread hatred of the Jews.

What was behind this enmity of the masses? Baron theorized that it was some kind of religious factor whose particulars we do not know.[27] I feel that it would be better related to socio-economic competition, and especially because of the highest senior positions of authority which Jews achieved. We have not found a fanatic religious fervor in the Fatimid Caliphate. Al-Hakim was an exception in being a Shi'ite. The masses were Sunnis. On the other hand, the writer twice stressed that one of the purposes of the outbreak was to loot the possessions of the Jews. A third factor, which supports my interpretation, is that the Muslim sources have preserved evidence relating to that period which contains serious charges against the Jews because of their socio-economic success. Their pinnacle is described in the poem of any anonymous contemporary:

> The Jews in our time have achieved their fondest desires and have gained authority; theirs is the honor and the money; from them come government advisors and the highest of officials. O, people of Egypt! Let me advise you: Become Jews, for even the Heavens have converted to Judaism.[28]

The extravagant life-style of some of Egypt's Jews of that time, with its occasional haughtiness as well,[29] contributed to the development of these hateful feelings. Even if they were few, the poisonous propaganda presented these Jews as the true rulers of Egypt and as representative of the entire Jewish community. If we are correct, this *megilla* contains most valuable testimony to the strength of the hatred which stemmed from the socio-economic situation and which, in particular, successfully reached so many sections of the population (which the author specifically emphasizes!) in every region of Egypt.

4. The Events in Spain

In Spain, we know of two large anti-Jewish outbursts in the first half of the eleventh century, as against the three in Egypt, but their consequences were much more severe and many Jews were killed.

The first occurred at the beginning of the eleventh century at the time of the continuing wars in Cordoba, about 1011, at the end of the Umayyad rule. The second occurred fifty years later, in Granada. In Spain, as in Egypt, the persecutions were accompanied by bitter anti-Jewish propaganda. Its main motif was "the wealth of the Jews as against the poverty of the Muslims," the positions of authority which the Jews had achieved, and "their intention to oppress the Muslim masses." The bitter attack by Abu Ishaq al-Tujibi of Elvira, who had composed a long poem (forty-seven rhymed verses) in which he explicitly called for the assassination of Jehoseph Ha-Nagid b. Samuel and other courtiers as a religious duty, had an especially strong influence. He levelled various religious and social charges at the Jews. On the one hand, according to him, they mock Muslims and their faith and, on the other, they exploit Granada's wealth for their own benefit and oppress the Muslim masses:

> I have seen them (=the Jews) do whatever they wish there (=Granada). They have divided up the city and its residential courts, and everywhere one of these accursed (rules). They collect its taxes and dine gluttonously, they dress magnificently while you are dressed in rags . . . [30]

The land is atremble, as it were, at the crime of the Jews, and all of Granada is on the verge of collapse as a result. The Jews exploit the trust of the Muslims, learn their secrets, but, in actuality, betray them. This is one of the most poisonous poems ever penned against the Jews. It contains most of the antisemitic charges made against them in medieval and modern Christian Europe. There is no doubt that the propaganda was intensified precisely at that time because of the profligate and ostentatious life-style of Jehoseph and his court colleagues which was, in great measure, contrary to that of their predecessors.[31] The fact that this socio-economic motif was so greatly stressed in al-Tujibi's propaganda indicates the extent of the envy and hatred of the Jews because some had attained positions of authority and because of their financial status. The writer knew that this motif would win the masses and stir their hatred to the point of rioting against the Jews. For this reason he wrote his poem in simple language intelligible to all, without the rhetorical and poetic flourishes so dear to the Arab poets of that time.

It is difficult to assume that this propaganda first surfaced in the days of 'Abu Ishaq, that is, in the mid-eleventh century. At the end of the tenth and the beginning of the eleventh, one can find similar propaganda and for identical reasons. A most bitter personal attack was launched against five Jews who had achieved greatness and high position in Muslim Spain between 950–1050: Hasdai Ibn Shaprut, Jacob Ibn Jau, Jekuthiel b. Isaac Ibn Hasan, Samuel Ha-Nagid, and Jehoseph b. Samuel Ha-Nagid. Sometimes the attack was accompanied by charges and polemics against the Jews and Judaism, and in two instances it helped bring about the downfall of these courtiers.[32] Even though the Jewish courtier was clearly doing his best for the country (as in the instance of R. Samuel Ha-Nagid), it was not enough to silence his detractors. The fact that charges against the Jews and Judaism were added (as in the cases of Hasdai Ibn Shaprut and R. Samuel Ha-Nagid) shows that it was assumed from the start that these would strike a sympathetic chord with the masses – and this was in the tenth century.

The polemics, the propaganda, and the atmosphere of hate against those in authority and the Jewish community in general, also found their expression in the works of a number of the contemporary Jewish poets. A study of these works indicates the force of the charges directed against these courtiers in particular and the Jewish community in general, and the special sensitivity to them by these poets. It is a near certainty that they expressed not only their own sensitivity but that of the entire Jewish community.[33]

5. Socio-Economic Factors

These accusations and propaganda against the Jews were grounded in reality: Over the years the Jews had reached the most senior positions, but when the wheel of fortune turned in the second half of the eleventh century and these positions were taken away, the propaganda which called for harming the Jews and their wealth diminished drastically. At the same time, the aim of degrading them (and the Christians as well) and lowering their image in the eyes of their Muslim neighbors remained in force. Clear testimony to this is preserved in the "ideal" constitution for Muslim Spain proposed by Muhammad Ibn 'Abdun at the end of the eleventh or beginning of the twelfth century.[34] Five of its paragraphs refer to Jews and have recommendations to forbid Muslims from cleaning in Jewish or Christian homes ("they are more suited for such tasks which are for lower-grade people"). Likewise, a Muslim may not greet them because they belong to the "cult of the Devil." Jews and Christians were not permitted to dress as did respectable folk and were obliged to wear a badge of shame upon their garments. Anyone selling clothing which they wore – or that was worn by a sick person – must so inform the buyer. It is not advisable to allow Jewish or Christian physicians to heal Muslims because they conspire to harm them. It is surprising that despite the fact that the aim of degrading the Jews and Christians came to so powerful an expression in this suggested legislation, Ibn 'Abdun stopped short of suggesting that they be forbidden to serve in senior positions of authority or that severe economic measures be taken against them (the suggestions in this realm are quite mild). This, it would seem, is attributable to the fact that by that time the Jewish involvement in the royal courts of Muslim Spain had declined greatly (as was also the case in the Christian courts). On the other hand, the fame of their physicians had become widespread and many Muslims sought them out; therefore Ibn 'Abdun suggested limiting the use of their help as far as possible, since they are enemies of Islam, but he also had to be realistic and did not suggest this as an actual law.

Similar accusations against Jewish physicians, doubly caustic, recur in Arabic sources of the twelfth and thirteenth centuries, among them in Razi Ibn al-Wasiti and 'Abd al-Rahim al-Dimashqi. The latter is especially acerbic: According to him, the Jews are the worst of all creatures and hate the Muslims most of all. Outwardly they seem submissive and pathetic, but given the chance, they poison Muslim food. Their physicians are the most heretical of all. According to al-Rahim, they order patients to take harmful medicines and in curing them of one illness cause them another.[35] Among the charges raised against them is one that the Jewish religion requires them to kill the Muslims because they do not observe the Sabbath.[36] Undoubtedly, this poisonous propaganda also springs from the success of the Jewish physicians and fits with the basic facts which emerge from our study: the Muslim envy of the success and rise of the Jews and Christians and the hate propaganda which this jealousy engendered.

There are two possible reservations about the above conclusions:

(a) Perhaps the outbreaks at the end of the tenth and the beginning of the eleventh centuries were primarily nurtured by other factors – religious or political – which were at the basis of this development and connected only coincidentally with the economic and social rise of the Jews and the Christians.

(b) A number of the important Arabic sources dealt with here are late, and the earlier traditions upon which they claim to have relied were written in the context of the polemic literature against the Jews and Christians in the Mamluk period in Egypt. In that case, are these traditions dependable?

Clearly, the socio-economic factor is not to be isolated from the religious and political reality, and certainly there was a close interrelationship between the three. The temptation to exploit the religious component to strengthen unity within their camp, was extremely great for the Abbasid caliphs, most of whom had difficulty imposing their authority upon the vast and varied areas of the caliphate. This was especially so when new tribes and peoples penetrated the lands of the caliphate (Berbers, Turks, and others). There is no doubt that in great measure the religious fanaticism, the anti-infidel propaganda, and the laws against them, were already affected by this reality as early as the ninth century. But two facts argue to the contrary: that the socio-economic factor was no less significant than the other two. The *masses* did not riot against the Jews until their rise to authority was at its peak; in most of these sources the main motif in the propaganda against them is social. This factor is given much greater weight than the religious. The various polemicists and agitators knew that its effect upon the masses would be greater. The events in the Fatimid Caliphate – which, as stated, was not characterized by religious fanaticism – clearly lead one to the same conclusion. It is instructive that in some of these sources the calumniators did not even feel the necessity of resorting to those Koranic texts which were often contrued as commanding Muslims not to permit infidels to amass wealth but to leave them in poverty.[37]

The second reservation, about the reliability of the sources, is also insufficient to refute our conclusions. The extent of the identity between these sources, which like a number of the traditions about the anti-Jewish and anti-Christian measures, indicates that they drew in part from a common source. We cannot determine if that source is indeed early, as they say, but the Jewish literary sources – mostly written at the time of the events themselves – contain enough to teach us the basic accuracy of that picture. This is so with the restrictions and measures of al-Ma'mun, with the attempt to harm the Jewish courtiers in Baghdad at the end of the ninth century, and with the persecutions in Egypt at the start of the eleventh century and in Spain at mid-century.

Another objection to the conclusion of our study – that the economic and social rise of the Jews became their impediment – can possibly be raised from the writings of al Jahiz who, as mentioned, flourished in the first half of the ninth century and was considered among the most important of the early Arab authors. He listed the Jews' low economic and social standing as one of the important factors in their Muslim neighbours' looking upon them less kindly than upon the Christians:

> I shall begin by listing the reasons which have made the Christians more beloved to the masses than the Majus and more acceptable to them than the Jews, more liked, less feared as traitors and untrustworthy, and less deserving of punishment. For this there are many clear reasons and motivations . . . and the greater respect (=of the Christians) by the masses and fondness for them by the community stems from the fact that there are among them secretaries to sultans and servants of the Kings and physicians of the nobility, and spice merchants and money-changers. Among

ATA—G

the Jews [on the other hand], there are only dyers or tanners or blood-letters or butchers or harness-makers. And when the masses saw this among the Jews and the Christians, they assumed [the worth] of the Jew-ish religion among the other faiths to be as [degraded] as their occupations among the other occupations, and that their heresy is the greatest of all since they are the filthiest of the nations.[38]

In this account it is precisely the economic-social rise in status of the infidels which was sufficient to raise their value and the respect for their faith in the eyes of the Muslim masses and to improve the latter's relationship with them. This is how an astute contemporary writer saw it.

A judge may only act on the evidence. The sources I have cited, which deal with actual facts, paint a different picture. Al-Jahiz produced different reasons in his attempt to explain the Jews' being less liked by their neighbors in the mid-ninth century than the Christians,[39] and perhaps because of the difficulty of pointing to a single clear factor he made other claims, part of which were appa-rently in the realm of pure hypothesis. His treatise is intended to make a point and is not noteworthy for its accuracy in other matters either.[40]

Yet, it may be that the difference is actually in the nature of the occupations which al-Jahiz listed, of the kind to improve the status of the infidels. All are in the realm of service to the state or the aristocracy. Though they may have some influence, they certainly do not possess real authority or great wealth. These two factors are the ones which increased the Muslim hatred, for all the honor they carry. If this explanation of al-Jahiz' is correct, then he sketched for us the desirable path for minorities to take in the Muslim Caliphate in order to establish their economic-social status: the middle road, the golden path, which can increase honor but not envy and hatred.

6. Summary

The strong impact and influence of the social and economic status of the Jews on the development of attitudes of hatred toward them in the Muslim Caliphate emerges clearly from the sources dealt with above. The first clear evidence of the appearance of this phenomenon can be found as early as the beginning of the ninth century, when economic development began in various parts of the Muslim Caliphate – a development which by its very nature gave birth to a greater competition between the successful strata of the society. The effect on the masses was less. They joined the cycle of hatred when the Jews were given the opportunity of gaining senior positions of authority, though such Jews were few. The devotion and achievements of these court Jews were to no avail. The xenophobia was deeply rooted in the people's consciousness, and emerged especially when these strangers adopted a life-style for themselves of ostentation and even haughtiness. The hatred was not limited to these foreigners alone but was also directed against all of their coreligionists.

The Jewish society also took this popular hatred as directed toward the entire House of Israel, and this hatred resulted in a similar reaction toward the Gentile, Muslim environment. Hence the praise for Manasseh for his attempts to degrade the "B'nei Kedar" and increase "their degradation," "their rejection," and "their shame." This motif of degrading the Muslims is one of the outstanding ones in the lengthy paean. This is also the source of the hatred of the Muslim environment as it finds expression in various places in the poetic works of Rav Saadiah Gaon, Rav Hai Gaon, and the poets of Israel in Spain.

The Jewish sense of degradation in the Ishmaelite exile is one of the central motifs of these poems. This feeling and the complaints about the difficulties of exile were seen as expressing a general emotion deriving from the fact of the nation's being in exile. They did not seem to have a connection in fact with any specific reality. See, for example, the poem of Rav Hai Gaon in which this sense of degradation is expressed.[41]

From our discussion here it appears that these feelings were also nurtured by specific events, and they are not to be seen as merely a general description. The relationships between the Jewish courtiers and their Muslim environment had a great influence upon the political and social status of the Jews in general in the Muslim lands during that period.[42]

Notes

1. Three main factors molded the (relatively) positive attitude of Islam toward Judaism at the outset: Firstly, the stand of the Koran in principle toward "the people of the book," the Jews and the Christians; secondly, since the Muslims were a small conquering army they needed the services of the Jews and Christians in the administration of the Caliphates and thirdly, the Jews helped the Muslims conquer many areas. In the nature of things, this was a conditional love: the memory of their assistance in the conquests gradually faded and a local Muslim bureaucracy developed (which included many Persian converts to Islam) which looked askance at the Jewish and Christian share in the institutions of government. Even the tolerant stance toward the *dhimmis* ("the protected ones") weakened, and for other reasons – some political – religious fanaticism arose and gradually developed. Only three generations after the appearance of Islam, there were clear signs indicating the decline of the Jews' position. This deterioration and the development described herewith to a great extent parallel (but are *not identical* with) Islam's attitude toward Christianity. On this matter, Islam's attitude toward the *dhimmis*, there is an extensive research literature. See bibliographic listing appended to the entry: "*Dhimma*" in *The Encyclopedia of Islam*, New Edition, II (Leiden, 1965), pp. 230–231. For the subject under discussion here, also see the studies of W. Fischel (n. 6 below); S. Baron (n. 27 below), pp. 120–172; M. Perlmann (n. 31 below); E. Ashtor (n. 29 below); S. D. Goitein, *Jews and Arabs* (New York, 1964).
2. Thus, for example, in the chaotic period in Spain, between 1010–1013, many hundreds of Jews were killed (mainly in Cordoba), and there are those who think the toll was in the thousands (see N. Aloni, "Songs of Zion in the Poetic Works of Rabbi Shmuel Hanagid" (Heb.) *Sinai* 68(1971): 210–234. This event is almost unmentioned in the literature. During the riots in Granada in 1066, according to the figures of the Arab geographers, three to four thousand Jews were killed. The author of *The Scepter of Judah* (Heb.) listed more than fifteen hundred families. R. Abraham ibn Daud of Toledo writes in his *Book of the Kabbalah* (Heb.) "the entire Granada community was killed." Even though logic tells us that these numbers were exaggerated, hundreds of Jews were certainly killed in these outbreaks. The degree of harm done to this important community is not less than that done to the community of Mainz in 1096. Yet what a great difference there is in the research literature dealing with the two of them! Though

this difference is attributable in great measure to the religious, political, and social foundations of the Crusaders' movement of 1096, as well as to the heroic martyrdom of many members of the Ashkenazi communities in those persecutions – two factors which, in the nature of things, claimed the attention of the scholars – there is no doubt that the fact that these scholars were in Europe greatly influenced the character of their research.

3. " . . . that because of our many sins God has confused and agitated us amidst this people, that is, the nation of Ishmael, which does its utmost to disturb us and plan our evil and our hatred when the Blessed One has frightened us and our enemies are mighty, and since a more hating nation has never risen against Israel nor one which has come to degrade us and decimate us and make hating us their chief desire" (Maimonides, *Epistle to Yemen* [Heb.], ed. A. S. Halkin, [New York, 1952]), p.94). But here Maimonides was greatly influenced by the difficult events of the eleventh and twelfth centuries and especially by the al-Murabitun and al-Muhahidun persecutions.

4. The main sources for this edict are: *Letter of Rav Sherira Gaon* (Heb.), ed. Lewin, (Haifa, 1921) p.105; *Gaonic Responsa, Hidden Treasure* (Heb.), paragraphs 22, 65, and in ms. Cambridge, G2; *Thesaurus of the Gaonic Respons and Commentaries, 8: Tractate Ketubot* (Heb.), (Jerusalem, 1938), Responsa section, par. 534. This last source further supports the argument that the edict is a result of the reality in many broad areas: "But Mar Rav Nahshon, of blessed memory, taught us that for the last eighty two years the Exilarch, the two yeshivots, the judges, and the heads of the Kallah are agreed that debts and the *Ketubah* ("marriage contract") are collectible from movables. And letters are written to all the Jewish communities with the authorization of the Exilarch and the four seals of the heads of the yeshivot that any judge who does not collect debts and the *ketubah* from movables is removed from office."

5. On this, see S. D. Goitein's classic essay, "The Rise of the Middle-Eastern Bourgeoisie in Early Islamic Times," in *Studies in Islamic History and Institutions* (Leiden, 1966), pp.217–241.

6. See especially what W. Fischel wrote about them in *Jews in the Economic and Political Life of Medieval Islam* (London, 1937). The Jewish society's great political power is clearly evident in the account of R. Nathan ha-Bavli, in *Medieval Jewish Chronicles*, (Heb.), ed. A. Neubauer 2 (Oxford, 1895), pp.78–88.

7. *Gaonic Responsa* (Heb.), ed. S. Assaf, (Jerusalem, 1927), par. 2.

8. See: S. D. Goitein, *A Mediterranean Society 1: Economic Foundations* (Berkeley, 1967). The source published by Goitein, "Early Letters and Documents from the Collection of the late David Kaufmann" (Heb.) *Tarbiz* 20(1949):197–198 is very important. Important evidence about this structure of the Jewish community in North Africa is also preserved in the responsa literature of the Babylonian geonim.

9. This work of al-Jahiz *The Refutation of Christianity* (Arabic) was published by J. Finkel, (Cairo, 1926). The source was treated by him (and even partially translated into English) in *Journal of the American Oriental Society* 47(1927):311–334. Finkel already sensed the imprecision of the description of the Jewish occupations as given in this work, even though he had only partial sources. See his comments, ibid., at the end of p.319 and p.320. It seems that all al-Jahiz intended to say was that there were more Christians than Jews in the free and "respected" professions. On the other hand, commerce was not yet recognized by everyone as a respectable occupation. See Goitein, n. 5 above.

10. On this pact and its connection with the period of 'Umar II see, in particular, A. S. Tritton, *The Caliphs and Their Non-Muslim Subjects* (London, 1930).

11. Al-Qalqashandi quotes the text of this oath in his book, *Subh al-A'sha*, vol. 13, (Cairo, 1918), pp.266–267 (at the beginning of his discussion of the oaths that were imposed upon the Jews, ibid., p.265). Most of the threats against the Jews if they were to break their oath, originate in the Koran and the Bible (as interpreted by the Koran), such as: "God turned him into an animal as he did the Sabbath-violators, and made them monkeys and pigs . . . and if not (=if the oath is not true) God will decree that you meet someone emerging from the water on Sabbath eve, and God will change your food into pork . . . " On the use of such oaths in the Mamluk period, see: L. A. Mayer, "The Status of the Jews under the Mamluks" (Heb.) in *Magnes Anniversary Book*, ed. F. I. Baer et al. (Jerusalem, 1938), pp.161–167; E. Strauss (Ashtor), *History of the Jews in Egypt and Syria under the Mamluks* (Heb.), 2 (Jerusalem, 1951), pp.197–199. On the text of this oath, attributed to Charlemagne, see: J. Aronius, *Regesten zur Geschichte der*

Juden . . . . (Berlin, 1887–1902), No. 77. On Basil, see: A. Sharf, *The World History of the Jewish People: The Dark Ages*, ed. C. Roth, (Tel-Aviv, 1966), p.65. Though we have no proof of the mutual interrelationship of the three different centers, it is hard to assume that this oath was adopted by the three of them in the same period – if the testimony is at all authentic – strictly by coincidence.

12. Al-Qalqashandi there describes the oaths special "for the members of the Jewish faith" in connection with the swearing of witnesses who are to testify or take on some festive obligation within the context of the Abbasid Kingdom. See Subh al-A'sha (above, n. 11), pp.265–266.

13. The first tradition is cited by Ibn al-Naqash. See: M. Belin, "Fetoua relatif à la condition des zimmis," *Journal Asiatique* 4ème serie 18(1851) pt. II: 444. The quotation was taken from the book of Ibn Qayyam al-Jauziyah (Damascus, 1961), p.219. As for the Samaritans, according to the version in Ibn Qayyam, it is clearly the Samaritans who are meant. Belin, on the other hand, who did not quote the Arabic text of Ibn al-Nakash, translated it as *Juif de Samâra*, and the text is not unequivocal. Their context however tends to an identification with the Samaritans who apparently played an important role at that time in the administration of the caliphate as well. If this tradition is reliable, important information is preserved herein on their status at the beginning of the ninth century. Also see what is written on this elsewhere (n. 18 below).

14. The source was published by R. Gottheil, *Journal of the American Oriental Society*, 41(1921):396. Also see what E. Strauss (Ashtor) wrote on this, *History of the Jews in Egypt and Syria* (Heb.) 1 (Jerusalem, 1944), p.104ff.

15. Razi ibn al-Wasiti: Gottheil, ibid.; and this *hadith* has been preserved in various sources.

16. See I. D. Markon, "Wer ist der in einem Responsum des Natronai Gaon II, erwähnte Karäer Daniel?" in *Festschrift zum 70 Geburtstage von Moritz Schaefer* (Berlin, 1927), pp.130–136. The source for this: *Gregorii Barhebraei Chronicon Ecclesiasticum*, ed. Abbeloos et Lamy, I. (Lovianii, 1872), p.365. For a discussion of this source see the lliterature cited by Markon, ibid., in n. 10, and also Sh. Abramson, *In the Centers and the Diaspora in the Gaonic Period* (Heb.) (Jerusalem, 1965), p.13. A. Grossman, The Babylonian Exilarchate in the Gaonic Period, (Jerusalem, 1984), pp. 53–56.

17. "And in the middle of the rule of the Ismaelites [in] the days of David b. Judah the Exilarch, they were deposed by the government and there was no further heads of the yeshiva of Pumbedita there . . . " (*Letter of Rav Sherira Gaon*, ed. Lewin, [above, n. 4] p.93). Of course, the example of degradation chosen by Rav Sherira is in an area close to the hearts of the Jewish scholarly world, which clearly cannot be taken as an absolute indication of degradation. R. Samuel b. Ali also wrote, in a general context, but providing the same picture: "In the days of David b. Judah the Exilarch, they were removed from the King's service and rejoined the sages and the yeshivot and they were not accepted until the conditions of the yeshiva were imposed upon them . . . " "The Letters of R. Samuel b. Ali Cohen" (Heb.), ed. Assaf, *Tarbiz* 1(1930):67.

18. Perhaps this should be linked to al-Ma'mun's rationalist tendency (his connection with the doctrines of the Mu'tazila), or perhaps he was of the opinion that the Jews had not sided with him sufficiently in his struggle with his brother for the rule, but there is no proof nor support for these hypotheses. The Arab authors mentioned above see his negative attitude to the *dhimmis* in general as a result of the influence of his teacher, Kisa'i. On the other hand, if these traditions are correct (the expulsion of the Jews and the *hadith*), there is enough to show that he had a deep hatred especially toward the Jews. For Al-Ma'mun's attitude toward the Jews, including the matter of the reliability of the above-mentioned sources, see my article, "The Attitude of the Caliph Al-Ma'mun to the Jews" (Heb.), Zion 44(1979): 94–110.

19. This directive is mentioned in various sources of the early eleventh century on. See the sources cited in *The Book of the Jewish Community in Eretz Israel* (Heb.) 2, ed. S. Assaf and L. A. Mayer (Jerusalem, 1944), pp.71–72, and B. Dinur, *Israel in Exile* (Heb.) A, 1(1958), p.91–93.

20. About this family, see W. Fischel, *Jews in the Economic* . . . (n. 6 above), and J. Mann, "Varia on the Gaonic Period, I: On the History of the Gaonate in the X Century" (Heb.), *Tarbiz* 5(1933): 148–179.

21. A. Harkavy, "The Scroll of Netira and his Sons" (Heb.), in *Festschrift zum siebzigsten Geburtstage A. Berliner's*, ed. A. Freimann and M. Hildesheimer (Frankfurt a.M., 1903), Hebrew section, p.39. The writer's style suggests the possibility that he may be (as J. Mann, ibid.

believes,) R. Nathan ha-Bavli (see 6. above).

22. Also in al-Tanuhi's detailed description of the Jewish bankers' activities (including the corrupt dealings which he attributes to them) there is no evidence that they were detested by the masses. See W. Fischel, *Jews in the Economic* . . . (n. 6, above).

23. See Fischel, ibid. and also *The Book of the Jewish Community* 2, pp. 73–74. Especially serious is Ibn Ayas's charge, ibid., about the great harm done by Manasseh to the people of Damascus and by Nestorius the Christian in general because of these two who had achieved greatness.

24. See: *The Book of the Jewish Community* 2, p. 75ff. However, the reference here is not to these persecutions of his; see below.

25. See Fischel, *Jews in the Economic* . . . , pp. 68–69.

26. J. Mann, "A Second Supplement to 'The Jews in Egypt and Palestine Under the Fatimid Caliphs'," *Hebrew Union College Annual* 3(1926):259. The conclusion according to version A, ibid. Also see his work *The Jews in Egypt and in Palestine under the Fatimid Caliphs* 1 (2nd. ed.: Oxford, 1969), pp. 29–33. About the hymn composed upon the Jews' being saved, see B. Z. Halper, "Descriptive Catalogue of Genizah Fragments in Philadelphia, III," *Jewish Quarterly Review* n.s. 14 (1923–24): 255.

27. *A Social and Religious History of the Jews* 3 (Philadelphia, 1957), p. 122.

28. This poem is quoted in various sources and in different periods. See Fischel, *Jews in the Economic* . . . , pp. 88–89, and the three versions of the poet's name in n. 1.

29. These accusations were made frequently as part of the Muslim attack on the Jewish courtiers. In the case of Jehoseph, Samuel ha-Nagid's son, there certainly was real cause. See: E. Ashtor, *The Jews of Moslem Spain* 1 (Philadelphia, 1973), p. 147ff. It could be that there was some sort of basis to the claims that Manasseh preferred Jews and harmed the Muslims. In a paean in honor of Manasseh's son, Adaiah, Manasseh is described as degrading the "Bnei Kedar." (J. Mann, *The Jews in Egypt* 2, pp. 11–12). But it may be that these are only stylistic flourishes of the poet who wrote as a sort of court-poet, not to be taken literally.

30. The poem was published in E. Levi-Provencal's book *Kitab A'amal al 'A'alam: Histoire de L'Espagne Musulmane* (Rabat, 1934), pp. 265–267. See also: E. Garcia Gomez, *'Abu Ishaq de Elvira: Texto arabe de su Diwan* (Madrid, 1925), n. 25.

31. Also see what was written about him: M. Perlmann, "Eleventh-Century Andalusian Authors on the Jews of Granada," *Publications of the American Academy of Jewish Research* 18(1948/49):284–290; M. Perlmann, The Medieval Polemics between Islam and Judaism, in: S.D. Goiten (ed.), Religion in a Religious Age (Cambridge, Mass, 1974), pp. 103–138; E. Ashtor, *The Jews of Moslem Spain* 2 (Philadelphia, 1979), pp. 186–187.

32. See M. Perlmann, ibid., p. 269ff.; S. M. Stern, "Two New Data about Hasdai b. Shaprut" (Heb.), *Zion* 11(1946):141–146; E. Ashtor, *The Jews* 1, pp. 181–182 and 2, p. 41ff; N. Aloni, (n. 2 above): 215ff.

33. See N. Aloni, ibid.

34. Published by E. Levi-Provencal, "Le traité d'Ibn 'Abdun," *Journal Asiatique* 224(1934):177. (A Hebrew translation is quoted by N. Aloni, n. 2 above, pp. 213–214).

35. See: Gottheil and Ashtor, (n. 14 above).

36. See ibid. This is an example of the absurd claims among those raised against the Jews for, according to the Halakha, a non-Jew is forbidden to be scrupulous about Sabbath observance (a pagan who kept Sabbath is deserving of death). See *TB Sandhedrin* 58b.

37. Sura, 2, verse 58 (regarding the Jews); Sura 3, verse 108.

38. Cairo edition (n. 8 above), p. 17.

39. Even if we do not accept his testimony about the occupations of the Jews, nor all of the factors to which he ascribes the negative attitude toward the Jews, it is difficult to argue with his evidence that at that time the Jews were considered less desirable in their Muslim environment than the Christians. The main thrust of his propaganda there is against the Christians, whom he sees as the main competitors of Islam in his day, helping the growth of heretical movements. Therefore, it is inconceivable that he should have deviated from the truth in this testimony. He is supported by another Arab author active in that period in Babylonia (the beginning of the ninth century): al-Harith al-Muhasibi also testified, as something clearly understood, that in his day the Jews "are in the eyes of all Muslims worse than the Christians." *The Book of the Patronage of the Law of Allah* (Arabic) ed., M. Smith [London, 1940], p. 256). In his opinion, this was because the Jews denied Muhammad though they knew the truth, i.e., that he is God's messenger. In this case, as well, the reason (doubtful in itself) should not be

connected with the evidence about the actual situation. The evidence of these two authors about the inferior status of the Jews in their day in the eyes of their Muslim surroundings is of great value.

40. On this tendentiousness and its causes, see Finkel, *"The Refutation . . . "* (n. 9 above), pp.318–319.

41. H. Brody, "Religious and Laudatory Poems of R. Hayya Gaon" (Heb.), *Yediot Ha-Makhon le-Heker ha-Shirah ha-Ivrit* 3 (1936): 12–13.

42. This phenomenon also recurred later in Christian Spain. See H. Beinart, "The Image of Jewish Courtiership in Christian Spain," in *Elite Groups and Leadership Strata* (Heb.) (Jerusalem, 1967), pp.55–71.

13

"Blood Libels" in the Ottoman Empire of the Fifteenth to Nineteenth Centuries

JACOB BARNAI

In the sources and studies of the Ottoman Empire from the fifteenth through nineteenth centuries, about eighty "blood libels" are mentioned, and apparently there were more. We know of about ten Turkish firmans from this period against "blood libels," but though these libels abounded in the Empire during this period, especially in the nineteenth century, it does not mean that the Ottoman authorities' attitude toward the Jews was negative. The opposite was the case.

1. Background

The Ottoman Empire extended over vast areas and many countries of Europe, Asia, and Africa. We shall here treat only of the area which can be designated "the heart of the Empire": Turkey, Greece, and the Syrian Province which includes Palestine. In these districts, the central government was more efficient and more centralized than in the distant European and Asiatic provinces. From many points of view, these countries constituted a unit in other matters as well. The Ottoman Empire was a Muslim state and the religion of Islam was a deeply ingrained part of its being: in its law, in its regime, and in every facet of its life. Islam guided its course, and the chief differentiation which the Ottoman government made between the population over which it ruled was between the Muslims and the non-Muslims (the *dhimmis*), in the best classic Muslim tradition.

The Ottomans conquered many lands with mixed populations: Muslims, Christians, and Jews, together with their various sects. This empire was founded mainly on the ruins of two kingdoms: one, the Mameluke, chiefly in the

ATA=G'

189

regions of Syria and Egypt and with a population which was mainly Muslim with a Christian-Jewish minority; the second, the Byzantine Empire, primarily in Turkey and the Balkans, whose population was Christian-Greek Orthodox and Armenian, with a Jewish and Muslim minority. Legally, in principles, there was no difference between Jews and Christians: They were included equally in the *Ahl-al-Dhimmah* framework, as separate groups normally designated as *millets*. In practice, however, one can generalize and say that for several reasons the Christians were discriminated against more than the Jews.

Though there had been Jews in the territories of the Empire since the Byzantine period, who were called the "Romaniots," most of them had come after the expulsion from Spain at the invitation of the Ottoman state and at a time when Europe's gates were closed to them. The Ottoman state was interested in those Jews for it benefited from them economically. They brought with them the progress which Spanish Jewry had enjoyed in all walks of life. Another factor in this preferential status was the fact that the Jews did not constitute a factor dangerous to the Ottoman Empire, unlike the Christians against whose nations the Turks fought in Europe and saw as a constant, threatening foe. In official Turkish documents we find a clear distinction between the Christians, who are termed "infidel," and the Jews who are not.[1] This clearly shows the distinction made by the authorities between the two faiths and is at variance, we feel, with what is usually found in the scholarly literature which includes all non-believers in one category.[2] Withal, one must remember that the Ottoman Empire was generally tolerant of other faiths and groups – an attitude which stemmed from its economic and political needs as well as from the pressure of the European countries, especially from the beginning of the seventeenth century on, when the European influence and pressure grew ever stronger. The heterogeneity of the population also brought about official tolerance. The Jews and the Christians were active participants especially in many areas of the economy and the society, but not on the senior political levels. Many Jews and Christians served in important political and economic advisory capacities in the court of the "Sublime Porte" and those of the local rulers in the provincial cities and provinces. One can say that from a practical standpoint the policy was generally one of tolerance in spite of the exceptions which showed up in the provinces; yet in this relatively stable system there were very many outbreaks of "blood libel." To study this, the period must be divided into two parts: Until the middle of the nineteenth century there were very few; from the second half of that century there were many.

2. The Blood Libels

The blood libels occurred primarily in cities with a Christian concentration, especially a large Greek concentration: in Smyrna, Constantinople, and other cities. Almost all, of course, took place around Passover time, and originated in the disappearance of Christians – children, clerics, and others – with the Jews being accused of killing them in order to use their blood in the baking of *matzot*. At times, actual pogroms resulted – for example, in Smyrna in 1872 and in Constantinople in 1874 – and only the intervention of the Turkish police kept matters from deteriorating. In 1870, in Constantinople, Jewish merchants' sacks were opened in the *suq* (the public market) because it was thought that they held Christian children; and in 1872 a synagogue on the island of Marmara was razed to the ground by the Greeks. The Jews on this island, fearing a pogrom, found refuge with the Turks. They turned to the rabbi of Constantinople and the culprits were apprehended. Three months later, the Greeks continued to shoot at the Jews, looted their food and wine stores, and there were many other similar incidents.[3]

Two main factors seem to explain the penetration and spread of the blood libel in the nineteenth century:

1. The growing influence of Europe in the decaying and deteriorating Ottoman Empire. This was a political influence which was followed by cultural and financial penetration, along with modern antisemitism. This is the reason that the phenomenon occurred in the nineteenth century and in the Mediterranean port-cities where the influence of the European consuls, especially of the representatives of the Catholic countries such as France, was great. Since the sixteenth century the French had been recognized as the protectors of the interests of the Christians in the Empire, and this also strengthened their position in defending the interests of the other churches until the mid-nineteenth century.

2. The wars between the Greeks and the Turks contributed to the development of the blood libels. These wars, begun at the end of the eighteenth century at the instigation of the European powers, continued with the attaining of Greek independence in the 1830s and, as the century wore on, with the Greeks' struggle to free more territories from the Turks. In the nineteenth century, the Greeks in Turkey began to become an agitating factor. The Jewish problem and the blood libel were exploited as a means of creating political unrest in Turkey. This explains the epidemic of blood libels, especially in Smyrna and Constantinople, starting in the sixties of the nineteenth century. During this period, there was hardly a year without a blood libel of Greek origin.

One must also remember that the Greeks and the Armenians saw the Jews, almost from time immemorial, as competitors in many economic areas of the Ottoman Empire. For example, the production of textiles, almost a Jewish monopoly in the Ottoman Empire of the sixteenth and seventeenth centuries, slowly passed into Armenian and Greek hands, and the competition between them, primarily in the eighteenth century, was very fierce.

In international commerce, in tax-farming in the Empire, and in other areas, the competition between Jews, Greeks, and Armenians spread as well. Smyrna, which was a prime economic center in the Ottoman Empire and the most important Turkish port of that period, served as the base for the econo-

competition of the Jews and the Greeks. Europeans who spent time in Turkey in the late eighteenth and early nineteenth centuries attest to the strained relationships which prevailed between Jews and Greeks in the Turkish cities of that period. At the beginning of the nineteenth century, a Greek Orthodox monk named Neophytos, who claimed he was an apostate Jewish rabbi, wrote a bitterly antisemitic tract called *The Confutation of Judaism and its Customs.*[4] The book was disseminated in a number of Balkan and other European languages and gained great acclaim and distribution among the Greeks in Turkey. A large portion of the book described the use of Christian blood in the baking of *matzot* (the unleavened bread of Passover). Among other things, he wrote of his Jewish childhood and said: "When I was thirteen, my father revealed to me the mystery of the blood and warned me and made me swear by heaven and earth that I would never reveal the secret. If I should marry and have ten children, I should reveal the secret only to one."[5] Further on he wrote that this matter of blood which the Jews take from the Christians for Passover use is known only to the rabbis, and he detailed the religious and social reasons for its use. As stated, his claim that he had been a Jew in his youth and knew the religious secrets of Judaism from within was very effective in spreading the blood libel among the Greeks in nineteenth-century Turkey.

It is of interest to note that while the initiative for most of the blood libels was Christian, a small number Armenian, but mainly Greek, the reactions of the foreign consuls in the cities of the Ottoman Empire were not identical. Protestant consuls, especially British and Prussian, attempted to fight the blood libels, whereas the tendency of the Catholic consuls, such as the French, was to support them. For example, the French consul supported the Damascus libel while the British and Prussian consuls in Palestine fought libels of this kind. In another case, before Passover 1871, the British stationed a frigate off the port of Smyrna at the request of the British Jews to prevent an expected blood libel.

What was the position of the Turkish government? From the outset of the phenomenon of blood libels in the fifteenth century, the Ottoman authorities rejected them and, apparently, so did the Muslim population of the Empire. The firmans issued by the Sultans unequivocally condemned the blood libels. The firman from the beginning of the seventeenth century[6] which was published by the late Uriel Heyd and the firman which Montefiore received at the time of the Damascus Affair[7] are only samples of the regimes' absolute rejection of these charges. However, as the European intrusion and the Greek rebellion against the Turks grew stronger, the importance of the Turkish firmans generally diminished and the Empire totally declined.

These firmans were of help to the Jews till the nineteenth century, but then they had to fight the blood libels primarily by seeking the intervention of the Jews of Europe. In the nineteenth century, the trend for Jews to organize internationally continued to grow. When the Western Jews began to organize, they came to the aid of the Jews of the East in their struggle against the libels.

Renowned for their activities in this regard are Montefiore, Cremieux, and the "Alliance," as well as personalities such as members of the House of Rothschild, Baron Hirsch, and others, who participated in the effort to prevent blood libels in Turkey, but were not always successful. Noteworthy, also, is the important role played by the European and Jewish press which contributed greatly to publicizing the blood libels in the Empire and helped to create a public opinion sympathetic to the struggle.

3. Summary

In sum, the Ottoman Empire government's tolerant and sympathetic attitude toward the Jews is clearly indicated when dealing with the blood libels. Most of these libels came from Greek Christians, nurtured by the traditional and modern Christian anti-Jewish influence. Likewise, the charges stemmed from the economic competition between the Christians and the Jews. The Jews were no danger to the Ottoman Empire whereas the Christian factor was ever hostile; hence the preferential attitude enjoyed by the Jews in the Empire. This certainly caused Christian jealousy of the Jews. It should be noted that until the nineteenth century the blood libels were very few and could be defined as an anomaly, whereas in the nineteenth century they proliferated. The numerous blood libels in the Ottoman Empire caused an increased interest of the European Jews in their eastern brethren. The involvement of the representatives of the European powers in this problem indicated this region's importance in nineteenth-century international affairs. One can say that along with the Enlightenment, modernization, and the spirit of the new times, modern antisemitism penetrated the Ottoman Empire from Europe. In the Empire's Christian population it found an infrastructure which was prepared to absorb it.

Notes

1. See, for example, a 1577 firman about the garb of the Christians and the Jews in the Ottoman Empire in A. Refik, *Istanbul Hayati* (Istanbul, 1930–35), p. 51.
2. See, for example, S. J. Shaw, *History of the Ottoman Empire and Modern Turkey* 1 (Cambridge, 1976), pp. 163–164.
3. See the following bibliography for additional examples of blood libels.
4. E. G. Jab (pseud.), *Le sang chrétien dans les rites de la synagogue moderne*, (Paris and Reims, n.d.).
5. According to R. Walsh, *Narrative of a Journey from Constantinople to England* (London, 1828).
6. U. Heyd, "Ritual Murder Accusations in 15th and 16th-Century Turkey" (Heb.) *Sefunot* 5(1961):140–144.
7. A. M. Luncz, *Erez Yisrael Almanach 1896* (Heb.) (1895):9–12.

For Further Reading

A. Ben-Yaakov. "Firman against Blood Libels of 1866", (Heb), in *Sinai* 55(1964): 169–170.
A. J. Brawer, "New Material on the Damascus Affair" (Heb.), in *Shmuel Krauss Jubilee Volume* (Jerusalem, 1937), pp. 260–280.

H. J. Cohen, *The Jews of the Middle East 1860–1972* (Jerusalem and Toronto, 1973), pp.9, 16–17.

B. Z. Dinur (Dinaburg), "The Political Character of the Damascus Affair" (Heb.), *Hashiloah* 41(1924): 518–528.

S. Dubnow, *History of the Jews* 5 (South Brunswick, N.J., 1973), pp.392–394.

S. Ettinger, *Modern Times* (Heb.) [=*History of the Jewish People, 3*], ed. H.H. Ben-Sasson (Tel-Aviv, 1969), pp.131–137.

M. Franco, *Essai sur l'histoire des Israelites de l'Empire Ottoman* (Paris, 1897), pp.220–223.

A. Galanté. *Histoire des Juifs d'Anatolie*, 1 (Istanbul, 1939), pp.183–199.

A. Galanté, *Histoire des Juifs d'Anatolie*, 2 (Istanbul, 1939), pp.125–135.

U. Heyd, "Ritual Murder Accusations in 15th and 16th Century Turkey" (Heb.), *Sefunot* 5(1961): 135–150.

E. G. Jab (pseud.), *Le sang Chrétien dans des rites de la synagogue moderne* (Paris and Reims, n.d.).

J. M. Landau, "Ritual Murder Accusations and Persecutions of Jews in 19th Century Egypt" (Heb.), *Sefunot* 5(1961): pp.415–460.

A. M. Luncz, *Erez Yisrael Almanach 1896* (Heb.) (1895):9–12.

A. R. Malachi, *Studies in the History of the 'Old Yishuv'* (Heb.) (Tel Aviv, 1971), pp.79–89.

M. Maoz, "Changes in the Situation of the Jewish Community in the Land of Israel in the Mid-19th Century". (Heb.), *Keshet* 48 (Summer, 1970): 5–16.

M. Maoz, *Ottoman Reform in Syria and Palestine 1840–1861* (Oxford, 1968), pp.189–240.

14

Antisemitism and Economic Influence: The Jews of Morocco (1672–1822)*

SHALOM BAR-ASHER

1. Introduction

An important new element has been introduced into the study of the history of antisemitism in Europe. Earlier scholars explained antisemitism as the result of anti-Jewish prejudices, such as that Jews are exploiters and parasites, or that they are essentially evil. Other explanations were that Jews served as scapegoats for the frustration of the masses at the injustices of the authorities, or that there is an innate hatred of them. All of this was before the characteristics of the Jews as a group had become clear. Even if the explanation for the hatred is, for example, real differences between Jews and their environment, the results seem to be all the same. For why was it, then, that when Jews in the eighteenth and nineteenth centuries "improved" themselves – in their concepts, their life-styles and their religious practices – and became integrated into their environment, they still continued to be the target of hatred. The "reformed" Jew was hated even more than the traditional Jew. Therefore scholars now explained that the hatred was the fruit of the general anti-Jewish stereotype which has a long and multifaceted history. Its roots are to be found in Roman writings, in the fact that the Jews were the only ones who rejected idolatry and emperor-worship; then the stereotype was transmitted through the Church Fathers in the Middle Ages to the eighteenth and nineteenth centuries; and is to be found in all phases of life – in the economy, in society, and in all aspects of culture: thought, literature, art, theatre, folk-humor, and so forth. In times of actual economic, social, and political crises, these stereotypes have erupted in hatred and violence against the Jews. The continued expression and crystallization of this antisemitic stereotype has been treated most thoroughly by Professor Shmuel Ettinger.[1]

---

* To my teacher and mentor Professor Shin'ar on his 70th birthday.

The question is whether this explanation fits the relationship of Jews and Muslims in eighteenth-century Morocco and, if so, to what extent.

This discussion relates primarily to the images of the Jews as seen through the eyes of their Muslim neighbors in their daily interrelationships. For a full description of this pattern of relationships we need, on the one hand, many and varied literary sources: From the Muslim side, for example, *fatwas* (responsa of the Islamic law), *khutbat* (sermons, especially those preached in the mosque on Friday), the description of the Jews in Arab historiography, in the folk literature, in tale and legend, and the other areas of folklore; and on the other, sources for the history of these relationships in actuality, about mutual meetings in the Muslim city and the Jewish neighborhood, joint business ventures, mutual aid and contacts against a background of social and religious confrontation. But this is precisely the problem. The sources available for the period under consideration are too meager to provide a complete and reliable picture of these interrelationships.

We must therefore make do with a few remarks for the most part based on Hebrew sources (legal decisions, responsa, sermons, rabbinic decrees, and the like) which shed some light, albeit very one-sided, upon this set of relationships,[2] and on the works of the European travelers who tend to generalize[3] and sometimes even exaggerate in their theories.[4] The result, then, is that we learn of the Muslims' attitude toward the Jews not primarily from their own words but from the way in which the Jewish society depicted them or by Muslim behavior as seen by outsiders (for example, the travelers).

Here we should point out that the set of relationships was not very complex because every group lived in a separate section of the city[5] and tended to live out its life within its own confines. The relationship, therefore, was carried out at a distance and was not the result of close, continued contact. What is more, from the religious standpoint, there was in Muslim-Jewish relations no sense of grave competition over being the divinely chosen – and this was also true in Morocco – for which reason the religious polemic, characteristic of Christian-Jewish relations in the Middle Ages, and the modern ideological debates, were generally absent.[6] Hence, our comments will be generally limited in character and restricted to periods of severe pressure by the authorities and society when the savants loosened their tongues and denounced their opponents without restraint, in contrast to periods of normalcy when their hatred was generally suppressed.

2. Islamic Images of Jews

The earliest images of the Jew in the eyes of the fathers of Islam and its adherents are already found in the Koran and *hadith* (the body of oral tradition transmitted in the name of Muhammad and subsequently committed to writing). Jews are seen first and foremost as infidels and the Koran has a specific commandment to degrade them.[7] These images almost certainly influenced not only the Muslim religious establishment but also the masses who fulfilled the Koran's commandments, albeit only perfunctorily. They also heard the oral traditions which generally refer to the Jews even more severely than does the Koran.[8] In part of the traditions the Jews are debased forever, cursed and anathematized by God to the end of time, and so rejected by Him that they can never repent; some of them were even turned into monkeys and pigs. They have been frightfully execrated, but, since they are by nature cheats and traitors, they denied Muhammad and were jealous of his success. From then on and ever after they have been defiant and stubborn, rebelling against the true prophets and killing them. "Jews are never found in any land but that they are the lowest of its inhabitants." The Jewish sages falsified the Torah, and the Jews in general are liars, take bribes, and eat carrion. In many of the traditions, the Christians are preferred to the Jews because the latter are the stronger in their hatred of the Muslims.[9] Since the people of Morocco and the Maghreb generally are known for their extreme religiosity and attachment to the Koran and its traditions, these images of the Jews undoubtedly took hold among them.

The few mentions that remain from the period under discussion indicate that the Jew (and the Christian as well) was treated as an infidel[10] or as one who is unclean. For example, there is the account of a Muslim who returned from the *Hajj* to Mecca and, upon being asked by Jews to deliver some letters for them, refused lest he impair the purity he had acquired through the pilgrimage. The same phenomenon is found in nineteenth- and twentieth-century Morocco: A pilgrim who wished the blessing which had enwrapped him at the *Hajj* not to leave him, should not go to the market lest he be seen by a Jewish eye (apparently for the first period after his pilgrimage to Mecca).[11] Jew and Christian are accursed especially when the holy spirit envelops the "faithful." For example, upon concluding prayer, a Moroccan Muslim will say "Allah curse the Christians and the Jews."[12] Likewise, one may assume that the close watch kept upon the movement of Jews in the vicinity of places holy to Islam also stems from this attitude. As we know, one of the restrictions particularly enforced by the Moroccan authorities until the latter part of the nineteenth century was that Jews must remove their shoes when passing a mosque.[13] However, our concern is not with the occasional practical expression of prejudices and stereotypes but with their crystallization in the religious tradition and their eruption in times of crisis.[14]

The Jew was also seen as a sinner who causes drought and famine in the land. The English traveler Windus tells of a ceremony held in Meknes in 1680, the year of a severe drought in Morocco. The Muslim religious leaders conducted a service to induce rain, and when they were exhausted from their prayers they called upon the Jews: "To be sure, God will not heed their prayers but he will send rain in order to be rid of their supplications, to purify the foul air which they exude and cleanse their stinking feet."[15] If these words are correctly quoted, we have not only the Muslims' image of the Jews but also their dual attitude: Though God does not listen to the Jews' prayers, they should be still turned to[16] as a last resort. In another source, from 1737 (also a year of serious drought in Morocco), the Jews of Fez are informed that the Muslims have convened a meeting to clarify the causes of the drought, and from the tenor of the remarks it seems they wish to blame the Jews.[17]

This duality is also well known in Europe. The depiction of the Jews as debased and degraded is characteristic of the Middle Ages. For example, in the pair of statues placed at church entrances, a beautiful, victorious woman symbolized Christianity while the other woman, the Congregation of Israel, has her face covered, her staff broken, and her head hung in shame. Yet on the other hand, there is the stereotype of the Jews' lust for unjust gain by which they have amassed fortunes through usury, exploiting society, and dominating it; or their practice of bribing innocent Christians to hand over the holy wafer, which in Christian tradition is transmuted into the body of Christ, in order to desecrate it and to stab it till blood flows forth.[18]

The same is true of Morocco: The Jews are sometimes presented as weak, sometimes as omnipotent; they are infidels, but God sometimes heeds their prayers more than those of others, and there are many more such contradictions.[19] In all honesty, however, one must differentiate between Europe and the Islamic lands in the strength of the relationship and its consequences: Whereas in Europe it often led to pogroms and horrible slaughter, in Morocco and elsewhere its practical impact was relatively minimal.

The first source mentioned above contains the image of the Jews as exuding a foul odor. When I was growing up, an expression widespread among Moroccan Muslims was *ulad zifa* or *bni zifa*, the sons of carrion. One may assume that this expression was also common in earlier centuries. In a letter of another period, from 1887, in which the sages of Fez and its residents recount their tribulations, we are told that the new ruler in Fez, shortly after his recent appointment, decreed that Jews may not buy flowers because "fragrance and perfumes are unbecoming to Jews."[20]

3. Folk Tradition

Literary and folk works of another period which were committed to writing in the twentieth century are sources of another sort and are likely to reflect the reality, not only of the time they were compiled, but also of earlier periods including the eighteenth century. A genre which has certainly retained a kernel of truth is that of the folk traditions. The origin of the term *mellah* is an example: It seems to lie in the name of the site upon which the new Fez was built, part of which was the first Jewish quarter in Morocco. And the roots of that seem to be in the mines of salt (*milh* in Arabic) near the city. However, none of this is completely certain.[21] But the reasons given by Rabbi Yosef Mashash, one of the greatest of the Moroccan rabbis of the last generation, based upon a tradition preserved over the generations, attest to the Muslim attitude toward the Jews. And since no sects developed in the nineteenth century, obviously these were in existence earlier. "First, it is said that the Jews used to salt the heads of the king's enemies killed in battle which the king would bring back, and this is still the practice (as I myself have seen); the one doing the salting is called in Arabic *al-mallah* and the Ishmaelites deprecatingly call the street of the Jews after this despicable work. Second, it is said that the meaning of *mellah* in ancient Arabic is cast away," which is a derogatory term to indicate that the street of the Jews is something tossed away like an unwanted item."[22] True, according to the rules of Arabic etymology there is no basis for the last explanation, but this is no concern of folk-etymology.[23] These traditions may also be explained by the fact that, since the twenties of the eighteenth century, thirty rebels against the kings were hung upon the gates of the mellah at Meknes.[24]

A source which has been partially investigated, the folk-tale, hints at an interreligious, intersocietal tension which existed in Morocco. A study of seventy-one tales from Morocco revealed that a third of them contain descriptions of all sorts of intergroup, interreligious contact which for the most part is tense and contentious. The Jew, who is sometimes of high station – an administrative leader or a rabbi – is always required to carry out some task, to answer questions, to pay the highest tax, and the like. As is the case in many folk-tales, the Jews succeed in vanquishing the evil lord or having the decree cancelled, a motif which is often more wish than fact.[25] One story begins as follows: "In the city of Meknes there lived a wicked king who hated the Jews very much and caused them much trouble. How? He would levy heavy taxes upon them, forbid them commerce, force them into the mellah . . . "[26] Part of this description reflects the historical reality of the eighteenth century.[27] But whether it is true or not is unimportant. More important is the fact that if this tale was told around that time it attests to a certain image of the Moroccan authority held by many of the Jews. The same apparently is the case for folk tales among the Muslims, of which we have no knowledge.

The popular play also presents informative descriptions of how the Jews looked to their neighbors, and their interaction. However, for the time being, only one Moroccan play is known: on the legend of "Ibn Meshal." Its possible influence is reason for citing it here. The widespread version tells of a Jew by that name who terrorized the Muslims in the region of Taza, northeast of Fez, became king, and was wont to exact an annual tax from the residents of Fez in the form of a beautiful young Muslim maiden whom he would add to his harem, until along came Moulay Alrashid, founder and first king (1666–1672) of the 'Alawid dynasty, and killed him. In a comprehensive study, the prominent French scholar Cenival has proven the entire tale to be contrived, that is, so that the oppressed victim became "king." The fact is that Rashid, who was in need of money, did not recoil from murdering a wealthy Jew from the village of Dar ibn Meshal on Mt. Beni Sensasen in northeast Morocco. The distorted recollection in this legend is the basis for the annual holiday of the students in Fez – "'Id Sultan a(1)Tulbah" – in which they select a student sultan who receives gifts from his subjects. There is no doubt that the annual presentation of this legend in an elaborate ceremony enforced the anti-Jewish stereotype.[28] And since Fez was a central city in Morocco, especially in matters of religion and faith, this festival certainly had repercussions in other places.

A detailed study of the proverbs prevalent among the Moroccan populace in the twentieth century shows that Jews and Muslims view each other negatively. One of the common stereotypes in these proverbs is of the Jews as untrustworthy and hostile to both Islam and Muslims. They are always scheming against the Muslims and seeking ways to cheat them. One of the Arabic proverbs, for example, was that "when a Jew cheats a Muslim, his day has been made." At the same time, among the Jews there was a very common saying that "you cannot trust a non-Jew even after forty years in the grave." However, one of the conclusions of this study was that it was difficult to find fixed, widespread stereotypes of Muslims in the Jews' proverbs to the same extent that the reverse was true among the Muslims.[29]

4. Attitudes towards Christians and Jews

There would be an added dimension to this discussion were it possible to compare the attitude toward the Jews and other groups in the population, especially other religious minorities. But during this period, unlike elsewhere in the Ottoman Empire, except for groups of merchants who spent short periods of time on business in the cities of the region, there were no large Christian groups in the North African countries. Still, there is some testimony that is of interest in this matter. In an eyewitness account of a member of a British delegation which visited in the twenties of the eighteenth century, we have: "The Moroccans think that they have a natural right to mistreat Jews and Christians." From his other descriptions, it appears that this primarily meant humiliation and vilification.[30]

On the other hand, another traveler in Morocco at the end of the eighteenth century is more specific. He notes that the Muslims had different attitudes towards Jews and Christians. For example, when talking about the death of a Jew they said: "The fellow with the horns died," horns being the symbol of treachery and obsequiousness. However when a Christian died, if he had been of good character and not particularly disliked, they said: "The poor fellow died" or at worst: "The infidel died,"[31] expressions of commiseration and alienation. If this is so, then in this period there was a clear differentiation in favor of the Christians. It may be that the growing interest in contacts with Europe at this time, to the extent that it was commonly realized, also had some influence on the general public. Or perhaps the attitude toward the groups of European traders (who were Christian), stemming from the desire to encourage trade with their countries and from political considerations, led to a different attitude towards Christians. There was probably also the influence of the long tradition against the individual or main *dhimmis* whom the masses knew, that is, the

Jews, so that the arrows of calumny and scorn were aimed at the Christians to a lesser degree. Furthermore, from Muhammad's time on, in certain traditions, scorn for the Jew is inestimably more prominent than for the Christian.[32] At this stage of research, there is no definitive answer on this for the period under discussion. Still, it is worth comparing with the situation in the Ottoman Empire, which did contain a large number of Christians and other minorities, and with the situation in other periods in the Maghreb, where there were congregations of Christians and Jews.

5. Jewish Attitudes

Generally, historiography has much about the Jews as objects of their surroundings while ignoring how they saw this environment, its strata, its rulers, and institutions. The picture would be complete if we saw both sides, even though the attitude of the Muslim environment toward the Jews was, in actuality, much more significant. Here, too, we should point out that the description of the Jewish attitude toward Muslim society in the Jewish sources, and particularly in the rabbinic literature which constitutes the lion's share, is not central, though not as meager as it is in the Muslim sources. In the nature of things, the spiritual leaders of the community were interested in Jewish society, its values, and institutions.

The attitude of the Jews to their environment is first and foremost a result of its attitude to them. The image of Morocco in the writings of the sages was generally negative. They saw it as one of the lands to which, because of their sins, the Jews had been exiled to be enslaved among the nations.[33]

This sense of oppression finds expression in the poetry and *piyyut* current in eighteenth-century Morocco. Some contain a strong yearning for the Land of Israel;[34] some conclude with prayers for a return to Erez Israel.[35] This longing did not remain abstract: In every generation there were individuals who "went up" (returned to settle), among them a leading sage, R. Hayyimm ben Attar.[36] The Yazid period (1790–1792) had left its impression not only in the atmosphere of utter dejection of the time. The Messianic tension came awake again and there were sages who were busy calculating the date of the Messiah's coming. Tens and perhaps hundreds of Jews left Morocco at the end of the eighteenth century and emigrated to the Land of Israel.[37]

Islam was depicted as the antithesis of Judaism: the religions of the Muslims (and Christians as well) were stolen from the true faith;[38] and some considered them idolatry. An example of the latter is R. Judah Halevi, one of the great rabbis of Tetuan in the eighteenth century. He apparently accepted the opinion of the Rambam (Maimonides)[39] on the relationship of Islam and Christianity to idolatry. As we said, Jews were forced to remove their shoes whenever they passed a mosque or other holy places. On this R. Judah says: "When we pass their houses of prayer and remove our shoes we do not bend down to do so since we would appear to be bowing to their houses of worship; but one raises his left foot and removes the shoe, then lifts his right foot and removes the shoe, and thus Jews act in such matters."[40] About the way God was revealed to Muhammad and the meaning of the name "Allah," a Meknes sage, R. Pethahiah Berdugo, wrote:

> What do I want with a people to whom God's name was not revealed and to whom He did not divulge it, for "Allah" as you call Him, (and he turns to his disputant, the Muslim fiqh) means "God." But what the name of God is you do not know . . . and [I heard] from my father in the name of R. Simeon ben Zemah Duran in his work *Magen Avot*[41] that since His blessed Name is not known to them, the Ishmaelites call him by a doubtful, confused name. For, the word "al" (=the definite article) serves for all definite words in the tongue of Ismael ("al-sadur," "al-qaght," etc. And the term "Allah" is used as a result of doubt, as when a person wondering at something beyond his grasp says "lah, lah"; and thus the Ishmaelites called Him "Al lah", i.e., the one who is hidden and whose name they did not know . . . "[42]

The source of "alah," as we know, is in the root A-L-H common to the Semitic languages, but this did not keep the rabbi from adopting this interpretation, divorced from reality. In other words, R. Pethahiah had a certain image and this interpretation served as his justification. The courts of the *shari'ah* are, first of all, "registries of idolators" and their judges are mentioned in a negative tone[43]. In the terminology of the sages of Morocco, the *madrasa* took on the meaning not only of a "house of learning" but also of a "house of trampling" [a play on the root d-r-s], that is, a place of impurity.[44] But all of these things must also be treated with caution because of the negative attitude evidenced by the sages in principle toward other faiths, their founders, and their present servants, which does not always reflect a hostile, negative reality.

The rabbinic literature from Morocco sometimes describes high government officials, especially its soldiers and officers, as rough and aggressive and "as just plain spiteful and harmful gentiles, especially with a sense of authority which will brook not the slightest infringement of it, and only one in a thousand who gets involved emerges unscathed."[45] And their anger knew no bounds whenever the government descended upon a community and imposed a very heavy tax. The rulers of Fez who made the lives of the Jews a hell at the start of the century are "birds of prey," "vicious vipers," and "wild beasts."[46]

On the other hand, the Jewish attitude to the central government is totally different. Characteristic is the affection they felt for the kings of Morocco, especially, understandably, for those who were concerned with the Jews' welfare. In general, the Jews had a fundamental interest in the stability of the government because they feared they would be the first victims of its overthrow. A similar strain is heard in a source from 1669 when al-Rashid successfully established his rule in northern Morocco and smashed a number of the rebels there "at a time when the kingdom was renewed and the families of the officials in every city were utterly destroyed."[47] However, one should remember that, as a rule, most of the Muslims at that time were also dependent upon the caprice of the local *ka'id* or official. That is to say, it was not only the lowly status of the Jews which led to their being discriminated against but also the nature of the society in which they lived and functioned.

The phrases "elevated be his glory" or "may the Almighty be merciful to him" were added to the names of all the sultans and ka'ids who dealt properly with the Jews. Even Sultan Isma'il, who was not always kind to the Jews, was generally designated in the Hebrew documents as "Moulay Sma'il, may the Almighty be merciful to him," because they apparently recognized his contribution to their improved security and that, in general, like every king, he was a factor in protecting them.[48] On the other hand, in their letters, they expressed their attitudes to those who treated them harshly. An example of this is the designation *ha-mezid* (Hebrew for "the one who wilfully does evil") which they added to the name of the sultan, Yazid,[49] whenever it crossed their lips. As we know, the Jews suffered greatly under this sultan.[50] Interesting, as well, is the change that took place in their custom of prayer after Yazid's death. Starting with the reign of Suleiman who, as we have said, cancelled Yazid's decrees and even lowered the tax quota imposed upon the communities, the Fez congregation began to bless the king "who is deserving of blessing from the Lord of the kingdom."[51]

The sages of the period properly appreciated the religious and communal autonomy granted them by the government. R. Samuel Amar, at the end of the nineteenth century, stated specifically – and the same conclusion could be derived from eighteenth-century sources – that "under the rule of Ishmael, despite all the decrees, there is always a concern for the existence of our faith and they are commanded by their prophet (meaning Muhammad, of course) to support us in strengthening it."[52]

6. Relationships between Muslims and Jews; Jewish security

What was the day-to-day contact between the Jews and their environment? Again, we must remember that it was limited and, except for the shared cultural infrastructure and the ramified economic relationships,[53] each group lived its life within its own society. All the travelers who visited the Moroccan cities from the end of the seventeenth to the beginning of the nineteenth centuries described the life of the Jews as terrible, continuous combination of humiliation, degradation, contempt, and oppression. One writes that the Jews "are open to beatings and humiliation by everyone."[54] Another: "The Jews live in fear and are abject before the Moors."[55] A third noted that Jewish children ran away from him because they thought he was a Moroccan and "fear of gentiles is deep in their hearts."[56] And, in general, "Anyone who opens his mouth takes his life in his hands because of the religious zealotry."[57] However there is almost no doubt that these descriptions are more than slightly exaggerated: either because of their general character – even a traveler regarded as reliable and moderately disposed to the Jews generalizes that "everywhere in Morocco the Jews are regarded as second-class creatures. Nowhere in the world are they as degraded as in Barbary"[58] – or because their accounts reflected the European stereotype of the Jew. One of them wrote: "The Jews here are like all the Jews everywhere, the vilest under the sun, and the Moors seem to know them better than other nations and treat them accordingly."[59] Hence, one must be doubly careful in dealing with this material and consider it valid only when there is evidence of actual physical harm done to Jews.

Another area reflective of the relationships between Jews and Muslims is the Hebrew of the spoken language as recorded in the twentieth century.[60] Many of the words and combinations are part of a need to conceal words or meanings or actions from the Gentile hearers. Many of the expressions are extremely caustic: the Muslim ruler in Tafilalet was called "eunuch" and the prophet of Islam "the flawed one." A few expressions are from the economic sphere in which the Jews wished to conceal their intentions from those around them *lamed kametz* which is *la* in Arabic, meaning "no." The Jews of Tafilalet and Fez[61] constantly used as a curse the Hebrew passage (from Ps. 119:18): "May he be clothed in a curse like a garment," and in Tafilalet they also used the verse (from Ps. 72:16) "And may they sprout up in towns like country grass," or (from Deut. 29:22): "(May) all its soil (be) devasted by sulfur and salt," whenever they passed a Muslim cemetery.[62]

Since language preserves old linguistic forms, there is no doubt that many of these expressions were also prevalent in the eighteenth century. Also of interest is the Hebrew word *zorerut* meaning Jew-hatred, which developed from the biblical word *zorer*.[63] If the reality was such that it gave rise to the need to create a new abstract noun to describe it, then Jew-hatred must have been prevalent. The new meaning of "apostate" (*meshumad*) – one who left Judaism for another faith – given to the word "insane" (*meshuga*)[64]indicates the Jewish attitude toward the renegades.

Let us focus primarily upon the state of Jewish security in this period about which, relatively, we have more reliable evidence; "security" in the most basic sense of the word, that is, how dangerous was it to be a Jew in Muslim society. One must assume that the suppressed enmity toward the Jews sometimes came to practical expression for no reason at all. But the Jews who were harmed were mainly the itinerant peddlers, and there were some who were murdered for plunder as they made their way from village to village. That there were a number of such occurrences we learn from the responsa of the rabbis of Morocco. There is the general report, from the end of the nineteenth century, of R. Raphael Moses Elbaz to the Alliance Israélite Universelle in Paris about his community of Sefrou, that "there is almost no year in which two or three Jews are not robbed and killed, God knows the hidden things."[65] In the eighteenth century as well, the same had been the case for this community and the others.[66] Also involved in such activities were the Barbary tribesmen, who plundered wayfarers and against whom the government was powerless.

Instances of rape were less common, apparently because women seldom left their homes and would not go out without their husbands or parents. But perhaps we do not hear of such things because the victims would not report it from fear of becoming compromised, especially maritally, for example, being slandered for fornication.[67] On the other hand, there is evidence of women being raped, primarily when riots spread throughout the city, including the Jewish quarter. For example, in Meknes in 1728: "they entered the mellah of the Jews, looted everything and left them naked – the men, the women and children, the sages and the righteous – and killed 180 of them, leaving the rest alive, but beaten and tortured . . . then they looked to the women and the virgins, and defiled them all in front of all Israel, Heaven forbid!"[68]

The Muslims, to be sure, were also victims of such violence, but the degradation of the Jews exposed them relatively more. This explains the wonder of the Muslims of Morocco in the eighteenth century at the daring of the Jews in traveling the roads alone.[69] In fact, Jews did occasionally hire bodyguards for routes which were known to be dangerous. The French Ambassador St Olon made a general statement that "Jews do not travel in the country without Muslim bodyguards."[70] In any case, the general comments of the Moroccan chronicler Al-Zaiani may be valid for the specific period of Isma'il (1672–1727) who was especially concerned with the security of the main roads for the passage of troops, officials, and couriers, but it was not true of every period and every place. "Matters were settled, the subjects were at ease, the country was quiet, the sultan was busy building his palaces and planting his orchards, and the land was secure and peaceful. A woman and a Jew could go from Oujda (in northwest Morocco) to Wadi Nun (in the southeast) with none stopping them to ask where from and where to."[71] Furthermore, Al-Zaiani's words themselves show how exceptional was the situation he described. His pairing of "woman and Jew" is of interest because it indicates that these two were considered the weakest elements in the society. Ibn Khaldun had already mentioned this motif, adding that both are sly and hypocritical. This stereotype, also widespread in the nineteenth and twentieth centuries, proves its strength and continuity.[72]

There are instances in which the government very severely punished Muslims who harmed Jews. At the beginning of the eighteenth century, five Muslims were hanged for the robbery and murder of a Jew.[73] But he was a distinguished person who may have been close to the court and whose family had enough influence to demand an investigation and punishment. In other cases, the sultan indemnified the family of the victims[74] and, in a few instances, to mention the name of Asma'il was enough to deter Muslims who sought to harm Jews.[75]

Attacks upon the Jews in periods of anarchy were apparently among the decisive factors in establishing a specific Jewish neighborhood for purposes of protection. But this was not always an effective solution to the problems of Jewish security and we know of attacks upon the Jews within the mellah itself. It happened in Meknes in 1703, 1720, 1728, and 1790.[76] In one of these instances "gentiles invaded us, burned the houses of worship and study in this city, the flower of the Maghreb in learning and piety, tortured a number of women and girls, and left us naked and barefoot." In one instance, the mellah was plundered. Muslim friends of Jews had warned them "to mount a special guard on the mellah because the Ishmaelites have plotted against you to plunder and loot." However, this guard was obviously of no avail because "they plundered and looted, particularly those houses known to belong to the Jews." The last apparently refers to the Meknes mellah pogroms of 1790.[77] There was one sharif who used to enter the mellah of Meknes to attack the Jews and the city's kadi set up guards against him.[78] However, proper conclusions in this matter can be drawn only after studying the specific circumstances in each instance.

Still, the Muslim population also had different attitudes about the security of the Jews; for example, there was a kadi who saved Jews from the wrath of a furious ruler. Thus we learn that in the bitter days of Sultan Yazid's reign, the Kadi of Tetuan urged the Sultan that "it is not proper to kill all the Jews, because their *palil* (as mentioned before, a derogatory term for a judge; the reference here is to Muhammad) did not say so."[79] He was alluding to the words of the Koran, that Muhammad commanded that the Jews were not to be killed if they paid a special tax.[80] Sometimes Muslim neighbors afforded Jews protection during pogroms.[81] In general, writes R. Raphael Berdugo (one of the leaders of the Jews of Meknes at the end of the eighteenth and beginning of the nineteenth centuries), when the Jews foresaw trouble they entrusted their possessions to their Muslim acquaintances.[82] There is also interesting evidence that after the death of Hafid, the ruler of Fez at the beginning of the eighteenth century, Muslims who had belonged to the rival faction and feared the vengeance of his heir found refuge in Jewish homes.[83]

Mutual relationships between Jews and Muslims did develop sometimes. The Jewish peddlers who went from village to village stayed with their Muslim friends. Most of the sources are about the Jewish peddlers who made their way among the Berber tribes[84] and sometimes even spent the Sabbath among them.[85] Naturally such relationships are not to be expected in the cities where there were Jewish communities. There were Muslims and Jews who visited back and forth on holidays and festivals and family celebrations. This was normal in times of trouble or family bereavement and so forth.[86]

Extended relationships between Jews and Moslems were primarily in the economic sphere: business partnerships, mutual loans, house rentals and the like. This was found not only with the great merchants but also with the middle level businessmen, peddlers, and the plain folk, and is expressed mainly in the collections of responsa of the period.[87]

At times Muslims lent Jews money even in times of oppression and did not use this as an excuse to turn them away.[88] In normal times, the Jews worked in the *madina* (the Muslim city) and their absence caused a slackening of economic activity. A French priest who spent time in Meknes at the beginning of the eighteenth century points out that "no business was transacted on the Sabbath because the Jews observe it scrupulously."[89] He of course exaggerated when he said that no business was done in the city but it is a near certainty that economic activity was much less on that day. On the other hand, there were Muslims in the mellah for economic reasons, especially commercial purposes.

In certain instances this sort of relationship made its imprint upon the entire economic activity of a city, as for example, in Mogador in the second half of the eighteenth century.[90] There was a particularly close economic connection between the large merchants who dealt with the court and royal family and the other officials of the *makhzan* (the Moroccan government).[91]

On occasion there were exchanges of ideas in various areas. As we have said, the Jewish society did indeed generally function independently but, as everyone knows, the Jews were influenced by their environment. This is evident in locales and periods when the non-Jewish society was preeminent in concepts and values which the Jewish society wished to adopt.[92] On the other hand, in those periods of decline and general isolation in the surrounding society, the effect was especially noticeable in outside areas. Thus, for example, in the period under discussion we find influences upon the Jewish community organization which are partially a result of the external environment: Increasingly the eighteenth-century Jewish community was dependent upon an indirect tax on products and merchandise to finance its expenses, especially for purposes of social welfare. This indirect tax was probably imposed more and more widely because this system had also become increasingly widespread in the Muslim society of Morocco.[93]

There were clear influences in the cultural area. For example, there is definite evidence of environmental effect upon folk customs, and the sages often protested against distortions and strange practices which had adhered to the Jewish community. Especially did they fight those who turned to the non-Jewish courts, but this was not a very common phenomenon.[94] Likewise they again and again railed against the practice of gashing oneself in mourning over the dead.[95] The repetition of decrees and warnings against such things proves that, at least in the long run, they were ineffective.[96]

The limited social contact did not bring in its wake any noticeable instances of apostasy from Judaism, though there were some such. The fraternization of the Jews at court with their Muslim colleagues was apt to cause their estrangement from the Jewish community. The above-mentioned R. Raphael Berdugo spoke harshly of the Jews involved with the court: "And to this day the only one who scorns positive and negative commandments, Sabbaths, and festivals is the one who is a familiar of the government."[97] But this must be accepted with reservations because of its moralizing tone, and it should be pointed out that this circle generally was steeped in the tradition of its people. A more common phenomenon was that of individuals who, because of their close ties with Muslim government ministers and officials, shirked the obligations the community imposed upon its members, especially in matters of taxation.[98] However, the Jewish community did not generally tend to create tension with individuals but preferred other means of returning them to the ranks of responsible community members.

We conclude this section with a unique example from the sources[99] which, because of its importance, must be cited. From the responsa of R. Pethahiah Berdugo, who also lived in Meknes at the end of the eighteenth and beginning of the nineteenth centuries, we learn of an interesting theological debate he had with a Muslim religious sage (*fiqh*). The subjects were similar to those of the earlier medieval debates between the sages of the three great faiths: the election of Israel, its exile and suffering; the coming of Jesus and Muhammad; the importance of the various religions, and the like.[100] There does not seem to have been any new material presented in the argumentation, but the very holding of such a debate attests to the fact that there were instances of clear religious tolerance also on the part of the Muslim religious doctors whose circle is usually known for its zealotry. Furthermore, in the debate itself R. Pethahiah Berdugo levelled some harsh words against the religion of Islam and against Muhammad himself, and one may assume that he did it knowing full well that he would not be annihilated. On the other hand, one can argue that this was a debate between two friends, with no official approval whatsoever, and its significance should not be overestimated.

7. Other Areas

A comparison with other periods and places in the Maghreb and Morocco in general will give some of these matters further significance. Two contrasting approaches explaining the development of Muslim-Jewish relations mainly in the nineteenth and twentieth centuries have taken shape in the research literature about this period. (In recent years, this has apparently been the most developed topic of study about the Jews of the Maghreb). Most scholars today are of the opinion that the Jews were integrated to an appreciable degree in the Muslim society of the Maghreb, especially in its economic life. Research dealing with the period of 1880–1930 in Sala, an important Jewish center on the Atlantic coast of Morocco, reveals that both groups led modest, religious, and ethical lives, and shared a common language. There was economic cooperation between them: The Jewish and Muslim merchants maintained close ties, jointly supplied credit to the residents of the area, and shared the village lands and pasturages in the Sala region. Some of the Jews did business as itinerant merchants in the Sala region and lived in the area most of the year. The Jews were granted a *mizrag* (literally: a javelin), a guarantee of free passage publicly announced on market days. This meant that one of the notables took it upon himself to sponsor the peddlers, or sometimes a specific family associated with them, or even an entire clan, and to see to their security. The "wards" bestowed gifts and great honor upon their patrons. Secure with their powerful *mizrag*, caravans of Jews from Sala moved through the Gharb region at the end of the nineteenth century. Many merchants and craftsmen belonged to the guilds which continued to function until the twenties of the twentieth century. The westernization of some of the Jews increased their numbers in the offices of the Protectorate and in the European economic sectors, weakened the close personal relationships with the Muslims, and even caused tensions.[101]

In the rural sections of Libya[102] and to some extent also in Morocco,[103] Jews were prominent as the economic brokers between the villages and the cities. In fact, there were instances when their being social outsiders made them preferable to the Arab traders. For example, in Libya and to an extent even in Algeria[104], the Berber women in the nineteenth century were ready to admit Jewish peddlers into their homes, something absolutely forbidden to Muslim men. In Libya, southern Tunisia, and southern Morocco, there was also the figure of the itinerant Jewish craftsman who would spend days and even weeks among the Berber tribes.[105]

The tendency to close economic ties between the large Jewish merchants and the royal family[106] continued to expand in the nineteenth century to other cities on the Atlantic coast and to additional cities such as Marrakesh.[107] For example, there were even personal relationships between the Corcos family and members of the court.[108]

A number of studies have pointed out the relative security in which Jews lived under the Berber sheikhs.[109] One scholar stressed the function of the Jews as brokers between the Berbers and the urban Arabs.[110] But others who have summarized this research, have cautioned against a one-sided description and have given examples from the Damnat region to show differences in the status of the Jews. Even very wealthy Jews had, at times, to show submission and obsequiousness toward their Berber friends. And, occasionally, they were subject to humiliations, injuries, sadism, and even murder.[111]

Folk culture is one of the clear indicators of national experience and in this regard there were many similarities between the Arabs and Berbers and the Jews who lived among them: in diet, garb, ornamentation, furnishings, as well as folk customs, such as the widespread belief in the evil eye and the open hand (the *hamsa*), or the belief in demons and spirits. There were also many similarities in the language and music of the two groups. A characteristic example of the similar cultural milieu was the veneration of "holy men." There were Muslims in Morocco[112] and Libya[113] who made pilgrimages to the graves of Jewish "holy men" because they were reputed to have the power to heal the sick. There were Muslims who would place donations in the charity boxes at the graves of the "holy men" or at ancient synagogues.[114] They were even partial to Jewish practices whose purpose was to benefit the entire society, such as the custom common in Libya on Shavuot when the children poured water upon one another so that it would be a year of abundant rainfall,[115] or the Muslim practice in Morocco of bringing the Jews the first leavened dough so they might observe the custom of the *maimuna* at the end of Passover.[116] Of course, there were sometimes quarrels between Jews and Muslims at the graves of the "holy men," with each side claiming they belonged to it.

To be sure, not everywhere and not at every time was the joint veneration of the same "holy man" a factor making for understanding and good neighborliness. There is much evidence that Jewish "holy men" were the targets of Muslim attacks;[117] and this proves the dual attitude. But in general, the prior, common infrastructure of language, beliefs, customs, and environment contributed to a certain unity.

In contrast to the first approach, there are scholars who believe that though there were periods when Jews enjoyed physical security, economic prosperity, and personal relationships with the Muslims, the Jews were essentially of inferior status: a weak group, for better or worse dependent upon the Muslim rulers and the arbitrary behavior of the Arab.

This is the conclusion of one scholar whose examples were drawn, in the main, from Libya of the nineteenth and early twentieth centuries. He centered his discussion on the traditional legal basis of the position of the Jews: the "Covenant of 'Umar" or the concept of the *dhimmah* (covenant). In the researches which he criticized, he found a number of weaknesses: For example, he saw as too simplistic the argument of one of the scholars that the Jews in the Maghreb were outside the social fabric and hence there was no competition between them and the Muslims. On the contrary: The Jews were not only a social, cultural group happening to live in Libya but were in fact an active part of that society, able to compete with the Muslim majority.[118] Evidence of this is the opposition of Zawia to the erection of a synagogue there and the burning of the one at Zlitan which had begun to be built in 1867. These events argued that the building of a synagogue would strengthen Jewish settlement in those places and become a threat to Muslim commerce.[119]

Even more interesting is his conclusion about the effect which the deviation of individuals from the conditions of the covenant had upon the whole: It was expected that a Muslim who deviated would be punished, but this in no way endangered the Muslim community; whereas an infringement by a Jew could sometimes be disastrous to the entire Jewish community.[120]

8. Conclusions

Based upon the existing sources, it is difficult to draw proper conclusions about the social interrelationship of Jews and their environment in eighteenth-century Morocco. Nevertheless, the following is a general sketch.

The Jewish and Muslim estimations of one another were rooted, first and foremost, in the religious differences between them – differences with a lengthy history, though the Muslim view of the Jew was also nourished by the former's sense of superiority in face of the Muslim law's definition of the latter as an inferior who must be tolerated. But herein lies an instructive distinction: When dealing with Jews or Muslims as a group, there is the usually negative, typological generalization; whereas in reality the stereotype dissolves into an ever growing variety of images. The officials of the *Makhzan* appeared in the general Jewish descriptions as arbitrary and violent, and there were, to be sure, officials who fit this description; but, on the other hand, there were also officials who treated the Jews kindly.

Beyond the images each held of the other, there was generally no broad social contact between Jew and Muslim in Morocco because of the social and religious differences and also because of the physical distance between the two groups who lived in separate areas of the city. The sense of the Jews' alienation was expressed negatively in practice, especially in periods between rulers or in high risk places such as major crossroads. At such times the reciprocally negative stereotypes burst forth, but the Muslims had the upper hand because of their status and numbers. The Jews became targets of physical abuse, humiliation, aroused passions, and even murder; whereas their "strength was only in their mouths." Then they would give vent to their wrath and disappointment mainly internally: in literary expression, in language, song, sermons, historiography, and so forth. The hatred and alienation existing in both camps surfaced and erupted in times of crisis such as, for example, when security was threatened or hostile rulers assumed power. This explanation is akin to that given by Ettinger of European antisemitism except that there is a great difference between it and antisemitism in Morocco. The long, historic continuity of ity of European antisemitism and the much more severe political, social, and cultural changes bred an unimaginable catastrophe. On the other hand, between Jews and Muslims we have another sort of relationship, especially in the economic sphere where they were partially dependent upon one another and where their religious affiliations did not interfere. These relations were especially prominent in the instance of the merchant families and the court people who had common interests. In the cultural realm, the influences during this period were casual, a result of living in the same environment.

The sources of the period can also be explained by the difference between the general image, which becomes concretized in time of tension, and the manifold aspects of daily life governed by a desire to survive in a basically shared culture. Religious traditions, proverbs, some of the literature of the travelers, and the like, of the eighteenth to the twentieth centuries, reflect the stereotype which generally was negative. Conversely, the responsa, the Jewish chronicles, and other parts of the travelers' literature, describe actual situations of attacks upon Jews on the one hand and economic cooperation on the other.

Modern research on the nineteenth-twentieth centuries tends to emphasize the involvement of the Jews in the society of the Maghreb and, especially, the economic role which they played not only as an economic élite but also in the areas of small business, as peddlers, as middlemen between village and city, and more. This conclusion is enforced by the continuity of what a study of the eighteenth century indicates. Anthropological research into the folk culture has also provided a broad basis for a number of conclusions drawn from this century in which the unity of folk culture shared by the Jews and the Muslims – in language, art, music, magic, foods, and the like – contributed to the self-confidence of the Jew. To this should be added another factor which has as yet not been discussed: the long, historic continuity of the Jewish existence in Morocco, for at least two thousand years. The expression common to the Jews of Morocco, "our Muslims," undoubtedly developed from a long life in the same environment. In general, the fact that people could say to themselves that their ancestors had been in Morocco for hundreds of years, bestowed a not insignificant fortitude.

Notes

1. See S. Ettinger, *Modern Antisemitism: Studies and Essays* (Heb.) (Tel Aviv, 1978).
2. See below.
3. Thus for example, the Frenchman, Mouette, devoted not more than one page out of one hundred and ninety-nine to the Jews of Morocco of his time. See: H. de Castries, *Les Sources Inedites de l'Histoire du Maroc* (=SIHM) (Paris, 1922–1960), *Serie 2* 2, p.176.
4. See below, n. 13; and the summary at the end of the article.
5. See Sh. Bar-Asher, *The Jewish Community in Morocco in the Eighteenth Century* (Heb.) [=Sh. Bar-Asher, *The Community*] (The Hebrew University of Jerusalem Ph.D dissertation, 1981), p.13.
6. For an example of an exception, see below, notes 17 and 18.
7. Characteristic is verse 29 of Sura 9.
8. G. Vajda, "Juifs et musulmans selon le hadith," *Journal Asiatique* 229(1937):57–127 and the "Ahl-Al-Kitab" entry in *Encyclopedia of Islam*, 2nd. ed., 1:264–266.
9. See Haggai Ben-Shammai's "Jew-Hatred in the Islamic Tradition and the Koranic Exegesis" in this volume.
10. See, for example, R. Berdugo *Upright Laws* (Heb.), 1 (Cracow, 1891), par. 202, p.40.
11. S. J. Abitbol, *Stones of Marble* (Heb.), 2 (Jerusalem, 1934–1935), par.99, p.1; and see note 72, p. 10.
12. S. Romanelli, "Arabian Journey," in *Selected Writings* (Heb.), ed. H. Schirmann (Jerusalem, 1969), p.106.
13. See Bar-Asher, *The Community*, p.12 and the sources in n. 33 there.
14. And see the summation below.
15. W. Blunt, *Black Sunrise: The Life and Times of Mulai Ismail, Emperor of Morocco 1646–1727* (London, 1951), pp.142–143; who quotes J. Windus, *A Journey to Mequinez* (London, 1751), unavailable in Israel at this writing.
16. See *Bension Cohen Yalkut Ro'im* Collection, Library of the University of Alberta, Ms. 174.
17. *The History of Fez* (Heb.), Ben-Zvi Institute, Jerusalem ms. 1742, p.20.
18. See S. Ettinger, *Antisemitism*, pp.4–6.
19. And compare Stillman, below, in n. 29.
20. See D. Obadiah, *The Community of Sefrou-Morocco* (Heb.) 1 (Jerusalem, 1975–1976), p.190.
21. See M. Gaudefroy-Demombynes, "Marocain mellah," *Journal Asiatique* Serie 11, 3(1914):651; and H. Z. Hirschberg, "The 'Mellah' and the 'Mesoos': the Jewish Quarter in Morocco" (Heb.), *Eretz Israel* 4(1956):228 and, in general, pp.226–230.
22. See Joseph Mashash, *Treasury of Letters* (Heb.) 1 (Jerusalem, 1968), n. 127, pp.47–48.
23. It should be pointed out that in Arabic there is a verb *lah* meaning "threw away." But the derivation of noun *mellah* from the verb is not plausible according to the accepted rules of grammar, as stated.
24. For example: J. Braithwaite, *The History of the Revolutions in the Empire of Morocco, upon the Death of the Late Emperor Muley Ishmael* 2nd ed., (Miami, 1969), p.200.

PLATE 1. Illustration depicting the Jews of England, from a manuscript dated 1233, in the possession of the Public Record Office, England (E 401/1565, m.1). The Jews are shown standing near the Fortress of Norwich. At the top center appears the face of the prosperous Jew, Isaac of Norwich, wearing the Crown of King Henry III. Beneath him is the horned devil, claiming for Satan the two Jews (agents of Isaac) standing on either side of him.

PLATE 2. Satanic figures identified with the Jew Badge. One figure rides a sow, common in many depictions of Jews in the Middle Ages. Title Page from *Der Juden Erbarkeit*, 1571.

PLATE 3. Satan Attended by Jews. Pierre Boaistuau, *Histoires Prodigieuses*, Paris, 1575.

PLATE 4. Blood libel – Conjuring the devil from blood secured through ritual murder. Pierre Boaistuau, *Histoires Prodigieuses*, Paris, 1575.

Wie die falſchen Juden das bild
Marie durch ſtachen vnd Blut vßher ran.

Wie die falſchen iuden die bildung
Marie verſpottet vnd verſpuwet haben.

PLATE 5. Wilhelm, the Jew, pierces the image of the Virgin Mary, causing her to bleed. Martin Hupfuff, *Entehrung und Schmach*, Strasbourg, ca. 1512–1515.

PLATE 6. Jews mocking and blaspheming a picture of Mary and Jesus in the Cambron Monastery. Martin Hupfuff, *Entehrung und Schmach*, Strasbourg, ca. 1512–1515.

PLATE 7. Jesus in disputation with Jews. Woodcut by the Swiss artist Urs Graf, from the Passional of 1506.

PLATE 8. Depiction of the sow as foster-mother of the Jew. An early seventeenth century version of a design engraved at the entrance to a bridge in Frankfort in the fifteenth century. Copper engraving, Frankfort, seventeenth century.

PLATE 9. Jewish types, Germany. This genre of Jewish caricatures was widespread in the nineteenth century, but it had eighteenth century precedents. K. B. A. Sessa, *Unser Verkehr*, Leipzig, 1814.

PLATE 10. Jews as soldiers. From: E. Fuchs, *Die Juden in der Karikatur*, Munich, 1921.

PLATE 11. Polish Jews and French soldiers. From C. W. Faber du Faur, *Blatter aus meinem Portefeuille im Laufe des Feldzugs 1812 in Russland*, Stuttgart, 1831.

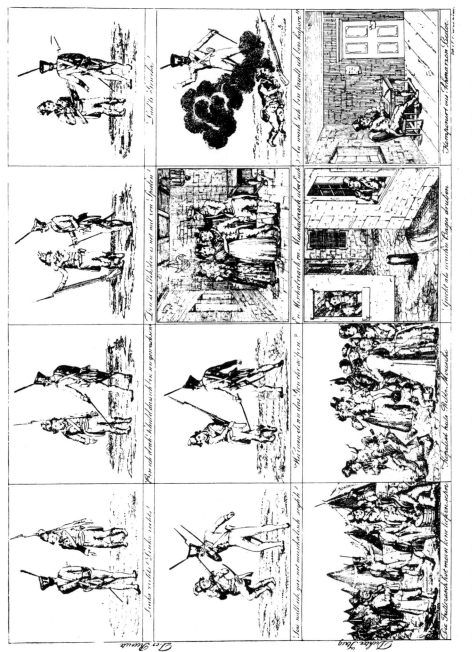

PLATE 12. "Jacob as Recruit and Jacob as Poet," Nuremberg, nineteenth century. E. Fuchs, *Die Juden in der Karikatur*, Munich, 1921.

Die Generalpumpe.

PLATE 13. The General Pump. Frankfort caricature of Amschel Rothschild's methods in gaining political influence through his financial dealings. The Roth-schilds were the subject of many venomous caricatures in nineteenth century Europe. *Die Juden in der Karikatur*, Munich, 1921.

PSST...!

Images par FORAIN CARAN D'ACHE

PARAISSANT LE SAMEDI

N° 28
13 Août 1898.

Le NUMÉRO : 10 centimes.
Abonnements : France, 6 fr.; Étranger, 8 fr.

BUREAUX
10, rue Garancière, Paris.

En revenant de Nantes

— Guel zale pays!
— Ya!...

PLATE 14. "Returning from Nantes." Below, a dialogue between two Jews, in Germanized French:- "What a dirty country!" – "Ja." Published after the second Dreyfus trial that confirmed his alleged guilt. From the front page of *Psst....* Paris, August 1898.

PLATE 15. Election poster of the German DNVP Party, 1919. Caption above: *"These are your present leaders!"* And below, *"Do you want others?* Then vote *German-National!"*

PLATE 16. The infiltration of German trade into the USA through the assistance of the "Bolshevik Jew, born in Russia, 'shaped' in Germany" – in the form of a dachshund. *Exporter's Review*, 1918.

PLATE 17. Anti-Bolshevik, antisemitic poster by Manno Miltiades, Budapest, Hungary, 1919.

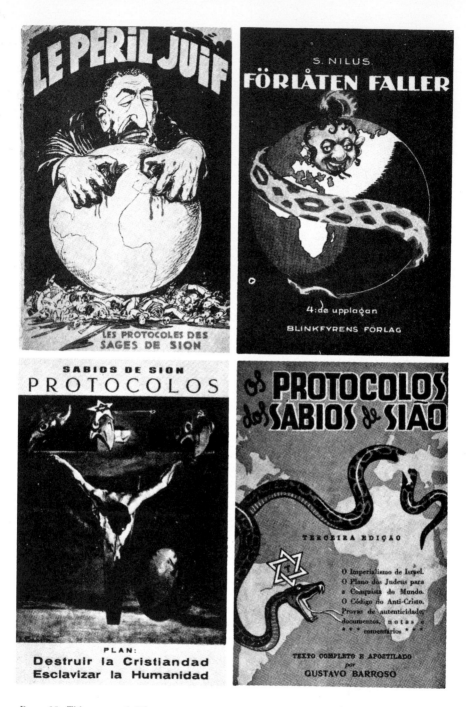

PLATE 18. Title pages of different versions of the "Protocols of the Elders of Zion." a) French edition, 1924. b) Swedish edition, 1934. c) Spanish edition, 1937. d) Brazilian edition, 1963. In the Spanish edition, atop the cross are three snake heads symbolizing the State of Israel, Communism and the Jewish religion. From Norman Cohen, *Warrant for Genocide*, London, 1967.

PLATE 19. Ahmed Haemad Alefko, *Zionism without Makeup*. Decisions of the Jews (1951).

PLATE 20. Abas Mahmud Al-Akad, *World Zionism*. Official publication of the Egyptian Government. Cairo, 1956. (The "Protocols" appear in the appendix of the book.)

PLATE 21. Shuki Abed Al-Nasser, *The Protocols of the Elders of Zion and Talmudic Teachings*. Cairo (1966–1967). The publisher of this edition was the brother of Nasser, the President of Egypt.

PLATE 22. The front page of Juluis Streicher's antisemitic newspaper *Der Sturmer*, Nuremberg, Germany, 1934. The headline at the bottom of the page reads: "The Jews are our misfortune." Quotation taken from the German historian Heinrich von Treitschke's "Unserer Aussichten," Preussische Jahr bücher 44/45, Berlin 1899.

Der Nürnberger Jude Otto Mayer

pflegte seine Opfer zu kreuzigen. In völlig nacktem Zustande band
er sie an ein eigens dazu angefertigtes Holzkreuz und schändete
sie, sobald aus den Wundmalen das Blut floß.

PLATE 23. National Socialist caricature. The caption tells of a
Jew who, after crucifying a woman, tied her naked to a cross
and raped her as the blood flowed from her wounds. Repro-
duced from S. Cohen (ed.), *Germany*, Jerusalem 1974.

25. See the introduction to the anthology *Jewish Folktales from Morocco* (Heb.), ed. Dov Noy (Jerusalem, 1964), pp.17–18.
26. Ibid., p.100. And see A. Marcus, *Israel and the Nations in Folk Tales of the Jews in the Islamic Lands* (Heb.) (The Hebrew University of Jerusalem, Ph.D. dissertation, 1978). See, for example, pp.17, 717.
27. Cf. Bar-Asher, *The Community*, pp.16–22.
28. P. de Cenival, "La Légende du Juif Ibn Mechal et la fête du Sultan des Tolba à Fés," *Hesperis* 5(1925):137–218.
29. N. A. Stillman, "Muslims and Jews in Morocco: Perceptions, Images, Stereotypes," in *Proceedings of the Seminar on Muslim-Jewish Relations in North-Africa* (New York, 1975), p.40–50.
30. Braithwaite, *The History of the Revolutions, pp.179, 348.*
31. J. G. Jackson, *An Account of the Empire of Morocco* (London, 1914), p.165; and see R. Dozy, *Supplément aux dictionnaires arabes* 2 (Leiden, 1927), p.339.
32. See the article by H. Ben-Shammai in this volume.
33. See Yaakov ben Zur, *Language of Instruction* (Heb.), Ben-Zvi Institute, Jerusalem, ms. 638, fol. 107. Likewise see Pethahiah Berdugo, *Honeycomb* (Heb.) (Casablanca, 1938), fol. 12b–13a. And see Raphael Berdugo's sermon for Shabbat Ha-Gadol, in *Passover Haggadah, Expanded Mouth of the Righteous* (Heb.) (Jerusalem, 1978), fol. 74b–85a.
34. For example, David Hassin, *A Psalm of David* (Heb.) (Casablanca, 1931), fol. 17–18.
35. For example, ibid., fol. 14, column 2 or fol. 37, column 2.
36. S. Bar-Asher, "The Jews of North Africa and the Land of Israel in the 18th and 19th Centuries," in L. A. Hoffman (ed.), *The Land of Israel*, (Notre Dame University Press, 1986), 297–315.
37. Joseph Mashash, *Treasury of Letters* (n. 22 above) 1, Introduction, p.13.
38. "The Book of Enactments" (Heb.) in *The Enactments of the Jews of Morocco* (Jerusalem, 1977), par. 148, p.73.
39. See J. Katz, *Exclusiveness and Tolerance* (London, 1961) pp.119–120.
40. J. Ben Malkah, *Western Candle* (Heb.) (Jerusalem, 1931), part 1, end of par. 143, fol. 161b–fol. 162b.
41. We have been unable to locate this source.
42. Pethahiah Berdugo, *Honeycomb*, (n. 33 above), fol. 13a.
43. See, for example, Obadiah, *Community of Sefrou* 2, pp.101–102.
44. See: Yaakov ben Zur, *Law and Justice among (the people of) Jacob* (Alexandria, 1895–1903), 2, par. 121, fol. 63b, and Raphael Berdugo, *Still Waters* (Heb.) 2 (Djerba, 1942), fol. 80b.
45. Obadiah, *Community of Sefrou* 1, p.107, according to the ruling of the sages of Meknes.
46. Ben-Zvi Institute Ms. 1742, pp.50–51; Ben-Zur, *Language of Instruction*, (n. 33 above) fol. 88a, and likewise see Obadiah, *Community of Sefrou* 1, p.30.
47. "Book of Enactments" (n. 38 above) p.80, and cf. J.-S. Gerber, "The Pact of 'Umar in Morocco," in *Proceedings of the Seminar on Muslim-Jewish Relations*, (n. 29 above) p.48.
48. Ms. 1742, (n. 17 above) pp.56–57 is one of many examples; but when, at the beginning of the eighteenth century, the Jews of Fez were being squeezed and came to complain about the heavy taxes levied upon them, the chronicler Samuel Abendanan, in *The History of Fez*, appended the strongest curses whenever his name was mentioned: "May his name and memory be blotted out," "May the name of the wicked rot." See, for example, ibid., p.51, ms. mentioned in n. 17.
49. See, for example, the letter published by J. M. Toledano in *Survivor and Refugee* (Heb.) (Tel Aviv, 1945), p.58.
50. See Bar-Asher, *The Community* p.6.
51. "A Reminder for the Children of Israel", Ben-Zvi Institute ms. 1742, p.76.
52. S. Amar, *The Word of Samuel* (Heb.) (Casablanca, 1940), fol. 28a.
53. See below, pp.[21–22].
54. *SIHM* 2, p.176.
55. Braithwaite, *The History of the Revolutions*, p.115.
56. Romanelli, *Arabian Journey*, (n. 12 above) p.91.
57. Ibid., p.59.
58. G. Lemprière, *Voyage de l'Empire du Maroc* (Paris, 1801), p.155.
59. Braithwaite, *The History of the Revolutions*, p.348.

60. See M. Bar-Asher, "The Hebrew Foundations of the Moroccan Jews' Spoken Arabic" (Heb.), *Leshonenu* 42(1978): 163–189 and especially pp.163–165.
61. Ben-Zvi Institute Ms. 1742, p.50.
62. On this, M. Bar-Asher, "The Hebrew Foundations," pp.175–176.
63. Ibid., pp.178–179; 184.
64. Ibid., p.175.
65. In Obadiah, *The Community of Sefrou* 1, p.163.
66. These things are found mainly in testimony before the Jewish court to clarify problems of *agunot* (wives whose husbands have disappeared without having divorced them), of inheritances and the like. On instances from Fez see: Yaakov ben Zur's *Law and Justice* (n. 44 above) 2, paragraphs 152–154, fols. 85b–86b; from Meknes, see for example, Raphael Berdugo's *Upright Laws* (n. 10 above) 1, par. 353, fol. 43a; for Sefrou, for example, see S. J. Abitbol's *Stones of Marble* (n. 11 above) 2, par. 23.
67. See, for example, *Stones of Marble* 2, par. 100, fol. 70.
68. Raphael Moses Elbaz, "Throne of Kings," (Heb.) Ms. Heb. 8° 1211 The Jewish National and University Library in Jerusalem, fol. 6a.
69. See, for example, *Upright Laws* par. 166, p.164; and cf. *Stones of Marble* 1, par. 4, fol. 3a; and also see *Law and Justice* 1, par. 65, fol. 63a.
70. *Law and Justice* 2, par. 21, fol. 11b; and cf. the general statement of the French Ambassador St. Olon that "Jews do not travel in the country without Muslim bodyguards," according to Blunt, *Black Sunrise* (n. 15 above), pp.34–44.
71. E. Levi-Provencal, *Extraits des historiens arabes du Maroc* (2nd ed., Paris, 1929), p.113 and cf. H. Terrasse, *L'histoire du Maroc* 2 (Casablanca, 1949–1950), p.264.
72. P. Shinar, "La recherche relative aux rapports Judéo-musulmans dans le Maghreb contemporain," in *Les relations entre Juifs et musulmans en Afrique du Nord, 19–20e siècle.* (Paris, 1980), p.12.
73. Braithwaite, *The History of the Revolutions, p.200.*
74. Ben-Zur, *Law and Justice* (n. 44 above) 2, par. 21, fol. 11a. Similarly, Moses Berdugo, *The Words of Moses* (Heb.), (Meknes, 1947), par. 71, fol. 16b.
75. *SIHM* 6, p.636.
76. For the years 1703 and 1720, see: J. Mashash, *Treasury of Letters* (n. 22 above) 1, paragraphs 191–192, fols. 82b, 83a; for 1728 see Bar-Asher, *The Community* p.124 n. 15; and for 1790, in the next note.
77. Berdugo, *Upright Laws* (n. 10 above) 1, par. 264, p.54 recounts that Muslim friends of Jews warned them "to mount a special guard on the mellah because the Ishmaelites have plotted against you to plunder and loot." However, this guard apparently was to no avail because "they plundered and looted, particularly those houses known to belong to the Jews." The last apparently refers to the Meknes mellah pogroms of 1790, and cf. the introduction to the Benaim Ms. Collection no. 37, Jewish Theological Seminary of America, New York.
78. Ms. of Eleazar Bahlul cited by Mashash in his introduction to the volume of Moses Berdugo, *The Chief Dispenser* (Jerusalem, 1975).
79. Ben-Zvi Institute Ms. 1742, p.63.
80. See above, n. 7.
81. Obadiah, *The Community of Sefrou-Morocco* 3, pp.145–146.
82. R. Berdugo, *Upright Laws* 1, par. 264, p.54.
83. Ben-Zvi Institute Ms. 1742, p.55.
84. Abitbol, *Stones of Marble* (n. 11 above) 2, par. 23, fol. 17a.
85. Ibid. 1, par. 14, fol. 2b; fol. 3a.
86. Obadiah, *The Community of Sefrou* 3, pp.145–146 and also see ms. 1742, p.61, about Muslims who came to spend time with Jews and to drink *mahyya* ("water of life"), the Moroccan strong drink, because of a miracle that happened to Ismail.
87. This is found not only with the large merchants but also with the middle level businessmen, peddlers, and the plain folk and is expressed mainly in the collections of responsa of the period. See, for example, the sources in Bar-Asher, *The Community*, p.97.
88. Ben-Zvi Institute Ms. 1742, p.57. And similarly in Ben-Zur *Law and Justice* (n. 44 above) 1, par. 78, fol. 68b.
89. *SIHM* 6, p.635.
90. D. Corcos, "Les Juifs au Maroc et leurs Mellahs," in *Studies of the History of the Jews of Morocco* (Jerusalem, 1977), pp.64–175; and on Mogador in particular, pp.123–175.

91. See the source in n. 108 below which undoubtedly also reflects the realities of the eighteenth century.
92. See E. Ashtor, *The Jews of Moslem Spain* (Philadelphia, 1973–1984), 3v.
93. See Bar-Asher, *The Community*, pp.113–114.
94. Ibid., pp.94–100.
95. See Obadiah, *The Community of Sefrou* 3, pp.46, 132–135.
96. Ibid., and particularly the second source in n. 28.
97. Raphael Berdugo, *Still Waters* (n. 44 above) 2, fol. 61a. Also cf. ibid., fol. 119b.
98. "Book of Enactments" (n. 38 above) par. 75 and Obadiah, *The Community of Sefrou* 1, pp.71–72.
99. Pethahiah Berdugo, *Honeycomb* (n. 33 above) par. 42, fol. 12b–13b.
100. On the polemics between Jews and Muslims in the early Middle Ages, see M. Perlmann, "The Medieval Polemics between Islam and Judaism" in *Religion in a Religious Age*, ed. S. D. Goitein (Cambridge, Mass., 1974), pp.103–138.
101. K. L. Brown. "Mellah and Medina, a Moroccan City and its Jewish Quarter," *International Conference of Jewish Communities in Muslim Lands* (Jerusalem, 1974). (mimeographed).
102. See H. Goldberg, "The Jews in the Rural Social and Economic Life of Tripolitania" (Heb.) in *Memorial for Abraham [Elmaleh]*, ed. H. Z. Hirschberg (Jerusalem, 1972), pp.176–194 and especially pp.179–185.
103. Thus I saw and heard in the area in which I grew up, in Tafilalet; another example is from Sefrou: see the source below in n. 110.
104. Ibid. p.181, and on Algeria, A. Cahen, *Les Juifs dans l'Afrique Septentrionale* (Constantine, 1867), pp.39–49.
105. According to what I saw in Ksar-El-Souk in Wadi Ziz in southeast Morocco and from what I heard from my grandfather Shimon Attia, of blessed memory, and my mother (his daughter), may she have a long life, Sarah Ben-Haroush.
106. See the discussion earlier in the article, and especially the sources in notes 90, 91.
107. See J. L. Miège, *Le Maroc et l'Europe (1830–1894)* 2 (Paris, 1961–1963), pp.86–89; 560–580.
108. M. Abitbol, *Temoins et Acteurs: Les Corcos et l'histoire du Maroc contemporain* (Jerusalem, 1978), pp.12–28 and especially the document on pp.40–41.
109. M. Shokeid, "Jewish Existence in a Berber Environment" in *Jewish Societies in the Middle East*, ed. S. Deshen and W Zenner (Washington, 1982), p.107.
110. L. Rosen, "Muslim-Jewish Relations in a Moroccan City," *International Journal of Middle East Studies* 3(1972):435.
111. In Deshen and Zenner, *Jewish Societies*, pp.107; 112.
112. On Morocco, see J. Ben-Ami, "Le culte des saints chez les juifs et les musulmans au Maroc," in *Les relations entre juifs et musulmans en Afrique du Nord, 19–20e sie* (Paris, 1980), pp.104–109.
113. Ibid., p.25.
114. *Jewish Folktales from Morocco* (n. 25 above), p.26.
115. H. E. Goldberg, "The Mimuna and the Minority Status of Moroccan Jews," *Ethnology* 17(1978):79.
116. Ibid., pp.77–78.
117. See the many sources cited by Ben-Ami in the expanded English version of the source in n. 71 above: "Relations between Jews and Muslims in the Veneration of Folk Saints in Morocco," *International Folklore Review* 3(1983):98.
118. M. HaCohen, *The Book of Mordechai, a Study of the Jews of Libya: Selections from the 'Highid Mordechai . . . '*, ed. Harvey E. Goldberg (Philadelphia, 1980), p.48.
119. Ibid., pp.51–52.
120. Ibid., p.55; and cf. P. Shinar, "La recherche relative . . ." (n 72 above) 1–31.

15

Anti-Zionist and Anti-Jewish Ideology in the Arab Nationalist Movement in Palestine

YEHOSHUA PORATH

1. Muslim-Christian Relations

Relations between the different religious communities in Palestine in the nineteenth century varied. While affairs between Jews and Muslims remained stable, those between the Muslim majority and the Christian minority steadily deteriorated, so that by the 1860s and 1870s there were constant clashes in their ordinary day-to-day encounters.

The primary cause for this development was the Napoleonic invasion. The invasion, perceived by some as having brought the light of modernity to the Middle East, in reality aroused the reverse of modern enlightened behavior – hostility of a majority towards the minority living in its midst.

The overwhelming enthusiasm with the Christians in Syria and Palestine greeted the advancing troops from Egypt enraged the Muslims. Neither community took note of the secular nature of the French Revolution. The tricolor of the revolutionary flag notwithstanding, France was viewed as a Christian power. The Christian minorities, especially the Maronites of the Lebanon who were allied with Rome, and the Christians of Galilee, waited with open arms for the arrival of Napoleon. When the French left, the embittered majority took its revenge.

A second cause for the deterioration in Muslim-Christian relations was the Egyptian invasion in the 1830s during the reign of Muhammad 'Ali who instituted new policies to improve the status of the non-Muslim. He revoked most of the restrictive legislation against all the communities; he instituted almost total equality of taxation, the exception being the poll tax; and, as he had in Egypt, he brought Christians into the ranks of public service, especially in financial and fiscal positions.

Mohammad 'Ali's reign quickly lost its popular appeal. He was too centralized and efficient. He collected too many taxes and tried to conscript the local populace into the army. The masses turned in anger against him and against all those who had cooperated with him. This time the Jews were not spared. However, the attacks on the Jews of Safed and Jerusalem in 1834, though part of the general uprising, were only minor episodes in a campaign whose wrath was directed primarily against the Egyptian conquest.

The third and most important reason for the change in relations between the communities were the reforms instituted by the Ottoman Empire in the mid-nineteenth century. These reforms continued the trend of equalization of status between Christians and Muslims. All official-legal discriminations were abolished including the poll tax, symbol of the inferior status of non-Muslims. To the consternation of local élites the central government in Istanbul imposed this policy upon all the major urban centers of the Fertile Crescent.

2. Attitude to Jews pre-World War I

However, the situation of the Jews was totally different from that of the Christians. For the Christians, this was a period of increasing affluence and economic growth. Their pride and self-confidence had increased as a direct result of the constant intervention of the Christian powers. These interventions also gave them a great sense of security. As a result, the Christian communities began to behave as if all restrictions and discrimination had been removed. They would go out in public with Christian symbols and toll the church bells, acts which had previously been prohibited. They even paraded through the streets in religious processions, holding aloft crosses. These actions especially infuriated the Muslim majority and its leaders and led, in 1860, to anti-Christian riots in Damascus. The rioters clearly differentiated between the city's Christians and Jews. The Jews were not hurt; and according to many accounts were not in the least unhappy with what the Muslims did to the Christians for the effects of the "Damascus blood libel" of 1840 had not yet been forgotten.

To understand what occurred from the end of the nineteenth century, one must understand that the traditional Muslim treatment of the Jews persisted, albeit in a more liberal guise. The fundamental concept of Islam's superiority was preserved. In everyday life, the Muslims continued lording it over the Jews, but stopped short of physical injury or attempts to force the Jews to convert.

By the second half of the nineteenth century this attitude of superiority in daily contact was no longer supported by official regulations. The Ottoman Empire from its beginning was much more tolerant than the Muslim régimes that preceded it, and this was certainly so by the end of the century. But the Jews at this time were not anxious to press for their legitimate equal rights. They kept their place on the fringes of society, thus creating a mutually acceptable pattern of relationships, and conflicts were kept at a minimum. Until the political issue connected with the Zionist enterprise in Palestine arose, a commonly accepted practical pattern of relationships functioned almost without hindrance. This was based, as stated, upon the acceptance of a tolerant superiority of Muslims over Jews.

Things began to change, of course, as the basic premises of the parties involved began to change. When the areas in which Jews could function in the society began to be more and more restricted, many Jews refused to accept their fringe status. They broke out of the boundaries of the "old settlement" and in the course of the first and second *aliyot*, from the 1880s until World War I, created the infrastructure of a new Jewish society in Palestine. The Arab community, especially the Muslims of Palestine, began developing an ideology, a system of responses to these developments, even as early as at the beginning of the "Hibat Zion" movement. The first glimmer appeared in the 1890s. There are those who, with some justification, treat the years up until World War I as one historical time period.

3. Objections to Jewish Settlement

Until the war, charges against Jewish settlement were based on four different viewpoints. First, from the Muslim perspective: The Jews are attempting to take the land over from the Muslims and alter its Muslem character in the face of a thirteen-hundred-year-old historic tradition.

A second objection, heard at various times from the general Ottoman point of view: The Jews are about to create a new minority problem in Palestine, and the Ottoman Empire already has enough such problems; there is no need to add a Jewish question in Palestine to the Armenian question or to what remains of the Bulgarian question.

The third objection began to develop a little later, especially after the revolution of the Young Turks. This was the start of a patriotic, Arab-Palestinian claim: It is the land of the Palestinians, an Arab land which must remain such; the Jews' attempt to change this must be prevented.

The fourth objection, voiced together with the third at the end of this period, was a more generally Arab one – if you like, the seed of a pan-Arab claim to Palestine: If the Jews should gain control of the land and reach the Gulf of Aqaba, it would sunder the geographic continuity of the Arab world and thus weaken the Arab nation by preventing future unification within a single territorial unit.

These are rational objections deriving from an historical or empirical assessment of the situation. They are not grounded in anti-Jewish or antisemitic feelings as we know them. But already at this stage charges were added to the empirical case from another constellation of feelings and beliefs antagonistic to Jews as such. These charges bore no relationship to what was happening in Palestine but were aired in that context. First of all, the charge was raised again that because the Jews are merchants by nature, diligent and talented, their immigration and settlement in Palestine must be prevented because they are liable to undermine the position of the local merchants. This charge was picked up to a relatively noticeable degree by the Christian elements, Christian merchants prominent in the commercial sphere. Christian newspapers frequently published it. Islam developed as the religion of a merchant society while the Christians' attitude towards commerce was very ambivalent and so this attitude could more easily appeal to the Christians.

To this was added the usual antisemitic claims, originating primarily from France, and from the Action Francaise school of those days. They were quickly transmitted and absorbed by the French speaking population (the majority of whom were Roman Catholics) and appeared in their periodicals. These were the old charges, repeated throughout the history of antisemitism, about the nature of the Jews, their practices, their characteristics and so on. One important charge should be mentioned here, for it took root, persisted for many years, and affected both the Christian and Muslim forms of expression. Starting with the Second Aliyah, the charge was raised that the Jews were introducing sexual promiscuity into the traditional society of the Middle East, a phenomenon aggravated, of course, by the Third Aliyah, which was much more revolutionary than the Second in everything concerning its life-style, especially in its collective organization – the kibbutzim.

We have in our possession the diary of a young Arab in Jerusalem during World War I. He was to have gone to study in Beirut but owing to the war was forced to remain in Jerusalem. His attitudes toward Jews as expressed in the diary is positive. He recounts that during the war the Ottoman military authorities caught Jews who had managed to avoid military service and forced them to do unpleasant tasks cleaning the city. The young man also describes their travail. It is interesting that when he mentions the new Jews, the Zionists, he does not excoriate or vilify them, nor does he even express any opposition to them, but he does mention their "shrewdness" "if they want to arrange something at some government office, they deliberately send one of their pretty girls. This way they get their matter attended to sooner." This description is indicative of the image which was created of the new life-style and place of women in the new Jewish society: their freedom to come and go, even to deal with government officials. This idea took root and was to reappear in the future.

During these years, a slight antisemitic tone was added to the charges levelled earlier. Charges began to be heard based upon the antisemitic infrastructure extant in Islam. This would be repeated in the future when the dispute intensified, the political tensions grew, and it was necessary to convince the public and the rulers of their validity. Verses were drawn from Islam which were interpreted as directed against the Jews, establishing their status among the nations of the world as lowly and miserable. This status must be preserved;

Jews must be prevented from daring to change this order of the world as set by Islam.

Despite everything, it must be said, that this same pre-World War I political opposition to Zionism or the Zionist endeavor did not re-appear after the war. The perception of threat and danger was still minimal. Zionism was seen as an experiment which would undoubtedly be nipped in the bud. It was even possible to appreciate and admire various practical achievements of the Zionist enterprise.

4. Attitudes after the Balfour Declaration

On the eve of and during the first years of World War I one could still find a factual balanced attitude toward the Jews in the Arab press. In the wake of the Balfour Declaration, as it became apparent that Britain had obligated itself to help the Jews establish their national home in Palestine, Arab society grew more wary. However, attitudes toward the Jews remained reasonable and opposition was not based upon an irrational pattern of Jew-hatred. A case in point is the fact that the first protest of the Arabs of Palestine was organized after the Jews celebrated the first anniversary of the issue of the Balfour Declaration with great ceremony and a mass rally. At the Arab protest, Zionism was sharply denounced and various reasons were offered why its fulfillment in Palestine should not be permitted. The protest was directed at the British, but it is important to note the fact, which was clearly emphasized, that they were protesting against the foreign Jews who came from outside and not against the established residents of the country, those who had been there from before the war or up till 1918, and who would enjoy the same full rights and obligations as all the other inhabitants. In this connection, let us add that the "Young Arab Movement," which had rallied around Faisal at the time and in which Palestinians played an active role, saw to it that Joseph Laniado (who later became the leader of the Syrian Jewish community) represented the Jewish community as a delegate to the Syrian Congress which enthroned Faisal. Under those conditions, it was conceivable that a Jew could become a journalist and even editor of a newspaper which was one of the clarions of this "Young Arab Movement" in Damascus in those years. This was Eliyahu Sasson, who later immigrated to Palestine and whose career blossomed particularly on the Jewish side; but in the years 1919–1920 he was editor of the newspaper *al-Hayah*, one of the organs of the Arab National Movement.

In general after the Mandate was confirmed and it became ever more evident that the danger was great, the anti-Zionist tone grew more strident. It was then that an entire set of arguments was developed which can be designated as the anti-Zionist ideology of the Palestinian Arabs. At first the principle of the right of peoples to self-determination was used. After World War I, this principle was accepted and almost sanctified, at least in eastern and southern Europe; and theoretically in the former Ottoman territories as well. The claim was that the right earned by Serbia should also apply to the Palestinian and other Arabs. Another interesting phenomenon which also developed at that time in the Arab National Movement was the adoption of a secular point of view, which was taking hold of the masses more and more, that is, that the Arabs are in the country not by dint of the seventh-century Muslim conquest but by virtue of the continuity of the Arab population ever since the Canaanites. Without getting involved in arguments about the extent to which the Canaanites truly were Arab as the term is defined by Arab nationalism, one can examine the linguistic kinship of the Canaanite and Arabic languages, and find that this investigation actually supports the Jewish argument more than the Arab. But in matters ideological the beliefs and the claims which are aired are more important than tested facts.

In that period and in the years thereafter, the claim to the right of national self-determination reappeared and was bolstered by the factual presentation of the relative numerical strengths of the groups in the country after World War I: Ninety percent or more of the population in Palestine were Arabs, mainly Muslims, with a Christian minority, and the Jewish population was not more than eight or nine percent. Another argument heard at that time was that Palestine was a Holy Land. This was a new argument, later to be developed in another fashion: Palestine is holy to the three faiths, including the Jews. But there are hundreds of millions of Muslims and hundreds of millions of Christians in the world and only fifteen million Jews. Therefore, because the country is holy to the three groups, its government should reflect their relative numbers in the world as a whole. It is inconceivable that authority over the land be given to the Jews or that an infrastructure for future Jewish rule be created there when it is sacred to a much greater number of Christians and Muslims.

As with many other concepts and symbols, in the ideational infrastructure the concept of the land's being holy to the three faiths was put aside. Instead, what was stressed was that the land is holy to Islam and contains holy sites whose care and protection are entrusted to the Arabs of the country – the country's Muslims – together with the Muslims of the world. This stance is related to the activity of Hajj Amin Al-Hussaini in the Supreme Muslim Council in his support of the mosques in Jerusalem. The concept, heard to this day, that Jerusalem is the third holy city of Islam, was furthered by this Council. Needless to say, there was also an attempt to cope with Zionism by analyzing it rationally. This approach did not try to prove that Zionism is a hopeless, illogical phenomenon; that an analysis of Zionism and the Jewish condition in the world makes it unthinkable. Rather, it resorted to an adaptation of the European Liberal and Socialist argument: The Jews are not a nation, they are a sect. Their rights are guaranteed in their lands of residence, and where these rights are not yet assured, they should be striving to attain them. A Jew cannot at one and the same time be a British, American, German, or Polish citizen and lay claim to Palestine on grounds of nationalism, and so forth – a full array of arguments of European origin.

An analysis of Jewish history added another layer to the argument: Even if we admit that theoretically there is something to the Jewish claim, in the final analysis it is baseless because the Jews, of all the peoples connected with Palestine, have lived in the country for the shortest time – only a few hundred years, and that not continuously; have left almost no trace; and what they did build was destroyed. On the other hand, in the thirteen centuries of Islam, beautiful mosques have been built in Jerusalem while almost no trace remains of Jewish civilization. Claims that the period of Jewish rule was one of anarchy and others in that vein have held up for many years and can still be read today. Even had the Jews lived in the land uninterruptedly, so the argument goes, and been a majority, and had an ordered government, thirteen hundred years have elapsed since then; the hands of the clock cannot be turned back nor the order of the world changed. For if such a thing could be done in Palestine, why not in Spain, in the United States, or in other countries?

5. 1920–30s

By the 1920s, seeds of anti-Jewish polemics were added to these pre-World War I contentions. These anti-Jewish themes have continued to develop. They are based not upon a rational or empirical analysis of reality or history but upon anti-Jewish myths featuring the evil qualities of the Jews. In the 1920s, it centered more specifically in the charge that the Jews brought Bolshevism to Palestine and the Middle East. There was a basis in fact to this argument, of course, because the Palestine Communist Party was established by Jewish immigrants, a Jew was behind the establishment of the Egyptian Communist Party, and emissaries of the Palestinian Communist party – even though they were not the moving spirits – helped establish the Communist Party of Syria and Lebanon; but this was not the thrust of those making the charges, because they were unaware of these facts. They saw only the kibbutzim and the communal life-style, and the charge that the Jews brought communism was intertwined with the earlier one that the Jews had introduced sexual and social license. The kibbutz, it was alleged, epitomizes all of these things: It has both communal living and sexual freedom. The kibbutz life-style is one of license and societal anarchy and make it difficult to determine who a child's parents are.

There is also an interesting semantic curiosity. In the early 1920s, the Arabic translation for "communist" was *ibahi*, which means permissive. Thus, when the Arabs charged that the Jews had established the Communist Party, it meant at one and the same time that they were the source for a party that is destructive of society and licentious in its social mores. There were those who justified the charge that it was the Jews in particular who had introduced Bolshevism by saying "Look at what they did in Russia – they imposed this blight there." But more important in this argument is the contention that the license, the destruction, the striving to demolish, are all inherent in Jews by their very nature.

This was the approach till approximately the end of the 1930s. In World War II the star of the Soviet Union rose: It became a major power and fairly strong Communist Parties, unrelated to Jews, also developed in the Arab countries. When Socialism became an acceptable goal there, the charge of the Jewish-Bolshevist connection disappeared. (Now, of course, the charge is reversed: The Jews represent Fascism and imperialism). Till the end of the 1930s, the charge was basically anti-Zionist with occasional antisemitic tones, the main thrust being that Zionism should not be implemented in Palestine. The distinction in principle between Jews and Zionists, between the old settlers and those who had recently arrived, though still retained, had by the 1930s become progressively blurred. The enormous growth of Jewish settlement understandably made Zionism a most frightening matter. After the large aliyah of the 1930s, there was no longer any point in the distinction between the established Jewish settlers and the new ones, because now almost all of them were new. The number of old settlement of First and Second Aliyah "veterans" comprising the country's population was small. It was then that, alongside the anti-Zionist argument which continued, the antisemitic charge grew stronger.

6. Nazism and Fascism

In this connection it is interesting to examine the effect of the rise of Nazism and Fascism in Europe. First, it is interesting to see how the Arab National Movement saw itself, and the similarity it found with German nationalism after the rise of Hitler. From the time of the early nineteenth-century romanticists, Arab emphasis had been upon language and culture as the basis of national unity, upon seeing the glorious past as the springboard for the re-formation of the nation. From the start, Arab nationalist thinkers headed by Sati al Husri saw the German model, both in its ideology and path to fulfillment, as one from which to learn; but understandably more important for their claim from a political point of view was that the Nazis, after coming to power, had successfully damaged Britain and France, the two detested imperialistic countries. Everything that happened in Europe, from the violation of the demilitarization of the Rhine region on, aroused great admiration among the Arabs. That Hitler, whose power in the early 1920s was so small, had managed to garner such great strength; to tear up the Versailles Treaty; to impose his will upon Europe – all this stirred the admiration of the Arabs who were at that time very much aware of the events in Europe.

Nazi antisemitism constituted a problem. It of course created feelings of identification and rejoicing at the calamity of the Jews. The "great power" had harmed the Jews, put them in their place, and given them what they deserved. But the Nazi rise to power had a concomitant difficulty of which the Palestinian Arabs were not unaware: the clear connection between the Nazi rise to power in 1933 and the great aliyah to Palestine. The Jewish community in Germany became a great potential for aliyah – which was different from the past situation. German antisemitism was very influential in the growth of antisemitism in Eastern Europe in the 1930s and in the mighty surge of Jews wanting to leave; therefore the Arabs were not drawn into a position of total identification with Nazism.

This was also true of Italy. The Arab attitude to events there was ambivalent: To be sure, the Italian Fascist Movement was worthy of emulation. It had succeeded in achieving national unity and rescuing Italy from the abyss of collapse and the anarchy of the early 1920s; but this movement was imperialistic and the Arabs felt themselves under attack. The conquest of Libya, the very ruthless suppression of the revolt there in 1931, and the hanging of 'Umar al-Mukhtar – the main street of Gaza is named after him to this day – all of these roused hatred, and the feeling was that the Italians were trying to expand in the Mediterranean area, also potentially detrimental to the Arabs. They therefore adopted a somewhat reserved stance. But, in the end, after the Nazi rise to power, what was mainly decisive was the Jewish aliyah, for the country was swept by ever-greater waves of immigrants. When this aliyah became a fact, the only remaining consolation was German antisemitism and the vitriolic Jew-hatred of the Nazis. From this point of view one can see that as the fear of aliyah grew, as German antisemitism developed, as echoes of the damage to the Jews in Germany reached Palestine – to these antisemitic accounts were added rejoicing at the catastrophe and attempts to find verification in the East for the charges levelled by the Nazis in Germany against the Jews and their way of life.

In this same period, one can read in Arab newspapers and books that the Jews received what they deserved, for trying to do to Germany what they had done to Russia twenty years earlier. This approach affects the Arab historiography of the Holocaust. Politically the position is one of neutrality: We are not responsible for the Jewish question in Europe and it should be solved where it was created, not at the expense of the Palestinian Arabs. To be sure, on the main political level, one can find a slight expression of regret in the post-World War II Arab League pronouncements; but if we examine the *belles-lettres*, the press, and the propaganda, we find that the chief reaction was silence. The political development in Palestine and the struggle over it were also analyzed without reference to the events taking place in Europe. Whenever the Jewish problem was mentioned, it was claimed that the Holocaust was inflated out of all proportion by the Jews for propaganda purposes, for it is unimaginable that so many Jews had been murdered. There were also those who claimed that far fewer Jews had been killed, and that those who were killed had been put to death legitimately because they had tried to injure Germany in wartime.

As for the question of the Nazis' ambivalent attitude to the fact that the Arabs are Semites, it seems that the Arabs understood that German antisemitism was directed primarily against the Jews, and were unenthusiastic about the attempts of the British in World War II to explain to them that antisemitism is part of the general concept of Aryan racial superiority. It is my impression that to the extent that the Arabs could express themselves freely, this explanation was not accepted and their attitude to the Germans during that period was not hostile. Antisemitism was understood in its anti-Jewish sense only. Incidentally, the day after Hitler came to power in the run-off elections in March, Hajj Amin al-Hussaini went to the German Consul in Jerusalem, proposing that they join in a treaty against the Jews, and that Nazi Germany and the Muslims announce a joint boycott against them. The Arabs even managed to gain some gestures of sympathy from Hitler, though not to the extent they wished. Shortly after the liquidation of Czechoslovakia in March 1939, Hitler did deliver a famous speech praising the struggle of the Arabs of Palestine but did not go very far in support their political aims.

7. The Canaanite Question

The question of the Canaanites and historic continuity were not part of the mainstream arguments at first. In Muslim historiography the Canaanite matter is not relevant at all because real history begins with Islam, and the only historic continuity to be found is that of the Arabs, not of the non-Muslim or non-Arab peoples. The Canaanite trend came chiefly from the Christians and developed with the predominance of secularism. At first, when the quarrel in Palestine was just budding, the Hebrews were considered part of the peoples who had emerged from East Arabia, from the Arabian Peninsula, and had settled in Palestine. But this attitude vanished quickly, and as the conflict in Palestine became more acute, the claim surfaced that the Arabs are the continuation of the Canaanites whereas the Hebrews are strangers who conquered and tried to destroy them. From this point of view, the Arabs have been, as it were, historical victims of the Jews ever since the latter's entry into Palestine. The view of the historical linkage with the Canaanites did not include the Jews or the Hebrews; they were not considered as being among the ancient peoples of Palestine of whom the present population is the continuation.

16

On Arab Antisemitism
Once More

YEHOSHAFAT HARKABI

1. Introduction

On the eve of Rosh Hashanah 5726 (Fall 1965), I published an article in
the newspaper, *Ma'ariv*, entitled "Arab Antisemitism." My purpose was to
alert the Israeli public's attention to the fact that a large number of antisemitic
books had been published in the Arab countries. Furthermore, what gave these
books greater significance was that many of them were officially sponsored by
governmental publishing houses.

Certain circles within the Israeli public were not pleased with this revelation
and the reaction to the article was first and foremost one of anger. To me
this seemed strange: it seemed that while antisemitism in a distant country is
intolerable and Israelis protest against it bitterly, for some reason, in the Arab
countries it is tolerable and to be passed over in silence. What was personally
even more upsetting was to discover that in Israeli and Jewish circles there was
a tendency to self-deception, to ignore Arab antisemitism as I described it,
despite all the evidence I specified, and even to deny its very existence. I was
especially upset since such a tendency to gloss over the Arab position involved,
at least in my opinion, a distortion of the truth and of reality. I was also grieved
to see how Israelis unwittingly abet Arab propaganda by such a stand.

I have tackled the phenomenon of Arab antisemitism in several books and
articles so that to reconsider it here gives me a degree of discomfort lest it
appear repetitious, for I do not pretend to offer anything new and have for
some time stopped exploring this subject and following its developments.[1]

2. Characteristics and Sources of Arab Antisemitism

In my writings on Arab antisemitism I have tried to stress some of its chief
characteristics: that this antisemitism is primarily ideological and political, a
political weapon in the struggle against Israel; it comes from above, from the

ruling circles and from the literary and political elite in a number of the Arab countries; it is not social, emerging from below. It is directed first and foremost against Israel and not necessarily against world Jewry; or more precisely, because of Israel it is directed also against the Jews. Its barbs are not so much against the Jewish race but against the culture and history of the Jews. It is not antisemitism which caused the Arab-Israeli conflict but the conflict which caused this sort of antisemitism. Its ideas are not particularly original, for similar ideas have appeared in foreign societies and even in the Arab countries, but the Arab-Israeli conflict infused them with vitality. The publication of such literature in the Arab countries does not mean that the Arabs are antisemites, but there is the danger that if these ideas take hold with the Arab public they could give birth to a tendency to antisemitism. The main significance of the antisemitic manifestations, their frequency and intensity, is that they provide a gauge for the strength of the opposition to Israel.

I have explained the logical evolution of the growth of this antisemitism: that is, the Arab goal in the conflict – the elimination of the State of Israel – is by its very nature unique in international political life, where normally the goals of countries in conflict are limited. In most conflicts, both contesting parties assume the other's right to exist and are not fighting for the elimination of one or both of them. This goal of elimination made it necessary to present the State of Israel is uniquely despicable so that it would warrant the verdict of death decreed for it. Israel's establishment was described as aberrational, and the claim was that only a community so deeply and radically depraved could have perpetrated so foul and outrageous a crime as stealing a country from its inhabitants and turning it into a homeland for itself. The odium of this people is not only superficially revealed in the present but is embedded in its history and interwoven in its culture.

Furthermore, during the Nasser period, all-out war was decided upon as a means by which the Arabs would achieve their goal – as a primary programmatic principle. The concept of the elimination of a country by all-out war, by an act of annihilation of great proportions, required a hardening of the hearts, dehumanizing the Israeli community and presenting it as unworthy of compassion. This aim, too, reinforced the antisemitism. It is not accidental that the literature used for the indoctrination of the Egyptian Army abounded in antisemitic ideas.

I have attempted to shed light upon the sources from which the Arab antisemitic ideas drew. Since the mid-nineteenth century, antisemitic books in Arabic had been published in the Middle East by Christian Arabs who had drawn their teachings from western, mostly French, works. This followed upon the Damascus Blood Libel of 1840 and continued. In those days the sources of Arab antisemitism were Christian, but of late there is an evident tendency to "Islamize" Arab antisemitism by giving it a Muslim ideational color, stressing the negative characteristics of Jews and Judaism as found in the old

Muslim literature. Indeed, there are many manifestations in Islam from which an antisemitic tendency could draw motifs and ideas without European sources. One idea, it seems to me, which became basic to Arab antisemitism is clearly western: the Jewish conspiracy derived from the *Protocols of the Elders of Zion*. The Jewish plot is presented as giving the Jews malevolent power whereas the dominant image of the Jews in Islam is one of degradation and weakness. It is possible that there was also a role for the plot idea within the framework of the Arab-Israeli conflict – as an explanation of the Jewish victories. Such an explanation also mitigates the Arabs' self-reproach; that is, their vanquishment was a result of a satanic force such as a world-wide plot and the victory is not indicative of Israeli skill or ability.

3. Antisemitism and Zionism

The connection between the Jews and Zionism is semantically expressed in Arab writings by the fact that "world Jewry" and "world Zionism" are used interchangeably as synonyms. For example, Abbas Mahmud Al'Aqad, one of the great modern Egyptian authors, used the term "anti-Zionism" when he meant antisemitism (in the pamphlet *World Zionism* in the official Egyptian series "We Have Chosen You"). Sometimes we find Arabs referring to Jews who lived in early times as "Zionists" without at all being mindful of the anachronism of this charge. In the Egyptian Army they taught that "the *Protocols of the Elders of Zion* is the most prominent of Zionist writings as far as its political planning."[2] One should note that such a stand implies an endorsement of the truth of the Protocols; and in changing the attribution to "Zionists" rather than to "Jews" there is no moderation of the antisemitic position which underlies it. Such an approach is common and is heard from many Arabs, including residents of Judaea and Samaria. The derogatory qualities which the antisemitic literature attributes to the Jews are thereby transferred to Israel and the Israelis. Zionism is termed "the executive arm" or "the executive apparatus" of the Jews. This too is a logical development. If the Jews are depraved, then their State, their creation, is also inherently debased; and conversely, the depravity of Israel is transferred to the Jews. Thus a cycle is formed: reinforced depravity from the Jews to Israel and from Israel to the Jews.

In this desire to complete the circle of debasing both the Jews and Israel, the Arabs were the pioneers and trailblazers for European and American antisemitism where there has recently been evidence not only of Jew-hatred but of hostility towards Israel as well, and support of the Arab side. In the past there were antisemitic circles which saw Zionism as a way of getting rid of the Jews and which therefore, to a certain extent, were sympathetic to it. Thanks to the Arabs, antisemitism today outside the Middle East, in its social and cultural manifestations, is assuming a political dimension in the form of opposition to Israel, its policies, and even its existence. In this respect, antisemitic circles in the West are becoming an extension of Arab antisemitism and of the most militant anti-Israel Arab position.

To be sure, an anti-Zionist stand unentangled with antisemitism is possible. There are Jews who oppose Zionism who cannot be accused of antisemitism. The matter becomes problematic, by Arab argument, when Zionism is defined as "Jewish nationalism" which, according to them, is forbidden to Jews because they are not a national entity but only a religious community. Therefore, those Arabs argue, Zionism is a perversion of Judaism. As individuals, Jews and Israelis are entitled to all rights; but as a group, to none. In the past, before the establishment of the State of Israel, such a position was tenable; but it is a different matter now, after the State has been established as an expression of nationalism. Today, such a concept negating Israeli nationalism, even if unintentionally, degrades Jews and to a certain extent Israelis, implying them to be inferior human beings undeserving of statehood. If this is not antisemitism, it is a step in that direction.

Antisemitism, one suspects, may be expressed by heaping opprobrium not only upon Jews, their culture and history, but also upon Israel and Zionism. The critics of Israel and Zionism tend to attribute to them the negative qualities which antisemites were wont to attribute to the Jews in general – aggressiveness, corruption, scheming, and the like. Furthermore, there is no country in the world nor any political movement which is perfect and all are deserving of criticism for some act or other. There is no country without sin, and human existence contains both the good and the evil. But when Israel, whose deeds are certainly also not to be measured by a purely moral standard, is singled out for a spate of reviling accusations, there is reason to suspect antisemitic influence. The stereotypes which nations apply to the peoples around them are usually summed up in a single derogatory quality – the Scots are excessively frugal, and the like – or in a few. Antisemitism singles out the Jews for an infinite catalog of negatives. They are the hopeless representatives of evil and the Devil. The same is the case with the State of Israel's being seen as different from all the others by levelling endless charges against it. People have some hesitation before they leap from an accusation related to a certain action to finding fault with the perpetrator's very being, from accusing people of an aggressive act to attributing aggressiveness to them as part of their character and essence. Yet Israel and Zionism are described not only as having failed in a specific particular or detail but as the embodiments of a group of reprehensible characteristics. Such descriptions, it seems, lean toward antisemitism. It is not antisemitism because of a single accusation but because of the accrual of charges.

Arab opposition to the establishment of Israel was understandable, but meanwhile Israel exists and has firmly established itself. Many of the world's political facts, even those established by violence, have – once established – become part of the international tapestry and they are not forever denounced. In most instances, countries accept the fact of one another's existence; at most there are those who demand a change of régime in a rival country or make territorial claims on some area.

It is futile to argue with the Arab stand demanding the elimination of Israel for that is a matter of Arab will. But a position which insists that one's will must prevail is arbitrary and cannot therefore be convincing. This is not generally the Arabs' *modus operandi*. They try to justify their demand for Israel's elimination by the claim that its existence is unjust. However, the longer Israel continues to exist, the more difficult it becomes to base the demand for its elimination on reasons relating to the circumstances of its establishment. Its establishment in the past becomes irrelevant to its present existence, as in other historical instances. For this reason as well, the Arab motivation for demanding that Israel cease to exist has turned to the argument that Israel is negative in its very being and nature. That is to say, the mere possibility that Israel may be good or tolerable in any way is rejected out of hand as self-contradictory. Herein, it seems, lies a covert antisemitic approach similar to that which claims that the evil quality of the Jews is immutable and is, as it were, a transhistorical factor.

The Protocols of the Elders of Zion has been published in Arabic many times as well as in a number of different translations and they have left their mark upon the image of Israel and the Jews in Arab eyes. There is much evidence of this. For example, Anis Sayegh, former director of the PLO's Research Centre in Beirut, explains in the introduction to Adiv Qa'uad's book, *The Jewish Woman in Occupied Palestine*: "Most of what has been published in Arabic about the Jewish woman and her role in Palestine during the past fifty years is restricted to one aspect of the Zionist female's activity, that aspect whose origins go back to the ancient period of the Pentateuch and relies upon the roll spelled out for the Jewish women in the building of the kingdom of Zion in the *Protocols of the Elders of Zion*."[3]

Alongside the *Protocols* there is another book whose influence has perhaps been no less: the Austrian antisemite August Rohling's *Talmudjude* which was translated from French into Arabic and appeared in Cairo in 1899 as *The Buried Treasure of the Talmud (Al-Kanz al-Marsud min qu'ad al-talmud)*. The book was republished in 1938 as *The Barbarity of the Instructions of the Talmud* and, in both its forms, was reissued in Beirut in 1968 and 1970. Its advantage over the *Protocols* is that it relies upon Jewish sources such as the Talmud; thus its defamation of the Jews is deep and culturally based, not the fruit of any hidden conspiracy. It also allows for the Zionism-Talmud linkage. (The book's influence is evident in the Egyptian Army indoctrination of the pre-1967 years. See the lecture of Sabari Al-Huli in my *How the Arab Position Was Explained in the Egyptian Army*.) The tendency to connect Zionism and the Talmud was criticized by Dr As'ad Razuq in his book *The Talmud and Zionism*.[4] But in his critique he listed a lengthy series of books in Arabic based upon Rohling. In fact, it is doubtful that a book such as Rohling's could have been published again in any language except Arabic.

4. After the Holocaust

In the 1950s and 1960s the Holocaust cast its shadow over Western antisemitism; the memory of the Holocaust lessened its possible influence. Arab
antisemitism suffered no such inhibition; it even contained bitter charges that
the Jews were lying and grossly exaggerating what Hitler had done to them or
that his action was a just retribution for what the Jews had done to Germany. It
seems that denial of the Holocaust in Arab writings started much earlier than in
Europe. What is more, the charge recurred in Arab writings that the Jewish
Holocaust hyperbole was intended to serve them in their conflict with the
Arabs, that is, that the Jews are trading on their history in order to create an
atmosphere in which the world would recognize its obligation to them and
weigh the scales in their favor in that conflict. Already at the Bandung Conference in 1955, when Nehru mentioned the matter of the "five" million Jews
who had been killed in Europe in World War II, Dr Charles Malik of Lebanon
replied that the slaughter of the Jews is only "Zionist propaganda."[5] Arab antisemitism is largely a post-Holocaust development and its fervor testifies that
the Holocaust did not diminish it. Thus it was a fact that in the years when
Western antisemitism declined, Arab antisemitism flourished. Apparently, it
even took the lead ideationally, especially in linking the defamation of Jews with
the State of Israel. The practical contribution to antisemitism by the Arabs is
also depicted by the fact that many of the antisemitic publications were printed
in the Arab lands and disseminated upon Arab initiative. Arabs could place at
the disposal of antisemitic groups throughout the world the amenities which the
latter lacked and thereby also help them gain status and influence. This same
phenomenon recurs in the infuence of the PLO organizations upon international
terrorism which comes from their ability to provide means, training camps,
arms, documents, and refuge which are unavailable to underground organizations, thus, in exchange, gaining their assistance and support in the struggle
against Israel. The phenomenon of antisemitic circles maintaining intimate
relationships with Arabs and at times even being supported by them financially,
is commonplace: for example, the negotiations between Shad'hali, when he
was Egypt's military attache in England, and Mr Colin Jordan (a British right-
winger).

Even more, Arab antisemitism, by being official and supported by Arab
circles of international standing, helped give the anti-Israel and anti-Jewish
positions a measure of *respectability* in the world. The world's memory of the
Holocaust faded and a new generation arose which did not know its horrors. To
be sure, it was possible to continue and sustain the stigma which marked antisemitism by fighting Arab antisemitism. For this reason there is a real significance in the constant denunciation of antisemitism by world public opinion.
Precisely because Arab antisemitism has abounded in manifestations of overly
abusive language, this aspect could have been used to create a spiritual climate
of antidote to the spread of antisemitic ideas, to make antisemitism repulsive at
least to the more enlightened segment of public opinion in the Western world.

Most regrettably no effort whatsoever was made in this direction. Manifestations of Arab antisemitism were met by an almost forgiving stance on the part of the Israeli government and public. How could the world be expected to be impressed or repelled by antisemitism if the Israeli public remained unimpressed? How could one expect the world press to deal with it or decry it if the Israeli press dealt with it only perfunctorily?

Since Arab antisemitism is political and not necessarily social, the struggle against it should also have been political. Pamphlets did appear in Israel which dealt with Arab antisemitism and denounced it, but these were presented as informative pieces – their influence is minimal and they seldom get beyond dentists's waiting rooms. My own pubications have had no effect, and some Israelis' criticism of them made Arab antisemitism a controversial subject. The review of a pamphlet or book does not make newspaper headlines. Only a political topic which occupies a parliament, or a political pronouncement by prominent personalities, grabs the headlines. For example, the manifestation of Arab governmental antisemitism did not even lead to the Knesset's devoting a session to a discussion of the matter which could have drawn world attention. No Israeli prime minister saw fit to devote a political statement, speech, or even a single line of speech, to these manifestations – at most it was mentioned incidentally. The Knesset protested against the hanging of Jews in Iraq, but when the government of Iraq published the *Protocols of the Elders of Zion* Israel was silent. Perhaps this tolerance of Arab antisemitism was among the factors which enabled Western antisemitism to raise its head. This was a failure for which Israel is to blame.

There is another aspect to this matter: Israel's relation to the Jewish people. There is no comparing the publication of an antisemitic book by a private party in some small city to the publication of an antisemitic book by a government. It is Israel's *duty* to the Jewish people to protest against every instance of any government's show of antisemitism.

My impression from symposia on antisemitism is that Israeli scholars share the responsibility for this attitude of ignoring Arab antisemitism. They did not credit it as a manifestation of antisemitism either because it did not develop from below as a social phenomenon, or because it was not Christian, as if antisemitism can stem only from Christian sources. These, however, are arbitrary restrictive conditions and there can be a species of antisemitism without them.

The Arabs have also revealed a great sensitivity to their antisemitic manifestations; they recognized it as a point of weakness in their position, should Israel exploit it in the contest for world public opinion. It is no accident that they have published apologies for these manifestations. What brought that about was precisely the condemnation of their antisemitism; yet the perception which prevailed in many circles in Israel was that to emphasize the gravity of the Arab position is undesirable; that the Arabs will mellow if presented as moderate (in the magic manner of self-fulfilling prophecy). The reverse is true.

The Arab position can be moderated if its gravity is stressed in a way which forces them to apologize for it and retreat from it.

5. The Effect of the Six-Day War

After the Six-Day War the standing of the Arab position in the conflict, as far as world public opinion went, slowly began to change. Previously, the Arabs had to admit that their purpose was the annihilation of Israel. This aim of eliminating a political state seemed eccentric and anachronistic, a return of humanity to the barbarism of ancient history. The results of the 1967 war enabled the Arabs to claim other goals: a return to previous boundaries and the right of self-determination for the Palestinians. There is room to assume that for many of them these were only interim goals leading to the old goal, that of eliminating Israel. But their advantage was that these goals freed the Arabs of the necessity of clearly enunciating their final aim. These intermediate goals also fit into the universal norms which shaped the spirit of the post-World War II period – the negotiation and suspicion of territorial changes, for people had learned the lesson that these are the first cause of wars; that the way to prevent wars is to build a hard and fast territorial order. The right of self-determination was the chief slogan of the Third World and of the entire period.

The change in the standing of the Arab position in world public opinion did not come about only as a result of political and economic interests. Circles uninfluenced by oil and petro-dollar considerations began to support the Arab position, and especially the Palestinian stand, for ethical reasons. In some quarters, the complaints and the denunciations began to be directed against Israel, for to come out against Israel was not as extreme as supporting its elimination, which by its very nature is anachronistic. Furthermore, when different circles in the world began to show an understanding of the Arab position and to support it, some of them actually went the full route to negating Israel's right to exist.

This possibility of denouncing Israel as an occupying power or as depriving the Palestinians of their rights, broke the dam and made it also possible to come out against Jews and find fault with them. Certainly there are deep and independent reasons for Western antisemitism and its awakening, but we are not sufficiently aware of the extent to which events in the Middle East in the realm of Israel-Arab relations effect it, albeit indirectly. Certainly, Soviet anti-semitism is helped by charges and examples of Israeli behavior in the Middle East. It also maligns the Jews, decries Zionism, and evidences hostility to Israel. Criticism of a particular piece of British or French behavior does not lead to heaping scorn upon the British or the French. Britain and France, as it were, are the fruit of a long history whereas Israel is the product of the Jews, with some of its founders still alive. We are not conscious enough of the peculiarity of our situation. It is no wonder that among the despicable traits imputed to Israel there appear, in a new guise, those which had previously been imputed to the Jews.

The rout of the Arabs in 1967 brought many of them to introspection and self-criticism. In some circles the stimulus of the crushing defeat caused a spate of antisemitic motifs. A specific connection between the defeat and the *Protocols of the Elders of Zion* can be found in the book by the Jordanian Prime Minister of those days, Sa'ad Jum'ah, *The Conspiracy and the Battle of Fate.*[6] The defeat brought an upsurge of Muslim antisemitic expressions in Al-Azhar circles, of which the Fourth Congress of the Muslim Academy, convened in Cairo in September 1968, was a prominent example. (There is a photograph of segments of the English translation officially issued in Egypt in D. F. Green's book, *Arab Theologians on Jews and Israel.*[7]) In the Lebanese paper *al-Anwar* of 8 March 1970, the *Protocols* headed the list of that week's best-sellers in Lebanon.

On the other hand, after the war, Arab intellectuals published articles denouncing antisemitism and reproaching Arabs for resorting to it. In his introduction to the Arabic translation of Herzl's diaries, Anis Sayegh explains that the Arabs are losing the battle for world public opinion because of their reliance upon the *Protocols*: "The Zionists, with their renowned slyness, in order to rally world public opinion against the Arabs, are spreading the word throughout the world that some of the Arabs are relying upon the *Protocols* and their publication locally."[8] Dr Sadiq Jalal Al-'Azm spoke out harshly against the Arabs' use of the *Protocols* and criticized the Arab stand which attributes detestable qualities to the Jews as permanent ones; he even pointed out that such a stance leads to a genocidal position: "If the Jewish people in its on-going essence is always and everywhere evil, aberrational, degenerate, and characterized by all the detestable qualities, the hope of rectifying this disgraceful state disappears. There is no avenue of influence open to us other than to uproot this abominable nature, that is to say, its elimination and eradication. A manifestation of this logic is implicit in some of the Arabs' irresponsible demagoguery about solving the Palestinian problem by killing, slaughtering, and throwing into the sea."[9] One should remember that the same argument leading to the Holocaust has been analyzed by Norman Cohn in his book *Warrant for Genocide.*[10]

The standing question is: What is the current trend of antisemitic publications in Arabic? My general impression is that the official publications are fewer. This is especially evident in the books published by the Egyptian information institutions: In the 1950s and 1960s there were many such publications, even accusing the Jews of human sacrifice and the use of human blood, which is foreign to Islam. On the other hand, in Islamic pronouncements anti-Jewish concepts are being expounded persistently. In the publications of the "Muslim Brotherhood" which began to appear again in the latter half of 1976, the motif recurs that the Jews are the enemies of Islam, and a similar theme pervades

Khumeini's speeches. To be sure, Islam does contain some harsh anti-Jewish components. To excise them from the religion is difficult for the faithful; but it is possible to consign them to oblivion – for even if there are elements in a religion which, because of their sanctity are not to be cancelled out, the faithful can minimize or submerge them, and a prolonged submergence can result in their being forgotten, which is tantamount to cancellation *de facto* if not a denial *de jure*.

There were manifestations of Muslim anti-Judaism, for example, in Anwar Sadat's speech at the mosque on the Prophet's birthday, 25 April 1972:

> Now they talk of direct negotiations. They were the Prophet's neighbors in Medina: He negotiated with them and they reached an agreement but, in the end, they proved to be liars and traitors for they made a pact with his enemies to strike at him in Medina and attack him from within. The most magnificent thing which the Prophet Muhammad did was to drive them from the entire Arab Peninsula. This is what God's messenger Muhammad did. We will never negotiate directly. We are aware of our history and the life of the Prophet Muhammad. They are a nation of liars and traitors, a people of plotters, a folk created for treacherous deeds . . . Last year I promised you this and I promise it to you this year: that on the Prophet Muhammad's next birthday we shall celebrate here not only the liberation of our land but also the removal of the Israeli arrogance and lack of restraint so that they shall again be as described in the Koran, living as they are fated to live, in degradation and impoverishment. We shall not give in on this. The issue no longer is only the liberation of our land but it concerns our honour and the destiny in which we believe. We shall restore them to the condition in which they were. If they thought in a moment of distraction that they have achieved a modicum of power, we shall return them to their condition. For power lies not in arms; power comes from within.

The linkage Sadat finds between historic memories (the Jews' relationship to Muhammad) and current events is typical of the Muslim writings relating to the conflict in which historic memory is given actual meaning.

Anis Mansur, the journalist apparently close to Sadat and considered by Sadat as an expert on matters of the Jews and Israel, invoked antisemitic ideas in his articles, even ones relating to the blood libel (the Jews as "bloodsuckers"). He did not even shy away from proclaiming that "Hitler was right." Mansur also called for the republication and dissemination of Rohling's book.[11]

6. Peace Negotiations

From the variety of evidence, one may conclude that antisemitic concepts have made inroads in the consciousness of many Arabs even though they disguise them as anti-Zionist ones. This raises the question of how to relate to this phenomenon especially in the light of peace negotiations and the possibility of peace. It is not a simple one.

It would be an error to say that the annoucement by Egyptian leaders of their desires to create a real peace is proof that they have spurned their earlier anti-Jewish concepts. Such ideas may still have a hold on their thinking. The desire of the Egyptian leaders for peace is not derived from any conclusion that they have erred in denigrating Israel, but rather from their conviction that they themselves are in need of peace as an internal Egyptian interest and as a condition for the development of Egypt. As a result, they are ready to distinguish between their policy in the conflict and their image of Israel. This is a new factor. In the past, their image of Israel was negative and their policy was the denial of Israel's existence. It can be claimed that there is a certain consistency of a sort to this stand, whereas the present situation is inconsistent. However, if a peace agreement is reached and can actually be implemented without crises and disruption of relationships because of differences in interpretation of the details of the agreement, there is reason to hope that these images will be changed over time and that direct meeting between the peoples may improve their mutual stereotypes.

The complexity of the situation is that peace is likely to bring about a change of images, but if this change is made a requisite for peace, then peace will be long delayed. Once the Arab-Israeli conflict is settled, there is room to hope that many of the antisemitic manifestations aroused by the conflict would disappear. True, the life expectancy of antisemitism in Europe has shown itself to be considerably long. However, there is a sort of "historicistic" arrogance in imposing rules upon history by deciding that antisemitism in the West is permanent and thus differentiating between it and Arab antisemitism. Let us remember that in the West there is also friendship toward Jews and Israel and that we Jews share the Bible with Christianity, which is not the case with the Muslims.

Even if there are factors of bitter opposition to Judaism within Islam, in regard to Jews the Muslim religious factor is not only an aggravating factor but an ameliorating one as well. True, when an aim becomes a religious one, the aggressiveness in its pursuit may grow; yet, on the other hand, the realization of national goals becomes less urgent as responsibility may be passed to the Almighty.

Islam as a religion also allows for explanations which support peace. The Egyptian writer, 'Aishah Abd Al-Rahman, known as "Bint Al-Shati," published some very harsh writings of a religious nature against Jews, including a book called *The Enemies of Mankind*,[12] the appellation she applies to Jews. In the light of Sadat's initiative, she published an article in the *Al-Ahram* of 16 December 1977 in which she repeated the line taken in her book: viewing current events in the light of the Jews' attitude towards Muhammad. Then, too, there was no need for the Prophet to make a pact with the Jews of Medina. He did so from a position of strength as an expression of his generosity and magnanimity.

238   *Yehoshafat Harkabi*

So too with Sadat, following the Prophet's path. To be sure, the Jews caused the breakdown of the agreement because of their arrogance (*Ghurur*), but one can make peace with them not as a reward for their actions but rather as an expression of the greatness of the Muslims.

A similar motif is heard again, for example, in the words of Ahmad Al-Hufi that peace suits the supremacy of Islam and expresses it. "Islam is the religion of peace," and here he cites a verse from the Koran: "If they turn to peace, you do so also and trust in God." Islam, he explains, sees peace as a commandment so long as the rights of the faith are not impaired.[13]

It is not the change of images, then, which will lead to peace but peace which will lead to the change of images. It should be noted that in the official Egyptian media such as the radio, antisemitic motifs are no longer appearing, apparently upon instruction from above. However, these motifs do continue to appear, as of old, in the publications of the "Muslim Brotherhood" and Islamic fundamentalists in Egypt.

The matter of Arab antisemitism should be raised in the negotiations with Egypt. The fact that the political élite in Egypt harbors antisemitic perceptions should be raised at least in the discussions with the United States as a problem related to the stability of the existing order. Manifestations of malice among the Arabs are the best, and perhaps the only, justification for Israel's requests pertaining to its security. This claim of Arab antisemitism underscores the debt which the Arabs owe Israel and not only what Israel owes them, as they are wont to argue. Raising this claim will be effective if there is no suspicion that it is an Israeli excuse to avoid concessions. There are Israelis who fear that broaching Arab antisemitism will provide an excuse for a hawkish Israeli position. It is not necessarily so. In Israel, not only the moderates, but also the extremists have tried to paint the Arab position as more moderate than it was; Arab radicalism upset their argument that the Arabs, in the end, will accept Israel's conquests. It is possible to take the most dove-like of Israeli stands and still speak of the evidence of Arab malice as antisemitism, as a justification for the Israeli demands. In Israel's circumstances, such a combination constitutes the best political formulation.

Notes

1. I have dealt with Arab antisemitism in: *Arab Attitudes to Israel* (Jerusalem, 1972), ch. 5; *The Position of Israel in the Israel-Arab Conflict* (Heb.), (Tel-Aviv, 1968), pp. 29–30, 43 (and the need to condemn Arab antisemitism, pp. 62–63); *Between Israel and the Arabs* (Heb.), (Tel-Aviv, 1968), pp. 16–20, the first article "Arab Antisemitism" and "Some Introspection on Arab Antisemitism"; "Our Delusions and Arab Antisemitism" (Heb.), *Ma'ariv*, October 29, 1965; *Fundamentals in the Israel-Arab Conflict* (Heb.), (Tel-Aviv, 1971), sub-chapter: "Antisemitism as a Political Instrument"; *How the Arab Position was Explained in the Egyptian Army* (Heb.), (Tel-Aviv, 1968); *The Arab Lesson of Their Defeat* (Heb.), (Tel-Aviv, 1969) – Al-'Azm's criticism of the Arabs' dependence upon the Protocols, p. 85, and of Nadim Al-Jasr calling for a war of annihilation against the Jews as a commandment of Islam, pp. 251–254.
2. Y. Harkabi, *How the Arab Position was Explained in the Egyptian Army* (Heb.) (Tel-Aviv, 1968), p. 23.

3. A. Qa'uad, *The Jewish Woman in Occupied Palestine* (Arabic) (Beirut, 1968), p. 7.
4. A. Razuq, *The Talmud and Zionism* (Arabic) (Beirut, 1970).
5. Quoted by G. H. Jansen, *Zionism, Israel and Asian Nationalism* (Beirut, 1971), p. 257.
6. S. Jum'ah, *The Conspiracy and the Battle of Fate* (Arabic) (Beirut, 1968).
7. D. G. Green, *Arab Theologians on Jews and Israel* (Geneva, 1971).
8. Th. Herzl, *Yaumiat Herzl* (Arabic) (Beirut, 1968), introduction.
9. S. J. Al-'Azm, "The Arabs and the Marxist View of the Jewish Question," (Arabic) *Dirasat 'Arabiyah* (January 1970), p. 10; repr. in his *Leftist Studies of the Palestinian Problem* (1970).
10. N. Cohn, *Warrant for Genocide* (New York, 1969).
11. *Al-Ahram*, April 13, 1977.
12. 'A. Abd-al-Rahman, *The Enemies of Mankind* (Arabic) (Cairo, 1969).
13. *Al-Ahram*, November 25, 1977.

A Personal Note

In the past when I analyzed Arab antisemitism I was encouraged by the realization that it was one-sided and that symmetrical denigration of Arabs and their culture is almost non-existent among Jews. Now I am not at all sure of it, as anti-Arab ideas expressed by Jews have emerged. This development should grieve and worry us. We can no longer find fault with Arabs without finding fault with ourselves.

17

From Radicalism to Antisemitism*

MOSHE ZIMMERMANN

Antisemitism is generally regarded as a regressive trend in a world undergoing industrialization and a change of values. Therefore one does not expect political forces engaged in modernization and seeking rational and practical solutions to indulge in antisemitic or anti-Jewish activities. Nevertheless, we encounter a considerable measure of antisemitism among the enlightened of the eighteenth century, among the revolutionaries of the twentieth century, and among the democrats or radicals of the nineteenth century, who were the heirs of the enlightened and the inspiration for the twentieth-century revolutionaries.

In the present essay I shall not attempt to give a general description of the interaction between radicalism and antisemitism in the nineteenth century. Rather I shall concentrate upon one biographical aspect of this subject only. On first thought it would seem that the biography best suited for this purpose would be that of Richard Wagner, the man who during the revolution of 1848-9 stood on the barricades beside Bakunin and who, two years later, mounted a general attack against the Jews in music. However, I am convinced that the most significant and interesting biography to throw light upon these developments is that of Wilhelm Marr. It was in the year 1878 that he coined the term *antisemitism*, thirty years after he himself had fought with his pen, if not with his sword, the battle of the revolutionaries of 1848.

When discussing this man, we need not hesitate to use the term radicalism – since he called himself a radical – as well as the term antisemitism, for he was the original antisemite. We might even claim that he was the only one of his generation to whom the term fully applies, since he himself regarded his successors as degenerated antisemites. Before he died he was even convinced that antisemitism, as he understood and promoted it, had passed away and disappeared.

* This translation first appeared in a slightly different form in *The Jerusalem Quarterly* 23 (Spring, 1982): 114–128.

Marr's successors themselves regarded the radical, democratic tradition of 1848 as the source of their master's antisemitism. They were not far from the truth. I shall attempt to demonstrate how consistent this 1848 radical was in his ideology, how he transferred his radicalism from one area of political and social thinking to another, until he became a sheer reactionary in terms of the late nineteenth century. I wish to emphasize here the *continuity* rather than the turning points in the road from radicalism to antisemitism.[1]

1. Wilhelm Marr's Radical Background

The radicalism of the 1840s has five main characteristics: democracy, emancipation, secularism, revolutionism, and the protest against the accepted norms of society and social thinking.

The connection between radicalism and democracy is so close that we find the combination "radical-democratic" in the name of a party (Marx), and "radical" and "democratic" as interchangeable terms in the definition of Wilhelm Marr's own party. This radical democracy is in the first place distinguished by numerical terms: it is concerned not only with individual citizens as entitled to determine their own fate, but the *majority* as the decision-maker for all, a distinction that clearly differentiates between the liberals and the democrats of that period.

Ever since the 1830s, the slogan of emancipation had been applied in various contexts: It was meaningful for relations between social classes, between the sexes and between churches. This last point in particular led to heated arguments among radicals. Outside the Church (Feuerbach) as well as within it (Wichern), radicals not only contested the status of the church within the state but even its place in human relations in general. The combination of democracy, emancipation, and anticlericalism necessarily led to revolutionism, to the demand for radical change in the governmental institutions and in the foundations of social activity, using force and violence to a greater or lesser extent. The revolutionary drive was searching for as many outlets as possible, from basic principles of government to matters nowadays termed women's liberation, quality of life, and so forth. Therefore it was regarded by friend and foe alike as calling for a change in the basic norms of society. Only thus can the semantics of the term radical be justified.

First of all, let us consider Wilhelm Marr's way of expressing his radicalism. He was born in Switzerland in 1819 and started his radical activity at an early age. His father, the well-known actor Heinrich Marr,[2] sent his son to study trade, but the latter soon got involved in politics. In 1843 he was active in a group called "Young Germany in Switzerland" which was widely regarded as communist and by some as related to the "Young Germany" movement which had previously been operating in France and elsewhere. The movement was indeed close to both these trends; nevertheless it had a character of its own.

Wilhelm Marr surveyed the history of this movement in a book published in

1846, after his expulsion from Switzerland.[3] In this book he emphasized the uniqueness of his movement as well as its similarities to the two others. In this context it is important to point out Marr's connections with Weitling, the father of German communism, and his indiscriminate criticism of Karl Marx and Moses Hess, the two great mentors of German communism at that time.

The activity of "Young Germany in Switzerland" was diffuse, its organization loose, and its ideology nebulous. Yet the radical element was dominant, and this was why Marr himself was expelled twice from one canton to another, until his final deportation from Switzerland. We can trace his way through the articles he published during 1843-44 in Berne and in his first journalistic attempts in the *Blätter der Gegenwart* which he edited. But his first piece of writing in our possession is a letter he wrote to his father in June 1843. In this letter he tried to play down the practical significance of his political activity, but he did not conceal his radical leanings.[4]

In the simplest and most characteristic sentence of this letter he says that "a new world must be built on the ruins of the old," and there can be no doubt that, when he wrote the letter, Marr was convinced that this destruction was a task still confronting him and his fellow revolutionaries. At that stage Marr was looking forward to a war between socio-political classes: "there are only aristocrats and democrats." He regarded the polarization of society as an established fact, as the point of departure for revolutionary acts of the democrats, of "the people." Like a true radical, Marr did not think of a struggle for political power only, but also for economic power, and in this context the subject of the Jews came up in his writings for the first time. Marr saw in Rothschild the personification of economic injustice and asked his father whether it would not be desirable to strip Rothschild of his riches and to distribute them among the 3,333,333 hungry weavers to feed them for 360 days a year (it should be recalled that the time was just before the famous weavers' revolt in Silesia). This question might not be considered as particularly reflecting Marr's views on the Jewish question, for it was posed in the spirit of the 1840s. And yet, the type of Jew outlined here was not just a passing preoccupation with Marr as can be seen in the sarcastic cartoons and articles in his paper *Mephistopheles* which appeared in Hamburg between 1847 and 1852, while he was politically active there as a radical.

While to him the Jewish question was a side-issue at the time, this was not the case with his anticlerical, even anti-Christian, position which he loudly proclaimed both in its political and its social context. It is important to mention here that Marr was working then on an abridged and simplified version of Feuerbach's book *The Religion of the Future* for the larger and less educated public. From Marr's identification with Feuerbach's ideas we can already guess at his future attitude on the subject of religion as a social phenomenon. And indeed his reactions in times of crisis – in 1848, in the early 1850s, and to a certain degree at the end of the 1870s – were consistent with this point of departure. In retrospect it is clear that his anticlerical polemics prepared the ground for his anti-Jewish attacks, not a rare development for the radicals of the period. We shall be looking into this later.

One basic principle adopted by the radicals, at least as a means to their ends, was nationalism or – mainly in Germany – national unity. In the 1840s, the unification of Germany in the form of a German republic was also an intermediate aim for a man like Marx. Marr considered nationalism as an end in itself, although he felt obliged to justify this in his book of 1846. That nationalism, wrote Marr, was the black, red, and gold nationalism[5] which meant the sort of nationalism that enjoyed the support of both German liberals and democrats, who were trying to rid the country of the restoration régime since the Congress of Vienna.

It was just this subject, which had no connection to the basics of radicalism, that troubled Marr at a later stage, and precisely in this matter he expressed his fear of showing a lack of consistency in his radicalism. As we know, Marr the antisemite acted within the political framework of the Second Reich – the reich whose colours were black, white, and red and not those of the flag of the republic and the revolution. From the early 1860s onward Marr became, by reason of political logic, one of the supporters of the idea of unification on that basis (it is said that he even received financial aid from Bismarck for writing in praise of the Prusso-German solution). So he had to find an explanation or justification for his support of this sort of national unification which was so different from that for which he had striven in the 1840s. In his memoirs, which he wrote in the last decade of the century, but which were never published, he actually misquoted the parts from his book dealing with his earlier years (the 1840s) by eliminating all the paragraphs in which he glorified red, black, and gold nationalism. But most important of all, he explained why he no longer approved of the nationalism which he had championed in the past: Black, red, and gold nationalism was the nationalism of romantics and its colors were those of the flag of Barbarossa – that is, of the spirit of the Middle Ages[6] – and that was why he ultimately rejected it. With this argument he seems to be saying that the liberal-democratic nationalism in which he had erroneously believed in the past did not go well with the modern radical approach, and that paradoxically his later conception of nationalism was more consistent with its radical roots. As we shall see, by the same method Marr changed his stand in the matter of the Jews in the direction of an antisemitism that, according to him, was compatible with the principles of the radicalism he had upheld from the very beginning.

2.   Marr's Conclusions from the 1848 Revolution

The year 1848 was a critical one for Marr personally and for radicalism generally. The events of that year had a traumatic effect on Marr and on his comrade-in-arms, Richard Wagner. These events proved to them that the road to the realization of the principles of radicalism was blocked, at least within the political and social frameworks in which they wanted to operate. Marr summarized the relevant conclusions in his long and detailed reminiscences.

His first conclusion relates to two elements of radicalism – democracy and revolution – in redefining the term "people." His point of departure had been democratic-liberal in the past, and the people were defined as a collection of rational individuals who preserve their own personalities in a collective framework. After 1848 Marr became convinced that this was not an apt definition. The people, he stated somewhat crudely, usually acts instinctively, preferring cheap potatoes – and that is all. It is not a sum total of rational and individual aspirations, but a mass – perhaps resembling an organism, perhaps a conglomerate – that can be manipulated. This utterance was a result of his disappointment of 1848. The next revolution, said Marr, must be conducted in a different way. But not only did Marr change his liberal-rationalistic definition of the term "people" into an organic-psychological one; as a result of this, he also placed stronger emphasis on the element of majority. It is, no doubt, easier to defend the theoretical rights of a minority in accordance with the liberal-rationalistic definition of "people" than according to the later definition which only refers to the weight of the masses, to the majority as against the minority. And henceforth Marr could rid himself easily of the shackles which liberalism had imposed on his democratic convictions and bestow the crown of all democracy on the "majority" (disregarding the rights of the individuals constituting the minority), thus opening the road for his democratic radicalism to launch the battle against a minority – in this case the Jewish one.

Another conclusion concerns the separation between Church and State. In the final analysis the theoretical radical, and even liberal, assumptions on this subject hardly made any difference in political practice, despite the efforts made in this respect before the revolution and in its wake. Consequently, there were only two ways open to Marr – to intensify his struggle or to find a compromise. Marr chose both; surprisingly he pulled the rope at both ends, and the Jews were the main victims of this lack of consistency, for they became the lightning rod of his anticlericalism, and he thereby cooperated with Christianity as theology and state religion.

The conclusion which is most relevant for us and at which Marr arrived after 1848, concerns emancipation. This conclusion was closely connected with his personal fortunes. Marr had expected to reach great heights on the tide of the revolution – either on the all-German level or on the local level in Hamburg, his own state. His expectations remained unfulfilled, for he failed in both cases. In the overall German arena he did not succeed in making an appearance at all; and within a few months his party and his views were defeated in Hamburg. This defeat aroused his personal wrath against the Jews, for the men who succeeded where he had failed were Gabriel Riesser and Isaac Wolffson, both belonging to the liberal camp.[7]

Between 1848 and 1863 we witness the contest between Marr and the other two in which Marr attacks while the others ignore him. This contest is not so

ATA—I

important in itself; it is of greater importance in connection with a concept which concerns the success of his two Jewish opponents and his own failure, that of emancipation. The strange development of the revolution explains the distortion of Marr's attitude towards radicalism and towards emancipation.

3.   Emancipation and the Bremen Letter

In the eyes of the radicals the revolution of 1848 was a defeat for emancipation – neither the lower classes nor the bourgeoisie had attained it, and the people had not been liberated from autocracy, nor the State from the Church. The only exceptions were the Jews, and this fact was particularly conspicuous to Marr in his city. The Jews attained their emancipation, leaving everything else behind. Still worse, the Jews, whom he had known to be liberals and even radicals in the historic times between 1848 and 1851, retired from the general battlefield with their loot, leaving him and his comrades to continue the battle alone. This feeling of Marr's was completely unfounded, when one considered the events in Germany as a whole. But if one looked at the revolutionary events as seen from Hamburg, one could on the face of it agree with him: Of all the binding resolutions of the Frankfurt parliament which had been ratified by the revolutionary authorities of Hamburg in 1849, only *one* remained in force two years later – that concerning equal rights for the Jews. Under the circumstances it was only to be expected that – even barring the factor of personal animosity – Marr and his kind would go into battle, not for the sake of emancipation as a whole but for non-Jewish emancipation, and ultimately for anti-Jewish emancipation, to the detriment of the Jews.

As a consequence of the conclusions drawn by Marr from the outcome of the revolution, he also changed his views about the Jewish question. But for Marr this change did not come about as quickly as in the case of Wagner. This was because circumstances made him slow in reaching conclusions and because, after the failure of the revolution, he left Europe and spent the next seven years in America. Having returned to his city and to political life, he did not change his views immediately – this time also due to special circumstances. In 1859, after a period of reaction, a thorough constitutional reform was introduced in Hamburg, and the prospects of the radicals (that is, the democrats) looked rosy. In seemed that amends would be made for what had happened ten years earlier. Yet in the early 1860s Marr realized that the disaster was going to repeat itself. The new constitution had given expression to the success of the moderate liberals, and the radicals' electoral victory did not bring about a corresponding change in policy. More aggravating to Marr was the fact that the Jews prevailed again and were granted rights and privileges as an independent group, while the general implementation of radical principles and the overall emancipation was not carried out.

Marr's sharp reaction, unexpected as it may have been, was understandable. It was expressed and published in Bremen's newspaper *Courier an der Weser*[8] in a letter addressed to his friend Hobelmann, who was a supporter of the emancipation of the Jews. Hobelmann had sought Marr's backing for a law granting equal rights to the Jews of Bremen. He saw in Marr's letter a parallel to Balaam's words to Balak – the opposite of what was intended.

Wilhelm Marr was known as a democrat, as a fighter for emancipation, and even as a friend of the Jews (at that time he was married to a woman of Jewish extraction), and therefore, despite his opposition to Gabriel Riesser, he could be expected to lend his support to the granting of equal rights to the Jews of Bremen. However, by June 1862, all the conclusions at which Marr had been arriving in the course of the previous years and months found their expression in a surprising letter which we quote below *in extenso*:

Hamburg, 4th June, 1862

Dear Sir,

I hasten to answer your letter and regret to tell you that I cannot be your ally in the matter mentioned therein. Without intending to influence your view in any way, I still consider it my duty to reward your trust in me by explaining the motivation of my opinion, and you may use these lines in any way permissible among honest men, i.e., publish and oppose them, as you may wish.

In the first place, there is no question of emancipation in the case of the Jews. This is not a matter that concerns only them (the Jews) and not us. In every body politic the minority has to obey the rules of the majority, and I consider it foolish if the latter wants to grant the former exceptional legal privileges. If the Jews want to live in our state and enjoy equal privileges with us, they have to live as we do, to be as we are. Above all, not to form a religious or political state within the state. But I can tell you in advance that the Jews will refuse to live in Bremen as a non-Jewish community, i.e., to leave their temple [synagogue] to the discretion of the individual. They will demand of the State protection and privileges of the sort that every Jew will be compelled to become a member of the Jewish state within the state, and with their official temple they have founded an official substate which must become detrimental to their civil liberties, not by reason of religion – this is of secondary importance – but as a necessary consequence of their innate tribal peculiarity (*Stammeseigenthümlichkeiten*). That mixture of all sorts of human races, as confirmed unanimously by science as well as by the Jews' own tradition (Isaiah, Jeremiah, Ezekiel), is incompatible with the Germanic elements in the pure, better sense. And our instinctive antipathy to the Jews is based on history and experience. That race which under Joseph's ministry introduced slavery, which under Mordechai's ministry committed mass slaughter of men, which even to this day celebrates the memory of these horrors in the political *Purim* festival, is not entitled – don't get me wrong! – as Jews to equal civil rights. Just as we had been incapable, and therefore ineligible, for freedom until we had emancipated ourselves from our prejudices and slavish peculiarities, thus also the Jews.

If I wanted to live according to my principles in any particular state, the externality of a religion, believe me, would not deter me, and as I leave the nexus of one state, I never would have the cheek to demand of the majority of that state to legislate special regulations in my favor.

But the problem lies deeper. According to my opinion, Judaism, which is the same today as it has always been, since it is a tribal particularity, is incompatible with the life of our state. By its very nature it must always strive to form a state within a State. You cannot exterminate the instinctive popular aversion against Judaism through so-called emancipation, and it takes its revenge by becoming a satellite of reaction, of which we have distinctive proof here in Hamburg. The oriental element is politically and socially incompatible with ours, just as black and white will never produce a color other than gray. At one time I, too, dreamed about this question, but later on I found only renegades in politics, and in social life only . . . and the few exceptions among the Jews had simply ceased to be Jews.

In one word: Don't look at this question from the religious side; examine it from the aspect of cultural history, and you will discover a tribe of mongrels whose vital principle, from the time of the patriarchs who traded away their wives, to this day is – selling to the highest bidder. The honorable exceptions (who anyway have better blood in their veins) should not induce a state to allow its own element to be affected for sake of an ideological conception. You would not permit 10,000 monks to settle in Bremen. Not for religious reasons, oh no! But because monasticism endangers the common weal. Judaism, however, is nothing else than a social congregation, the congregation of a tribe whose whole essence is beyond our morals and who, once they have struck root, will strive to take hold of everything for themselves. Religiously they are commanded to do so, socially this is their nature, politically this is a consequence of both.

You are asking: where is the freedom of religion? And I answer: if material interests are dearer to the Jew than his religion, let him give it up; if his religion is dearer to him, how can he demand of us to adapt our state to it?

If you can prevail upon emancipation to stipulate formally that no Jew may be compelled to contribute to the upkeep of his temple, but that he must also contribute his share to the levies borne by all other citizens – just you try it. But as soon as you accord official recognition to Judaism in your state, you will experience the bitter consequences in less than three years!

I am making no secret of my aversion to the Jewish character; as a rule and almost always I have found among the Jews only masks instead of real human beings. The religion and its precepts are nothing but products of their consciousness, their particularities are manifestations of their organism. And now to the end, for one could write a book on this subject.

Emancipation can only be the fruit of one's own effort. If the people, the plain, simple people, inexperienced in the arts of dialectics, demands emancipation with equality for the Jews as emphatically as it demands political or social reform, then this has become a necessity. *It depends on the Jews to make themselves so popular that the demand is raised as a necessity in the consciousness of the people*: It is not up to us to enforce emancipation. Emancipated by us, but remaining isolated in the consciousness of the people, the reaction is as inevitable as it is certain. You will create allies for despotism and through the exclusivity inherent in the tribe you will form a limited company which *viribus unitis* will also be detrimental to the economic life of your state. Tribal particularities cannot be legislated away with the stroke of a pen. But there is still something else, and this you cannot dispute. So long as the separation of the Church from the State has not been consistently introduced and carried out by us, it would be self-contradictory to talk about the emancipation of the Jews.

But if a state religion, viz., a Christian state, is not enough for you, then you may, as far as I am concerned, allow a temple and synagogal state by its side. I wish you success.

Don't be angry with me for being so frank. I am doing nothing against the Jews, because people learn most quickly from experience, and here with us nine-tenths of the population – and the most intelligent radicals at their head – are cursing the artifical and spurious emancipation. But I can do even less for a tribe whose best critics are its own prophets! I and several congenial friends no longer attend the local citizens' council, our "constitutional caricature," where Abraham's descendants play the role of faithful satellites of reaction.

When the party which, like ours, is being oppressed, wants to spill its cornucopia over others, it is being pulled instead of doing the pulling.

I should like to cry out: If you, Jew, are disgusted with your temple as I am with my church, then attach yourself to me, not I to you. Do not shy away from a few drops of water, when it is a matter of replacing orthodoxy by free humanism. If you are a hydrophobiac, then you are orthodox, and I have nothing in common with orthodox people.

Adieu!

Yours sincerely,
W. Marr

What is most significant about this letter is that Marr does not renounce his democratic radicalism, but makes use of it as a boomerang to hurl at the Jews. The democratic system is reduced here to the principle of the supremacy of the majority and thus to an argument against any form of Jewish existence in a non-Jewish state. He interpreted the demand for granting any rights at all to a minority as an assault against the majority, that is, against democracy. And emancipation, like democracy, is presented as a deviation in favor of the Jews and of their very existence in non-Jewish society. No wonder that already at the beginning of his letter he declares that the Jews are not at all interested in emancipation. Thus he can conduct his fight for emancipation without bringing the Jews into it, and he can even attack them as opponents of emancipation or at least as not being ready for it. He admits that at a certain stage non-Jews were not entitled to freedom and emancipation either, since they had not yet cast off their preconceived ideas and slavishness. But this admission was mainly to serve the inference he was interested in making: that the Jews were not entitled to emancipation because they have not yet abandoned their old beliefs. The hitch is that in the context of this inference Marr spoke about the non-Jews in the past tense, whereas he used the present tense concerning the Jews, so that from this formulation of his principal position one must draw the correct conclusion that the Jews, in contrast to the non-Jews, do not deserve emancipation, nor are they fighting for it, in the final analysis. Theoretically he is faithfully sticking to radical-democratic thinking; in practice this is a selective democratic proposal which excludes the Jews as such from the community.

4. The Development of Marr's Antisemitism

Marr knows full well that his definition of the term Jew may be the Achilles' heel of his argument. Indeed an anticlerical spirit permeates the whole letter: Granting rights to Jews is compared to rights given to a group of monks; the fight is presented as a fight against religion of any kind, for separation of Church and State in principle, and directed against orthodoxy as such. There is actually a certain consistency in his argument that, so long as the Church is not separated from the State, the emancipation of the Jews would only be part of the total imbalance in relations between Church and State. Yet Marr is in a dilemma. It is not his attack against religion as such that can straighten out the distortions of his argumentation. Throughout the letter we find a discrepancy between the attitude which differentiates between Jew and non-Jew in the religious context and adduces arguments of a religious character for or against emancipation on the one hand, and the impression that this explanation does not sufficiently prove the distinction between Jews and non-Jews. It is insufficient, in the first place, because the principal claim of the Jewish fighters for emancipation had been that they were no longer a "Church," a "state within a state," and that they did not support a theology that militated against real social and political partnership in a modern state. Consideration of this claim would have taken the wind out of his sails, but Marr would not agree to its necessary consequences, because his intuition told him that there existed a difference between Jew and non-Jew, and this difference was of great significance. Secondly, this distinction would place Marr, the anticlerical radical, into a position where he would have to do the work of the Christian Church and theology in the battle against granting the Jews equal rights.

Although for the sake of the provocative effect and as a *ballon d'essai*, Marr recommended conversion as a solution, there can be no doubt that this was a mere stratagem. Therefore, Marr reported that he had found a better method for distinguishing between Jew and non-Jew: a method based on race. At that stage he formulated this method mildly, but the implications of his still traditional terminology – the use of such loaded words as *Stamm* (tribe) and *Stammeseigenthümlichkeiten* (tribal characteristics) rather than *Race* (race) – are clear. Just after the Jews had achieved recognition of their claims for equality between people of different religions living within a state and had even attained emancipation, Marr's assertion could have turned the clock back. This was a typically postemancipatory declaration made by Marr after the emancipation of the Jews in Hamburg, and fifteen years later it characterized the general assault in and outside Germany against the equality of rights attained by the Jews on a wider scale at a later stage. Let us say right now that there was a process of escalation in Marr's exploitation of the subject of race. In the Bremen letter and in his book *Der Judenspiegel*, published immediately thereafter in 1862, his conclusions were not unambiguous. Although the oriental background was presented as the opposite of political and social life in Europe, there was still a possibility of emerging from orientalism into the "light." Thus Marr in 1862. In 1878 this premise is totally abandoned by the denial of the possibility of erasing the racial provenance through any act of will: conversion, adaptation, or renunciation of religious customs. This was his position in his book *Sieg des Judenthums über das Germanenthum* ("Victory of Judaism over Germanism") written in 1878, which became the battle cry of the antisemitic movement in Germany. Paradoxically, this attitude was not only radical in the full literary sense of the term, but if we disregard some irrational and romantic expressions, we can trace it back to the enlightenment of the eighteenth century, which looked for connections between the natural environment and the political configuration as did Montesquieu, for example. Consequently, if the accusation had been made against Marr that in his racist doctrine of 1862 he was unfaithful to his radical-democratic principles, he could have refuted it. As we shall see below, at that time this was not the main point of the arguments against Marr.

In only one respect did Marr, in the letter and in the book written immediately thereafter, appear to pursue his radical-democratic line explicitly, rather than just implicitly. This matter is connected with the above-mentioned political developments in his immediate environment in Hamburg, and from which he drew conclusions about what was happening abroad. As already mentioned, Marr had come to the conclusion that, immediately after the revolution and after they had attained their ends in Hamburg, the Jews had become reactionaries. At first they had only fought for their own interests, in a democratic-radical guise; when they had achieved their purpose, they showed their true colors: They could not be anything but a state within a state. Society, Marr was convinced, had proved incapable of absorbing them even in the new constitutional situation, and the Jews sensed this. Therefore the Jews deserted their former allies and took their revenge against the people, democracy, civilian society, and the radical ideas by taking the reactionary road. As we have said, this description of the specific case of Hamburg contains a grain of truth, but no more than that. A more balanced view of these developments reveals that there existed a general tendency to revert from the support of radical principles to that of liberal ones – a logical tendency in light of the political developments in Hamburg and of the attitude towards the Jews following these developments. On the other hand it cannot be said that the Jews in general supported the radicals from the outset; neither can one say that the liberal Jews went over to the reactionary and conservative camp in Hamburg, even though the radicals could have got this impression.

5. Marr's Later Years

Marr's letter as well as his book *Judenspiegel* gave rise to an echo and to opposition. These did not come from the Jewish camp under attack but from the radical-democratic camp which felt itself compromised by a member such as Wilhelm Marr. The majority of the Jews at that time reacted to the sudden attack by adopting the tactics of "silent death sentence," but the radical-democrats had to take active steps, especially in view of the fact that new elections were imminent. Marr's fellow radicals understood that with his anti-Jewish utterances he had not renounced the party, but created a deviant stream within it, and for this they wanted to have him expelled. And indeed Marr was excluded from the directorate of the Hamburg Democratic Association. He nevertheless announced his candidacy for the elections and was roundly defeated – not by the liberals but by the democratic-radicals in his district. The radical citizens of Hamburg rejected Marr's strange brand of radicalism.

Thus ended Marr's political career as a radical democrat. In the ensuing sixteen years he worked mainly as a journalist, but despite his talent remained an obscure member of the profession until 1878. Then the barrier between his democratic-radical past and his anti-democratic and reactionary convictions broke down. The concept of race became a dominant concept which swept away all values of human logic and human will. Nevertheless, the split between these two periods of his life should not be overemphasized; even in the second stage there persists a basic continuity. Firstly, a perusal of Marr's writings of the 1870s reveals that his conclusions were, at least indirectly, derived from the attacks of 1862. Secondly, his writings over the years after 1862 show his ever-increasing interest in the subject of race in its national context. "Genuine nationhood," stated Marr in one of his articles written in the late 1860s, "is the race." He did not make this statement, though, for destructive purposes; on the contrary: he joined three races – the Latin, the Slavic, and the Germanic – as carriers of the future, the equilibrium guaranteeing peace and order in Europe. But at a certain moment, partly as a result of the feeling of personal frustration which had been growing in Marr ever since 1862, the knowledge he had acquired on the subject of race was turned in the direction of antisemitism and concentrated upon what he considered to be the central and perhaps only goal, the fight of the German nation against the Jews.

A careful reading of Marr's published works since 1879 will show clearly that even at this stage he was still giving an account of himself as a radical of past years. Attacks were still leveled at Gabriel Riesser in these pamphlets, even though he had been dead for more than fifteen years. The defeats which Marr had suffered in 1848 and 1861 still hurt. And this is borne out more by the lively correspondence he conducted during that period than by his published writings. One example will suffice: Among the abundant mass of letters in the Marr archive there is a lengthy correspondence with one of the pillars of German antisemitism from its very beginnings until Hitler's rise to power, Theodor Fritsch. The archive does not contain Marr's own letters, but Fritsch's answers disclose the general spirit. Thus Fritsch calls Marr "one of the impractical men of forty-eight"[9] and attacks him for his numerous and, in his view, old-fashioned proclamations in favor of revolution. No doubt, Fritsch was right: Marr's contentions, as we can infer, were based upon the ideology and experience of the radical forties as translated into antisemitism.

In the course of the correspondence between the two, Fritsch's expressions of his opinion grew increasingly caustic and aggressive over the years, until Marr finally became disappointed in his successors to the antisemitic leadership. He regarded them as traders in antisemitism (*Geschäftsantisemiten*) and in his opinion this bode ill for the future of the movement which he himself had launched. To the former radical the antisemitism of Fritsch and his companions looked too pragmatic, too narrow, too closely connected with money and organization, and too far from the ideals of 1848 – those ideals which, in his view, should have formed the basis for a better world, for democracy and for genuine radicalism. With the passing of time one can discern Marr's growing embitterment over the fact that the new antisemites, whose world view was not radical enough for him, were casting him aside. After five years of fighting in the front lines of the antisemitic ranks, Marr and his friends disappeared from the leadership. And if Marr, the gifted writer, had felt in the past that the Jews were outmanoeuvering him, he now had the feeling that they, the antisemites, were doing the same with even greater ruthlessness. He was so deeply offended that in his late, unpublished, articles[10] he pronounced antisemitism dead and paid compliments to the Jews.

In one newspaper, the *Oesterreicher Volksfreund*, where Marr was still given an opportunity of publishing his letters in his later years, we see the aim of his fight and the consistency of his methods. Marr saw two ways for social revolution – the one was based upon the state and the other on its destruction. The first is the road of antisemitism; the second is the social-democratic one. Thus, even at this late stage, Marr did not regard antisemitism as "yet another" of the foundations of the state, a narrow-minded form of social critique, but as an all-embracing and radical solution to all the problems that are the subject of social critique. With this Marr continued in 1892 the dispute with the communists in which he had been involved fifty years before as a young man in "Young Germans in Switzerland." In those days even his friends showed antagonism to the state but, unlike the communists of that time, they did not regard the very concept of the state as an obstacle on the road to social revolution. Now Marr saw antisemitism as the basis of the modern state, as opposed to social democracy which strives for betterment at the expense of the state. It irked Marr that ultimately his enemies had won out and that too many people were seeking the radical solution in social democratic ways. Therefore Marr spared no effort to show that his battle against the Jews was a continuation of his radical road, a continuation of the fight for the basic social norms, by showing that it was the Jews who were undermining genuine democracy, the emancipation of the lower classes, the oppressed nationalists, and revolutionary ideas. There are doubtless many discrepancies and contradictions in his words which are irreconcilable with all the radical principles that characterized the start of his course, such as his appeal to Christian feeling and the emphasis on the role of the Christian state. It would seem that these were owing to tactical considerations and, to a certain degree, to the lack of consistency in an aging man. Yet despite all this, it is clear beyond doubt that until the end of his life his antisemitism sprang from the "radicalism of the forty-eights," only that this radicalism no longer served the process of change and modernization but had turned into an obstacle to it and its proponents.[11]

Notes

1. Cf. E. Sterling, *Er ist wie Du* (München, 1956); and J. Toury, *Turmoil and Confusion in the Revolution of 1848* (Heb.) (Tel-Aviv, 1968).
2. The fact that Heinrich Marr sometimes played Jews on the stage gave rise to rumors that he was Jewish, and thus also Wilhelm Marr was "suspected" of belonging to the Jewish race. This insinuation is completely baseless, as confirmed by research into the family history in the archives of the State of Hamburg during World War II.
3. W. Marr, *Das junge Deutschland in der Schweiz* (Leipzig, 1846).
4. W. Marr to H. Marr, State Archive Hamburg, Marr estate, A. 149, letter No. 1.
5. *Das junge Deutschland*, p. 79.
6. Marr estate B.I.c. *Memoirs*, 3rd Part, p. 20.
7. Cf. M. Zimmermann, "Gabriel Riesser und Wilhelm Marr im Meinungssteit," *Zeitschrift des Vereins für Hamburgische Geschichte* (1975):59–84.
8. Supplement to No. 161, June 13, 1862, Bremen.
9. Th. Fritsch to W. Marr, April 28, 1886, Marr estate, A. 67.
10. "Im Philosemitismus" and "Testament eines Antisemiten," in Marr estate, B.V. a and b.
11. Cf. M. Zimmermann, *Wilhelm Marr – the "Patriarch of Antisemitism"* (Heb.) (Jerusalem, 1982).

18

The Racial Motif in Renan's Attitude to Jews and Judaism*

SHMUEL ALMOG

Since Eugen Dühring and Houston Stewart Chamberlain, the concepts of *racism* and *antisemitism* have become to some extent synonymous. The merger of antisemitism and racial ideology has been so striking that one hardly remembers now that these were originally two independent factors. Racism as a school of thought came into being with the appearance of the book by Joseph Arthur de Gobineau *Essai sur l'inégalité des races humaines* (1853-55), unrelated to the Jewish question. Nevertheless, the work contained seeds of anti-Jewish significance which did, in fact, fall upon the fertile soil of the antisemitic movement of the seventies and eighties of the nineteenth century.

1. Ernest Renan – Biographical Background

Even in the very coining of the term *antisemitism*, attributed to Wilhelm Marr, there was certainly a move toward a racial perception. The connections between Richard Wagner and Gobineau also helped merge the racial outlook originating from France with the anti-Jewish movement in Germany. However, the ideological reworking of these two elements into a single, combined system was still to come. In searching for the missing link, it is worthwhile to examine the work of Ernest Renan, a contemporary and compatriot of Gobineau, who concerned himself extensively with matters of race and was instrumental in shaping the modern image of the Jew.[1] A close look at Renan's teaching is relevant to our concern, both from the theoretical point of view and because of the great influence he had on the intellectual life of France and Europe at large.

Renan was born in 1823 in a small town in the region of Brittany in the north-west of France. Till the age of twenty-two he was educated in Catholic institutions and prepared himself to take holy orders. After much soul-

* A previous version appeared in Hebrew – *Zion: Quarterly for Research in Jewish History,* *32*(1967):175–200.

searching, he decided in 1845 to leave the seminary. His withdrawal from Catholicism was a slow, gradual process. The more he matured, the more he drew away from dogmatism and rejected clericalism. But he never ceased to regard himself as a Christian. Moreover, despite his clash with the Church and a certain sympathy which he had for Protestantism, he maintained some spiritual connection with Catholicism.

In 1862 he was appointed to the chair of Hebrew at the *Collège de France*, but Napoleon III removed him from this position under pressure from Church circles. Only in 1870, upon the establishment of the Third Republic, did he regain it. His most important work, the one which made him famous, was *Vie de Jésus* (1863). During the Empire, he was politically active for a time and was aligned with the moderate Republicans. He stood for the 1869 elections but lost. Thereafter he left politics but continued to engage in public affairs and was close to many leading personalities of his time. In 1878 he was elected to the French Academy, and in 1883 became head of the *Collège de France*. He died in 1892.

Renan was twenty-five when King Louis-Philippe's reign ended in 1848 and the Second Republic was established. In that year he wrote the work of his youth, *L'Avenir de la science* ("The Future of Science") which was not published until about forty years later. This work was an important milestone in his intellectual progression and reflects the development of his world-view. In 1870-71, he was witness to France's defeat at the hands of Germany, the fall of the Empire, and the Paris Commune. These events left their impression upon his views, especially as regards his attitude toward Germany. Till then he had believed that Germany embodied all the values he held dear.[2] During the war he made some futile efforts to come to an understanding with German colleagues, especially David Friedrich Strauss, but concluded that he had erred in his previous estimation of the Germans.[3]

For years Renan had admired Strauss and had considered him as his guide to the appreciation of Christianity. Strauss' book on Jesus (1835-36) had influenced him greatly. In it he found a critical spirit which still preserved a close connection with Christianity.[4] Renan adopted Strauss' method of interpreting the New Testament as a myth but claimed that Strauss was too abstract and overly Hegelian.[5] His own book was essentially intended to complement what was lacking in Strauss and present an image based upon historical fact and psychological analysis from that selfsame point of view.

In spite of his affinity for Strauss, he clearly took exception to other Young Hegelians. He was sharply critical of Ludwig Feuerbach's anti-Christian approach and his "chauvinistic Germanism."[6] As for Bruno Bauer, Renan especially rejected his attempt to cut off the Gospels from their Jewish soil.[7] From the 1870s on, Renan distanced himself from Strauss as well, not only because of their political differences resulting from the Franco-Prussian War, but also because of some more profound mutual changes. Strauss had abandoned Hegelian philosophy and began to support the Darwinist perception,[8] whereas Renan gradually outgrew his old world-view and turned in his later years towards a sceptical relativism.[9]

Renan's studies reflected the prevalent ideas in linguistics, emanating from the discovery of the relationship between Sanskrit and European languages.[10] In his writings on language[11] he based himself upon the comparative linguistics of Franz Bopp[12] and the philosophy of Wilhelm von Humboldt, who saw each language as an expression of the particular character of its speakers.[13] The combination of these influences led to a two-fold result: a view of the Indo-European languages as an independent grouping of languages distinct from other groupings, foremost among which is the Semitic; and a definition of the common character of the Indo-European peoples in contradistinction to the Semitic character.[14] This can be seen as an impetus to Renan's views on race. The French historian Augustin Thierry must also be credited with some influence on Renan's view of race. Thierry claimed that the different origins of the Germanic conquerors and the Celtic population respectively had a lasting effect on the history of England and France.[15]

In his evaluation of Judaism, Renan was fairly close to the ideas of another French historian, Jules Michelet, who was his senior. To young Renan, Michelet was an exemplary author who had impressed him greatly.[16] Later on, they came to know one another in Paris. Like Renan, Michelet had also changed his outlook on Christianity. At about the time Renan left the seminary, in 1845, there was a clearly evident, sharp change in Michelet's evaluation of Christianity and, as a result, in his approach to Judaism. Previously Michelet had considered Judaism as a positive factor because it had produced Christianity. Although he spoke of the ruthlessness of the ancient Hebrews, he justified it as belonging to a young and savage world. He saw the Israelites as the embodiment of unity and freedom in an ancient world rife with fatalism. In 1840-45 he underwent a spiritual crisis after which he levelled bitter criticism at the Judaeo-Christian enslavement to an arbitrary God. He saw in both religions a sort of feminine surrender to a capricious deity that bestowed its favors arbitrarily and without justice.[17] Renan also shared the perception of Christianity (but not of Judaism) as a feminine faith, but related lovingly to its female softness.[18] Renan was apparently influenced by Michelet in negating the idea that Israel was chosen by God. As for race, in the 1860s Michelet regretted his rather slipshod use of the concept in the 1830s.[19]

Renan was not consciously antisemitic. In the last stage of his life he even had occasion to denounce antisemitic manifestations (he protested against the Tisza-Eszlar blood libel in 1882 and joined Victor Hugo in organizing relief committees for the Jews of Russia), and was himself a target of antisemitic attacks. What is more, his enemies accused him of being in the pay of the Jews. One of his biographers mentioned rumors that Renan had received a million francs from the House of Rothschild and was even said to have been a Jew himself.[20] In the political-legal realm he stood for equal rights for the Jews and for their integration into society. Thus he approved of the status bestowed upon French Jews since the reign of Napoleon.[21] In brief, Renan apparently sided with the heritage of the Enlightenment and the Emancipation against clerical conservatism and racial antisemitism.

As we shall see below, Renan came to this position after inner struggle, yet he clung to it strongly despite the growing skepticism of his later years. Renan's attitude developed, then, in the reverse direction of the Young Hegelians in Germany. Starting from a rational humanistic position, some of them embraced antisemitism and even racism,[22] whereas he gradually freed himself of their influence and became more and more opposed to antisemitism and racism. Notwithstanding, his ambivalent attitude toward the Jews remained in force to the end. Even in 1882 he still wrote about the Jews in a vein which very clearly indicated this:

> A peculiar people, in very truth, and created to present all manners of contrasts! This people have given God to the world, and hardly believe in Him themselves. They have created religion, and they are the least religious of peoples. They have founded the hopes of humanity in a kingdom of Heaven, while all its sages keep repeating to us that we must only occupy us with the things of this earth. The most enlightened nations take seriously what this people have preached, while the latter laugh at the former.[23]

2. The Laws of History

Renan was an eclectic *par excellence*, open to different influence but not totally accepting any of them. Yet having received a Catholic education, he sought for most of his life an all-encompassing world-view. The philosophy at which he arrived in 1848 was based upon two main influences: positivism and the ideas of Hegel.[24] Like Auguste Comte, Renan also built an edifice of three stages. Instead of the theological stage, the lowest one, Renan had the spontaneous stage of primitive syncretism – humankind was religious but not scientific. For Comte's metaphysical stage, Renan posited the analytical one in which humankind was scientific but not religious. In place of Comte's scientific stage, Renan placed that of the perfect synthesis, the fusion of religion and science.[25]

The fundamental difference, then, between Renan and Comte lay in the importance Renan attributed to religion and the positive role he assigned to it. Renan was dissatisfied with Comte's schematic perception of human nature.[26] He himself used the concepts of religion and science rather loosely and was therefore able to arrive at a combination such as "the religion of science." Renan borrowed the framework of the historical process from positivism, and its purpose from Hegel. "The human purpose" for Renan was "to realize the highest possible human culture."[27] And this was obviously a rather superficial formulation of the purpose of history in Hegel.[28]

This is not the place to deal with the various nuances which one can find in the development of Renan's thoughts. He loved to play with ideas and delighted in the effect of the clash of opposites.[29] Yet for most of his life he remained true to the outlook which he had formulated in his youth. In 1889 he was still interested in publishing the forty-year-old manuscript of his book *The Future of Science* and, for all of his reservations, said in the later preface: "My religion is still the progress of reason, that is to say, of science."[30]

The concept of progress was central to his outlook[31] and was one of the fundamentals to which he remained faithful most of his life. The advance toward perfection takes place dialectically.[32] The process has a deterministic, involuntary character.[33] It is a complex of contrasting forces, each of which fulfills its specific role.[34] The process is objective and each stage is measured in relation to the entire pattern, not by any moral standard.[35] The principle guiding the human spirit is the principle of *becoming*.[36]

The inescapable conclusion of these premises was one's submission to the objective course of history and the acceptance of reality as the final arbiter. "Morality is thus reduced to submission,"[37] he pronounced. Renan himself was unable to live with the severe conclusion his system imposed upon the human will. He wrestled with it and revised it from time to time until he finally broke free of it completely. He lost faith in humankind's ability to fathom the goals of history and to judge it. Instead, he moved towards ethical relativism and hedonism.[38] Earlier, Renan submitted to reality through the acceptance of a preconceived pattern of history;[39] now, he merely yielded to reality as such. First, he gave up moral judgment in favor of a dialectical notion of progress; now, he gave up moral judgment due to the loss of values. Experience taught Renan that there was no basis for his philosophical presumptuousness, but he retained the fundamental sense of resignation.

Within Renan's perception of the pattern of human history, there was a special and unique place for Jewish history. Israel – according to Renan – had a mission, both in itself and as a part of the Semitic race. It was destined to give the world monotheism and socialism.[40] and to be the leaven in the struggle for progress.[41] But Israel's main function apparently was to bring forth Christianity: "Christianity and the conversion of the world to monotheism being Israel's essential creation, overriding everything else, anything in its history which detracted from this supreme goal was but a frivolous and dangerous deviation.[42]

Elsewhere in that same work, he presented Israel's mission even more explicitly in the spirit of Church tradition: "Has Israel fulfilled its vocation? Has it preserved among the great muddle of peoples the post entrusted to it of old? One can without hesitation respond affirmatively! Israel was the stem upon which mankind's faith has been grafted." Again: "And after Judaism produced its fruit, it had to continue its long, tenacious existence though the ages but the spirit of life has henceforth gone."[43] This is apparently an echo of the interpretation which Hegel had received at the hands of the Young Hegelians.[44]

When he wrote the history of Israel at the end of the 1880s, Renan had a comprehensive theory of Judaism's contribution to human culture – Judaism was the counter-weight to Hellenism and they complemented each other: "The movement of the world is the outcome of the parallelogram of two forces, liberalism, upon the one hand, and socialism upon the other" (liberalism of Greek origin, socialism of Hebraic origin), "liberalism impelling its adepts to the highest degree of human development; socialism accounting above all else justice most strictly interpreted and the happiness of the greatest number."[45] In another volume of his history of Israel Renan again presented the two opposing forces, but this time they were not Greeks and Hebrews, but Aryans and Semites; nevertheless it seems that the basic meaning was the same: "The Semite believes in God too much; the Aryan believes too much in the eternal man. Both conceptions were necessary for the founding of civilization. The Semite gave God; the Aryan gave the immortality of the individual. No one to this day has been able to pass over these two postulates."[46]

Renan held that the Aryan cultures, especially Hellenism, were based upon the immortality of the soul and therefore the Aryans believed in the future of the human race. Out of this faith they were able to achieve wonderful things in culture and science, but they lacked a developed sense of justice. The Semites, especially the Hebrews, did not believe as yet in the immortality of the soul,[47] but in the immediate and tangible, and therefore rejected the notion that God could suffer foul deeds: "The ardent genius of a small tribe established in an obscure corner of Syria seemed created to supply this void in the Hellenic intellect. Israel never stood idly by to see the world so badly governed, under the authority of a God reputed to be just."[48]

Faithful to his dialectical system, Renan was ready to acquiesce in methods which may appear invalid to the modern observer, in order to achieve the historic purpose. In describing Israel's past he listed some vile deeds but emphasized at the same time that the kingdom of France, the unity of Christendom in the Middle Ages, as well as Protestantism and the French Revolution, all came into being through various criminal acts: "The work of Israel was accomplished, like all human undertakings, by means of violence and perfidy, amidst a tempest of oppositions, of passions, and of crimes without number. The Jewish intellect derived its strength from its least sympathetic characteristics, from its fanaticism and from its exclusive tendencies."[49]

In a previous work of 1859 he spoke of the dialectical change in evaluating the qualities of the Semites. At first it seemed that the Semites were superior to the Aryans, whereas in the course of time the wheel turned: "The Semites could then rightly pity them (the Aryans) as senseless, worshipping passing shadows; and, for all that, the privilege of which the former were proud did not amount to real superiority. The character trait which preserved them from the fables and superstitions of paganism would forbid them one day any rich and varied civilization. Thus they became a stumbling block in the march of humanity after having been the cause of its great progress."[50]

The reference here was to the contrast between biblical monotheism and Hellenism. Semitic monotheism was made superfluous, as it were, by the ruthless laws of the historical process. Characteristics vital to the development in the early stages became a stumbling-block at a higher stage. Semitic theology, said Renan, certainly approximated to reason more than did paganism, but in the later generations it fell into the hands of the scholastics, which indicated again its primitiveness: "The inroad of the scientific mind within the last century has made a great change in the relation of things. What was an advantage has become a drawback. The Semitic mind and intellect have appeared as hostile to experimental science and to research into the mechanical causes of the world."[51]

One can perhaps take issue with Renan and ask why he attributed such great importance to the influence of Jewish scholasticism in its clash with science and did not refer to Christian scholasticism as well. A possible explanation for this may be found in the perception of the Young Hegelians,[52] in which he was caught up, despite the changes in his thinking. Essentially it was a further aspect of his general picture of Judaism after the rise of Christianity – its advantage became a detriment! Renan was contending with a problem which threatened to undermine his entire system: If indeed there is a purpose to history, and if the historian is really able to fathom its nature, why is it, then, that Judaism survived ("Judaism . . . had to continue its long, tenacious existence through the ages") after having completed its task, only to become a stumbling-block to progress; for does not every component have a role in the total complex?

Renan, therefore, tried to establish what the role of Judaism was after the rise of Christianity. Israel became a wanderer among the nations, but no longer in order to fulfill the role assigned to it by the Church – as a living witness – rather in order to fulfill a social mission which emanated from its original socialist character: "The end of its political life, the destruction of its national framework, far from entailing spiritual ruin upon Israel, will be the means of developing its destiny. While Persia, Greece, and Rome occupy the foreground of the world's history, little Israel – like the white ant of Africa – works its way silently through the structure of ancient society and will bring the subsoil to the surface. The Prophets and the Law (*Torah*) fulfill their slow task of working as the leaven of coming ages. Above the ruins of the Oriental, Greek, and Roman civilizations spring two mighty trees, Christianity and Islam; each an offshoot of Judaism."[53]

There is no doubt that he accorded the Jews a social function after the appearance of Christianity, and he also said as much in the following volume of that work: "The Jew was designed to serve as leaven in the progress of every country, rather than to form a separate nation on the globe," and in this connection he explained that "the Jew of the 'dispersion' fulfilled his vocation far better than the Jew of Palestine who was always trying to create a national government, and then working to destroy it."[54]

Gradually Renan moved away from the Christological view of Jewish history, and at the completion of his five-volume work, near his death in 1892, he stated that not only is Judaism destined to come to an end but so is Christianity. Only the Greek values – light, reason, and truth – will remain, but the memory of Israel will also last because Hebrew justice is due to exist alongside Greek liberty: "Judaism and Christianity will both disappear. The work of the Jew will have its end; the work of the Greek – in other words, science and civilization, rational, experimental, without charlatanism, without revelation, a civilization founded upon reason and liberty – will last forever; . . . The trace of Israel, however, will be eternal."[55] Renan here perceived the religions as an intermediate stage towards the rule of universal and eternal values. Against Judaism and Christianity, whose contribution was impermanent, he wished to bequeath to humankind the reason and freedom of Greece and the justice of Jewish origin.

3.   The Election of Israel and its Universality

It is no wonder that Renan, deeply rooted in Christianity, resorted to the central motif of the clash between the Church and Judaism: Israel's divine election and its validity after the appearance of Jesus. This was obviously related to the question mentioned earlier of Israel's place in history after the rise of Christianity. The Church's attitude to the election of Israel was to affirm it but claim it for itself. Renan's presentation of the question attempted to undercut the very concept itself.[56]

Here one can discern Michelet's influence upon Renan. In his book, *The Bible of Humanity* (1864), Michelet objected to the election of Israel on two counts: (1) because the principle itself was exclusive and discriminated against those not elected; (2) because the choice fell upon an unworthy object – petty and feeble Israel.[57] Renan took up both of these points. In the second volume of his history of Israel, reflecting Michelet's views on the choice of the small and weak, he said: "Among so many mountains which in appearance were better designed for the purpose, it was the little hill of Zion which had been chosen by Iahveh. And why? Because it was little, and because Iahveh, being very mighty and strong, loves the small and the weak, who do not dare to display pride towards him."[58]

Michelet's position was a denial of the common heritage of both Judaism and Christianity and he opposed Judaism while denying Christianity.[59] That was not Renan's approach. Christianity, for him, remained a positive value and the "petty and feeble" motif was not characteristic of him. On the other hand, he made more of his attack upon the exclusivity inherent in Israel's election: "The God of Jesus is our Father . . . the God of Jesus is not the partial despot who has chosen Israel for his people and specially protects them. He is the God of humanity."[60]

This was essentially a return to the classic Christian concept,[61] in modern terms, whose form ("the partial despot") reminds one of Michelet's metaphor[62] and whose content was reminiscent of the Hegelian Absolute Spirit. Jewish history exhibited grand characteristics – according to Hegel – but was limited by its exclusive relationship to the Jews.[63] Renan reiterated the Church's view in its Hegelian interpretation and attributed it to Jesus himself: "The pride of blood seemed to him the main enemy to be fought. In other words, Jesus was no longer a Jew . . . He called all men to a worship founded solely on the fact of their being children of God."[64]

He offered no historical proof of Jesus's leaving the Jewish fold and depended upon a speculative claim: "There is no doubt that Jesus proceeded from Judaism; but he proceeded from it as Socrates proceeded from the schools of the Sophists, as Luther proceeded from the Middle Ages, as Lamennais from Catholicism, as Rousseau from the eighteenth century . . . far from having continued Judaism, he represents the rupture with the Jewish spirit."[65] The verb *sortir* was used here in its two-fold meaning of "emerging" from Judaism and "leaving" it.

It is but a step further to the central issue in the history of Christian anti-semitism – the charge of deicide. Renan, to be sure, did not recognize the divinity of Jesus but worshipped him all the same – if Jesus constituted a break from Judaism, then Judaism took its revenge on him and caused his crucifixion. Renan indicated that the modern view does not blame the son for the sins of his father and that the individual Jew is not to be blamed for the death of Jesus; however such is not the case with the Jews as a nation: "But nations, like individuals, have their responsibilities, and if ever crime was the crime of a nation, it was the death of Jesus."[66] With dialectical skill Renan played upon the collective indictment of the Jews. He saw the crucifixion of Jesus as an example of the Jews' zealous dogmatism, which incidentally was inherited by Christianity as well.

According to Renan, the exclusiveness of Judaism, related to Israel's election, deepened the opposition between Jews and others over the course of history.[67] Renan stressed the point that the Jews had almost always been hated by their neighbors: "Full of a sense of their own superiority, harsh in temper, quarrelsome, brought by their law to separateness that seemed disdain, the Jews were held bad neighbors, and indeed were so. They were detested by the populations that lived about them. This has been the case in all ages, too constantly not to have its cause."[68] The isolationism of the Jews and their negative qualities accompanied them wherever they went. Yet lo and behold! The Jews barricaded themselves behind their faith and withstood all the on-slaughts – "The fanaticism engendered by the Torah survived all attempts to kill it. The best energies of the race were engaged in mad squabbles of mere casuistry. The Talmud, that bad book, which to this day is the evil genius of Judaism, took life from the Torah, and then in great part filled its place, becoming the new law of Judaism."[69] Thus, in spite of the changes in his thinking, Renan still adhered to the basic Christian concepts of Judaism.

The election of Israel and its survival against superior forces continued to fascinate Renan. His concept of history as a pattern within which every pheno-menon had its special function, put Judaism to the ultimate test of survival. According to Hegel, a nation could exist vegetatively after its spirit had already died.[70] Renan did not allow for such duality. Furthermore, his knowledge of Jewish history would not permit him to consider Judaism after Jesus merely as a petrified relic of the past. Renan could not ignore its vitality and had to acknowledge its universality as well. Compared to Jewish isolationism, he con-ceded that the admired Greeks segregated themselves even more – "Greece, that created so many beautiful things, disdained the barbarians too much. The Jews certainly despised the non-Jews too, but the Jewish disdain did not pro-duce such disastrous consequences as the Grecian contempt. It did not prevent Christianity; whereas the Greek contumely prevented Constantinople from assimilating the barbarians etc."[71]

Taking exception to some ideas of the German scholar, Christian Lassen, regarding the Semites' lack of tolerance,[72] Renan justified their zealousness on clearly universal grounds: "The intolerance of the Semitic peoples is the necessary consequence of their monotheism. Before the Indo-European peoples converted to Semitic ideas (Jewish, Christian, or Muslim) they never took their religion as the absolute truth but as a familial or tribal heritage, and had to remain alien to intolerance or proselytism . . . Yet the Semites, hoping to realize a cult independent of provinces or lands, had to proclaim all the religions different from theirs as evil."[73]

The yardstick of universalism was the central touchstone of rationalism and of Hegel's philosophy. Those of Hegel's disciples who wished to divorce Christianity from Jewish influence saw Judaism only as a primitive faith of the ancient Hebrews. This was also Michelet's perception before his attitude to Christianity changed. The later Michelet denied Christianity while recognizing its link with Judaism and naturally saw Judaism as a universal phenomenon. Renan, on the other hand, remained more faithful to Hegel's own original approach. To him, Judaism was the cradle of Christianity and therefore uni-versal from the start, but its attachment to the Jewish people prevented its all-inclusiveness. Herein also lay the difference between Renan and Lassen. Lassen looked upon Judaism as a tribal Jahweh-faith, whereas Renan again and again revealed its relationship to the general development of history. When sketching the image of an ideal religion, in 1883, he stressed this motif: "In a word – the pure religion, which we see as capable of rallying all mankind, will be the realization of Isaiah's religion, the ideal Jewish religion, purified of the dross which could have become mixed into it."[74] Or elsewhere: "Not separat-ing the lot of humanity from that of their little race, the Jewish thinkers were the first who sought for a general theory of the progress of our species."[75]

This perception was not limited to antiquity only; Judaism had the capability of nurturing humankind even in its later periods. Renan in many instances pointed out the affinity between the Reformation and Judaism. He saw common aspects between John Calvin, John Knox, Oliver Cromwell, and the prophets of

Israel – puritanism, dangerous simplification, inability to separate politics and religion – but none of these could detract from Judaism's universalism: "Hebrew literature is the *Bible, the Book par excellence*, the universal reading. Millions scattered throughout the world know no other poetry. Without a doubt, this astounding fate is attributable to the role of the religious revolutions which caused the Hebrew books – especially since the sixteenth century – to be considered the source of all revelation. But one could affirm that had these books not contained something profoundly universal, they would have never arrived at such fortune."[76]

When, according to Renan, does this Jewish universalism come to an end? The social mission of the Jews in the modern period, replacing their religious function of the past, was seen by him as a universal mission in the full sense of the word. That means that Jewish universalism was still in full force, but one should distinguish between the function Jews fulfill as individuals in society and Judaism's historic contribution as a group.[77] Infinite universalism, according to Hegel, is given to the "rational State only."[78] Even according to Renan, the Jews as an historic phenomenon cannot continue to have universal significance. Therefore he had to find the link connecting historic Judaism to the universal function of the Jews in the modern period. Is this connection one of race? Renan did not offer a clear-cut answer to this, but we shall see that he did seek the answer in this area.

4. The Concept of Race

Renan's field of specialization, philology, was the impetus for his views on race.[79] For him, philology was "the science of mankind" through which one could discover the phases of the human spirit's development. However the human spirit could not be grasped through methods such as befitted geometry; psychological insight, empathy, and intuition were required.[80] The criticism that Renan levelled at Comte in the area of philology indicated his line of thought with regard to race as well – while Comte was searching for the principle uniting all the languages, Renan was interested in their variety.[81]

Variety was the starting point for a series of perspectives which took shape during the 1850s in the debate over the origin of human language. According to Renan, language was not the result of historical development but was produced *ex nihilo*.[82] He did not see the various languages as branching off from a common source[83] but as relating to a number of archetypes with defined, fixed boundaries between them.[84] Each linguistic group equaled a specific race.[85] Along with its language, each group also created its characteristic religion.[86] Renan divided his system into two stages: the early, biological stage in which race was the decisive factor in human development,[87] and the historical stage, in which the racial influence was pushed aside by the cultural[88] but never disappeared completely.[89]

Thus he did not set a clear limit to the influence of each stage; from time to time the center of gravity shifted from one to the other, as for example: "Races are originally physiological facts, but they tend more and more to become historical ones which have almost nothing in common with blood."[90] Or: "Language, religion, laws and customs came to constitute the race far more than blood."[91] On the other hand, he remarked that those confined within the circle of French culture had difficulty in understanding the great importance of the ethnographic matter because in France itself the racial differences had been blurred and racial theories seemed to be exaggerations or paradoxes.[92]

Contrary to what Renan had thought in 1848 about the course of progress, he now rejected any all-embracing system and insisted upon different closed circles, each subject to its own laws of development.[93] He accompanied this claim with examples from nature, which pointed indirectly to a contest with Darwinism.[94] The argument was directed at the German philologist Max Müller, to whom Renan imputed a unified system, which required that all the linguistic families pass through the same stages in the course of their progress.[95] Renan, on the other hand, held that each language – like each natural species – was to achieve its own perfection.[96]

According to him, languages developed along independent lines within the frameworks of the different families; but here he suddenly admitted that there was no direct relationship between the level of language and that of its speakers.[97] It would seem, then, that the philologist overcame the philosopher, but this was only a passing hesitation often found in Renan.[98]

At bottom were the basic premises about deterministic creation and the immanent link between race and language, so that little room was left for development in the historic-cultural stage. Renan's framework led him to establish a clear racial hierarchy. He divided the races into two major groups: civilized and savage.[99] The cultured races again subdivided into various groups, each of which bore its particular genius – the Indo-European race was at the top of the ladder, followed by the Semitic, and subsequently the Hamitic and the Chinese races. At the bottom were the inferior races that could hardly be called human anymore.[100]

This thinking threatened to destroy the basic values common to the Christian and humanist traditions about the unity of the human species. Renan, incidentally, distinguished between abstract values and scientific analysis, and claimed that it was possible to embrace the view of a common humanity despite the racial conflict.[101] He resorted to two parallel sources of inspiration – science versus values – and claimed autonomy for each: "For science to be independent it must not be encumbered by any dogma."[102]

Here it seems that we can see the roots of Renan's concept of race – in the static creation of language; in the connection between race, language, and religion; in the way each racial group is subject to its own laws; and in the clear distinction between human values and scientific truths. Here was the key to Renan's attitude to race and not in the racial explanations then prevalent among

French historians with regard to the conflict between the Franks and the Gauls[103] (nor in his own connection in the 1880s with the so-called Celtic Association).[104]

Renan admitted that the use of the term *Semites* was essentially based on an error. The Semitic family, according to the modern division into linguistic families, included groups not listed in the Bible among the children of Shem (Genesis 10), whereas some of Shem's descendants spoke languages not considered Semitic by modern linguistics. The biblical table, according to him, indicated a geographic and not an ethnographic division. Therefore he clarified who was included in the group which (for the sake of convenience) he called the Semitic race: "Here this term designates not the peoples that appear in Genesis as the children of Shem but the peoples that speak or spoke the languages erroneously called Semitic, i.e., the Hebrews, the Phoenicians, the Syrians, the Arabs, and the Abyssinians."[105] The group which he called the Semitic race was related, in his opinion, to the Indo-European or Aryan group. Human history was created by them jointly and they complemented each other. This was not the case with the other races, such as the Negroes or the Tatars; or the Chinese, who created a separate civilization for themselves: "Viewed from the physical side, the Semites and the Aryans constitute but one race, the white race; viewed from the intellectual side, they are one family, the civilized family."[106]

When discussing the Jews, he went much further. The Jews had gradually moved away from their original race until, in the modern age, they became "European." The racial heritage gave way to the cultural to such an extent that Islam (which he considered a perfect example of the Semitic spirit) set its mark upon all the non-Semitic races that had adopted it, and therefore "the Turk, a devout Muslim, is now much more of a true Semite than the Israelite who has become French, or even better, European."[107]

Lecturing to the Saint-Simon Circle in Paris in 1883, Renan related[108] that when he worked in the National Library he met all kinds of Jews and, as a result, concluded that there was no single Jewish type. Even in their external characteristics, Jews were not alike; there were numerous Jewish types. He believed that the Jews did not constitute a single ethnic group and that they had, in addition to their original blood, a noticeable mixture of non-Jewish blood. However, the Jewish way of life has imprinted itself upon them because they had married for centuries within a closed circle.[109]

In saying that the Jews were no longer pure Semites, Renan apparently intended to compliment them. In any case, he found no fault in their being a mixed race as he was no proponent of racial purity.[110] By the time he delivered his Saint-Simon lecture, the racial doctrine had become a ready-made political instrument. In the dispute between France and Germany over Alsace-Lorraine, the Germans used the claim that these provinces should be annexed to Germany because their inhabitants were of the Germanic race. Renan changed his mind about race at the beginning of the Franco-Prussian War and in his second letter to Strauss, in 1871, he reproved the Germans for their aggressive policy, warning them that the racial principle (in his words, the result of German comparative linguistics) would eventually be turned against themselves – a Slavic front would come into being and raise similar claims about areas in the east of Germany. Renan suggested, instead, a policy of international amity: "The overly extreme division of mankind into races cannot but lead to 'zoological' wars of extermination . . . like those the various species of rodents or carnivores wage among themselves for survival."[111]

At the end of his life, Renan took a clear stand against the political utilization of the racial principle. In a famous lecture on the essence of nationhood, in 1882, he based national identity upon voluntary partnership and not upon determinism and said: "The truth is that there is no pure race, and to have politics repose upon ethnographic analysis is to have it carried away by a chimera."[112] How, then, does one explain his boasting one year later that he had always understood the dependence of religion on race? "Here is the best proof of the great axiom which we have often proclaimed, namely that the value of religions equals that of the races which profess them."[113] Now he returned to what he had said half a century earlier when he argued that the purity of Islam was upheld by the Arab race and that Jewish reformers (Maimonides, Spinoza) purified Judaism of the foreign anthropomorphism which had stuck to it.[114]

His return to the racial concept in 1883 completely contradicted his public career over the years. But with Renan one must distinguish between scholarly truth and current affairs. When he talked of languages and religions in their broad historical perspective, he was incapable of breaking away from the molds he had set for himself in his youth. In his later years, there was a change in his outlook, but he did not revise the basic premises which had guided him in his early work. What he wrote with the toil and enthusiasm of a young researcher in the forties and the fifties of the century remained fixed. The antideterminism he acquired later, his penchant for individual freedom, his negation of clericalism – all of these appeared on the surface, but did not always penetrate into deeper levels; furthermore, they applied only to European society.[115] To this may be added his extreme flexibility, or indecision, which led him to contradictory positions without his being able – as he himself attested – to untangle the knot.[116]

5. The Racial Characteristics of the Semites

In keeping with the theory of race and the particular roles of various races within the general pattern of humankind, Renan determined the characteristics of the Semites. Comparing the Semitic to the Aryan race, he argued: "Well, I am the first to recognize that the Semitic race compared to the Indo-European race clearly represents an inferior combination of human nature."[117] He was gratified to find similar sayings by Christian Lassen, considered then the doyen of Indian studies. It turned out that each, working in different fields – one studying the Semites, the other the Aryans – had independently reached similar conclusions, scientifically proven as it were, on the nature of each of the two races. Renan was especially impressed by Lassen's views on the subjectivity of the Semites,[118] which he, Renan, derived from history and religion as well as from language and culture. Subjectivity, according to him, was tied to a lack of creative ability, to simplistic perceptions, insufficient curiosity, and monotony. The Semites, according to Renan, lacked a sense of discipline and were incapable of proper political organization. Subjectivity was at the root of Semitic morality, different in essence from conventional morality: "The Semite hardly knows any duties except to himself. To avenge himself, to demand what he believes to be his right – is to him a kind of obligation. On the other hand, to ask that he keep his word, that he carry out disinterested justice, is to ask of him the impossible."[119]

Uniformity and simplicity were to Renan clear indicators of the Semitic race. These were not outstanding qualities as such, but rather a primitive state, or the sheer absence of qualities: "Thus the Semitic race is recognizable almost uniquely by negative characteristics. It has no mythology, no epic, no science, no philosophy, no fiction, no plastic arts, no civic life; there is no complexity, nor nuance; an exclusive sense of uniformity."[120] As a philologist, Renan found the typical attributes of the Semitic race in language – sensuality and no gift for abstract thinking: "This physical and sensual character seems dominant in the family of languages we are studying,"[121] and in another work thirty years later: "The Semitic languages do not lend themselves at all to the expression of exact ideas; they affect brisk action, mere glitter. They decompose trains of thought and scatter their parts to the four winds."[122]

Thus far Renan was speaking of the Semites in general, including the ancient Hebrews. The difficulty arose when he approached the Semitic faith and its connection with Christianity. There he made a clear distinction between Semitic monotheism as such and one of its later derivations, Islam. Islam was roundly detested by Renan. This did not find its fullest expression in his formal writings but was well reflected in his literary estate.[123] The Semitic faith should have shown all the faults which Renan attributed to the Semites in general, yet he could not ignore their contribution to the faith of the Aryans, as he himself repeatedly stated. This contradiction gave him apparently no rest: "It was fitting that monotheism be the product of a Jews with exalted religious ideas. In fact, it comes from a race with few religious needs. It is a minimal religion, both in dogmas and external practices."[124] As we have seen earlier, Renan always tended to come to terms with reality. Although he was not ready to retract his evaluation of Semitic monotheism as primitive, towards the end of his life he conceded that perhaps primitivism was but an early stage of Semitism. In 1887 he suggested that nomads of all races usually embraced a simple sort of faith and the contrary was the case with non-nomadic Semites.[125]

The reference here was to a qualitative contrast between the developed Christian religion and the primitive Semitic sources; but Renan also had a genetic criticism which was clearly racial: "It is strange that Europe adopted as the basis of its spiritual life books which are the least suited to it – the literature of the Hebrews, a product of another race and another spirit, but it adopted them only by turning them inside out. The Veda, much more than the Bible, deserved to be the sacred book of Europe. That is really the work of our fathers."[126] Against this background it is no wonder that Renan asked himself if Jesus was a Jew by race: "The conversions to Judaism were not rare in these mixed countries [Galilee]. It is therefore impossible to raise here any question of race and to seek to ascertain what blood flowed in the veins of him who has contributed most to efface the distinction of blood in humanity."[127]

All the faults Renan attributed to the Semites applied in one degree or another to the ancient Hebrews, but how much they applied to modern Jews was questionable. This makes doubly valuable the following extract in which Renan contrasted the Jews and the Aryans, depicting their racial characteristics with the aid of imagery borrowed from the Aryan myth: "This ideal of material comfort without military nobility and of middle-class vainglory not founded upon the heroism of the masses, appears very small to our sentimental, romantic races . . . Whatever we may do we are the adepts of a wild chivalry, pursuing dreams and fundamentally reposing upon the belief in immortality."[128] To this Renan juxtaposed the "servant of the Lord" and said: "But the genius of great races always reasserts itself. Let the so-called materialist, the seeming egoist, say what he likes. His own life will be one of perpetual self-devotion. He has a gift which belongs to him only, that of hope."[129] Here Renan again raised the racial confrontation to a spiritual contrast between faith in the human race and the kingdom of heaven.

As a dialectician, Renan essentially reached some kind of synthesis: "The Semitic race was inferior to the Aryan. The Aryan produced civilization. The Semites were primitive, of narrow horizon, sensuous and subjective. What need did history have to send the superior race to learn its faith from them? But if such was decreed by the Lord of History, it was no doubt decreed wisely. Therefore one must set up the dialectical construction and the problem will be solved:

- thesis – the Semites were limited;
- antithesis – their limitation prepared them for monotheism;
- synthesis – only when Semitic monotheism permeated Aryan civilization did it achieve its true meaning.

The human race, then, rose to a higher stage: "To the Indo-European race belong almost all the great movements in the history of the world – military, political, and intellectual; to the Semitic race, the religious movements. The Indo-European race, preoccupied by the variety of the universe, would not have come to monotheism by itself. However, the Semitic race, guided by its firm and certain views, immediately stripped the divinity of its veils and without reflection and reasoning arrived at the purest form of religion mankind has known."[130] The two races, then, complement one another.

6. The Jews in Society

The study of Jewish history gave Renan a specific, set image of the traits of the Jews. Even when he was harshly critical of their historical characteristics, he saw them above all as the proponents of a spiritual struggle. Experience apparently taught Renan a lesson that contradicted this characterization and he reacted with biting irony: "Go then and make trouble in the world, make God die on the cross, endure every kind of suffering, set fire to our (your) country three or four times, insult every tyrant, overthrow every idol, and finish by contracting a disease of the spine in a richly furnished hotel on the Champs-Elysées, regretting that life is so short and pleasure so fugitive. Vanity of vanities!"[131]

For the romantic Renan, disappointment was compounded by a shade of xenophobia. Not only did modern Jews turn their backs on their glorious past, but they sought to gain a vested right to a heritage which was not theirs: ". . . how easily he adapts himself to the requirements of modern civilization; how exempt he is from dynastic and feudal prejudices; how he knows to enjoy a world he has not made, to gather the fruits of a field he has not worked, to supplant the simpleton who persecutes him, to render himself necessary to the fool who despises him. It is for him, believe it or not, that Clovis and his Franks struck dull thuds with the sword, that the race of Capet unfurled its political banner a thousand years ago, that Philip Auguste conquered at Bouvines and Condé at Rocroi."[132]

The exploitation of the political and military achievements of others was, to Renan, a part of the Jewish heritage, for he did not consider the Jews capable of political life: "In spite of this seeming superiority, the Jewish people never had a political life and the Jewish institutions that so greatly served the religious progress of mankind, did little to the service of progress in public life. It can even be said that they did it harm by spreading everywhere a people detached from any homeland, too much inclined, as we already see in the book of Esther, to furnish the sovereigns with docile servants against their subjects."[133] This dispersion among the nations, which Renan saw as positive in view of the universal mission of Israel, was presented here as an antisocial act. The Jews as strangers everywhere fulfilled an unwholesome social function,[134] attesting to the parasitic attitude of the chosen people.[135] The Jews depended on others to carry out the military chores which were disagreeable to them: "The great empires founded upon the military classes are entrusted with this work. This leads to an approach which jars our instincts. Israel always says to itself, in the final analysis, that it has the best part, and in spite of its subordinate position the world really exists for it alone."[136]

In this, Renan was the disciple of Michelet. Michelet has said that the Jew was essentially not a warrior. According to him, the Jew's ideal was the sly shepherd, Jacob, who submitted to Esau like a woman.[137] Renan admitted that the Jew was capable of martyrdom but not of battle: "Jewish pietism is too reflective. It might make martyrs, it could never make an army . . . the Jew in the day of battle only thinks how he may escape. He offers his purse to the soldier about to kill him; and when he sees that this will not serve, he sees no sense in a game where a prudent man can make no use of all his means, and he decides never again to expose himself in battle."[138] Other assumed traits of the Semitic race could well match the Jewish image: "The abnegation of one's personality and the sentiment for hierarchy, necessary conditions for any militia, are deeply antipathetic to the individualism and the ungoverned pride of the Semites."[139] Renan did not sense any contradiction between such exaggerated individualism and the socialist role which he attributed to the Jews.

The racial character of the Jews along with their spiritual tradition, then, prepared them for their historic fate. The absence of political ability brought on the loss of their national independence and their dispersion among the nations. Their dependence on others made them the servants of the rulers against the peoples. Through their diligence the Jews penetrated the interstices of society and here revealed one of their particularly characteristic traits – their clannishness. True, Renan was not overtly critical of this but he bolstered the antisemitic claim by his description: "The synagogues corresponded with one another, and exchanged letters of recommendation. They formed a vast secret society, a sort of freemasonry."[140]

Only a few features were now missing to complete the picture drawn by modern antisemitism – the Jews as Mammon worshippers and as fomenters of revolution.[141] Michelet had explained that it was natural for the Jews, due to insecure conditions, to regard wealth as their sole guarantee and as a means to bribe the high and mighty.[142] Renan, in his book *Ecclesiastes* (1882) which contained some virulent passages against modern Jews, said: "This is the man who has overthrown the world by his faith in the kingdom of God, who now believes in nothing but wealth."[143] On the other hand, he also explained that Judaism originally opposed cupidity and it was the Christians' fault that Jews became tradesmen and middlemen.[144] However, Jewish law which forbade them to loan money at interest to one another permitted usury as far as Gentiles were concerned and thus they came to be branded as usurers.[145]

As to the revolutionary movement, Renan's position was completely different from Michelet's. Michelet reproached Judaism for supporting reaction and was consistent in this position. Renan joined in this reproach but at the same time also placed the Jews in the camp of social progress; first of all in the past: "The most exalted democratic movement of which humanity has preserved the remembrance . . . had long disturbed the Jewish race;"[146] and likewise in the modern period: "Abuses and violences to which the Christian patiently submits, disgust the Jew; and this is why the Israelitish element has, in our time, in every country in which it resides, become an element of reform and progress. Saint-Simonism and the industrial and financial mysticism of our days result in great measure from Judaism. In the French revolutionary movements the Jewish element plays a capital rôle."[147]

Even though Renan did not support revolution politically, he greatly valued its historic function and there is no doubt that what he said about Jews in this connection was laudatory. On the other hand, it is clear that he thereby added another layer to the antisemitic structure; and not only because he strengthened the conservative claims against the Jews. By stating that the Jews worshipped money, that they served the ruling power yet also constituted a revolutionary element, Renan contributed to the stereotype of the Jews aspiring to destroy society by every means at their disposal.

7. Summary

Renan was full of contradictions. Without being an out-and-out antisemite, and even though he was not an avowed racist, he played a significant role in the creation of racial antisemitism. Interestingly enough, Renan was far from any extremism. It is thus pertinent to ask: how did he arrive at his views and what made him into the springboard of a certain kind of antisemitism?

Intellectually, Renan drew from many sources, each of which contributed to the climate of opinion that shaped modern antisemitism. In this context, one should mention the pattern of history, at the center of which was the idea of progress, as manifested by the philosophy of Hegel. By means of this perception one was able to judge history and issue death sentences upon weak nations that faltered in the face of progress. This perception as applied to the Jews was reminiscent of the Church's view of their status in Christian society. The Jews' debased position was taken as proof that divine grace had deserted them. Were the Christians to allow them to raise their heads, it would refute this proof. The result was a self-fulfilling prophecy in the hands of Christian society. Thus if the assumption that Judaism had lost its vitality should come into conflict with reality, there would be room for one of two conclusions: Either the theory would be rejected in the face of reality, or its adherents would actively fight against the vitality of Judaism.

On the one hand Renan was influenced by the Young Hegelians via Strauss, and on the other he was close to Michelet. These two influences reflect various stages in his attitude to Christianity. The Young Hegelians tended to negate Judaism's contribution to Christianity. The later Michelet rejected Christianity and objected to Judaism precisely because of its connection with Christianity. In spite of the difference between the two approaches as regards Christianity, they were close in their negative attitude toward Judaism.

But all of these influences are still not enough to explain Renan's racial views. The main source for these are the outlooks prevalent in philology at the time, which legitimized racial thinking under the guise of "positive science." Comparative linguistics established the basis upon which developed the sense of "Aryan" superiority. The discovery that there was presumably a connection between Sanskrit and Greek allowed for the notion that there had been an ancient connection between the conquerors of Greece and those of India. It undermined the accepted European lineage, which was fundamentally a cultural-spiritual heritage (Israel-Greece-Rome) and replaced it with the pedigree of a common origin.

It should be pointed out that there was a marked contrast between the conclusions drawn by Renan from the doctrine of race and the Hegelian perspectives which guided him in the area of history. According to Renan's grasp of racial matters, there was no room for the dynamic development of the human species; there was merely a static hierarchy of superior and inferior races. The two-stage division (the early biological stage and the historical-cultural stage) somewhat mitigated his theoretical rigidity, but the absence of a clear line of demarcation between the two stages made Renan slip easily into racial determinism. This process found its justification in the separation of science and values. Also note that Renan derived his racial theory from a non-Darwinist point of view, whereas racial theories very often relied specifically on Darwinism.[148]

Renan was influenced by many sources but he did not mold them into a total outlook. Therefore he was obliged to reconcile the internal contradictions of his teaching. He claimed that the Semites were inferior to the Aryans, that they were subjective, primitive, and self-centered; that the people of Israel were not capable of creating a state, that they escaped from battle, worshipped Mammon, and were obedient servants of authority against the people; that they were fanatic, arrogant, and justifiably despised by others; that they sought positions which were not theirs, stirred up revolutionary movements, and conspired with each other.

But Renan himself contradicted almost each and every aspect of these accusations. He pointed out that the basic concept of a Semitic race was erroneous, and that the very concept of race had changed its ethnic meaning and was to become primarily a cultural attribute. He thought that the Jews were far removed from their original race, that their blood was mixed, and that they had become Europeans. He saw Judaism as one of the two forces upon which rested civilization as a whole. He believed that the Jews gave humankind religion and social justice, that they had a universal mission to fulfill and were destined to promote social progress. The contradiction between the anti-semitic elements in Renan and his positive assessment of Judaism was to some extent resolved by him through dialectics. According to this, Judaism had a role in human history as a necessary counter-weight to other historical forces. The very duality of his approach marks the peculiarity of antisemitic thinking, which allocates to Jews and Judaism a central role, far beyond their position in real life.

There is also a certain difference in his perception prior to the Franco-Prussian War and its development in the later years of his life. His growing away from Strauss and his change of attitude toward Germany contributed greatly in this direction. His ever-growing scepticism and finally his drifting towards moral relativism undermined the entire theoretical structure by which he dared judge history, and Judaism with it. It must be emphasized that Renan was never an antisemite in the full sense of the word; he never drew the logical conclusions from his criticism of the Jews nor did he advocate any measures against them. His racism also never led to any practical conclusions, perhaps because racism is basically a monistic system[149] and Renan was by nature far from monism.

Renan's personality was particularly fit to influence his generation. He was a gifted popularizer and was listened to far and wide. His words also carried weight because of his scholarly prestige. The contradictions in his position (which he himself acknowledged and attributed to indecision and good manners), provided opposing movements with an incentive to adopt him as their patron saint. His moderation, it should be added, further strengthened his authority because he could not be dismissed as a fanatic. This facet of his character was also important in relation to his views on the Jews. His activity as an opponent of antisemitic excesses strengthened his theoretical teachings and inadvertently bolstered their antisemitic charge.[150] He could not fully comprehend as yet the ramifications of what he had written on this subject, but he had already some vision of the future. He saw what use could be made of antisemitism by clerical politicians in France and even grasped the danger of racism in Germany, and came out openly against both.

Notes

1. See I. Schapira, *Der Antisemitismus in der französischen Literatur* (Berlin, 1927); R. F. Byrnes, *Antisemitism in Modern France* (New Brunswick, N.J., 1951).
2. E. Renan, *L'Avenir de la science (pensées de 1848)* (Paris, 1890), esp. p. 459.
3. H. W. Wardman, *Ernest Renan: a Critical Biography* (London, 1964); E. Renan, *Souvenirs d'enfance et de jeunesse* (Paris, 1883), p. 166.
4. D. F. Strauss, *Essais d'histoire religieuses et Mélanges litteraires*: Introduction E. Renan (Paris, 1872), pp. X–XI.
5. E. Renan, *Etudes d'histoire religieuse* (Paris, 1864), p. 162.
6. Ibid., pp. 408–409.
7. Ibid., p. 184: cf. B. Bauer, *Philo, Strauss und Renan und das Urchristenthum* (Berlin, 1874), p. 126.
8. D. F. Strauss. *Der alte und der neue Glaube*, Introduction, E. Zeller (Bonn, 1881), p. IX; W. Kaufmann, *Nietzsche* (Cleveland & New York, 1962), p. 142.
9. D. G. Charlton, *Positivist Thought in France* (Oxford, 1959), p. 123.
10. R. A. Wilson, *The Miraculous Birth of Language* (London, 1937), Chap. 5: "From Herder to Darwin."
11. E. Renan, *De l'origine du langage* (Paris, 1848), (1864 edition quoted here is an augmented version); *Histoire générale et système comparé des langues sémitiques* (Paris, 1855), (="*Histoire des langues sémitiques*"); *Nouvelles considérations sur le caractère général des peuples sémitiques* (Paris, 1859) (="*Nouvelles considérations*").
12. *Histoire des langues sémitiques*, preface, p. I.

13. W.v. Humboldt, *Uber die Verschiedenheit des menschlichen Sprachbaues* 2 (Berlin, 1876), p. 18; cf. E. Renan, *De l'origine du langage*, p. 86.
14. F. Hertz, *Rasse und Kultur* (Leipzig, 1915), p. 85.
15. G. P. Gooch, *History and Historians in the Nineteenth Century* (Boston, 1962), p. 165. (Renan assisted in his youth the blind Thierry.)
16. E. Renan, *Souvenirs d'enfance et de jeunesse*, p. 160.
17. G. Monod, "Michelet et les Juifs," *Revue des Etudes Juives* 53(1907):1–25. (The antisemite Toussenel served as Michelet's secretary for a while.)
18. H. Psichari, *Renan d'après lui-même* (Paris, 1937), p. 131.
19. C. Jullian, *Extraits des historiens français du 19ème siècle* (Paris, 1898), p. 313, note 3; p. 316.
20. J. Pommier, *Renan* (Paris, 1923), p. 164.
21. E. Renan, *L'Histoire du peuple d'Israël* 5 (Paris, 1887–1893), p. 238.
22. E. Sterling, *Er ist wie du* (Munich, 1956), Chap. V; N. Rotenstreich, "For and Against Emancipation: The Bruno Bauer Controversy," *Leo Baeck Yearbook* 4(1959):32–36.
23. E. Renan, *Cohelet or The Preacher* (London, n.d.), p. 37.
24. D. G. Charlton, *op. cit.*, pp. 111–112; R. M. Galand, *L'Ame celtique de Renan* (Paris, 1959), p. 46; F. A. Hayek, *The Counter-Revolution of Science* (London, 1964), pp. 191–206.
25. E. Renan, *L'Avenir de la science*, pp. 301–318.
26. Ibid., p. 149.
27. Ibid., p. 364.
28. F. Hegel, *The Philosophy of History*, translated by J. Sibree (New York, 1956), p. 53.
29. E. Renan, *Souvenirs d'enfance et de jeunesse*, p. 63.
30. E. Renan, *L'Avenir de la science*, préface, p. VII.
31. Ibid., p. 422.
32. Ibid., p. 375.
33. Ibid., p. 370.
34. Ibid., p. 384.
35. Ibid., p. 379.
36. Ibid., p. 380.
37. E. Renan, *Dialogues et fragments philosophiques* (Paris, 1876), p. 43. (This may also be a literary device.)
38. E. Renan, *Feuilles detachées* (Paris, 1892), pp. 382–383.
39. E. Renan, *L'Avenir de la science*, préface, p. XIV.
40. E. Renan, *Histoire d'Israël 3*, p. 251.
41. Ibid. 5, p. 221.
42. E. Renan, *Etudes d'histoire religieuse*, p. 102.
43. Ibid., p. 131.
44. B. Bauer, *Die Judenfrage* (Brunswick, 1843), p. 81.
45. E. Renan, *History of the People of Israel* 2 (London, 1889), p. 454.
46. E. Renan, *History of the People of Israel* 3 (Boston, 1905), pp. 402–403.
47. Cf. Voltaire, *Oeuvres complètes* 35 (Basel, 1784), p. 246; G. E. Lessing, "Erziehung des Menschengeschlechtes," in *Freimaurergespräche und anderes* (Munich, 1981), p. 91.
48. E. Renan, *History of the People of Israel* 1 (Boston, 1905), preface, p. VIII.
49. Ibid., p. XV.
50. *Nouvelles considérations*, p. 97.
51. E. Renan, *History of the People of Israel 1*, p. 50; *Coup d'oeil sur l'histoire du peuple juif* (Paris, 1881).
52. B. Bauer, *Die Judenfrage*, p. 83; see also S. Ettinger, "The Young Hegelians: A Source of Modern Anti-Semitism?," *The Jerusalem Quarterly* 28(1983):73–82.
53. E. Renan, *History of the People of Israel* 4 (Boston, 1895), pp. 8–9.
54. Ibid., 5 (Boston, 1907), p. 189.
55. Ibid., p. 361.
56. Cf. Voltaire, *Oeuvres complètes* 33 (n. 47 above), p. 17.
57. J. Michelet, *La Bible de l'humanité* (Paris, 1864), p. 374.
58. E. Renan, *History of the People of Israel* 2, p. 44.
59. Cf. F. Nietzsche, *Jenseits von Gut und Böse* (Leipzig, 1886), pp. 118–119.
60. E. Renan, *The Life of Jesus* (London, 1904), p. 49.

61. *Galatians*, III, 28.
62. Cf. P. H. d'Holbach, *L'Esprit du judaïsme* (London and Amsterdam, 1770), avant-propos, p. XXI (pseud. Anthony Collins).
63. F. Hegel, *op. cit.*, p. 197.
64. E. Renan, *The Life of Jesus* (New York, 1927), p. 225.
65. Ibid., p. 390.
66. Ibid., p. 358.
67. Cf. F. W. Ghillany, *Die Judenfrage* (Nuremberg, 1843), pp. 19–20.
68. E. Renan, *History of the People of Israel* 4, p. 321.
69. Ibid., p. 53; cf. S. Munk, *Palestine* (Paris, 1845), p. 565A; J. Derenbourg, *Essai sur l'histoire et la geographie de la Palestine* (Paris, 1867), p. 191.
70. F. Hegel, *op. cit.*, p. 75.
71. E. Renan, *History of the People of Israel* 3, p. 410.
72. Ch. Lassen, *Indische Alterthumskunde* 1 (Bonn, 1847), p. 416.
73. E. Renan, *Etudes d'histoire religieuse*, p. 87.
74. E. Renan, *Discours et conférences* (Paris, 1928), p. 337.
75. E. Renan, *The Life of Jesus* (New York, 1927), p. 101.
76. *Histoire des langues sémitiques*, p. 124.
77. E. I. Kose, *Ernest Renan and the Jewish World*, 1955 (Ph.D. Thesis, Columbia University).
78. *Hegel* Selection F. Heer (Frankfurt. M. and Hamburg, 1955), p. 233.
79. D. Bierer, *Renan's Role in the Culture of Modern France*, 1951 (Ph.D. Thesis, Columbia University).
80. E. Renan, *L'Avenir de la science*, p. 298.
81. Ibid., p. 506, note 70.
82. E. Renan, *De l'origine du langage*, pp. 99–100.
83. Ibid., p. 203.
84. Ibid., p. 202.
85. Ibid., préface a l'édition de 1864, pp. 44–45.
86. J. Darmesteter, *Notice sur la vie et l'oeuvre de M. Renan* (Paris, 1893), p. 24; *Nouvelles considérations*, pp. 69–70.
87. Ibid., p. 98.
88. Ibid., ibidem.
89. Ibid., id.
90. *Nouvelles considérations*, p. 99.
91. E. Renan, *History of the People of Israel* 1, p. 3.
92. *Nouvelles considérations*, p. 99.
93. *Histoire des langues sémitiques*, p. 476.
94. E. Renan, *De l'origine du langage*, préface a l'édition de 1864, p. 44.
95. Ibid., id.; L. Noiré, *Max Müller und die Sprachphilosophie* (Mainz, 1879), pp. 16, 31; Renan approved of A. F. Pott, *Die Ungleichheit menschlicher Rassen* (Lemgo, 1856), who was influenced by Gobineau; see also: L. Poliakov, *Le Mythe arien* (Paris, 1971), p. 209; J. Barzun, *Race: a Study in Superstition* (New York, 1965), p. 62.
96. E. Renan, *De l'origine du langage*, préface de l'édition de 1864, pp. 44; cf. A. F. Pott, *op. cit.*, p. 80.
97. Ibid., p. 45; A. F. Pott, *op. cit.*, p. 86.
98. E.g., E. Renan, *De l'origine du langage*, p. 203.
99. *Histoire des langues sémitiques*, p. 468.
100. Ibid., p. 476.
101. Ibid., p. 448.
102. *Histoire des langues sémitiques*, p. 449.
103. *Nouvelles considérations*, pp. 99, 101.
104. R. M. Galand, *op. cit.* (n. 24 above), p. 57; E. Renan, *Judaïsme et christianisme*, preface J. Gaulmier (Paris, 1977), pp. 22–23.
105. E. Renan, *Etudes d'histoire religieuse*, p. 85 (note).
106. *Histoire des langues sémitiques*, p. 464.
107. *Nouvelles considérations*, p. 101.
108. However, he also admitted that he was always eager to please: E. Renan, *Souvenirs d'enfance*, p. 132.

278   *Shmuel Almog*

109. E. Renan, Le judaïsme comme race et comme religion, 27.1.1883, *"Discours et conférences"*, pp. 369–370.
110. See T. R. (Reinach), *Revue des Etudes Juives* 11(1883):141–147.
111. E. Renan, *La Réforme intellectuelle et morale de la France* (Paris, 1871), p. 199.
112. E. Renan, *Discours et conférences*, pp. 293–294.
113. Ibid., p. 403.
114. *Nouvelles considérations*, p. 41.
115. E. Renan, *La Réforme intellectuelle et morale*, p. 197.
116. E. Renan, *Souvenirs d'enfance*, p. 101.
117. *Histoire des langues sémitiques*, p. 4.
118. Ch. Lassen, *Indische Alterthumskunde* 1, p. 414.
119. *Histoire des langues sémitiques*, p. 15.
120. Ibid., p. 16.
121. Ibid., p. 18.
122. E. Renan, *Cohelet or The Preacher*, p. 45.
123. H. Psichari, *op. cit*, (n. 18 above), p. 214; cf. D. Chwolson, *Die semitischen Völker* (Berlin, 1872); Th. Noldecke, Über die Begabung der Semiten, *Im neuen Reich* 2(1872): 883.
124. *Nouvelles considérations*, p. 40.
125. E. Renan, *Histoire d'Israël* 1, pp. 42–43.
126. E. Renan, *L'Avenir de la science*, p. 515, note 124.
127. E. Renan, *The Life of Jesus* (New York, 1927), p. 83.
128. E. Renan, *History of the People of Israel* 3, p. 403.
129. Ibid., ibidem.
130. E. Renan, *Etudes d'histoire religieuse*, p. 85.
131. E. Renan, *Cohelet or The Preacher*, p. 54.
132. Ibid., pp. 52–53.
133. *Nouvelles considérations*, p. 92.
134. Cf. J. Michelet, *La Bible de l'humanité* (n. 57 above), pp. 382–383 (note).
135. Cf. A. Bein, The Jewish Parasite, *Leo Baeck Yearbook*, 9 (1964): pp. 3–40.
136. E. Renan, *History of the People of Israel* 3, p. 354.
137. J. Michelet, *op. cit.*, p. 366 seq.
138. E. Renan, *History of the People of Israel* 4, p. 167–168.
139. *Histoire des langues sémitiques*, pp. 14–15.
140. E. Renan, *Histoire d'Israël* 4, p. 221.
141. Cf. M. A. Bakunin, *Gesammelte Werke* 3 (Berlin, 1924), p. 209.
142. J. Michelet, *op.cit.*, p. 379.
143. E. Renan, *Cohelet or The Preacher*, p. 53.
144. E. Renan, *Histoire d'Israël* 4, p. 190.
145. E. Renan, *History of the People of Israel* 3, pp. 356–357.
146. E. Renan, *The Life of Jesus* (New York, 1927), p. 195.
147. E. Renan, *Cohelet or The Preacher*, pp. 23–24.
148. See e.g., H. Conrad-Martius, *Utopien der Menschenzüchtung* (Munich, 1955), G. L. Mosse, *Toward the Final Solution: A History of European Racism* (London, 1978), pp. 72–73.
149. E. Cassirer, *The Myth of the State* (Garden City, N.Y., 1955), p. 291.
150. E.g., H. S. Chamberlain, *Die Grundlagen des XIX Jahrhunderts* 1 (Munich, 1907), p. 383.

19

The Preparatory Stage of the Modern Antisemitic Movement (1873-1879)

JACOB KATZ

Our topic, the period which paved the way for the outbreak of modern anti-semitism in 1879, may be termed micro-history. The general background of antisemitism from antiquity to our time is macro-history. One may well ask: Is modern antisemitism part of a continuum or something new? Simply put, the answer is – both. Clearly there are motifs which come from antiquity through the Middle Ages to modern times. But history is not so much interested in what different stages share as in those elements which change over the course of time and in their effects. This is so for macro-history and micro-history alike. Even in the limited 1873-79 period there were at least three stages – which make it history.

1. Historical Background

In broad perspective, I feel that the first antagonisms toward the Jews in antiquity resulted from the fact that the Jews appeared as a closed group with a unique religious consciousness, whose faith compelled its withdrawal from the surrounding society. The world reacted to this withdrawal with hostility, at which Jewry withdrew even more. One can debate at length about how it began, but both sides undoubtedly contributed. This situation persisted throughout the Middle Ages, especially in the Christian world, but assumed a completely new form. What took place in medieval times is essentially different from what happened in antiquity.

Professor Ettinger has stated that the European cultures have a heritage of antisemitism. That, of course, is correct, but the question is how this came about. It is not an outgrowth of the local tribal traditions but the result of Christianity's encounter with Judaism. There is a vast difference between the ancient world's opposition to Judaism and that of the Middle Ages. In antiquity,

279

neither Judaism nor its opposition were of major importance. The opposition broke out sporadically and, most importantly, never received any substantial religious sanction. There is a great difference between specific accusations leveled by an historian such as Tacitus or an advocate such as Cicero and the material in the Christian scriptures that degrades Jews and Judaism. The words of the Gospels carry a weight different from those of a secular author. The religious connection not only deepens the awareness of the opposition psychologically but also bestows upon it an entirely different social significance. Opposition to Judaism became a principle of Christianity, rehearsed annually in the sacred texts, and this principle became firmly entrenched within its educational and religious doctrine. In this way opposition to Judaism penetrated the most basic cells of society and it is no wonder that at the end of the Middle Ages the Jew appeared as one diabolic and doubtfully human, who could be treated as one wished with no twinge of conscience.

Ostensibly, this sort of opposition ended with the start of the Modern Era; for, from the moment that the Jews could look forward to emancipation, and especially after achieving it, Christian society discarded the bases for its reservations about the Jews. Many said, and rightly so, that in the old régime the Jews could at best achieve some relief from the authorities and an improvement of their situation; they were not deemed fit to be citizens or subjects with equal rights and obligations. The very fact that the state of the kingdom was tied to Christianity precluded this. Only a secular state, entirely independent of the Church, could grant equal rights to the Jews; in fact was compelled by its own internal logic to do so. It was therefore supposed that antisemitism, that is, the Church's opposition, would disappear. We know, however, that from the start of the emancipation process there were already new sources of opposition developing. Contemporaries sensed it but thought of it as an inheritance from the distant past which would vanish as emancipation developed. This feeling was widespread among both Jews and non-Jews, Reform Jews and Orthodox Jews, at least from the time that emancipation also began to be implemented in lands beyond France, that is, Austria, Hungary, and Germany, in the 1850s and 1860s. Everyone thought that the world was breaking away from the past. Therefore, when the antisemitic movement suddenly burst upon the scene and swept the public, it was very shocking. In retrospect, historians have decided that it did not happen with absolute suddenness; that for a few years prior, there had been a sort of preparatory process. This brings us to the microhistoric subject of this paper.

2. Reaction to the Economic Crisis

Generally 1873 is seen as the pivotal year. The preceding period had been one of great economic growth, especially in Germany. After the War of 1870, Germany received reparations from France which led to the establishment of economic enterprises on an unprecedented scale. The country had been swept by a wave of economic prosperity which had ended in a tremendous collapse. The economic crisis was most severe, and the depression continued with its ups and downs until 1896.

The antisemitic eruption more or less coincided with the crisis and one can find a connection between the two. Jews had been part of what preceded the economic collapse and could therefore be blamed for the crisis which befell the country. Every book dealing with modern antisemitism mentions this. But, in fact, the connection is not that simple. We mentioned that the brief 1873-1879 interim consisted of three stages; but there were really four. When one mentions 1873, the impression is that the antisemitic movement erupted immediately upon the great crisis. This is not so. First, one must remember that the great crash began, not in Berlin, but in the stock market of Vienna in May 1873 and spread from there to the other stock markets, the other enterprises and the other countries. The shock in Germany was great but antisemitism was not the immediate result. There were those, to be sure, such as Paul Massing, who ascribed to 1873 the appearance of Wilhelm Marr's book *The Victory of Judaism over Germanism*. He does so, as if in all innocence, in his *Rehearsal for Destruction*, written after World War II, one of the first books to deal with antisemitism.[1] This is an error that flows from the mistaken assumption that modern antisemitism began as a reaction to the crisis. The truth is that Marr's book first appeared in February 1870.[2]

Marr does have a role in the antisemitic movement, but the central figure in the birth of the movement was Otto Glagau, who is often mentioned in the history of antisemitism but whose role is much more decisive than the literature indicates. Antisemitism is often related to developments in the lives of individuals and this is the case with Glagau. One can summarize the main stages of this development: first, silence; second, journalistic incitement (and here Glagau's name appears); third, an amalgam of anti-Jewish propaganda and denunciation for political and economic ends, and an attack upon Liberalism and Liberals, even upon Bismarck himself who at that time enjoyed Liberal support; and, fourth, the emergence of antisemitism as an independent slogan claiming to replace the other social and political goals.

The first stage, as we have said, was silence, a lack of reaction to the economic crisis. In Austria there was no reaction even in 1879. Karl von Vogelsang, later to be the ideological leader of Austrian antisemitism, was asked in 1876 whether it was worthwhile waging an attack on the Jews of Austria in his newspaper *Vaterland*, as was being done at that time in Germany in its Catholic counterpart, the newspaper *Germania*. He rejected the idea, claiming that there was no point to it in Austria where the situation was different; that the remedy could not come from attacking the Jews. Austria must recuperate from within. In 1879 a lengthy article appeared in the scientific monthly which Van Vogelsang edited.[3] It contained an in-depth analysis of social conditions in Austria, plus a sharp critique of the Liberal régime, as one concerned not at all with the workers but entirely with the capitalistic exploitation of their labor. Though the article dealt with various aspects of the economy, including those in which Jews were actively involved, it contained not a word about the Jews. The critique was strictly social. Austrian anti-semitism was late in coming, though there was no lack of antisemitic Catholic denunciation which later became an important basis of political antisemitism.

3. Glagau's Journalistic Writings

In Germany as well, the first anti-Jewish reaction did not come for a year and a half. The crisis began in May 1873 and Glagau's first article appeared in the weekly, *Gartenlaube*, in December 1874. Its title was "The Swindle of the Bourse and Promotion and Berlin."[4] This article is often mentioned in the literature, but what is not mentioned is the fact that, before he published the article, Glagau had written a play called *Stocks*[5] which he was only able to get published later, after he had become known through his articles. The play has two central characters, a Jew and a Christian, and the blame is equally divided between them. Nothing indicates that Glagau saw the Jews as the chief or exclusive culprits. They were only part of the picture, and there is no doubt that his first articles were not aimed specifically at the Jews.

The editor of the weekly *Gartenlaube* was a Liberal and the weekly had a very wide circulation: 400,000 subscribers with an estimated readership of 2,000,000. Glagau succeeded in convincing the editor that his articles exposing the background of the economic crisis – how the promoters trapped the public by setting up false enterprises – were in the public interest. They showed him to be a very talented journalist: One of his colleagues, Helmut von Gerlach, who after a time spurned the antisemites, in his memoirs justifiably compared Glagau to the Frenchman, Edouard Drumont. Both described events in vivid colors and a flowing style, with detailed characterizations of personalities which made for reader credibility. Glagau exposed the exploits of the promoters who established unsound companies and issued worthless stocks. The public, attracted by the promoters, bought the shares, invested in the enterprises, and finally were entrapped. To the argument that everyone was caught up in the speculative fever, grabbing at the opportunity to become rich, Glagau replied that the ordinary folk were not to blame; it was the fault of those who initiated these activities and functioned deceitfully. Economists, in explanation, proposed the periodicity of economic crises but Glagau scoffed at them, arguing that whoever tries to provide a scientific explanation is only protecting the guilty. In short, Glagau appeared as a defender of morality, always able to pinpoint the culprits.

The promoters, Jews and non-Jews alike, were to blame. However, Glagau's first descriptions gave the impression that the Jews played the decisive role. When asked why he particularly blamed the Jews, he replied: "I mention the Jews and the Christians in the same breath." How is it then that the reader got the impression that Glagau was specifically blaming the Jews? The truth is that he did mention Christians as well, but in writing of the Jews he made a point of their Jewishness.[6] In a section describing what happened in Berlin, he had four characters: three well-known Christian Germans and a Jew. No mention is made of the social background of the three non-Jews. The fourth character, "Herr Munk," is not only described as a Jew but comments are made about the Jews of Berlin in general. Munk is portrayed as one of those Jews who had come to Berlin from Posen and amassed fortunes. "There is no poor Jew in Berlin; they are all wealthy."[7] Such comments, and his derision of the Jews, underscored his assessment of their share in the blame. For example, he mentions a Jewish apostate named Strousberg who built railroads and made a huge fortune in partnership with aristocrats. He was known as a member of the Reichstag and "king of the railways." As a youth he had lived in England and had Anglicized his name. Glagau poked fun at Strousberg, divulging to his readers that Henry had once been Heinrich. He identified him as a Jew and blamed his actions upon his Jewish origin. Again and again such things were repeated in his articles, and though originally they had not been intended as anti-Jewish, the reaction of Jews and non-Jews focused on the Jewish aspect.

A sharp attack on Glagau appeared in a Breslau newspaper.[8] To the question: "Why do you put the Jews at the center of your accusation?" Glagau responded: "Is it my fault that ninety percent of the promoters are Jewish?" This answer of course contradicted his claim that he was not particularly singling out the Jews. Suddenly they are ninety percent to blame. This figure itself is the result of a deception worth noting. The number is not of the supposed promoters who defrauded the public; at that point he was speaking of both promoters and stockbrokers. For the preponderance of Jews among the latter he had proof: "Do you know that on the Day of Atonement the stock exchange is closed, not only in Berlin and Frankfurt, but also in Paris and London?" That was correct. The Jews conducted the lion's share of the financial activities, and the stockmarkets of those cities sometimes took on a Jewish character. But were the stockbrokers of London and Paris, and even Berlin, identical with those who headed the promotion and the swindle? Glagau combined the two as if inadvertently, and by similar juxtapositions convinced himself and his readers that there was a Jewish hand in the entire economic disaster.[9]

This led to the slogan: "Ninety percent of the promoters are Jewish," which was taken up by the press and used by Glagau again. He reissued his articles as a book,[10] sharpened their tone, restored all the anti-Jewish expressions which had been deleted by the editor and, to bolster his anti-Jewish indictment, added details drawn from newspapers whose copy echoed his own words.

4. The Conservative Attack

As we have said, Glagau's activity remained journalistic. But as early as 1875, when the anti-Liberal Conservatives joined the fray, the third phase of his antisemitic development had already begun. The Conservatives opposed economic and political liberalism and were for denying full Jewish emancipation even after it had been granted. The attack began with an article by Franz Perrot in *Kreuzzeitung*, a Conservative organ. In his title, Perrot combined the name of the Jewish banker, Bleichröder, and those of two government ministers, Delbrück and Camphausen, who headed the country's political and economic leadership.[11] The combination was intended to provide the basis for the contention that the Gentile ministers, unsophisticated in matters economic, were but the banker's tools. To be sure, Bleichröder was not as well-known as the ministers, but this was only because he also controlled the press and deliberately concealed his role in the conduct of the state's affairs. The standard charge against the Jews was that they exploited the press for self-glorification. Here we have the exact opposite: Bleichröder is able to hide behind the backs of the non-Jewish ministers precisely because he controls the press.

We are familiar with Perrot's opinions from his earlier books. He was opposed to the Liberal régime in principle and was especially critical of Bismarck's conduct of the government. However, in his previous articles he had never touched on the Jewish matter. Now he lent his pen to the Conservatives' attack, although from his brother's testimony we know that his articles were not written on his own initiative but were dictated by the party leadership. They also reflect the Conservatives' position on the Jews. The end of the last article specifically states that they oppose the emancipation granted the Jews; that they are prepared to give the Jews a place to live in the country, but do not agree that there should be Jews in the army, administration, or politics. They knew that the time was not ripe for changing the Jews' legal status but they did not give up their intention of doing so in the future.

The Conservative camp never denied these positions. The innovation was that now the Jewish aspect was added to the main thrust of their policy against Bismarck's connection with Liberalism. The Jewish issue was politically useful. Like Glagau, the Conservatives felt that the public would react negatively to anything with a "Jewish" association. This stratagem was to appear and reappear in various forms thereafter. At that time, the social critics were very severely attacking the Liberal régime along familiar socialist lines but not necessarily directed to socialist conclusions. Rudolph Meyer had written a few books in this vein but had not especially connected his critique with the Jews. From 1875 on, however, he made the association clear, nor was he alone.

Better known is the Reichstag member Wilmanns who wrote *Die "goldene" Internationale*.[12] The book is divided into two parts: The first is pure socioeconomic criticism directed at the unbridled activity of capitalism and its devastating results. In the second part, with no logical connection to the first, he shifts to an anti-Jewish stance. In the first part, Wilmanns stresses that the economic crisis had resulted from the nature of capital as an economic factor; in the second, the economic activity of the Jews is to blame. This is a repetition of what we saw with Glagau: Even though the criticism was directed at general social phenomena, the book gained attention for its anti-Jewish tone. There were six editions in rapid succession; the book became a public conversation piece and *Die "goldene" Internationale* an anti-Jewish slogan. Wilmanns suggested forming a new party to make basic social and economic changes.

The third stage of the antisemitic development had not yet attracted attention. Here and there the Jewish press noted an increase of antisemitism but it was not taken seriously. It was seen either as a journalistic ploy or was attributed to the Conservative party whose anti-Jewish stance held no surprise.

5. Emergence of the Antisemitic Movement

The fourth stage came with the appearance of Marr's book mentioned above which, for the first time, called for severing antisemitism from general political goals. The Jewish presence was a disease of the previous generations, and to be treated as an independent issue. Once the Jewish matter is rectified, all the other problems will take care of themselves. Marr blamed the characteristics of the Jews on their race; religion was insignificant. Marr has therefore been seen by some as the representative of racial antisemitism and hence his importance. Yet many before him had spoken of race. His innovation was that he wanted to build a party based upon antisemitism. The atmosphere, he felt, was so saturated with anti-Jewish feeling that antisemitism could become the basis for widespread public activity. Because he wanted to build a new party, or at least a new action organization, his book is pessimistic: Germanism is lost; Germany has been defeated; the Jews are taking over more and more, building their Jerusalem on the ruins of Germany; Germany is beyond despair; and the Germans themselves are to blame for having allowed the rise of the Jews. He suggested the formation of an Antisemitic League from which he hoped would come the healing of all of society's ills.

It is interesting that Glagau who, meanwhile, had published some books against the Jews, also underwent a development similar to Marr's. Whereas in the first stages he appeared as an indicting moralist, now he came out with a slogan linking the Jewish and the social question: "The social question is nothing but the Jewish question." That is to say, there is a social problem but it does not require a special solution – when we solve the Jewish problem, the workers' problem will be solved. Few note that this oft-quoted slogan appeared not in *Gartenlaube*, but in a book first published in 1879.[13] Thereafter, the antisemitic idea became a major issue. It was the result not just of incitement. As Glagau saw the positive reactions to his anti-Jewish comments originally intended merely as goads, he took that course more and more. This was also the case with Wilmanns: The anti-Jewish aspect of his book evoked a very strong response. We must conclude, therefore, that it was not the anti-Jewish propaganda which created the antisemitism; it was the anti-Jewish sentiment of the public which encouraged the propaganda.

Now, of course, a chain reaction began. Adolf Stoecker, the court-preacher and leader of Berlin's antisemitic movement is a case in point. He began as founder of the Christian-Socialist party, totally unrelated to the Jewish issue, because he felt that the workers, especially in Berlin, were being attracted to the Socialists, which he saw as a danger to their Christian souls, and he wanted to satisfy both their social and Christian needs. The party gained no support. The working masses and the citizenry did not join it. After the publications we have mentioned, Stoecker's friends urged him to say something about the Jewish question which was engaging public opinion. Remember that Marr's book, *The Victory of Judaism over Germanism,* had appeared in February 1879. By the Fall, it had appeared in a number of editions and received very wide press reaction. In September, Stoecker yielded to his friends' requests to touch upon the Jewish question in his addresses. From the very first, he showed himself to be a theologically based anti-Jewish Christian but with a pragmatic social and political platform. His words drew an enthusiastic response and the movement was well on its way.

6. A Historical Analysis

We do not subscribe to the popular theory that antisemitism is a product of economics, a claim to be found in Hans Rosenberg's important work on the Bismarck period, the economic depression, and the continuing economic crises in the ups and downs of the 1873-96 years.[14] He also ascribed the fluctuations in the antisemitic movement to the economic ones. However, Rosenberg himself said that the year of 1879 was a relatively good one: For the first time since the economic collapse of 1873, the economy had begun to recover. So there is no simple correlation between the economy and antisemitism. The economic factor did lend strength to the Conservatives' attack upon the Liberals and the Jews. However, in time, as we have seen, the opposition to the Jews became removed from its original context, became an independent matter, and was even presented as a substitute for the general social and economic criticism.

The explanation of this process lies in Theodor Mommsen's reply to Treitschke, who had followed Stoeker in the bitter critique of Judaism. Mommsen, Treitschke's colleague at the University of Berlin, as a Liberal, angered by the phenomenon of antisemitism in general, wrote his famous treatise *Auch ein Wort über unser Judenthum*[15] in which he said:

> We have always known that the Jews have remained a distinct entity within German society. We knew that they have peculiarities which are not easily reconciled with their citizenship in the country. The correct and proper attitude toward this phenomenon was to wait with patience and tolerance to see how things would develop. These peculiarities were

bound to disappear, and the assimilation, i.e., the absorption of the Jews by the German society, was slowly but steadily progressing. And now, along come the vulgar antisemites who are disturbing the integration process.

This diagnosis of Mommsen's agreed precisely with that of Ludwig Bamberger, a Jewish leader of the Liberals who had not converted. He even compared the process to that of crystallization, which is disturbed if a foreign body is introduced into the solution.

Their diagnosis aids our historical analysis. We stated at the outset that with the Emancipation, society had discarded the old Christian ideologies and opened the way to the integration of the Jews. Judaism, or the independent existence of a minority Jewish community, were not meant to be positive values. The intent was that, with integration, the signs of Jewish peculiarity should disappear. Everyone constantly monitored the process and asked: Are they truly making progress? Are their Jewish traits continuing to disappear? Until the crisis came, they had waited patiently, according to Mommsen. But when attention focused on the Jews, the defense of silence crumbled. Now, when it was discovered that too many signs of Jewishness still remained in full force, their patience vanished, and all the dormant and suppressed anti-Jewish elements erupted. For some, these related to old Christian arguments; for others, though no longer so closely tied to Christianity, these feelings returned and were roused to action.

Earlier, we compared the anti-Jewish approach of antiquity with that of the Middle Ages. The medieval period, unlike antiquity, was dominated by religious zealotry. The new antisemitism seemingly had nothing to do with religion. The antisemites proclaimed that it was not because of the Jewish faith that they attacked Jews, for religious tolerance was a principle no one dared deny. They found their motivations in available ideologies, notably that of racism, which is a product of the modern period and not necessarily related to Judaism. After the racist doctrine had been developed, it was transferred to the anti-Jewish sphere, with recourse to religion no longer necessary. It would seem, then, that in the modern period we have returned to the situation which prevailed in antiquity.

There is no comparison, however, between the non-Christian, pre-Christian anti-Judaism of antiquity and the modern age's post-Christian anti-Judaism which, though nonreligious in its inception has, in historical perspective, resulted from two thousand years of Jewish exile among the Christians. First, it is not true that Christian ideology was entirely neglected. A number of the major antisemites were Christians in the full sense of the word: Stoecker, in Germany; Vogelsang, in Austria; and others who, while not exemplary Christians, were Christians nevertheless because their world-outlook was based upon Christian premises.

Even in antisemites like Dühring, who was also anti-Christian, the opposition is not identical. Dühring's anti-Christianity was directed against Christianity, not against Christians; his anti-Judaism was specifically directed against Jews. Furthermore, even while opposed to Christianity, he still employed Christian premises against the Jews. He was not embarrassed to libel the Jews with the blame for the killing of Jesus. According to him, their guilt has metaphysical, philosophical significance. The Christians did not need Jesus; the Jews did, so that he might save them from their vile essence. Instead of being saved by him, they killed him. This is dialectics, of course, but one can recognize the remains of Christianity and the immense residue which it left in the culture of the European nations.

Comparing modern antisemitism to that of antiquity and of the Middle Ages, we find that the modern form carries within it the worst of its two predecessors. In the Middle Ages the Jews were persecuted and degraded, but the Church remained open for individuals who could accept Christianity if they so desired, and the option remained for all Jews to repent at the end of days. According to Christian belief, they were destined finally to accept Christianity. Thus the future remained open. In antiquity there was no such expectation and the Jews had no main avenue of rescue. The opponents of the Jews in antiquity were vehement and at times radical in their opposition. As far as they were concerned, the Jews had no right to exist among the nations. Antisemitism at that time, however, was not central, not a religious issue, not deeply imbedded in the consciousness, and not widespread in society. Modern antisemitism is doubly smitten. On the one hand, it has inherited the breadth and depth of medieval Christian antisemitism. On the other hand, there is no avenue of escape or solution left open for the future. If Jews are inferior, alien, and neither worthy nor equipped to assimilate, then they are an irredeemable vexation. The question has become: What is to be done with this group which society must not tolerate? The unique seriousness of modern antisemitism lies in the very fact that this question could even be asked.

Notes

1. P. Massing, *Rehearsal for Destruction* (New York, 1949), p. 6.
2. W. Marr, *Der Sieg des Judenthums über das Germanenthum* (Bern, 1879).
3. A. Tschoerner, "Die materielle Lage des Arbeiterstandes in Oesterreich," *Oesterreichische Monatsschrift für Gesellschaftswissenschaft* 1 (1879).
4. O. Glagau, "Der Börsen- und Gründungs-Schwindel in Berlin," *Gartenlaube* (December, 1874). This was the first in a series of articles in that journal later republished in book form as *Gründungsschwindel in Berlin* (Berlin, 1876).
5. O. Glagau, *Aktien: Historisches Schauspiel aus der allerjüngsten Vergangenheit* (Leipzig, 1877).
6. Glagau, *Gründungsschwindel*, introd., *passim*.
7. *Gartenlaube* (1875), p. 525.
8. *Schlesische Presse*.
9. Glagau, *Gründungsschwindel*, pp. xxiii-xxv.
10. See n. 4 above.

11. Reprinted together with other articles as F. Perrot, *Die Aera Bleichröder – Delbrück – Camphausen* (Berlin, 1876).
12. C. Wilmanns, *Die "goldene" Internationale und die Nothwendigkeit einer sozialen Reformpartei* (Berlin, 1876).
13. O. Glagau, *Des Reiches Noth und der neue Culturkampf* (Osnabrück, 1879), p. 282.
14. H. Rosenberg, *Grosse Depression und Bismarckzeit* (Berlin, 1967), pp. 88–117.
15. Th. Mommsen, *Auch ein Wort über unser Judenthum* (Berlin, 1880).

20

The Dreyfus Affair and the Jews

RICHARD I. COHEN

Hardly any other event in France's contemporary history can challenge the continuous attraction of the Dreyfus Affair to the mind and imagination of writers and scholars.[1] There has been no let-up in the constant flow of articles and monographs on the Affair, which spread over such a wide range of areas that at times the connection with Dreyfus seems completely accidental.[2] The historical literature concentrates on two basic topics: French society and its relationship to the Affair; and the Jewish aspect. Countless studies have focused on the attitude of divergent social and political elements to the Affair, emphasizing the imprint left on French society for generations, which is also well reflected in the historical writing of those years.[3] Many different ideas and theses have been proposed regarding the Jewish aspect, though few have been properly anchored in research of the phenomenon. This is rather surprising considering the deep impression which the Affair left upon the Jewish community and in light of the fact that in the course of time it became a symbol of Jewish vulnerability even in a Western society with a liberal tradition.

Unfortunately, these two lines of inquiry developed with little cross-pollination. That is to say, for the writers on French society, Dreyfus's Jewishness was an insignificant circumstance bearing only slightly on the Affair, while those interested in the Jewish problem confined themselves almost exclusively to the Affair's implications for Zionist history. The exception to this generalization is a monumental study of the antisemitic atmosphere in France during the Affair which integrally relates to the Jewish community's perception of, and response to, the antisemitic manifestations.[4]

1. Central Issues in the Jewish Aspect of the Affair

In its Jewish aspect, the Dreyfus Affair touches on three central problems. The first is the reaction of the Jewish community in France to the Affair. More than a decade and a half ago Michael Marrus offered the first scholarly analysis of the relationship between the Affair and the Jewish community's integration in French society. Without reservation Marrus concluded that though Western countries and world Jewry were shocked by the display of antisemitism in France, French Jewry remained steadfast, continued to proclaim its loyalty to the homeland and the values of the French Revolution, and recoiled from any overt action on behalf of their coreligionist Alfred Dreyfus.[5] For Marrus, as for others who preceded him, French Jewry was thoroughly involved in a process of assimilation which compelled acceptance of the surrounding society's behavior patterns and a passive reaction until the storm subsided.

According to this point of view, organized Jewry was prepared to sacrifice Dreyfus in order to assure its place in French society. Here the historiographical understanding fitted in with the feeling of two contemporary onlookers, Léon Blum and Theodor Herzl.[6] Troubled and aggravated by the Jewish reaction, both of these figures condemned the pusillanimity of the community leaders and disassociated themselves from their behavior. Though there is ground for such an interpretation, it requires certain qualification.

The second matter relates to the place of the Dreyfus Affair in the development of antisemitism in France and abroad. Historians' interest in French antisemitism has grown considerably since the Holocaust, and particularly in the last decade and a half. Partially in search for an answer to the chilling question of why the Holocaust emanated from Germany and not France, and partially in an attempt to uncover the precedents of the Vichy period, scholars have delved deeper and deeper into the roots and "uniqueness" of French antisemitism.[7] For most, the Dreyfus Affair remains a major turning point. Some have argued cogently that in stirring up lively public controversy over the Jewish question, and placing the fate of the Republic on the scales of a judicious solution to the trial, the Dreyfus Affair succeeded in shifting antisemitism to the back burner.[8] Moderate and radical political elements, writers, intellectuals, and the clergy, joined in the public struggle over the essence of France, wherein the specific "Jewish problem" figured intrinsically, though in an indirect manner. This social and cultural upheaval sharpened the persistent clash between two competing French traditions: that of the French Revolution, on the one hand, and that of the monarchy and Church, on the other. Generally speaking, one can say that those who fought for continuing the revolutionary tradition championed a retrial of Dreyfus, whereas those seeking a return to a monarchical/clerical regime regarded this with horror as an act of blasphemy against the State and the army. The rout of the latter, according to certain arguments, led to the rejection of antisemitism as an acceptable ideology in French society.

The third matter is the Affair's effect upon the Jews outside France. Interestingly, while in the case of the Damascus and Mortara affairs, the impact on international Jewry has been well traced and widely discussed, revealing much about certain Jewish communities, this has not been achieved vis-à-vis the Dreyfus Affair. Here attention has focused mainly upon the leaders of the Zionist movement who, as we know, reacted sharply. It seems, moreover, that their dramatic response became the ideal and yardstick for those writers who dealt with the reactions of other Jews.[9] In this framework, we shall concentrate on the first two topics and only allude to the third.

Three main periods distinguish the Dreyfus Affair: the first, from the imprisonment of the Jewish captain from an assimilated family, till the publication of Emile Zola's famous letter *"J'accuse"* in Clemenceau's paper *L'Aurore* on 13 January 1898. The second period extends from Zola's bombshell until Dreyfus's second condemnation in Rennes in September 1899. Within these two years the Dreyfus trial became a major internal issue, moving from a heated public controversy to a boiling political event which threatened the very fabric of French society. The court's reaffirmation of the validity of the first decision, with a large majority, somewhat helped the cauldron to simmer down. But the affair was not totally laid to rest, not until the presidential pardon came in 1906. These intervening years constitute the third period. Dormant during those six years, interest in the trial rose only infrequently, but the shadow of the Affair hung over France as a Sword of Damocles and precipitated the separation of Church from State in 1905. With this chronological division at hand the course of the reaction of the Jewish community of France can be traced.

2. The Consistory's Attitude

By the end of the nineteenth century French Jewry had completed its demographic revolution, having transferred its concentration from Alsace-Lorraine to Paris, where the community was still organized in the hierarchical consistorial system – the government structure established in the days of Napoleon I. Immigration of East European Jews into France had begun, but their involvement in communal affairs and organization was minimal. The reins of the community were controlled by native French Jews, *de vieille souche*, often of Alsatian origin, who were well assimilated into the French bourgeoisie and distanced from a strict religious life-style.

Intermarriage was a common occurrence both among the leadership and the rank and file members, while involvement in French society and politics in all of its aspects was by no means exceptional. Since Jews moved freely in the French state the Central Consistory's direct influence was weak, though as an official public body it could prevent the establishment of religious institutions not to its liking. Reflecting a certain consensus within the Jewish community, the Central Consistory was regarded as its representative and it entertained a modicum of public leverage.[10] However, its *raison d'être* was to placate the French, blur the differences between the Jews and their neighbors, and create a Judaism in which the French element predominated. Illuminatingly, synagogue architecture, which the Consistory encouraged in Paris in the last quarter of the nineteenth century, as well as certain rituals, rabbinic dress, and sermons were bent on intensifying these tendencies.[11] These were rudely jolted when antisemitic publications and manifestations rained down on France during this period. French Jewry's quest for a comfortable integration into French society had to be postponed.

Cautiously and with little public support, individual Jews and non-Jews began to call for Dreyfus's retrial a year after his court martial; a few, more audacious, argued that he was not guilty of treason or responsible for turning over secret material to the Germans. Yet a rare communal response preceded all Dreyfusard initiatives. Spurred on by the Chief Rabbi of France, Zadoc Kahn, a Committee of Defense against Antisemitism (*Comité de défense contre l'antisémitisme*) originated in December 1894, and included respected members of the Jewish community. Here too trepidation prevailed and the Committee opted to function behind the scenes, in limited areas, and did not become publicly known until 1902, when the tide of antisemitism had calmed down. Among the Committee were individuals who had, from the beginning, doubted Dreyfus's guilt and were shocked by the multiplicity of antisemitic events in France, but feared lest open intervention would cause a backlash.[12] The Central Consistory, the community's bastion of conservatism, showed even greater reticence in relating to the public controversy. In vain, one combs the protocols of the Consistory during the years of the Affair for a glimpse of its response. No reference is made, even in its closed sessions, to the ensuing agitation and the wave of antisemitism. The Consistory, guided by its strict definition of the Jews as "French citizens of the Mosaic faith," did not deviate from this principled stand. It had the authority to represent the Jews but it was not interested in broadening its narrow religious definition and refused to take sides. Dreyfus was unable to gain its support. The Consistory adhered to this definition of Judaism in other times of crisis for French Jewry, before and after the Affair, and was often strictured for it by opposing forces in the community. For example, during World War II the Consistory refused to represent French Jewry before the authorities politically, on the grounds that Judaism is only a religion, and the Consistory merely a religious body.[13] A firm believer in the state apparatus, the Consistory was convinced that problems of the Jews and the Jewish community could best be solved within the framework of the French Republic. By refraining from entering the fray the Consistory certainly reflected the view of a large Jewish constituency, but it was by no means a consensus of the Jews in France. Discontent with the Consistory's apparent complacency was expressed by Jews associated with the community and those on its periphery. Both French language Jewish newspapers, *L'Univers israélite* and *Archives israélites*, weeklies at the time of the Affair, closely followed the trial's development and, as evidence of a mistrial grew, published resounding attacks against the Jewish leaders.

3. Bernard Lazare

But in the forefront of the agitators for Dreyfus was, of course, Bernard Lazare.[14] Lazare, who in the 1890s, while associated with the anarchist movement, began to publish articles on Judaism and antisemitism, became eventually the stalwart of the Dreyfusard cause. In his early articles Lazare issued a scathing criticism of that category of Jews which he designated as *"Juifs"* and which he differentiated from another category of Jews identified as *"Israélites."* The *Israélites*, according to Lazare, make every effort to contribute to the country they inhabit, to integrate into the host society and assimilate to its life-style. The Sephardi Jews were his example of such behavior, held up as a model for all Jews. But the *"Juifs,"* the East European Jews, who were beginning to migrate to France, epitomized the opposite. Lazare views them in the mythical negative image of antisemitic literature: Driven by egoism that knows no satiety, the "Jews" with suspect plans constitute a foreign element in the country, forcing society to expel them in one way or another. This crude distinction between Sephardim and Ashkenazim and its accompanying value judgment was not an original perception and precedents ranged from de Pinto to Oliphant, but Lazare gave it an acute slant.[15]

The negative opinion of the *Juif* guided Lazare in his first analyses of antisemitism, whose source lay in the Jewish inability to assimilate; the Jews' behavior was the cause of society's opposition to them – especially since the Jew was always and everywhere an antisocial being. The decisive period, of course, was that of the Second Temple and the Talmud. It was then that the detailed, all-encompassing pattern of laws was fixed which necessitated for its fulfillment isolation and the arousal of hatred. But in his important book *L'Antisémitisme, son histoire et ses causes* ("Antisemitism, its History and Causes") which was published in 1894, Lazare had already moderated his opinions of the "Jew." Abandoning the original premises of the antisemitic camp, headed by Drumont, he no longer saw the isolationist and detestable characteristics of the Jews as an integral part of their being.[16] Now he advanced the Utopian view of the Emancipation ideologues, which saw a possibility of changing the Jewish situation through assimilation into society – in other words, by the disappearance of the Jews. However, this was not conceived as an easy process. As a result of his research Lazare concluded that the Jews are not a nation like the other nations, yet they maintain a strong national consciousness; thus, only a drastic change in the home society's attitude to them and a revolutionary change in the structure of the economy would allow the Jews to strike roots in society. Lazare had reversed the tables. This time he allotted the surrounding society an important role in the assimilation of the Jews.

As can be seen, Lazare's interest in the Jews and the history of antisemitism was constantly evolving, and preceded the Dreyfus Affair. A month before the court's first verdict he published an article "The New Ghetto," in which he argued that the Jews are rejected by society, not only of their own will, and find themselves faced with a sort of social quarantine and hostile atmosphere, far more pressing than the physical ghetto. Having abandoned his original premises, Lazare was now prepared to take a further step, to enter the active fight against antisemitism. His target was the workers' movement, to whom he directed his pamphlet, "Antisemitism and Revolution" published in March 1895. [17]

Part of his continuous writings on antisemitism, in which the image of the Jew had become more positive, the pamphlet made no reference whatsoever to the Dreyfus trial. Here Lazare concentrated on the interrelationship between antisemitism and socialism, coming down squarely against a commonly held view that antisemitism served the interest of the working class. Antisemitism, he contended unequivocally, was an effective tool of the bourgeoisie, the Church, and reactionary elements, and therefore the removal of the Jews, most of whom were downtrodden and impoverished, would only enrich the Christian bourgeoisie and strengthen the hand of the clerics and the reactionaries – but would not improve in the least the lot of the proletariat. His view of modern antisemitism as an outgrowth of economic competition between Jews and Gentiles shifted the spotlight of blame from Jewish separatism to the prevailing capitalistic system. In liberating himself from the negative image of the Jews maintained by the Left (and accepted at this time by even Jean Jaurès), [18] which identified the Jew with capital, Lazare was now able to defend Dreyfus as an oppressed and persecuted *Jew*. It also enabled him to join his political rival, a bourgeois Jew Joseph Reinach, on this mutual basis. Lazare's first work on the trial appeared at the end of 1896, after a year of deliberation wherein he lashed out against the many inconsistencies of the trial's evidence and the injustice of the verdict. [19] Immediately he catapulted into the first rank of Dreyfusards and remained throughout one of the strongest fighters for Dreyfus.

Unlike many of his fellow Dreyfusards, Lazare kept the Jewish element in proper perspective, constantly referring to the specific Jewish nature of the Dreyfus scandal. This attitude went hand in hand with his rejection of antisemitism and growing identification with the oppressed and downtrodden Jewish people, on his way to endorsing Jewish nationalism. By 1897, Lazare had indeed turned full circle, and in a Barrèsian spirit called on the Jews to reappraise their assimilatory orientation: "We should absolutely not take the path which the peoples among whom whom we live would perhaps like us to take; we must strive for that spiritual strength implanted in us; by no means should we Christianize Judaism, but, rather, Judaize the Jew, teach him a life for himself and an existence faithful to himself." [20]

. The struggle on behalf of Dreyfus had clarified for Lazare the bankruptcy of the assimilation he had professed in the early 1890s and helped him crystallize his changing understanding of antisemitism which, as we have seen, had begun prior to the trial. Moreover, it would seem that it was this unique combination of a consistent intellectual quest to uncover the roots of antisemitism and the nature of Jewish integration into modern society, together with an active public defense of Dreyfus, that moved Lazare to embark on a national course – one which hardly had resonance within French Jewry. Lazare was truly a unique

French Jewish phenomenon. The Jewish establishment distanced itself from him and his activity, while the Jewish press initially had serious reservations. Only as it underwent a clear shake-up in the wake of the Affair, did the press reflect a change of attitude, though not with regard to his nationalist position.

4. Influence of the Jewish Press

During the first period of the Affair, French Jewish journalists were full of anxiety, though not as obviously as was Lazare, about every aspect of the trial and were troubled by its harmful effect upon Jewish integration into French society. Sensitive to manifestations of antisemitism, the Jewish newspapers did not shy away from reporting them nor from drawing certain conclusions about Jewish life. Strong opposition to the structure of Jewish society was a major outcome. In calling for Jewish solidarity and an explicit defense of the status of the Jews in French society against the attacks of the antisemitic sector of French clericalism, the Jewish newspapers were in effect taking a public stand for a reshaping of the Central Consistory and its institutions. Such outright pronouncements gathered force at the height of the Affair, and grew sharper as French intellectuals entered the Dreyfusard camp.

Buoyed by their support for Dreyfus, the Jewish journalists joined at the beginning of 1898 the moderate Dreyfusard voices while at the same time condemning the impotence of the Consistory and its negative effect on Jewish solidarity. But they did not stop there. The Jewish newspapers launched a vigorous attack upon the Catholic Church which it saw as the prime factor in fostering antisemitism in France. In these incisive articles against clericalism the Jewish press showed no sense of being the representative of an indecisive religious minority. Catholicism was portrayed on innumerable occasions as a tyrannical, belligerent, arbitrary, and intolerant religion which denies freedom of thought. Such a forceful and resolute attack against the religion of the majority of French citizens had not been aired in the Jewish press for decades.

From a communal Jewish point of view the journalists' perception of the threat of clericalism and antisemitism to the Jewish community on the one hand, and the silence of the Consistory and the *Alliance Israélite Universelle* on the other, encouraged them to take issue with the exclusive right of the Consistory to represent Judaism.[21] As a corollary, they advocated Judaism's liberation from the Consistory and religion's liberation from the State as a vital means of invigorating and deepening the internal life of the Jews of France. In this vein, Hippolyte Prague, the editor-in-chief of *Archives israélites*, wrote a programmatic article in 1901 on granting funds to religious institutions. Clearly under the impression of the Affair, the article provides an indication of how the spread of antisemitism effected the Jewish press and prodded it into taking up the cudgels for the separation of Church and State. After reviewing the sucessful process of Jewish emancipation in France from the time of the French Revolution until the days of Louis-Phillipe in 1846, when the legal status of Judaism was put on a par with that of the other faiths, Prague took issue with the idyllic view of the past. Instead of gratefully acknowledging this unique achievement and praising the glorious French tradition, Prague looked wryly at these laws, blaming them for holding back Judaism's development. These laws, universally acclaimed and seen as the beacon of humanity, were now held responsible for retarding the fruitful productivity of Judaism and linking it to the State:

> In a country where Judaism is not dependent upon the tutelage of the state and is free in its decisions, one can expect the encouraging sight of on-going development and feel the true spiritual strength revealed in the productive proliferation of religious or literary creations. Judaism in France is chained and can cope with its needs only with great difficulty, reluctantly and unenergetically. It is sick and at the mercy of events. Judaism lacks trends of thought which could foster activity in the communities by pitting conflicting ideologies against one another. There is no impetus to healthy competition between members of the communities in ideas concerning matters of ritual, no impetus to defend them; there is no turbulence in the calm lake of French Judaism. The institutions and rabbis are floating with the current and devoting their self-respect only to the punctilious fulfillment of their prescribed duties.[22]

Prague was not alone in decrying the Jews' submissive attitude to the authorities in gratitude for their goodness and graciousness toward the Jews, exemplified by the official standing of the rabbis. He, and others like him, invoked the separation of Church and State as an imperative in order to save Judaism from destruction, for religion cannot flourish without freedom. This spirit, pulsating within the Jewish press circles, fit the post-Affair atmosphere prevailing in broad circles of the French parliament and moved them to realize one of the Third Republic's central goals – the separation of Church and State. The Jewish press saw the Affair as proof that the official position of the Consistory and the rabbis, and their dependence upon the State, denied them freedom of activity and prevented their active involvement on behalf of truth and justice. Notwithstanding the criticism of the State and the Jewish institutions, no dramatic turnabout ensued as we have seen with Lazare; neither did it end the aspiration of being absorbed into French society, nor did it lead to an acceptance of the Jewish nationalist idea. What we have, so it appears, is a firmer belief in the right and duty of the Jews to express openly their concern for their fellow Jews, without fear of placing the private interest before the general. Preoccupation with a parochial Jewish issue was by no means incommensurate with French citizenship. An interesting example from 1903, when the Socialist leader Jean Jaurès sought to reopen the trial, is a case in point.

Emile Cahen, the grandson of the founder of the *Archives* and a leading opponent of Drumont's and the antisemites of his day, thought otherwise. Arguing in a traditional manner that those who did not accept Dreyfus's innocence would not be convinced by new proofs, Cahen preferred to let sleeping dogs lie and advised the Jewish community to refrain from mixing in the matter. His motto was taken from Gambetta's famous phrase about Alsace-Lorraine: "*Y penser toujours, n'en parler jamais*" (To think of it, always; never to speak of it"). Coming from the mouth of Cahen, this approach is surprising, and it supports the notion that a religious minority must not intervene in delicate political questions, so as to avoid any reprisals. But Cahen was reproached by his counterpart, the former prefect and editor of *L'Univers*, Isaïe Levaillant. In full support of Jaurès's position, he called for political intervention for Dreyfus. Contrary to Cahen, Levaillant looked to the Affair as a future guideline for Jewish life. The Affair taught that inactivity is futile and Jews must prove that their support for Dreyfus was not only directed against the foes of Judaism but was also a general struggle against the enemies of freedom and liberty. This opinion was in perfect keeping with Levaillant's perception that Dreyfus was not the victim of a miscarriage of justice but of the corruptions of the time, which must be fought. Levaillant's attack on the *Archives* proved successful. Cahen retreated from his earlier position and rejoined the fray.[23] This interaction is indicative of the growing sensitivity of the Jewish press to the complexity of Jewish life in French society, further apparent in the more thorough reporting of antisemitic manifestations in France. Thus, without generalizing from these developments or granting the Jewish press more influence than it actually had upon the Jewish public, an overall assessment of the impact of the Affair on the Jews in France must take it into account.

It may be claimed, by way of summary, that the Dreyfus Affair barely altered the central processes within the French Jewish community, but it cannot be maintained that it left no impression upon its representatives. Adherence to the principles of the Revolution persisted, but judging from the response of the Jewish press, a change had taken place in the degree of reliance upon the law as the exclusive guarantor of Jewish security. Criticism of the Catholic Church and repudiation of the Consistory's form of leadership indicated an uneasiness within certain Jewish circles and a quest for a redefinition of the Jewish role in French society. Some desired to breathe new content into Judaism even to the extent of minimizing the contacts with the French state and questioning the value of the legal achievements which had made French Jewry the symbol of successful emancipation. As such, the wholehearted support of the separation of Church and State was a manifest statement of an evolving existential reality, which the Dreyfus Affair clearly sharpened. Whether this reassessment contributed to the evolution of Zionism in France is an issue worthy of study, though at the time the radical solution of Zionism was criticized by these elements.

5. The Affair and the Republic

In 1907, Isaïe Levaillant, by now former editor of *L'Univers* and a member of the same Central Consistory which he had mercilessly attacked in the first years of the century, published a lecture which he had delivered before the Society for Jewish Studies in Paris. After broadly surveying the dissemination of antisemitism during the Third Republic until the Dreyfus Affair, Levaillant raised an important question: How was it possible that after antisemitism had reached its peak in the Affair, the Affair itself should, of all things, bring about its decline. Levaillant's answer was clear:

> The decline of antisemitism began when, in light of the events, its true character and purpose were revealed to the entire community. Over a long period, the country and even the country's republicans, did not grasp that antisemitism was only a mask for the rejected clericalism to wear, and that disguised as a war against the Jews the battle was really being waged against the Republic. But owing to the lessons of the Dreyfus Affair, and the useful warnings that emerged in characteristic and serious affairs, such as the rebellion at Fort Chabrol and the altercation at the Reuilly barracks, the country's eyes were opened and it saw clearly that anti-semitism constituted a danger, not only to a religious minority, but also to all the achievements of modern France.
>
> From the day people recognized the danger of antisemitism, which until then had not been properly appreciated, the Republican faction returned to its principles and traditions that negate antisemitism in their very essence. It admitted the fact that the principle of freedom of conscience, realized by the Jews, at times in honor and at times in sorrow, is insep-arable from the general concept of the French Revolution. Thus the struggle was no longer between antisemitism and the Jews, but between antisemitism and the principles of the Revolution. From that moment it was inevitable, by virtue of the events that antisemitism would be vanquished and banished.[24]

Levaillant was convinced that the principles of the Revolution could block the attempts of reactionary elements to change the face of France; yet, as long as the Republicans hesitated and did not establish antisemitism as one of the forces opposed to the principles of the French Revolution, the breach existed for the undermining of the Republic. However, when the Republicans realized that antisemitism was not a private affair between the Jews and their enemies but a universal concern which pitted the principles of freedom and equality against those of order and authority, they joined the battle. Within this context they realized that in protecting the rights of the Jews they were safeguarding not only a Jewish concern but a link in the history of France, and sometimes even a significant link, which could be ignored only at the risk of endangering the entire society.

Let us take a closer look at the significance of Levaillant's thesis that the liberal forces joined the struggle for Dreyfus in order to save the fundamental values of the Republic. An essentially similar pronouncement had been made almost a decade earlier by Ludovic Trarieux, then president of the "League for the Defense of Human Rights."

> We are people of justice and law. When protesting on behalf of Dreyfus or Picquart or upon demanding the rights of the Algerian victims to live, we do not shout "Long live the Jew" or "Long live the Christians"; we shout "Long live Justice," "Long live the Law," and we turn our faces to the great sun of mankind.[25]

Prior to Zola's "*J'accuse*," declarations of this nature were few and far between and the Jewish community stood alone as antisemitism encompassed different circles, even those which were mutually antagonistic. Certain Jewish observers were particularly pessimistic and reported each antisemitic incident as if it were part of an overwhelming epidemic.[26] Yet recent research has seriously revised the contemporary view, limiting the intense antisemitic atmosphere to certain urban centers, particularly Paris. Rural areas of France showed little or no interest, let alone knowledge, of the Affair's development.[27] But in those areas where it proliferated, French antisemitism tried to capitalize on the economic crises, France's decline as a political power, and the internal instability of the Republic. The Jew was perceived as a dominant factor in all of these, theoretically or actually. The classic French antisemitic traditions, the Church, and French Socialism played a certain role, but it was the work and efforts of Edouard Drumont which galvanized these ideological currents into an organized movement. More than any other individual figure in France, it was Drumont in his *La France Juive* (1886) who pounced on the widespread involvement of Jews in the French state administration and later associated Dreyfus's "treachery" with the Jewish plot to rule France. His argument had definite appeal. Few antisemitic tracts, including those of Theodor Fritsch[28] and Adolph Hitler, ever reached the outstanding success of Drumont's *La France Juive*, disseminated in hundreds of thousands of copies during the succeeding years.

Drumont's untempered harangue against Dreyfus as the apotheosis of Jewish connivance was adumbrated by less vociferous antagonists. Prior to "*J'accuse*" (and even after) important elements in French socialism saw the Dreyfus trial as a struggle to gain strength and influence in the middle class, with no bearing whatsoever on the working class. Others went so far as to contend that the release of Dreyfus would only strengthen the Jewish bourgeoisie and further encourage their scheming to undermine the foundations of the Republic. Therefore socialists were cool even to Lazare's struggle on Dreyfus's behalf, dubbing him "Rothschild's faithful admirer." The tradition, begun by Alphonse Toussenel, found its heirs here, and it is no wonder that

Lazare saw it necessary, in 1895, to direct to the socialist camp his treatise "Antisemitism and Revolution." Yet, while the anti-Jewish tradition had persisted among the socialists and found new adherents in the 1880s and 1890s, it became much more widespread in clerical and royalist quarters.

In the 1890s, various Conservative groupings were attempting a reconciliation with the French Republican ethos in order to become a decisive factor in French politics.[29] Aligned together in a single union (*Ralliement*), these conservative and clerical figures were bent on bringing the Church out of its isolation and restoring it to the authority it had possessed before the establishment of the Third Republic. Pope Leo XIII was an enthusiastic supporter of this movement, anticipating that its success would improve his diplomatic standing and establish a center for his war against the "subversive" elements of society (e.g., the Liberals, Freemasons, etc.) in the European countries. In the life of the Third Republic this was truly a historic moment. Vilified for its outright opposition to clerical associations and its secular educational laws, the Third Republic had been a constant source of contempt for conservative elements who rejected its basic principles. In crossing the Rubicon and accepting the legitimacy of the Third Republic, this Conservative wing minimized its opposition, especially on the subject of religion.

As a political body the *Ralliement* constituted a possible rival for the Republican forces, and though it did not publicly parade its antisemitic ideas, several personalities emerged from it, who were to figure prominently in the antisemitic outburst during the second period of the Affair. Yet this Conservative alignment must not be overemphasized since it did not include most of France's Catholics. For many Catholics the Third Republic continued to be anathema, and wide sections of French Catholicism rejected the submission to the Republic and took forceful action against it and its anti-Christian goals. Many remained attracted to those religious orders and associations which had come under attack during the Third Republic, and whose publications – *La Croix* (The Cross), *Le Pélérin* (The Pilgrim), and others – were read by some hundreds of thousands of readers. Taking issue with the antisemitism of Drumont, who saw race as the basis of the "Jewish problem," these organs reverted back to the classic Christian idea: "We believe the question to be a religious one, since the mystery of the persistence of the Jewish race among the nations, despite the punishments meted out to it throughout history, is a religious phenomenon."[30] These French Catholic circles continued to welcome warmly any Jew who was prepared to accept Christianity, in complete contrast to the approaches of Drumont or of Jules Guérin. Their proselytizing tendencies did not go unmentioned by the Jewish press in France, which as we have mentioned feared the ultramontane tendencies in French Catholicism and warned against them. More troubling was the lack of French public response to the antisemitic edge of these movements. Very few French figures openly discussed the wave of antisemitism in the first years of the Affair. Two of those who did, Emile Zola and André Leroy-Beaulieu, will be treated here.

6. Zola and Leroy-Beaulieu

Two years before *"J'accuse"* disrupted the French political scene, Zola had openly discussed the Jewish presence in French society. Unlike the bold accusatory style of *"J'accuse," "Pour les Juifs"*[31] (On Behalf of the Jews) offered an objective analysis of antisemites' arguments against the Jews and attempted to refute them. According to Zola, two major contentions were levelled at the Jews – one, that they constitute a state within a state and do not assimilate; and the second, that the Jews control the power and rule the finances of Europe. While ridiculing the notion that two hundred million Catholics should fear five million Jews, Zola proceeded to defend Jewish behavior in every form, both on the basis of the principle of freedom and from the point of view of adaptability as a religious minority. His solution to the tension between the Jew and European society was, however, no different from that of the eighteenth century European thinkers, who advocated the complete integration of Jews into society in order to eliminate the charge that they constituted a "state within a state." Following the Enlightenment approach, Zola placed the blame on Christian society which refused to allow the Jews to assimilate. The equation was simple – had Christian society behaved otherwise, the Jew would have integrated and naturally disappeared. In effect, Zola was reiterating a classical Christian notion that the perennial hostile attitude towards the Jews was the ultimate factor in preserving their existence. Almost echoing Abbé Grégoire's appeals on behalf of French Jewry and foreshadowing Jean Paul Sartre's reflections on the "Jewish Question," Zola offered a simple, one-dimensional solution: "Stop talking about him. The day the Jew will be a human being like we are, he will be our brother. Open your arms wide and put into practice socially what is recognized by law. Embrace the Jews in order to assimilate and absorb them among us."[32] At this stage Zola viewed the Christian tradition as the source of the conflict with the Jew and he inveighed against it; he had not yet assessed antisemitism as a danger to the existence of the Republic, which went beyond the traditional Christian invective.

In turning to Anatole Leroy-Beaulieu, a liberal Catholic, we encounter a rather rare species – an outspoken Catholic Dreyfusard, a member of the Catholic Institute, and one of the founders in 1899 of the *Comité Catholique pour la Défense du Droit* (Catholic Committee for the Defense of the Law).[33] Certainly Leroy-Beaulieu was not the only Catholic Dreyfusard, as Wilson and Pierre Pierrard have shown,[34] but few Catholics dared to take the involved and public course that he undertook. A versatile author, who wrote on many subjects, Leroy-Beaulieu was particularly drawn to the deteriorating relations between Church and State which inevitably impinged upon the "Jewish Question" in society. Leroy-Beaulieu's interest in the Jews was not limited to the Dreyfus Affair alone as his *Israël chez les nations* (Israel Among the Nations) indicates, yet it is his views on antisemitism in the midst of the affair which deserve special observation. Speaking in February 1897 before an audience at the Catholic Institute of Paris, unaccustomed to hearing a defense of the Jews, Leroy-Beaulieu unmasked antisemitism and expanded its ulterior motives.[35] He argued that antisemitism embraced wider worlds than meet the eye and that it appears under the sanction of three principles – defense of religion, defense of the native land, and defense of society. Antisemitism was thus a guise for those who opposed different views on religion, France, and society, making not only the Jews victims of antisemitism, but sometimes even Christians or Liberals. Moreover, Leroy-Beaulieu sensed correctly that it was not only the antisemitic ideology which posed a danger to the Jews and society, but the recourse to violence, and vulgar instincts and impulses. Attentive to the changing political climate, Leroy-Beaulieu warned against the danger hidden in the popular nature of French antisemitism and advocated a more vigorous opposition. His liberal perspective was unswerving, and after refuting the religious, national, and social claims which served as a basis for antisemitism, he returned to his point of reference: For the well-being of France all citizens must equally enjoy the legal basis of society. The slightest infringement of this principle will not only harm the Jew, so he contended, but endanger the welfare of other minorities and especially Catholic bodies which are in any case subject to severe attack by society. Ruling out all other avenues for solving the problem, from restrictive legislation, at one extreme, to the establishment of a Jewish state, at the other, Leroy-Beaulieu upheld the tradition of the Revolution together with the principle of humane, universal nationalism.

Leroy-Beaulieu's treatise on antisemitism remained an almost solitary Catholic response to the heated political atmosphere during the Dreyfus Affair. No other book was written by a Catholic pen which defends the Jews *as Jews* and attempts with such diligence to counter the charges against them.[36] Other Catholics joined the League for Human Rights and supported the Dreyfusard position, but they were few in number and influence and their main thrust was to preserve the Republic. Little thought was given to the problem of antisemitism as a recurrent Jewish issue. Moreover, Leroy-Beaulieu went even beyond Zola and, rather than advance assimilation as a solution to the Jewish presence in society, he fully accepted their existence as a unique minority.

Most Dreyfusard writers did not join the specific defence of the Jews and the explicit attack on antisemitism presented by Zola and Leroy-Beaulieu, and during the stormy time of the Affair, between January 1898 and the end of 1899, works dealing with antisemitism from the Liberal viewpoint were few and thinly spread.

7.   Effects of the Affair in France

At this point we must return to the opinion of Isaïe Levaillant, that antisemitism peaked with the Dreyfus Affair by virtue of the Liberal forces, which converted the Affair into a power struggle over the essence of the Republic.

The Dreyfus Affair and the Jews   305

During 1898-1899, the opposing camps of Dreyfusards and anti-Dreyfusards created a model "affair," setting up a host of rival associations and public forums: civil liberties leagues countered by antisemitic leagues; splinter groups and new political creations, especially in the anti-Dreyfusard camp; mass street demonstrations, sometimes accompanied by violence, against Jews and between the antagonistic camps. Each camp had its guiding spirits and fearless protagonists willing to pursue their cause to the end: Clemenceau, Péguy, and Lucien Herr stood beside Zola and Lazare and were joined at the height of the Affair by influential political figures in the Radical and Socialist wings of the French parliament. But they had their stalwart counterparts in Drumont, Jules Guérin, Léon Daudet, and Paul Déroulède who knew no inhibitions in their anti-Dreyfusard campaign. With such volatile figures as each other's antagonist, it is no surprise that the Affair sharpened the problems which had divided France since the Third Republic in matters of religion and education, the army, and its supervision, and questions of class. During these two years the antisemitic literature concentrated on all those matters, receiving important help from the anti-Republican literature which the conservative elements, disappointed with the achievements of the alignment (*Ralliement*), disseminated. The well-known antisemitic newspapers of Drumont (*La Libre Parole*), Henri Rochefort (*L'Intransigeant*) and Jules Guérin (*L'Antijuif*) were supplanted by a sudden surge of antisemitic publications, among which was the poisonous illustrated weekly *Psst!* which appeared regularly for a year and seven months with the antisemitic caricatures of two of France's foremost caricaturists, Emmanuel Poiré (*Caran d'Ache*) and Jean-Louis Forain.[37] *Psst!* appeared until the court verdict was issued at Rennes, indicating the founders' belief that Rennes vindicated their campaign and consolidated the anti-Dreyfusard position. But, as we know, they underestimated the persistence of their opponents. In energetically upholding the principles of the French Revolution as the basis of the Republic, the Dreyfusards successfully countered the rash of antisemitic publications. The anti-Dreyfusards failed to turn back the clock and Zola's aphorism that "the truth is on the way" became a reality. Furthermore, the struggle against antisemitism, undertaken in the form of a struggle for the Republic, strengthened the Radical party in parliament, and brought as a corollary a decline in the influence of the Catholic Church.

From the retrial at Rennes to Dreyfus's presidential pardon in 1906, the moderate Left in France enjoyed a glorious period, wherein the Church was attacked at every turn, both for its antiliberal ideology and its isolationist institutions. Again and again, members of the National Assembly demanded reductions in the budgets and restrictions on the behavior of religious organizations and orders, until they gained sufficient nerve to grab the bull by the horns, that is, to confront head on the issue of the separation of Church and State. Separation (1905) was one of the direct internal outcomes of the Affair and its most vociferous protagonists were found among members of the *Ligue des Droits de l'Homme* (The League for the Rights of Man) established in

February 1898, at the height of the Affair.[38] (One of the architects of the separation law, François de Pressensé, was one of the pillars of the League.) With separation, the victory of the Dreyfusards would seem to have been complete and to verify Levaillant's description of antisemitism's deterioration following the Affair, yet a certain qualification is nevertheless in order.

The year 1900 marks a turning point for the antisemitic movements of western and central Europe, the political eclipse of antisemitism, and its confinement to specific social and cultural organizations. A similar process transpired in France after the Dreyfus Affair, as the nationalist movements and certain trade union organizations continued to court antisemitic ideologies and became the bearers of antisemitic ideas, replacing the prominent figures of the former decade (Drumont, Guérin, etc.). As government circles were celebrating the Dreyfusards' victory, there was in the years 1905-1914 an awakening of the nationalist forces, best expressed in the activity of the *Action Française* and the *Camelots du Roi*, nurtured by the combination of nationalism, militarism, and antisemitism, characteristic of the anti-Dreyfusards of the *fin de siècle*. Even Catholic populism, which grew in the 1890s and was hard hit by the anticlerical atmosphere in the first years of the twentieth century, was also still flourishing, and now and again these circles renewed their demand to drive the Jews out of France.

Antisemitism found its outlets in other areas as well. In literature, the works of Ernest Psichari and Henri Massis, and especially Romain Rolland's *Jean Christophe*, published in ten volumes (1905-1912) with the widest distribution, were an important instrument for preserving negative Jewish stereotypes. Rolland's masterpiece contained many Jewish figures, almost all of them depicted quite negatively, giving substance to his anti-Dreyfusard stance during the Affair. Rolland did not hesitate to express his antisemitic opinions and his hostility to the "brazenness of the Jewish race" and "the corruption of the Jews to well-known Dreyfusards."[39] Nonetheless, the overal antisemitic scene hardly reached the dimensions of the antisemitism of the 1890s even though the French Republican press in these years – and especially during 1908-1914 – often evoked the dangers lurking for the Republic in the outbreaks of the various nationalist forces, and at times sensed that it was facing a return to the days of the Affair.[40]

In summary, it appears that during the decade prior to World War I, antisemitism in France was pushed to the sidelines and its political support severely curtailed. In this process, the Affair had made a definite contribution, yet at the present stage of research it is too early to say whether the decline of antisemitism was peculiar to France as opposed to other countries on the continent. Levaillant's description may well have been accurate for its time (1907), but it seems that from 1907-1914 antisemitism became ensconced in France's right-wing radical bodies, eliciting from the French Jewish and republican press a constant and anxious riposte.

8. Effects of the Affair on World Jewry

In turning to the third aspect of the Affair's impact on the Jewish world – its reverberations among Jewish communities outside of France – we shall limit ourselves to a few general, methodological remarks. Stemming from the fact that, for the Jewish world, France represented the ideal of a liberal country, Jewish interest in the Affair was far more intense and persistent than in any other antisemitic incident in the last quarter of the nineteenth century. France's historic role in Jewish emancipation was repeatedly mentioned in the reactions to the Affair, bespeaking a certain trepidation that if France could fall prey to antisemitic outbreaks, world Jewry has to take stock of its status. But the conclusions were far from being uniform. Emphasis has primarily been on the Affair's implications for the renaissance of Jewish nationalism, but to examine its impact on the Jewish community solely from the perspective of the Zionist movement is wholly inadequate, nor is it proper to use the nationalist conclusion as the criterion for assessing other reactions. Every Jewish community anxiously followed the Affair, thereby enabling us to look at the Affair as a touchstone for the lives of different Jewish communities and to discern their way of dealing with France's impaired ideal. Thus far, little study has been done on the reaction of Jewish communities, though an excellent primary source exists for this purpose in the Jewish press.[41] The Jewish newspapers across the globe covered the Affair closely and in their reportage resides much important material for evaluating the attitude of elements in society to antisemitism and emancipation.

A mere glance at the Hebrew press in Eastern Europe illuminates the research potential in such an effort. Two leading Hebrew newspapers revealed a blunt, bitter reaction to the Affair from its very outset, long before anyone had any doubt whatever about Dreyfus's guilt. Following Dreyfus's public degradation, an editorial in *Ha-Maggid* openly challenged on 17 January 1895 the entire procedure:

> And lo, unintentionally, straight into our hearts comes the question: Was there not a foreign hand at work in this deed? Was this entire machinery not set up by hostile, villainous, satanic scoundrels who wanted to plunge a Jewish soldier into the depths so that he should be unable to rise again? Alas, who knows if he was not attacked from afar by one of those anonymous people who are proliferating and multiplying like locusts in France these days, who shot a honed arrow at this unfortunate Jew and also at the entire Jewish people![42]

The editorial left no room for conjecture as it stated explicitly: "Dreyfus is not a criminal. The hand of Israel's enemies has been at work here." Clearly, the Hebrew press in Eastern Europe had no delusion or any doubts whatsoever about Dreyfus's innocence. On the contrary. Its immediate conclusion was that antisemitism had even managed to penetrate that idyllic world where "the sun of freedom shone." No less shameful was the response of French Jewry, which failed to rally to Dreyfus's defense, as *Ha-Meliz* put it that same day: "Our brethren in France, asleep with a storm round about them, will still not stop being in their Eden of pleasant dreams. If they would only wake from their deep sleep now, they would see the heavy cloud coming up on the sky of their lives, but they lie there . . . dreaming!"[43] In these spontaneous responses, highlighting the sensitivity of certain Jewish circles to the court martial, we have a fine indication of the possible benefits of a thorough analysis of the Jewish press.

Future research on the Jewish press in those countries where antisemitism penetrated least in those years (England and the United States), and in the countries where it penetrated more, such as Germany and Austria, could provide an interesting, comparative picture of the reactions of these communities to several key issues of the day: for example, the level of concern about their standing in the surrounding society, and their apprehensions of the East European immigration which, in their eyes, was tied to the increase of antisemitism. Through such an examination we will come closer to a more accurate picture of the effect of the Dreyfus Affair on the Jewish world outside of France.

In studying the Dreyfus Affair as an intersection of various processes within the Jewish community of France and abroad, the impact of the Affair looms wider than certain historiographical perspectives have intimated. In unsettling elements within the French Jewish community and putting into question France's image in the eyes of Jews abroad, the Affair provoked an intense response to the Jewish situation in modern society in which the Zionist riposte was by no means singular. The termination of the Dreyfus Affair, in upholding republican principles, constituted a major victory for French liberal society and reinforced the trust in the French state, yet was unable to squash all antisemitic manifestations nor to anesthetise Jewish sensitivity to these expressions.

Notes

1. See Robert L. Hoffmann, *More Than a Trial: The Struggle over Captain Dreyfus* (New York and London, 1980); Jean-Denis Bredin, *L'Affaire* (Paris, 1983); Michael Burns, *Rural Society and French Politics: Boulangism and the Dreyfus Affair 1886–1900* (Princeton, 1984). For a recent revisionist, albeit antisemitic view, see André Figueras, *Ce canaille de Dreyfus* (Paris, 1982).
2. Michel Winock, "Les Affaires Dreyfus," *Vingtième Siecle: Revue d'histoire* 5(1985): 19–37.
3. Léon Lipschutz, *Bibliographie thématique et analytique de l'affaire Dreyfus* (Paris, 1970); Frederick Busi, "A Bibliographical Overview of the Dreyfus Affair," *Jewish Social Studies*, no. 1 (1978): 25–40.
4. Stephen Wilson, *Ideology and Experience: Antisemitism in France at the Time of the Dreyfus Affair* (London and Toronto, 1982).
5. Michael R. Marrus, *The Politics of Assimilation: A Study of the French Jewish Community at the Time of the Dreyfus Affair* (Oxford, 1971). The book appeared in French translation in Paris in 1972. See Nelly Wilson's review, "The Dreyfus Affair and French Jews," *Wiener Library*

Bulletin 26 (1972): 32–40, in which she questions several of Marrus's conclusions and raises the doubt whether there existed a community awareness of a "politics of assimilation."

6. See Léon Blum, *Souvenirs sur l'Affaire* (Paris, 1935); Herzl's article on the Dreyfus Affair in *Die Welt* 24 December, 1897; and see A. Bein, *Herzl and Dreyfus: Herzl's Reports and Articles on the Dreyfus Trial* (Heb.) (Tel-Aviv, 1945); idem., *With Herzl and in his Footsteps* (Heb.) (Tel-Aviv, 1954), pp. 25–33. For Herzl's first reports of the Affair, see *Boulanger to Dreyfus, 1891–1895* (Heb.) 3 (Jerusalem, 1974).

7. *Inter alia*, Robert Byrnes, *Anti-Semitism in Modern France* (New Brunswick, N.J., 1950); Eugen Weber, *Action Française* (Stanford, 1962); Robert Soucy, *Fascism in France: the Case of Maurice Barrès* (Berkeley and Los Angeles, 1972); Zeev Sternhell, *La droite révolutionnaire 1885–1914: Les Origines française du fascisme* (Paris, 1978); Pierre Pierrard, *Juifs et catholiques français: De Drumont à Jules Isaac (1886–1945)* (Paris, 1970).

8. Shmuel Ettinger, Foreword, in Uriel Tal, *Christians and Jews in Germany: Religion, Politics, and Ideology in the Second Reich, 1870–1914* (Ithaca and London, 1975), pp. 12–13; Yehuda Bauer, "Trends in Holocaust Research," *Yad Vashem Studies*, 12 (1977): 13–15.

9. Bein, *Herzl and Dreyfus*, passim; Marrus's attitude to the Jewish community seems to emanate from this perspective. Cf. Wilson, *Ideology and Experience*, chapter xix.

10. Phyllis Cohen Albert, *The Modernization of French Jewry: Consistory and Community in the Nineteenth Century* (Hanover and London, 1977).

11. We are referring especially to the synagogues in the fourth and ninth *arrondissements* of Paris, and to the elaborate ceremonialism observed in the rue de la Victoire synagogue in the ninth. See Carol Krinsky, *Synagogues of Europe: Architecture, History, Meaning* (New York, Cambridge, Mass., and London, 1985).

12. Marrus, *Politics of Assimilation*, pp. 240–242; idem., "Le Comité de Défense contre L'Antisémitisme," *Michael* 4(1976): 163–175.

13. On the reaction of the Consistory to the establishment of the Alliance Israélite Universelle in 1860, see Michael Graetz, *From Periphery to Center: Chapters in 19th Century History of French Jewry* (Heb.) (Jerusalem, 1982); its negative reaction to the establishment of an umbrella organization under the Vichy regime is discussed in my book *The Burden of Conscience: French Jewish Leadership During the Holocaust* (Bloomington, Indiana, 1987), chapters 3, 7.

14. Nelly Wilson, *Bernard-Lazare: Antisemitism and the Problem of Jewish Identity in Late Nineteenth Century France* (Cambridge, 1978).

15. Cf. Israel Bartal, " 'Old Yishuv' and 'New Yishuv': Image and Reality," *Jerusalem Cathedra*, 1(1981): 216–217.

16. Bernard Lazare, *L'antisémitisme, son histoire et ses causes* (Paris, 1894). Unlike Drumont, Lazare's "*antisemitism*" drew its strength from the Socialist conceptions of Jewish behavior in modern society, but both were in general agreement about the image of the Jew.

17. B. Lazare, *Antisémitisme et révolution* (Paris, 1895). Due to a bibliographical oversight, this work has often been discussed as if it had been written in 1898 (the date of its reprinting), resulting in a misreading of an important stage in Lazare's development. Meant to be the first of a series of writings on the proletarian revolution, the work had no sequel. See Nelly Wilson, *Bernard-Lazare*, pp. 218–219.

18. Robert S. Wistrich, "French Socialism and the Dreyfus Affair," *Wiener Library Bulletin*, 28(1975): 9–20; cf. Harvey Goldberg, *The Life of Jean Jaurès* (Madison, Milwaukee, and London, 1968); idem., "Jean Jaurès and the Jewish Question: The Evolution of a Position," *Jewish Social Studies* 20(1958): 65–94; Wilson, *Ideology and Experience*, pp. 330–340.

19. Bernard Lazare, *Une erreur judiciaire: la vérité sur l'affaire Dreyfus* (Brussels, 1896).

20. Bernard Lazare, "*Nécessité d'être soi-même*," *Zion*, 3 (no. 4, 30 April 1897).

21. *Archives israélites*, 1896–1899, passim; *L'Univers israélite*, 1896–1899, passim; Wilson, *Ideology and Experience*, p. 412.

22. Prague continued: "If indeed they would consider the true usefulness to our sacred religion, and if the only concern were assuring that it shed its light upon people and offer an outlet for the munificent powers latent within it, then it would be necessary to aspire to sever the ties which bind Judaism to the state in France. Such a separation might cause rather vexatious troubles for those in prestigious positions who might be forced to lose them because of the new situation. But in the highest interests of our faith there is no doubt that it would be a blessing." Hippolyte Prague, "Sur le budget des cultes," *Archives israélites*, LXII (19 De-

cember 1901): 402; similar articles were published in 1902 and 1903 in the *Archives* and the *Univers*.

23. Echoes of this debate were heard in both newspapers during the course of 1903.
24. M. I. Levaillant, *La genèse de l'antisémitisme sous la troisième république* (Paris, 1907), pp. 27–28; also *Revue des Etudes Juives*, 53(1907): c. The antisemitic writer Raphaël Viau reached a similar conclusions in his *Vingt ans d'antisémitisme 1889–1909* (Paris, 1910).
25. Ligue Française pour la Defénse des Droits de l'Homme et du Citoyen, *Compte-rendu de l'assemblée générale, 23 Décembre 1898* (Paris, s.d.), p. 20; Wilson, *Ideology and Experience*, pp. 59, 704.
26. See especially *L'Univers israélite* in the first months of 1898.
27. Burns, *Rural Society*, chapter vi; Wilson, *Ideology and Experience*, passim.
28. E.g., Theodor Fritsch, *Antisemiten-Katechismus* (25 Auflage, Leipzig, 1893).
29. See A. Sedgwick, *The Ralliement in French Politics, 1890–1898* (Cambridge, Mass., 1965).
30. Quoted in Pierre Sorlin, *"La Croix" et les Juifs (1889–1899)* (Paris, 1967), p. 150.
31. Emile Zola, "Pour les Juifs," *Le Figaro*, 16 Mai 1896.
32. Ibid.
33. Wilson, *Ideology and Experience*, passim.
34. Ibid., passim; Pierrard, *Juifs et Catholiques*, passim.
35. Anatole Leroy-Beaulieu; *L'Antisémitisme* (Paris, 1897). And see his book *Les doctrines de haine: L'Antisemitisme, L'Antiprotestantisme, L'Anticlericalisme* (Paris, Troisième edition, s.d., [1902]).
36. Léon Chaine's *Les Catholiques français et leur difficultés actuelles* (Paris, 1903) is worthy of note. Written when the Church was under attack from every quarter, it contains a relatively lengthy discussion of antisemitism as one of the problems harming the Catholics' image in France.
37. Robert F. Byrnes, "Jean-Louis Forain: Antisemitism in French Art," *Jewish Social Studies*, 12(1950): 247–256.
38. For a skeptical view of the relationship between the Affair and separation, see Maurice Larkin, *Church and State After the Dreyfus Affair: The Separation Issue in France* (New York, 1973); Wilson, *Ideology and Experience*, pp. 59–64.
39. Robert J. Smith, "A Note on Romain Rolland in the Dreyfus Affair," *French Historical Studies* 7(Fall, 1971): 284.
40. Eugen Weber, *Action Française*, passim; idem., *The Nationalist Revival in France, 1905–1914* (Berkeley and Los Angeles, 1968). See the various studies of Sucy and Sternhell.
41. For an example of such usage, see Jonathan Frankel, *Prophecy and Politics: Socialism, Nationalism, and the Russian Jews, 1862–1917* (Cambridge, 1981), pp. 464–473; Deborah Yellin Bachrach, *The Impact of the Dreyfus Affair on Great Britain* Ph.D. Thesis, University of Minnesota, 1948.
42. *Ha-Maggid* (Heb.) 21 Tevet 1895 (Cracow).
43. *Ha-Meliz* (Heb.) 4 Shevat 1895 (Petersburg).

21

The Two Continuities of Antisemitism in the United States

LLOYD P. GARTNER

Attempts to probe the roots of antisemitism usually focus on Europe. Recognizing the place of the United States within the social and cultural development of the European world is undoubtedly important for understanding antisemitism in the United States. With American antisemitism yet to receive the thorough study it warrants, one result has been some lack of clarity about antisemitic phenomena in the western world as a whole.

Antisemitism or Jew-hatred, or both, did and do exist in the United States. We know of a long line of written and oral antisemitic expression, and of discrimination against Jews in social life, education, and employment. These have recurred throughout the history of the United States and lead to the apparent conclusion that American antisemitism is a link in the historic continuity of antisemitism and Jew-hatred.

Yet, what is historic continuity? Investigators are apt to assume that antisemitism always exists and receives some expression. If they have not found it, then it is due to their faulty research or lack of insight. But such a presumption of continuity is unhistorical. It seems to me that in this case continuity means causal regress, that is to say that the causation of a given phenomenon – in this case antisemitism – is far removed in time, and in the course of time its effects repeat themselves again and again under different conditions. Continuity is not infinite and can even come to an abrupt end one day, although this possibility is hardly to be expected of antisemitism. History is such that it cannot accept that a social factor may exist to eternity. Above all, one must remember the profound truth Gerschenkron expresses: "At all times and in all cases, continuity must be regarded as a tool forged by the historian rather than as something inherently and invariantly contained in the historical matter. To say continuity means to formulate a question or a set of questions and to address it to the material."[1]

In my opinion, antisemitism in the United States can be studied by means of this concept of continuity. One might add from the outset that in spite of hostile statements and acts, some of them serious, antisemitism in America has remained largely passive and latent. No antisemitic movement in the United States has ever grown, endured and made substantial political headway. Hence the possibility should be raised of another continuity in the United States, another causal regress, which did limit, though it did not prevent, the growth and spread of antisemitism. We should consider, therefore, two continuities: One is the continuity of antisemitism on American soil, and the other is the continuous operation of causes within American society which have thus far limited the scope of antisemitism, as compared to antisemitism in other modern societies where Jews live in large numbers.

1. Attitudes of the Christian Churches

The United States is a Christian country, if only because the overwhelming majority of its population is Christian. One may also contend that essentially the country is strongly Christian in spirit, difficult as that is to define. Herein lies the practical importance of our earlier discussion. True, the New Testament is the basic text of the Christian faith and the constant source of hostility and antisemitic motifs. Yet this alone cannot explain how it happens that in one place or another, at one time or another, people draw large quantities of poison from this source, whereas at other times and places they draw little. Moreover, it is not enough that the historical conditions which bring Christians to use or disregard their sacred text change from time to time. One must also remember that the Christian tradition itself is not of one piece. We quote, for example, a scholarly political leader who was perhaps America's greatest nineteenth century orator, Senator Daniel Webster (1782–1852): "Christianity — universal, tolerant Christianity – Christianity without sects and groups – that Christianity which knows neither sword nor fire – universal, tolerant Christianity is the law of the land!"[2]

Webster's claim would have received the approbation of the Founding Fathers, though some of them would have had reservations about proclaiming Christianity "the law of the land." From the very beginning of the American Republic, equal rights in matters of religion was a fundamental principle in its life, and all people who considered themselves patriots supported it. This equality, strengthened by the separation of Church and State, also explains why Jews in the United States defined themselves specifically as members of a religion. The main point however, is that the New Testament is subject to many interpretations. How American Christians interpreted it is of importance when dealing with the historical framework of antisemitism in America, just as in studying the history of the Middle Ages it is important to know how the popes interpreted the gospel. Here is something said, not by a famous statesman, but by a forgotten daily newspaper in 1846, when the Jews of Cleveland dedicated that city's first synagogue: "A scattered and persecuted people, they with faith await the coming of their promised Messiah, and at the end of 6000 years confidently expect to be restored to the privileges, the blessings, and the land of the Fathers."[3] This is a specific Christian view of Jews and Judaism, and it is doubtful whether the Jews present there on that day really wanted all that! But another newspaper reacted differently to the same event: "These deluded people are no doubt the genuine remnants of Israel. They have resisted the influences of Christianity for 1800 years and are still hoping for the restoration of the Holy City and the country of their promised Messiah."[4]

What may be derived from these two reactions to the same local event? The origin of both, like Webster's speech, lies in the Christian faith, yet they are quite different. Christians in the United States also differ in the ethnic groups to which they belong, the regions in which they live, their social strata – and all these are also functions of concrete historical circumstances.

Thus, in Christianity there is an approach connected spiritually to the English dissenting churches. It stresses religious individualism and the personal experience of religion solely by means of acquiring faith in the direct redeeming power of Jesus. It considers itself free of Church tradition and hierarchy. From this conception there later developed the point of view which champions good deeds in this world, as exemplified by the philanthropic deeds of Jesus himself. Through such deeds the individual may gain salvation. Satan holds a conspicuous place in religious individualism, but only unusually radical minorities were prepared to identify him with the Jews. To adherents of religious individualism the Jew was generally perceived as a mythic figure, different from the flesh-and-blood Jew many of them knew personally. In its secular transformation the identification of the Jew with Satan is fertile soil for the most radical antisemitism, but within the framework which occupies us here Satan and the Jew are still in the realm of symbol and myth.

These main streams in American Protestantism contributed much to shaping the spiritual character of the land. Using symbols and traditions derogating the Jews has been avoided or rejected, but the ancient reservoir is still there ready to be tapped should the appropriate movement or circumstances arise.

The American Christian churches also served as home and bastion for ethnic groups which sought to preserve their individual identity. The language of prayer and preaching was that of the country of origin. Church schools educated their youth in the ethnic language and its culture. An example is the Lutheran Church as it functioned among German, Swedish, and Norwegian Americans. In the middle of the nineteenth century this Church split, primarily because of ethnic differences among its members. There were also sharp differences within the Catholic Church among its ethnic components. Since ethnic identity is in large measure expressed religiously, it is difficult to differentiate between religious and ethnic antagonisms. In the mid-nineteenth century, hatred of the Irish immigrant was expressed in rabid anti-Catholicism to the extent of riots and bloodshed. In the large cities, relations between Jews and

Catholics were tense enough until recent years, but not only because of ancient traditions. The Catholic church was composed of many ethnic groups: Poles, Italians, Slovaks, and others, who had reached the new land on the same ships as the Jews. The hardships and frustrations of adapting to American life exacerbated the enmity. Furthermore, many of these groups brought an antisemitic tradition with them to America.

Our point is that, just as Christianity is multifaceted, so are the conceptions of the Jews which it harbors. Undoubtedly they are mainly negative. However, as a result of the particular character of American Christianity, they are not only part of antisemitic continuity in the sense of causal regress mentioned above. They are also indicative of the second continuity, that which prevented the spread of antisemitism or limited its scope.

2. Economic, Social, and Political Aspects

Antisemitism in economic and social matters is much more tangible than religious enmity. Characteristic of the United States was the sense of a developing country with unlimited possibilities. The opposite feeling – that the size of the economic pie was limited and everyone had to fight desperately for a piece – was generally absent. However, there was sharp competition for jobs and business success. Even though the labor market was free, jobs were subject to the whims of employers. Employment was not one of the areas in which the ideals of equality applied; there was no limitation on the employers' freedom to employ, promote, or dismiss as they saw fit. They could deliberately discriminate on the basis of religion, nationality, or race. Labor unions contributed to improving the situation though some, especially the smaller craft unions, functioned almost as exclusive clubs. Only in the past thirty years has the concept of "fair employment practices" become part of civil rights, although it has met with opposition and evasion. More recently, there have been established such programs as "affirmative action," which means direct government intervention in the employment market. Earlier, especially during periods of mass unemployment, above all during the 1930s, widespread systematic discrimination against Jews in employment was the rule. To cite a small but telling example, a Cleveland high school teacher reported to the Jewish manager of a large department store about the plight of Jewish young people who had finished secondary education and sought employment: " . . . in almost seventy-five per cent of the cases where a request is made [by employers] for graduates, the stipulation is made that they will not take Jewish students, and that at least half of the Jewish firms themselves make this stipulation."[5]

It was no different in higher professions, especially medicine and law, where difficulties were heaped upon Jews both in admission to professional schools and in finding places of employment. It was well known that for such reasons young Jews avoided studying engineering, and it was the same with the chances of teaching in an institution of higher education.[6] In short, until the

New Deal the American economy was one of economic liberalism, meaning nonintervention by governmental agencies. One result was the untrammeled expression of antiliberalism and hatred in American society. Consequently, many Jews found employment in government, where there was no discrimination, established independent businesses, and worked in "Jewish" sectors of the economy such as the clothing industry. For thirty prosperous years, from 1940 to about 1970, economic conditions were favorable for Jews and other minorities who previously had been discriminated against in employment. During the last decade, conditions have worsened slightly in a few areas.

In the social sphere we find that Jews who had reached the economic summit a century ago were not allowed to do so socially. For example, they were not admitted to exclusive clubs and salons or to boards of élite cultural, educational, and charitable institutions. They found themselves shut out of the high society created by the new plutocracy of the 1870s and 1880s, even though some Jews belonged to this plutocracy. John Higham has compared the situation in the United States to that in England, where Jews could be accepted on the fringe of entrenched aristocratic society and in its salons. According to Higham, such a comparison demonstrates that in the United States, unlike England, high society was in a state of formation and self-definition, and one of the means towards self-definition was to prevent Jews from joining its ranks.[7] The new plutocracy, based primarily in New York and Chicago, thrust aside the old political-commercial-intellectual aristocracy. This was most evident in Boston, the hub of New England, a region which also relatively declined. The brothers Henry and Brooks Adams, grandchildren and great-grandchildren of American Presidents, furnish fine examples. Both these significant thinkers and historians complained throughout their lives that American society deprived them of their rightful public position. Jewish bankers supposedly controlled society, a state of affairs the brothers detested. In short, they were out-and-out antisemites. As Henry Adams put it in 1892, at a time of deflation and economic crisis: "As for myself, more than at any other time am I different from all my contemporaries and my beliefs are contrary to theirs. I detest them and everything connected with them, and I live only and solely with the hope of seeing their demise, with all their accursed Judaism. I want to see all the lenders at interest taken out and executed . . . "[8] Four years later, the reclusive aristocrat stormed: "The Jew has penetrated to my soul. I see him – or her – everywhere, and everywhere that he – or she – goes there remains a taint in the blood forever."[9]

Others of the old aristocracy were prominent in movements to limit immigration. From their milieu the American version of racist theory emerged, with no evident connection to the racist theories prevalent in Europe at that time. What their efforts and the theory they espoused achieved was criticial, for the drastic immigration law of 1925 was based on their racist principles: the superiority of the Nordic over the inferior Slavic and Semitic "races."[10] There are two sets of relations here, and together they exemplify a familiar irony in the history of antisemitism. Many of the declining élite detested the Jews as a symbol of the forces which brought about the élite's descent. Yet at the same time the ascending élite, which the Jews supposedly symbolized, refused to admit them socially. The first Jew to encounter open rejection was the banker Joseph Seligman, who was publicly denied entry to an élite resort hotel in 1877. This incident brought a wave of protest throughout the country, but what was then the exception gradually became the accepted rule.

At the less fortunate end of the social ladder were those who had not risen, or who felt that relative to the new ethnic groups clustered in the industrial cities they had gone down. Those at or close to the bottom who lived in the towns and villages were, for the most part, unsophisticated Protestants and the New Testament anti-Jewish tradition was close to their hearts. From their midst sprang the Ku Klux Klan, which was more concerned with anti-Catholicism and Negro subjugation than it was with antisemitism. A more constructive response to their problems was the populist movement, which constituted a political force in the last quarter of the nineteenth century. In 1896 the populists captured the Democratic party and nominated William Jennings Bryan for the presidency. Populism was the voice of the ordinary people, especially farmers, workers, and small business people in the west and south. They rose up against the overweening power of the monopolistic railroad companies and concentrated bank capital, and proposed far-reaching social reforms. The movement's extensive propaganda and some of its leaders' speeches did not lack the image of the Jew as banker and symbol of capital which, by its control of money and credit, was strangling the masses of ordinary, simple folk. Yet despite these images, there was no actual incident of antisemitism among the populists. A few Jews were active in the movement and some were appointed to public office by populist officials. In general, the attitude to the flesh-and-blood Jew was not hostile. Some populist leaders identified the concentration of economic power with the mythic Jew, but the populists lived in peace with the local Jewish merchants and showed understanding for the Jewish workers.[11]

However, the emotions and conditions which produced populism did not always find their outlet in political movements of reform. There are always xenophobic sentiments, at times quite powerful: natives against newcomers in a land to which new people are always coming; conformists against nonconformists in their thinking; traditional isolationism versus cosmopolitan tendencies. Clearly, American xenophobic feeling is likely to harm Jews, the strangers *par excellence*. Xenophobia's last powerful expression came during the McCarthy period of the early 1950s. But there was no overt antisemitism in McCarthyism. One reason is that this was a period of economic prosperity. Some scholars have also provided a social interpretation of McCarthyism as a counter-attack of anti-intellectuals and Catholics, especially Irish, against the northeast Protestant establishment which had looked down upon them and had discriminated against them. This establishment, or a few prominent personalities within it, was supposedly "soft on Communism." In the name of anti-Communist patriotism, the despised and downtrodden of yesteryear could avenge the humiliations of several generations. In any case, though McCarthyism did not harm the Jews, they and the Jewish establishment were its avowed opponents.

3. Two Periods of American Antisemitism

American antisemitism was especially prominent in two periods. The first was from approximately 1875–1896, a time of deflation and economic crisis. It was then that social ostracism commenced and spread and populist rhetoric employed religious antisemitic symbols. The second period, much more serious than the first, was from approximately 1920–1940 and then during the tense days of war prosperity till 1945. During that period, the earlier America of the agricultural economy and rural town declined completely in face of the growing superiority of the large city and industry. This gave rise to a bitter and prolonged reaction, again using Christian symbols in an antisemitic, xenophobic version resembling the racist ideology which had been developed by the aristocratic old-timers. The foremost advocate during the 1920s was the famous automobile tycoon Henry Ford, who disseminated *The Protocols of the Elders of Zion* and the entire antisemitic mythology by means of a weekly magazine and other propaganda publications. Despite his great mechanical and business talents Ford was a simple man, almost primitive in his general outlook, and although he was the symbol of modern industrialism he remained throughout his life true to the outlook of the rural society in which he had grown up.[12] The Immigration Law which was passed in 1925 was aimed primarily against the continued immigration of the "inferior races" from Eastern and Southern Europe. It was explicitly racial legislation.

The position of the Jews in the large cities was also difficult. As long as they were poor immigrants who remained in their neighborhoods and in their special sectors of the economy, the reaction to the Jews was more tolerant than when they, or more likely their children, aspired to be accepted to the exclusive universities and professions. At that point tolerance vanished. The administrators of universities and the leaders of professions cleverly erected barriers to reduce to a minimum the number of Jewish admissions. Obstacles were put in the way of Jews seeking to rent or purchase homes in fine residential areas. These phenomena were conspicuous during the 1920s and they continued into the 1930s when, in addition, there was a bitter struggle for economic survival as well as the threat of Nazism which was gaining supporters in the United States. The leading spokesman of populist xenophobia which became antisemitism in its full sense was the Catholic priest Charles E. Coughlin. He emitted slogans of popular, isolationist, antisemitic Christianity and accused the Jews of trying to drag the United States into World War II. Father Coughlin attracted millions, not only Catholics, until he was silenced by the archbishop of his Detroit archdiocese when the United States entered World War II.

AIA–K*

As we have said, at the end of the 1930s, in face of the spread of Nazism and Fascism, United States foreign policy was fiercely debated until the Japanese attack on Pearl Harbor. The debate did not lack antisemitic overtones, for example, in the views expressed by the national aviation hero, Charles A. Lindbergh. At heart he admired the Nazi spirit and, like Coughlin, held that the Jews were pulling the United States into the war. At the height of the war, popular opinion polls showed the frightening strength of antisemitism in the American community. It is not easy to explain why antisemitic tension subsided in great degree after 1945, but it is reasonable to assume that it resulted from the end of the war, revulsion at the sight of Nazi antisemitism, and above all continued economic prosperity.[13]

An important subject, studied but slightly, is the reaction of the Jews to antisemitism. Without exploring it further one may say there has been a spectrum of responses: conciliation, requests that fellow-Jews improve their behavior, systematic refutation of the charges, counter-attack, silence, and avoidance. For an example of all these we again turn to the city of Cleveland. At the beginning of November, 1938, there was a proposal that the city be asked to introduce Hebrew as one of the languages offered in the high schools. Several Jewish community leaders debated whether or not to request this. One argued that teaching Hebrew in the schools "is likely to have a good will effect upon our general population" and would dispel any impression that the Jews were "secretive." Another replied: "We are going to fan the certain unreasoning elements, the rising tide and flame of antisemitism." Still another agreed: "The Jewish community should not make itself too conspicuous, too demanding and too assertive . . . We should try to be good citizens and make no private and individual demands." The final word was spoken by Alfred A. Benesch, a member of the city's Board of Education, highly respected and possessing long experience in public life. He emphatically dismissed the opposition to Hebrew, saying that he regarded these views as "of the same type with the complaint about the unduly large immigration into this country, and the complaints of too many Jews in public life. I have no sympathy with the public relations argument [against Hebrew] at all." He continued: "The concern lest Jews be too conspicuous is an admission of an inferiority complex . . . Nor am I worried about the argument that too many Jews are seeking public office. If they are the right kind of Jews, they deserve support. That argument emanates more from our group than from the non-Jewish group."[14] Three months after these forceful words well-known Jews appealed to President Roosevelt not to appoint a Jew to the Supreme Court in place of the aged Brandeis who was retiring. But the President thought it particularly fitting to appoint a Jew, Felix Frankfurter.

4. Summary

Everything thus far compels still another question: How did it happen that antisemitism, which does exist in the United States, never became a viable, lasting movement with political power? It appears to me that five answers have been intimated in our discussion:

1. There developed within American Christianity, alongside the tradition hostile to the Jews, a clear liberal and humanitarian trend which explicitly rejects – if not always whole-heartedly – any expression of hostility.

2. Within the multifaceted American society, there are many inner antagonisms and tensions and the Jews are not the only target for hatred. The Jews were hated particularly by those who were intolerant of the variegated society and wished to preserve the familiar social structure which had benefited them.

3. The United States is a wealthy country. For most of its existence, all levels of the nation have felt expansively optimistic about their economic future. As long as these feelings of optimism and abundance were dominant, antisemitism was not a serious force in public life.

4. The "committed" antisemites belonged to different social classes with completely differently interests and cultural styles. They never joined forces, perhaps because there was never a leader acceptable to them all. However, it is more probable that for most antisemites their hatred was not so intense that they would be ready to forego their other political and social interests to join the ranks of a one-plank antisemitic movement.

5. In the United States, an American patriot is defined as one loyal to the American political tradition as defined by the Founding Fathers and continued through personalities like Webster, Lincoln, Wilson, and the two Roosevelts. The founders and heroes of this tradition unanimously preached equal rights, religious tolerance, and equal opportunity for every person as a human being. In such an outlook there is no place for antisemitism. Since the antisemites make their claims in the name of pristine American values, the Jews and the opponents of antisemitism were able to present it as contradicting traditional American ideals, a betrayal of unsullied "Americanism."

The prophetic power of historians is limited to their ability to see the near past from a perspective of the more distant past. They cannot foretell the future. But one may risk saying that so long as the traditions exist which have proven themselves able to reject antisemitism or limit it, and so long as economic conditions satisfy most of the citizenry, it may be that antisemitism in the United States will remain limited and latent.

Notes

1. On the subject of continuity, see the important work of Alexander Gerschenkron, *Continuity in History and Other Essays* (Cambridge, Mass., 1968), pp.11–40 esp. p.38; John Herman Randall Jr., *Nature and Historical Experience* (N.Y., 1958), pp.66–69; Robert A. Nisbet, *Social Change and History* (N.Y., 1969), pp.287–294; Arthur O. Lovejoy, *The Great Chain of Being* (N.Y., 1960), pp.331–332.
2. James Fulton McClear, "The True American Union of Church and State: The Reconstruction of the Theocratic Tradition," *Church History*, XXVIII, 1, (March, 1959): 41.
3. Lloyd P. Gartner, *History of the Jews of Cleveland* (Cleveland, 1978), p.7.
4. Ibid., p.32.

320   *Lloyd P. Gartner*

5. Ibid., p.302. The practice of Jewish employers not employing Jews was widespread though not extensive. The reasons offered were that Jewish employees are less disciplined than non-Jewish; Jews tend to join unions and strike; they only want to learn the business so that they can open businesses of their own.
6. On antisemitism in the legal profession see: Jerold S. Auerbach, *Unequal Justice: Lawyers and Social Change in Modern America* (N.Y., 1976); Melvin M. Fagen, "The Status of Jewish Lawyers in New York City," *Jewish Social Studies*, I, (January, 1939): 37–104. See Dan A. Oren, *Joining the Club: A History of Jews and Yale* (New Haven, 1985).
7. See the two basic articles of John Higham: "Ideological Anti-Semitism in the Gilded Age" (1957) and "Social Discrimination Against Jews in America" (1957) in his book: *Send These to Me: Jews and other Immigrants in Urban America* (N.Y., 1975), pp.173ff.
8. Ernest Samuels, *Henry Adams: The Middle Years* (Cambridge, Mass., 1958), p.129.
9. Ibid., p.168.
10. John Higham, *Strangers in the Land: Patterns of American Nativism, 1860–1925* (2nd ed., N.Y., 1970), pp.131–157, 300–330.
11. The attack on populism came primarily from two historians: Oscar Handlin, "American Views of the Jews at the Opening of the Twentieth Century," *Publications of the American Jewish Historical Society* 40(1951): 323–344; Richard Hofstadter, *The Age of Reform: From Bryan to F.D.R.* (N.Y., 1953), pp.77–81. Their charges were answered by Walter T. K. Nugent, *The Tolerant Populists* (Chicago, 1963); Norman Pollack, "The Myth of Populist Anti-Semitism," *American Historical Review*, LXVIII (1962): 76–80, and other articles by him. See also C. Vann Woodward, "The Populist Heritage and the Intellectual," *American Scholar*, XXIX (1959–1960): 55–72.
12. For a discussion of Ford see Morton Rosenstock, *Louis Marshall and the Defense of Jewish Rights* (Detroit, 1965), pp.128–200.
13. For Coughlin and his movement see: Seymour Martin Lipset and Earl Rabb, *The Politics of Unreason: Right-Wing Extremism in America, 1790–1970* (N.Y., 1970), pp.67–189. On the Second World War period and thereafter see: Charles Herbert Stember and others, *Jews in the Mind of America* (N.Y., 1966), pp.110–208, 259–403.
14. Gartner, *History of the Jews of Cleveland*, p.303. See Naomi W. Cohen, "Antisemitism in the Gilded Age: The Jewish View," *Jewish Social Studies*, XLI, 3–4 (Summer-Fall, 1979): 187–211, and "American Jewish Reactions to Anti-Semitism in Western Europe, 1875–1900," *Proceedings of the American Academy for Jewish Research*, XLV (1978): 29–65.

22

Argentina: A Case Study in Dimensions of Government Antisemitism

HAIM AVNI

"It is high time. Whoever does not blind himself to visible signs must perceive that the situation has undergone an ominous change for the worse." With these words did the founder of the Zionist organization, Theodor Hcrzl, react to the pogroms at Kishinev.[1] The unrestrained rioting of mobs in a district capital, where army troops are stationed and the head of the district resides, could not have occurred without governmental protection. The revelations of the London *Times* reporter, that the local authorities took no action on direct order of the Minister of the Interior, Von Plehve, only confirmed what was logically certain. The forty-nine casualties and the hundreds of wounded in Kishinev shocked the western world; and most of all the shock was over the fact that this pogrom was a clear expression of government antisemitism.

Only thirty years after Kishinev, state antisemitism reached its fullest manifestation. The Nazi rise to power in Germany turned the aspirations of a large antisemitic movement almost overnight into the official government policy. The slogan "The Jews are our misfortune," which was the plaint of the antisemites in Germany from the beginning of the nineteenth century, became the basis of legislation and governmental action in Nazi Germany. The removal of the Jews from public life, from all branches of the economy, and finally, from the human landscape, was carried out by the government, and because of this could be so systematic and all-encompassing. When the rulers of the Nazi state decided first to drive out, and then physically to wipe out, the Jewish population under its control, they had all the means to execute these evil designs. During that period, official antisemitism was not confined to Germany only. As a result of internal political changes, antisemitism came to power in other states as well. In a number of places the local antisemites were strengthened by their overt

321

and covert relationships with Nazi Germany. When their government failed in the political arena or on the battlefield, they became the rulers of their nation with the patronage of the antisemitic power. Thus the state antisemitism "exported" from Germany became a helpful factor in establishing government antisemitism beyond its borders and so the stage was set for the comprehensive scope of the Holocaust.

In its programs and excuses, state antisemitism is no different from "popular" antisemitism. Religious zealotry, economic frustration, national chauvinism, and the kindred factors which motivate the individual antisemite, are also likely to be the programmatic basis of state antisemitism. Furthermore, the very existence of antisemitic feelings, open or dormant, in the population, and especially the existence of movements, organizations, or political parties with an antisemitic platform – directly or indirectly – constitute a background for the antisemitic activities of the government. Government antisemitism differs from popular antisemitism in two dimensions only, though these are of fundamental and decisive importance: the nature of the *instrumentalities* at its disposal and the force of its damage. The injury wrought by the governmental bodies when *they* are directed against the Jewish individual or community is inestimably more severe than that which could be inflicted by hostile individuals or an aroused mob. This is symbolized by the attitude of the police and other security forces toward the Jews. These factors, whose function it is to preserve law and order, are meant to be the refuge of all those whose enemies are plotting against them. Therefore, so long as the government itself is not infected with antisemitism, its victims will seek its protection. However, when state antisemitism is put into effect, the governmental bodies themselves will be among the first to implement the antisemitic policy, and the Jews will, in practice, be outside the law and fair prey for all.

Clearly, then, from the standpoint of Jewish existence past and present, this distinction between manifestations of "popular" feelings of hatred and antisemitic government acts is of supreme importance. Because of the programmatic connection between them and the possibility that the transition from popular movement to state policy need not necessarily come about through open, dramatic, political upheaval but through evolutionary process, we must sharpen our study and look in particular at the possible intermediate stages between these two forms of evil. Also, in the reality in which the Jewish community lives, the possibility that state antisemitism may hide behind a "popular" tradition compels us to attempt to uncover its first symptoms so that we can gauge the degree of its danger.

Antisemitic manifestations and occurrences have prominently taken place in each of the Latin American countries in one period of its history or another. During the Nazi peak in the world – from the 1930s to the mid-1940s –antisemitic occurrences and incidents multiplied in all the Latin American countries. But in that period, and even more so thereafter, the Argentine Republic was especially outstanding in the activity of its antisemites.

This reality has accompanied Argentine Jewry almost from its start, and if a connection exists between the size of the Jewish community and the opposition which it rouses against it, then the number of Jews in Argentina, with the largest Jewish population of all the Latin American countries, can be one of the starting points for an understanding of the phenomenon. Other factors are surely in the Republic's political history, in the pace at which its national awareness was crystallized, and so forth. We find clear evidence of Argentina's prominence in everything relating to antisemitic occurrences in the chronicles which systematically attempt to register their frequency. A cursory perusal of one of them, of recent years, indicates that there were more antisemitic incidents reported in Argentina in 1983 and 1984 than in all the other Latin American states, and in Latin America, from 1970–75, four times as many such incidents were reported as in the United States and Canada.[2]

Does this fact stem from the reality of a deeply rooted *popular* antisemitism or might it also result from attempts by the régime to use antisemitism as a means to achieving one of its goals?

Below, we shall detail the reflection of this problem in the most serious antisemitic incident in the history of Argentine Jewry prior to the military régime which ruled Argentina from March 1976 to December 1983. On the basis of our findings in this affair, we shall spell out its necessary conclusions for an investigation of the essence of the other antisemitic developments in Argentina.

1. The Pogrom in Buenos Aires

On 16 January 1919 the heads of the Jewish community in Rosario, Argentina's second largest city, made the following entry into the minutes book of the community:

> A full-blown pogrom, greater almost than anything known before in the antisemitic world [took place in Buenos Aires]. Juan José de Soisa Reilly, a reporter for the [illustrated] newspaper *Caras y Caretas*, its special war-correspondent and writer, wrote in the popular journal *Revista Popular*: "I visited a number of Jewish homes where the blood cries out. I saw innocent old men whose beards had been plucked out. I saw scientific libraries burned. I saw a plucky woman forced to eat her own excrement. I witnessed the calamities caused by these mobs of well-dressed young men, many of them public school students who, protected by the swords of the police, fell upon the quiet, Russian Jews, killed old folks, raped women . . . When I saw all this – I shuddered from fear and love of culture and country . . . and thus into the history of the Republic of Argentina there is written a page full of Jewish blood seen [spilled] in the streets, the blood of innocents."[3]

The leaders of the Rosario community added that disturbances had been planned in their city as well but had been thwarted thanks to preventive actions that were taken, including intervention by the local French consul.

That same month, the president of the Zionist Federation in Argentina sent the Zionist Organization at The Hague a detailed description of what he called "the bloody events suffered by the Jews of Argentina and especially those of Buenos Aires":

> It will certainly not be news to you that there has been an antisemitic movement in Argentina for the past thirty years. Antisemitism appeared in this country immediately upon the arrival here of the first Jewish immigrants. Since then it has gradually grown with the addition of new immigrants . . . In spite of all this, we never believed that antisemitism could come to an actual eruption in Argentina . . . The storm burst upon us suddenly and surprised us all with its bloody scope. This is how it happened: On the ninth of the month, a general strike broke out in Buenos Aires and some of the provincial cities . . . no one knows how and where from – but a rumor immediately spread of a revolution of the "maximalists" [a common term in Argentina at that time for left-wing revolutionaries, anarchists, and others]. The fire of patriotism was kindled among the Christian youth along with hatred for all strangers, especially the Jews (who especially) in their opinion must be responsible for the uprising. The students organized in a group called the "White Guard" which assumed the role of helping the keepers of the law save the country . . . From that first day of the general strike it was very clear that the disturbances were of antisemitic character and the Jews would be the scapegoats for the sins of others. What would happen was not yet clear. Every Jew was terrified and despairing. But certainly no one even imagined the half of what happened. It started in the streets mainly occupied by the Jews. The "White Guard," which was permitted to move through the streets freely and do whatever it wished, exploited this freedom particularly against the Jews. Any Jew who chanced along the street – anyone who looked Jewish – was stopped, beaten mercilessly, and dragged off to the police station. His only crime was his Jewish origin. Each one was seen as a "maximalist." There were instances when pedestrians, stopped by riders on horseback, were forced to run along behind the horse, and when tired, were beaten by sword or clubs until, wounded and half-dead, they were dragged to the police. Young or old, it made no difference. All were accused of maximalism – the seventy-year-old or older and the fifteen-year-old alike. These onslaughts were called "the Russian hunt," "Russian" and "Jew" being synonymous. This lasted a few days.
>
> In order to voice its protest against the maximalist uprising and demonstrate its general xenophobia, especially its Jew-hatred, the "patriotic" "White Guard," with the approval and participation of the police,

organized patriotic demonstrations which passed through the Jewish
streets. When they reached the clubhouses of Jewish organizations, they
broke into them and destroyed whatever they contained or set them afire.
The smashed items were brought out to the street and burned – as was
done in the past at an *auto-da-fé* . . . In the process, they ruthlessly beat
up the neighbors, Jew and non-Jew, men, women, and children. They also
arrested the men. All this took place in broad daylight, with the national
flag flying at their head and with cries of "Long live our fatherland – death
to the Russians!" and the like. Even small synagogues were nests of maximalism to them. In one of them, Jews were praying. The police broke in
and searched them at gunpoint, finding nothing of course. When the police
saw the phylacteries, it occurred to them that they contained dynamite.
One of the Jews was forced to tear open a pair of phylacteries to show
them what was inside. Only then was he taken to the police station . . . During the night and into the daytime hours, when endless
sounds of gunfire were echoing – the most terrible evil was taking place in
the Jewish quarter. Under the pretext of searching for maximalists, the
police, the army, and the "White Guard" attacked the Jewish homes, destroyed them, and mercilessly beat the men, women, and children, and
arrested the former. They also arrested many women. Hundreds of those
arrested were so severely beaten on the way to prison that they were
half-dead on arrival. They were beaten again, tortured with all the inquisi-
torial methods, and thrown into cells. For the duration of their detention,
they were not fed. When some women and children tried to bring food to
the imprisoned men, they were gruffly chased off with threats of also
being beaten and imprisoned. The prisoners were dragged from their cells
a number of times a day so that the police, the army, and the "White
Guard" could beat and humiliate them . . . [4]

This detailed description, which was later quoted extensively in the Jewish
press,[5] seems to present a classic picture of government antisemitism: State
security forces, with an antisemitic militia by its side, run riot against Jews
beating them up in broad daylight with no interference. Yet, an entirely different picture emerges from a summation of the events of 1919 in Argentina in
The Annual Register. A Review of Public Events, Home and Abroad published
in London, 1920, which echoed the reports in the Argentine and foreign press:

The year was marked in Argentina by the occurrence of very serious labor
troubles due in the main to the spread of definite Bolshevik doctrines
through the large number of Russian immigrants in Buenos Aires and elsewhere. The most serious outbreak occurred in January. Early in the
month a general strike was declared in Buenos Aires and this appears to
have developed into a deliberate attempt to bring about a political and
social revolution and the establishment of a Bolshevik régime. On 9 Janu-

ary, the revolutionaries were able to seize control of the city, and it was notable that on the following day the only newspaper to appear was the socialist organ. Thefts and murders occurred on all sides; and by a concerted movement the strike spread on 11 January to every town in the Republic. For several days it appeared that the Russian and the other foreign workmen would be able to seize control of the Argentine capital. President Yrigoyen and the Government acted decisively. On 11 January, General Dell Epiane [Sic; Luis Dellepiane] was appointed Military Dictator of Buenos Aires with full powers. He immediately imposed the most severe form of martial law and severe street fighting between the troops and the revolutionaries occurred in the Capital. A serious battle took place outside the general Post Office in which there were nearly a thousand casualties. The fighting in the Russian quarter was even more severe; and much blood was shed before General Dell Epiane was able to carry out his instructions of interning the Russian ringleaders on the warships anchored in the harbour. After a few days of what was virtually civil war, however, General Dell Epiane's vigour had the desired result and the revolutionary movement collapsed.[6]

This was not an account of a criminal pogrom of government forces against the Jewish population, but rather of a military array against a revolutionary uprising which was put down with great effort after some bloodshed. Along with this, for all of the contrast between this version and the testimony of the Jewish sources, we find that the events of the second week of January 1919 are considered of central importance both in the history of Argentina and Argentine Jewry. As such they have warranted comprehensive historiographic attention.

A labor leader who was one of the heads of the moderate trade unions;[7] a police official who was on duty in the police station of one of the quarters most heavily populated by Jews;[8] writers of the history of the Argentine labor movement;[9] biographers of Hipolito Yrigoyen,[10] president of Argentina at that time – all of them were to describe and evaluate the events of the second week of January. In addition, there are writers of research monographs especially on this event, designated in Argentine historiography as "The Tragic Week" ("*La Semana Tragica*").[11] All of these are on the non-Jewish side. On the Jewish side there were also many who dealt with that week. The first of them was the journalist-author Pinie Wald who was involuntarily destined, as we shall see, to play a central role in that week's events. His book, *Koshmar* ("Nightmare"), written on the tenth anniversary of the January 1919 events, and even more, his summary article, written more than a generation after the event,[12] were the partial basis for a small pamphlet published in Spanish[13] and then for a comprehensive chapter in a research study which was also published.[14] Yet, for all of this abundance of documentation and research focused on this one week, we still find partial, blurred, contradictory versions in some of the comprehensive histories of Argentina. Some of them do not mention the attacks upon the Jews at all and in others it is swallowed up in a blurred account.[15]

What, then, did happen in "The Tragic Week"? Was it in fact an expression of government antisemitism?

2. Proletarian Struggle and Antisemitic Attacks

The bloodshed began on Monday, 7 January 1919, far from the quarters in which the Jewish population was concentrated. That day, groups of workers in the factory owned by Pedro Vasena and his partners (mostly wealthy Englishmen), and other steel-plant workers were positioned at the gates of the operation's warehouses trying to prevent the strike-breakers from getting raw materials from them. The factory was, to be sure, one of the largest in the country, but the strike which had been called there was only one of many which had broken out in Argentina in the months after World War I. That afternoon, a number of wagons driven by strike-breakers were moving toward the warehouses. They were escorted by an armed police guard. As they neared the plant's warehouses, they were met with words of dissuasion, jeers, and finally with a shower of rocks. The police guard responded by firing in every direction, and when the panic subsided there were four workers and passers-by dead and another thirty wounded.

News of the victims infuriated the labor community. The two rival trade federations – one syndicalist, the other anarchist – united in a decision to proclaim a general strike on the day of the victims' funerals. The two rival Argentinian Socialist parties also joined in support of the strike. 8 January was spent in preparing for the funerals and the general strike set for the next day. All the unions were agreed that bringing the economic life of the capital to a halt was intended to be more than merely a demonstration of the strength of the working class. The organizers, however, disagreed on its specific goal. The syndicalists and the socialists wanted to see it as a springboard for advancing the negotiations to improve working conditions. The anarchists, on the other hand, a minority among the organized workers, wanted to exploit it as a stage in their political struggle to undermine the capitalistic system. They also prepared for armed confrontations with the security forces.

By noon of 9 January 1919 the strike was general and complete. In the early afternoon, the funeral cortège left the workers' neighborhood at the edge of Buenos Aires with tens of thousands of workers filing behind the coffins. At the same time, all along their route, in the side streets and the central avenue, there were a number of attacks on stores which sold weapons, and a monastery was violated and set on fire as well. About two hours later, the throngs reached the cemetery which was at the other end of the town. They stood massed at its gates listening to the speakers and then, with no prior warning, the security forces, concentrated on the cemetery walls at strategic vantage points, opened fire upon them. In a short time, dozens of workers were injured as they sought cover among the tombstones. Many other were injured in the massive attempt to flee. At about the same time, an armed clash took place at the gates of Vasena's plant. Thousands of workers who had been besieging the factory since early morning were enraged at the news of the cemetery slaughter. A few of them opened fire upon the building in which there were, at that time, the plant directors and a number of the heads of the manufacturers' and employers' association (*Asociación Nacional del Trabajo*), who had come to mediate the labor dispute. The police returned the fire and again many workers fell.

That night a state of siege was proclaimed and army units entered the capital. The President of the Republic gave the command to General Luis Dellepiane and also placed the police under his command. The soldiers' intervention ended the siege of the Vasena plant but their presence on the streets did not prevent violent clashes between anarchist bands and police and soldiers which lasted the whole night between 9 and 10 January.

Till Friday morning, 10 January, none of what was happening was directed against the Jews. True, there were some Jews among those who fell at the cemetery and the propaganda about the large number of "Russians" among the labor demonstrators did not cease; but there were not as yet any attacks aimed at the Jews in particular. These actions began that day and grew most intense on 11 January and the following day and followed in the wake of the organization of the civilian "volunteers."

Their organization began on the morning of the 10th on the initiative of leaders of the major economic corporations, grouped together in 1918 in the *Asociación del Trabayo* (Association of Labor) – as well as the nationalist university youth who had organized during World War I in the "National Youth Committee" (*"Comité Nacional de la Juventud"*). These organizations sent their representatives to a meeting convened on the morning of 10 January by a high naval officer (Admiral Domecq García) and one of the Radical leaders (Manuel Carles), who had, almost until January, held an important public office. They all enjoyed the support of the clergy, which was prominent throughout the decade before the "Tragic Week" in its efforts to swing the mass of workers away from the influence of the socialists and the revolutionaries. There was some bitter antisemitism in the activity of the priests, which was expressed in the books which they published – including school textbooks – and in their street-corner oratory on the outskirst of the most heavily populated Jewish quarter. Hatred of the Jews for nationalistic, xenophobic, and Christian-Catholic reasons and also because of the class struggle with the so-called "standard-bearers" of the revolutions, was also basic to the thinking of the other factors.[16] The common denominator they all shared was their conservative-rightist leanings and the fear lest the government not act with the severity and force necessary to suppress the strikers and eliminate the root of their rebelliousness. They therefore offered the government their assistance in maintaining law and order, and their offer was accepted.

That day the young people of the well-to-do families, the students, and others organized into groups of "Defenders of Order" ("*Defensores del Orden*") of the "White Guards." They were provided with arms and given a free hand to function within the police stations for the detention of suspects. Such measures could be taken only by the decision of those in charge of the army and the police. Immediately thereafter, members of the civilian guards appeared on the streets of the capital, in private cars and on foot, some of them accompanied by groups of naval men or other security forces and the rest operating with no escort whatever. At once the systematic, comprehensive hunt began, ostensibly to catch the leaders of the strikes and the proletarian struggle, and especially the leaders of the anarchists among them. Actually, German immigrants, Catalan Spaniards, and others suspected of maximalism were grabbed and dragged off to prison amidst abuse and beatings. However, in the centers of Jewish population, in the center of the city and in a number of the suburbs, the action was directed against the entire population indiscriminately, with the police and the soldiers participating alongside the civilian guards. This fact, to which Nathan Gezang attested in his report to the Zionist Organization at The Hague, as we have seen, is clearly verified in all the sources, Jewish and non-Jewish alike. Thus an anti-Jewish pogrom became part of an inter-class confrontation.

On 13 January, when the general strike was finished and done with, the activities of suppression against the workers and the pogrom in the Jewish sections received a "sensational" justification. According to official police announcements, the security forces and their assistants had succeeded in uncovering the existence of a revolutionary plot intended to make Argentina a Soviet republic. According to the testimony of one of the newspapers published subsequently, the Argentina police had received information from the Uruguay police of a pan-Latin-American plot for a communist revolution and, upon its discovery, four Jews had been arrested in Montevideo. In Buenos Aires, the police announced the capture of the intended "Soviet government" of Argentina, headed by the Jewish journalist, Pinie Wald. And indeed, Pinie Wald, one of the outstanding Bundist activists in Argentina, had already been arrested on 10 January and, according to him, he first heard of this charge on 15 January, the eve of his release from prison. Meanwhile, this information became the basis of a version about a Bolshevik revolution which supposedly threatened Argentina, and whose traces were evident, as we have seen, not only in newspaper accounts of that year but even much later.[17] These revelations – and the suppressive actions in Buenos Aires – quickly led to the spread of such actions to other cities of Argentina (as well as to Montevideo, Uruguay), and thus the "Tragic Week" brought to many communities of Jewish immigrants in the La Plata region the sensations of pogrom-fear which they had hoped to escape when they emigrated from Eastern Europe.

There are conflicting accounts of the total number of "Tragic Week" casualties. Two accounts were published immediately after the end of the events, on

14 January: According to the socialist newspaper *La Vanguardia* there were about 700 killed and 2000 injured; according to *La Nacion* – the organ of Argentina's upper classes and the largest of the dailies – 100 were killed and over 400 injured. A police official, who wrote about the "Tragic Week" as an eye-witness and was able to present official data, presents a daily report of the dead and wounded which comes to 141 killed, 108 seriously injured, and 413 slightly injured; whereas the ambassador of the United States in Argentina testified that, when it was all over, another police official had boasted to him that the mortuaries held 193 bodies: "14 of them Catalan Spaniards and the other 179 – 'Russian Jews'." The number of those arrested throughout Argentina reached the tens of thousands.[18]

What was the number of Jews injured in the pogrom and the labor demonstrations? The Jewish institutions did not yet have exact information about this more than two weeks after the riots ended. Nathan Gezang, who was at the center of Jewish organization at that time, noted at the end of January:

> To date, exact statistics cannot be compiled [on the number of imprisoned, injured, and killed]. It may not be possible in the future either. Many disappeared during the days of bloodshed and no one knows where they are. The police themselves do not know. The reason for this is that the "White Guard," the police, and the army in many instances acted entirely independently with no one knowing what the others were doing. From the data which is available, we know that there were over 1,000 imprisoned. There were also tens of injured and many dead. It is thought that many of the Jewish dead did not receive Jewish burial . . . [19]

This general estimate has not been changed by the research done since then. A number of the polemical articles in the Jewish press, to be sure, spoke of "many widows and hundreds of orphans" left by the pogrom among the Jews[20], but the blurred lines between the general and the specifically Jewish make it difficult to accept these generalizations as starting points for estimating the number of those affected in the specific attacks upon the Jews.

3. The Government and the Pogrom

In January 1919, Hipolito Yrigoyen, the President of Argentina, was the leader of the Radical Party. His coming to power in 1916 was a revolution of sorts in the history of the republican régime. In contrast to the previous governments which had ruled the country till then, both the President and the Congress had that time been chosen in general, democratic elections with no fault to be found. The masses of voters of the lower and middle classes thus rewarded Hipolito Yrigoyen and his party for having struggled tirelessly for a generation as members of the opposition and having gained them the possibility of actually exercising their civil right to vote without fear and without distortion. The desire of the President and his party for reforms and changes in a number of areas of life had already been proven in the years preceding the "Tragic Week," most prominent of these changes being their support of the university reform of 1918 which brought about the democratization of the institutions of the national universities and student partcipation in their administration. The President's popular personality and his nationalist, populist leanings somewhat strengthened, to be sure, the tendency to emphasize the Catholic tradition in the lines of the Republic's national image; but, in all of this, there was not an iota of Jew-hatred.

The circles that united to form the "White Guards" for the most part came from the conservative right-wing of the Argentine political spectrum; and it was this wing particularly which had been routed with Hipolito Yrigoyen's rise to power. But the régime of the Radical party did not wish to rid itself of the economic and social order which had preceded it, and for all its desire for a certain improvement in the workers' condition, it was very far from the position of the small socialist parties.

On the other hand, the heads of the capitalistic sectors, for all their opposition, were indirect, necessary, and desirable allies. The influence of the economic élite upon the army officers and perhaps also upon other segments of the administration and police, increased the tendency of these arms of government to respond to the "spontaneous" organizing of the citizenry to enforce "law and order."

Added to these internal circumstances at that time were other, external ones. In January 1919, in those very days of the "Tragic Week," the capitalist world was in shock at the momentum of the communist revolutions. Beside the Bolshevik revolution in Russia, which was still going on under a banner of world-wide revolution, during that very week, the Spartacus rebellion led by Rosa Luxemburg and Karl Liebknecht in Berlin was being put down, and this news was being published in the daily press in Buenos Aires. The terror at the spread of the revolution was great among the foreigners with economic interests, no less and perhaps even more than among the Argentinians. Under these circumstances, if outside pressure was in fact exerted upon the central government in Argentina, it was certainly to increase the suppression of the proletarian disturbances and not merely to block it. More than that: The prominence of the Jews in the revolutionary movement was at that time considered a proven fact. Jewish names were conspicuous at the head of the rosters of the revolutionary leaders and activists not only in Russia, Hungary, and Germany, but in Argentina as well. The trade unions and the anarchists found it proper, as a condition for halting the general strike of the "Tragic Week," to stipulate the release from prison of a young Jew. The man in question was Simon Radowitzky who, on 14 November 1909, had killed the Buenos Aires Chief of Police, Ramón L. Falcón, after the latter had been responsible for firing upon a workers' demonstration on 1 May of that year.[21]

The Jewish proletariate was seen, then, not only as involved in an attempt to undermine the world's capitalistic order but as its instigator. Once the persecution of the Jews in Buenos Aires was linked to the "Red scare" which, at that time, gripped public opinion in the United States and western Europe, one could not expect that considerations based upon the attitude of world public opinion would especially work to the advantage of the Jews of Argentina. In contrast to the riots taking place at that very same time in the Ukraine and in Poland which were denounced by the West, there was no such moderating factor regarding the occurrences in Buenos Aires.

The antisemitic forces in Argentina which were enlisted to suppress the workers' disturbances, then, gained government support: Arms, police authority, and the direct cooperation of the security forces were all put at their disposal. With all this, the commanders of the army and the police did not reach a point of principled, open support for the attack upon the Jews. On the contrary: When the rabbi of the *Congregacion Israelita de la Republica Argentina*, the oldest communal organization in Buenos Aires, on 12 January turned to the chief of police, the latter disassociated himself from the pogrom and asked the rabbi to calm the Jewish community and promise them, in his name, that the lives of the Jews would be assured. Another delegation saw General Dellepiane, Commander of the Army, on 13 January, and this meeting resulted in the issuance of a circular in which the general announced that a distinction must be made between "the criminals whose attacks we are still suppressing" and "the peaceful, diligent members of the Jewish community who are contributing in every way to the progress and greatness of the Republic." However, these pronouncements, made as the troubles were almost ended, did not keep the commanders of the police and the army from praising the work of the rioters and the help they gave the security forces, though the scope of the pogrom was already clear to everyone.[22]

The stand of the President of the Republic was also ambiguous. A Jewish community delegation which met with him on 25 January heard him say that, had he known of the riots as they occurred, he would have stopped them at once. According to the President, the country's tradition, the spirit of its laws and culture, and the character of its inhabitants all stand in clear opposition to the hatred and persecution of Jews. Therefore, he promised them, they need have no fear of renewed attacks. Yet, for all that, against his specific promises, the President did not take any legal steps whatever to discover the perpetrators and try them.[23]

4. The "Tragic Week" Riots and Government Antisemitism

To what extent, then, can the antisemitic attacks which occurred in January 1919 be considered as manifestations of government antisemitism?

In the course of this study we have seen that there were broad, influential, antisemitic circles in existence before the events of "Tragic Week." These came especially from the upper strata of Argentine society and their Jew-hatred was based upon a nationalist, Catholic self-identity; upon general xeno-phobia; and primarily, upon class motifs. The violent eruption of this hatred occurred in a period of economic crisis which heightened the social tensions within Argentine society and brought the interclass relationships to the point of explosion. The Jews in Argentina, at that time mostly among the lower strata economically speaking, were prominent not only because of their concentration but also because of the attachment that many of them had to proletarian ideolo-gies. And these three factors – popular, deeply-rooted antisemitism, a time of national crisis, and the Jewish prominence – constituted the immediate background for the antisemites' scheming against the Jews.

However, alongside these we have another triad: The high social-economic level of most of the antisemites brought them especially close to the govern-ment and its security arms. The class base of antisemitism, the fear of com-munism, and the identification of Russia as the source of the revolutionary evil were shared by the antisemitic rioters and those responsible for the existing order. This partial concensus was enough to give the rioters not only protec-tion by the security forces but also their direct assistance. The international conditions prevailing were not such as to act as a deterrent to government antisemitism; on the contrary, they were such as to encourage it, and thus was stifled one of the important factors which might have acted against the open cooperation of the rioters and the security forces. The liberal principles of the central government – as well as the broad strata of Argentine public opi-nion – were strong enough to prevent antisemitism's becoming a clear and open government instrument for solving the problems of the emergency in which it found itself by dint of a seemingly local labor dispute. Therefore we have not found clear and openly proclaimed government antisemitism. Yet, these principles did not have enough power to block the government's being dragged after the antisemites at the height of the crisis, nor to shake loose of them and prosecute them under the law after the tumult had subsided.

It is only within these parameters that the greatest, most comprehensive, pogrom against the Jews of Argentina is to be seen as a manifestation of government antisemitism.

The power of the antisemites and their proximity to the government; the direction and limitations of outside influence; and the ideological tendencies of those at the helm of the central government – these three factors, then, deter-mined the extent of the activation of government antisemitism in the events of January 1919. Together with the three background factors for the course of this event, which we have noted above, they can serve as guidelines for research into the history of antisemitism in Argentina even in the period thereafter.

5. A Yardstick for Further Studies

The reign of the Radical party was ended in 1930 by a military revolution. After a year of military rule, a president was elected and the parliamentary system was restored, but it was done while barring some of the leaders and parties from political life and with serious irregularities in the electoral process. This perverted democracy came to an end in a second military revolution, in June 1943. This time the military officers wanted to keep control and did so for three years. In 1946, after a dispute which undermined the military caste, free and democratic elections were held which brought the populist leader and general Jaun Domingo Peron to the helm of government. His reign, which deteriorated into a populist dictatorship in democratic guise, ended in a new military coup in September 1955. After a very tense transition period, the Radical parties came to power in May 1958. But their division into two rival camps and the army officers' barring of the supporters of the ousted President Peron from political life, placed the régimes of the Radical presidents under the shade of the military. Accordingly, the two presidents did not serve out their terms, which were cut short by military coups in March 1962 and June 1966. Then the army again resumed direct control of the government, and its officers held power, with tensions and military court upheavals, until March 1973. Free and democratic elections held that month restored the aging leader Peron to the helm after eighteen years of exile. Three Peronist presidents, his assistant, Peron himself, and after his death, his wife, managed to serve for three years, until March 1976. Then the military rebelled once more: Its commanders abolished the republican institutions and a new and heretofore unprecedented period of state-terrorism was inaugurated.

Twenty-one presidents have passed through the "Pink House," the presidential palace in Buenos Aires, in the years from the "Tragic Week" and until General Videla and the Junta occupied it. Thirteen of them came to office by virtue of the constitution, but only five of them were chosen in proper democratic elections. On the other hand, eight army officers – who seized power with their colleagues – have held the presidency of the Republic.

During this long and stormy period, did those conditions exist which had prepared the ground for the evils of the "Tragic Week"? The chronicle information and the few studies that have been done in the realm of antisemitism in Argentina indicate that they in fact did exist.[24]

The popular antisemitism which we found to be the basis of the events of January 1919 did not disappear after things quietened down. On the contrary. That same month the circles which had perpetrated the riots established the nationalist "Patriotic League" ("*Liga Patriotica*") whose platform included xenophobia – toward both the new and the old immigrants – among its basic tenets. This social-political factor has continued to accompany the political changes in Argentina from then till now. Furthermore, active antisemitism also spread to other, more popular, strata. Echoes of the publication of *The Proto-*

cols of the Elders of Zion in the 1920s and the spread of racial antisemitism in the 1930s also added some variety to the antisemitic motifs. During the Nazi period, the activities of the Argentine antisemites enjoyed the active support of the German state antisemitism. Through its governmental extensions, the Nazi power made active Nazis of most of the German emigrants and their offspring and used its governmental resources to support the Argentine antisemitic organizations and their organs.

A further diversification and expansion of antisemitic motifs and circles took place from the mid-1950s onward, thanks to additional government antisemitism. This came from the "Arab League" and depended upon the representatives of this Arab umbrella organization, as well as upon the representations of the major Arab states. With their help, anti-Zionism was added to the collection of antisemitic motifs and charges and, alongside the other allegations, that of "dual allegiance" was underscored from then on. In addition to this, anti-Zionism served as a much needed cover especially in the period when naked antisemitim was unacceptable to public opinion. Since the Six-Day War and especially the Yom Kippur War, this activity has consistently expanded the antisemitic circles. On the one hand, they have gained a certain number from among the immigrants from the Arab countries and their descendants, whose Arab identity was stimulated first by the military defeat, and then by the power of oil. Also added to the supporters of antisemitism were new factors who saw their identification with its anti-Zionist version as part of their "Third World" identity.

A period of national crisis, such as we saw as one of the background factors of the "Tragic Week" events, has occurred again and again during the five and a half decades which followed them. The beginning of every pivotal period was characterized by internal and international crisis conditions. Each of the political changes – even when they followed proper constitutional elections as was the case in 1946 and 1973 – were the result of great inner tension which was accompanied by acts of violence or authorized them. Under such circumstances, these hours of decision and turnabout could have been the antisemites' greatest hour.

The prominence of the Jews, another of the background factors, did not disappear after the 1919 events, but actually became greater and more varied. The extreme economic changes in Argentina served as the setting for the economic emergence of many Jews from the working and lower-middle classes to the upper-middle and wealthy ones. These changes were of special significance for the opposite process which was taking place in the spread of antisemitism. In contrast to its exclusive concentration in the upper strata of Argentine society in the "Tragic Week," thereafter it trickled down to the popular levels and the proletariate, and the new economic prominence of the Jews fed these new rivulets of hatred considerably. The yearning for higher education on the part of many Jews during this period greatly increased their presence in the free professions and the country's cultural life. At the same time, Argentina's political system, polarized between left and right, made many Jews visible particularly in the leftist movements and parties, especially in those which emphasized their international socialist character. This prominence in spiritual and professional life, on the one hand, and left-wing political activity on the other, further strengthened the hatred of the right-wing, conservative circles.

In the course of the Holocaust and the establishment of the State of Israel, the attachment of Argentine Jewry to Zionism grew stronger, and its communal institutions were outstanding in their support of the Jewish State. Furthermore, among all the other Jewish communities outside Israel, the Jewry of Argentina was the only one which faced a severe confrontation on the issue of "dual loyalty", when, in May 1960, at the height of the national festivities celebrating the 150th anniversary of the Republic's independence, the capture of Adolf Eichmann by Israeli agents and his removal to Jerusalem for trial became public knowledge. This reality was another important excuse for the hatred of the antisemites in all circles and classes.

In spite of the paucity of comprehensive studies, we can state with a great degree of certainty that the three background factors which existed at the time of "Tragic Week" – deeply rooted popular antisemitism, national crisis, and Jewish prominence – not only have continued to exist since, but have even grown very much stronger. Did these also produce government antisemitism in the ensuing years? And if so, was it of the same kind and scope as that of the "Tragic Week" or was it more severe and direct?

Apart from attempts to interpret antisemitic manifestations as expressions of government antisemitism, and an initial investigation of the period following the Yom Kippur War, we have thus far no answers to these questions.[25] To be sure, in seeking them, the investigators will not only have to examine carefully the manifestations of antisemitism in general but also painstakingly weigh the factors which we have found to be the determinants of the actual existence of government antisemitism and the measure of its strength: How close to the central government and its extensions are the Argentine antisemitic personalities and forces; the direction of external forces – world public opinion, international pressures, and so forth – and their impact upon the considerations and freedom of action of the state government; the extent of the central government's identification with or opposition to the antisemites' charges and the degree of its readiness to act upon these considerations against the Jews or their persecutors.

The pogrom of the "Tragic Week" shocked the Jewish community of Argentina not only because of the victims, the damage, and the humiliations which it engendered, but because of the foundations of government antisemitism which it revealed. The Jewish leaders complained of this in all of their statements and they were set at ease only when they heard the President, the Commander of the Army, and many political leaders disassociate themselves from the events and their perpetrators.[26] These declarations seemingly returned the violent antisemitic outbreak to the category of popular antisemitism. However, the echoes of the shock have not been forgotten and still constitute a conscious – though subdued – experiential base for the history of Argentina's Jewry. The serious consequences which flowed from the government's placing its police and army at the service of the Jew-haters for a brief moment in history, tangibly demonstrated the powerful danger of government antisemitism even in a partial form. This experience also points up the importance of carefully checking the existence of partial government antisemitism in the reality of the lives of the Jews of Argentina and the other diaspora lands.

In Argentina it has become even more significant now that the most recent, and darkest, era of its history is to be studied: the era of the Military régime of 1976–1983, the years of state terrorism, of the "Dirty War," and of the *"Desaparecidos."*

Notes

1. From Herzl's address opening the Sixth Zionist Congress at Basel, 23 August, 1903. *Stenographisches Protokoll der Verhandlungen des VI. Zionisten-Kongresses in Basel: 23, 24, 25, 26, 27, und 28, August 1903* (Wien, 1903), p.4. [Eng. translation by Nellie Straus in Th. Herzl, *The Congress Addresses . . .* (New York, 1917), p.33].
2. See: *Reseña de Sucesos Antisemitas* Jan–Feb 1985 p. 3 and *Boletín de Sucesos e Incidentes Antisemitas* 27 (March, 1976):3. In 1983, of the 260 antisemitic incidents reported in Latin America, 151 occurred in Argentina, and in 1984, 89 out of 151. The total number of incidents recorded in Latin America from 1970–1975 reached 628 and in North America – 167.
3. See the minutes of the *Asociacion Israelita de Beneficencia, Rosario* Libro de Actas No. 1, Acta No. 186, Jan. 16, 1919, p.283. The fear that gripped the Jewish community of Rosario still was evident a few months later when, in preparation for the national holiday in May, flyers appeared in the city streets "calling to order" the leftists, the foreigners, and especially *the Russians.* At that time, the community leaders even devised a strategy for defense against possible attacks. See ibid., meeting No. 188 of May 8, 1919, p.288.
4. Nathan Gezang to the Jewish National Fund at The Hague, January 31, 1919, *The Central Zionist Archives, Jerusalem, Z3/770.*
5. *Die Juedische Rundschau,* May 13, 1919.
6. *The Annual Register: A Review of Public Events, Home and Abroad for the Year 1919* (London, 1920), p.290. The United States' Ambassador in Buenos Aires, Frederic Jessup Stimson, in 1931 still wrote of the Bolshevik plot which had been thwarted in Argentina thanks to the army's intervention. Quoted by Victor Mirelman, "The Semana Trágica and the Jews in Argentina," *Jewish Social Studies,* 37 (1975):65.
7. Sebastián Marotta, *El Movimento Sindical Argentino, su Génesis y Desarrollo,* 2 (Buenos Aires, 1961).
8. Octavio A. Piñero, *Los Orígenes de la Trágica Semana de Enero de 1919* (Buenos Aires, 1956) as well as the book of another police official, José Romariz, *La Semana Trágica: Relato de los Hechos Sangrientos del Año 1919* (Buenos Aires, 1952).
9. Diego Abad de Santillan, *La FORA: Ideología y Trayectoria del Movimiento Obrero Revolucionario en la Argentina* (Buenos Aires, 1933).
10. Félix Luna, *Yrigoyen* (Buenos Aires, 1964); Gabriel del Mazo, *El Radicalismo: Ensayo para su Historia y Doctrina* (Buenos Aires, 1967).
11. Julio Godio, *La Semana Trágica de Enero de 1919* (Buenos Aires, 1972).
12. P. (Pinie-Pedro) Wald, *Koshmar* (Yiddish) (Buenos Aires, 1929); "Los Judios en la Semana Trágica" ("Jews in the Tragic Week") (Yiddish, with Spanish summary), *Argentiner YIVO Shriftn* 4 (Buenos Aires, 1947):5–55.
13. Nahum Solominsky, *La Semana Trágica* (Buenos Aires, 1971).
14. Victor A. Mirelman, *The Jews in Argentina, 1890–1930: Assimilation and Particularism* (Ph.D., Columbia University) (New York, 1973), pp.91–101 as well as his article, above n. 6).

15. Three examples of this: a. the author of the article on the presidency of Hipolito Yrigoyen in the multi-volume work on the history of modern Argentina of the National Academy of History, does not mention the Jews at all and swallows whole the revolutionary uprising version. Arturo Capdevila, "Primera Presidencia de Yrigoyen," in *Historia Argentina Contemporánea* 1, 2nd Sec. (Buenos Aires, 1963), ch. 15, p.257. b. In the classic volume by José Luis Romero, the event are mentioned in foggy fashion and without an explicit mention of the attacks on the Jews. See: Jose Luis Romero, *A History of Argentine Political Thought* (Stanford, 1963), p.224. c. Arthur Whitaker, one of the most important American researchers, took a similar course. See: Arthur Whitaker, *Argentina* (Eglewood Cliffs, N.J., 1964) p.74.

16. The "Association," which had been established in 1918, brought together the heads of the commercial market, the association of land owners, the grain exporters, the shipping company owners, representatives of the railroad companies, etc. Many of the economic enterprises represented by these corporations were owned by foreigners, primarily British. The university youth organization was right-wing. Prominent among the clergy was the spiritual leader of the Catholic workers' circles, Miguel de Andrea; see: Julio Godio, *La Semana Trágica*, pp.179–181; Victor Mirelman, *The Jews in Argentina*, pp.97–100. Later, Bishop de Andrea was outstanding in his democratic struggle and his sympathy for the State of Israel, which he visited in 1954. Upon his death, in 1960, he was eulogized by the leaders of the Argentine Jewish community as "a friend of the Jewish people." (*Mundo Israelita*, June 25, 1960, p.3.)

17. This is detailed in both of Pinie Wald's works (n. 12 above).

18. See: Julio Godio, *La Semana Trágica*, p.79 and also Beatriz Seibel, "La Semana Trágica: Recopilatión de Documentos," *Crisis* (Buenos Aires) 21 (enero 1975):69. The American Ambassador is quoted by Victor Mirelman in his article "The Semana Trágica."

19. See Nathan Gezang's report, n. 4 above.

20. See the article "Vida Neustra" quoted by Nahum Solominsky, *La Semana Trágica*, p.40.

21. See: Julio Godio, *La Semana Trágica*, p.101.

22. See: *Vida Neustra* II, No. 8 (Febrero 1919): 169. General Dellepiane's answer to a survey conducted among public figures on their attitude toward the Jews; and see Nahum Solominsky, op. cit., pp.39–40 on the police commander's praise of the "White Guards".

23. See the report of the meeting in *La Prensa*, Jan. 26, 1919 and in that day's daily Yiddish press, *Die Presse* and *Yiddishe Zeitung*.

24. For the most recent research see Leonardo Senkman, *El Antisemitismo en la Argentina*, 1–2 (Buenos Aires, 1986). It analyzes the periods of the constitutional regimes between 1959 and 1975. For earlier publications see Juan José Sebreli, *La cuestión judia en la Argentina* (Buenos Aires, 1971) which is an anthology of sources and studies, some of which are quoted extensively by Robert Weisbrot, *The Jews of Argentina from the Inquisition to Peron* (Philadelphia, 1979), chap. 8.

25. On the attempts at an ideologically tinted historical interpretation of Argentine antisemitism, see Israel Viñas, "Los Judíos y la sociedad Argentina," in *Controversia de ideas sionistas* (Buenos Aires, 1983), pp.70–112; and also Juan José Sebreli, *La cuestion judía* , pp.223–255; and see Haim Avni, "Anti-Semitism in Latin America after the Yom Kippur War: A New Departure?", in *World Jewry and the State of Israel*, ed. M. Davis (New York, 1977), pp.53–82.

26. See *Vida Neustra* II, No. 9 (Marzo 1919), the Jewish monthly's summary.

23

Hungarian Antisemitism: Ideology and Reality (1920–1943)

NATHANIEL KATZBURG

1. The Political Background

The year 1920 marks the beginning of the new Hungarian régime which was established after the revolutions which shook the country in 1918–1919. In the early 1920s the new régime was consolidated and it retained that form until the German occupation in March 1944. During this entire period Admiral Miklós Horthy was the head of State.[1] Constitutionally, Hungary remained a kingdom, but its rulers—the kings of the House of Hapsburg—were stripped of the monarchy, and the royal privileges and responsibilities were bestowed upon Horthy, as regent.

In the period between the two wars, Hungary was immersed in a deep sense of the national disaster which had befallen the country after World War I and the peace treaties which followed it. The lion's share of the lands of the prewar Hungarian kingdom was taken from it and ceded to the neighboring countries – some of them new, like Czechoslovakia to the north and Yugoslavia to the south, and some of them countries which were considerably extended at Hungary's expense, like Romania, to the east. This experience of national disaster accompanied the Hungarians throughout the 1920s and 1930s and shaped their political thought. The hope of revising the peace treaties was the main impetus of Hungary's political orientation and, from the mid-1930s, pushed her toward rapprochement with Italy and Germany.

The national catastrophe of the disintegration of the old kingdom was associated in the consciousness of the Hungarians with the further experience and tribulation which occurred close upon the end of the war – the Communist régime. This régime, to be sure, lasted only about four months, but it had a decisive influence upon the image of the order which arose in Hungary after the régime was smashed and upon Hungary's internal policy. The hatred for com-

339

munism and anything associated with it was one of the characteristic features of the Hungarian régime between the two wars. This also had a Jewish aspect for, as is well known, there were numerous Jews among the leaders of the communist revolution in Hungary. What caused so many persons of Jewish extraction to play so prominent a role in Hungarian communism[2] is beyond the scope of the present discussion; what is important to our subject is that in the eyes of the society at large communism was the work of the Jews. Ignoring the complexities of the political and social circumstances which gave rise to the 1918–1919 revolutions, and employing superficial generalizations, Hungarians put the blame on the Jews for the passing of the old régime. This had an immense impact on Hungary's Jewish policy throughout the interwar period. Therefore, when we deal with the Jewish question and antisemitism in Hungary in the period between the two wars, we must remember the communist experience of the Hungarians and the Jewish associations which accompanied that experience and could not be divorced from it.

2. The Numerus Clausus Law

As the title of this paper indicates, ideology and reality in Hungarian antisemitism went hand in hand; and reality here means acts of legislation by means of which the antisemitic outlooks and attitudes were put into actual practice. This was already evident at the beginning of the period in the *Numerus Clausus* law enacted in 1920 and designed to limit the admission of Jews to institutions of higher learning.[3] The formal motivation for this legislation was that because of the territorial shrinkage of prewar Hungary, many fewer professionals were needed than before and therefore there must be a limitation of student admissions to the universities; this to be accomplished by establishing a system of quotas. As the law stipulated: "The number of students of different races and nationalities shall be in proportion to the number of such races and nationalities in the country." Accordingly, the Jewish share was set at five percent, their proportional part of the population.

The true motivation for this legislation, however, was the part played by Jews in the postwar revolutions, and especially the prominent number of intellectuals of Jewish origin. The *Numerus Clausus* law, then, was intended to limit severely the entrance of Jews to the professions and the intellectual life. From here on, the goal was, on the one hand to "punish" the Jews for their role in the revolution and, on the other, to decrease the number of Jewish intellectuals likely to engage in revolutionary activities. But beyond the practical aspect, there was another side to the limitations which this legislation placed upon the Jews. For several years past, especially from the second decade of the century, Jewish intellectuals had come under attack for their allegedly negative role in the national culture. They were charged with disseminating destructive ideas such as liberalism, socialism, and cosmopolitical ideas, and thus exerting a baneful and corrupting influence on the morals and spiritual life of the non-Jewish society. In prewar Hungary there was little chance that such agitation would result in any practical steps to remove Jews from intellectual life. In the early postwar years, however, the time was ripe for such measures when the revolutionary activities of Jewish intellectuals provided a suitable ground for taking measures to eliminate the Jewish influence in the culture.

Numerus Clausus was of significance not only for Hungarian Jews but for Jewry as a whole, for it was feared, and with good reason, that other countries would follow Hungary's example and legislate similarly. To deter any such measure in other countries, the Jewish organizations in the western countries embarked upon an international political struggle against the Hungarian *Numerus Clausus*. In the forefront of this struggle stood British Jewry's Jewish Joint Foreign Committee of the Board of Deputies and the Anglo-Jewish Association[4] and the *Alliance Israelite Universelle*. The two bodies complained against Hungary at the League of Nations[5], and after years of discussions the law was amended in 1928. To be sure, anti-Jewish discrimination was not eliminated completely but those elements in the law which had stirred harsh complaint, especially among Hungary's assimilated Jews, such as their being defined as a race and nation for the purposes of the law were.

Two principal points must be noted in the intervention and international activity of the Jewish organizations: Their intervention was without the consent of the leadership of Hungarian Jewry. The latter argued that the law is a matter between themselves and their government which they expect to correct by their own activity without external intervention. The Jewish organizations, which generally refrained from acting on behalf of a Jewish community without the latter's consent, in this instance adopted a different course based on the premise that Hungarian Jews are not at liberty in this matter, that is, that they are subject to governmental pressure to abort foreign intervention. The second principal matter – perhaps even more important than the first – is that the activity of the organization was successful in bringing about a certain change in the Hungarian government's position. This success is attributable, on the one hand, to the persistence of the two organizations and, on the other, to Hungary's position in the 1920s, when it was in need of the good will of the international community, especially of the western countries, for its economic and political rehabilitation.

3. Components of Hungarian Antisemitism

The ideology of Hungarian antisemitism between the two wars had two basic elements: the coupling of nationalism and Jew-hatred, and the attempt to introduce the racial principle.

Hungarian nationalism was not prominent in the antisemitism of the nineteenth and early twentieth century.[6] In that period, antisemitism was mainly professed by the German minority, especially the German urban bourgeoisie, and the Catholic, pro-Hapsburg, political circles. On the other side, the Hungarian nationalists favored the absorption of the Jews, for they strengthened the Magyar element in the kingdom, almost half of whose entire population were of non-Magyar nations. In postwar Hungary there were almost no national minorities; consequently this problem ceased to be an issue of importance. Jewish identification with Magyar nationalism, which had been highly valued in the multinational Hungarian kingdom, lost its political significance in the situation produced by the unitary national complexion of postwar Hungary. The carriers of antisemitism now became the right-wing nationalists, and thus antisemitism and nationalism went hand in hand. This is one of the significant characteristics of the new course of Hungarian antisemitism in the 1920s and 1930s.

A dominant component of Hungarian antisemitic ideology is its anti-Bolshevist character, and it goes without saying that in the popular image Jews and Bolshevism were synonymous. In the commonly accepted thinking of the international political reality of the 1920s, anti-Bolshevism was the accepted currency; therefore, under the anti-Bolshevik banner, the Hungarians sought to give their battle against the Jews a pan-European, international character, saying that their war upon the Jews in Hungary was a war for Europe and European civilization in order to protect them against the Bolshevik menace and its Jewish carriers. For this reason, those who espoused this ideology argued that the war against the Jews in Hungary was a struggle of universal significance and should be the concern of the entire western, Christian world. The Hungarian Right, especially the "Awakening Magyars" organization,[7] strove to act according to this conception and established connections with right-wing movements in other countries. Especially important is the close contact which the movement established with the Nazi movement in Germany, then in its early stages.[8]

Another innovation in Hungary's antisemitic ideology of the period under consideration is racism. Here too, the difference between the prewar and postwar periods is instructive. Hungary before 1914 was a multinational state, and the national Magyar interest required the submergence of the various races and ethnic groups in the Magyar nation. This interest in assimilation ceased to exist after the war; now the time was ripe to adopt the racist ideology, and antisemitic scholars and writers tried to establish a theory of a pure Magyar race. From a scholarly standpoint these theories had no basis, for even if in the distant past there had been such a race, over the thousand years of Magyar settlement in the Danube basin it had become assimilated and intermingled. Yet, in spite of the doubtful content of the "Magyar race" concept, it was accepted and was able to serve actual needs, that is, to emphasize the contrast between the Magyar race and the Semitic one.

Nationalism and racism, then, are the two basic components of the Hungarian ideology of antisemitism. From this point of view, Hungary is no different from other central and east European countries, but there are differences rooted in the political and social condition of Hungary in the interwar period.

4. "The Jewish Question"

Throughout this period there was a deep awareness within the national leadership and public opinion of the seriousness of the Jewish question. This awareness kept the Jewish question constantly on the agenda and was a cause of political and social tension. To be sure, the consciousness of the existence of a Jewish question, and even critical approaches to Jewry, do not necessarily lead to antisemitism, though they are likely to foster it and contribute to its continuation.

The sense of the gravity of the Jewish question flowed from a series of factors: The first of these was the number of Jews in relation to the total population. The Jews of Hungary in 1920 numbered 473,000 (5.9% of the population); in 1941, their number had reached 724,000 as a result of Hungary's annexation of parts of Slovakia, Carpathian Russia, and northern Transylvania. Without the annexed territories, however, the number of Jews was only about 400,000 (approximately 4.9%). In the period between the two wars, then, we find that there had been a gradual decline in the number of Jews both absolutely and relatively. However, in spite of this growing decline of the Jews demographically, the reference to their great numbers did not cease. To a certain extent, this can be attributed to the prominence of the Jews' presence. This was especially accentuated by the discernible number of Jews in the capital city, Budapest: 216,000 in 1920 (about 23%). But here too the absolute and relative Jewish decline is evident: In 1941 the capital's Jews numbered only 184,000 (15.8%). Admittedly, even this is a discernible number; and if we remember that the Jewish impact in the capital city was not only the result of their numbers but also influenced by their economic and social position, one can easily understand that the public pictured them as much more significant than was actually the case.

The awareness of the seriousness of the Jewish question fed the antisemitism, and from the mid-1930s, with the Nazi rise to power in Germany, it was reinforced in Hungary as in the other central European countries. We find this given specific attention in a letter written by the well-known Hungarian statesman Pál Teleki[9] in February 1939:

> The growth of German power and the repeated political successes of Hitler played their part of course. Many people were influenced so much that they became enthusiastic admirers of Germany and of Hitler's system. There is nothing astonishing in this; every expansive idea, every successful leader, has enthusiasts. There are still thousands of people who keep a portrait of Napoleon in their rooms. Nevertheless, Hungarian antisemitism is not simply a copy and surely not a carbon copy of German antisemitism; and surely it will never be a copy because it will never grow to such cruelty, even if the Hungarian Law[10] were made as severe as the German or even more so. It would not grow to such cruelty in conse-

quence of our temperament – I would like to say, our happily Oriental temperament.[11]

The evolution of events in Hungary during the Holocaust period proved that Teleki's prognosis did not stand the test; however his diagnosis of the influence of the Nazi example in Hungary was accurate.

This influence is seen first and foremost in the proliferation and self-assertion of the various parties and factions of the radical Right, whose common denominator was the adoption of the National-Socialist ideology. The most important of these was the Arrow Cross Party led by a former army officer, Ferenc Szálasi.[12] He developed an ideology based upon a strange mixture of Magyar mysticism and a political-social program for the restoration of the Hungarian kingdom within its ancient borders, while guaranteeing the equality of the various nations. The Jewish question did not have an important place in Szálasi's political program. The principle which he championed as far as the Jews were concerned was that they should be removed from the national Hungarian body politic. The question of course is what the concept of "removal" meant. There are those who claim that originally the intent was to see to their orderly emigration. In the view of the well-known British scholar of Hungarian history, C. A. Macartney, Szálasi was not afflicted with the same morbid antisemitism of Hitler, Streicher, or the Hungarian Endre László.[13] But the Jewish policy of the Arrow Cross should not be judged by Szálasi's early ideological tenets alone. Rather it should be assessed in the light of his party's general attitude and its record as a whole until 1945. Szálasi's underlings, the rank and file of his party, and not least, the press organs inspired by him, all disseminated throughout the country crude and unrestrained anti-Jewish propaganda. In so doing, they poisoned the political atmosphere, injected the public with an intense anti-Jewish venom, and persuaded the nation that the Jews had to be excluded from the fabric of national life. This goal was systematically implemented after the late 1930s, and the Arrow Cross and other right-wing groups played a major role in preparing the ground.

From the mid-1930s, the influence of the radical Right parties in the formulation of policy vis-à-vis the Jews is evident. The source of this influence, which grew constantly, was rooted to a large extent in the ability of those parties to attract that public opinion which was highly conscious of the Jewish question and to activate it to pressure the government on the Jewish question. However, the parties exerted pressure on the government not only from the standpoint of the Jewish question but also from an economic-social aspect. For the rightist parties were not antisemitic only; they were also antiestablishment, and almost all of them were striving to change the existing order. Therefore, from the government's point of view, it was important to neutralize the radical Right, which could be done by adopting an anti-Jewish policy which, while not fully satisfactory to the extreme right, would content those who aspired to a limitation of the Jewish position. This was the point of departure for the anti-Jewish legislation from 1938 on.

5. Anti-Jewish Legislation 1938–42

The legislation against the Jews marked a new stage in Hungarian Jewish policy. Characteristic of this stage was the fixing of a defined framework for the place of the Jews in the economy and in the society. This was the purpose of the 1938 law, entitled "For a More Effective Safeguard of Equilibrium in Social and Economic Life," commonly known as the first Jewish Law.[14] The law fixed the participation of the Jews in the economic life of Hungary and the professions at twenty percent. This was a relatively moderate law and, once promulgated, the Jews acquiesced and made their peace with it because they realized that, given the political circumstances at the time, it could have been much worse. The government, increasingly pressured by the radical Right, felt that this law would take the wind out of the antisemites' sails, that the social tension of the Jewish question would subside, and that this issue would be put to rest. However, the spirits were not calmed, and a few months after the law came into force, the government turned to the enactment of a new anti-Jewish law, more severe than its predecessor. The second law was promulgated in May 1939 and is officially called: "The law for restricting the place of the Jews in public life and in the economy." The difference in the names of these two laws is instructive. The first law speaks of a balance, and the intent ostensibly was to restore the balance which allegedly had been disturbed by the Jews' penetration of society and the economy beyond their proper extent; on the other hand, the second law speaks explicitly of restriction. But the principal innovation in the second law was that the Jews were defined by racial criteria, that is to say, the law applies not only to Jews by religion but also to Jews by origin, even though they were Christians by religion. Jewish participation in economic life was fixed by this law at six percent.

The second law created a new problem and in essence brought to the fore a problem which had existed but of which people were not aware – the problem of half, third, and quarter Jews. Estimates place about one hundred thousand in this category at the end of the 1930s. The source of this problem was in the phenomenon of intermarriages which, along with conversions, had increased rapidly from the end of the nineteenth century. The legal definition of this group as Jews was a decision of principle about the very matter of Jewish assimilation. Already in the nineteenth century the charge was being levelled at the Jews that their assimilation is only external; that inwardly, in their pattern of thought and their mentality, they remain Jews. This charge was made not only by out-and-out antisemites but also by politicians and thinkers who cannot be defined as antisemites. The second law included alike those who had accepted Christianity and those whose origin was only partly Jewish. This was a decision that vindicated the charge that Jewish assimiliation is solely external.

The second law did not placate the spirits on the question of the Jews either, for in the meantime there had been a radicalization in this matter. The source of this was the ever-increasing German influence in Europe generally, and particularly in Hungary, some of whose territorial demands had been satisfied with

German help. A second factor influencing the development of extreme opinions about the Jews was the political achievements of the extreme Right – especially of the Arrow Cross Party – in the general elections of 1939.[15] As these things developed, a new, more radical perception of the Jewish question and its solution emerged. According to this perception, the solution to the question of the Jews would be achieved by removing the Jews from the life of the society and the nation. This perception went much beyond that which underlay the anti-Jewish legislation. The legislation's purpose was to fix the place of the Jews in society and the economy, not negating the fact of their right by law to a place within the framework. In contrast, the extremist Right denied this very right and was therefore dissatisfied with the Jewish laws. When the radical Right gained political and parliamentary strength after 1939, it increased its pressure on the government for the enactment of more radical measures against the Jews. Such a measure was the 1941 Race Protection Law which forbade marriages between Jews and non-Jews. This law was a decisive step in segregating the Jews and designating them as a separate social entity.

The final piece of anti-Jewish legislation came in 1942, with the abolition of the establised status of the Jewish religion. This law rescinded that of 1895 which had granted recognition to the Jewish faith and by which the Jewish religious community enjoyed privileges similar to those of the Christian Churches, such as representation in the upper house of Parliament and government support of education and welfare institutions. The Law abolishing the established status of the Jewish confession was designed to legalize an already existing situation whereby Jewish equality was practically annulled. While this law had no direct effect on Jews as individuals, as it was concerned with communities as such, nevertheless it was not without indirect effect on their members. Now that state aid was withdrawn, the financial burden on the communities and on the national Jewish bodies increased. And it should be noted in this context that, owing to the war, no aid was forthcoming from abroad.

6. Before the Holocaust

Antisemitism and anti-Jewish legislation had far-reaching effects on the fate of the Hungarian Jews under the Holocaust. Antisemitic ideology, which had permeated all levels of society, provided the political and moral justification for the attitude of nonintervention and the passive stance of the greater part of Hungarian society in the fateful summer months of 1944 when Hungarian Jews were deported. In the first stage of this process, the Jews were segregated and isolated from the general population. The conditions for segregation had already been prepared, step by step, by the anti-Jewish laws and other measures enacted between 1938 and 1943. During those years Hungarian Jewry had in fact gradually been relegated to a politically and socially separate community, governed by discriminatory laws. The first step had been to restrict Jewish participation in the economy and the professions. This was accomplished in two stages: the first moderate (the first Jewish Law), the second more severe (the second Jewish Law). Then followed social exclusion, through the Race Protection Law, which stigmatized Jews as elements harmful to both the Hungarian nation and the Magyar race. Thereafter, the last remnant of equality had been removed by the abolition of the established status of the Jewish confession. To these measures was added the labor service, which classified Jews in an inferior category with regard to national service and was, at the same time, a punitive measure. The result was that by the time of the German occupation, Hungarian Jews had already been excluded from major areas of national life. The measures taken after the occupation, such as the compulsory wearing of the Yellow Star and the concentration in ghettos, were therefore logical sequences of principal policies and legislation enacted previously.

Segregation was followed by deportation. This, too, was the product of the evolution of the Hungarian conception of the Jewish problem and its solution. The prevailing view in the 1930s was that the Jewish problem was primarily a socio-economic issue, to which the appropriate solution was the limitation of the proportion of Jews in particular occupations. The very existence of Jews in Hungary was not questioned at this stage. The second Jewish Law, which also provided for Jewish emigration, did indicate a shift of attitude, but not a radical transformation. Only with the forceful emergence of the extreme Right in 1939 did the challenge to a continued Jewish existence in Hungary attain prominence. Thereafter, however, the notion of total Jewish expulsion from the country gained rapid and wide acceptance. It is significant that this view, hitherto advocated almost exclusively by the extreme Right, now gained adherents in senior government quarters as well. As much was indicated by Prime Minister Teleki's reference to the removal of Jews from Europe during his talk with Hitler in 1940.[16] From now on, subsequent Hungarian governments referred from time to time to the deportation of the Jews as an eventual solution. Thus, though deportations on a large scale did not commence in Hungary until 1944, the idea of such a measure had gradually permeated the public mind from 1940 on and had become acceptable.

The continuity of antisemitic theory and practice in Hungary from the early 1920s up to and including the Holocaust is one of the characteristic signs of Jew-hatred in this country; and it is this continuity which gained Hungarian antisemitism its place among the enemies of the Jews in Europe in the period between the wars.

Notes

1. See N. Katzburg, *Hungary and the Jews 1920–1943* (Ramat Gan, 1981) (= *Hungary and the Jews*); *The Confidential Papers of Admiral Horthy*, eds. M. Szinai and L. Szücs (Budapest, 1965). The survival of these papers was unknown to Horthy when he wrote his memoirs – Nicholas Horthy, *Memoirs* (London, 1956) – which contain several references to the Jewish question.
2. See William O. McCagg, Jr., "Jews in Revolutions: the Hungarian Experience," *Journal of Social History* 6(1972):78–105.

3. *Hungary and the Jews*, pp.60–93; Victor Karady – Istvan Kemeny, "Antisemitisme Universitaire et Concurrence de Classe: la Loi du *numerus clausus* en Hongrie entre les deux Guerres," *Actes de la Recherche en sciences sociales* 34(1980):67.

4. The Committee's secretary, Lucien Wolf (1857–1930) was the moving spirit in the struggle against the Hungarian *Numerus Clausus* law.

5. For the petitions and other relevant material concerning the intervention with the League of Nations, see *The Jewish Minority in Hungary* (London, 1926).

6. On nineteenth century Hungarian antisemitism, see Jacob Katz, *From Prejudice to Destruction: Anti-Semitism 1700–1933* (Cambridge, Mass., 1980), chs. 20 and 24.

7. The principal political and military organization of the extreme right in Hungary in the 1920s. It stood behind the White Terror and was the main bearer of antisemitism in that period; see *Hungary and the Jews*, pp.41–46.

8. The connections between the Hungarian and German extreme right-wing movements go back to the early 1920s; see Johann Weidlein, *Die ungarische Antisemitismus*, (Schorndorf, 1962), pp.39–42. The "Awakening Magyars" also strove to spread their ideology in the western countries, and published a pamphlet entitled *Antisemitism in Hungary* Budapest, 1920). This is a printed memorandum presented by the Association to the representatives of Britain and the United States in Budapest.

9. Count P. Teleki (1879–1941) was prime minister in 1920–1921, when the *Numerus Clausus* Law had been enacted, and again in 1939–1941. For his views on Jews and the Jewish question, see *Hungary and the Jews*, pp.133–136.

10. The reference is to the Second Jewish Law (see below), which was then debated in Parliament. Teleki participated in its preparations and drafted its preamble. The Law was enacted when he was prime minister.

11. The letter, dated February 13, 1939, was published in *Soviet Jewish Affairs* 2(November, 1971):105–111. The quotation appears on p.107.

12. Born in 1899, Szálasi was put on trial as a war criminal and executed in 1946.

13. C. A. Macartney, *October Fifteenth: A History of Modern Hungary 1929–1945*. 1(Edinburgh, 1957), p.165. Endre was secretary of state in the Ministry of the Interior after the German occupation and directed the ghettoization and subsequent deportation of the provincial Jewry. After the war he was tried and executed.

14. On this and the Jewish laws which followed, see *Hungary and the Jews*, chs. 5–8.

15. In the 1939 general elections the Arrow Cross Party gained 42 out of 260 mandates, and together with other right-wing groups, the extreme right parties in Parliament totalled 49 mandates. They received their votes mainly from workers and the lower middle class.

16. It took place in Vienna on November 20, 1940, when Hungary joined the Tripartite Pact of Germany, Italy and Japan. See *Documents on German Foreign Policy*, Series D vol. 11, p. 635.

24

On the Character of Nazi Antisemitism

YISRAEL GUTMAN

1. Introduction

It is well known that in the study of the phenomenon of antisemitism it is relatively easy to gather the factual details, that is, to trace the outbreaks of antisemitism and ascertain the immediate cause of its outbreaks; but it is very difficult to penetrate to the roots of the hatred as a continuous historical phenomenon, to understand its *élan vital* and its persistence through changing times and political systems. And as for many generations antisemitism has been accompanied by many extraordinary and shocking manifestations, how much more difficult is it to shed light upon the phenomenon of National Socialism, a radical antisemitic-racist doctrine which was adopted by a populist party and became the guiding and dominant concept in a very highly cultured, twentieth-century central European country. This hatred did not remain theoretical nor confined only to a set of discriminatory laws which nullified the gains of the Emancipation and equality; it resulted in death and destruction unprecedented in Israel's long history of exile among the nations.

We shall not deal here with the various modern research methods employed by different disciplines such as the dynamics of psychology and sociology to find the answer to the sources and essence of antisemitism. Without underestimating the motivating factors indicated by the social scientists, and even assuming their special significance in modern life and the social situation which spawned National Socialism, they cannot provide a definitive, comprehensive answer; at best they can shed some light on one or another aspect of this complex historical phenomenon.[1]

It is natural for an historian seeking the origins of ideas that have existed for hundreds of years, and have been a powerful motivation for dramatic events and intergroup relationships, to examine historical developments. To an historian it is basic and self-evident that one cannot separate National Socialist Jew-hatred from that which had been shaped over the ages. Yet it appears that not only those scholars studying the subject from a sociological perspective, but also certain historians conclude that Nazi antisemitism, in decisive measure, was a reaction to the contradictions and dissatisfaction evident in German society since the middle of the previous century. They totally, or almost totally, ignore the heritage of the conflict between Christianity and Judaism and the later stages in the development of antisemitism. Thus, for example, the German historian, Friedriech Meinecke, in the short section which he devotes to the Jews and antisemitism in his work on *Die deutsche Katastrophe* ("The German Catastrophe"), written toward the end of his life, claims:

> The Jews, who were inclined to enjoy indiscretely the favorable economic situation now smiling upon them, had since their full emancipation aroused resentment of various sorts. They contributed much to that gradual depreciation and discrediting of the liberal world of ideas that set in after the end of the nineteenth century. The fact that besides their negative and disintegrating influence they also achieved a great deal that was positive in the cultural and economic life of Germany was forgotten by the mass of those who now attacked the damages done by the Jewish character. Out of the anti-Semitic feeling it was possible for an anti-liberal and anti-humanitarian feeling to develop easily – the first steps toward National-Socialism.[2]

Another German historian of repute, Gerhard Ritter, does not blame the Jews for their easy and ostentatious wealth, but argues for the existence of an "instinctive hate" of the Jews. In his opinion, these "instincts" were stronger in Germany than in the other western European countries but, on the other hand, were not as strong as in Eastern Europe. This hatred became politically linked even prior to 1914 but the antisemitic movements of that period were short-lived in the postwar period, however, antisemitism became strong again due to many aggravating circumstances, especially the immigration of eastern European Jews, which helped in the formulation of National Socialism.[3]

Hannah Arendt, in her book *The Origins of Totalitarianism*, attacks the premise of the existence of perpetual antisemitism, with the Jews as the permanent scapegoat. To her, modern antisemitism is a result of a decline in the importance of the national state, the competition of the Jews and the middle class in the developed nations of Europe, and also of the fact that the Jews are a propertied group but lacking political power and authority; all of which, according to Arendt, attracts the scorn and hate of the masses.[4] In his essay *The Non-Jewish Jew*, Deutscher claimed that Marx was right in defining the Jews as "the bearer of the money-economy," the . . . "Jewish religion as the religious reflection of a bourgeois thought process," and he saw the essence of the tragedy in that "as a result of long historical development, the European masses were used to identifying the Jews, above all, as a nation of commerce, stock-market brokering, money-lending, and the amassing of money."[5] Incidentally, Deutscher does not stop at determining the factors which nurtured antisemitism, but also says that antisemitism and the Holocaust pushed the Jews in the erroneous direction of seeking an escape from their situation by establishing a national state of their own. Though, he feels, they are not to be blamed for this longing, a result of the wrong done them by the world, the reality of the times in which the Jews have begun to build their state – when the day of the national state is over, when the national state is declining and crumbling and retrogressive in character – dictates that the Jews are devoting themselves to their national independence and are enthusiastic about it despite the fact that "from an historical point of view it is obsolete."[6] Throughout the essay, Deutscher discusses Jewish radicals and those of Jewish origin such as Marx, Lassalle, Luxemburg, Trotsky, and even Freud and others whose intellectual lives and personal identities were formed, as he puts it, on the frontiers between nationalistic cultures and groupings. This gave them the ability to see the long view and move society forward away from all the limitations of conservative, particularistic frameworks. He goes on to analyze the causes of antisemitism and the Holocaust and points out lessons, erroneously as it were; but he does not bother to note, nor even hint, that a number of his heroes caused inestimable harm to their compatriots, the Jewish nation, which they often reviled and, at best, completely denied. This avoidance is characteristic. In the eyes of their detractors, these revolutionaries who pretended to be saviors of mankind remained Jews and, albeit unintentionally, added a very significant and powerful dimension to modern antisemitism and the Jewish tragedy in Europe.

Is there a common denominator in these various conceptions briefly reviewed here and, if so, what is it? Meinecke does not feel that after the Emancipation the Jews ceased being a separate human entity in the German state, and does not see that the attempt to indicate them as a separate and different body in circumstances of complete equality, as it were, is a flaw from the liberal point of view. Furthermore, Meinecke attributes provocative characteristics and actions to the Jews; and even though, in his opinion, the masses ignored certain positive aspects of the Jews' activities in Germany, the hatred was a reaction based upon real, negative foundations and was reinforced by a fortuitous conjunction of circumstances. Both Arendt and Deutscher – though they start from different yet not dissimilar points of view – describe the Christian-Jewish confrontation as a conflict against a background of real socioeconomic events and developments in which the Jew played a negative or subordinate role.

And yet, the radical antisemitic claims which gave modern antisemitism its zealous, terroristic nature, such as racism, a description of all Jews as a group of conspirators scheming to gain control of the world under the leadership of the "Elders of Zion" or by the dissemination of radical ideas, revolutionary chaos, and communism – these claims are rooted in the realm of fantasy, not in a framework of concrete social conflicts. This does not mean that there is no reality to the economic competition between Jews and non-Jews or that it is of no consequence in the development of antisemitism. There is also no ignoring the specific traits of the Jews or their dealings which are liable to cause anti-Jewish sentiments. But all of these in no way whatever provide the basis for the ideational load, the dynamics and the ruthless force of National Socialism's hatred. There is no doubt that the ideas upon which the picture of the Jews was based in Nazi eyes, their dissemination and their power, were not restricted to contemporary conflicts but drew upon inciting motifs and libels of the past.

Hitler's excellent biographer, Allen Bullock, defines the Nazi leader's antisemitism, which all agree was decisive in the shaping and spread of National Socialist hatred of the Jews, as follows:

> In all of the pages which Hitler devotes to the Jews in "Mein Kampf" he does not bring forward a single fact to support his wild assertions. This was entirely right, for Hitler's anti-Semitism bore no relation to facts. It was pure fantasy; to read these pages is to enter the world of the insane, a world peopled by hideous and distorted shadows.[7]

Occasionally one hears among Jews and non-Jews alike that the Holocaust – and perhaps the entire National Socialist period – is a deviation in European history, an eclipse, a madness which struck the modern world. True, this thesis is not generally put forth by people involved with historical analysis, but it has made its way in popular perceptions and in fiction. Not long ago I chanced upon an official publication, guidelines for information officers in the Israel Defense Force, containing two approaches – historical and metahistorical – one alongside the other, as legitimate ways to explain the essence of the Holocaust period.[8] From this point of view, it makes no difference whether one tends to attribute the ahistorical dimension of the Holocaust to the murderous manifestations of its perpetrators, or tends to see the fate of the victims and their sufferings as a phenomenon which should be excluded from the regular historical process. In either case, from this point of view the period is described as an event outside of human history and society. It is impossible to understand the sources, nor is there any point in trying to understand them or the background to the development of the events and ideas which led to the catastrophe; there is no lesson to be learned from what happened during that period, not for the Jew nor for contemporary society.

In other, rarer, instances, one hears a hint of "justification and acceptance of the judgment" coming from those who are searching for the theological meaning of the period or clinging to rigidly deterministic explanations. I do not intend to go further into such views or dwell upon those explanations which see the Holocaust with all of its horrors as containing a purpose hidden from the human mind. In my view, such interpretation deprives human beings of a conscious, active role in the adventures of their lives and determination of their destiny, and turns not only the victims themselves but the murderers as well into instruments moved by power orchestrating processes beyond our understanding.

2. Why the Holocaust was not Foreseen

From time to time, even people guided by an historical approach question whether Nazi antisemitism is only a stage in the evolution of antisemitism, or if we are perhaps facing a reality which, though it grew and came to fruition against an historical background, has a nature and dimensions which allot it a place apart and is essentially unique. Ben-Zion Dinur, in one of his works, brings us a sketch of "Five Beginnings from the Day of Mourning and Outcry" in which a philosopher, a Hasid, an historian, an author, and a soldier participate. The historian in the group, who undoubtedly expresses Dinur's opinion, says, among other things:

> Did this evil really come upon us suddenly? Have we not for generation after generation been sitting upon smoking volcanos, and every time the earth quakes beneath us and the volcanos spew forth their flame which destroys us, we stand shocked and dumb-founded, because we shut our eyes to seeing and proclaim loudly again and again that the volcanos are long extinct, that it is not smoke issuing from their craters but rather the morning mists which cover them and are no danger at all? "Suddenly!" Is this the first frightful holocaust which has come upon us in the thousands of years of our exile and wanderings? Did not great Jewish centers fall "suddenly" and cover with their ruins hundreds upon hundreds of thousands of Jews, old and young, women and children – who became as if they had never been? Did not these centers, by their fall, seal the chapter of the life's works and soulful tribulations of tens of Jewish generations who entombed their bodies and souls in the walls of "Pithom and Raamses" throughout the world? . . . [9]

One can conclude from Dinur's words that he sees the history of the Jewish people in exile as a recurring drama of delusion and destruction, toil and servitude in foreign fields with eyes closed to the horror lying in ambush. Therefore, the Holocaust is just another manifestation in the dialectic process of slumber and sudden awakening which always takes its toll of innumerable victims and possessions amassed through the generations. And though there are many who subscribe to the view of Jewish postexilic history as the rise and fall of population centers which adapt and are self-confident until the outbreak of wrath and ruin caused by their non-Jewish neighbors – the question remains as to whether Dinur's bitter and sharp indictment of his compatriots for not having sensed the approaching Holocaust of our time is not more an expression of searing pain in face of the immense catastrophe and loss than a sober, systematic analysis. It has already been noted that the breast-beating and the attributions of blindness and guilt are in great measure the result of shock and an attempt at hasty soul-searching. [10] It has been proved that wise distant observers, as well as those actually in the countries affected by the Holocaust, did not foresee nor imagine what the future held, and certainly did not conceive of programmed and unrestrained murder. A Dutch historian, Louis de Jong, who has been dealing for years with his country's history during the war and the Nazi occupation, noted that "for most people the Nazi extermination camps became a psychological reality – and even this not yet entirely – when they ceased to exist and perhaps precisely for that reason."[11] Dinur himself wrote, after dealing with the character of World War II as a total war which caused an immense loss of life and destruction:

> Nevertheless, what happened to us is unique and totally different. Something unprecedented in the world. It had never before happened that "open season" should be publicly proclaimed upon the blood of an entire people. In front of the entire world we were read out of the human race. In front of the entire world we were taken out to death and destruction by every manner and means. Let us see things as they are and let us not blur them. This is not like anything that ever happened in the darkest days of the Middle Ages of which the German chroniclers write simply and succinctly: "In this year all the Jews in all the cities of all of Germany were burnt."[12]

At the opening of the Eichmann trial in Jerusalem, Salo Baron stated as the considered opinion of an expert historian:

> . . . that the Nazi movement not only turned the wheels back, that is, the wheels of modern progress which championed greater emancipation, greater freedom, and greater equality, but it brought the world new and unprecedented fundamentals different from the entire two-thousand-and-more year history of antisemitism.[13]

Whereas Jacob Katz pointed out that as the information about what was taking place in the ghettos and the death camps filtered out to the free world:

> . . . it penetrated the world's consciousness that we were facing events far beyond the limits of our old concepts garnered from history. For Auschwitz and Treblinka there were no historical parallel, nor was there any related philosophical or theological system able to encompass and abosrb them.[14]

The German historian, K. D. Bracher, notes that *"Die Judenpolitik des Dritten Reiches ist ein Phänomen sui generis."*[15]

Let us now see what the factors were that prevented the contemporaries from sensing the approaching storm and danger. First, one must consider the fact that the evil came out of Germany. It is well known that racist and political antisemitism had struck root in Germany and spread. It is common practice now, after the fact, to collect opinions and slogans and trace the antisemitic legislation in Germany, and the impression is of a unidirectional line of development, becoming increasingly acute until its climax in the Nazi régime. Furthermore, those who have retraced the growth of anti-Jewish manifestations in Germany have found that the programs proposed by the earlier extreme antisemites already included all the elements later carried out in the National Socialist campaign of persecution: discrimination, expulsion, and eventual extermination. [16] On the other hand, scholars expert in German history have often claimed that the prominence of antisemitism, especially in its racist form, as a fixed and growing component of German culture and political thought, does not reflect the complex and multifaceted reality and offers a simplistic picture instead of explaining complex facts and development. And indeed, the political map of Germany during the Weimar Republic and the years prior to the Third Reich was marked by the radicalization of both the Right, with the increase of National Socialist power, and of the Left, with the strengthening of communism. The very fact that the Nazis rejected and concealed important parts of German culture and erased the names of its creators because, as they put it, they were foreign to the German spirit, is indicative of the selective, purposive system which adopted only that which agreed with, or at least did not contradict, the Nazis' conceptual world. It is doubtful that, prior to the forceful rise of National Socialism, antisemitism can be considered to have been a dominant factor in Germany's conceptual and cultural spectrum, with the exception of marginal groups. One must also bear in mind the great gap between the verbal slogans and crude expressions of scurrilous antisemite literature and the systematic acts of murder of the Nazis. Shaul Esh, in his article "Between Discrimination and Extermination," pointed out that there are investigators and writers who have found "proofs of the extermination idea" in Germany and Austria as early as the first half of the nineteenth century, and notes in connection with these manifestations:

> We suspect that all of those digging that deeply for antisemitism – even the most bitter and extreme of its expressions – tend to ignore the vast difference between words and thoughts on the one hand, and programs worked out to the last detail, on the other. [17]

On the same matter, Jacob Katz writes:

> It is not only the half-century which separates Dühring from Hitler but also the psychological abyss between the man of the spirit, cut off from the world of action, giving free play to his thoughts and illusions, and a wilful, unbridled person prepared to realize these fantasies. [18]

From German society we turn to the German Jews. The Jews of Germany, perhaps more than any other Jewish group in Europe, were prepared to pay a very high price for emancipation. Most of them had left their traditional life-style and blurred their identity and heritage in order to be full Germans. These changes which took place among the German Jews should be seen not only as a reaction to outside pressures or as an acceptance under duress of conditions imposed as prerequisites to equal rights, but also, and perhaps primarily so, as an honest desire to be absorbed into the German nation and its culture. Ludwig Bamberger thought that "The Jews did not reach, nor even approximate, so great a measure of a common life and identification with any people as they did with the Germans. They were thoroughly 'Germanized' not only in Germany but far beyond its borders."[19] "The unfortunate love of the Jews for Germany and its culture" was famous, and when the Nazi period took hold, there were not a few instances of suicide as a result of frustration and inability to accept the expulsion from participation in German national life. Orthodox Jewry, which had sought to preserve the tenets of the faith and the Jewish way of life, was also outstanding in its civic loyalty, and demonstrated a very close connection with German nationalism and loyalty to German interests. Analyzing the pro-tracted Jewish-German symbiosis, at a 1966 conference in Brussels dealing with the complex of post-Holocaust relationships between the Jews and the Germans, Professor Baron said: "For a thousand years, the German and Jew-ish peoples were so closely related that despite the injuries and suspicions, they are seen as twins in the eyes of the historian."[20]

Paradoxically, Germany was seen by the Jews of other lands, especially by the east European Jews, as a country in which the Jewish position was sound both economically and socially, where all were accustomed to obeying the law and respecting it. Therefore, not only was full confidence placed in the legal position which the Jews had achieved in Germany as a fact of life, but the prevalent opinion among Jews was that the process of expanding the dimension of equality and rights was constant, progressive, and irreversible. The at-tempts to block or impinge upon Jewish rights were seen as the necessary birth-pangs of the historical development of emancipation, or as temporary reversals ultimately doomed to failure. The Jews tended to adopt liberal ideolo-gies and placed their trust in liberal principles even when forces championing freedom of the individual, liberalism, and justice were clearly in retreat.

It is true that most of the known antisemitic spokesmen during the period of political antisemitism, such as Von Treitschke, on the one hand, and Stöcker, on the other, concentrated on levelling specific claims and accusations against the Jews: They are not fit to be part of the German culture and society and represent alien and corrosive elements; they should be removed from their positions of authority and influence in public, cultural, and economic life; the east European Jews must be prevented from pouring into the Third Reich and recent arrivals should be removed. However, they still did not dare to demand the outright repeal of Emancipation. That is to say, those who spoke openly in terms of the "expulsion" or "liquidation" of all of Germany's Jews were for the most part seen as eccentrics challenging the accepted social norms or speaking for relatively youthful circles whose extremism was rejected even by the right-wing parties which had adopted "moderate" antisemitism as part of their general platform. Many in Germany relied upon the fact that the Jewish community was declining demographically (in the eight years prior to Hitler's rise to power, for example, the number of Jews in Germany had declined by forty thousand due to a mortality rate greater than the birth rate, emigration, and the abandonment of Judaism), and that therefore the Jews were not to be seen as a troublesome problem for, in one way or another, they would disappear in the foreseeable future.

3. The Doctrine of Racism

The central component of the National Socialist ideology in general, and of the Nazi version of antisemitism in particular, is racism. This became the determining factor in their theoretical formulations and in great measure created the dynamic for the implementation stages of the anti-Jewish policy in the Third Reich and occupied countries.

Ever since the mid-nineteenth century, there has been a widespread tendency in Europe to examine individuals and define human groups and their histories according to their racial origin and separate racial essence. We know of the attempts to classify population groupings by the Social Darwinist system. In the last quarter of the nineteenth century, the followers of Herbert Spencer tried to apply the Darwinian principles of conflict in nature to their contemporary society. Such concepts were intended to provide the seal of approval and authorization for free competition, the existence of class differences, and even the neglect of disabled or hereditarily afflicted people by organized society and its institutions. Social Darwinism also granted imperialists the desired legitimization for ruling over peoples supposedly inferior from a racist viewpoint.[21]

From an historical perspective we must clearly differentiate between racist trends intended to explain and perpetuate social contrasts and imperialistic tendencies, from historical/philosophical racist concepts in which the history of nations is the arena, and the conflict is between racial blocs struggling for material and ideational rule of the world. However, the combination of theories representing race as a determining factor in history, and racism in a perverted Darwinist version, succeeded in giving racism the weight of a theory built upon a scientific basis.

Let us now dwell briefly upon the role of the race factor in history. A few of the scholars who have investigated the introduction of racist theory into modern antisemitism have distinguished between Gobineau's concept of racism and that of its later disseminators, especially H. S. Chamberlain.[22] In his treatise on the inequality of the races, Gobineau tried to convince his readers that the French aristocracy was the outgrowth of a pedigreed racial stock superior to the country's masses and thereby was the expression of a specific tradition in France.[23] Therefore, Gobineau's racial theory had a clear class significance and sought to legitimize the extra privileges of birth and the aristocrats' authority to rule. Withal, Gobineau's claims were basically apologetic. He was aware of the fact that the Revolution had radically changed France and that there was no restoring the past, hence his brooding pessimism and his clinging to times past and gone forever. Gobineau's ideas had little response in France itself, but in Germany racism gained a circle of devout adherents.

Chamberlain's concept is different. According to him, the Germans, who constitute an admirable racial bloc, contributed the decisive share in the formation of European culture and the building of modern civilization. The racial antithesis confronting the Germans and the Aryan race are the Jews. The Jewish race is the embodiment of sterility, absence of imagination and creative force, but its ability and its wiles are directed toward undermining the position of the master race, destroying its achievements, and causing unrest and rebellion against it. According to him, in the nineteenth century there was a great penetration of Europe by Jewish elements and Jewish-Semitic domination became strong. The "Aryan" race, superior by virtue of its physical characteristics and spiritual qualities, was constrained to do battle in order to overcome the destructive influences of the Jewish race. Chamberlain sees the main danger of the modern period in the alliance of the Jews with the revolutionary radicals threatening the world. In contrast to Gobineau's spirit of resignation to the inevitable and its acceptance, the ideational motifs which Chamberlain cites as being at "the foundations of the nineteenth century" are in the nature of a call to arms for the racial forces, and contain a strong faith in the victory of the Aryan race.[24] In contrast to the apologetic strain in Gobineau, who addresses the conservative circles and their devotees, Chamberlain is seeking to recruit the masses.

Racism was not confined to discussions of the place and contribution of the races in human society and of the essential interracial contrasts. It soon became linked with people's appearance, their facial contours, the structure of their limbs, the movements of their body, and the like. George Mosse writes:

> Theories of racial distinctions were to be comprehended not only in a mystical sense; on the contrary, they could be made popular through the use of stereotypes. The Aryan was distinguished by a physical form that typified the Germanic idea of beauty; the Jew was his very opposite. Symbolically, . . . the two represented the polarization of God and the devil.[25]

Since the start of this century, following the essay contest sponsored by Alfred Krupp on the topic: "What can be learned from Darwin's theories for use in developing domestic policy and state legislation," an all-encompassing racist world-view (*Weltanschauung*) began to crystallize in Germany. This constellation was the result of a combination of components – the ideology of racism; a loose, broad interpretation of Darwinism's significance for the organization of society; and the actual application of racist concepts to the body and soul of the individual.

The innovative and most sinister aspect of racism is its attribution of fixed behavioral and psychological patterns to biological structure and identifiable biological indicators. If, indeed, the excellent and the inferior, the harmful and destructive, are carried within the body and blood of people of a defined racial origin, then there is little value in educational methods, in the concept of acquired characteristics, or in experiments of social improvement. The separation of the races and the preservation of their original form is a sort of imperative of nature which the human race must manage and direct. Human intervention working toward blending the races is liable, then, to damage the master race, diminish its value, and harm the purposes destined for it by nature.

There is no point in wasting words on the supposed scientific basis of the race doctrines developed from Gobineau to Hitler. Race is an accepted category for classifying the earth's peoples into groups with similar, defineable, physical-natural characteristics. The racial blocs were divided by anthropologists into many major classifications and subclassifications; but the attempt to attribute common characteristics and a common psyche to these blocs, though it has found a place in popular perceptions, has had little acceptance among biologists though, here and there, some have also held these opinions. A person like H. F. K. Günther, a recognized authority on Nazi racist theory, rejected the existence of "the Jewish race," whereas Hitler opened almost every discussion on Jewish matters with the assertion that the Jews are not primarily a religious community but a race.[26] There is of course nothing at all scientific or rational in attributing to the "Jewish race" concepts about the essence of morality, political and ideational outlooks, or efforts to achieve domination of the world. (Perceptions and aspirations which are completely within the realm of the conscious are acquired by people, and can have nothing hereditary about them.) These theories of moral racial characteristics are at best, mythical concepts or form a part of nationalistic, political demagoguery which has adopted such theoretical concepts as a camouflage or out of sheer ignorance. Thus there is no basis for the term "Jewish blood" which is constantly repeated in Hitler's writings and speeches and which is also used in the formulation of laws in the Third Reich. Actually, blood groups are generally spread among various racial groups and no solid proof has been found to connect physical characteristics, such as the color of hair or eyes, with blood groups. Even more is it impossible to speak of any relationship whatever between traits of the psyche in someone of a specific racial group, and the known blood groups. The concepts "Nordic" or "Semitic" do not designate racial blocs *per se* but rather linguistic groupings which share a common basis.[27] Clearly, then, "the racist *Weltanschauung*" is nothing but a hodge-podge of prejudices and pseudoscientific concepts which were exploited for evil and which penetrated historical thought, social life, and politics.

The crystallization of radical, nationalist perceptions and the spread of the racist world view were also influenced by original German thinkers, such as Spengler, who had abandoned liberalism and the striving after egalitarianism. They prophecied the "decline of the West" or, like Nietzsche, called for rebellion against the accepted norms and the Christian ethic fettering humankind, for the release of the inner impulses, and the worship of power. According to Neitzsche:

> . . . whenever the German reaches the state in which he is capable of great things, he invariably raises himself above morals! And why should he not? Now he has something new to do, viz. to command – either himself or others! But this German morality of his has not taught him how to command! Commanding has been forgotten in it.[28]

According to the racist world outlook, Judaism insinuated into the western world, mainly via Christianity but in other ways as well, beliefs and opinions on the essence of the human race, on people's accountability to their Creator and to each other, on ethical imperatives and social norms – and all of these contradict the laws of nature and the basic heritage of the "Nordic-Aryan" race. The concepts from the Book of Genesis on humanity created in God's image, on life as a sacred treasure, on mercy, and on the expectation that good will overcome evil – these were the beliefs and social perceptions which constituted the ideational common denominator of both the believers of the monotheistic faiths and the supporters of most schools of modern secular humanism. These concepts were interpreted by racism as offshoots of the alien Jewish spirit which is concerned with stifling the free and unhampered competition of humanity's racial blocs, with weakening the assurance and self-confidence of the master race, and robbing it of its preferential status on earth. The development of physical strength, courage, and a sense of mastery unfettered by mercy toward the weak and deformed as well as an affirmation of war – such views and behavior patterns constitute a return to the proper order of things as befits both innate human compulsions and instincts as well as the logical course of history.

Perfecting the world and humanity, then, according to the racist perception, demanded the removal and banishment of the Jewish influence from the arena of Europe. The racists taught that the phenomena of mixed families and sexual relations between Jews and non-Jews is a diabolical plot of the Jews who are thus attempting to damage the purity of the "Aryan" race, knowing that only the pure race is the carrier of the values and strengths which the master race embodies. Again, from a scientific point of view it has been determined that there is no such thing as a pure race and that it is a product of the racists' imagination. But the proponents of the racist theory, especially the Nazis, succeeded in forging the slogan of safeguarding racial purity and turned the Jewish threat lying in wait, as it were, for innocent young Germans, into a propaganda weapon which fired the imagination of the common people.

In sum, the conclusions of the racist doctrine led to a zealous struggle against the Jews. The Jews, as described by the racists, cannot free themselves of the accusations against them and of their faults. The possibilities of changing their vocations were barred to them if they were engaged in what was considered one of the despicable Jewish callings. They were prevented from ridding themselves of those provocative outlooks which were disseminating discontent in the poisoned nation. For the racist, there was no longer any point to the Jews' foregoing their traditional customs and adapting to the lifestyle of the environment. Even the radical and decisive step of changing one's faith – none of these could change or "improve" the Jews. On the contrary. Any step which the Jews took to distance themselves from their setting and come closer to the environment only increased the danger and was construed as a sign of tactics and scheming on their part. Since the dangerous and harmful elements in the Jews lie in their bones and blood as well as in their spirit and soul, their faults are fixed and unchangeable; they make the very physical existence of the Jews harmful and dangerous to other human beings. This definition of the Jews was the basis of the policy which led to the insane idea of total extermination in the days of the National Socialist régime.

Racism, therefore, is different from the antisemitic ideologies which preceded it. The difference is expressed not only in that it left Jews no escape. In fact, in its first stages racial antisemitism did not infect large masses, but it was outstanding for its zealousness, and its propaganda was injected in many indirect ways. When the Nazis came to power, the racist doctrine became an official article of faith as a component of the policy of the ruling party and the state institutions. At this stage, racism became a universal disease. Gobineau had given expression to a sense of contempt and rejection regarding the Slavs, but when racism found its expression via the German government, a hierarchy of nations was established in which the Germans and the nations "close to them by blood" were destined to rule and preside over the "New Order," whereas the others would be the "hewers of wood and drawers of water," with no right of national or human freedom.[29] Antisemitism, which had existed in European society for many generations, became in its most extreme and perverted version an all-inclusive doctrine destroying principles of equality among nations and the human race. Though racism, in its beginning, was a theory which included all human beings and was not clearly anti-Jewish, it has been proven beyond a doubt that only when it turned its barbs against the Jews in particular and was presented as a form of antisemitism, did it spread and acquire many faithful adherents. And, as stated, after the triumph of Nazism and especially during the war, racism became a destructive system of political ideas which threatened to undermine the foundations of the civilized world, the position of the nations, and the individual in human society.

4. Hitler's Racist Ideology

Let us now deal with the nature of the racist-antisemitic perception of Adolf Hitler. In the twenties and thirties of this century, many sought to trace the subjective motivations for the Nazi leader's blazing, obsessive hatred of the Jews. There is no conclusive evidence for the premise that contacts with Jews in the stages prior to his political rise, a searing personal injury, or disappointment in everyday life, are what kindled the zealous, constant, flame of hatred. Hitler himself, in *Mein Kampf*, claimed that he knew no Jews at first hand nor had he imbibed antisemitic feelings in his home or in his youth. According to him, this hate grew as a result of his observations as he crystallized his ideational development in Vienna. Chance encounters in the streets of the capital with Jews wearing long garments caused him to ask himself whether these are Jews; then, on second thought, whether they are Germans. As he puts it, he discovered their two-faced role, of paralyzing German-nationalist desires and introducing cosmopolitanism, which was infiltrating the Viennese central press, owned and influenced by Jews. Thus he came to understand the nature of the Jewish leadership of the Austrian Social Democratic party which managed to lead the German workers astray and harness them to foreign international political programs.[30]

Hitler's biographers think that he adopted his ideas about the Jews, and shaped his hatred of them, from his obsession with reading the cheap pamphlets and popular antisemitic gutter literature which was widespread in Vienna at the beginning of the century.[31] In any case, it may be possible, then, to give credence to Hitler's words that "in Vienna, he learned to hate the Jews."

It is generally accepted that Hitler's ideological-political teaching was eclectic, that is, that he took the main points of his doctrine from the views of others and tailored them to the social and political circumstances of his time. He succeeded in making racism part of the plank of a populist political party, thus putting antisemitism at the center of both political ideology and political action. Walther Hofer, a Swiss scholar, makes the point that "without antisemitism the entire structure of the National Socialist *Weltanschauung* collapses. The doctrine of the racial enemy belongs to National Socialism in an essential way, just as the doctrine of class struggles is identified with Bolshevism."[32] Nolte points to the fact that Hitler focused his various and contradictory accusations leveled against the Jews in the various antisemitic ideologies, and argued that their origin is in the Jewish race.[33] Many researchers have underscored the fact that Hitler adhered to antisemitism throughout his political career, from his first steps in the arena (the first political document of September 1919) until his end in beleaguered and destroyed Berlin in April 1945 (his words in his will about preserving the race, and the Jewish enemy as "the poisoner of the nations").

Hitler was often confronted by the conflict between his declared ideological principles on the one hand, and his realistic political interest on the other. In such instances he was sometimes forced to compromise or to retreat from the ideological line. This is the only way one can understand his pact with Stalin, or Japan's inclusion in the broad political-ideational coalition.[34] Only as regards the Jews and racial antisemitism was Hitler unprepared for compromise or discussion except for temporary tactical deviations, such as tempering the blatant show of antisemitism for the 1936 Olympic Games in Berlin.[35] Eberhard Jaeckel, in his work on *Hitler's Weltanschauung*, points out that after the 1923 Munich *"putsch"* and his stint in jail, a change took place in Hitler's political premises and his tactics directed toward gaining power, but "the conceptions of racial policy remained surprisingly constant."[36] In the stage prior to his gaining power and in the first years of the Third Reich, Mussolini strongly criticized Hitler's racism and his extreme antisemitism. *Il Duce* was at that time considered the senior and experienced partner in the pair of leaders of Fascist Régimes, and he tried to restrain Hitler, because of his reservation in principle about the Aryan-Nordic myth, and the fear that world Jewry might use its strength to harm Fascism. Mussolini offered to mediate between the Jews and the Nazi leader and a number of times raised the Jewish question in his contacts with Hitler and his coterie. In the final analysis, however, Hitler was not influenced by Mussolini's pleadings – on the contrary, *Il Duce* subsequently adopted the racist-antisemitic legislation.[37]

Now to some of Hitler's basic ideas about the Jews. The matter of the Jews occupied Hitler incessantly and he constantly returned to it in writing and in his speeches: in *Mein Kampf* and in his second, unpublished book,[38] in *Hitler's Secret Conversations or Hitler's Table Talks*,[39] and in his many speeches and discussions with statesmen and assistants.[40]

According to Hitler, the Jews are not a religious community nor a nation in the accepted sense of the term, but a race. The structure of a religious community helps the Jews to organize and demand rights of the nations among whom they dwell. Jews are not fit to establish a state of their own and maintain it because they lack the ability to work and to create, and they are especially far removed from nature and agriculture which is the nurturing infrastructure of the human strength of the nation. The Jews have no creative ability of their own and adopt as theirs the achievements of the creative Aryan race, and therefore they are clearly an element of secondary importance. The ability of the Jews lies in preserving their racial purity, in penetrating into the arteries of the economic lives of foreign nations, and in the spreading of ideas which advance their goals. The Jews aim at world domination through economic power and political enslavement. "The Jew as a race," said Hitler in a 1923 speech, – "has eminent powers of self-preservation, but as an individual he possesses no cultural gifts. He is the demon of the disintegration of peoples, he is the symbol of the unceasing destruction of their life."[41]

The parasitic Jews living among the nations were never able and never desired to assimilate or to blend into their host nation. "As a matter of fact," says Hitler, "the Jew can never become a German however often he may affirm that he can. If he wished to become a German, he must surrender the Jew in him. And that is not possible: He cannot, however much he try, become a German at heart, and that for several reasons: first, because of his blood; second, because of his character; thirdly, because of his will; and fourthly, because of his actions."[42] The external signs of identification which the Jews have assumed, such as the language of the land in which they live, are only a pretense to hide their true Jewish image and goals. The Jew has no other way of blending in and "therefore his whole Germanism rests on the language alone. Race, however, does not lie in the language, but exclusively in the blood, which no one knows better than the Jew, who attaches very little importance to the preservation of his language, but all importance to keeping his blood pure."[43] The great danger in the Jew disguised as a non-Jew is in the violation of the blood and the race. In various contexts Hitler returned to the purity of the blood; blood was like a fetish to him, the essence of the person and the secret of the nation's vitality and power. "All great cultures of the past perished only because the originally creative race died out from blood poisoning."[44] " . . . for men do not perish as a result of lost wars, but by loss of that force of resistance which is contained only in pure blood."[45]

Hitler further claimed that, as a rule, the Jewish race wants to rule the nations. Jews made their way among the nations of Europe as business people and brokers, and in the course of time gained "a monopolistic position in commerce and finance." Then the Jews sought equal civic rights, and when that was given them they asked for special rights. In modern times the Jews became active in politics and the *Protocols of the Elders of Zion* reflects the worldwide Jewish conspiracy. The Jews do not wage their campaign openly but conceal their designs behind theories and various and conflicting political movements such as capitalism and liberalism on the one hand, and socialism and communism on the other. They combined all of these in order to blur their authentic racial-nationalistic characteristics and to set up humane, international interests and values in their stead. Within this all-encompassing framework of theories, doctrines, and political organizations, Jews of different backgrounds – people of great wealth on the one hand, and renowned revolutionaries on the other – function with one mind and toward one goal. According to Hitler, the Jews had already gained some of their ends in a few European countries and had achieved a complete victory in Bolshevist Russia. The Germans, who are the most laudable and least damaged racial branch among the European nations, bear the responsibility of fighting to the end against the Jews. Time is of the essence, for the contest between the "Aryan" race and the Jewish race has reached a decisive stage. Hitler saw himself as the man of destiny upon whom rests the mission of leading the "Aryan" race to victory. However, should the Jews realize their plot and succeed in gaining world domination, all will end in total disaster which will include the Jews, because after the object upon which the parasite feeds is destroyed, the parasite can no longer sustain itself. This mix of untenable opinions and prejudices fed the spiritual world of the leader of the National Socialist Party and created an eschatological world-view with him as the uniquely gifted one appointed to save the world from destruction and to establish firmly the naturally chosen master race as savior and ruler.[46]

This is not the place to discuss at length the subject, interesting in itself, of Hitler's duality: on the one hand, a captive of an ideologically dogmatic perception replete with fantasies and stubborn, irrational opinions; on the other hand, a clear-eyed, skilled statesman who knew how to operate with agility and shrewdness in critical situations. Of course, in Jewish policy matters it was mostly the first Hitler who spoke and acted, the Hitler welded to the racist ideology.

From the Nazis' rise to power, their Jewish policy was conducted along two tracks: the concrete and the abstract or long-range ideological. They moved along the first track in the implementation of the anti-Jewish laws and measures. However, in the background, beyond the matter at hand, there was always the general, ideologically significant system with the need for an absolute or "final solution" of the Jewish question. In the various stages, this solution was not actually clearly defined, but it was clearly more radical than any step actually being taken, each of which was only a piece, as it were, of the overall solution.

Those who review the history of the Third Reich sometimes posit that the program for the physical extermination of the Jewish people was clarified and prepared by the Nazis from the very outset of their assumption of power, and that they perpetrated their evil design step by step until the act of total murder. As has been stated, a careful study of the Nazi policy of the first years reveals that it was not always single-tracked and clear. In any case, the abundant documentation at our disposal proves with certainty that the program for the murder of the Jewish people as a realistic method for the "solution of the Jewish problem" was not raised until 1941.[47]

On the other hand, it is absolutely imperative to invalidate the opinion, heard from time to time even now, that the antisemitism of Hitler and the Nazis served at first only as an effective propaganda point, and later on as a factor in establishing the régime, and as a diversion from the real problems besetting Germany. In no way, shape, or manner is this opinion acceptable, and the secret documentation available to us, revealing the innermost thoughts of Hitler and the Nazi élite, indicates that racial antisemitism and the "Jewish problem" occupied the leaders of the régime and the Party as a most central problem. (In addition to Hitler's "table talk," this is revealed in Goebbel's diaries, in Frank's daily work-log and others). The opposite is the case. The very private expressions were always sharper and more extreme than those used publicly. Furthermore, it is known that Hitler and his henchmen adhered to the antisemitic line and made it ever harsher even after they were solidly in power and no longer in need of demagogic propaganda. The truth is that the Nazis continued their anti-Jewish campaign not only when it was no longer of any use to them but even when it harmed them and compelled them to conduct the murder campaign in utmost secrecy, hiding it as much as possible even from the knowledge of the Germans themselves. In the "final solution" phase of the Jewish problem, people who were working under slave conditions for the Nazi war effort were murdered and at a time when the Third Reich was faced with a constantly growing labor shortage.

In the above-mentioned political document of September 1919, Hitler emphasized that he was not on the side of emotional antisemitism's being expressed by outbreaks of rioting, but that he was for "rational antisemitism," that is, for putting into effect a continuous, persistent anti-Jewish line bearing the character of a system leading by a planned process to the complete solution of the problem.[48] This does not mean that Hitler recoiled from the vulgar antisemitism of *Der Stuermer* or from the "Crystal Night" initiative. What it does mean is that sporadic anti-Jewish actions or persecutions from below were not Hitler's final aim; he sought to provide the anti-Jewish campaign with a format of political activity leading to a planned "solution" of the Jewish question.

5. Nazi Measures against the Jews

Let us now turn to the main stages in the National Socialist policy on the Jews in the 1933–1945 years.

During the first stage, from the time the Nazis came to power until 1938, a system was put into effect against the Jews of legal discrimination, of removing Jews from the community of citizens with rights, from public office, from cultural life, and finally, even from the economic life of Germany. During that period, Germany's new rulers were interested in the emigration of the Jews, but the economic policy which kept the Jewish emigrants from taking their possessions with them slowed the pace of the exodus. Another most important factor which prevented emigration on a much larger scale was the controlled quota policy of immigration of the United States and other overseas countries, as well as unemployment and fear of economic crisis in the European countries. "The great Arab revolt" and the restrictions on entry to Palestine imposed by the Mandatory Government limited that possibility.

In the second stage, which began with a series of severe anti-Jewish edicts and the strengthening of Nazi Germany's political status in 1938, Jewish matters were turned over to the S.S. and the German police, the voluntary emigration became a forced one, and legal discrimination was to a great extent replaced by violence. After the outbreak of World War II in September 1939, a further development in Jewish policy occurred. The new situation was characterized by two basic changes: With the annexation by Germany of most of Poland and a series of west European countries, the number of Jews within its jurisdiction rose very greatly; on the other hand, the chances for emigration declined completely. As a result, the suggestions for a solution of the Jewish problem, especially their removal from the Third Reich, centered on the idea of concentrating the Jews in the east, in the area which in the past had belonged to

Poland, or in an overseas settlement (the Madagascar plan).[49] The first suggestion was an improvization with no foundation in reality, whereas the implementation of the Madagascar plan was not even begun. In the middle of 1941, with the start of the invasion of Russia, the Nazis began to implement their program of the murder of the Jewish people in Europe, and ultimately the plan for "the final solution of the Jewish question." In the first period, the mass murder was executed by the *"Einsatzgruppen"* which accompanied the troops of the eastern front; whereas from the spring of 1942, the Nazis activated a series of death-camps in the area which had been Poland. (The first camp, at Chelmno in the Lodz area, was established at the end of 1941.) Jews were brought there from Poland and the various countries of Europe and gassed to death there. During the mass murder stage, the Jews were denied exit from the lands conquered by the Nazis, and every attempt was made by the administrators of the plan to capture all of the Jews and exterminate them to the very last one. In the fall of 1944, in view of the expected imminent collapse of Germany, the total mass murder was halted,[50] but at that time, in the occupied countries and within the Nazis' sphere of political influence, there were only remnants left, the survivors of European Jewry at the end of World War II.

There is a reciprocal connection between the political strengthening of the Third Reich, the ideological buttressing of the order and the Party, and the policy toward the Jews. It seems that every real gain in the political realm and every act of massive support of the régime by the German nation, very quickly found its expression in anti-Jewish measures. Another important factor influencing the restraint or the hastening of the political anti-Jewish process, was the reaction of foreign countries. Thus, for example, the Nazis interpreted the results of the Evian Conference in 1938 as a lack of desire on the part of the western democratic countries to join in activities on behalf of the Jews and to accept Jews into their countries or into countries within their sphere of influence.[51]

Hitler pointed out that he was not an exporter of racism, which fixes a hierarchy of nations and sets the Germans in a position of mastery over the others; rather he was an exporter of antisemitism.[52] And, indeed, radical antisemitism did without a doubt help Nazism's political penetration into the various countries of Europe.[53] During the period preceding the outbreak of World War II, changes took place in the emigration policy of the Third Reich. During the first years in which the régime was establishing itself, the Germans did not distinguish between the countries of destination of the Jewish emigrants. In a later period, as Nazi Germany's political position grew stronger and the Third Reich's circle of interests broadened, the German régimes were not complacent about the lands of immigration and tried to steer the Jews to distant countries where they could not amass economic power or harm Germany on the propaganda or political level. For a time, the findings of the Peel Commission on Palestine also influenced the Third Reich's emigration policy. The Germans considered whether the establishment of a Jewish State in Palestine of any size would not necessitate a change in the Haavara ("Transfer") agreement with the settlement in Palestine. According to the Nazi perception, the Jews were not capable of establishing their own state, but a formal Jewish State in Palestine, a sort of "Jewish Vatican," could provide a legal basis for activities against Germany.[54]

In general it can be said with certainty that the policy toward the Jews was constantly becoming more and more severe. A few times, to be sure, a sort of temporary respite was announced, but in pivotal points there was a drastic worsening, which was actually a shift from one stage of policy toward the Jews to a new, more severe level. One cannot find in these measures any deliberate planning or gradual process. It is more plausible that what we have is the constant momentum of a tense political line breaking out, conditioned by ideological and political circumstances, internal and external alike. The German researcher, Martin Broszat, in his book *Der Staat Hitlers* ("Hitler's State"), also deals with the Jewish policy;

> . . . there was no room for discrimination endlessly. Therefore, the "movement" had finally to end in physical destruction. The mass killing of the Jews was unplanned in the same degree that the legal discrimination, which sometimes prompted and sometimes prevented step after step, was unplanned. Here, as in the steps toward the final irrational goal of *"Lebensraum"* in foreign policy, the National-Socialist leadership was unable to foresee the results of the dynamics [of the process]. More characteristic was the fact that again and again they had to formulate a *Weltanschauung* on the "Jewish question" and again and again they dealt with the question of partial "solutions" until only the "final solution" remained as the way to proceed.[55]

On 30 January 1939, in Hitler's annual speech on the anniversary of his rise to power, and in this instance, the last months of peace on the eve of World War II, the following, among other things, was said:

> . . . and I wanted to say one thing today which wants remembering not only by us, the Germans: Throughout my life I often was a prophet and most people laughed at me. During the days of struggle to achieve power, it was first and foremost the Jewish people which greeted my prophecies with guffaws, when I said that one day I would gain the leadership of the German state and people, and then I will solve, among other things, the Jewish problem. I think that the Jews' gales of laughter have already been stifled in their throats. Today I wish to prophesy again: If the Jewry of international finance in Europe and beyond it will again succeed in drawing the nations into a world war – then the result will not be the Bolshevization of the world and, with it, a victory of Judaism, but the destruction of the Jewish race in Europe.[56]

This fateful prophecy and subdued denunciation sound like a libel against a helpless victim. The truth is that the Jewish people, in the hour of greatest danger for its survival – on the eve of the outbreak of World War II and at the height of the war – was in an absolutely weak and almost helpless position. This is not the place to discuss the combination of circumstances which led to this weak Jewish position. What is important, however, is the fact that Hitler believed, or had convinced himself, that the Jews were the instigators of war, and he often repeated this senseless charge in his public speeches and within the intimate circle of his cohorts.[57] There is evidence that, after the victory over France, that is, at the peak of the Third Reich's political and military might, Hitler was in favor of concentrating the Jews on the island of Madagascar.[58] A decisive change took place at the beginning of the preparations for "Operation Barbarossa" – the invasion of the Soviet Union. Hitler saw this war as a confrontation between two world-views, and the crusade against Bolshevism as the realization of National Socialism's ideological imperative. From then on, Jews or "the Jewish-Bolshevik foe" were part of the actual front. In later years, after the *Blitzkrieg* had failed and the scales of the contest had slowly begun to tilt toward the Soviet Union, there were added to the dark prophecy and dastardly accusations, a raging fury and compulsion to wreak his vengeance upon the victim at hand. On 23 January 1942, in *Table Talk*, Hitler said:

> One must act radically. When one pulls out a tooth, one does it with a single tug, and the pain quickly goes away. The Jew must clear out of Europe. Otherwise no understanding will be possible between Europeans. It's the Jew who prevents everything . . . But if they refuse to go voluntarily, I see no other solution but extermination. Why should I look at a Jew through other eyes than if he were a Russian prisoner-of-war? In the p.o.w. camps many are dying. It's not my fault. I didn't want either the war or the p.o.w. camps. Why did the Jews provoke this war?[59]

And Josef Goebbels, one of Hitler's loyal aides, noted in his diary for 27 March 1942:

> . . . the verdict against the Jews is being implemented. True, it is a barbaric one, but they thoroughly deserve it. *Der Führer's* prophetic words about them are beginning to be fulfilled in the most frightful fashion. In such matters there is no room for sentiment. The Jews will destroy us if we do not defend ourselves against them. This is a war of life or death between the Aryan race and the Jewish virus. No other government, no other régime, was able to muster the force to solve this problem in a general way. Here too *Der Führer* is the first to do battle, fearless, bearing the word of a radical solution which reality inevitably requires given things as they are. As of today, in war-time, it is our good fortune to have a whole series of possibilities unavailable to us in peace-time.[60]

As is well known, no written document or order signed by Hitler has been found directing implementation of the general slaughter of the Jewish people. There are a number of different assumptions about this: There are those who believe that such an order was given in the spring of 1941, in advance of the invasion of the Soviet Union. Others surmise that this general order was not issued until the fall of 1941, when it became clear to Hitler that there was no possibility of transferring the Jewish masses to the depths of Russia. One also hears the opinion that there was no single order but rather a series of partial instructions which, *in toto*, added up to a general order.[61] We shall not treat this matter in detail here. However, one must deal briefly with the executing forces, the S.S. command and the S.S. units who were put in charge of "the final solution." There is no doubt that the broad authority delegated to the S.S. in Jewish matters, especially in the "final solution" stages, gave the S.S. a position of power in the Third Reich, the conquered countries, and their satellites. Through the Jews and their murder, the S.S. took control of much Jewish property and workers and learned to function in the various countries as a factor independent of the local government and the local Nazi authorities. Thus Himmler, who was always contending for influence and favors from the omnipotent leader, was able to strengthen his position among those close to *Der Führer*. The material wealth plundered by the S.S. and the concentration camps which served as an unlimited labor pool, helped fortify the economic power of the S.S.

The S.S., and especially those directly in charge of the murder operation, had great independence of action. They set the times of the actions, their scope, and the *modus operandi*. There is no doubt that the dynamics of the activity conducted by branches of Eichmann's department and the units in the death-camps had an effect on speeding up the entire process. The S.S. and Police Leader for the Lublin district, Odilo Globocnik, who was in charge of the major death-camps in the Lublin area, is reported to have spoken of the fact that the murder must be speeded up because in the course of the war things may occur to prevent the completion of the job.[62] The murder fever was accompanied by a claim with which the Nazis involved in the matter had been imbued, that the secret operation which they were carrying out and which they would never be able to divulge nor boast about in public, was vital ideologically and vital to the future of the Reich.[63] It may be that the S.S. was also pursued by that feeling characteristic of criminals – that they must try to eliminate every witness and anyone who suffered from their crimes, and thus all traces of the deeds can be obliterated. Be that as it may, the S.S. which, more than any other organization in the Third Reich, was beyond any legal responsibility, had an important role in the process of carrying out the murder of millions of Jews.

To summarize this section it must be said that, by the stage of mass murder, the partial steps on the road to "the solution" of the Jewish problem merged with the longed-for ideological goal of National Socialism into one frightful entity.

5. Antisemitism of the German People

Finally, let us examine, in general outline, the importance of the antisemitic factor in Germany society at the time of the Weimar Republic and in the context of the National Socialist state. Did antisemitism help the Nazis win the masses and take over the government? Did the German masses agree – or even identify – with the government's course vis-à-vis the Jews: the legal steps and the campaign of persecutions which followed them, ending in the total murder of the Jewish people; and did they see this as an ideological and political goal of the highest importance for the régime? Were they aware of the scope of the killing and its methods, and what were their reactions and behavior in light of the information which filtered out to the population?

The German historians do not deal with these questions much and those few who do touch upon them are of different opinions. The fact that there was no free press in Germany and one must discover the opinion of a community which was not free to express it, makes it very difficult for the researchers and leaves room, of course, for differing and sometimes contradictory interpretations. Generally, the German historians claim that the character of German antisemitism was not vocal or violent and therefore there is no reason to posit that the antisemitic currents in Germany were stronger than in Poland, Romania, or even France. In our opinion, this claim, seemingly based upon correct facts, is misleading because it avoids coming to grips with the essence of the problem. Yes, it is true that in a few countries of eastern Europe there was an open, brutal attitude toward the Jews, and the hatred, the damage, and the violence were sometimes felt in everyday life. This was not prominently so in Germany until the National Socialist stage. On the other hand, the east European antisemitism was tangible, for the most part with concrete denunciations and goals, and therefore, for all of its paradoxes, it was also more "rational." In Poland or Romania the Jews were portrayed by the antisemites as economic competitors controlling all the key economic and urban branches, blocking the advance of the indigenous population, conducting their affairs unfairly, being isolationist and scornful of the ruling nation, its culture and the like. Ideologically this antisemitism was generally nurtured by a network of prejudices and accusations against the Jews, already deeply rooted in those countries. But in Germany, where political and racial antisemitism struck root, the Jewish problem did not appear mainly as an economic one nor as a pattern of interpersonal relationships, but rather as a comprehensive, ideological base with many ramifications for the fate of Germany and even of all humanity. Without a doubt, of the two forms of antisemitism, each with its different dominant focus, the ideological or *Weltanschauung* antisemitism proved itself of much greater social and political influence, inestimably threatening and dangerous. In this connection, the difference emphasized by Hitler should be pointed out: between the spontaneous, pogrom antisemitism more characteristic of the east European model, and antisemitism as a state goal, striving for "an inclusive, absolute solution," as it grew and became dominant in Germany.

The German historian, Golo Mann, minimizes the role of antisemitism in paving the way for Hitler's régime, basing his case upon the fact that in the last free elections before Hitler took power and became entrenched, he restrained the antisemitic slogans and demogoguery. [64] Again, these facts are only apparently correct. It is true that in their first years of political party activity the Nazis adopted a more aggressive tone than when the sphere of influence of their movement expanded throughout Germany. It is also true, apparently, that after the Nazis felt that they had squeezed the last advantage from certain charges (including antisemitism) they provided other motivations for attracting potential supporters and votes and temporarily emphasized the latter. Yet the fact that they slanted the propaganda to take advantage of circumstances still does not indicate the depth of the influence of antisemitism in the long run.

Professor Werner Jochmann, in a work of systematic research, concentrates on the fluctuations and significance of the antisemitic moods in Germany 1914–1923. [65] With the outbreak of World War I, a spirit of conciliation and an atmosphere of harmony between different groups reigned in the Second Reich. Kaiser Wilhelm II spoke of removing the barriers in view of the gravity of the situation and said that all the citizens of the country were Germans. Yet, as the difficulties on the fronts and at home multiplied, the antisemitic strain surfaced once again. At first as a whisper from mouth to mouth and then openly and aggressively, the denunciation was heard that the Jews were sitting in the offices too much instead of serving in the military, were involved in the black-market, and the like. In 1916, the war offices in Prussia conducted a census of the Jews serving in the armed forces to ascertain their roles and activities in the military ranks. [66] The Jews made an evident apologetic effort, published numerous articles and books to prove that their share in the army and at the front was no less than that of the general population. They listed their dead and wounded to convince the world that their love of country and readiness to sacrifice did not fall short of the others. These attempts, of course, did not achieve the desired results. In face of the total military defeat, antisemitism grew apace. The Jews were presented as responsible for the weakness at home, as "stabbing Germany in the back," as if the war had been begun as a result of the shadowy intrigues of the Jews. Jews were also considered to be those who had devised the Republic system which had been imposed by foreigners and was contrary to the national character and tradition of Germany. And lastly, the Jewish pollution had come with the Bolshevik revolution and the revolutionary torrent in Germany.

Z. Barbu, in a treatise on the psycho-social aspects of National Socialist antisemitism, indicates that the first time-span of the Weimar Republic was characterized by bitter antisemitism. [67] The economically and politically relatively placid years in Weimar Germany also saw a kind of regression in the antisemitic mood, but with the start of the deep economic crisis, there was again a steep rise in the antisemitic perversion. According to Barbu, in the last years prior to the Nazi seizure of power, antisemitism had embraced large masses and was at the center of general public concern.

Barbu finds that the various strata of German population were influenced to different degrees by the antisemitic penetration. Thus, for example, according to Barbu, the aristocratic and the wealthy were skeptical of Hitler's racial theories but supported the Nazis and their leaders for pragmatic reasons, since Hitler could represent a popular rightist alternative against the Left. On the other hand, the middle classes gave massive support to Hitler and Nazism and were the breeding ground of authentic radical antisemitism. The German workers, says Barbu, did not join the antisemitic wave when it began, but adapted to the reality which had been penetrated by Nazism and, with time, they also showed signs of making their peace with the new force.

We shall now concentrate on another aspect and try to trace the approach of the German people, or of strata among them, to Nazi racism and antisemitism. It has already been pointed out that various German authors express general, single-dimensional evaluations to characterize the German population's support of the Nazis' policy toward the Jews and their identification with it. Usually the German historians posit a population most of which opposed the Nazi systems against the Jews, but in face of the terror and nature of the régime, could not demonstrate its opposition in deeds. There are those who think that the Germans did indicate their reservations about the anti-Jewish steps of the Party and the government by their actions.

Certainly it is neither accurate nor responsible to posit that all of the Germans or even all of the loyal Nazi supporters thoroughly studied Hitler's teaching or digested the far-reaching significance of racial antisemitism. We have no way of examining these matters – but one may theorize that most of the Germans who voted for Hitler and put him in power and, even more, those who supported Hitler afterwards, did not see antisemitism as a particularly important issue on the regular agenda, and antisemitism was not the main, key factor in the Nazis' list of promises and changes which they said they would institute. Yet, antisemitism was almost no deterrent at all in keeping the Germans away from the Nazis.

The claim of the Germans, heard since the end of the war and until now, that they had not read *Mein Kampf*, that they had not paid any serious heed to Hitler's speeches, that they did not see or were not aware of anything beyond their immediate ken – does not stand the test of reality. Hitler's ideas about the Jews and the principles of the racist creed, Nazi version, were disseminated through the media and all sorts of sophisticated propaganda systems directed at a spectrum of levels and at all ages. Racism as an ideational perception and as a behavioral guide was infused into the school, the youth movements, the army, the press, *belles lettres* and theoretical literature, films, and so forth. It is more reasonable to speak of mass brain-washing – which succeeded in Nazi Germany, and to a great extent even before that, in ousting the Jews from human society, in making them a detestable and harmful object whose blood might be shed with impunity – than to talk of unawareness.[68]

Withal, one must remember that we are dealing with a totalitarian state in which an open reaction or a public demonstration against the régime, especially on the sensitive Jewish topic, were liable to make a person suspect in the eyes of the governing bodies and the Party and even to bring about tangible results. And yet there is still a prevalent and worrying amazement that the Nazi persecutions were met with almost no opposition, and except for some few, truly exceptional people, there were no Germans who took the firm decision to endanger themselves and courageously express their condemnation or their reservation. The lack of reaction and the absence of any expression of opposition, in this respect, cannot apparently be interpreted as merely fear of the régime. It stems from the fact that the masses demonstrated their identification with and support of the removal of the Jews from the various areas of life so that there was broad community support for the anti-Jewish policy and the anti-Jewish steps. One often finds mention of the population's activities and demands to strengthen and sharpen the anti-Jewish line and of the fact that the administrations and the police had to control the hot-heads and calm the dissatisfied.[69] Instances are known in which women married to Jews demonstrated their identification with their husbands, but such manifestations of daring and loyalty are not the same as a public reaction; rather they are indicative of an outburst of fury on the part of unfortunate people whose family lives and homes were being destroyed by the wickedness of the régime. The public protests and preachings of the clergymen, as well, were not generally directed at the discrimination and the injuries done to the Jews in general, but were objections to the inclusion of Jews who had converted to Christianity or their descendants in the legislative process and the anti-Jewish policy.[70]

A wave of protests swept Germany at the beginning of the war when, as a result of a close adherence to the racial concept, the mentally ill and other sorts of chronically ill among the German population were put to death in "Operation Euthanasia." There is a theory that this spreading wave of opposition compelled the régime to stop these killings. The German historian K. D. Bracher points out that "for all that, in contrast to the policy against the Jews, the attempts to kill the sick were faced with stronger immediate opposition by the broad population as well, and especially by the churches and the medical circles."[71] Instructive is the fact that even the small cells of opposition that had been formed in the Third Reich received secret documents about many wrongs and injustices of the régime, but one can hardly find in their writings any expressions of resentment or opposition to the persecutions, and later, to the murder of the Jews.[72] E. L. Ehrlich, an author residing in Switzerland, says definitively in his work *Jew-Hatred in Germany*:

> . . . it is precisely from the acceptance of the anti-Jewish steps, from the almost absolute absence of oppositionary forces, from the silence which is so perplexing, that we learn not only about normal human fear, but can discern most clearly the special German traditions. When Hitler quietly began to eliminate the mentally ill in the "Euthanasia" program, there were loud complaints among the populace. The protest, supported by the

bishops, priests, and attorneys, achieved noteworthy results. But the voice against the Jewish persecutions was only rarely heard. Too few were those who dared, who proved that humaneness and ethics were not completely destroyed in Germany. Nationalism or antisemitism as a political movement is not a German invention or an exclusively German phenomenon, but it is only in this country that they were permitted to vent their brutal fury to the fullest because the moral forces did not stand against them almost at all.[73]

It is clear, then, that the various stages of the anti-Jewish policy and the brutal injuries – the dismissal from their jobs, the ousting from social and cultural life, the legal discrimination, the confiscation of property, and finally the expulsion to the east – did not arouse countermeasures nor even serious expressions of opposition. German authors most often point out the fact that the German populace did not know what was awaiting the Jews expelled to the east. And it is indeed true that the process of extermination was a guarded state secret and no hint of it was published or officially released. But should not the very act of expelling the Jews have raised vexing questions among the neighbors, friends, classmates, and intimates of many Jews? Did this not demand that the interested and concerned raise questions and demands about the fate of tens and hundreds of thousands of the expelled? Is the not knowing not to be understood as abandonment, lethargy, or a lack of a desire to know? From the few indicators available for examining the moods of the Germany community, one also gets the impression that there is no way of accepting the unequivocal conclusion of unawareness. Logic dictates that despite the wall of secrecy much information filtered through to Germany, and if things were not perfectly known, there were at least many who surmised, and many who also knew, that masses of Jews were being slaughtered in the east.[74]

One who studies the thousands of testimonies of the Jewish survivors, trying to learn from them about the opinions and behavior of the rank and file Germans – the soldiers, camp guards, or German work-supervisors in places where Jewish prisoners were used – is confronted again and again with merciless rigidity, uncompromising obedience to instructions, and on occasion even sadism and brutality beyond the call of duty and instructions. Even if one takes into account the known German submission to discipline and legitimate authority, these characteristics are still not enough to explain the enthusiasm, the envy, and the rejoicing at the fall, which accompanied the carrying out of the persecutions and the murder. This phenomenon is only to be understood as an ideational and spiritual identification with these deeds. The German diligence in the process of executing the anti-Jewish policy and "the final solution," and the identification with them, is especially outstanding when we compare the manner of the Germans' behavior with that of the Italians when both were required to carry out pursuits and expulsions. We find that the Italians, both in their own country, in the conquered lands and, according to information we have, even in the army, often recoiled at carrying out the anti-Jewish orders or turning Jews over to the Germans.[75] This opposition to fulfilling orders has been discovered among officers, soldiers in the ranks, senior officers and commanders in the Fascist echelons. It is instructive that the out-and-out Polish antisemites, who openly admitted that the results of the German actions were to their liking because they removed the Jews from Poland forever, added, at the same time, that personally, they were revolted by the murderous deeds and the way they were executed, and that no Poles would do such things in their free country.

On the occasions that there was a sign of resistance by Wehrmacht officers or the administrative régime in the conquered countries to the uprooting of Jews and their murder, this opposition did not as a rule stem from humane motives or from a nonacceptance of the systems of the régime; the various resisters rebelled against the waste of the Jewish work force when this force was most necessary for the Reich's war effort, and only on rare occasions was a protest expressed about the murder of specific groups of Jews. Involvement in saving Jews, or an attempt to bring word of the danger or the significance of what was happening to the knowledge of those whom it concerned, or to the free world – were expressions of "swimming against the stream" by a few rare, exceptional people,[76] and a large measure of optimism is needed to believe that it is precisely these solitary ones who represent the European in general and the German in particular.

Notes

1. See, among other things, in this field: T. W. Adorno and others, *The Authoritarian Personality* (New York, 1950); N. W. Ackerman and M. A. Jahoda, *Antisemitism and Emotional Disorder* (New York, 1950); N. Sanford, "The Roots of Prejudice: Emotional Dynamics," in *Psychology and Race*, ed. P. Watson (Harmondsworth, 1973), pp. 57–75; S. Friedlander, "Some Aspects of the Historical Significance of the Holocaust," *The Jerusalem Quarterly* 1(1976):36–59.
2. F. Meinecke, *Die deutsche Katastrophe* 2(Wiesbaden, 1946), pp. 29–30.
3. G. Ritter, "The Historical Foundations of the Rise of National Socialism," in *The Third Reich* (London, 1955), p. 415.
4. H. Arendt, *The Origins of Totalitarianism* (Cleveland and New York, 1966), pp. 11–88.
5. I. Deutscher, *Non-Jewish Jews and Other Essays* (New York and Toronto, 1968), pp. 32, 38.
6. Ibid., p. 41.
7. Alan Bullock. *Hitler: A Study in Tyranny* (New York, 1961), pp. 16–17.
8. Sheet No. 16, "For Holocaust and Heroism Day," (Heb.) Chief Education Officer, Information Branch of the Israeli Army, Nisan 5738 – May 1978.
9. B. Z. Dinur, *The Holocaust and its Lesson* (Heb.) (Jerusalem, 1958), p. 19.
10. S. Ettinger, *Antisemitism in the Modern Age* (Tel-Aviv, 1978), p. 9.
11. L. De Jong, "Holland and Auschwitz" (Heb.) in *European Jewry in the Holocaust*. A collection of articles edited by Y. Gutman and L. Rothkirchen (Jerusalem, 1973), p. 234.
12. Dinur, *The Holocaust*, p. 36.
13. The Attorney General, v. Eichmann, *Testimony* (Heb.) 1 (Jerusalem, 1963), p. 29.
14. See J. Katz, "Could the Holocaust have been Foreseen?" (Heb.) *Bi-Tefuzot Ha-Golah* 75–76 (1976): 64.
15. K. D. Bracher, W. Sauer and G. Schultz, *Die national-sozialistische Machtergreifung* (Koeln-Opladen, 1960), p. 284.

16. On this subject, see among others: G. L. Mosse, *The Crisis of German Ideology* (New York, 1964); F. Stern, *The Politics of Cultural Despair* (Berkeley and Los Angeles, 1963); P. W. Massing, *Rehearsal for Destruction* (New York, 1949); E. Sterling, *Er ist wie Du* (Muenchen, 1956).
17. S. Esh, *Studies in the Holocaust and Contemporary Jewry* (Heb.) (Jerusalem, 1973), p.262.
18. See J. Katz, "Could the Holocaust . . . ", p.67.
19. See the segment from: L. Bamberger, "Deutschtum und Judentum" (1880), in *Selbztzeugnisse des deutschen Judentums, 1870–1945* (Frankfurt am Main, 1962), p.18.
20. *Deutsche und Juden, Beitrage von S. W. Baron, E. Gerstenmaier, K. Jaspers* (Frankfurt am Main, 1967), p.88.
21. There are those who believe that Darwin intended to implement the laws of evolution and their implications with the human species. This position is expressed, for example, in Ya'akov Talmon's "European History as Background to the Holocaust," in *The Age of Violence* (Heb.) (Tel-Aviv, 1974), pp.276–278. On the other hand, in his lecture on "Darwinism and Ethics," Saul Adler claims that, to be sure, Darwin accepted the premise that human development is based on biological heredity and that the social instincts are also transmitted hereditarily, yet he still emphasized the ethical foundation and considered ethical attainments of great importance. He hoped that a prolonged high level of morality would leave its mark on all of humankind forever since, in his opinion, both physical and spiritual characteristics developed through use are inherited and become part of future generations. See: Saul Adler, *On Darwin and Darwinism* (Heb.) (Jerusalem, 1960), pp.17–32.
22. On this, see: E. Nolte, *Der Faschismus in seiner Epoche, Die Action Francaise, der Italienische Faschismus, der Nationalsozialismus* (Muenchen, 1963); G. L. Mosse, *The Crisis of German Ideology*, (n. 16 above), pp.88–98.
23. On the racist ideas prevalent in France and their social significance, see: S. Almog, "The Racist Motif in Ernst Renan's Approach to Judaism and the Jews" (Heb.) *Zion* 32(1967): 175–200.
24. H. S. Chamberlain, *Die Grundlagen des XIX, Jahrhunderts* (many editions). On Chamberlain's conceptions, see: Jean Deal, "The Religious Conception of Race; Houston Stewart Chamberlain and Germanic Christianity," in: *The Third Reich* (London, 1955), pp.243–286.
25. G. L. Mosse, *The Crisis of German Ideology*, (n. 16 above), p.95.
26. Guenther writes: " . . . *die Juden sind ein Volk und wie jedes Volk, ein Gemisch verschiedener Rassen . . . Die Juden sind also nicht etwa Angehörige einer 'semitischen Rasse'. Es gibt Voelker semitischer Sprache, und zu ihnen haben ursprünglich die Juden gehört; diese Völker stellen aber sehrverschiedenartige Rassengemische dar . . . "* H. F. K. Guenther, *Kleine Rassenkunde des deutschen Volkes* (Muenchen, 1934), p.55. Also: *"das Judentum ist demnach weder als Rasse noch als Glaubensgemeinschaft, noch als irgendeine Kulturerscheinung, sondern als Volktum aufzufassen."* H. F. K. Guenther, *Rassenkunde des jüdischen Volkes* (Muenchen, 1931), p.16; whereas Hitler, in *Mein Kampf*, sees the Jews as a race and primarily so: *"Den gewaltigsten Gegensatz zum Arier bildet der Jude. Bei kaum einem Volk ist der Selbsterhaltungstrieb stärker entwickelt als beim sogenannten Auserwählten. Als bester Beweis hierführ darf die einfache Tatsache des Bestehens dieser Rasse allein schon geltern . . . " "Daher ist auch der jüdische Staat – der der lebendige Organismus zur Erhaltung und Vermehrung einer Rasse sein soll – territorial vollständig unbegrenzt . . . " "Das Judentum war immer ein Volk mit bestimmten rassischen Eigenarten und niemals eine Religion,"* A. Hitler, *Mein Kampf* 16th ed. (Muenchen, 1932), pp.329, 331, 335.
27. See: the "Race" entry, written in part by Yeshayahu Leibovitz, in *Encyclopaedia Hebraica* (Heb.) 10, cols. 563–578.
28. F. Nietzsche, "The Dawn of Day" in *The Complete Works of Friedrich Neitzsche* 9, (New York, 1964), p.221. On Neitzsche and National-Socialism, see: Wilhelm Grenzmann, "Nietzsche and National-Socialism." in *The Third Reich*, (n. 3 above), pp.203–242.
29. On the racial criterion relating to forced laborers in Germany during the war, see my article, "Forced Labor in Occupied Germany during the Second World War" (Heb.), *Zion* 43(1978): 119–127.
30. A. Hitler, *Mein Kampf* (München, 1941) (671–675 Auflange), pp.54–70).
31. See, for example: Alan Bullock, *Hitler* (n. 7 above), p.39.
32. *Der Nationalsozialismus, Dokumente, 1933–1945*, ed. Walther Hofer (Frankfurt am Main, 1957), p.268.

33. E. Nolte, *Der Faschismus*, (n. 22 above), pp.405–408.
34. On the racial evaluation of the Japanese, A. Hitler, *Mein Kampf*, pp.318–319.
35. Thus, for example, in the first years of the Nazi régime, steps were also taken to limit the disturbances when the administration wanted to control unsupervised outbursts from below or was interested in undisturbed economic activity and, for a time, when it was concerned with foreign criticism of the Jewish persecutions. On Hindenberg's demand, the "Law for the Restoration of the Professional Civil Service" of April 1933 did not apply to the employment of Jews in the government apparatus dealing with the World War I wounded and relatives of the deceased. As stated, before the 1936 Olympics in Berlin, deliberate action was taken to blur the antisemitic campaign, including the removal of signs that Jews were unwelcome, etc.; and Jewish athletes were even granted permission to participate. In 1922, a separate fifteen-year treaty had been signed between Germany and Poland for the protection of minorities in the area of Silesia, part of which was Germany and part of which had been handed to Poland. The League of Nations was entrusted with supervising the treaty's implementation. In May 1933 the League of Nations was presented with a petition by a Jew named Bernheim, a resident of German Silesia, who complained that the paragraphs of the treaty were being violated by Germany in the legislation discriminating against the Jewish minority. Following this complaint, the Nazi authorities excluded the Silesia area from the discriminatory laws and this condition continued until 1937, when the term of the treaty expired. Immediately thereafter, all the anti-Jewish laws and decrees of the Reich were also instituted in Silesia.
36. E. Jaeckel, *Hitler's Weltanschauung* (Middletown, Conn., 1972), p.52.
37. On this matter, see: M. Michaelis, *Mussolini and the Jews: German-Italian Relations and the Jewish Question in Italy 1922–1945* (London and Oxford, 1978).
38. *Hitlers zweites Buch*, ed. G. Weinberg (Stuttgart, 1961). Hitler's second book written in 1928 was not published in his lifetime, and was discovered among materials captured by the Americans at the end of World War II and transferred to the United States. The reasons Hitler hid the manuscript and did not publish it when written do not concern us here. In the last chapter he deals with "the Jewish question" in concentrated form and especially with its political aspects.
39. The reference is to collections of conversations, or more precisely, monologues of Hitler's which were delivered during mealtimes and meetings with his close colleagues. These talks were taken down and published in various editions. See for instance: *Hitler's Secret Conversations, 1941–1944*, New York, 1953.
40. H. Rauschning, *Gespraeche mit Hitler* (Zürich, 1940).
41. E. Calic, *Ohne Maske: Hitler – Breiting Geheimgespräche*, 1931, (Frankfurt am Main, 1968). *The Speeches of A. Hitler*, ed. N. H. Baynes (New York, 1969), 1, p. 68. In a May 1, 1923 speech, Hitler returned to this motif as well as to others similar, often in almost identical formulation. See, for example, in *Mein Kampf*, pp.300–303.
42. *The Speeches of Hitler* 1 p.59. It is important to note that Hitler did not talk much of the evolutionary-Darwinian principle . . . The premise about evolution on the racial plane was contrary to his perception of the unchanging and stable hierarchy of races. On this matter Professor Mosse notes (n. 16 above). "As National-Socialism and the Voelkisch movement claimed that the German Race was perfection incarnate, that its greatness was immutable, the idea of racial evolution and progress had to be rejected."
43. *Mein Kampf*, ibid., p.342.
44. Ibid., p.316.
45. Ibid., p.324.
46. Hitler, in a February 1942 conversation with his intimates at which a Danish S.S. officer was a special guest, said: "If Germany hadn't had the good fortune to let me take power in 1933, Europe today would no longer exist." See: *Hitler's Table Talk 1941–1944*, transl. by Norman Cameron and R. H. Stevens (London, 1973), p.328.
47. On this see: H. Krausnick, "Judenverfolgung," in *Anatomie des SS Staates* (Muenchen, 1967), pp.297–300; U. D. Adam, *Judenpolitik im Dritten Reich* (Duesseldorf. 1972), pp.305–316. Martin Broszat, "Hitler and the Genesis of the 'Final Solution'" *Yad Va-Shem Studies* (Jerusalem, 1979), Vol. *XIII*, pp.73–127.
48. See the formulation of Hitler's first political document of September 1919 in *Hitlers Briefe und Notizen*, ed. W. Maser, (Duesseldorf, 1973), pp.223–226.
49. On the programs of a reservation in the eastern sections of Poland and Madagascar, see: Philip

Freidmann, *Roads to Extinction: Essays on the Holocaust* (N.Y. and Philadelphia, 1980), pp.34–58; Leni Yahil, "Madagascar: Phantom of a Solution for the Jewish Question," in *Jews and Non-Jews in Eastern Europe*, ed. by B. Wago and J. L. Mosse (N.Y., Toronto and Jerusalem, 1974), pp.315–334.

50. We have no document ordering the cessation of the systematic and total destruction of Jews, but we do know of verbal instructions by Himmler in the fall of 1944 and the beginning of 1945 to stop the general annihilation of the Jews.

51. On the Evian Conference and its after-effects see: H. L. Feingold, *The Politics of Rescue*, 2nd ed.; (New York, 1980), pp.22–44; A. D. Morse, *While Six Million Died* (New York, 1968), pp.199–220; Katz. Z. Schlomo, "Public Opinion in Western Europe and the Evian Conference of July 1938," *Yad Va-Shem Studies*, (Jerusalem, 1973): 9, pp.105–132.

52. Krausnick, "Judenverfolgung," (n. 47 above), p.280. See also: J. Tenenbaum, "The Crucial Year 1938," *Yad Va-Shem Studies*, (Jerusalem, 1958), Vol. II, p.61.

53. In this connection, the conversation held with Hitler in September 1938 by the ambassador of Poland to Berlin, J. Lipski, is of interest. In that conversation Hitler said to Lipski that he intended to solve the Jewish problem by sending them to settlements, in coordination with Poland, Hungary, and perhaps with Rumania as well. To this the Polish representative replied that if Hitler succeeded in this, the Poles would erect a magnificent statue in his honor in Warsaw. See: J. Lipski, *Diplomat in Berlin* (London, 1968), p.411.

54. See: D. Yisraeli, *The German Reich and Palestine: The Palestine Problem in German Politics, 1889–1945* (Heb.) (Ramat-Gan, 1974), pp.154–158.

55. M. Broszat, *Der Staat Hitlers* (Muenchen, 1969), p.437.

56. A. Hitler, *Reden und Proklamationen, 1962–1963*, ed. M. A. Domarus (Neustadt a.d. Aisch, 1962–63), 2, p.1058.

57. See Domarus, Ibid., the speech of 30 January 1941, p.1663; the speech of 30 January 1942, p.1829. See also *Hitler's Table Talk* (n. 46 above), pp.238–239.

58. See n. 36, the material pertaining to Madagascar.

59. See: *Hitler's Table Talk* op. cit, p.238.

60. See M. Broszat "Hitler and the Beginning of the Final Solution," (n. 47 above), p.85.

61. Ibid.

62. See: *Nuremberg Documents* No–205.

63. See Himmler's speech to the Senior Officers in Posen in October 1943, *Nuremberg Documents* Ps–1919.

64. See G. Mann in *Deutsche und Juden*, (n. 20 above), pp.60–62.

65. W. Jochmann, "Die Ausbreitung des Antisemitismus," in *Deutsches Judentum in Krieg und Revolution, 1916–1923: Ein Sammelband* (Tuebingen, 1971), pp.409–510.

66. I. Elbogen, *A Century of Jewish Life* (Philadelphia, 1966), p.457.

67. Z. Barbu, "Die Sozialpsychologische Struktur des national-sozialistischen Antisemitismus," in *Entscheidunsjahr 1932: Zur Judenfrage in der Endphase der Weimarer Republik, Sammelband* (Tuebingen, 1965), pp.157–181.

68. On the dissemination of the racist doctrine and racial antisemitism among scientists and their part in the active antisemitic campaign, see: M. Weinreich, *Hitler's Professors: The Part of Scholarship in Germany's Crimes against the Jewish People* (New York, 1946).

69. On this see: *Bayern in der NS-Zeit: Soziale Lage und politisches Verhalten der Bevoelkerung im Spiegel vertraulicher Berichte*, ed. Martin Broszat, Elke Froelich, Falk Weisemann (Muenchen and Wien, 1977).

70. See, for example, B. Forrel, "National-Socialism and the Protestant Churches in Germany," in *The Third Reich* (n. 3 above), ibid., p.830.

71. Bracher, Sauer and Schultz, *Die national-sozialistische Machtergreifung* (n. 15 above), ibid., p.285.

72. See, for example, F. V. Schlabrendorff, *Offiziere gegen Hitler* (Frankfurt a.M., 1965). (The material cited on pp.62–63 about the officers' activities against the murder of Jews is unfounded); G. Ritter, *Carl Goerdeler und die deutsche Widerstandsbewegung* (Muenchen, 1964). (Especially see the documents in the book's appendix).

73. *Judenfeindschaft, Darstellung und Analysen* (Frankfurt am Main and Hamburg, 1963, p.254.

74. *Bayern in der NS-Zeit* (n. 69 above), p.638; *Meldungen aus dem Reich: Auswahl aus den geheimen Lageberichten des Sicherheitsdienstes der SS, 1939–1944* (München, 1968), p.314. G. Mann, *Deutsche Geschichte, 1919–1945* (Frankfurt am Main and Hamburg, 1958), p.174.

75. On this see: D. Carpi, "The Rescue of Jews in the Italian Zone of Conquered Croatia," in: *Rescue Attempts During the Holocaust* (Jerusalem, 1977): 456–426. See also: E. Brand, "The Attitude of the Italians towards the Jews in the Occupied Territories," *Yad Va-Shem Bulletin* 6/7 (1960):17–18.
76. Most well-known is the complicated affair of Kurt Gerstein, who was present at the death-camp in the Lublin area and tried to alert free-world public opinion. There is great importance, also, in the role of the member of the German Foreign Ministry, F. G. Dulckwitz who, in September 1943, warned the Danish leaders and the personnel of the Danish Foreign Ministry of the imminent deportation of the Jews. Even the information about the mass murders which were being carried out and which were being planned, disseminated by the World Jewish Congress representative at Geneva, G. Rigner, in the summer of 1942, were transmitted by an unidentified German personality.

25

Antisemitism in Western Europe

YEHUDA BAUER

In recent years, a movement has developed in western Europe and the United States called Neo-Nazism. We are not sure, however, that the concept "neo" is apt, for what is being spoken of is Nazism. To be sure, biologically it is a new generation, these are new people – but this does not essentially change the picture: It is the same Nazism. However, there are two aspects to the new Nazism which, we feel, are new: One, it is an international movement. Whereas previously, during the Third Reich, though the S.S. was explicitly a transnational organization, it was German. Nazism today considers itself a European, or if you will, a worldwide "white" movement. One of its centers is in Brussels, with a publication called *Nation Europa*; and another center is located in Lincoln, Nebraska. The aim of the movement is to transcend national boundaries and to speak on behalf of all the white nations. The second aspect, most prominent in the new Nazism and characteristic of it, is the claim, by those whose spiritual parents organized the murder of the entire Jewish people, that this murder, which succeeded to such a great extent during the Hitler period, never took place at all. This is a paradoxical claim to which we shall return.

From the political standpoint, the Nazi movements are peripheral. In the last German elections, they received no more than three-tenths of one per cent of the votes. In England, apparently one of the world centers of the Nazi movements today, the "National Front" has in a number of places reached over five per cent of the votes, but it has disintegrated lately into a number of factions. The problem, therefore, is not quantitative and there need be no fear that tomorrow morning we will witness a wave of Nazism. The problem is a different one: We know from the past that when there are organizations with political apparatuses, they are available for exploitation when the political, economic, social, or cultural picture changes. That is to say, there is a danger in the very existence of these organizations even when they are a negligible minority and do not constitute any immediate political threat whatsoever.

In the basic anti-Jewish charges which include the antisemitic tradition which the Nazis inherited from the past, and mixed into their own special concoction, a central place is held by the claim that the Holocaust never took place at all. Until the end of the 1960s, this claim did not penetrate the public's consciousness, but it is now beginning to make headway, and this is an essential change. This claim was first heard in the 1950s from the French Nazi, Paul Rassinier, a former French Socialist and concentration camp inmate who for some reason "changed his spots" and became a defender of the S.S. and Nazism. In the 1950s, his claim sounded weird and astonishing. In the meantime, however, he acquired heirs: the Englishman who signed himself Richard Howard, the German Manfred Roeder and others. They published pamphlets and leaflets, the ideas were disseminated, and they began in most serious fashion to make inroads in the awareness of the public. The book by Arthur R. Butz of Northwestern University in Chicago, Illinois, *The Hoax of the Twentieth Century*,[1] "proved scientifically," as it were, that a million Jews reached the United States and the State of Israel; a million disappeared somewhere in the Soviet Union; and a million, to be sure, died – as did many other millions during the World War II period. The Holocaust was invented by the Jews in order to extract monies from West Germany and in order to establish, in the State of Israel, the international Jewish center which would dominate the world. Jamil Baroody, Saudi Arabia's ambassador to the United Nations, repeated this charge from the U.N. rostrum on 24 and 25 March 1976. Of all those present, only the British ambassador rose to protest.

The charge began to penetrate. Butz is impossible to read because the book is unreadable – but so was *Mein Kampf.* We are now witnessing a wave of such publications. The Institute of Contemporary History in Munich, which devotes most of its energies to investigating the Nazi period, each week receives, without exaggeration, hundreds of requests from West German teachers. The children come from home with questions: Did this happen or not? Are the stories true or not? These same questions are heard in London, in Chesterfield, in Liverpool, in York, and in Hull. Such questions have also appeared in readers' letters to the *New York Times*.

Another point in connection with antisemitism today is the matter of anti-Zionism and antisemitism. One need not be enthusiastic about the policies of one government or another in the State of Israel or the policies of the Zionist Movement; and, indeed, those who have reservations about them are not necessarily antisemitic. But the moment one moves from criticizing a particular act or series of acts to a negation of the very right of the Jewish people to exist in its state and in its land, one is crossing the line into antisemitism; and this line is easily crossed. It is particularly happening today, especially in intellectual groups, and that includes media people. There are a few examples of this relating to definitions of *The Protocols of the Elders of Zion* and events which preceded *The Protocols*. Zionism is described as a movement enabling the Jews to dominate the world. In South America these accusations appeared in the guise of "the Andinia plot" which claims that the Jews intend to separate off sections of Argentina in order to establish the world Jewish authority there after they will have been driven from the State of Israel.

On 27 November 1977, a member of Parliament in London, Eric Moonman, saw fit to rise and charge that antisemitism has reached such proportions in thirteen of Britain's universities that certain Jewish organizations are not able to function. From one of these universities, antisemitic propagandists were sent to schools in the neighborhood to advise their Jewish students not to register for the university. In a number of these universities "Z-R" (Zionism-Racism) resolutions were passed – copies of the infamous resolution passed in 1975 by the automatic Arab-Soviet-Third World majority at the United Nations which denounces Zionism as a "racist" movement. On the basis of these resolutions, the general student-body organizations in those colleges prohibited Reform Rabbis from speaking to the Jewish student organizations at a number of these colleges about Jewish ethics; for as one knows, from ethics the speakers will move to Zionism, and from Zionism to Fascism, and such things may not be heard at a British university. These were the decisions of the students, not of the lecturers. The university staff were furious, shocked, and shaken by these events but were powerless, because the students have their own autonomous organizations.

In this particular example we have the union of several factors: the nationalistic movement in England, the student organizations with P.L.O. influence, and the young radicals. In England, the young radicals are usually counted among the leaders of these movements. To all this, there is the added factor of an historical revisionism which is making headway, especially among western intellectual circles, different from and more sophisticated than the blatant neo-Nazi type of the Butz book. This revisionism sees the Nazi period from another angle: It deals with the trivialization of the entire period, that is, with the claim that Nazism is essentially an incidental phenomenon and completely marginal. Nazism, so it says, is a deviation in modern history and is of no significance beyond its own time and place. There are those who say that there should be a new investigation of who was to blame for World War II. Thus, for example, there is David Irving's book *Hitler's War*[2] which was the basis of a television program with David Frost, seen by many millions of viewers. During this program, David Irving succeeded in convincing the viewers that Hitler is really a banal figure: Hitler, so he said, was a fifty-five year old man with false teeth and chronic stomach problems who was not in control of his environment, and did not know of the murder of the Jews.

Here the phenomenon of the "Hitler fad" should be noted. This will subside. It seems to be ebbing already. In the last few years, serious books have appeared correcting the distortions of Irving and his associates. But, alongside these, there has also appeared the well-known film of Joachim Fest, the West German, pro-Israeli journalist, who sought to prove that Hitler was an ordinary man, a German dictator who, like Napoleon in France, finally brought a catastrophe upon Germany. In his film there are neither Russians nor Poles, and certainly no Jews. Nor do French or any others appear in it. Hitler brought catastrophe upon Germany as Napoleon did upon France. The French had Napoleon and the Germans had Hitler, and the problem is: How did he succeed in winning the German nation? This is a philosophic, historico-political problem, and Fest does not consider the ethical problem at all. This precludes the possibility of dealing with the Holocaust for, as far as the world is concerned, this is a moral issue, and moral problems do not enter into the arguments put forth by these writers and film-makers as "realistic" problems. This could of course strengthen the antisemitic virus for renewed activity.

The same attitudes can be discerned in films and books that are not directly political in content. Such works present a sometimes romantic, sometimes nostalgic picture of Nazism and the Holocaust. The book by D. M. Thomas, *The White Hotel*,[3] could serve as an example of this, as could the film "The Night Porter." Both are serious attempts, from different angles, to analyze victims' reactions to the events of the Holocaust. They try to uncover psychological truths, to disclose to the reader or viewer elements such as the identification between victim and perpetrator, or the suicidal desires of many of the victims. But the – perhaps incidental, most probably unintended – message is to set the victim and the perpetrator on the same level, and in effect to make the Holocaust altogether trivial, and thus deny its function as a warning to a humanity which still suffers from chronic diseases such as Jew-hatred.

The danger lies in the union of neo-Nazism, historical revisionism, anti-Zionism, and cultural antisemitism, for the effect of such a union can snowball. This is not an immediate but a relatively distant danger. Yet we must recognize that the period is past when we, too, perhaps felt that antisemitism and its remnants are only a subject for historical research. We must consider the problem we are confronting as not only historical but actual; that without serious study of antisemitism's results we will be unable to cope with it. The fundamental problem is that, until recently, there was no research institute whose function and concern was to investigate these phenomena so that institutions and organizations could come forth – on the basis of this research – with proposals for specific action to be taken. It seems to us that a number of the influences creating this picture, apart for the ethical influences to which we have alluded, are coming to the western, democratic world first and foremost from the Soviet bloc. In the popular, weekly, Soviet press, these antisemitic charges appear openly, in the crudest form, and from there reach and penetrate the Arab and Muslim world, but their traces are also to be found in the West.

Notes

1. Arthur R. Butz, *The Hoax of the Twentieth Century* (2nd. ed.; Brighton, Sussex, 1977).
2. David Irving, *Hitler's War* (London, 1977).
3. D. M. Thomas, *The White Hotel* (London, 1981).

26

From Overt Philosemitism to Discreet Antisemitism, and Beyond

Anti-Jewish Developments in the Political Culture of the Federal Republic of Germany

FRANK STERN

There is a fine line between an antisemitic mood and a rising, steadily intensifying wave of anti-Jewish sentiment. Such a phenomenon in the Federal Republic of Germany deserves some consideration.

Countless publications, and numerous public forums, including some that were hardly appropriate, have dealt with the issue: What is the link between current manifestations of antisemitism and German history prior to 8 May 1945? The responses elicited vary from complete to partial acknowledgement of guilt; from accepting responsibility to ignoring or denying it. The once passionate acknowledgment of guilt is now increasingly resigned, leaving only a faint echo that can be heard in the fruitless "Brotherhood Weeks" dedicated to German-Jewish understanding, officially celebrated once a year in many German towns and cultural centers.

While for some, the immediacy of the mass murder of the Jewish people cannot be minimized, for others it is receding into the annals of German history. It is becoming embedded in the past – a past for which subsequent generations appear to have been relieved of responsibility – because of what Helmut Kohl[1] has termed, with obvious historical detachment, "the gift of later birth" (*"die Gnade der späten Geburt"*).

Jews who, especially in Germany, will remain the children of Auschwitz for generations to come, are confronted with those German "fellow citizens" who seem to be constantly "dropping out" of history. This contradictory development leads to a second question: How are contemporary manifestations of antisemitism actually connected with the history of Germany after 8 May 1945 – that is, with the history of the Federal Republic of Germany?

1.   An Antisemitic Atmosphere and Latent Antisemitism

One of the concluding remarks made at the International Seminar on Present Day Antisemitism held at the end of December 1985 in Jerusalem was: "We are not faced with an antisemitic wave but an antisemitic mood" (Yehuda Bauer). Given the present conditions in the Federal Republic of Germany, Willy Brandt's remark on the occasion of the Berlin Festival screening of Claude Lanzmann's *Shoah* is not inappropriate: "German-Nationalist obtuseness and political speculation on antisemitic resentment are surfacing uninhibitedly once again."[2] Let us consider a few recent events. The scandal evoked by R. W. Fassbinder's antisemitic play[3] is no more a wave of antisemitism than the radical, verbal anti-Zionist invectives of some Germans who seek to relieve themselves of the burden of their own history. Both are an expression of West Germany's return to "normalcy" in the 1980s. Latent antisemitism follows this pattern. It is no longer confined to smoky beer halls frequented by right-wing Conservatives, old and new style Nazis. Now endorsed by many people, it is emerging in the political institutions of parliamentary democracy – despite the fact that politicians of the governing Conservative Party, the Christian Democratic Union (CDU), occasionally deplore its verbal expression as an "inept choice of words." Let us harbor no illusions. The public outcry will be shortlived, as it often is, and will refer only to the surface of antisemitism.

Those who wish to take up arms and combat the current manifestations of latent antisemitism should first ask themselves: What am I fighting? What are the underlying causes of these antisemitic phenomena? What should be the objectives of investigation?

In the past, it was not difficult to express moral indignation whenever right-wing extremists or neo-Fascists produced one of their masterpieces of antisemitism. Such incidents could be put in perspective, the roots of Nazism traced, and Hitler's heirs unmasked. The legitimate rage against avowed antisemites, however, has often left no room for calm consideration of their acceptance by wide sectors of the population. Moreover, perceptions of them have been narrowed as a result of preoccupation with organized right-wing extremism. Hence, one must ask: What changes have occurred in the grey zone that links right-wing extremism and Conservatism; what induced the Conservative mode of thinking, both in the large democratic parties and in the spheres of culture and the media? Finally, what does the "silent majority" think?

The key term "antisemitic mood," mentioned at the outset of this article, is applicable here. Primarily, it indicates a variable state of mind, a spontaneous reaction to stimuli, associations, or prevailing opinions. While moods may fluctuate, they always leave a residue – an inkling of what is to come. They can prevail for extended periods, or develop cyclically. They may seem superficial, but in fact are deeply entrenched, and cannot be traced exclusively in the mind of the person or persons concerned. Moods can be expressed through emotional or cognitive patterns as relatively stable views, thought patterns, and attitudes. At the same time, they may overcome their irrational origins, and find expression in prejudices and stereotypes. Beyond the individual, however, moods can assume a collective character, affecting larger groups and social strata, as well as entire nations in certain historical instances. As moods gather momentum, perspectives and ideas long considered outdated may reactivate the potential for prejudice inherent in the social consciousness until a wave of antisemitism is generated.

The Fassbinder affair is a case in point. In 1974, R. W. Fassbinder wrote an overtly antisemitic play entitled *The Garbage, the City, and Death* which was not staged at that time. Based on a novel by the West German author Gerhard Zwerenz, the play focused on the financial speculations of a rich Frankfurt Jew in the 1970s. In 1985, the Frankfurt Theater arranged for a performance of this play, which evoked vehement protests from Jewish communities and negative public reactions in Germany and abroad. Since these international protests were apparently ineffective, Jewish demonstrators staged a sit-in inside the theater at the time of the scheduled performance in October 1985. After more than two hours of debates and demonstrations in and outside the theater, the performance was cancelled, and the entire production curtailed. The essence of this affair was not dictated by the antisemitic play itself or the public protest staged by the Jews, but rather by the offensive anti-Jewish reactions that accompanied the ensuing debate in the media.

It is now clear how, after a few weeks of tension and publicity in 1985, the age-old image of the odious, wealthy, perverse Jew was revived with unprecedented intensity among the population. The mood was conducive to confirmation of a stereotype that, while vaguely outlined, had not as yet been clearly articulated. It was first expressed in an insolent remark by a representative of the Frankfurt theater, referring to the "end of the close season" for Jews. This remark could be understood as if permission to resume the hunt had been granted. A member of parliament, representative of the Christian Social Union (CSU)[4] depicted the mood as such: "Jews are quick to respond when they hear the jingle of German cash-boxes." Another conservative politician, Graf Spee, added: "A few rich Jews would (have to be) killed to balance the budget"; and a local chairman of the Christian Democratic Youth Union complained: "How arrogant of Israel to make our democratic constitutional state responsible for the murder of the Jews in the Third Reich!" Numerous statements in this vein followed in letters, telephone conversations, and so on.[5]

In other words, anti-Jewish prejudice, long considered overcome, has resurfaced in West Germany among the intellectual underground and – despite all protestations to the contrary – is now socially acceptable in every way. This phenomenon is, however, contingent upon a wider susceptibility, a disposition that did not suddenly materialize in the 1980s but developed in literature, arts, and political culture over a long period of time. Public opinion polls conducted during the past forty years repeatedly attest to the prevalence of the view that Jews have too much influence – yet totally fail to consider the Jew's actual status in Germany. The extent to which this anti-Jewish dogma is accepted is not determined by education, knowledge, or personal experience.

In 1949, the first president of the Federal Republic of Germany, Theodor Heuss, stated in an interview:

> Real antisemitism no longer exists in Germany. "Against whom would antisemitism be directed? There is no longer any rivalry between Jews and non-Jews, nor any other grounds for envy. So why should antisemitism exist?" Foreign and German Jewish leaders have confirmed this. Some Germans still harbor somewhat confused National Socialist sympathies – but these sentiments are harmless. These Germans are far more concerned with developments in other countries . . . There has been a public outcry and great concern in Germany and abroad following a number of incidents in which Jewish cemeteries were desecrated. "This was not a manifestation of antisemitism, since there were never any Jewish residents there whose feelings might have been hurt as a result of the vandalism."[6]

The fact that this interview took place in 1949 should not lead one to resort to that popular, hackneyed cliche that "the Germans have always been and will remain antisemites." The antisemitic mood, causing latent antisemitism to become so clearly manifest, is common to all Western countries – as the findings of the Jerusalem Seminar have indicated. This latent antisemitism, increasing in the West, by no means rules out mitigation of the manifest, virulent antisemitism expressed in militant anti-Jewish activities and publications. The more brutal forms of aggression are currently directed against other ethnic groups, primarily foreign workers and their families: Turks in Germany; Algerians and black Africans in France; blacks and Asians in Britain; non-whites in Holland, and so on. Nevertheless, it is clear that hostility toward Jews, or, at the very least, anti-Jewish prejudice that can be exhibited at any time, is inherent in any form of xenophobia and can always be employed for political purposes.

To sum up: The essential argument in response to latent antisemitism is reference to Germany's crimes under the Third Reich. Some West Germans call for cool normalcy; others engage in historical trivialization or produce vague, noncommital confessions of guilt; and many Jews are content to emphasize the historic uniqueness of the crimes against the Jewish people, and their universal significance. While this is correct, one can neither understand nor combat contemporary antisemitism – that malicious, yet discreet antisemitic mood – by disregarding the past forty years and dealing exclusively with the crimes of fascism. Exclusive reference to the tradition of prejudice is academic:

We must trace the origins and causes of latent antisemitism among the German population during the forty years following Auschwitz, that is, during the evolution of postwar Germany.

2. Old Prejudice and a New Understanding of History

Young Germans can hardly be denied the right to a natural feeling of kinship and identity with their homeland. The trouble with German history and lately also with German historiography is that, sooner or later, such endeavors have always led to extreme views, essentially depicting the enemy through implicitly anti-Jewish images.

The search for identity, homeland, and past began in the 1970s, when German memories of the Nazi period had begun to fade. As early as 1959, Max Horkheimer remarked: "Kowtowing to resistance fighters, official denunciations of antisemitism, from synagogue visits by mayors to the silence concerning Anne Frank – all this fuss about guilt simply allows rightist patriotism to flourish once again with a clear conscience . . ." And in another instance: "The German admission of guilt after the defeat of National Socialism in 1945 was a splendid scheme for carrying over the popular feelings of community (*völkisches Gemeinschaftsempfinden*) into the postwar period."[7]

The changes that have since occurred in this "splendid scheme" will be discussed below. Effective modification, neutralization and re-evaluation of the official concepts of history – including current images and clichés about Jews – began at the end of the 1960s, continuing through the 1970s, and becoming socially acceptable in the 1980s. Where there had previously been at least some acknowledgement of responsibility, a version of history stressing "normalcy" is now becoming predominant. The twelve years of the Third Reich have been discarded, filed away as no more than an unpleasant episode, a dark chapter in Germany's glorious thousand-year history. Trivializations and re-evaluations abound in the media and book stores.

For a number of years "pseudoscientific" paperbacks and magazines have been propagating a historical perspective which views the crimes committed during the Third Reich as a relative phenomenon. Reference is made to the heinous deeds of other countries and governments, body counts are tallied up and German history, in effect, decriminalized – something right-wing extremists have been demanding repeatedly over the years. Ernst Nolte, considered an élite contemporary West German historian, initiated the most recent historiographic debate by posting the question: "Wasn't the Gulag Archipelago a prior event to Auschwitz? Wasn't the class murder of the Bolsheviks in actual fact the logical and concrete predecessor of the race murder carried out by the National Socialists?"[8]

Anti-communist stereotypes from the Cold War period reappear in modern guise. Once again, we find Nazi Germany being equated with the Soviet Union. The horrible singularity of Nazi Germany's crimes against humanity becomes the "normalcy" of just another historical mischief. Germany's past is thus redefined in terms of collective innocence.

This relative view of German history is often accompanied by its personalization. The existence or nonexistence of orders issued by Hitler, for instance, serves as the topic of entire conferences; and this is no longer confined to the realms of right-wing extremist historiography, for these tendencies can now be encountered among established, professional historians, who have been teaching for years at West German universities. The somewhat vehement public discussions on these matters ensue from scholarly developments extending over a period of many years and at the same time from a nonscholarly process which spawned a new popular self-righteousness coupled with anti-Eastern and anti-Western sentiments.

The essential issue is the historiographic legitimization of a "German normalcy," defined in terms of "national identity" rather than democratic, liberal, anti-Fascist or humanistic identity. Such an apologetic approach to contemporary historical reality carries to extremes what the President of the Federal Republic of Germany, Richard von Weizsäcker, singled out in his address to the 16th International Convention of Historians in 1985 in Stuttgart as the task now facing German historians: "clarification of the truth . . . but not by means of a history of one's own national failures."[9]

Writing in the conservative journal *Criticon* in late 1984, the conservative social philosopher Günter Rohrmoser argued that "national identity" should not be based on "an abstract democratic identity devoid of history." Quite aside from the fact that, in this way, one would render the democratic forces in Germany after 1945 a historical non-entity, it must be borne in mind that "democratic identity" clearly played an important part, ideologically and politically, in the establishment of the Federal Republic of Germany.

Just as conservative circles in the Weimar Republic appealed to the "ideas of 1914" – defense of the fatherland, German glory, German culture, *Volk*, and community – and not to the founding of the 1919 republic, influential West German historians are now defining the democratic consensus of 1945 as a relative phenomenon. Once again, German scholars are developing a historical perspective in which the nation becomes the all-embracing principle. This is not merely an incidental development, but rather conforms with prevalent ideological trends. The new German communal spirit, after its various confessions of guilt and verbal reconciliations with the past, has come up with a new formula: collective absolution (*kollektiver Schlusstrich*), that is, a call to stop regarding the years 1933-45 as historically singular. Another closely linked historiographic trend is to write about everyday life in the German homeland during that period and, going further back than 1933, to recount romantic lore and heroic epics of Germany's distant past. With such a historical perspective, one can gaze into a future completely detached from the Nazi experience of the twentieth century. At the Jerusalem Seminar one participant, Martin Stöhr, former director of the Arnoldsheim Evangelical Academy in West Germany, criticized this mode of thinking, stating:

> It is not the criminals or the bystanders and their children who feel obligated today to explain what happened, and perhaps penetrate deeper, asking why it occurred and whether something similar could eventuate again . . . Not only are the victims of Nazi terror required to recount and expand on their past ordeals . . . they must often justify the fact that they or their children discuss the experiences they suffered. The victims are a living reminder, embodying experiences and unresolved questions for those who deny collective guilt but would gladly accept collective absolution.

Bearers of evil tidings in ancient Rome were as unpopular as today's living witnesses of Germany's misdeeds, which no longer trouble those who do not want to be reminded of them. One has to consider how the German population reacts to those Jews who actively oppose re-evaluation, trivialization, and neutralization of fascism and antisemitism. Once again, it is suggested that critics of anti-Jewish pronouncements should consider whether they are not essentially cultivating a new wave of antisemitism. The *Frankfurter Allgemeine Zeitung*, for instance, submits that the statements quoted by West German politicians should be taken more lightly:

> The antisemitic expression that in order to obtain money one first has to "kill a rich Jew," has been used colloquially for generations in the Rhineland and Westfalia. Ugly as it may be, it merely attempts to figuratively describe the inexpedience of certain financial claims.[10]

In these "figurative" and "colloquial" terms, we are assured once again of the continued existence of latent antisemitism and its overt manifestations. As it turns out, such statements are by no means novel. In an article published in 1983 upon the death of a well-known Frankfurt Jew, the same paper described him as a "businessman of Jewish descent and the best German conviction,"[11] leaving no doubt as to what is expected of us.

Taken together with the Fassbinder affair, which involved a Jewish speculator and has long since spawned similar local incidents throughout West Germany, such statements have brought us right back to the immediate postwar period. It was between 1945 and 1949 that the stereotype of the wealthy Jew assumed its post-Nazi character. Jewish Displaced Persons flocked to the large towns; Jewish survivors returned from concentration camps and emerged from the underground, moving into the apartments of former Nazis. They claimed their property, which had been seized by the Nazis, demanded restitution and financial compensation. They arrived unexpectedly and were received accordingly. The writer Peter Edel,[12] who survived Auschwitz, summed up the shock of that return: "They had forgotten to gas us."

A tormented society applied age-old prejudices to a Jewish minority that, while infinitely larger than the contemporary community, had little in common with traditional German Jewry. The inception of postwar antisemitism cannot be rationalized by the abstruse, quasi-mystic "antisemitism without Jews" slogan; rather, it can be traced to the renewed establishment of Jewish communities and revival of Jewish activities after 1945. The stereotype of the Jewish speculator, the profiteer, the rich Jew, materialized when Jews resumed commercial activity.

Along with the stereotype of the "rich Jew," and "Jewish capital," we are currently witnessing the resurrection of yet another antisemitic prejudice. In May 1985, on the occasion of an official visit by US President Ronald Reagan, the German government chose to commemorate the Armistice at a Wehrmacht and SS cemetery in the small town of Bitburg. The Christian Churches participated; the Jewish community protested by refraining from participation. Bitter letters were exchanged between Jewish community leaders and representatives of the Federal Government. One might say that Bitburg (and not the Fassbinder affair) marked the end of a fairly calm period in official German-Jewish relations. Bitburg was a nightmare not only for Jews in Germany but for Jews the world over, as well as surviving resistance fighters and survivors of the concentration camps. It threatened the survival of the anti-Fascist and democratic principles which had been widely accepted in 1945.

In Germany of 1986, the declaration that "the Jews" had too much influence in the American media and even in Germany is not limited to extreme right-wing circles. The century-old stereotype of the intellectual Jewish critic, the destructive anti-German Jew who allegedly has too much power and influence in the media and political press – and now even in the theater – has been reinvoked.

Ironically, the prevalent anti-Jewish mood has turned a short-lived victory in the battle against antisemitism such as the protest against the Frankfurt Theater production into a quasi-confirmation of the stereotype of Jewish influence. Anti-Jewish prejudice runs a vicious circle: When Jews in an anti-semitic atmosphere become politically active as Jews, then prejudices against them are not refuted but rather confirmed. Again, however, it should be borne in mind that prejudices do not arise overnight, but are rooted in the past, with their own history. In 1965, Hannah Arendt described the situation in West Germany in a letter to philosopher Karl Jaspers:

> . . . no trace of any revolution in their way of thinking! The first signs of it were eliminated by Adenauer consciously, and solely to serve his own political interests, his theory being: The majority of the population was involved, and it is therefore in their interests not to recall the past. The greatest danger of interference lies in the Jewish camp, considering its

influence on world opinion. Hence we must do all we can to avoid the danger.[13]

Along with the two stereotypes mentioned above, which are currently prevalent and have a historical basis, another antisemitic prejudice is becoming evident in the context of the general German search for identity, in almost all spheres of the political spectrum: The destruction of the German town Dresden during World War II is being equated with the massacres at Auschwitz, and Beirut under Israeli occupation with the Warsaw Ghetto; hysterical assertions are made that the Jews invented the atom bomb; it is suggested that the installation of US rockets in Germany is a delayed act of Jewish vengeance; and the Jewish lobby in Washington as well as the Israeli government are regarded as a sinister, insidious threat. Hence, it is not only in right-wing periodicals that the old stereotype of an "international Jewish conspiracy" has been restored. The *Frankfurter Allgemeine Zeitung* was careful to place Bitburg and "influential circles in Washington" in close juxtaposition. The West German reader could then infer the identity of those "divisive circles" who had foiled attempts at a harmonious graveyard conciliation.

A disturbing phenomenon, repeatedly confirmed at the Jerusalem Seminar on Present-Day Antisemitism, is the prevalence of the "conspiracy" thesis and increasing distribution of the *Protocols of the Elders of Zion* in various forms. Anyone who has been following the press since the Frankfurt Theater affair can affirm that this is certainly the case in Germany. Once again, the figure of an anonymous, powerful Jew has been conjured up, and the conspiratorial element in this secret power is fully employed. The insidious social legitimization of these antisemitic prejudices raises an additional question. Was the deletion of the world "Jewish" from the traditional German formula of a "Jewish Bolshevik world conspiracy" after 8 May 1945 final? The replacement of "the Jews" by "the Communists" as irrational targets for hostility since the Cold War may not be permanent if, with the aid of an appeal to the common national denominator, German culture (*Kulturnation*), and its "undivided" history – popular feelings against sources of evil in the world are revived.

Until now, these may have been mere passing trends, but the rejection of everything foreign, contrary, alien, and "un-German," is becoming increasingly accepted. The sad truth is that the various historical identities that make up the current political spectrum consider the 2,000-year-old history of the Jews in German lands a *quantité négligeable*, appropriate for museums. This history has largely been replaced in the political culture by a revival of anti-Jewish stereotypes. No one should be deceived by the occasional exhibition or Sunday school lectures on Jewish themes.

In short, primeval antisemitic prejudices and stereotypes are emerging in modern guise, sometimes in other spheres and frameworks that had confidently been considered democratic and therefore immune. Stereotypes such as "Jewish Power" and "the Jewish conspiracy," once prevalent in politics but since laughed off as a thing of the past, are suddenly enjoying the same comfortable status in the realm of culture as the myth of the "rich Jew," and are now infiltrating political institutions. The essential elements of antisemitism do not change – the arsenal was filled to overflowing during the nineteenth century – although the cause, milieu and social context of action are subject to change. The prejudices are, so to speak, being shifted into the more relevant domain of social psychology. This is hardly surprising, considering the role of culture (*Kulturnation*) and historical tradition in the public consciousness of the German people. The various theories concerning antisemitism have not as yet developed any viable explanation of this phenomenon. Psychology is helpful, but not sufficient in itself. It should be stressed that any Jewish attempt to fend off these manifestations of antisemitism must pay more attention to the historical dimension. Not every new German identity crisis need necessarily be duplicated by the Jews.

3. Antisemitism as a Stowaway

Among West Germany's current intellectual trends and principal political ideologies, antisemitism has assumed the role of a stowaway on a train. Sitting in his compartment, the passenger had remained unnoticed until the train reached its destination – around the mid-1980s – at which point he walked out of his compartment and in passing kicked all the Jews in the shins. They let out a shriek, having forgotten in their excitement that by ignoring him all this time they had helped boost his self-confidence. Certainly other passengers had seen the stowaway but they had disregarded him.

In German history, overt political antisemitism has often been accompanied by other ideological concepts and goals ranging from socio-economic objectives to power politics and aggressive militarism. Yet the reverse also holds true. The sparkling new brand of nationalism in West Germany can be seen as the train compartment in which antisemitic trends have comfortably ensconced themselves. However, the antisemitism now coming to the fore is not, as a rule, the same as the traditional racial antisemitism. The latter was totally discredited after 1945, and eked out a stunted existence in rightist niches. Only with the advent of the blatant racism manifested against Turkish workers could racial antisemitism resurface.

Racial antisemitism, however, may not be the most prevalent expression of today's antisemitic mood. The fact that the antisemitic mood of the 1920s shifted from political movements and parties to other domains should not be regarded as a simple analogy. The current increase in cultural, social, sexual, and emotional anti-Jewish prejudices is linked to the intellectual climate of the Weimar Republic. The increasingly accepted perception of foreigners, outsiders, and Jews is not rooted in the state-sponsored racial antisemitism that prevailed between 1933 and 1945, but rather in pre-1933 antisemitism and post-1945 philosemitism. Before 1933, antisemitism was socially acceptable;

after 1945, there was a transition from ordained philosemitism to a collective absolution of national guilt and an end to "resti-jew-tion." Again, however, this is not the same as racial antisemitism.

In other words, the battle against contemporary antisemitism calls for appropriate weapons. The weapons used to resist racial antisemitism will not stem the tide of cultural antisemitism; nor is incessant harping on the crimes of the Nazis and the guilt of the German people effective. The production of Fassbinder's play was not meant to propound a second "Final Solution," but simply to portray a nasty Jew on stage once again.[14] It is misleading to invoke Hitler and the question of responsibility. The existence of a completely "normal," autochthonous, antisemitic mood must be recognized and dealt with.

This mood is fostered and sustained through lectures, publications, debates, and contexts in which the word "Jew" never appears, nor are Jews attacked directly; nevertheless everyone is well aware who is being discussed. The implications, rather than the actual statements, are clearly antisemitic; and the antisemitic association sits discreetly in the train compartment. This phenomenon is not confined to the Federal Republic of Germany. It also exists, for example, in France's political culture. There is a smooth transition from an antisemitic mood to antisemitism as a cultural code, a key to self-assurance, logical reasoning, analysis of the past, and, increasingly, a framework for social attitudes and activities. Latent antisemitism is emerging as a sociopsychological and ideological package-deal between West Germany's contemporary culture and her past. Its current effectiveness stems primarily from its interaction with three influential intellectual and social trends: Nationalism, Christian Fundamentalism, and Conservatism.

4. National Dawn and Antisemitic Mist

Once again, everyone has begun to rally around *"Deutschland."* Germany is reflected as an entity deeply rooted in history, a cultural and literary identity, a regional and historic achievement. Once again, German identity becomes a state of mind. By this I am not referring primarily to the extreme chauvinism of right-wing groups, but to that indigenous atmosphere in which Germany's national identity is vigorously promoted. This trend ranges from films about the homeland, ceremonious addresses, Refugee Day, commemorations in the Bundestag, Homeland Day, reunions of former members of the SS, veterans of the Nazi Party and the Wehrmacht, to a short-cut oral history, Mother Earth shops, and newspapers and journals such as the *Frankfurter Allgemeine Zeitung, Tageszeitung, Bunte,* and *Quick,* all woven into a shining popular nationalist fabric.

In certain instances, the indigenous environmentalist movements that defend the German *Heimat* have the upper hand. In other cases, the scales are tipped in favor of German neutrality and reunification, and public opinion is mobilized against the super-powers by a patronizing glance at some of their

German relatives in the East who also seem to be having reservations about the "super-power" in which they live. The question is whether a nationalist synthesis of anti-Americanism and anti-Communism provides a new vehicle for antisemitic perspectives. Furthermore, Germany's location in the heart of Europe may again become a real "place in the sun." The Deutsche Bank, the iron and steel giant Krupp, and the new German missionary zeal will no doubt guarantee this. All these factors are combined by what Jürgen Habermas in the Hamburg weekly *Die Zeit*[15] defined as "disposal of the past," that is to say, an escape from "poisonous" history. Thus Bitburg is systematically transformed into a Jewish problem although it is, in the truest sense of the word, a problem that affects the Federal Republic as a whole.

Only in this light can one understand how and why intellectual right-wing extremism affects the political center, the Conservative establishment. The crux of the issue is not the numerical influence of the extreme right – which itself claims to be a national opposition and is regarded as insignificant by the reports of the Federal Office for the Protection of the Constitution – but the fact that Christian Democrats and the Free Democrats are increasingly attracting a rightist public. In 1985-86, these parties' internal policies became increasingly right-wing. The President of the Federal Republic and leading intellectual of the Christian Democratic Union, Richard von Weiszäcker, pursued a seemingly moderate foreign policy while also demanding the release of the last Nazi prisoner, Rudolf Hess (since deceased) as a concession to a rightist-oriented electorate and to popular historical consciousness. In certain instances, one has to consider why extreme right-wing institutions are necessary when expatriate organizations, associations of former members of the SSand Wehrmacht officers, CDU/CSU high school and student organizations and their affiliated scientific institutions by their nationalistic tone and actions, represent right-wing extremism rather than the conservative political center. For example, the difference between certain groups in the Christian Democratic High School Union and the professed extreme right-wing school initiatives is very marginal. It must be emphasized that the appeal of this political trend lies in its nationalist orientation.

This fundamental trend – by no means limited to any particular generation – is not only inherently conducive to antisemitic prejudice but encourages antisemitism more or less spontaneously. Everything alien is emphasized aggressively or emotionally as the reverse of German and then rejected. Incidentally, some of the associations generated by the terms *foreign, Turkish,* or *Jewish* can send cold chills down one's spine. In the 1950s, when the word "Jew" or "Jewess" was taboo in West Gemany, I heard the term "your fellow countrymen" applied to my family in every conceivable context. Today, some thirty years later, the term "fellow-countrymen" is heard once again – no longer, however, in the saccharine sweet tones of philosemitism, but disapprovingly, as a reference to Israeli tradesmen in Frankfurt or Berlin.

Jews can try to be assimilated into their German surroundings, but to no avail as long as the majority of Germans are prepared to do everything except accept them. From a Jewish standpoint – however it is defined – one can observe the detachment, the growing alienation of West German society from its Jewish citizens, who are still looked upon as "Jewish fellow-citizens," the "Jewish community of fate," and "victims of Hitler's racism." Heinz Galinski, chairman of the Jewish community of West Berlin, remarked on 9 November 1985: "We Jews are almost as isolated as in 1938." This is, in my opinion, no mere figure of speech. While there is no question of history repeating itself, historical mistakes may well be repeated. Past experiences do not have to be repeated by every generation of Jews in Germany. Certainly one can always stage a demonstration in a theater. But can one portray historic memories, so adamantly rejected by the others; can one propound democratic humanism, other people's guilty consciences, and the ideals of equality common to all great revolutions in every smoky German pub?

5. The Christian Counter-Offensive or "To Tolerate is to Hate"

I would like to discuss another cultural-intellectual process closely linked with the general nationalist mood in the Federal Republic, whose intrinsic logic is forcing Jews into the role of outsiders in today's society. This process of a multifaceted, profound religious breakthrough primarily takes the form of Christian Fundamentalism. It is constantly capturing new sectors of society, promising perennial individual and collective well-being in the face of the fragility of prosperity and the political and ethical values that characterized the reconstruction of the Federal Republic of Germany.

During President Reagan's visit to Bergen Belsen, a Protestant clergyman, viewed by millions on television, quoted Psalm 85, verses 5-6:

> Restore us, O God of our salvation, and cause Thine indignation toward us to cease. Wilt Thou be angry with us forever; wilt Thou draw out Thine anger to all generations?

After weeks of public discussions and Jewish protests, millions of viewers must have gained the impression "that the German people would like to be restored to favor, and that the victims are also victims of God's wrath."[16]

The Church's ambivalent attitude towards Jews and Jewish history is problematic, not only because of the Christian response to brownshirt Germany but because it is linked to much more basic, constitutional questions of Christian identity. For centuries, Christianity was the main vehicle for anti-Jewish opinions, attitudes, and actions. The postwar period saw an admission of guilt on the part of the Christian Churches and forty years of attempts to overcome anti-Jewish aspects in the Christian creed and dogma. We know today that these attempts – as demonstrated by the passion play tradition of Oberammergau in Bavaria, by existing antisemitic church decorations, religious instruction, and Christian school songs – actually reached a deadlock. Apart from that, I doubt whether Christianity would have been able to maintain its former status had it voluntarily divested itself of fundamental points in its dogma. The lukewarm attitude expressed in such concepts as "tolerance," "Christian-Jewish dialogue," or the unsuccessful attempt to revive the chimera of "German-Jewish symbiosis" is, in any case, limited to a marginal sector of committed Christians. (In politics, for instance, the unchanged attitude of the Catholic Church is typified by its refusal to recognize the State of Israel.)

Significantly, the fact that many well-meaning Christians maintain that Jesus was a Jew may help pave the way towards enlightenment. It does not, however, negate the Christian gospel, which portrays the Jews as culprits and victims, survivors who are living evidence of the truth of the New Testament. The Jews are witnesses, sufferers, and, as victims, they must be loved. Here lies one of the roots of German postwar philosemitism. However, philosemitism reaches its limit when the victim becomes a viable, active personality; when the stereotype of the suffering Jew comes to life in a non-Jewish society, emerging as a politically active individual or social group, or even as a nation among the nations.

This should not be interpreted to mean that secular German society has been overcome once again by puritanical zeal. The modernization of religion, and Christianization of the younger generations is a gradual process in which basic individual psychological trends and the formation of values, attitudes, and needs converge with the general ideological trends of society as a whole. An excerpt from a songbook used in German elementary schools – to teach music, and not religion – may illustrate this tendency:

> Between Jericho and Jerusalem lies the path of mercy. It is steep, treacherous, and cheerless. Once a band of robbers surrounded a man and threatened him. Soon he lay at the side of the road, beaten, robbed, half dead. Hear his cries on the path of mercy! A priest came riding along followed by a Levite. They had come from holy places and pitied the man, but could not save him because the time was not right. Oh, how wide is the path of mercy.[17]

From this song schoolchildren have come to learn that the Levites must be really bad; and many other songs in this highly recommended booklet were written between 1933 and 1945.

Now what is happening in other sectors of society where Christian ideology is emphasized in leading, influential institutions of the German Federal democracy? Official statements, speeches by top political representatives, publications, and the media state unequivocally that modern German society is founded on Christian values. The Federal Republic of Germany is being propagated, popularized, and recognized increasingly as a country in the "center of

Europe," belonging to the Christian occident. This indicates a certain shift in values. The definition of the Federal Republic as democratic, Western country is being voiced less frequently, despite constant references to Germany's membership in the Western alliance. *Mitte Europas*, an old term referring to German super-power aspirations, is not merely a geographical expression, but a geo-political definition implying that postwar borders are not irrevocable and dreams of reunification are not merely an illusion. If all this can, moreover, be enhanced by a framework of occidental values, then it conforms not only with the individual search for identity, but also with the legitimization of the body politic. The term "occidental Christianity," less susceptible to criticism, has replaced secular aspects of German ideology, and provides a comprehensive framework for authoritarian structures, xenophobia, social prejudices, and socio-psychological predispositions. This may be one of the most significant and widely accepted guiding principles of future cultural-intellectual, internal, and external political development. The nationalist dawn that promises prosperity for Germany has a deeper spiritual basis in European variations of Christian fundamentalism than might be inferred, let us say, from the 1949 Basic Law of the Federal Republic.

The related concept of a New European Order – dangerous as it may be – is less relevant in this context than the danger inherent in anti-Jewish attitudes, viewpoints, and modes of thinking that may be strengthened by the synthesis of nationalism and religious renaissance. In this framework, latent antisemitism becomes a part – less problematic than it was in the past – of Germany's political culture. "The Jew" – with few exceptions – is certainly not Christian, and even less a German nationalist. In addition, those generations which, by virtue of "later birth," are relieved of the burden of guilt and thus, as it seems, of any prejudice, may re-evaluate their attitude toward "the Jews" and notions about "characteristic Jewish behavior." Hitler's heirs are proud. That is to say, the antisemitic mood mentioned above is not an aberration peculiar to former Nazis; it is neither the consequence of neo-Fascist activities nor of the revisionist rewriting of history by extreme right-wing authors – it is part of the daily antisemitic routine. This antisemitic mood cannot be completely counteracted, at least in the first place, through education. It is not mitigated through angry comparisons with the Third Reich or vain appeals to a guilty conscience – which actually never existed. This mood has been fostered by processes described above and by the developments of the past forty years.

On 25 November 1949, in an interview with the Jewish *Allgemeine Wochenzeitung*, Konrad Adenauer, first Chancellor of the Federal Republic, was asked if "the emphasis on the Christian character of the CDU was indicative of an anti-Jewish trend." He replied that the work of the first Federal government would be sustained by "the spirit of occidental Christian culture . . . As Christians, we want to revive the concept of consideration for others, regardless of religion, race, or nationality. In this spirit of tolerance, we consider our Jewish compatriots fellow-citizens with full rights."

But this can only come to pass in a "spirit of tolerance" and with the Jews as "fellow citizens." No doubt there is a trend within Christianity that creates Jewish "fellow citizens." Nevertheless, this question must be answered once more by the forces that motivate political and social conservatism.

6. On the Philosemitic Charm of Conservatism

Conservatism incorporates the above-mentioned trends of current German consciousness: nationalism; Christian values and beliefs; minimization of responsibility for the crimes of the Third Reich; maximization of the importance of Germany's future, aiming – as yet tacitly – towards establishing a reunited Fourth Reich. Conservatism embraces the ideological and political concepts and programs which the West German conservative establishment is striving to implement in politics and society. At the same time, Conservatism is now increasingly the common denominator of various cultural and political trends in Germany. This was emphasized in the case of Beirut and Bitburg, in the Fassbinder affair, and in the endorsement of a Federal penal code amendment that equated the murder of millions of Jews with the flight and expulsion of Germans from former German territory. It was expressed by Christian Democratic politicians through such actions as attendance of funerals of prominent former Nazis; and through statements such as that of a prominent Christian Democrat leader that as a Wehrmacht officer he was actually protecting the West from Bolshevism.

The same spirit was reflected in the remarks made by Helmut Kohl in Israel about the new, guiltless generation and the debate over a national memorial which would commemorate the mass murders and their victims as "victims of fate." Moreover, Conservatism seeks to preserve the German past as a state of normalcy, to maintain an identification with a glorious past that outshines little Austrian-born Hitler, rendering him an aberration that took a bitter toll but taught the German people a lesson; and the world is kindly requested to accept this.

Conservatism should not, however, be equated with antisemitism, nor are all Conservative politicians antisemites. After all, there was a change in the Conservative attitude toward Jews and Jewish concerns after 1945. From the period of the German Monarchy to the Weimar Republic's Conservative Revolution, initiated by intellectuals such as Ernst Jünger,[18] Conservatism was a political-cultural vehicle for anti-Jewish attitudes and values. In 1945, however, Conservatism seemed to be discredited precisely because of its antisemitic past and its intellectual political support of Hitler's rise to power.

Horkheimer,[19] however, called the German acknowledgement of guilt a splendid scheme to legitimize postwar Conservative policies; another such scheme was philosemitism. A statement issued in 1946 by a representative of the Christian Democratic Union illustrates these tendencies: "We . . . wish to inform our Jewish compatriots that our doors are wide open to them, and that we hope they will contribute the wisdom gained by their people throughout the millennia towards rebuilding a better Germany." The Jewish newspaper in which the above was published in 1946 contained an article by a Jewish writer responding to the CDU's pathos: "Everyone maintains that after this crime, no decent person will ever again 'do anything antisemitic . . .' but it is not overt antisemitism that one must look out for: dangers never recur in the same form."[20]

To understand why and how latent antisemitism is flourishing as the antisemitic mood prevails, the rise and fall of Federal German philosemitism must be considered. With the advent of philosemitism, Germany's political culture began to whitewash antisemitism whenever the ordained, democratic, anti-Nazi character of the Republic was questioned. Philosemitism provided clear moral legitimization for the Conservative era of rebuilding and restoration, while anti-Communism provided political legitimization.

The American High Commissioner in Germany, John McCloy, stated in 1949 that renunciation of antisemitic traditions was "a touchstone of democratic development in Germany." Philosemitism subsequently became an external and internal political device, confirming the existence of a new, democratic, humanistic Germany. Many Germans now paid lip service to "the victims," claiming that after all, they had helped Jews at some point, thus denazifying themselves and turning their anti-Jewish prejudices into pro-Jewish expressions. The emergent Federal Republic "aryanized" the stereotypes; nevertheless they remained stereotypes.

In 1963, the philosopher Ernst Bloch warned that philosemitism "itself implied something akin to an outgrown, yet immanent form of antisemitism."[21] In 1966, political scientist Eleonore Sterling anticipated a further decline in philosemitism,[22] which occurred in fact after 1967, despite annual celebrations of "Brotherhood Week."

The essential role played by philosemitism during the late 1940s and 1950s now is no longer relevant in the 1980s. Other western countries are dealing with their own manifestations of antisemitism and racism. The world does not consider West Germany's attitude towards "its" Jews particularly alarming. Relations with the State of Israel are a partial substitute – for the time being. Normalcy prevails; nevertheless this attitude has been and remains a touchstone, and political Conservatism still has difficulty convincing the Germans to forget this fact, as evidenced by the 1986 Bundestag debate on antisemitic trends. Every year, however, the process becomes a little easier.

In sum: The antisemitic mood of the mid-1980s, which has allowed latent antisemitism to come to the fore, is the product of German history after Auschwitz. Much has transpired during the forty years since 1945. The conflicts of that period have seen the vast majority of the Federal Republic's citizens rescind their ostensibly "eternal responsibility." Contemporary antisemitism, and this is my final point, is the historical response to the Conservative philosemitism prevalent during the establishment and restoration of the Federal Republic.

Philosemitism had not been successfully resisted. Indeed, no one had really wished to do so. It remains to be seen whether social forces are at hand to resist the transformation of conservative philosemitism into a generally acceptable form of antisemitism.

Notes

1. Helmut Kohl, born 1930, has been active in the CDU-Youth Union and the CDU since 1947. In 1973 he became chairman of the Christian Democratic Union which is the most influential conservative party in West Germany. Led by Konrad Adenauer in the first decade, the CDU remained the governing party until 1969, when a coalition of Social Democrats (SPD) and Free Democrats (FDP, a small liberal party) succeeded in the elections. In 1982, when the FDP left the coalition and turned to the CDU, Kohl was elected Chancellor. He suceeded in the 1983 as well as in the 1987 elections.
2. *Der Tagesspiegel* (West Berlin daily newspaper), 19.2.1986.
3. Rainer Werner Fassbinder, 1945–1982, West German author, movie-director and producer, actor and since the sixties influential representative of the New German Cinema. Produced many controversial movies, among them several dealing with the German past ("Lili Marlen").
4. The Christian Social Union (CSU) is the Bavarian sister of the CDU, which does not exist in Bavaria. The CSU is led by Franz Josef Strauss, and can always be found on the political right of the conservative spectrum. In the federal parliament the CSU and the CDU constitute one parliamentary party.
5. See among countless articles Robert Leicht, "Das Tabu zerbricht," *Die Zeit*, 14.2.1986.
6. *Frankfurter Allgemeine Zeitung*, 9.12.1949. The FAZ is the most important and intellectual influential conservative daily newspaper in West Germany.
7. Max Horkheimer, *Notizen 1950–1969* (Frankfurt/M 1974), pp. 106–200. Max Horkheimer, 1895–1973, Professor of Social Philosophy, together with Th. W. Adorno and others one of the founders of the Critical Theory which combined Marxist theory and psychological approaches. From 1930 until his emigration in 1933 Horkheimer was director of the Frankfurt Institute of Social Research, which continued its work in New York. 1943–44 Horkheimer became director of the science department of the American Jewish Committee. In 1949 he returned to Germany and became once more director of the refounded Institute. In 1951 he became Rector of the Johann-Wolfgang-Goethe-Universität in Frankfurt. Major works: *Anfänge der bürgerlichen Geschichtsphilosophie*, 1930; *Eclipse of Reason*, 1947; *Dialektik der Aufklärung*, together with Adorno 1947; editor of *Studies on Authority and the Family* and of *Studies of Prejudice*.
8. Ernst Nolte, "Vergangenheit, die nicht vergehen will," *Frankfurter Allgemeine Zeitung*, 6.6.1986. This article and other similar historiographical publications were answered by the prominent social philosopher Jürgen Habermas, "Eine Art Schadensabwicklung: Die apologetischen Tendenzen in der deutschen Zeitgeschichtsschreibung," *Die Zeit*, 11.7.1986. Almost all prominent West German historians participated in the following months in this discussion. Articles were published in *Die Zeit, Frankfurter Allgemeine Zeitung, Frankfurter Rundschau* and several journals. For further reading see *New German Critique* 13(1986/87) and the forthcoming article by Saul Friedländer in *Tel Aviver Jahrbuch für deutsche Geschichte*, 17(1987).— Ernst Nolte, born 1923, is Professor of History at Free University, Berlin; major works: *Der Faschismus in seiner Epoche*, 1963; *Theorien über den Faschismus*, 1967.
9. Richard von Weizsäcker, "Geschichte, Politik und Nation," *Geschichte in Wissenschaft und Unterricht* 37, 2(1986), p. 70.
10. *Frankfurter Allgemeine Zeitung*, 14.2.1986.
11. *Frankfurter Allgemeine Zeitung*, 28.11.1983.
12. Peter Edel, 1921–1984, grew up in Berlin, where Nazi race laws forced him to leave school. He studied painting and was acquainted with the artists Max Liebermann and Käthe Kollwitz. Forced to work at the Siemens factory like over 100 Berlin Jews he began to be active in the resistance in 1942. Peter Edel was caught by the Gestapo and sent to several concentration camps. He survived, lived for three years in Austria, and returned to Berlin in 1948. He worked as a journalist and editor in the German Democratic Republic. Major works: *Die Bilder des Zeugen Schattman*, 1969; *Wenn es ans Leben geht*, 1979.

13. Hannah Arendt, Karl Jaspers, *Briefwechsel 1926–1969* (Frankfurt/M, 1985). Hannah Arendt, 1906-1975, grew up in Germany, studied philosophy with Karl Jaspers in Heidelberg. She emigrated in 1933, became chief editor of Schocken Books, New York, in 1946 and later Professor of Political Philosophy at several universities. Major publications: *The Origins of Totalitarianism*, 1951; *Rahel Varnhagen: The Life of a Jewess*, 1958; *Eichmann in Jerusalem: A Report on the Banality of Evil*, 1963. Karl Theodor Jaspers, 1883–1969, German-Swiss philosopher. Until removal by the Nazis, Professor of Philosophy in Heidelberg. After the war until 1948 he taught again at the University of Heidelberg, but left in 1948 disappointed about the development of postwar Germany. From then on he taught philosophy in Basel, Switzerland. Major publications: *Allgemeine Psychopathologie*, 1913; *Die geistige Situation der Zeit*, 1931; *Philosophie*, 1932; *Nietzsche*, 1936; *Vom Ursprung und Ziel der Geschichte*, 1949; *Wohin treibt die Bundesrepublik*, 1965.
14. See Josef Joffe's commentary "Der Müll, die Stadt und die Republik," *Süddeutsche Zeitung*, 5.11.1985.
15. Jürgen Habermas, "Die Entsorgung der Vergangenheit; Ein Kulturpolitisches Pamphlet," *Die Zeit*, 17.5.1985; English translation now in *Bitburg: In Moral and Political Perspective*, ed. G. H. Hartman (Bloomington, 1986). Jürgen Habermas, born 1929, is Professor of Philosophy and Sociology at the University of Frankfurt. Today he is the most important representative of the "Frankfurt School" of critical theory within philosophy. Major publications: *Strukturwandel der Öffentlichkeit*, 1962; *Theorie und Praxis*, 1963; *Erkenntnis und Interesse*, 1968.
16. Martin Stöhr at the International Seminar on Present Day Antisemitism in Jerusalem, December 1985.
17. *Die Mundorgel* (Waldbröl, 1984), no. 77. This song was written in 1963.
18. Ernst Jünger, born 1895, German writer, served in the German Army in both World Wars, in the Weimar Republic author of the national right, in West Germany today leading conservative author, received many prizes and was honored by Chancellor Kohl on his 70th birthday. Typical for his glorification of war, death, and his elitarian concept is *In Stahlgewittern*, 1919, reprinted ever since.
19. See the above quoted texts.
20. *Jüdisches Gemeindeblatt für die Nord-Rheinprovinz und Westfalen*, 25.6.1946.
21. Ernst Bloch, "Die sogenannte Judenfrage," *Frankfurter Allgemeine Zeitung*, 14.3.1963. Ernst Bloch, 1885–1977, grew up in Germany, emigrated from Germany in 1933 and returned to East Germany in 1949. He was Professor of Philosophy at the University of Leipzig until 1957. In 1961 he became visiting Professor at the University of Tübingen, West Germany. Major publications: *Erbschaft dieser Zeit*, 1935; *Freiheit und Ordnung*, 1946; *Das Prinzip Hoffnung*, 1954–1960.
22. Eleonore Sterling, "Judenfreunde – Judenfeinde: Fragwürdiger Philosemitismus in der Bundesrepublik," *Die Zeit*, 10.12.1965. Eleonore Sterling, 1925–1968, grew up in Germany, emigrated in 1938 to the USA, returned 1952 to West Germany and became in 1956 faculty member of the University of Frankfurt, Institute for Political Science. She worked mainly on the history of antisemitism. Major publication: *Judenhass: Die Anfänge des politischen Antisemitismus in Deutschland (1815–1850)*, 1969.

For Further Reading

Pierre Aycoberry, *The Nazi Question: An Essay on The Interpretations of National Socialism (1922–1975)* (New York, 1981).
Wolfgang Benz, (ed.), *Rechtsextremismus in der Bundesrepublik* (Frankfurt, 1984).
Volker R. Berghahn, *Modern Germany: Society, Economy and Politics in the Twentieth Century* (Cambridge, 1982).
Saul Friedländer, *Reflections of Nazism: An Essay on Kitsch and Death* (New York, 1984).
Alfred Grosser, *L'Allemagne en occident: La République fédérale 40 ans après* (Paris, 1985) [German edition: *Das Deutschland im Westen: Eine Bilanz nach 40 Jahren* (Munich, 1985)].
Edvin Hartrich, *The Fourth and Richest Reich: How the Germans Conquered the Postwar World* (New York, 1980).
Walter Laqueur, *Germany Today: A Personal Report* (London, 1985).
Heiner Lichtenstein, (ed.), *Die Fassbinder Kontroverse oder Das Ende der Schonzeit* (Königstein/Ts, 1986).

New German Critique, Special Issue: Germans and Jews, 1–3, nos 19, 20 and 21 (1980); Special Issue on Heimat, no 36 (1985); Special Issue on the German Question, no. 37 (1986); Special Issue on the German Jewish Controversy, no. 38 (1986).

Raymond Poidevin, *L'Allemagne et le monde au XXe siècle* (Paris, 1983), [German edition: *Die unruhige Großmacht: Deutschland und die Welt im 20.Jahrhundert* (Darmstadt, 1985)].

Monika Richarz, "Jews in Today's Germanies," in: *Yearbook of the Leo-Baeck-Institute*, XXX, 1985, pp. 265–274.

Hagen Rudolph, *Die verpaßten Chancen: Die vergessene Geschichte der Bundesrepublik* (Hamburg, 1979).

Carl-Christoph Schweitzer et al., (eds), *Politics and Government in the Federal Republic of Germany: Basic Documents* (Leamington Spa, 1984).

Alphons Silbermann, *Sind wir Antisemiten? Ausmaß und Wirkung eines sozialen Vorurteils in der Bundesrepublik Deutschland (Köln, 1982).*

Alphons Silberman,, Julius H. Schoeps, (eds), *Antisemitismus nach dem Holocaust: Bestandsaufnahme und Erscheinungsformen in deutschsprachigen Ländern* (Köln, 1986).

Sinus-Studie, 5 Millionen Deutsche: "Wir sollten wieder einen Führer haben . . .": Rechtsextremistische Einstellungen bei den Deutschen (Reinbek, 1981).

Index

About the Contributors

SHMUEL ALMOG (b. 1926, Berlin); Director, The Vidal Sassoon International Center for the Study of Antisemitism; teaches Jewish History, Institute of Contemporary Jewry, The Hebrew University of Jerusalem. Recently published: *Zionism and History, The Rise of a New Jewish Consciousness.*

HAIM AVNI (b. 1930, Vienna); Professor of Modern Jewish History, Head of Division for Latin America, Spain and Portugal, Institute of Contemporary Jewry, Hebrew University. Among his publications: *Spain, The Jew and Franco.*

SHALOM BAR-ASHER (b. 1944, Ksar es-Suk, Morocco); teaches Jewish History, Hebrew University and Haifa University. Among his publications: "The Jews in North Africa and Egypt," in *The History of the Jews in the Islamic Countries*, ed. Shmuel Ettinger (Hebrew).

JACOB BARNAI (b. 1941, nr. Haifa); Senior Teacher of Jewish History, Hebrew University. Among his publications: *The Jews in Eretz-Israel in the 18th Century* (Hebrew).

YEHUDA BAUER (b. 1926, Prague); Jonah M. Machover Professor of Holocaust Studies, Institute of Contemporary Jewry, Hebrew University. Head of the Vidal Sassoon International Center for the Study of Antisemitism. His most recent publication: *A History of the Holocaust.*

HAGGAI BEN-SHAMMAI (b. 1939, Tel-Aviv); Senior Lecturer, Arabic Language and Literature, Hebrew University. Among his publications: "The Attitude of Some Early Karaites towards Islam" in *Studies in Medieval Jewish History and Literature*, ed. I. Twersky.

ROBERT BONFIL (b. 1937, Karditsa, Greece); Associate Professor of Jewish History, Hebrew University. Among his publications: *The Rabbinate in Renaissance Italy* (Hebrew).

MORDECHAI M. BREUER (b. 1918, Frankfurt); Professor Emeritus of Jewish History, Bar-Ilan University. Recently published: *Judische Orthodoxie im Deutschen Reich 1871–1918: Die Sozialgeschichte einer religiosen Minderheit.*

417

RICHARD I. COHEN (b. 1946, Montreal); Senior Lecturer of Modern Jewish History, Hebrew University. Among his publications: *The Burden of Conscience, French Jewish Leadership During the Holocaust.*

SHMUEL ETTINGER (b. 1919, Kiev); Rosenbloom Professor of Jewish History, Hebrew University. Chairman, Historical Society of Israel. From amongst his publications: *A History of the Jewish People: The Modern Period,* ed. H. H. Ben-Sasson.

LLOYD P. GARTNER (b. 1927, New York City); Abraham and Edita Spiegel Family Foundation Professor of European Jewish History, Tel-Aviv University. Published inter alia: *The Jewish Immigrant in England 1870–1914.*

MICHAEL GLATZER (b. 1946, Dallas); Academic Secretary of Ben Zvi Institute in Jerusalem. Area of interest: History of the Jews in Medieval Christian Spain.

AVRAHAM GROSSMAN (b. 1936, Tiberias); Ethel Backenroth Professor of Jewish History, Hebrew University. Among his publications: *The Early Sages of Ashkenaz* (Hebrew).

YISRAEL GUTMAN (b. 1923, Warsaw); Max and Rita Haber Professor of Holocaust Studies and Modern Jewish History, Hebrew University. Head of Institute of Contemporary Jewry. Among his publications: *The Jews of Warsaw, 1939–1943; Ghetto, Underground, Revolt.*

YEHOSHAFAT HARKABI (b. 1921, Haifa); Maurice B. Hexter Professor of International Relations and Middle Eastern Studies; Director, Leonard Davis Institute of International Relations, Hebrew University. Among his publications: *The Bar-Kokhba Syndrome: Risk and Realism in International Politics?*

MOSHE DAVID HERR (b. 1935, Tel Aviv); Associate Professor of Jewish History, Second Temple, Mishnaic and Talmudic Periods, Hebrew University. Contributed to and edited a ten-volume *History of Eretz Israel* (Hebrew).

JOSEPH KAPLAN (b. 1944, Buenos Aires); Associate Professor of Jewish History, Hebrew University. Among his publications: *From Christianity to Judaism: The Life and Work of Isaac Orobio de Castro* (Hebrew).

JACOB KATZ (b. 1904, Magyargencs, Hungary); Professor Emeritus of Jewish Social History, Hebrew University. Among his publications: *From Prejudice to Destruction, Anti-Semitism 1700–1933.*

NATHANIEL KATZBURG (b. 1922, Budapest); Professor of Modern Jewish History at Bar-Ilan University. His publications include: *Hungary and the Jews.*

YEHOSHUA PORATH (b. 1938, Tel Aviv); Professor of Islamic and Middle Eastern Studies, Hebrew University. His most recent book: *In Search of Arab Unity, 1930–1945.*

DAVID-ROKÉAH (b. 1930, Safed): Associate Professor of Classical History, and Jewish History during the Second Temple Period, Hebrew University. His publications include: *Jews, Pagans and Christians in Conflict.*

ZEFIRA ENTIN ROKÉAH (b. 1938, New York City); has taught at Brooklyn College, Haifa University, and Hebrew University. Among her publications: "Crime and Jews in Late 13th-Century England."

FRANK STERN (b. 1944, nr. Königsberg); lectures at Tel-Aviv University. Research fellow, The Vidal Sassoon International Center for the Study of Anti-semitism. Author of "Altäglicher Antisemitismus — Zur Analyse von Anlassen and Ursachen."

MENAHEM STERN (b. 1925. Bialyslok; Haim and Segula Razily Professor of History of the Second Temple Period, Hebrew University. Member of The Israel Academy of Sciences and Humanities. Among his publications: *The Greek and Latin Authors on Jews and Judaism.*

KENNETH R. STOW (b. 1944, Philadelphia); Professor of Jewish History, Haifa University. Among his publications: *The "1007 Anonymous" and Papal Sovereignty: Jewish Perceptions of the Papacy and Papal Policy in the High Middle Ages.*

MOSHE ZIMMERMANN (b. 1943, Jerusalem); Associate Professor, occupies the Richard Michael Koebner Chair of German History, Hebrew University. Among his publications: *Antisemitism and Democracy: The Biography of Wilhelm Harr.*